WILLIAM WELLS BROWN

WILLIAM WELLS BROWN

An African American Life

Ezra Greenspan

W. W. NORTON & COMPANY

New York   London

For information about permission to reproduce selections from this book,
write to Permissions, W. W. Norton & Company, Inc.,
500 Fifth Avenue, New York, NY 10110

For information about special discounts for bulk purchases, please contact
W. W. Norton Special Sales at specialsales@wwnorton.com or 800-233-4830

Manufacturing by Courier Westford
Book design by Helene Berinsky
Production manager: Julia Druskin

Library of Congress Cataloging-in-Publication Data

Greenspan, Ezra.
William Wells Brown : an African American life / Ezra Greenspan. — First edition.
pages cm
Includes bibliographical references and index.
ISBN 978-0-393-24090-0 (hardcover)
1. Brown, William Wells, 1814?–1884. 2. African American authors—Biography.
3. Fugitive slaves—United States—Biography. I. Title.
PS1139.B9Z64 2014
818´.409—dc23
[B]
2014027984

W. W. Norton & Company, Inc., 500 Fifth Avenue, New York, N.Y. 10110
www.wwnorton.com
W. W. Norton & Company Ltd., Castle House, 75/76 Wells Street,
London W1T 3QT

1 2 3 4 5 6 7 8 9 0

CONTENTS

ABBREVIATIONS

AASS—American Anti-Slavery Society

AFASS—American and Foreign Anti-Slavery Society

BFASS—British and Foreign Anti-Slavery Society

MASS—Massachusetts Anti-Slavery Society

NEASS—New England Anti-Slavery Society

PASS—Pennsylvania Anti-Slavery Society

WNYASS—Western New York Anti-Slavery Society

Introduction

W. E. B. Du Bois famously observed in 1902 what may be called the problem of the problem. "How does it feel to be a problem?" he reports being asked by a well-meaning but unknowing white acquaintance.[1] He answered on behalf of all African Americans in book after book that charted the strange course of racial relations over the nineteenth and twentieth centuries.

The same question applies to his nineteenth-century predecessor, William Wells Brown (1814–1884). For many decades now, Brown—in all his names, personas, and fictionalized incarnations—has been a problem. He was a problem at birth to his white father and cousins. He was a problem throughout his boyhood and adolescence to his slave masters. He was a problem to his colleagues—white and black—in the antislavery movement, and later, after the Civil War, to those in the temperance movement. He was a problem to defenders of slavery. He was a problem to audiences across the United States and the United Kingdom, the tens and tens of thousands of people who could not fathom the complexity or complexion of the man whose slyly humorous stories and understated homilies transfixed them. He was even a problem to himself, a man of such dramatic makeovers he was neither wholly black nor wholly white, slave nor free, American nor English, creative nor professional. It is no wonder Brown often struggled to know how to take himself, to unify the wildly incongruous, disparate parts of his experience as he moved back and forth across the color line with a facility few others had. Finally, he has been a problem ever since his era to readers of American literature, who know him—if they know him at all—only as a marginal writer of sundry books, not as the most pioneering and accomplished African American writer and cultural impresario of the nineteenth century. Even those who do know him face a further complication: a writer who composed habitually in the autobiographical mode, no matter whether writing fiction or nonfiction, so fictionalized "fact" and "history" that it is impossible to draw a straight generic boundary around any of his works or to connect them simply to his actual life. Autobiography becomes history and history becomes autobiography; like their author, they are never quite what they seem. Nor are his books, which current scholarship is demonstrating he compiled, to one extent or another, by appropriating and remaking portions of other printed works, sometimes his but many other times not.

Brown has been a problem in a different, collective sense. Like African Americans historically, he has been an absence—an invisible man—moving about in a world of recorded presence. Until the post–Civil Rights era, the historical record of his native region, the South, and the nation whitewashed away not just his presence but also that of his people. To this day, the historical signage surrounding the municipal park in his boyhood home in Marthasville, Missouri, proudly identifies his master as the pioneer founder of the town but makes no mention of Brown. Ironically, the signs are located on the premises of the very farm on which he grew up. The irony is greater yet: Brown was the leading African American historian of his era and devoted himself in one pioneering book after another to recording his people's presence in North America in common with people of European origin. As a student of the public record, whether engraved on public memorials or recorded in state archives, he so frequently encountered the pattern of deliberate or casual omission that he developed a term for it: *colonization*.[2]

Speaking to an African American church congregation in 1854, shortly after returning home from a five-year self-exile in Great Britain, Brown described their common experience as one of "being put on an experimental voyage" already of two hundred years' duration.[3] The metaphor came out of an eventful life of journeys and travels by river and ocean. In his pioneering novel *Clotel*, an epic story about the degraded lives of Thomas Jefferson's enslaved daughter and granddaughters as they descend into the depths of American slavery, he interjected an account of two ships that sail into early seventeenth-century North American waters. One is the *Mayflower* transporting Pilgrims to Massachusetts; the other is a slave ship transporting its human cargo on the Middle Passage to Virginia. Each carried a portion of the ancestry not just of Clotel and Brown but also, he repeatedly insisted, of the nation, neither portion sufficient without the other to serve as the foundation of the whole national story.

His own life was an experimental voyage so extraordinarily incongruous it matches for unlikelihood the lives of Benjamin Franklin, Walt Whitman, Abraham Lincoln, and Mark Twain, as well as his comrades Frederick Douglass, Harriet Jacobs, and Josiah Henson. He was born into slavery on a farm in Kentucky's Bluegrass Country, spent his boyhood on the Missouri frontier on the farm adjacent to Daniel Boone's, and in adolescence was "rented" out to a succession of steamboat captains who took him on runs up and down the Mississippi and Missouri Rivers. During one of those seven years on and off the river, the adolescent Brown was leased to a notorious Missouri slave trader named Walker who took him on three circuits of the trade—upland to purchase dozens of slaves in the Missouri interior, then down the Mississippi River to trade them at intermediate ports before disposing of the rest at New Orleans. He attempted several escapes, the second with his mother just months after completing his service to the slave trader. They were apprehended in central Illinois and returned in chains to St. Louis, where his mother was immediately sold down the river to the New Orleans market. At age nineteen, functionally illiterate and unaccompanied, he jumped his final master's ship at Cincinnati and this time successfully ran to freedom in Cleveland, renaming and educating himself in preparation for a life of freedom.

He immediately joined the Underground Railroad, smuggling fugitives on Great Lakes steamers and steering them to Canada. In time he joined the antislavery movement, becoming the leading black lecturer for the Boston-based radical abolitionist organization led by William Lloyd Garrison. He lived five years as a fugitive slave in England, lecturing extensively, exhibiting a pioneering African American antislavery panorama across the British Isles, and moving in leading intellectual and activist circles. By the time he returned to the United States in 1854, his freedom purchased by English supporters, he was the author of the earliest African American travelogue (*Three Years in Europe*, 1852) and the earliest African American novel (the now canonized *Clotel*, 1853). Over the next decade, he added a series of major works, including two plays, one now lost and the other the earliest printed African American play (*The Escape*, 1858), which he performed as a one-man show before audiences across the Northern states up to the Civil War. During the war, he lectured across the North, advocated emigration to Haiti on swings through Canada, recruited for the Fifty-fourth Massachusetts Regiment, and wrote a pioneering history of African Americans (*The Black Man*, 1863). That was soon followed by the first history of African American military service in the Civil War (*The Negro in the American Rebellion*, 1867), a fuller history of peoples of African descent (*The Rising Son*, 1873), and his final published book (*My Southern Home*, 1880), a savagely perceptive, rollicking account of the South looking both backward and forward from a Jim Crow–era vantage point. All the while, he practiced medicine back home in Cambridge, Massachusetts; ran for public office on a third-party temperance ticket; and toured the postwar South repeatedly campaigning for black uplift, temperance, and civil rights.

And then he died, the leading African American man of letters, a category that then had no clear status or precedent. Shortly afterward, so did his reputation, as a wave of Jim Crow reaction swept across the country. The Poplar Farm, as he called it, of his days in Missouri and later of his imagination faded into Scarlett O'Hara's Tara, and the achievements of the great generation of African Americans that spanned slavery and emancipation got whitewashed nearly, though not entirely, into oblivion. But Brown's ship is today coming back into general sight—and it is past time that it did. His life and writings are a test case for the far-reaching appeal of the twentieth-century poet Langston Hughes, "Let America be America again." It is time for William Wells Brown to be America again. But for that to happen, one has to go on a far-reaching exploration of what America was in his time, and what African Americans have to do with what it was then and is today.

To accomplish that task, one "must make the archives talk."[4] What more appropriate way can there be to engage a man who devoted his life to playing variations on a favorite instrument, the American archives? That question, however, is less rhetorical than it may at first seem. Brown was the most prolific black writer of his century, but even the existence of his large print corpus does not mean his life is readily recoverable. To gain access to his biography, both writer and reader must negotiate an evidentiary paradox characteristic of pre-twentieth-century minorities: He wrote books nonstop to the day he died, but he left behind no known personal archive—no family letters and little correspondence of any sort, no working books and papers, no library, and just a few scraps of literary manuscript. The sum total of material by and about him in established depositories fills out the picture, but only very partially. More complicating yet, he put more distance than meets the eye between his personal self and his published works, even those written in his shifty first person. A trickster of uncommon guile who brought north some basic lessons about identity mastered in slavery, Brown does not reveal himself simply or unequivocally even in his autobiographical writings.

To do Brown justice, writer and reader must be prepared to stretch "truth" to all reasonable limits, as Brown did over four decades of writing. The challenge of comprehending him is considerable, though not insurmountable. It begins with the biographer, who, when he cannot enter Brown's life through the front door due to lack of documentary evidence, must find additional points of entry. Often that means accessing the lives and archives of his friends and the African American community as a whole, a practice necessitated not only by documentary scarcity but also by Brown's governing logic, which took his life as continuous with his community's and his work as absorbing and reclaiming any other printed texts that could be made to fit. Gradually, the biographer hopes, a comprehensive portrait takes shape. How fully, how accurately it represents William Wells Brown, and how persuasively it makes the life and letters tally—let the reader decide.

MARTHASVILLE

The oldest village in Warren County, it succeeded the French village, La Charrette. Dr. John Young named this village for his first wife, Martha.

1817 - This village was part of Dr. John Young's farm and part of the William Ramsey Spanish Land Grant #1688.

1818 - A post office was established at Marthasville with Warren Swain as postmaster.

1820 - Daniel Boone, age 86, died at the home of his son, Nathan, and was buried in the Bryan Cemetery near Marthasville.

1826 - Dr. Young sold most of his property to Harvey Griswold.

1830's - German settlers began arriving on farms nearby.

1840 - Marthasville was the main landing place on the Missouri River for Warren County.

1855 - Griswald died. Augustus F. Grabs became Justice of the Peace and Postmaster.

1865 - Grabs died. In later years, Helen Rusche, great-granddaughter of Grabs, donated his house to the city of Marthasville.

1893 - The M. K. T. Railroad came to Marthasville. The depot is the oldest on the railroad.

Historical sign adjacent to municipal park of Marthasville, Missouri, indicating acquisition of the land by Brown's master, Dr. John Young.

PART 1

From Life to Letters

1

Antecedents in Black and White

The first commandment for authors of fugitive-slave narratives was well known: Thou shalt not lie. A pioneering generation of African American writers understood that readers expected their accounts of life in slavery to be strictly, verifiably factual. Even the authors of the most accomplished fugitive slave narratives complied. The fiercely independent-minded Frederick Douglass opened his immediately influential *Narrative of the Life of Frederick Douglass, an American Slave* (1845) with the familiar recitation of birth details common to the genre: "I was born in Tuckahoe, near Hillsborough, and about twelve miles from Easton, in Talbot county, Maryland." So did William Wells Brown in the opening words of his first book, *Narrative of William W. Brown, A Fugitive Slave* (1847): "I was born in Lexington, Ky." And likewise Brown's fellow Kentuckian Henry Bibb, founding editor of the first African Canadian newspaper, in his *Narrative of the Life and Adventures of Henry Bibb, An American Slave* (1849): "I was born May 1815, of a slave mother, in Shelby County, Kentucky, and was claimed as the property of David White Esq." Fifty years later, long after race slavery had been abolished in the United States, Booker T. Washington still honored the convention in *Up from Slavery*.[1]

Douglass was in fact born in Tuckahoe, on Maryland's Eastern

Shore; and Bibb in rural Shelby County, as stated. By contrast, Brown was born not in Lexington or its vicinity but two counties and about thirty-five miles to the east in the vicinity of tiny Mt. Sterling, seat of Montgomery County.[2] He no doubt retained little if any memory of a locale from which he was uprooted at age two or three and to which he never returned. His youth notwithstanding, he presumably had heard enough details from his mother and elder siblings about their old Kentucky home that he was deliberately obscuring the literal truth of the first fact of his life and authorship. As a writer, William Wells Brown was born different.

He sometimes wrote differently, as well. In one of his more audacious autobiographical claims, he repeated without comment a rumor that his mother was the daughter of Daniel Boone.[3] Whatever reason Brown might have had for recasting his ancestry, he was obliquely expressing one of the most profound truths about his formative years. To an extent rare among the African American leaders of the antislavery movement, Brown grew to maturity as a participant in the great frontier drama unfolding across the interior of nineteenth-century North America. Move by move, he and his relatives were pushed westward on a route running just south of the Mason-Dixon line, their master following in the footsteps of Boone and other pioneer settlers. In 1817 they would catch up to Boone at the western edge of settlement in the Missouri Territory. Evidence of their intersection survives to this day at a municipal park situated along the Katy Trail, the Missouri-to-Texas railway right-of-way, on the edge of the small town of Marthasville. Historical markers placed around the park commemorate three seemingly unrelated early nineteenth-century events: Meriwether Lewis and William Clark passed and returned through the nearby French hamlet of La Charrette on their transcontinental Voyage of Discovery; Boone lived his last years just outside the settlement and was buried on its outskirts; and a certain Dr. John Young, an opportunistic settler from Kentucky, purchased a large portion of the surrounding land and established on it the town he named Marthasville.[4] Nowhere do the official markers indicate, however, that Young was the master of a scrawny, light-skinned slave boy familiarly known as Sandy who grew up on his farm but in time freed himself and, as the self-fashioned William Wells Brown, notched his name into American history.

IN A SUCCESSION OF BOOKS, Brown would have much to say about Young—"the man who stole me as soon as I was born"—and his shrewish second wife, Sarah Scott, none of it complimentary. In actuality, Young was a more important person in Brown's life than he could comfortably state publicly or even admit to himself. A first cousin of Brown's biological father, Young owned Brown for seventeen years but exerted lifelong influence, not least on his eventual development into a writer and doctor. By contrast, his biological father, George W. Higgins (1785–1835), was a ghostly figure in Brown's life, as white men of his class and position typically were to their disposable offspring. Soon after Brown's birth, Higgins moved on, settling for a time in Tennessee and later permanently in Alabama.[5] A late bloomer, he married an acquaintance named Nancy Smith from a reputable Montgomery County family around 1814 and had a dozen white children with her. He lived out his last two decades chiefly as a respected doctor in Winchester, Tennessee, and founding father and leading citizen of Bellefont, Alabama.[6] Restless to the end like his respected cousin John, he moved one final time about seventy miles westward to Decatur, seat of Morgan County, where he was serving as president of the local branch of the Alabama state bank when he died suddenly in 1835, leaving his family insolvent and forced to sell off their slaves and other property.[7] Brown had virtually nothing to say about a man he probably never set eyes on, but he was outspoken about his feelings toward all of Higgins's cohort, the men who preached racial purity while practicing "amalgamation" not just sexually but also commercially by trafficking in "white" slaves: "If Jeremiah were still living, and believed that the Ethiopian could not change his skin, he would, at least, have been satisfied that the slave-holder could change it for him."[8]

The most important person in Brown's early life was his mother, a field slave likely of mixed racial heritage who comes down to us only through her son's telling as "Elizabeth." Sold down the river during her son's teens, she subsequently vanished from history—retrievable, to the limited extent possible, by the lifeline of her son's words. The intersecting lives of these three people formed the familial basis of Brown's birth and childhood. More closely examined, their tangled histories tell a story of slaves in the family that replicated itself across the American South.

The narrative of Elizabeth deserves priority in telling, but the facts about her origin and life are so obscure that her story must be one largely of inference and conjecture. Brown provided virtually no details about her background, an omission partly explained by Frederick Douglass's generalization about US slave lineage: "The reader must not expect me to say much of my family. Genealogical trees did not flourish among slaves."[9] Elizabeth's family history was one of those stunted genealogical trees that sprouted from slavery yet somehow endured. So few credible facts survive about her life that its larger trajectory can be plotted mostly only indirectly through an account of the family histories of Young and Higgins, which by contrast left a rich evidentiary trail in local archives. Following such evidence, one can closely track the pioneering history of the Young and Higgins families across the early South and West and, in the process, compose a rich genealogical history of this multiracial family. Separating the black from the white, to the extent they can be untangled, one can gradually make out the shape of Brown's family history from beneath the overhanging canopy of the Young–Higgins family. It was—and to this day remains—a family history that communicated an inconvenient truth, complicating even the most basic bureaucratic acts. When Brown filed for a marriage license in Boston in 1860, the local clerk wrote "George and Elizabeth Higgins" for his parents' names.[10] The reality was hardly that simple.

THE WHITE ANCESTORS of the future William Wells Brown, the Young and Higgins families, initially settled during the eighteenth century in the adjacent counties of Spotsylvania and Caroline in the area of today's Fredericksburg, Virginia. Both families moved westward along with the young nation in the years immediately following the American Revolution, as the line of settlement pushed over the mountains and across lands recently (and in some areas still) inhabited by Native Americans. The first Young to settle on American soil was John's paternal great-grandfather, Laurance, who immigrated to the New World early in the eighteenth century. He established a foothold in the area of Fredericksburg, where one source described him as "the first white person" to settle in the area.[11] His son, also Laurance (d. 1788), was an unlettered man who strove to improve the family's circumstances. He and his wife, Margaret, established an expanding homestead nearby in Spotsylvania County, raising numerous children and accumulating land and slaves. His presence survives chiefly in the form of land deeds in Spotsylvania County attesting to his hard-earned stake in colonial Virginia. His will, signed only with a cross, divided his estate into equal shares among their eight children, deeding them a combination of land and slaves—their goodly portion for themselves and their posterity.[12]

His son Leonard (1745–1821), father of John, was likewise a man of ambition and talent keen to improve the family lot. Searching for greener pastures, he followed the trail blazed by Daniel Boone and traversed by hundreds, soon thousands, of Virginians and other emigrants over the Cumberland Gap into a region of northern Kentucky still being "cleared" of Native Americans. Leonard Young eventually settled in the vicinity of Lexington and prospered along with the fast-growing city. Over the course of his three decades' residence, the frontier town grew into one of the most prosperous, cultured cities in the South. A semiliterate but industrious man, he was ill-equipped to enjoy the finery of upper-class Southern life, but he accomplished the next best thing: He made himself useful to local and regional families of importance as a civic leader, estate administrator, and land agent. One of his most important clients was General Jonathan Clark of Louisville, brother of Missouri territorial governor and Western explorer William Clark. Trusting in Young's integrity and capability, Clark appointed him to oversee his considerable landholdings and collect rents in Lexington, an important job Young managed for years. Always eager to serve the public, Young also played a multifaceted role in the swift development of the city. Among his various civic functions, he served as a commissioner for the construction of a new courthouse for Lexington, a new city jail, and a new brick meeting house near his home at Bryan's Station.

Leonard Young also played his accustomed good-citizen role in regulating an institution vital to him and his neighbors: slavery. In 1794, he was one of nine signatories on a notice published in the *Kentucky Gazette* protesting unregulated slave-trading practices in Lexington and surrounding Fayette County. Young evidently had a slave-management problem closer to home. On at least two occasions, Young family slaves staged escapes: John, "a remarkable black negro, with a bold look," in 1797; and Matilda, whom he advertised as a "bright mulatto girl" of twenty-two or twenty-three, who used her writing ability to forge a pass to facilitate her flight to Ohio or Virginia, in 1813.[13] During the next generation, the father's slave-management problem descended to three of his sons: John, Benjamin, and Aaron. Each one would have to deal with runaways or freedom suits brought against them by their slaves once they relocated to Missouri. John actually dealt with both.[14]

John Young (1779–1833) was one of thirteen children Leonard and his wife, Mary Ann Higgins (1744–1813), raised to adulthood. John was among their last born in the family home in Spotsylvania County but grew up in the vicinity of Lexington, Kentucky, to which his family had relocated by the early 1780s (1781, by one account), when Kentucky was still the westernmost county of Virginia.[15] By contrast with his father and grandfather, he was well schooled and highly literate, although details are sketchy. At some period in the 1790s, he studied medicine, probably at the Pennsylvania Medical College in Philadelphia, the new nation's first medical school. Before graduating, he returned to Kentucky to establish his practice, making his first appearance in the historical record in 1803 as a doctor in the pioneer town of Bardstown, Nelson County. Dissatisfied with that situation, he went looking for a more lucrative place to practice, eyeing "the falls" of Louisville, among other locations.[16] That same year, in nearby Shelby County, he married Frances Fuqua, a transplanted Virginian from Charlotte County and a woman of higher social class than he, who brought a number of slaves and other forms of property to their marriage.[17] Restless like his pioneer ancestors for better opportunity, Young moved his family and possessions in 1805 to the heart of Bluegrass Country in Montgomery County, home of his mother's well-established clan. Over time he became a large landowner, buying town lots in Mt. Sterling and larger tracts in outlying areas for farming. In the process, he established himself as Dr. John Young, physician, civic leader, and gentleman farmer, pursuing a medical practice and manufacturing in town and carrying on farming operations on his growing landholdings in the surrounding district.

Young possessed something of his father's public-service ethos. In 1807, he served a portion of a term in the Kentucky General Assembly as a representative of Montgomery County, a position he would also later fill for several terms in the Missouri General Assembly. In 1810, he addressed a letter to the editor of Lexington's leading newspaper warning about a smallpox outbreak in Mt. Sterling. A practitioner of the latest medical science, he proudly noted that the one person he had inoculated was tending to the sick with no risk of infection to himself.[18] In the three years after the death of Frances in 1810 or 1811, he and his second wife, Sarah Scott, took into their childless home at least three apprentices (one a four-year-old orphan girl). As their master, Young contracted not only to shelter, clothe, and feed them adequately but also to teach them the elements of literacy and numeracy, as well as a suitable trade.[19] We know nothing, however, about his actual disposition or conduct toward these children. During these years, he might also have begun the practice he would later pursue earnestly in Missouri of systematically distributing Bibles to the white community.[20]

His primary trajectory, however, in Montgomery County and wherever he resided in his far-ranging life, was the profit-seeking one of self-advancement. From the moment of his settling in Mt. Sterling, he vigorously pursued any opportunity. He ran his medical practice out of his Mt. Sterling home, keeping a carriage and horses to reach patients well out into the countryside.[21] In town he operated an apothecary shop stocked with the latest chemical and patent medicines (some of the former made by his slaves), as well as a gristmill and a hemp factory.[22] Casting his capital widely, he acquired extensive landholdings in both the town

and the surrounding countryside, presumably utilizing the land to produce additional income. And throughout his residence in Montgomery
County, he traded in the two valuable, interrelated commodities that, at
all times and locations, constituted the core of his estate: land and slaves.

The record of the former is clear and detailed. His landholdings and
dealings in Montgomery County are preserved in the deed books at the
local courthouse. He exchanged land too frequently to be interested
solely in cultivation; nevertheless, he did farm a significant portion of the
land he owned, presumably raising the crops best suited to local conditions, such as hemp, wheat, corn, and tobacco. To say that he farmed the
land is of course to engage in a figure of speech, since the farm labor was
assigned chiefly to his field hands, slaves superintended by overseers. By
contrast, the record of his slave dealings is difficult to establish. Brown
claimed that he heard that Young kept a plantation ledger, as masters
frequently did, and that his own birth appeared amid the roll call of
slaves, livestock, and other property-related data routinely registered in
such documents.[23] That claim is entirely plausible, but no such ledger
has survived. Nor has the John Young family Bible, which might have
contained the names and ages of his domestic slaves but passed out of
the family's hands after his widow's death.[24] Such had been the family
practice; Leonard Young had kept a record of the domestic slaves in his
Bible, listing their names close to but separate from the names and vital
dates of his own family members.[25]

Even without these sources of documentary proof, it is certain that
John Young occasionally bought and sold slaves, just as he had land,
strictly for profit. Like father like son, he professed to seek the best interest of his slaves, instructing them in the elements of religion, caring for
their basic needs, and attending to their medical treatment as necessary. When opportunity called, however, he sold them for gain, even
if doing so meant breaking up families. Young's doting father, a man
respected for his intense family devotion, had apportioned his estate in
as nearly equal divisions as justice would permit to his many children,
each one receiving a certain measure of land and other assets, including
one slave.[26] His son acted no more sentimentally, not during his active

years and not when near death in drawing up his own will. Nor, for that matter, did Young's widow in her last days.[27]

This genealogical chronicle is meant to historicize and contextualize the immediate questions about Brown's African American lineage: How, when, and for what purpose did John Young come to acquire Elizabeth; to hold her and, in time, her seven children; and eventually to dispose of her and them? Young and Elizabeth come down to us as silent on the subject; Brown's autobiographical writings provide limited but crucial help. The most revealing statement he makes about his mother, brothers, and sister is this clipped declaration, which he sets in the opening paragraph of his *Narrative*: "My mother's name was Elizabeth. She had seven children, viz: Solomon, Leander, Benjamin, Joseph, Millford, Elizabeth, and myself. No two of us were children of the same father."[28]

If Brown is speaking strictly factually and following the normal genealogical order of slave recording, as seems likely, his mother gave birth to her seven children in nearly the tightest interval possible. Calculating a precise sequence, however, is complicated by Brown's omission of dates and his limited knowledge. Frederick Douglass famously observed that slaves had as little knowledge of their exact birth date as horses about theirs, since ignorance about such matters suited their masters' need for domination.[29] Brown fit this pattern, giving such discrepant accounts of his birth year in his multiple memoirs that none can be taken as completely trustworthy. Whatever information about his birth date he got from his family would more likely have been by agricultural season than year. One can conclude with near certainty, however, that he was born in or around 1814, a date deducible from the deposition given by his third and final master, Enoch Price, in St. Louis Circuit Court. In the act of manumitting Brown on April 25, 1854, Price testified that his slave was "now in the fortieth year of his age."[30] If so, 1814 must have been approximately the last year Elizabeth gave birth, since Brown placed himself at the end of his genealogical recitation. His sister would likely have been nearest in age to him, consistent with the tight emotional pairing he ascribes to them in his *Narrative*, in which she figures as the closest of his siblings—so close that when she is sold down the river, he responds by planning his escape from slavery. Second from the top of that birth list was brother Leander, about whom Brown is generally silent in the rest of his *Narrative*. But Leander's birth year can also be construed; Young referred to him as nineteen in an 1828 document in which he "mortgaged" Leander and another slave to a creditor in partial payment for a debt.[31] No fewer than four and probably five of their siblings were born between Leander in 1809 and William in 1814.

What does that pattern of a birth per year tell us about Elizabeth? Strange though it sounds, it may help to date her birth and possibly even recover something of her early life story. In all likelihood, she was a "breeder" slave for Young, who stood to profit from her "increase" and would have wished to maximize it. In line with other female slaves trapped in her circumstances, Elizabeth probably had her first child nearly as soon as she was biologically able, very likely in her early or middle teens. If so, she herself must have been born roughly between 1790 and 1795 and likely in either Virginia or Kentucky, the two states associated with the Young and Fuqua families, as well as with most other first-generation white Kentuckians and their enslaved possessions. William Edward Farrison, Brown's assiduous twentieth-century biographer, surmised Virginia, based on his plausible acceptance of the statement made by Brown's dear friend William Cooper Nell in 1854 that Elizabeth was the daughter of a Virginia slave named Simon Lee who had fought with the patriots in the Revolutionary War before being returned for life to slavery.[32] Brown was generally guarded about his private life, which was full of skeletons, but if he exposed the story of his enslaved years to anyone, it would have been Nell, his nearest confidant in the mid-1850s.

How Elizabeth came to be Young's slave remains a mystery. The most likely possibilities are three: She was born into or purchased by the Young family and was passed by a sibling or parent to him at some date; she was born into or purchased by the slave-rich Fuqua family and came to Young along with his bride in 1803; or she was acquired by Young at a young age before or shortly after his marriage to Frances Fuqua, whether in Virginia or Kentucky. No known documentary evidence explicitly supports any of these hypotheses—no bills of sale, wills, family Bibles, guardianship papers, slave lists from either the Young or Fuqua families, or Virginia or Kentucky state records. She could not have come from the union with Sarah Scott, whom Young did not marry until 1814. His union with Frances Fuqua, however, is a more plausible possibility and does provide one tantalizing lead: A female slave named "Doll," left to Frances in 1790 in her father's will, was almost certainly the "Dolly" or "Aunt Dolly" whom Brown names in his recollections of life in the Young household in Missouri.[33] But there is no way to spot a future parent of the unborn Elizabeth in the Fuqua estate's slave inventory; and, more to the point, her name does not appear in the more extensive list of slaves in the 1809 case file accompanying the suit John and Frances Young brought against the estate's executor.[34] If both the Fuqua and Scott families are ruled out, the most likely possibility is that Young purchased her in either Virginia or Kentucky. Such transactions, however, rarely left surviving documentation.

Whatever her origin and path to Young, the basic fact remains that she was Dr. John Young's slave "for life"—as Kentucky slave documents typically spelled out—or, more exactly, for as long as Young chose to keep her. In the event, he held her for about three decades, long enough for her to yield him at least seven additional slaves and to raise them to maturity. Then he sold her—about which act and its consequences, more in due course.

One of the most tantalizing details in Brown's gnomic description of his family is that Elizabeth had each of her children by a different man. We know nothing about the identity of any of those men other than George W. Higgins—not their skin color, class, age, relation to Elizabeth or Young—and we probably never will. But we do know some bare facts about Higgins, as well as a fair amount about his family. Brown was inescapably mindful of his Higgins heritage; every time he looked in the mirror, he saw their reflection. Like the speaker in Langston Hughes's poem "Mulatto" who confronts his father—"I am your son, white man!"—Brown insisted he was a part of his white family and the obligation was mutual. While touring the British Isles and the US North as an antislavery lecturer in the 1850s, he took mock pleasure in boasting of his extended family's achievements, singling out his highly accomplished "Cousin Charles" and other members of the politically powerful Wickliffe family of Lexington: "My cousin Charles A. Wickliffe was Postmaster-General under John Tyler," he told an 1860 gathering of the American Anti-Slavery Society in New York City. "Probably many of you don't know anything about John Tyler, he filled such a small niche in our nation's history, but certainly you must have heard of my cousin Charles."[35] Say what he would about their common blood, he was their equal and opposite in one unmistakable regard: As eager as he was to shake the family tree to suit his emotional and polemical needs, his white relatives would have been equally eager to bury the "strange fruit" of any such relationship. Or, to switch the metaphor, like other proud Southern families, such as the Jeffersons of Monticello, they took care to wipe clean any blemishes on the family silver and passed down expectations to descendants to do the same.

CONNECTIONS BETWEEN the Higgins and Young families began in Virginia, where they interacted in occasional business and administrative dealings even before the marriage between Leonard Young and Mary Ann Higgins in 1765. The two families first arrived in Kentucky, however, at different times and in different fashions: the Youngs as farmers, the Higginses as fighters and pioneers. The Higgins vanguard consisted of two of Leonard Young's seven strapping brothers-in-law, who distinguished themselves for their military and pioneering exploits: Aaron, a redoubtable six-foot-three Indian fighter in Kentucky and subsequently in Indiana; and James, who earned a captaincy fighting the British in Virginia during the American Revolution. These two brothers pushed far into Kentucky, eventually reaching the area along Buck Lick Creek in the northern portion of the future Montgomery County. On April 20, 1780, they each received payment for their military service in Kentucky land grants and claimed preemption rights on additional lands, which they formally entered for registration two months later. With adjacent lots of 1,400 acres of prime land registered in their names, the brothers returned home to gather the family and prepare to lead them to their new home. For a few years, they bided their time, perhaps awaiting the end of the fighting with the British or a reduced level of hostilities with local Native Americans. Then the family embarked overland to Pittsburgh or Redstone, transferred their possessions to flatboats, and descended the Ohio River to Cincinnati, where they steered south down the Licking River to their land claims. For their common defense, they built Higgins Block House, a fortress of interlocking log cabins positioned on a bluff above the river.[36]

When conditions permitted, the brothers and their families fanned out onto the lands claimed by Aaron and James. In time they prospered, expanding their landholdings in Montgomery County and increasing their stock of slaves. The eldest of the seven Higgins brothers was William, the father of George W., who had struck out on a separate path from Virginia to Georgia for a time before reuniting with his brothers in Kentucky by the early 1780s. William and his young family lived first in or near Lexington, the likely birthplace of George W., before taking possession of land near Grassy Lick Creek, where he ran a gristmill and farmed land he acquired from one of his land-rich brothers. George W. grew to maturity there, although what he did subsequently as a young adult is not precisely known. He appears in the land records of Montgomery County only once, in 1808, when he sold a tract of 145 acres lying along Grassy Lick Creek for $400.[37] That document lists him singly as seller, which means he was not married at the time, nor is there any indication that he married during his remaining six years in Montgomery County. After 1808, his name appears in the county records only twice, but the timing is significant because it links Higgins to the area at the time of Brown's conception. In 1812, and 1813, "George W. Higgins" is listed on the tax rolls, the first year with seven slaves to his name. His name is thereafter absent from all surviving county documents.

There is one additional point of information about George W. Higgins's actions during his final years in Montgomery County before migrating to Tennessee, and it is decisive in linking Higgins to Brown's mother. The information surfaces in a remarkable genealogical letter that circulated around the family in the late nineteenth century. Today the document survives in modern typescripts in at least four Kentucky libraries, as well as among Higgins family genealogists and descendants scattered around the country.[38] Addressed in 1872 by a high-ranking Confederate officer named H. H. Higgins from Athens, Alabama, to his cousin and fellow officer, William J. Higgins, this long letter provides a detailed, rambling family chronicle ranging from "the old patriarchs of our name who left Virginia to settle in Kentucky" down to their own time. In executing this act of family devotion (and, at the time, Confederate patriotism), H. H. interspersed a wide range of acquired information with personal observation. One story of particular relevance concerned a memorable family visit H. H. paid sometime in the late 1810s to his native town of Mt. Sterling. Interrupting his long journey north, he stopped to lodge overnight outside Lexington at the fine house of a Young uncle, where his sudden, unannounced appearance moved a houseguest, his elderly great uncle Leonard Young, to tears. H. H. was brimming with information and stories about dozens of their Higgins relations, who were scattered across the South after the Civil War. He was noticeably silent, however, about George W., if for the simplest of reasons: William J. would need little information about the life story of his own father. But H. H. did mention one crucial fact about this elusive figure: He identified their great-uncle Leonard Young as "the father of Dr. John Young, of Mt. Sterling, with whom your father read medicine."[39]

During his numerous visits to his cousin's house and farm around 1813, the apprentice doctor George W. Higgins must have taken close notice of Young's slave woman Elizabeth. What subsequently happened between them happened, and the outcome was not simply the birth of a male child but also a tacit agreement between the cousins. Our source, speaking thirty-three years later, is Brown. In his *Narrative* he relates dispassionately the revelation his mother made to him that his father had extracted from Dr. Young a promise he would never sell Brown to "the New Orleans market."[40] What Brown did not know was that the tie between the cousins was so binding that, despite years of geographical separation, Higgins named a son after Young, one of at least several of Brown's half-brothers who fought with the Confederacy.[41] During seventeen years as Young's slave, the insubordinate young Brown repeatedly tested his master's resolve, but Young resisted the temptation to break his promise to Higgins. When, only after Brown's second unsuccessful attempt at escape, Young did finally dispose of Brown, he sold him to a St. Louis shopkeeper of his acquaintance named Samuel Willi. In the transaction, Young must have written the adolescent's name as Sandford Higgins, since that was the name under which Higgins/Brown was eventually emancipated.

George W. Higgins might seem to have tiptoed into, and then out of, the historical record. Such men as he, however, left behind indelible traces from their nocturnal forays into the slave quarters. These visits took place frequently across the nineteenth-century South, where everyday observation took note of the changing coloration of the enslaved population. Even in their own time, the fact and consequences of "amalgamation" became the subject of talk, hushed or bruited, everywhere from the slave quarters to the big house, from the printed works of Northern and foreign visitors in the South to the polemics of black and white opponents of slavery. White Southern tongues generally commented more guardedly but comment they did, as when well-heeled Mary Chesnut, South Carolina plantation mistress and wife of an ex–US senator, confided to her diary the thought on the minds of many of her neighbors: "The Mulattoes one sees in every family exactly resemble the white children."[42] Brown, who witnessed the same pattern through the other end of the looking glass, would likewise make scathing reference in his writings about Southern life to the rapacious conduct of self-styled "gentlemen" like Higgins and to the contorted ideological positions taken by defenders of the "peculiar institution." In time, the gaping incongruities between ideology and practice would afford him endless possibility for satire.

The sins of the fathers carried far and wide across North America and beyond. Brown was acutely aware he was one of thousands of mixed-race sons and daughters who fled over the Mason-Dixon line to new homes in the North. More particularly, however, he belonged to a specific cohort of civil rights and community activists with Kentucky slave backgrounds and racial profiles bearing marked resemblance to his own. One was his Boston friend Lewis Hayden, who was born in the Lexington area in 1811 to mixed African, European, and Native American heritage. Hayden and Brown would work closely together over the years in various civic and political endeavors and later during the Civil War as recruiters for the Fifty-fourth Massachusetts Regiment. At the end of a four-decade friendship, Hayden would speak at Brown's funeral. Another was Henry Bibb, born as mentioned in Shelby County in 1815 to an enslaved mother of mixed racial ancestry and a white father from the prominent Bibb family. Brown clashed with Bibb's brand of antislavery politics but valued his activism highly enough to include an admiring sketch of him in his first book on African American history.[43] Also well known to him were the Clarke brothers, Milton and Lewis, born within a few years of each other around 1815 in Madison County of a white father and a light-skinned (and possibly white) enslaved mother. Boston antislavery publisher Bela Marsh bundled the brothers' fugitive-slave narratives in a single volume several years before he published Brown's popular antislavery songster. Brown would come to know Milton particularly well—his neighbor in Cambridge, Massachusetts, for two decades beginning in 1860 and the city's first reputedly African American councilman.[44] More broadly speaking, wherever he went on his long speaking tours across the Northern states, southern Canada, and even the British Isles, he would find shades of his own life story in the looks and tales of the ex-slaves he encountered.

◆

William Wells Brown's birthplace was likely one of the creek-lined farms a few miles east of Mt. Sterling in the bucolic Bluegrass Country owned by his mother's master, Dr. John Young. Singling out which one must be a matter of speculation, since not one of the surviving deeds provides conclusive details about the use of the land or infrastructure. His one and only birth name was William, a name in circulation in the Young and Higgins families and assigned more likely by Young than by his mother, although he probably would have been known colloquially as Bill, Billie, Will, or Willie—Brown never specified which. He spent his first two or three years on the farm, sharing a cabin in the slave quarters with his mother, five brothers, and sister. With so many older siblings surrounding him, he would not have lacked for playmates, and the relative freedom given to very young slave children might well have permitted them opportunities for rural play.

Whatever stability Elizabeth and her family had in Kentucky would have been short lived. A man incessantly in search of greener pastures, John Young decided to relocate his family and possessions to the Missouri Territory, a portion of the Louisiana Purchase particularly attractive to settlers from the South looking for "virgin" land to cultivate. Ever since the conclusion of the War of 1812, a steady stream of Kentuckians had been flowing into the territory, with concentrations along the Missouri River, to take advantage of its favorable prospects—so many by the time of his arrival that Young would encounter a transplanted Kentucky on the Missouri. One of them was his Mt. Sterling neighbor Charles Younger, the grandfather of the four brothers who formed the junior partnership in the James–Younger Gang that began as Confederate bushwhackers before moving on to terrorize post–Civil War Missouri for profit.[45] An inveterate risk taker, Dr. Young made the same gamble as Younger and many of their neighbors: Economic opportunity would be greater out West than back home, where the soil was depleted and general financial conditions had grown unfavorable. In uprooting from Kentucky, he became the first member of his family to make the push westward, although within a few years he would be reunited at Marthasville with his enterprising brothers Aaron and Benjamin.

John Young planned his course of action deliberately. In the summer of 1816, he set out on a reconnaissance trip to sprawling St. Charles County, Missouri. Whether drawn by design or discovery, he fixed on Daniel Boone's neighborhood near the north bank of the Missouri River about fifty-five miles west of St. Louis, where land was cheap, abundant, and fertile. By this time, Young had resolved to acquire not just a homestead but enough land to establish a new town, calculating that a settlement so placed might in time become the administrative center of a new county to be split off from St. Charles. He eventually located a site suitable for his plan on a hillside above the river near the old French hamlet of La Charrette, now Americanized as Charrette Village. On October 29, he signed a contract with the owner of the land, William Ramsey, who had received it as an original Spanish land grant, for purchase of a large portion of his property. That historic deed specified that "John Young at present of Mount Sterling Montgomery County and State of Kentucky" had paid Ramsey $1,668 in exchange for a tract of 556 acres "on which said Ramsey now resides."[46] In addition, Young also bought a supplemental plot of twenty-five acres previously belonging to Ramsey's deceased son John.[47] He wrapped up that day's business by signing over a power of attorney to a local agent named Andrew Fort, authorizing Fort to represent him in any and all local transactions.[48] Given Young's ambitions for his new settlement, that would have been no nominal assignment.

His mission completed, Young headed back to Kentucky to wait out the winter before embarking for the West. Much of the winter would have been given over to preparations for the move. Slaves, so the prevailing master ideology would have it, were happily spared the trouble and anxiety left to their owners of planning for such consequential events, if not the physical toil of dismantling structures; packing equipment, furniture, and provisions; gathering food; and preparing whatever else would be needed for the trip and the construction of new homes on the frontier. In reality, such transitions would have been gut-wrenching experiences for slaves, who at all times of disruption feared for their own future as well as the possible breakup of their families. At this pivotal time, Elizabeth would have had everything to fear. As an unprotected adolescent, she had learned the bitter lesson of black female defenselessness, and now, as the mother of seven small children, she would have found herself among the most exposed of all of Young's slaves, no better equipped to protect her brood than herself. Worse yet, she would have known that with even the best possible outcome, the preservation of her family, she would be transported an additional, incalculable distance from the heartland of her family and early associations.

Young's attention turned in early 1817 to liquidation of assets, as he sold some but not all of his land in Montgomery County. Whether he also sold off slaves is unknown, although with an eye to future necessity or profitability, he left Elizabeth's family untouched. His largest transaction was the sale, on March 4, of a choice 186-acre parcel along Spencer Creek for $3,735, raising working capital for the move and the establishment of the village he had decided to name Marthasville.[49] A month later, he assigned a power of attorney to his friend Edward Stockton "to transact all my business in Kentucky," including renting out whatever property and lots he retained in Mt. Sterling and vicinity.[50] Probably within days of this agreement, the Young party would begin the journey westward.

Virtually no information survives of the migration of the Young party from Mt. Sterling. Young might well have struck out first on his own, with or without an advance party. Brown left no account of his family's experience, but he would later claim that among the household effects Young transported on the long, treacherous journey were forty-five to fifty slaves.[51] About all that is certain is that Brown and his family accounted for seven of them and that they left home early in spring. In those late pre-steamboat days, long journeys often involved travel by some combination of land and water. A water route comprising long stretches of the Ohio, Mississippi, and Missouri Rivers might have taken them part of the way, but they just as likely also traveled overland for much or most of the way. Just two or three years old at the time, Brown apparently retained no memory of the great expedition; in any event, the best he could have done was to stick close to his mother and siblings.

By June, the Young party reached its destination in the neighborhood of Charrette Village. The original hamlet of La Charrette was established as a French outpost dating back to the 1760s, before passing with the Missouri Territory through alternating periods of Spanish and

French administrative control until ceded to the United States in the Louisiana Purchase. It had been the westernmost village populated by Europeans when Lewis and Clark passed by with their Corps of Discovery in 1804, and it remained a sparsely populated settlement when John Young's party of Kentuckians arrived. They would have found old-time French settlers scattered around the area, but the new majority in the neighborhood and surrounding area was familiarly Kentuckian. Young's property bordered the farms of two Kentucky transplants, James Bryan and Flanders Callaway, several of the earliest English-speaking settlers in the region and both sons-in-law of Daniel Boone. Callaway was married to Boone's daughter Jemima, and the couple hosted Boone intermittently after the death of his wife Rebecca in 1813 until his own death in 1820. Young would almost immediately have made the acquaintance of Boone and various members of the Boone clan scattered around the area, and would have renewed acquaintance with various faces familiar to him from Kentucky. He would also have found comfortably familiar the local practices of slave-based agriculture, as these early transplants had been among the first to bring African slaves into a region previously habituated to Native American slavery.

No sooner did Young arrive than he ran an advertisement—phrased with a revealing touch of his sensibility—in the leading St. Louis newspaper announcing lots to be sold at auction in the new town of Marthasville he was laying out:

It is situated on a beautiful ridge, commanding an elegant view of the river, and containing two springs of as good and lasting water as ever ran from the earth. This town will be very suitably situated for the seat of justice, when St. Charles County is divided, as the country around it for many miles is thickly inhabited by industrious, wealthy persons, together with its being a very proper distance from St. Charles for a county line to run half way between these two places. The banks of the Missouri being so subject to wash away from the peculiar composition of the soil, and the omnific power of its current, nature seems particularly to have formed this beautiful eminence for a town. At and adjacent to this place there are inexhaustible timber for house and ship building. Charrette creek, a bold, lasting stream, runs within a mile of the town, on the west side, and on which there is a merchant and saw mill now building, and excellent seats for several others. On the east, about two miles, Duke creek is situated, affording several other seats for water works. The natural advantages of this place for a town, are so numerous that it would be tedious to enumerate them.[52]

The location, in short, was a settler's paradise: water and wood plentiful, soil fertile, location alluring but protected from river floods, lots presumably inexpensive—the future preordained by nature for growth and prosperity for white settlers. To promote communal comfort and sociability, Young announced he would operate a general store selling merchandise at prices 10 to 15 percent below the going rates in St. Louis and St. Charles, as well as a house of entertainment to function until he could find an entrepreneur willing to host a tavern. He met with measured success. A small number of lots were purchased at the September 1 auction, and the rudimentary village of Marthasville, the first town in what would become Warren County, subsequently began to take shape.

Young's advertisement notwithstanding, life on the Missouri frontier was arduous at best for everyone—Native American, European American, and African American—and sometimes brutal. As settlers made ever-deeper incursions into areas that had long been hunting grounds for local Native American tribes, tensions ran high, occasionally exploding in acts and cycles of violence. Young and his party would have heard enough about the area's recent bloody history to know their neighborhood was not entirely safe for settlers. Just two years earlier, a Native American raiding party attacked the family of William Ramsey's son Robert at their home near Charrette Village. They killed Robert, his pregnant wife, and two or three of their children in what quickly became memorialized as Ramsey's Massacre. That attack, and others in the vicinity, kept settlers on edge for months. So the situation remained until June 1816, when a group of territorial leaders, including William Clark and Auguste Chouteau, who had established ties among the warring tribes, negotiated a treaty at Portage des Sioux in St. Charles County. The treaty ended the fighting, allowing the tribes to retain possession of their lands while securing the area for current and future white settlers.[53] Relations between the two peoples nevertheless continued to be tense.

Like many of his fellow American settlers, Young saw the local Native Americans primarily in negative terms—preferable in their absence. Whatever wariness he felt about their proximity to his land, his over-riding concern was the success of his enterprise. He promptly set his people to an operation that would require massive labor. Most of it was performed by slaves, who carried out the backbreaking work of clear-ing the land, building the infrastructure of the farm, and preparing the first crop. Young harbored large ambitions for his farm, which sat on the rich bottomland below the emerging village and was soon produc-ing tobacco, hemp, and wheat. As in Kentucky, he kept his distance, relying on an overseer to run the operation. Persistent, backbreaking labor yielded results. Two years after his arrival, serving as Marthasville's Fourth of July orator, he celebrated with his neighbors "a bountiful har-vest" on the occasion of the "American Jubilee."[54]

Once his farm was operational, he devoted his primary attention to his medical practice, which he pursued in a partnership with a younger local doctor whom he might first have trained: John Jones, the grandson-in-law of Daniel Boone. On one occasion that first year, a friend of Young's from Kentucky but resettled in St. Louis summoned him to town on an urgent medical matter. He wanted Young to attend to a seri-ously ill Baptist missionary who had recently arrived off the river with a lingering fever but feared treatment by a frontier quack. The missionary was John Mason Peck, a native of Litchfield, Connecticut (home of the Lyman Beecher family), who had been deputed to the frontier to spread the faith among the white heathen of Missouri and Illinois. A few years earlier, his itinerant preaching had taken him to the Charrette area home of Flanders Callaway, where he excitedly made the acquaintance of "the veritable Daniel Boone." Peck survived his illness to disseminate God's word energetically across the Western territories for many years, becom-ing one of the frontier's leading evangelists. In his old-age memoir, Peck recalled encountering not only Daniel Boone but also John Young, "a regularly educated physician" from Kentucky whom he remembered as having "planted himself in the present county of Warren, and located Marthasville."[55]

Although Young's medical practice was located squarely in the Marthasville area, most of his patients came from the surrounding region. Others were brought to him from boats plying the Missouri River, which transported not just passengers and cargo but also disease. Like many of his fellow frontiersmen, Young also pursued a variety of supplementary profit-making enterprises, including operating a mill and experimenting with a stud farm. A proud Kentuckian with an interest in equine blood lines, he initiated the latter operation in 1818, when he purchased an expensive stallion named Black Prince in exchange for four of his Marthasville lots.[56] When time permitted, he retired to the large library in his house, which he kept well stocked with works in theology, medicine, political science, and the belles lettres. He might even have tried his hand at poetry—if by "my poems" he referred in his will to his own compositions rather than printed books.[57] Living among less well bred men and women struggling to establish a foothold on the frontier, Young must have stood out as a man of uncommon learning for his training and education, and Sarah as a woman of high cultivation for her fancy piano. People came from miles around to seek them out—Young for his medical services, Sarah for the pleasure of hearing the only piano in the region; but some would not have left without getting a whiff of the Youngs' self-importance.[58] For Young's part, he had no reservations about his abilities and accomplishments. Beneath the false modesty of his 1818 public letter requesting support for his candidacy for the legislature lay the cocksure certitude of a man who believed it was his right and duty to serve the white community.[59] Meanwhile, the slaves back in Marthasville served him.

ELIZABETH AND HER CHILDREN would live uninterruptedly during the years 1817 to 1825 on Young's large farm in the vicinity of Marthasville. Brown recalled that the slave quarters were located in the back of the property at some distance from the big house and populated by about forty slaves—if even remotely accurate, an exceptionally large number for an early Missouri farm. The family occupied a small, spare cabin, a squat wooden structure consisting of a single room stocked with rudimentary furniture and no beds. Everyone slept on the earthen floor. Food and clothing were simple, coarse, and cheap. Days were organized around the seasonal agricultural clock: Elizabeth labored as a field slave six days a week from before dawn until dusk. Brown's siblings presumably performed chores in the quarters and on the farm meted out to them according to age and ability. While a small child, Brown would have been spared such responsibility for a time, but he would have known that his day was coming. When it did, though, it came with a difference.

The facts about Brown's boyhood years on the frontier are scarce. His autobiographical writings would be numerous—he could hardly start a book without prefacing it with a memoir—but they provide little account of his personal or family life before the move to St. Louis. As a subject slave boy within the confines of a farm, his life lacked numerous external points of reference (names, dates, places, stories) or a clearly developing plot. Nor did a life lived within the confines of hereditary slavery typically contain a destination or outlet beyond the mundane. Just the same, the few scattered details that emerge from his writings communicate the story of a strikingly precocious boy jolted into consciousness of his existence as a slave. That fall from innocence awaited all enslaved children, but Brown's situation was in certain ways distinctive. In all likelihood, his skin color and blood relationship to Young separated him tenuously from the condition of most other slaves on the farm. Two events in particular support this hypothesis; both removed him physically from the rest of his family, not to mention his peers. One was the directive from his master to come up to the big house to serve him as a medical assistant, performing mundane tasks around Young's office and helping to prepare ointments and pills. At the next stage of his life, by which time Young had moved to the St. Louis area, Brown would be given the additional responsibility of tending to slaves from neighboring farms for whom his master's attention was not warranted.

The other incident, in Brown's telling, was more life determining. When he was about six, the childless Sarah and John Young took into their home the motherless baby of Young's brother Benjamin. In the pattern of mutant twinning sometimes generated by the institution of slavery, that white child (also named William) and Brown engaged each other in a complicated relationship. It began when the younger William reached a stage of development requiring companionship. In a scene that Brown recounted ritualistically, Sarah Young summoned the slave candidates to parade by her in a contest of the fittest:

> We were all ordered to run, jump, wrestle, turn somersets, walk on our hands, and go through the various gymnastic exercises that the imagination of our brain could invent, or the strength and activity of our limbs could endure. The selection was to be an important one, both to the mistress and the slave. Whoever should gain the place was in the future to become a house servant; the ash-cake thrown aside, that unmentionable garment that buttons around the neck, which we all wore, and nothing else, was to give way to the whole suit of tow linen. Every one of us joined heartily in the contest, while old mistress sat on the piazza, watching our every movement—some fifteen of us, each dressed in his one garment, sometimes standing on our heads with feet in the air—still the lady looked on. With me it seemed a matter of life and death; for, being blood kin to master, I felt that I had more at stake than my companions. At last the choice was made, and I was told to step aside as the "lucky boy," which order I obeyed with an alacrity seldom surpassed.

That evening, the older William was "scraped, scrubbed, washed, and dried" and the next day given a new suit of clothes and sent up to the big house. But first, as he tells the story, he received his mother's blessing: "My mother, one of the best of mothers, placed her hands on my head, and, with tears in her eyes, said, 'I knowed you was born for good luck, for a fortune-teller told me so when you was a baby layin' in your little sugar trough. Go up to de great house where you belong.'" That benedictory laying-on of hands and speech recorded in dialect are the most vivid, authentic portrayal Brown ever gave of his self-sacrificing mother as she actually acted and spoke, and they lead in directly to his new mistress's threatening malediction: "'I give your young master over to you,' said she, 'and if you let him hurt himself, I'll pull your ears; if you let him cry, I'll pull your ears; if he wants any thing, and you don't give it to him, I'll pull your ears; when he goes to sleep, if you let him wake before it is time, I'll pull your ears.'"[60]

If Brown ever formed a friendship with "the boy," as he referred to him, he was not telling. The only emotion he ever communicated was resentment. Two boys named William in his household proved one too many for Young, who unilaterally renamed the slave boy Sandford (or, familiarly, Sandy), a name the ex-William despised and shucked off the moment he escaped, but not before suffering whippings for expressing his bitter displeasure. The ex-William experienced the forced name change—then and there—as a violation of his personhood, as he had not yet learned that he had no personhood to lose. But the possibility exists that the older boy's resentment of the younger boy, who he would have known was actually his relative, came more tangled with other emotions—not the least envy—than he stated. Young raised the younger William as a foster son, schooling him in his library and, in time, preparing him for college. To ensure that his nephew would obtain knowledge of the "arts and sciences" suitable for a Southern gentleman, he bequeathed him tuition money and his "Literary Books."[61] It is not hard to imagine a recurring scenario of the younger boy being admitted to the library and the elder one sent away. In a variation on tales told in sundry stories of Southern life, such as Mark Twain's *Pudd'nhead Wilson*, this was one white boy who kept the most elementary secrets of the library's contents a mystery to his black companion. While the younger William received the Young legacy of letters and literature, eventually attending the Presbyterian college of his uncle's choice, the older one failed to gain admittance to knowledge of the ABCs.[62] Even as a boy he knew his deprivation and resented it keenly.

The slave boy's relatively privileged situation with the Young family removed him to a degree socially as well as physically from family and fellow slaves down in the quarters. It must have earned him and his mother some resentment from their fellows. It must also at times have offended his siblings, who with the exception of sister Elizabeth get only glancing regard in his *Narrative*. The mark of his difference was plain to all, white and black, family and outsiders. On the other hand, his new status was only temporary, reversible at a moment's call, and it left him missing the easy familiarity with family and friends he had known in the slave quarters. He still had friends among them, although no names have survived. One playmate about whom he later wrote was a girl, probably more or less his age, with whom he shared untroubled hours running around the grounds and meadows. Serendipity would reunite them thirty-odd years later during his 1861 speaking tour among African Canadians, many of them former Southern slaves now concentrated in first-generation settlements across southern Ontario. Sitting in that old friend's parlor with her youngest child perched on his lap, Brown passed hours in conversation, reminiscing about the life left behind on the Young farm in Marthasville. Letting their minds drift back over their shared past, they conjured a remote world of memories back into existence: the old familiar faces of their enslaved families and friends, amusing incidents on the farm, the pious exchanges between their mistress and the mean-tempered Reverend Pinchen who used to pinch their ears, and the "little family quarrels between old master and mistress." To the amusement of his hostess, Brown could still hear Sarah Scott Young's voice clearly enough to mimic its whinny petulance.[63]

The forced name change was traumatic. So was his growing separation from his mother, to whom he had been tightly—almost umbilically—connected through early childhood. He was in fact a mama's boy his entire life. The birth bond was reciprocal. He was her youngest and her chosen—if, as seems likely, the blessing she had invoked on his head replicated her words and sentiment rather than his retrospective self-elevation. And she provided his grounding in a shifting, dangerous world. Whatever security he felt as a small boy from her presence, however, diminished over time as he learned one of his most unsettling lessons—his mother's

defenselessness. If as a matter of course he witnessed her daily humiliation on the farm, one particular scene became fixed in his memory. One
morning during his boyhood, Elizabeth failed to arrive punctually at the
field and summarily received the common punishment: a whipping at the
hand of the overseer, Grove Cook. The adult son depicted the scene prominently in the opening chapter of his *Narrative,* where he pictures himself
as a small boy overhearing his mother's screams from the safety of the
cabin. In composing it, he echoed the analogous scene in the *Narrative of
the Life of Frederick Douglass,* which records his horrified witnessing of his
Aunt Hester's whipping, down to the drops of blood and dabs of gore.[64]
A more understated first-person narrator than Douglass, Brown, by contrast, presents his mother's punishment as overheard from the distance of
his cabin, where his position as a house servant purchased him a little extra
sleep time. The anguished tone of his mother's voice, he recalled, drew
him to the door, but no closer. More telling yet, he further distanced her
by recording her agitated pleas impersonally: "'Oh! pray—Oh! pray—
Oh! pray'—these are generally the words of slaves, when imploring mercy
at the hands of their oppressors."[65]

Brown rarely told a story without at least a single retelling; this scene
is no exception. When it was reprised in 1856, the ostensible teller was
sixteen-year-old Josephine Brown in her published biography of her
father. Josephine, who grew up free in the North, never set eyes on her
paternal grandmother and knew virtually nothing about her father's
childhood except what she had read or heard directly from his mouth.
In her account, which depended directly or indirectly on her father's, the
boy was physically present, a witness to the scene, but impotent to intervene. If this time his concluding words get us closer to his mother, they
still attach more directly to him than to her: "What could be more heart-
rending than to see a dear and beloved one abused without being able to
give her the slightest aid?"[66] Both versions leave Elizabeth a spectral figure
beyond the reach of her descendants. What may be more telling, they also
leave the little boy powerless to intervene. The quick-witted, smooth-
tongued adult ready with words for every situation would relive this
moment repeatedly but never find a way to talk away his basic impotence.

During his final years on the Marthasville farm, Brown grew into early adolescence, a tall but slight figure. Very near the end of this period, he claimed in his *Narrative,* he was removed from the big house and set to work for the first time in the fields. He disliked the hard manual labor, for which he lacked strength or skill. He had good reason as well to fear his exposure in the open air, where he knew the overseer was waiting with a hardened eye and quick whip to wield on an ex–house slave nicknamed "the white nigger" on the farm.[67] Indeed, by the mid-1820s, slavery had already left lasting marks on the youngster's flesh and spirit.

In the next phase of life, as a free adult, Brown would travel and read widely, compiling a remarkably comprehensive knowledge of United States, African, and general world history, geography, literature, and politics. But how much (or how little) did he know about his surroundings during his years as a slave boy in Marthasville? Did he ever set eyes on his supposed maternal grandfather? How much did he then know or understand about the looming political issues of the day, most particularly slavery, which would determine the future character and status of the Missouri Territory? How much did he know about Dr. Young's professional tribulations? Not long after they arrived, a former patient impugned Young's medical reputation in the pages of the leading territorial newspaper, a potentially damaging public attack requiring a quick, concerted counterattack by Young's friends. How much did Brown know about Young's legal entanglements? Did he know that Young was sued by the state of Missouri in 1821 for contractual failure to build a bridge on the road connecting the town of St. Charles to Marthasville? That failure elicited repeated complaints from settlers who could not conveniently get their animals across the creek that bisected that main road. Did he know that Benjamin Young, who had joined his brother in Marthasville in 1819, shortly afterward lost two runaway slaves, one carrying a gun, headed (he guessed) toward Illinois or Indiana?[68]

The most plausible answer to the overarching question of Brown's general awareness would be that at all times during these years he knew relatively little about the larger world—nearly as little as the Youngs could impose on him and his caste. But slaves always knew more than their masters allowed, and, given his intelligence and status as a house servant, Brown undoubtedly assimilated more information and gained sharper insight that most. On one occasion, he told an audience how as a child he had hidden behind a curtain to foil Sarah Young's attempts to keep secrets from her domestic slaves. That particular story was presumably apocryphal—he told it to a large assembly of Boston's black community on New Year's Day, 1863, as it anxiously awaited telegraphic delivery of Lincoln's Emancipation Proclamation—but its underlying point was true enough.[69] He knew, for instance, that the frequently absent Young, whom Brown derided as "a political demagogue," had been elected to and served in the Missouri General Assembly in 1820–21.[70] That body met in tense assembly in the Missouri Hotel in St. Louis in September to debate the terms on which the Missouri Territory would petition Congress for admission to the Union. Young had already announced his views to the public on the central question of the future state's basis as slave or free; his constituents could trust he was a firm proslavery man who "opposed[d] any plan of emancipation whatsoever."[71] Those discussions had sweeping life-determining consequences for the dozens of people Young held in servitude back in Marthasville, as their master joined the side of the majority proslavery element within the legislature. Local newspapers were of course filled with coverage of the momentous debates in St. Louis and Washington, and so were polite parlors across the territory. But did word filter down to the slave quarters?

Brown did not yet have a formal vocabulary to describe what he was seeing, but he had John and Sarah Young fixed clearly in his mind as religious and social hypocrites. He watched with wide-eyed fascination as they invited itinerant ministers to their house, enforced Sabbath observance on the farm, never failed to fill their pew at church, yet behaved "unchristianly" to each other, their neighbors, and especially their slaves. He observed with amusement the discrepancy between their professed adherence to a code of "honor" and the pettiness of their daily conduct. He took pleasure in sharing these impressions with his family and friends. The eyes and ears of the slave community implanted within the big house, he played communal spy, conveying stories back to the quarters that contributed to the general merriment at the Youngs' expense. The tenor of those reports can be surmised from one especially nasty story about the Youngs that passed down into local lore before being recorded in a nineteenth-century history of Missouri. An uncultivated legislative colleague accepted Young's invitation to come down from the state capital in St. Charles to Marthasville to hear the fabled piano and, mistaking the bedstead for the piano, asked Sarah "to perform on that instrument."[72] The local historians meant the story to come at the legislator's expense, but slaves in the quarters would have reveled in any story that deflated their mistress's hauteur. Sandy, who detested his "peevish" mistress, would certainly have seen it that way. Years later, Brown would skewer the Youngs' false airs and unscrupulous conduct in his historic play *The Escape; or, A Leap for Freedom* (1858), which he performed as a one-man show before thousands and thousands of people across the Northern states.

One can finally only guess what a perceptive but illiterate enslaved boy like Brown grew to understand about his surroundings and the people controlling his destiny. One does not have to guess, however, about the state of his mind once Young relocated his household from Marthasville to St. Louis. From that moment, the confines of the farm opened up onto vistas containing long sweeps along the Mississippi and Missouri Rivers. The expansion of his personal horizons, it turned out, corresponded to those of the American public, which took heightened interest in the vast American hinterland as the nation embarked on a course of manifest destiny. Published accounts of the Western expedition of Zebulon Pike, embarking from La Charrette down the Santa Fe Trail to the Southwest, and of Lewis and Clark across the Northern territories to the Pacific Northwest, stoked that interest; and widely circulating accounts of the legendary Boone, Davy Crockett, Mike Fink, and other Western heroes gave it a colorful vitality with mass appeal. So, over the course of the next generation, did a corresponding visual art of the trans–Mississippi River basin, painted by the likes of Brown's fellow Missourian George Caleb Bingham and the extravagantly successful artist/entrepreneur John Banvard, whose "three mile" panoramic painting of the Mississippi River brought him fame and fortune. Brown saw Banvard's painting exhibited in Boston in 1847 and was so provoked by what he considered its whitewashed representation of life in the Mississippi Valley that he felt compelled to respond with his own "original panoramic views." By the time he did, he was no longer the slave boy Sandy, but a new man with a new name and a broadened perspective on the world.

2

Down the River, Up the River

Brown lived in St. Louis for seven years (1826–33) at a relatively early stage in its growth into a major Western city. It had come into national existence only recently. Founded in 1764 as a trading post by the French and bandied between the French and Spanish colonial empires, it entered the American union in 1803 as part of Thomas Jefferson's purchase of the Louisiana Territory from a cash-starved Napoleon, who was willing to cede land on a distant continent to gain it closer to home. New Orleans was a crucial component of the transaction, St. Louis a relatively minor one. But the senior officer dispatched by Jefferson to oversee the territorial transfer from French to American control foresaw the town's great potential, reporting in 1804 that it was situated in "a position where the trade of the Missouri, Mississippi, and other rivers, was likely to center."[1]

Radiating from a small encampment established by Auguste Chouteau and Pierre Laclède on a bluff overlooking the western shore of the Mississippi River, the outpost was soon designated the administrative capital of Upper Louisiana. Over the next forty years, it grew exponentially, if in fits and starts. From its earliest years, its trade was based primarily on furs. French fur traders tracked far and wide into the wilderness during the late eighteenth century, trafficking extensively with

Native American nations spread out across the Louisiana, Illinois, and Western territories. These fur-trading operations gradually extended deep into the Southwest to Santa Fe and across the Northwest to the Pacific Ocean. By that time, the original French Creole town of St. Louis was administratively American, and Lewis and Clark had charted the way toward extension of the new nation's reach to the Pacific. The town's great strategic potential became clear to all on August 2, 1817, when the *Zebulon M. Pike* steamed upstream from Louisville and, cheered on by a large crowd gathered at the wharf, docked at the bottom of Market Street. The leading historian of St. Louis has called the arrival of this primitive vessel, which had to be assisted into port with poles, "a harbinger of the future."[2] A few years later, the Western chronicler Henry Rowe Schoolcraft foresaw St. Louis as a "seat of empire for the vast basin of land, situated between the Alleghany [*sic*] and the Rocky Mountains on the east and west, and between the northern Lakes and the Gulph [*sic*] of Mexico on the north and south."[3]

That imperial vision of St. Louis might then have had little direct bearing on the members of Elizabeth's enslaved family, which preceded the *Zebulon M. Pike* to Missouri by several months. But once Dr. Young moved his home base from Marthasville to St. Louis and assigned the adolescent Sandy to service on a Mississippi River steamboat, his awakening life would connect to the life of the river in a continuum whose outlet no one could then have predicted.

A VIVID PICTURE of this transitional St. Louis comes from the unpublished diary of James Essex, a successful antebellum era St. Louis bookseller who recorded his impressions of the old town he first entered as a teenager in 1825.[4] He had left his family home in Tennessee to seek his fortune in St. Louis, following in the footsteps of his older brother and sister. Crossing the Mississippi from the Illinois shore on Samuel Wiggins's ferry, he landed at the wharf on Market Street and walked up the unnumbered street, his saddlebag slung over his shoulder, looking for his siblings' bookstore. He boarded with them while he learned the bookselling and binding business. That city of his initial acquaintance, he noted in his diary, still had many French and some Spanish residents, but nearly everyone spoke English. Right at the center of what the visiting Charles Dickens referred to as late as 1842 as "the old French portion of the town" stood the Auguste Chouteau estate, and behind it Chouteau Pond.[5] They remained landmarks to the city's residents well into the American period. The Chouteau mansion, which occupied the center of the square on Main Street extending from Market to Walnut and back to Second Street, was a two-story structure ringed by verandas and surrounded by a high brick wall that enclosed its garden and fruit trees. Over the years, it hosted many distinguished guests, none perhaps more influential in determining its future than Lewis and Clark on the eve of their expedition.[6] Across the square stood the expansive house of Auguste's brother Pierre, also a leading figure in commercial and civic affairs.

Outside the French sector, Essex witnessed a fast-Americanizing city expanding to the north, west, and south. He quickly became part of it. By the early thirties, he had established himself on the corner of Main and Locust Streets as a bookseller and binder, selling a wide array of books, periodicals, and stationery from his store while also operating a full-service bindery. His stock consisted of local products and a fast-growing array of publications coming off presses all across the country, including Boston, Hartford, New York, Philadelphia, Baltimore, Richmond, Pittsburgh, Louisville, Cincinnati, and New Orleans. Shoppers could find in his store leading national periodicals, such as the *North American Review* from Boston, the *Knickerbocker Magazine* from New York, and the *Western Monthly Magazine* from Cincinnati, as well as the latest works of such popular American writers as Washington Irving and James Fenimore Cooper. But most of his stock consisted of the standard works of the day: schoolbooks, Bibles, almanacs, manuals, popular and imported novels, blank books, and stationery, along with a smattering of works from the higher professions. Some of his stock was printed locally, but the vast majority, as with other manufactured goods, came from distant locales via the rivers.

The boomtown Essex knew still retained traces of its rural origins.

A country boy himself, he enjoyed hunting and fishing just outside the expanding city center. His frequent companion was Thomas Cohen, a watchmaker and alderman who was also his former teacher in Methodist religious school. They combed the surrounding woods and fields for game—shooting deer, rabbits, quail, squirrels, and wild ducks. Essex also found the fishing good; catfish and bass abounded in Chouteau Pond and nearby lakes. In season, he routinely rose before dawn and went fishing on Rock Spring Pond with Cohen and their mutual friend Samuel Willi, another member of the young city's emerging middle class, returning home in time to be at work by 8:00 a.m.

Once he took over the family bookstore and amassed some savings, Essex purchased a residential lot on the north side of Franklin Street from John O'Fallon, one of the city's largest landowners.[7] With slaves inherited from his father and his business expanding, he was able to live in some comfort. Like many residents of St. Louis, Essex bought his bread from the well-known baker Daniel Page, who in Essex's estimation grew wealthy as a result of his "industry, economy, and perseverance." In 1829, Page became the city's second mayor, although it was not as a civic leader but as a slave master that Brown witnessed him chasing a male slave around his property with a whip.[8] In a small city characterized through the 1830s by tightly overlapping social networks of whites, Creoles, and blacks, Cohen, Willi, O'Fallon, and Page would all have connections directly with John Young and directly or indirectly with the future William Wells Brown. So did a younger generation of Chouteau descendants, whose family name (usually in the writing of Pierre's son Henry, the court clerk) appeared on various Young estate documents passing through St. Louis Circuit Court. One was Young's will, which spelled out a final dispensation for one of Brown's brothers.

Essex lived to see the rise of a modern commercial city, but one early building in particular caught his eye. That was the local courthouse, whose first structure was erected shortly after he arrived on land deeded to the municipality by city leaders Auguste Chouteau and Jean-Baptiste Charles Lucas. A bustling American city sorely needed such a facility to adjudicate its burgeoning affairs. Whereas lawyers had been viewed as a nuisance in the tightly regulated French municipality, they were regarded as a necessity in the rambunctious center of American enterprise. Of immediate concern were property rights. Lax compliance with Spanish and French registration requirements was so common that nearly all land titles were imperfect at the time of the Louisiana Purchase. Conversion of units of measure—French *arpents* to American acres, and French elongated tracts to American rectangular parcels—further complicated the smooth transfer of property.[9] Early nineteenth-century courts also handled a growing volume of other concerns requiring adjudication: general commercial conflicts, criminal cases (violent crime in particular increased exponentially after the American takeover), and, of course, slavery-related disputes. If the tie between a municipal courthouse and the institution of slavery was tight in all slaveholding regions, it was especially so in freewheeling St. Louis, where land, slaves, and all other kinds of property traded hands routinely, often with minimal regard for legality.

The growing volume of law cases necessitated by the late 1830s the construction of a larger structure on the same site. Over the next few decades, that handsome Greek Revival building grew into what is today the city's landmark historic structure, the Old Courthouse. That building's link to slavery was unusually direct: Right up to the outbreak of the Civil War, the city held public auctions of slaves from bankrupt or intestate estates on or near its eastern stairs. One of those numerous estates would be Sarah Young's, which the probate court ordered in 1846 to produce four slaves for auction from the courthouse steps.[10] The public sale of Robert, Jane, Sophonia, and Charles—each knocked off to a different master—took place between the hours of ten and two on October 21, earning the estate $1,460 to help defray its obligations.[11] That same day, while people with whom the enslaved Sandy had once lived were being disposed at auction, William Wells Brown was in upstate New York presiding over a meeting debating the merits of equal suffrage for African American males.[12] Slave sales from the courthouse steps continued even after the outbreak of the Civil War, though by then they were running up against a growing wave of public disfavor. The symbolic last sale of slaves was memorable enough to receive a harsh commemoration in the now-well-known painting of that name by Thomas S. Noble, a Kentuckian by birth and Confederate by choice who came to see the emotional devastation that slavery had wrought on black families.[13]

The main business of overseeing the institution of slavery took place inside the city's courthouse: disputes over contracts, routine matters of treatment and provision, and disposition of slaves in wills. More challenging to the system were the 301 freedom suits brought by slaves asserting their right to emancipation, culminating in Dred and Harriet Scott's in 1846. Among these were three from the Young estate, although none involved members of Brown's family. In all likelihood, none of Brown's relatives ever entered that building in any form except as a name on a document. Brown himself is a case in point. His fate was adjudicated there, though on a different basis from most cases. One day in April 1854, his final master entered the Old Courthouse to swear out manumission papers for his long gone but legally still reclaimable property, Sandford Higgins, at the time residing in London. The man who emerged from that transaction as the self-possessed William Wells Brown would see the Old Courthouse only once. When he returned to the city for a short visit in 1869, it is hard to imagine he did not enter the imposing building and conduct a self-guided tour.

At the time Young moved his family and slaves to St. Louis, the city's population was slightly more than 5,000; by 1834, it had grown to nearly 9,000. A writer for the *Missouri Republican* captured the city's demographic dynamic as well as its booster mentality: "Every steamboat that arrives at our wharves is crowded with passengers. Some of the Louisville boats [are] bringing three hundred at a time . . . many of these remain with us."[14] Although the main story of St. Louis was its increasingly pivotal role in the nation's westward expansion, a secondary narrative was one of escape, as from time to time a fugitive slave like Brown or Mark Twain's Nigger Jim lit out in the opposite direction.

BROWN'S SEVEN YEARS in early boomtown St. Louis were filled to overflowing with assigned tasks. Even the barest summary yields a lengthy list. By his account, he passed through the hands of three different slave masters; had his labor contracted by them to roughly a half-dozen steamboat captains; made multiple traverses of the Mississippi River downstream between St. Louis and New Orleans and upstream between St. Louis and Galena; traveled on the Missouri River westward to its then-navigable limits near Independence, Missouri; labored a hellish year as all-purpose servant to a slave trader preparing slaves for sale in markets along the lower Mississippi River; served as an all-purpose shop boy in the printing office of newspaper editor Elijah Lovejoy; did menial work among the large slave-labor force in the Missouri Hotel; and toiled for so unbearable a local tavern keeper that he ran away. That was only the first of two unsuccessful escapes he attempted during those years. Each time, he was brought back to town, verbally and/or physically punished, and returned to slavery. At the end of those seven turbulent teenage years, on January 1, 1834, he escaped to freedom.

So says Brown in his *Narrative*. Is his account accurate? Is it trustworthy? And is it sufficient? A single answer serves: partially, equivocally, problematically. Certainly the vast majority of the names, places, and events are verifiably authentic. The ships and captains he cites existed and plied the routes he mentions. The individuals in St. Louis he singles out for attention—such as his masters, employers, local businessmen, and civic leaders—show up nearly to a person in the historical record; and the events he ascribes to them are entirely plausible. Likewise, the various events he ascribes to his family and himself, right up to his escape, are not just credible but probable. A few, most importantly his final escape, are even documentable.

On the other hand, there are serious problems with Brown's reportage of these years. The most significant is that he gives no calendar dates for any of the events except his final escape. In the months following publication of his *Narrative*, he heard so much criticism about its lack of dates that he felt compelled to respond publicly: "It has been suggested that my narrative is somewhat deficient in dates. From my total want of education previous to my escape from slavery, I am unable to give them with much accuracy. The ignorance of the American slaves is, with rare exceptions, intense; and the slaveholders generally do their utmost to perpetuate this mental darkness. The perpetuation of slavery depends upon it."[15] His defense is credible; the overwhelming majority of slaves were partly or mostly innumerate. More to the point, he lacked knowledge of calendric time typical of a family that knew one another's birth dates, if at all, by agricultural season. (The closest guess he made about his own birth date was "about corn-cutting time," 1814.)[16] In telling the story of his early life as a narrative sequence, Brown was writing in 1847 at a double remove from his past—measured not just in specific months and years but also in the mode of their calculation. More problematically, he lists so many activities in so confined a time span that no mental effort can comfortably cram them all within the likely period of years.

In addition, a discerning reader needs to attend not just to what Brown says but also to what he does *not* say. This cautionary principle pertains to discussion of the hundreds of ex-slave narratives, which attempt to contain years of experience within pamphlet or short-book covers while responding to tight generic conventions and strict personal and textual surveillance. A much smaller percentage of fugitives also practiced the art of reticence for tactical reasons, keeping secret any information, such as escape routes and identities of "conspirators," whose revelation might aid defenders of slavery. Brown's was an extreme instance. Although he faced the normal generic expectations, he was writing from a position of extraordinarily rich observation and, quite possibly, extraordinary delicacy. Thus, a searching biographical account of his years in St. Louis must be the account not only of what he says he did, his facts closely sifted and rigorously scrutinized against external sources, but also of what he omits and why he chose a tactic of selective silence. The overriding reason is clear: He was writing a polemic against the institution of slavery, not simply or exclusively a personal memoir. Given such reticence, the underlying reasons and behind-the-scenes behavior require special scrutiny. So does the cumulative trauma of seven years of bonded servitude lived under conditions of unending trial by fire.

DR. YOUNG'S MOVE to St. Louis continued the restless pattern of itinerancy that characterized his life to the end. Whether motivated by economic problems or failing health, he began gradually in the mid and late 1820s to sell off most of his holdings in Marthasville and to buy land in and around St. Louis. In time, he set up a large household in town, as well as a farm in St. Louis County about three miles to the northwest. Precise dating is difficult. The move definitely did not take place before 1825, at which time Young was reported to be teaming with prominent landowner John O'Fallon in organizing a Bible society in St. Charles County.[17] He must already have established a residence in the city no later than that summer, however, when he was attempting to use his influence, despite health problems, to attract a minister from his Cumberland Presbyterian denomination to move from Kentucky to St. Louis.[18] His health was still not good the next summer, when a fellow Presbyterian from St. Louis, Stephen Hempstead, noted in his diary, "I visited Dr. Young who is sick."[19] In early 1827, William Carr Lane, a prominent St. Louis physician and the city's first mayor, who attended professionally to both John and Sarah Young, noted in a letter to his wife, "Old Dr. Young will decamp in the spring"—though from where to where is unspecified and open to interpretation.[20] No later than February 1827, Young was in possession of a lot between Second and Third Streets, one of the earliest settled sections of town and perhaps the site of his (and probably Brown's) first residence in town.[21] Until his final departure from the St. Louis area in December 1832, Young would continue his customary pattern of alternating town and country living, residing primarily in town for the first portion of the period and in the country for the remainder.

Brown's family must have moved to St. Louis along with their masters sometime in 1825 or 1826. Shortly thereafter, Young dispersed Brown's mother and siblings to work for him and Sarah in town or for local residents as contract laborers. That initial degree of displacement was but a prelude to the family's permanent division, as Young's worsening finances caused him to begin selling slaves. The adolescent Brown presumably wound up first as a domestic in the Youngs' fine city residence, where he performed menial services around the house and resumed his service to Young's medical practice. The duration of that service was limited, not lasting beyond late 1827. By that date, Young was once again on the move.

This time, the course of his wanderlust led up the Mississippi River to Galena, Illinois. Lead had recently been discovered in the surrounding hills, and the largest mining craze to date in American history was transforming Galena into a boomtown. It also turned the town into a familiar reference term in nineteenth-century American vernacular. Herman Melville, for instance, drew on it in characterizing the deep thinking of men like Ralph Waldo Emerson: "Any fish can swim near the surface, but it takes a great whale to go down stairs five miles or more; & if he dont attain the bottom, why, all the lead in Galena can't fashion the plumet that will.[22] Once steam navigation reached Galena in 1824, the town became a vital transit point for the transportation of lead ore to points south and east.

Hoping to profit from the latest outcropping of opportunity, Young set up a new household in Galena no later than the fall of 1827, while retaining his holdings in St. Louis. He undoubtedly knew the risks. Reports of fever from the Galena region were commonplace, and part of his medical practice consisted in treating patients passing through St. Louis via boats from all points, including the "Fever River" area surrounding Galena.[23] Sarah accompanied him, and the couple took along several of their female slaves to attend to their needs. Besides risking their health, the Youngs were also risking their property, since in transporting slaves over the river to a free state they were making the common slaveholders' gamble that their slaves would neither flee nor take shelter under the provisions of an 1824 Missouri statute. The Youngs had a copy of the 1824 Missouri statute book in their library but would hardly have needed to consult it over what was a matter of general knowledge: Slaves taken to a free state for an extended period of time had the right to sue for freedom.[24] One slave whom the Youngs did not choose to take—or perhaps whom they chose not to take—was Brown, whose loyalty might have been in question. But the identities of at least several of the chosen slaves are known. The most immediately relevant one was the previously mentioned house servant Dolly, who had been owned by Young for a considerable period—going back beyond Marthasville to Kentucky, and by his first wife's family back in Virginia. Indeed, it is due to Dolly that this episode in Young's life—and, possibly, in Brown's—has come to light.

After residing in Illinois with John and Sarah Young for approximately six months, from fall 1827 through late winter 1828, she upset their complacent calculations by filing a freedom suit against Young, heard in the March and July 1828 terms of St. Louis Circuit Court. Like all or nearly all of the Young slaves, she was illiterate, so the wording of the complaint was that of her court-appointed attorneys, who employed standard legal terminology in charging that Young "with great force and violence took and conveyed the said Dolly to fever river in the North Western Territory [Illinois] and then and there imprisoned the said Dolly and kept and detained her in prison . . . for the space of six months . . . contrary to the laws of the said North Western Territory."[25] Her suit was the first of three instituted against the Young family by their slaves—the others were against brother Aaron Young and the estate of Sarah—over the next fifteen years. Dolly was the only one of those slaves to lose her case. The consequence was a lifetime of slavery; she was still part of the Young estate when Sarah died in 1840.

What do these freedom suits have to do with Brown? According to his various accounts, nothing. He devotes not a single word to them in his *Narrative* or in subsequent memoirs. It is certain, however, that he knew Dolly well, since they lived on the same farm for most and possibly all of his early life. Moreover, she had been the nursemaid to young William during the same period Brown served as his guardian playmate.[26] During Brown's 1861 reunion in Ontario with his childhood friend from Marthasville, the old friends recalled the names of long-lost fellow slaves from the distant past, including "Aunt Dolly."[27] More to the point, he was well aware of Dolly's circumstances. It is likely that Brown had her specifically in mind when he wrote the subplot for his pioneering play *The Escape*, whose central character, a plantation owner and physician modeled on Young, kidnaps an attractive young slave woman and imprisons her on an outlying farm. Brown pursued the situation a good deal further by grafting onto his story a sexual-assault theme probably not drawn from Young's treatment of Dolly, who was older than Brown's mother. He would not have lacked for real-life originals; he had a large cast of male offenders from which to draw, starting with his own father.

The most immediate question concerning Dolly is not whether but what and how Brown knew about the bold course of action on which she embarked in spring 1828. Sometime in late winter, she left the Youngs' Galena residence to return to St. Louis, presumably with the intent to challenge Young's mastery in court. She understood the peril of her situation and took no chances in anticipating Young's likely reaction. Her lawyers quickly petitioned the presiding judge for a writ of habeas corpus—quickly granted—to ensure her physical safety in St. Louis.[28] But how did she manage to get herself to St. Louis in the first place? One possibility is she stole herself away by steamboat, with or without assistance. Another is she simply accompanied Sarah Young back to town, perhaps because Sarah had taken ill in the well-named "fever river" climate of Galena.[29] Whatever Dolly's course of action, an intriguing fact about her suit is that one of the four witnesses called to testify on her behalf was a veteran steamboat pilot named Otis Reynolds.[30] Why did the prosecution summon Reynolds, whose testimony unfortunately went unrecorded or has gone missing? The court's initial difficulty in delivering him a summons confirms his usefulness to their case: His profession took him away for long stretches on the river. During one of his voyages in 1827–28, he must have witnessed Dolly either in the possession of the Youngs in Galena or as a passenger on a boat—no doubt his own—in transit to or from the town.

His role in the suit would have been to provide information indispensable to the success of a plaintiff's case: eyewitness testimony that the plaintiff did indeed reside in a free state and that the person levying the suit was indeed the selfsame "kidnapped" individual. In the case of another Young family slave, Martha Ann, who many years after the event pursued and eventually won a freedom suit against the executor of the Young estate, the presiding judge issued the following charge to the jury: "If the Jury find that Dr. Young while the owner of the plaintiff as a slave took her to Galena in the State of Illinois to reside and held her there in service, the plaintiff thereby became entitled to her freedom and the jury ought to find for the plaintiff." On the other hand, he further instructed them, "Before the Jury can find for the plaintiff in this case, they must be satisfied from the evidence that the plaintiff is the identical one represented in the petition as having been taken by Dr. Young from this State to Galena in the State of Illinois."[31] Whether he transported Dolly on his boat or simply witnessed her in Galena, Otis Reynolds was in a position to provide this crucial information.

The teenaged Brown was well acquainted with Reynolds. In his *Narrative*, he referred to him as "a good man," one of the very few whites he treated with anything other than outright contempt.[32] His relationship with Reynolds dated from the period of months he worked as a steward on the *Enterprise*, the steamboat Reynolds captained on the upper Mississippi River. Although he assigns no date to this episode in the *Narrative*, Brown placed it in the early period after his move to St. Louis—which, if correct, would tentatively date this service to the late 1820s. One possibility is that Brown was serving on the *Enterprise* when Dolly was en route to or from Galena. If so, he might even have been involved in abetting her escape (just as he would help fugitive slaves get across Lake Erie shortly after his own escape to Cleveland). A more likely interpretation is that he simply heard about Dolly's ploy after her return to St. Louis, whether from her or from loose talk in the black community of St. Louis. Either way, he was undoubtedly apprised of Dolly's bid for freedom and would have responded with visceral sympathy, since his own yearning to be free began early and grew more consuming by the year.

Brown had only brief experience of domestic slavery in St. Louis. Because Young, like many other St. Louis residents of his class, had a surplus of slaves for his domestic and agricultural needs, he frequently "rented" or "mortgaged" his superfluous "people" as circumstances required. Or he simply garnished whatever wages they might have earned when he authorized them to hire themselves out in town. This altered economic environment had an immediate impact on Brown's family. Elizabeth was sent off to domestic service in a local house or establishment, while some or probably most of his siblings were hired out to local masters. Such was also to be the basic pattern of Brown's St. Louis years. Only during the intervals between his longer contractual assignments did he work in Young's city and country residences or, for very brief interludes, in his fields.

Brown presents his teenage years as a time of more or less unrelieved oppression. On a basic level, his portrayal was indisputably accurate. Even free blacks found their movements and actions circumscribed; slaves all the more so, with the added risk of beatings or sale if they strayed outside of prescribed rules and regulations. That said, there were also interludes of relatively free movement and unguarded communication among African Americans in the ways and byways of the city and its environs. There was, in addition, a subterranean world of black social interactions, with a unique coded language and signs. Brown rarely reveals this world to his readers, but it protrudes from the surface of his text at odd moments. A particularly interesting one occurs when he describes his return to St. Louis in chains after his second unsuccessful escape attempt: "On the way thither, I saw several of my friends, who gave me a nod of recognition as I passed them."[33] Although largely papered over in the *Narrative*, there was a lot of head nodding and tongue wagging going on around him during his St. Louis years.

HIS FIRST ASSIGNMENT, around 1826 or 1827, was one of his worst. Young hired him out to a particularly nasty, violent tavern keeper whom Brown called Major Freeland, one of many white authority figures from these years whose given name he possibly never knew. If the adolescent learned anything from his months with Freeland, it was to keep his distance from the effects of excessive liquor, especially on hot-tempered men like his employer. Freeland was a brute to his employees but seems to have taken sadistic pleasure in singling out Brown for special attention, a reaction that Brown seems often to have elicited, for good or bad, from his employers. Probably physically abused, Brown sought relief against Freeland from Young, but he miscalculated: Young cared about revenue, not fair treatment. Left unprotected, the adolescent Brown eventually fled to the woods outside of town in what sounds more like an act of desperation than a carefully planned escape. Instinct directed him toward the Young farm northwest of town, but he bypassed the farm due to his fear of the overseer. Instead he stayed in the woods a few more days, his direction uncertain. But he did not get very far before the bloodhounds of his master's friend Benjamin O'Fallon, brother of John, caught his scent and treed him. Tied, brought back to town, and incarcerated in the St. Louis jail, he was claimed by Freeland, who returned him to his quarters. He then led Brown out back of the tavern, tied him up in the smokehouse, and performed his well-practiced punishment: a severe whipping, followed for good measure by—Freeland's specialized form of torture—smoking in suffocating tobacco fumes.[34] Cured of nothing but his contempt for Freeland's savagery, and disillusioned by Young's apathy, Brown simply endured the remaining contractual time. His service ended only when Freeland's business failed a few months later.

Brown claims that he was next hired out to the captain of a Mississippi River steamboat. If so, that was the first of numerous terms of service that kept him employed on riverboats intermittently for much of this seven-year period. Looking back on these years of slave labor when he wrote his *Narrative*, he drew a broad distinction "between the work in a steamboat cabin and that in a corn-field."[35] Josiah Henson, the rumored original of Harriet Beecher Stowe's Uncle Tom, drew a similar distinction. A onetime Kentucky slave who escaped via Cincinnati in 1829 and later founded the Dawn Institute settlement for free blacks in Ontario, Canada, Henson remembered his time as a hand on the St. Louis–Galena route as a relatively "sunny spot" by contrast to the "painful" service he performed in a St. Louis hotel.[36] Brown, however, was a teenager, and the cumulative time he spent on the Mississippi and Missouri Rivers would prove to be a crucial component of his development into adulthood.

Author Lee Sandlin has richly evoked that early era by describing the nineteenth-century Mississippi River as a kind of composite artery, an ever-spreading body of water supplied by countless North American tributaries channeling their contents from points north, east, and west into one epic flow southward.[37] In its nineteenth-century heyday before the coming of the railroads, the great, amalgamated current of the Mississippi carried an astonishing wealth of goods down its central chute toward its main emporium at New Orleans. Millions upon millions of pounds of animals, produce, foodstuffs, raw materials, manufactured goods, printed products, and weapons coursed down its channel each year. So did multitudes of people, people of any and all sorts and configurations. Passengers on Mississippi River steamers routinely encountered planters, farmers, soldiers, families, migrants and immigrants, tourists, artists, fugitives, gamblers, prostitutes, servants, Native Americans (who sometimes tied their canoes to the stern), and—just about always—slaves, whether attached to individual masters or to one another in coffles. During nearly seven years spent on the river, Brown watched this ceaseless river traffic pass beneath his gaze. Eventually this current would course through his books, beginning with his *Narrative*.

As he quickly discovered, even a place of employment no wider than the space between deck railings on these fast-moving, steam-powered boats provided sharp relief from the cramped confines of life on a farm or in town—all the more so for a teenager with Brown's roving curiosity and ceaseless energy. Those years of river travel were to equip him with a breadth of insight into the trans-Mississippi region and the life of the black Mississippi that few ex-slave authors, and few Americans of any background, could match. The initial readers of his *Narrative* immediately perceived the novelty of an ex-slave whose experience spanned most of the Mississippi basin. Several particularly observant readers even compared his *Narrative* to *Robinson Crusoe*. From that point forward, Brown spent his life in proximity to water—the Missouri in Marthasville, the Mississippi in St. Louis, Lake Erie in Cleveland and Buffalo, the Atlantic Ocean in Boston, the Charles River in Cambridge, and the Thames in London.

Brown's years on the Mississippi took place when life on the interior waterways had barely passed beyond the frontier era, a dynamic period that became associated with such legendary figures as Mike Fink, river boatman; Mark Twain, cub pilot; and the hardy raftsmen who populate the paintings of George Caleb Bingham. Less visible in the collective imagination, then and now, have been the thousands of African Americans, slave and free, who staffed the riverboats as waiters, stewards, barbers, firemen, mechanics, and chambermaids. Historian Thomas C. Buchanan has aptly called his book on this long-neglected subject *Black Life on the Mississippi*, a twist on Twain's famous memoir of his years as a cub pilot on the Mississippi.[38] To emphasize the important role African American labor played in the commerce and transportation of the inland waterways, Buchanan opened his book provocatively by juxtaposing Twain's experience as a riverboat pilot and Brown's as a riverboat hand. Despite the clear role differential, ship practices resulted in no simple above-deck/below-deck dichotomy. Even servants like the teenaged Brown, laboring below the pilothouse, played a key role in the trans-Mississippi world of commerce, communications, and culture navigated by the steamboats. Their masters, captains, and onboard supervisors might not have admitted the fact publicly, but they could not have carried out their functions without command over black sweat and sinew.

The life of a hand on a Mississippi River steamboat was as close to a life of mobility as a slave's ever was on American soil. In mobility lay the prospect—or at least the lure—of freedom. Enslaved people came to associate waterways with release from bondage and, as Buchanan has noted, even salvation: "In slave spirituals like the 'Old Ship of Zion,' 'Deep River,' 'Down by the River Side,' and 'Roll, Jordan, Roll,' rivers and boats represented pathways to heaven."[39] During his years on the Mississippi, Brown would have heard and joined in the singing of these "sorrow songs," as W. E. B. Du Bois later characterized them. In maturity, he would collect hymns of slavery and freedom for communal singing, some of which he also performed. These songs had their printed counterparts in fugitive slave narratives, which likewise portrayed the life of the rivers and the magical ships that glided over them. Frederick Douglass memorably evoked the sails of "those beautiful vessels, robed in purest white" that haunted his vision of Chesapeake Bay from his enslaved position on the Eastern Shore.[40] Henry Bibb, who staged several escapes by river from slavery in Kentucky, reminisced about standing "upon the lofty banks of the Ohio River, gazing upon the splendid steamboats, wafting with all their magnificence up and down the river."[41] Such accounts expressed the yearning for freedom of many hundreds of thousands of people held in slavery. The daily experience of well-traveled slaves like Brown and Bibb, however, was that North American rivers flowed in mutually opposite directions: Boats that transported individual fugitive slaves up the river to freedom also carried multitudes of others down the river to irreversible bondage. The central fact of Brown's life on the Mississippi was that he precariously occupied both lanes of the two-way river traffic.

Brown's mobility was of two sorts. One, as already described, was geographic; the other was social. During these seven years, Brown made a partial ascent through the ranks of black steamboat society. Among the many onboard roles the large steamboats required, he never served in the lowest: mechanic, stevedore, fireman, or chambermaid. He presumably began as a waiter inside the cabins but quickly rose to the more respected position of steward. Though still inferior in legal status to free blacks and all whites, he earned a position of moderate responsibility. He wore a uniform, interacted with passengers, and had duties that carried over to land. In this sense, his service on board the ships corresponded to his service in St. Louis. Whether on water or land, obvious ability, light skin, and good fortune combined to position him relatively high within the slave hierarchy, just as it had in Marthasville.

His vertical mobility, however, was tightly capped; as a slave, he could not rise to the level of even the lowliest free black. Even in adolescence, Brown carried himself with the heightened sensitivity to social status typical of someone vulnerable on multiple fronts. He could sense black as well as white eyes all around him watching and monitoring, sometimes only to exclude. Some years after Brown's escape, the light-skinned, freeborn Cyprian Clamorgan wrote a vivid sketch of the free African American community of antebellum St. Louis that seemed to look right past slavery. Clamorgan was himself the descendant of a family whose crisscrossing racial history followed the meandering course of the Mississippi River as far back as their progenitor Jacques, a white French American adventurer on a grand scale.[42] Clamorgan cast a sharp eye on the color line, which he defined as "a line of division so faint that it can be traced only by the keen eye of prejudice—a line so dim indeed that, in many instances that might be named, the stream of African blood has been so diluted by mixture with Caucasian, that the most critical observer cannot detect it."[43] Clamorgan had little regard for slaves like Brown; his preoccupation was the local "colored aristocracy" of which he was a part. Most of its members lived and worked in the city, but at least four of the men he described were making their living on the river as stewards, where they worked side by side with slaves like Brown.

The fine shadings Clamorgan drew of the race-based color line accurately captured one aspect of Brown's doubly marginal status, but not another. Whereas his mixed-blood heritage gave him a particular status among fellow slaves, his classification as a slave located him on the opposite side of the St. Louis color line from freeborn blacks like the Clamorgan family, regardless of whether they were lighter or darker skinned than he. During his later years in St. Louis, Brown became well acquainted with Cyprian's sister-in-law Julia, a freeborn woman of color. Whatever the basis of their acquaintance, it was strong enough that he took pleasure in reestablishing it when he encountered her unexpectedly during the Civil War on a speaking tour in southern Ontario.[44] The old color line that had once divided them did not reach Canada, where they met on a wholly altered basis.

BROWN DEVOTED much of the middle section of his *Narrative* to a loose, free-flowing account of his service on at least half a dozen steamboats. The book's episodic structure corresponds to the checkered pattern of his labor on the rivers, when he worked for varying periods with one or another riverboat captain before being transferred to the next, each stint lasting a specified number of weeks or months—those assignments punctuated by periodic employment in St. Louis. Some jobs were more tolerable than others. But there was one extended period of service—a full calendar year he remembered as "the longest year I ever lived"—in which Brown worked continuously for a single employer, a hard-driving, implacable slave trader Brown referred to as James Walker. Brown had an extraordinarily retentive memory, but in this instance he was mistaken in identifying a man who resurfaced so frequently in his books and those of subsequent writers that he has gained notoriety in American history. The man was William Walker, the name under which he survives in the local court archive as defendant in no fewer than four of the city's 301 freedom suits.

The most consequential of those cases was *Rachel v. Walker*, a fairly typical freedom suit filed in St. Louis Circuit Court in November 1834.[45] Rachel was a roughly twenty-year-old woman (and mother of an infant born in a free state) whose life circumstances resembled not just Dolly's but also Dred Scott's—his so closely that it served his lawyers as a precedent in making their case for his freedom.[46] Rachel's master had taken her to live for a long period of time in Minnesota and Michigan, free states of the old Northwest Territory, before returning her to St. Louis and then selling her to another master. That person in turn sold her to Walker, a local slave trader who, according to Rachel's deposition, intended to take her "down the Mississippi River probably to New Orleans" for final sale—no more anticipating Rachel's preemptive act than John Young had Dolly's. Rachel pursued her case unrelentingly against Walker for several years, losing at the local court but eventually winning her freedom (and also her son's) by ruling of the Missouri Supreme Court. Her personal timing was fortunate; following the US Supreme Court's 1857 decision in the Dred Scott case, stripping all African Americans, free or enslaved, of any claim to citizenship, there would be no further basis for filing freedom suits before the Thirteenth Amendment abolished slavery in 1865.

Three or four years before Rachel took him to court, William Walker first laid eyes on Brown in the sleepy port of Hannibal, Missouri—town of Twain's blessed memory for *Tom Sawyer* and *Huckleberry Finn*. Brown was working as a steward on Otis Reynolds's steamboat when it made one of its usual downstream stops between Galena and St. Louis. Walker boarded the boat with a sizable coffle of slaves bound for Southern markets but would have had to switch boats at St. Louis, the transfer point for larger vessels headed to the deeper waters of the lower Mississippi.

Walker saw such potential value in the can-do competence of the young steward that he used the lag time between boats to ride out to see Young and inquire about his slave's availability. Young refused to sell Brown outright but agreed to rent him for a twelve-month period to run, as was customary, the calendar year. Just like that, Brown was soon heading down the river as Walker's right-hand assistant.

Brown recorded his time with Walker, a year in which they logged thousands of miles across the old Upper and Lower Louisiana Territory, as a year of hell. A onetime drayman, Walker had gradually worked his way up to the human flesh trade. As a rule, "soul drivers," as slaves labeled them, had little status among genteel whites. Good Southern society looked down on these traders in human flesh—all the more, perhaps, because their well-being depended on such people's services. Harriet Beecher Stowe's depiction of the vulgar slave trader Haley, whose entry into the Shelby family's plantation house to bargain over Uncle Tom registers as a social intrusion, accurately portrayed the prevailing sense of class inequality. John and Sarah Young would not have reacted any differently, nor does the fictional Gaines family in Brown's play *The Escape* at the entrance of the crude slave trader Walker into their fine home. The real-life Walker, as Brown rendered him in the *Narrative*, was if anything not just coarser but more dangerous than most of his peers. He violently separated infants from mothers, accosted attractive slave women, and sold his own mixed-race slave children and mistress down the river. Brown gave him no speaking role in the *Narrative*, but his characterization is so unremittingly harsh that it is not hard to sense the offensive quality of his voice, manner, and bearing.

Upstream Walker operated in the acquisitive mode, stopping to dicker at farms, villages, and towns wherever bargains were to be made. He pressed up the Missouri River to places far beyond Brown's known geography, buying up slaves all the way to the new capital of Jefferson City as well as into the interior of the state in pursuit of bodies. Downstream Walker turned to sales. Altogether that year, Brown would accompany Walker on three separate descents to New Orleans, each one yielding a large harvest as Walker stopped to deal slaves at prime slave markets that had sprung up along the river. The first trip was for Brown the most memorable, and not only because the shock of witnessing a slave trader in full operation registered fresh on a teenage conscience. While watching Walker dispose of enslaved men and women at intermediate markets in Mississippi, Brown secretly feared his own turn was coming as soon as they reached New Orleans—so little did he trust Young's or Walker's integrity.

As it turned out, Brown was relatively safe. The risks he ran during that trip and subsequent ones were more generally the normal ones all slaves faced in moving through their daily affairs. His lot was to witness—and, to a measured extent, to assist in—the sale of hundreds of slaves in Walker's possession. Brown served in constant attendance not just on Walker but also on Walker's growing population of slaves. He took the work achingly to heart, although it would have been even worse if he had had a previous acquaintance with any of the people placed under his supervision. That *did* happen, however, the following year. While working on the *Otto*, Brown spotted Walker taking down the river a man named Solomon he knew from St. Louis. On seeing Brown's friendly face, Solomon poured out his anguish at being separated from his wife and children, with no prospect of reunion. Brown knew him well enough to point out that this pious man, who had previously belonged to Dr. Young's brother Aaron, had attended the same church as his master.[47]

During one memorable march across central Missouri necessitated by their inability to find transportation by boat, Walker and Brown rode horses at the front and rear of the chained caravan on their way to Walker's farm north of St. Louis. That scene was so fixed in his mind that Brown included an engraving of it in the first illustrated edition of his *Narrative*. (Like the memory, that illustration trailed after him in subsequent works). His perch atop a horse signified his higher standing, but he grasped that even one false slip might land him in the middle of the captives he was overseeing. He also stood watch for many an hour over the chained slaves during the length of their transport. Slave escapes were such common occurrences on the river that one wonders how he would have reacted if any of Walker's captives had tried to flee. Suicides were also frequent, and that year one of Walker's captives, a woman distraught after being torn from her husband and children, leaped to her death in the Mississippi.

Once they headed downriver, Brown had a variety of roles on shipboard and on land to help ensure clear sailing and smooth transactions. Among his various duties, he remembered one as especially unsavory. Trained in the use of scissors, tweezers, razors, and blacking, he assisted Walker in preparing his slaves for market, making them look younger, nimbler, happier, and blacker in order to fetch higher prices. The goal was to turn real people with real ailments, to use the historian Walter Johnson's apt phrase, into "ideal slaves."[48] Brown played a further role yet in their transformation after they reached New Orleans. Once their jailer brought them out of the holding pens and into the yard for inspection, Brown later confessed, he "often set them to dancing when their cheeks were wet with tears."[49]

Slave trading, he observed, was a major operation. The collecting aspect of the work involved sweaty, hardscrabble hunting and gathering, as Walker went farm to farm and town to town, purchasing live souls by the unit of the individual, family, or group wherever supply was available. Once he had amassed the most profitable inventory permitted by conditions, he began the descent of the Mississippi with his cargo, stopping to sell at lively ports such as Rodney, Vicksburg, and Natchez en route to New Orleans. By the time Brown came into his service, Walker had worked out a routine. He would take rooms in a hotel close to the landing, put up his "merchandise" at a local facility such as a slave pen or some such enclosure large and secure enough to house and display them, and entertain potential buyers. He presumably handled the transactions personally in order to maximize profit, as well as possibly to dodge municipal regulations, although he could easily have found plenty of auctioneers ready to sell his slaves for a commission.

Partially lightened of his load, he arrived in New Orleans eager to sell off his remaining property and cash out. Here too he dispensed as many of his slaves privately, off the books, as he could. The remainder he sold en masse through Isaac L. McCoy, one of the city's most active auctioneers. McCoy operated seven days a week out of the Coffee Exchange

House, corner of Chartres and St. Charles, in the French Quarter near the river. He sold anything commercially movable: estates, steamboats, plantations, and slaves in any and all groupings. McCoy and his English- and French-speaking colleagues manned a last gathering point at the Mississippi River delta, through which the thousands of souls floated down the river or driven overland each year by traders like Walker passed through their hands toward final destinations. Brown probably did not actually witness those final sales, unless for some reason Walker commanded his assistance, but he had seen enough during that year on street corners and more fixed venues to be intimately familiar with the routine. Only with the conclusion of the last sale did the immediate horror of the experience fade into relief as their boat steamed northward. But not even safe arrival in St. Louis and the year's-end release from Walker could end the process, as the epic flow of human beings followed its inexorable course downstream the next year and the next.

If not then, in due course Brown would have internalized the haunting words of the Negro spiritual "Many Thousand Gone":

> *No more auction block for me*
> *No more, no more*
> *No more auction block for me*
> *Many thousand gone*

* * * *

> *No more children stole from me*
> *No more, no more*
> *No more children stole from me*
> *Many thousand gone*

* * * *

> *No more slavery chains for me*
> *No more, no more*
> *No more slavery chains for me*
> *Many thousand gone*

The song's meaning was all too personal for Brown. Just months after his release from Walker, two of those "many thousand gone" were his sister and his mother. Worse yet, for his mother's predicament, he of all people was indirectly responsible.

BROWN FOUND THE EXPERIENCE of working with Walker so repugnant that he implored Young after the first descent to end an arrangement that left him "heart-sick." Young, citing his contractual obligation, sent him back. Not until the end of the contractual year, sometime around Christmas, did Brown get his release. But even that year of lasting misery and accelerated maturation yielded Brown essential life lessons, the nearest approximation in his teens of Ishmael's "Yale College and . . . Harvard." Involved as the work was, it left him with more unassigned time and unsupervised movement than he had ever previously had. There are signs that Brown took advantage of his situation—this at a time when he was moving through a compressed adolescence into adulthood. Brown incorporated just a smattering of his countless experiences with Walker into his *Narrative*, but a close look at even a few of the particularly vivid stories gives some sense of the ways his teenaged body and mind got around on the Mississippi.

Walker routinely stopped for days at a time at river ports to conduct his business of buying and selling. While Walker's attention was turned to myriad details, Brown sometimes found opportunities to roam the wharves and streets. Once, in Natchez, supposedly posted as a lookout for the next steamer, he took the opportunity to search for an acquaintance from St. Louis, whose master had sold him to a Natchez merchant named Broadwell. Inquiring in Broadwell's store for his friend's whereabouts, Brown was informed: "They have got Lewis hanging between the heavens and the earth." Brown walked over to the warehouse to see for himself. Sure enough, he found Lewis tied to a crossbeam with his toes just reaching the floor, his punishment for having paid an unauthorized visit to his wife on an outlying farm one night after work. The conversation must have been intense, since Broadwell walked in and caught them completely by surprise. Agitated by what he took to be Brown's interference, he whacked him just over the eye with the tip of his whip (leaving a scar visible in the earliest known engraving of Brown). Broadwell would not have been the only slave owner who found Brown obtrusive, as Brown often pushed accepted limits in seeking out St. Louis acquaintances during his travels. Though generally silent about the fact, he was so frequently on the river that he must regularly have acted as a conduit passing greetings and news between family members and friends separated along the length of the Mississippi.

He likewise found time aboard ship to walk about, observe, and listen. The most revealing story he told in this regard was the tale of the beautiful quadroon Cynthia—"Poor Cynthia! I knew her well." Long before Brown read the "tragic mulatta" subplot in *Uncle Tom's Cabin* or created his own in *Clotel*, he was drawn to the figure of Cynthia. The unmarried Walker had purchased her in St. Louis with the initial intent of selling her in New Orleans, but, on closer consideration, he set her aside for personal use. On the first night on the river, he instructed Brown to find her a private compartment separate from the rest of the slaves. Brown knew exactly why. He did as he was instructed but also did more. After Walker entered the stateroom, Brown eavesdropped on the ensuing conversation. Cynthia, he reported, rejected Walker's "vile proposals." The next morning, she sought out Brown and confessed the terms of Walker's proposition: a life of comfort as his mistress or a life of toil in the deepest South. In confiding her dilemma to Brown, she presumably sought consolation. The ensuing part of her story, as Brown relates, was tragic. She eventually submitted to Walker, lived with him on his farm outside St. Louis, and bore him two children during Brown's residence in St. Louis. While living in the North, Brown heard—he does not state from what source—the final chapter of her story: She bore Walker two more children, and then he sold her and the children down the river, probably as a precaution, before marrying a white woman.[50]

Why did Cynthia confide in this slave and what did she expect from him? And what role, for his part, did the young Brown think he could play in her affairs by overhearing an intimate conversation and consoling her? Cynthia presumably was so desperate she would have welcomed the chance to unburden herself to any sympathetic ally, but perhaps she found in Brown a special quality. Other people in distress did. Over the course of time, many people unburdened themselves to this young man, whom they perceived to have a gift for listening and a capacity for empathy. Years later, he would say that the cumulative confidence fugitive slaves placed in him turned him into "the depository of their sufferings and wrongs."[51] At this time, his powerlessness would have been apparent to both Cynthia and him, but his lingering on the scene is curious. It is not out of the question that the adolescent slave took a slightly prurient interest in Walker's dealings with Cynthia.

An even more revealing scene took place in Vicksburg, according to the *Narrative*. Walker was using his hotel room to conduct business with potential buyers, tasking Brown to cater to their needs. On one occasion, Brown carelessly overfilled their wine glasses, causing at least one customer to spill some on his clothes. A quick glance at Walker's expression told him consequences would be coming. Sure enough, the next morning Walker sent him to the local jailer with a note and dollar. Brown suspected his motive but could not read the note, so he stopped a sailor and asked him to read its contents aloud. Already guessing it instructed that its bearer be whipped, a service routinely offered slaveholders by Southern jails, Brown schemed to trick an unwitting person into taking his punishment. He observed a number of people walking by, waiting until he found his look-alike, a free black man about his size who unwittingly accepted the note, dollar, and task. Brown even lingered to find out the results in order to know how to cover his deception with Walker.

BROWN'S VARIOUS STINTS on the Mississippi River were interrupted by one particularly memorable, if short-lived, assignment in St. Louis. Sometime before 1832, Young contracted Brown's labor to Elijah Lovejoy, the editor-publisher of the *St. Louis Times*.[52] Shortly after Brown worked for him, Lovejoy underwent a religious conversion that transformed his views of personal and social good. In 1832, he founded the *St Louis Observer* and, over the course of his five years of managing its pages, Lovejoy gradually drifted from a vague antislavery sentiment receptive to African colonization and repatriation to a tougher, take-no-prisoners abolitionism that antagonized and eventually infuriated much of the general populace of the slaveholding city. In 1835, he audaciously printed in the *Observer* the founding principles of the American Anti-Slavery Society, giving his explicit approval for all except immediate abolition of slavery and unconditional emancipation of all slaves.[53]

In due course, the people of St. Louis reacted to his editorial conduct by threatening to burn down his office. As his financial and moral supporters abandoned him, he felt compelled to relocate his operation to the Illinois side of the river.[54] The state of his affairs on free soil, however, went from bad to worse, as attacks repeatedly targeted the presses on which he published his stridently antislavery *Alton Observer*. Finally, on November 7, 1837, he was gunned down while trying to stop mob violence against his newest press. By the time Brown published his *Narrative* a decade later, Lovejoy was a hero to Brown's closest colleagues, including William Lloyd Garrison, Wendell Phillips, and Edmund Quincy in the Massachusetts Anti-Slavery Society. Phillips claimed it was news of Lovejoy's murder that prompted his first antislavery speech.[55] Other Northern abolitionists hailed Lovejoy as the first white martyr of their cause, a John the Baptist foreshadowing the coming of the messiah, John Brown, in 1859.

The Elijah Lovejoy whom Brown knew was but a remote precursor of this righteous antislavery crusader. Brown served for a period of weeks, maybe months, as one in a succession of slaves hired to perform menial work in Lovejoy's *St. Louis Times* printing office. The editor of that paper was a fairly straitlaced, middle-class young man who had arrived in St. Louis in 1827 following graduation from Waterville (now Colby) College in his native Maine. A circuitous search for a new home led Lovejoy eventually to St. Louis, where he opened a private school offering a classical New England curriculum to the rising generation of a rough-and-ready frontier city. That school afforded him solid standing in the community but left him, Yankee moralist to the core, hungering for a life of more consequential service. In the summer of 1830, he purchased part ownership of the *Times*, a Whig-affiliated sheet that carried more content than the better-established *Missouri Republican*. Under his editorial supervision, the paper expressed moderate views and advocated moral and behavioral norms well suited to the St. Louis middle class. Its position on the slavery issue was cautiously safe; sharp-tongued US Senator Paul Simon aptly characterized the *Times* in his Lovejoy biography as giving "more attention to the St. Louis Association for the Improvement of the Breed of Horses than the slavery issue."[56] In practice, it filled the conventional role of local newspapers in serving as a medium for the slave interest, routinely printing ads for auctions and runaways. On the last day the newspaper remained in his control, it ran a local resident's ad for "negroes wanted."[57] Brown would not have been the first or the last slave employed in the *Times* printing office.

In his *Narrative*, Brown would speak of Lovejoy—by that time a martyr in abolitionist circles—as "a very good man, and decidedly the best master that I had ever had. I am chiefly indebted to him, and to my employment in the printing office, for what little learning I obtained while in slavery."[58] That characterization may not be strictly accurate in several regards. Lovejoy probably did treat him relatively well, though decidedly not as the equal of his white apprentices. Even as editor of the *St. Louis Observer*, he conceded that he had no right to talk freely with slaves without the consent of their masters.[59] Brown also seems to have exaggerated the extent of his learning during his weeks with Lovejoy, since any attempt by Lovejoy to instruct an illiterate slave in the elements of literacy would have met with Young's vociferous disapproval. It seems unlikely that Young would have left a slave for long with an employer who was teaching him to read. What labor Brown performed around the printing office would presumably have been menial: cleaning the floor and equipment, attending to the needs of the editor and his staff, and running errands.

Brown was running a routine errand when events took a turn that landed him in serious trouble, verging on danger. Lovejoy frequently sent him to make deliveries to or from the printing office of the *Missouri Republican*, with whose editor, Edward Charless, he was on good terms. One day Brown was returning from the *Republican* office carrying some type when several race-baiting teens accosted him on the street. Angry words quickly escalated to violent acts, as they assaulted him with a barrage of snowballs, rocks, and sticks. Brown dropped the type and fought back, hurting one of the boys before racing off for refuge in Lovejoy's office. Apprised of the fight, Lovejoy went out to retrieve the type and encountered the enraged father of one of the boys, Samuel McKinney, a local bully who threatened to come after Brown with a whip. A few days later, McKinney made good on his threat, encountering Brown on Main Street and pummeling him over the head repeatedly with his cane. Brown was so seriously hurt that Lovejoy had to return him to Young's farm, where he remained bedridden for weeks. By the time he was able to resume work, Lovejoy had already replaced him.[60]

Another of his St. Louis assignments was at the Missouri Hotel, the prominent public house that in September 1820 had hosted the probationary state's first General Assembly with Young in attendance (as, in a further twist, during the Civil War it would house a school comprising mainly fugitive slaves).[61] Brown worked on the hotel staff at some indeterminate date in the late 1820s or early 1830s among a slave force numbering about two dozen women and men. Brown does not mention in his *Narrative* how he came to join that staff, but it is possible his assignment resulted from Young's acquaintance with the owner, Moses Bledsoe, from whom he had bought land.[62] The portability that landed him there can be inferred from that of a fellow slave named Abram, whose period of service at the hotel might have overlapped Brown's. Abram belonged to a master from St. Charles whose affairs in St. Louis in 1829 were overseen by the local jailer, John Simonds Jr. What was to be done with Abram had become a problem for Simonds, who wrote to the St. Charles master to explain that because Abram had grown too religious to do many other tasks, he had assigned Abram to work at Bledsoe's hotel. Abram proved himself so good an employee that Bledsoe now wished to hire him for a full year, and Simonds added his agreement contingent on the master's consent.[63]

Abram had no voice then or later in discussing the matter, but Brown did years later in discussing his own period of service at the hotel. He remembered it as a trying experience, the problem less the labor than the manager, John Colburn—"a more inveterate hater of the negro, I do not believe ever walked on God's green earth." Colburn abused anyone who crossed him—his wife, servants, tradesmen.[64] It did not take much to cross him, but one slave did in a way that not only she but also Brown never forgot. Her name was Patsey, and she committed the punishable offense of firing Colburn's lust when she was herself engaged to another slave. Once, after spotting the couple together, Colburn took out his frustration on Patsey with a whip, lashing her until boarders emerged from their rooms to implore him to stop.[65] Whether Colburn ever mistreated Brown goes unstated, but Brown made sure in his *Narrative* to give Colburn his public due. Violent men like the Marthasville overseer Grove Cook, William Walker, and John Colburn who assaulted slave women earned a special circle in Brown's hell. That circle grew more populous as Brown passed through adolescence.

BROWN'S GROWTH INTO early manhood coincided with the dismemberment of his family. As Dr. Young's fortunes fell into decline in St. Louis without a corresponding reduction of expenses, he began selling his chief assets: slaves and land.[66] The process probably began during Brown's year on the rivers with Walker and, once begun, accelerated. Brown's sole account of the most devastating trauma of his early life was severely foreshortened and tantalizingly brief: "My mother, my brothers Joseph and Millford, and my sister Elizabeth, belonged to Mr. Isaac Mansfield, formerly from one of the Free States, (Massachusetts, I believe.) He was a tinner by trade, and carried on a large manufacturing establishment. Of all my relatives, mother was first, and sister next."[67]

Their new master was Isaac Mansfield, a longtime acquaintance of Young's, possibly even from the time of his move from Marthasville to St. Louis. Mansfield had witnessed one of the Youngs' earliest land transactions, and he was named as a party in Young's final legal act in St. Louis, the drafting of his last will several months before his death.[68] All in all, Mansfield's role in the affairs of Elizabeth and her children was considerably greater than Brown acknowledged in his *Narrative*. A man to whom Young repeatedly turned in making slave deals, Mansfield was an uncanny presence in Brown's recorded adolescence, casting an ominous shadow over Brown and his entire family during the later St. Louis years. Although little is stated explicitly about their relations in the *Narrative*, one fact is clear: Mansfield disliked Brown, and Brown detested Mansfield.

The few facts about Mansfield are sufficient to bring his profile into focus. A hard-working, hard-driving Northerner who migrated to St. Louis no later than 1826, Mansfield devoted himself, as Brown claimed, to his work as a tinsmith and building contractor, carrying on his trade on a large scale.[69] One of his young workers remarked about him approvingly in 1830: "Mansfield has not wanted any work I think for 2 months, though I believe he would rather go peddling himself than discharge me for want of work. Business in our line was never known to be as dull as this season."[70] But later that year, Mansfield landed a large government contract for installing roof gutters and conducting pipes on the buildings of the Jefferson Barracks, a new federal military post about ten miles downriver from St. Louis. A year later, he contributed to the Missouri Auxiliary Bible Society, an organization dear to Young.[71] He was prospering during this period and might also have been achieving some local influence. Like Young, he was politically active, aligning himself with the city's Jacksonian Democrats and in 1831 even competing for a seat in the Missouri General Assembly.[72]

His success in business presumably provided the means for his gradual acquisition of the members of Brown's family, beginning in 1831 or 1832. What purpose he had in buying them, other than speculation, is unclear, since he was not a farmer and did not own a home. According to the 1830 census, he was unmarried, in his forties, and lived in the middle ward of St. Louis in a household consisting of five additional persons, all white males in their twenties and presumably the members of his work crew. Just several houses down the street lived the well-known Mississippi River steamboat captain J. C. Swon, a slave owner on whose boat Brown had accompanied Walker in transporting a coffle of slaves to downstream markets.[73] Next door to Swon lived "Nancy," likely a free woman of color; and next door to Nancy lived Lavinia Titus, a free woman of color liberated many years earlier via a successful freedom suit. Following in their mother's footsteps, Lavinia's children were engaged in 1832 in their own freedom suit about the time Mansfield took possession of Brown's mother and sister.[74] Since Mansfield was not housing his own slaves, it seems plausible that either Nancy or Lavinia was being paid to do so, and Brown's mother and sister might have been among them.[75]

Brown considered Mansfield a prime specimen of his view that Northerners made the worst masters. He was, of course, predisposed against anyone who came to own members of his family, particularly those closest to him, but Mansfield would give him special cause for spite. The purchases of his mother and his sister Elizabeth were the first in a series of transactions made between Young and Mansfield that in time came to include two of his five brothers (two more, Solomon and Benjamin, apparently died young, a fact of life not uncommon even among the affluent in a city plagued by disease). Mansfield did not hold the women long, Brown's sister being the first to go. Brown claims that he first heard word of her sale when he returned from a long steamboat trip; the news devastated him. For a time he was forced to make trips by night to visit her, a task made easier when he worked for masters in St. Louis rather than on Young's farm or on the river. Bad quickly turned to worse when, within a matter of months in 1832, Brown lost not only his sister but also his mother.

Mansfield's sale of the younger Elizabeth might have been strictly a business decision; a healthy teenager would have brought a good price. The going rate for young women in Natchez was $350 to $400, according to a leading slave trader doing business there around that time, but Elizabeth might have fetched an even higher price.[76] Mansfield dealt her to a man planning to take her and four other female slaves down to Natchez. Brown assumed the worst not just of the seller but also of a buyer who purchased five females (and only females) to transport to a city notorious as a center for the sex trade. Even if that was not the buyer's intention, Brown, who had come to know the city well from his time with Walker, could only have feared that the worst would be awaiting his favorite sibling at the end of her journey.

In the local practice typical following slave sales, Elizabeth was locked up in the city jail for safekeeping while awaiting deportation. At first chance, Brown headed to the jail and left a vivid description of their final conversation:

> She was seated with her face towards the door where I entered, yet she did not look up until I walked up to her. As soon as she observed me, she sprung up, threw her arms around my neck, leaned her head upon my breast, and, without uttering a word, burst into tears. As soon as she recovered herself sufficiently to speak, she advised me to take mother, and try to get out of slavery. She said there was no hope for herself,— that she must live and die a slave. After giving her some advice, and taking from my finger a ring and placing it upon hers, I bade her farewell forever, and returned to my mother, and then and there made up my mind to leave for Canada as soon as possible.[77]

The strong-minded teenager had already confided to his mother and sister—probably to them alone—his resolve to escape. Following his sister's incarceration, he lost no time in taking action, although now, given the altered family circumstances, he reconsidered his original intent to travel solo. Instead he urged his mother to join him, implored her that with her daughter already lost and her other sons powerless to help themselves, no less others in the family, she had no reason to remain in St. Louis. At this critical moment in the disintegration of their family life, he spoke with a new degree of authority. He might be her youngest son, but he was the nearest thing to the family caretaker. Reluctantly she agreed.

The timing for an escape, as Brown relates in his *Narrative*, was auspicious, since the sale of his sister coincided with Young's decision finally to sell him: When Brown demanded an explanation, Young claimed financial exigency, adding that in any case all other members of Brown's family had already been sold off. But in consideration of his pledge to Brown's father, Young was willing to allow Brown a week to arrange his own sale. The asking price was $500, a figure much less, Young added, than the offer he had rejected from Walker.[78] Why Mansfield's name as a potential purchaser did not come up goes unmentioned; perhaps Mansfield wanted no part of him. Brown countered by offering to raise the sale money himself by contracting out his services, but Young categorically refused. So, with Young's permission to go to town to look for a new master, Brown began making active preparations for an escape for two. Once again, as throughout this portion of the *Narrative*, he gives no dates, but the overwhelming likelihood is that the year was 1832.

They waited one evening until dark before stealing a rowboat and steering directly across the Mississippi River to the Illinois shore. Although Illinois was legally a free state, they anticipated they would be crossing a region not only densely populated by defenders of slavery but also crawling with bounty hunters. Brown's description of their flight is cagey—he provides no time of year, no landmarks, no flight path, no destination, no mention of (possible) accessories. Given the bare minimum of details, the reader is left to surmise how much they knew about the lay of the land across the treacherous no-slave zone of central Illinois. Although he had previously made multiple trips to Galena, in the northwestern corner of Illinois, it seems certain that they were headed on a northeasterly track, probably toward Chicago or Detroit and maybe beyond to Canada. They fled for about ten days, traveling by night, resting by day, and covering (by Brown's rough estimation) 150 miles. On the eleventh day, men on horseback rode up and identified them as runaway slaves by handbills put out by Young and Mansfield and offering a $200 reward for the pair—a top-dollar amount.[79] Taking no chances, his captors kept Brown's hands bound for the duration of their return to St. Louis, a four-day trip by carriage. Once they reached the Mississippi River crossing point, Brown exchanged words with the familiar ferryman Samuel Wiggins, who expressed surprise at seeing someone known to him as a creditable young man brought back to town in handcuffs.[80]

Brown and his mother were immediately taken to the same jail that had housed his sister until four days earlier. She had been removed from jail just about the time of their capture and placed on a boat already well on its way down the river. Brown never saw her again, nor presumably did their mother, whose turn was next. As soon as word of the captives' return reached Mansfield, the enraged man arrived at the jail to collect Brown's mother. He would have had anger to spare for Brown, a repeat troublemaker who had cost him time, money, aggravation, and probably an unwelcome and inconvenient trip to a printing office in Illinois. Brown remained confined for an additional week as slave traders poked around the jail making inquiries. The reason for his prolonged incarceration, he eventually ascertained, was that Young was seriously ill. Brown's spite for Young continued to boil fifteen years after the event: "I prayed fervently for him—not for his recovery, but for his death."[81] Once recovered enough to sit up in bed, Young sent a servant to town to retrieve Brown and take him to the farm. Despite his precarious position, Brown yielded no ground to his master, responding to Young's simmering resentment by asserting that he was simply following Young's orders by heading toward Canada in search of a master. This was hardly the first time he exercised a freedom of presumption, even insolence, toward Young, but it was the last. As soon as he was able to mount a horse, Young settled the matter definitively by riding into town and selling Brown to the St. Louis merchant tailor Samuel Willi for the modest sum of $300.

Willi, a transplant from western Pennsylvania, was in growth mode at the time he purchased Brown. Throughout 1832, he advertised in the *Missouri Republican* for journeymen and "boys of good morals" to work in his store on Main Street.[82] His store was located next door to the well-established auction house of Savage and Bostwick, whose commission business included a lively trade in slaves. The following January, for instance, while Brown belonged to Willi, they offered for sale "a likely Negro woman and child, a good cook and house servant"; and, five weeks later, "a likely Negro Boy, aged about twelve."[83] Brown walked by the storefront every day and undoubtedly knew people, possibly his own kin, who had passed through the hands of William Savage. At this time, Willi probably was looking for apprentices rather than slave labor, but he could not refuse the bargain he had gotten in his purchase of Brown— although Young did neglect to mention to Willi that he was buying damaged goods. The two men had known each other for some time; Willi had served Young as a tailor for years (one of his unpaid bills wound up in Young's probate file). By the same token, Willi and Brown also had prior acquaintance, since Young had hired Brown out to him a few years earlier.

Having no immediate use for Brown's labor around the store or house, Willi let Brown hire himself out to a steamboat owner. During the interval before his new boat's scheduled departure, however, Brown had the ultimate reckoning to perform. Mansfield had lost no time exacting retribution against his mother by selling her to a slave trader. Brown tried several times to visit her in jail, where she was being held pending departure, but he was rebuffed. The jailer and the parties to the transaction wanted no part in allowing a troublemaker like him to have access to her. As a result, he had no choice but to time his visit for the hour and place announced for her boat's departure. On boarding the steamer, he found her chained to another woman, the two of them part of a consignment of more than fifty slaves bound for the slave market of New Orleans. He knew the procedure all too well.

It was his second leave-taking in mere weeks, but this time he approached the dreaded reckoning weighed down by guilt: "On seeing me, she immediately dropped her head upon her heaving bosom. She moved not, neither did she weep. Her emotions were too deep for tears. I approached, threw my arms around her neck, kissed her, and fell upon my knees, begging her forgiveness, for I thought myself to blame for her sad condition; for if I had not persuaded her to accompany me, she would not then have been in chains." She forgave him unconditionally and urged him to lose no time saving himself. They got no further before Mansfield, spotting Brown from across the boat, hurried over and began kicking him repeatedly, while berating him for having cost him $100 to reclaim his "wench." As he retreated to the dock, Brown heard the bell tolling for the departure of the boat. He never saw his mother again, but her memory haunted him to the end of his life.[84]

BROWN WAS STILL WORKING for Willi in late 1832 when John Young prepared for what would be his final move. Things could not have been going well for the prematurely aged fifty-four-year-old man, whose health had been declining for some time. On a single day in early October, he sold most of his extensive landholdings, in two separate transactions, to a local merchant and municipal leader of his acquaintance named Edward Tracy. On November 30, he and Sarah appeared personally in St. Louis Circuit Court to finalize the sales.[85] The next day, he wrote his last will and testament. In a matter of weeks, he and Sarah moved to join her married sister and widowed mother in rural Lawrence County in northern Alabama, where he lived out his several remaining months. As luck would have it, the move likely placed him within twenty miles of his cousin George W. Higgins, probably by then residing in Decatur, Alabama. Perhaps the two men met one final time in Lawrence County, with one physician cousin attending the other. On January 25, 1833, Young signed a codicil to his will; in February or March, he died and was buried at his new home. Sarah did not find common cause enough with her relatives to linger in Alabama, moving back to St. Louis within several months with the ever-portable Martha Ann and whichever additional slaves the Youngs had taken with them.

Brown's reaction to these final days in his "old master's" life was silence. Once Young had sold him, Brown cut off all mention of his relative in the *Narrative*. Silence, however, was not ignorance; he surely heard the news of Young's death, which reached St. Louis within weeks. Nor was it indifference; Young remained a lingering presence in Brown's consciousness for decades. Brown never ceased to harbor bitter disappointment toward a man he felt had neglected the most fundamental responsibility toward him: the obligation to protect and provide for his cousin's son. Even this was not the entire story. The fatherless adolescent unconsciously saw in Young the substitute for the father he had never had, yet each time he appealed to Young for relief from unbearable conditions, Young turned his back. The pain for Brown was so elemental that it eventually erupted. A generation after Young's death, Brown reincarnated him as the status-conscious, slave-master doctor and plantation owner Colonel Gaines in his hard-hitting play *The Escape*, but in this incarnation he also makes Young double as the stand-in for Brown's biological father. That craven composite of John Young and George W. Higgins was the lingering bogeyman Brown could exorcise but, despite the play's title, could never wholly escape.

Brown's silence about Young was deceptive in a second regard. It obscured the fact that there remained one live connection between him and Young. The tally of his brothers in the St. Louis portion of the *Narrative*— two purchased by Mansfield and two deceased—came up one short. For some reason, Brown failed to mention that, at the time of his death, Young was still the master of Brown's older brother Leander. In the opening clause of his will, Young attended to Leander's final disposition: "I will that my negro man Leander be sold if he wishes to buy him to Isaac Mansfield of the province of Texas," the proceeds to go to the payment of Young's debts. Should Mansfield reject the offer, Young stipulated that Leander be sold, provided he consented, to another master. But should Leander reject his sale to anyone but Mansfield, Young directed that Leander and any other slaves who could be "spared from the family" be hired out to raise revenue. Leander apparently wanted no part of Mansfield or any other permanent arrangement; instead, he was mortgaged to a local acquaintance of the Youngs, Thomas Biddle.[86] What happened to Leander subsequent to the dealings between Sarah and Biddle is unclear, since his name disappears from local records after 1833.

Why was Brown not just silent but deliberately misleading about the status of this older brother? The most obvious reason seems to be that he was speaking rhetorically in his *Narrative* when he claimed he was the last member of his family to be sold by Young. Simplifying the actual dispersal of his relatives around St. Louis in a single convenient generalization allowed him as a professional antislavery lecturer to emphasize the catastrophic effect of slavery on African American families. Rhetorical leverage alone, however, would not account for his reticence about his own flesh and blood. Brown must also have felt a simmering personal disappointment, even resentment, toward older siblings who did precious little to help a family in acute distress. Even though they too presumably labored under arduous circumstances, he must have felt that the burden to take collective responsibility fell unnaturally on the shoulders of the youngest brother.

Willi turned out to be a less authoritarian master than Young, and their relationship was less fraught. Brown had relatively little to do with his new master, a man to whom he had no personal ties and from whom he was generally distanced by long periods of service on the river. Nor did Willi have any particular investment in Brown other than the expectation of good financial return, which must have accrued for at least a year from the labor of so productive an asset. Then, over a two-week period in autumn 1833, Willi closed his books with the Young estate. On September 16, he signed a receipt with Robert Renick, Young's brother-in-law and executor, acknowledging delayed payment for a suit he had made for Young.[87] Then, on October 2, he sold Brown to Enoch Price, a St. Louis steamboat owner and commission merchant. The price was $650, netting Willi a return on his investment too handsome to turn down.[88]

Brown represents himself as preoccupied at the time of that transaction with only one thought: his escape. He could not have abstracted himself, however, from the altered terms of his existence. Overnight he found himself in service to a new owner who, though well known locally and on the river, might have been a stranger to him. Price, a native of the river port of Maysville, Kentucky, had come to St. Louis in 1819 and been active for years as a steamboat pilot on the Ohio, Mississippi, and Missouri Rivers. Earlier in his career, he had conveyed troops up the Missouri to Fort Leavenworth and other western outposts, as well as cargoes for John Jacob Astor's American Fur Company.[89] One of the best-known pilots on the Mississippi at the time he purchased Brown, Price was vigorously pursuing the St. Louis–New Orleans trade, transporting merchandise and people (including slaves) on the new steamboat he owned, the *Chester*. He purchased Brown, however, not as a hand for his boat but as a household domestic. His family at the time comprised three people: Price; his wife, Almira, a native of Long Island; and their three-year-old daughter, Virginia, who died the following December. Brown joined the other two slaves, both female, in attendance on the family at its residence at 55 North Sixth Street in St. Louis.[90] Although he performed general service around the house, his primary occupation was as a coachman, driving this respectable family to church and other destinations around town in their newly purchased carriage.

Now about nineteen, Brown understood that he bore a potential multiplier value to Mrs. Price, who was eager to match and mate him with her slave "girl" Maria. Brown insisted he objected to that particular match but knew well enough not to state that his real opposition was to any slave match whatsoever. Having witnessed the fates of his mother and sister, and no doubt countless other female slaves transported in coffles down the river, he could not have seen Mrs. Price's matchmaking as anything but "a trap" for a young man resolved to attain his freedom and aware that the best way to gain it was to travel solo. Furthermore, he had already formed a romantic attachment with a young woman from town, one more person among the ranks of African American acquaintances from his past life who went unnamed in the *Narrative*. Knowing the delicacy of his situation, he allowed Mrs. Price to believe he was attracted to a local young slave named Eliza, whom Mrs. Price persuaded her husband to purchase.

The Prices had their calculations; Brown had his. From the moment he entered their household, he was carefully weighing his options for escape. Escape on foot from the city, he already knew from experience, was difficult. Escape by water, he knew from his time on the river, improved his chances. While waiting for his opportunity, he sought out the advice of a venerated figure among the local slave population, an emaciated seventy-year-old man known familiarly to both blacks and whites as Uncle Frank. The property of a well-known, French-speaking St. Louis merchant named Sarpy, Uncle Frank lived on his own in a hut in town and earned a little pocket money by telling fortunes.[91] Brown plunked down his quarter and listened earnestly to the old man, who peered into his gourd and told the teenager exactly what he wished to hear: One day he would be free, though not without suffering. As an older man distanced from his roots by self-improvement as well as time and space, Brown would remark that Uncle Frank had "the *name*, and that is about half of what one needs in this gullible age."[92] In 1833, however, he took the old man's forecast far more credulously than he was later willing to admit.

This wry story about Uncle Frank expresses something quite fundamental about Brown's mindset at the time: Those autumn days under the Prices' roof marked a period of deep soul-searching. The nineteen-year-old young man who had all but skipped from boyhood to adulthood sensed he was fast approaching a turning point in his life. For one so young, he had witnessed and suffered extraordinary emotional and psychic pain. He had lived for nearly two decades but could not recall a stable household he could regard as his own. He had been shuttled from master to master, situation to situation, with utter disregard for his feelings, wishes, or welfare. He had witnessed the routine commission of horrors, often from a vantage too close for personal or psychic comfort. He had lived with his deepest personal, emotional, and sexual longings unreciprocated. He had lost his beloved sister to the worst scenario of female trafficking his mind was capable of imagining. And, possibly more painful yet, he had lost his beloved mother to the worst scenario of servitude he could imagine for her—and by his own admission considered himself at least partly to blame. He was also losing what little contact remained with his brothers, those same brothers about whom he had said so little perhaps because he felt there was so little to say. Yet, for all his misery, he found himself among the fortunate few, as he, better than anyone else, must have known. He was a survivor. He had survived Young, he had survived Willi, and he meant sooner rather than later to survive Price. As autumn days came on, he sensed a better day might finally be coming.

Brown's term of service to the Prices proved short lived. Just weeks after purchasing Brown, Captain Price decided to take his family on a holiday excursion in which he mixed business with pleasure. His wife and daughter were to join him on the voyage down to New Orleans; Brown and his intended were to accompany them to serve the family needs. As the *Chester* pulled out of its berth in St. Louis the third or fourth week of November in 1833, Brown must have felt excruciatingly mixed emotions. The movement of the boat onto open water advanced him closer to freedom, but it also stirred agonizing memories about his mother's and sister's final trips down the river. The best testimony to the state of his mind came from the panoramic antislavery painting he commissioned in London in 1851 to exhibit across the British Isles. Among its twenty-four "views" was a richly symbolic one of St. Louis, conjured in surreal terms that anticipated a later St. Louis writer (T. S. Eliot's) imagination of an "unreal city." Its view of the city and river came from the Illinois shore, which Brown had witnessed just that one time as he and his mother were being forcibly returned to slavery. The city was vividly illuminated that particular evening by a combination of moonlight and fire from a burning flatboat, which silhouetted the city's vertical profile. In the painting's foreground was the steamboat *Chester*, just pulling out of port to begin its descent to New Orleans—but it was only one of two boats Brown fished up out of the depths of his memory. Just astern of the *Chester* was a small rowboat carrying Brown and his mother on their flight to freedom.[93] Even while living within smelling distance of the rancid Thames, Brown's nighttime memory was still roaming the Mississippi. Memory of life on the Mississippi was as inescapable for him as it would one day be for Twain.

The *Chester* arrived in New Orleans via Natchez on November 29, carrying 145 passengers and a cargo of the usual staples—buffalo robes, cotton, flour, mustard seed, beef, and rope.[94] Whether it was also transporting slaves to market, as it commonly did, is unknown. It remained in port for several weeks, taking on cargo for the return trip while the Price family enjoyed the shopping and allure of the city. Brown says nothing in his *Narrative* about what he did during this interlude, but a reasonable guess would be that, as soon as he managed to shake himself free from the Prices, he went looking for news or signs of his mother. Many slaves tried to find their lost relatives in New Orleans; very few succeeded. One who did was his future friend Milton Clarke, a Kentucky slave who secured employment on a Mississippi steamer expressly to find traces of his sister Delia, sold down the river in the early 1830s. It took Clarke numerous attempts, graphically told in *Narratives of the Sufferings of Lewis and Milton Clarke*, but against all odds he finally succeeded in 1838.[95] If Brown did a search, he had no such luck.

During their stopover in New Orleans, Price was offered an extravagant sum ($2,000, he claimed) for Brown, but, with his wife's likely objection in mind, he declined.[96] Before embarking on the return trip, Price made the calculated gamble to bypass St. Louis and head up the Ohio River toward Cincinnati, as he had done the previous winter.[97] This extended itinerary might not have been his original intention, to judge from the notice published by a St. Louis newspaper on December 20 that the *Chester* was expected home any day.[98] Before Price committed himself to transporting Southern cargo to Northern ports, however, he took the requisite precaution to have a slave master's frank conversation with his most valuable property. Brown recounted that classic interracial game of "puttin' on ole massa" with arch pleasure: "Captain Price had some fears as to the propriety of taking me near a free State, or a place where it was likely I could run away, with a prospect of liberty. He asked me if I had ever been in a free State. 'Oh yes,' said I, 'I have been in Ohio; my master carried me into that State once, but I never liked a free State.'" When Mrs. Price, no less suspicious, took her turn at probing Sandy's loyalty to her family, he responded just as coyly by reaffirming his love for Eliza: "Nothing but death should part us."[99] The Prices took the bait.

Throughout the first week of December, Price put out advertisements in both French and English for passengers and freight.[100] By mid-December, the *Chester* was steaming back up the river, stopping along the way to trade and to let off and take on passengers. At the intersection of the Mississippi and Ohio Rivers in Cairo, Illinois, it reversed the western turn that Brown might have made in 1817 when the Young party migrated downstream from Kentucky. It made a penultimate stop at Louisville on one of the last days of the year, discharging cargo and passengers. If Price's account is to be trusted, he was once again offered an extravagant sum ($1,500, he claimed) for his impressive male slave, and once again he declined.[101] He would have twenty years to rue his mistake.

Brown was unaware of this proposition. He was too busy to focus on Price while his imagination was already racing up the river, miles ahead of his circumstances. He had been readying himself for days, possibly weeks. He had saved whatever money he could before the departure, sewed a cotton pouch to hold his few possessions, and gathered his best clothes. He would tell a post–Civil War gathering of the American Anti-Slavery Society in New York City that he stole his master's coat, but it is more likely he made his escape wearing little winter clothing of any sort.[102] He paced the deck that last evening of the year with the ship docked alongside his native soil as he made his final preparations for escape.

———————◆———————

At the time of Brown's escape, Cincinnati was a thriving river port of nearly 30,000, the largest Northern city outside the Atlantic corridor and a major crossroads for the flow of goods and people between North and South, East and West. The city directory reported that 1,200 of its residents were "blacks and mulattoes," and another 1,500 a transient population comprising river men, travelers, and sundry others.[103] Of the many people who passed through the city, an invisible percentage would have been fugitive slaves, since, as a major river port and border town, Cincinnati was one of the most important interior stations on the Underground Railroad.

Given its strategic location and size, Cincinnati was bound to play a major role in the national conflict over slavery. Just a month after Brown's flight, one of the most important early nineteenth-century debates about US slavery erupted on Walnut Hill, a theological redoubt overlooking the commercial downtown from its northeast heights. They took place at the fledgling Lane Theological Seminary, founded in 1829 as an institution for training indigent young men for the Presbyterian ministry. Neither the Lane brothers of New Orleans who originally bankrolled it nor their trustees foresaw the radical fervor that broke out on their campus during its fifth winter. Word of the great slavery debates quickly circulated around the country through newspapers sympathetic and unsympathetic alike.

The president of the seminary was Lyman Beecher, a renowned minister fervent about divinity but not about slavery. In 1832, the seminary had lured Beecher west from Boston, along with his family, to add luster to the institution. Prominent among the seminary trustees was Arthur Tappan of New York, a recent convert himself to abolitionism and the president of the newly organized American Anti-Slavery Society. Beecher, however, took a backseat in the debates to a core group of talented, idealistic students zealous to serve God and the common good. These young men came from all across the country—from the East Coast to Arkansas and Missouri, and from both sides of the Ohio River. Among them was a black man, James Bradley, born in Africa and a slave in South Carolina and Arkansas before purchasing his freedom through extraordinary perseverance. Seven of the seminarians, by contrast, were the sons of slaveholders. Out of this diverse group, one extraordinarily talented student emerged as its leader: the charismatic Theodore Dwight Weld. Born in Connecticut and descended from a Puritan lineage running back to Jonathan Edwards and Timothy Dwight, Weld had come west fired by a mission, as a friend encouraged him, to convert the Ohio River Valley into "the great battlefield between the powers of light and darkness."[104] Weld combined two of the most potent ingredients of the time, each flammable but together combustible: messianic evangelicalism and radical abolitionism.

He leveled his attack against the moderate position held by Beecher and the seminary, which held that slavery was an evil inconsistent with American ideals but whose proper redress was for a people unequally endowed with whites and incapable of assimilation to return to its African homeland. Weld, Henry Stanton, and other radical leaders argued vehemently that the only moral solution was immediate abolition and subsequent preparation for African Americans to take their just positions in American society. Over the course of eighteen nights of speeches and sermons, that radical position, which had been held previously by few whites outside the just-formed American Anti-Slavery Society, converted the Lane student body en masse. Students who had considered themselves colonialists came over to Weld's views, and some students even moved from words to action. A Lane Seminary antislavery society was organized, with two sons of the slaveholding South in leadership positions: Alabaman William Allan as president and Kentuckian James Thome as treasurer. Putting into practice Weld's conviction that "faith without works is dead," some students forged connections as teachers with the African American community down the hill.[105]

Student leaders then took their case to the rest of the country. Thome and Stanton represented the seminary's antislavery society at the first annual meeting of the American Anti-Slavery Society, held that June in New York. There they interacted with national leaders, such as founding president Arthur Tappan and founding member William Lloyd Garrison, Boston's leading antislavery activist, who had covered the Lane Seminary developments with avid interest in his abolitionist newspaper, the *Liberator*. Thome quickly emerged as a center of attention at the New York meeting, a specimen convert from the slaveholding South who delivered one of its highlighted addresses. Speaking as "a living witness" from Kentucky, Thome attacked the institution of slavery from both inside and outside. He even revealed its intimate practices, such as the fact that slave quarters "are exposed to the entrance of strangers every hour of the night, and that the sleeping apartments of both sexes are common."[106]

Back on Walnut Hill and across Cincinnati, reaction soon set in. Beecher and most of the trustees were mortified by the debates, which not only challenged their principles but, worse yet, endangered the seminary's delicate relations with the downtown merchants, some of them Southerners and most of them engaged in business across the river. A rift was inevitable, and seminary authorities expelled many of the most outspoken students by year's end. A core group, including trustee Asa Mahan, eventually joined the progressive Oberlin Institute, which Mahan later served as president. Others, like Weld, spread out and traveled across the Northern states as antislavery lecturers. In time, Brown would come to interact with a number of the Lane Seminary outcasts. Influenced by Weld's bestselling *American Slavery As It Is* (1839), he quoted from it extensively in his *Narrative* and later books. He and Mahan would travel to Paris in 1849 as fellow delegates to the International Peace Congress. He would write *Clotel*, his antislavery novel, under the inspiration of Lyman Beecher's daughter, Harriet Beecher Stowe. And he would have to refute accusations made by Arthur (and Lewis) Tappan of personal and sexual impropriety that threatened his career as a public speaker.

THE ESCAPE took place on New Year's Day in 1834—the one entirely trustworthy date in this portion of Brown's *Narrative*. As the *Chester* neared Cincinnati, he paced the deck, scanning the riverfront for the best escape route. While Price, the crew, and passengers were preoccupied attending to the landing, Brown acted with dispatch. In the rush and confusion of disembarkation, he slipped clear of the family, lifted a trunk onto his shoulders, and headed down the gangplank and across the wharf. Dropping the trunk, he moved quickly beyond the crowd and, avoiding the city, headed toward the woods for cover. The most likely guess is that he veered off around the western side of town, the side less built up and the one he would have observed as the boat approached the Public Landing.

He waited in a marshy area until dark before setting out on the long trip north. His destination was Canada, probably via Cleveland. He had no map, compass, or guide—only, in line with the songs and lore he loved, the North Star. He moved fast that first night, later estimating his progress as twenty or twenty-five miles. But that was not a pace he could maintain for long, as his small supply of food grew depleted and his strength gave way. Worse yet, he had not anticipated the severe effect a northern climate would have on his progress. According to one local newspaper, the first week of the year brought the bitterest weather of the season. The temperature dropped to near zero Fahrenheit in the depths of the weeklong cold snap and did not rise above freezing. Canals and rivers froze, closing navigation across the region.[107] Ice blocks formed, turning the Ohio River into the land bridge vaunted in Underground Railroad fact and legend.

That first week, Brown suffered terribly from a combination of exposure and hunger as he made his way northeast. He eventually became sick, his feet probably frostbitten. Although afraid to trust any white person, he finally succumbed to desperation in venturing out for help. Hiding behind a pile of logs near the road, he let each of two white men pass by before he took his life in his hands by stepping out into the road and approaching a third, an elderly man in a Quaker-styled broad-brimmed hat who was leading a horse. The man took one look at the disheveled youth and asked point-blank whether he was a runaway slave. Brown conceded the point, but only after receiving assurance that the man would aid him. He so doubted the man's probity that the hours he spent waiting for his return with a covered wagon were the longest of his life. But Brown had found a white man true to his word, and in his later account of the story in his *Narrative*, that man and his wife saved his life. The old man took Brown in the covered wagon to his house, where he and his wife fed, clothed, fitted him out in proper boots, and harbored him two weeks until his strength was restored.

His rescuer was Wells Brown, a Quaker living somewhere in central Ohio, an area of the state containing scattered communities of Friends. Brown claimed in his *Narrative* that his "adopted father" lived about "fifty or sixty" miles from Dayton, but that assertion needs to be taken cautiously. He also claimed that he was then "between one and two hundred" miles from Cleveland.[108] Writing at a time when unprecedented numbers of fugitives were trekking north across Ohio in search of freedom, he might have been deliberately vague. Or he might simply have been unsure of his numerical units about a state with which he was unfamiliar. Either way, a safer unit of calculation is his count of days spent on the road, which would put the location of the Wells Brown homestead roughly midway along a shaky line between Cincinnati and Cleveland.

Besides giving humanitarian assistance and practical advice, Wells Brown tendered one special service, according to Brown's *Narrative*: He offered to rename the young man after himself, as though bestowing upon him a patrimony previously lacking. Whether or not he was a particularly discerning person able to read Brown's history and temperament, he found a young man in a keenly receptive mood. Deprived, like nearly all slaves, of self-determination and autonomy, Brown had felt the keenest connection between name and identity from the moment Dr. Young stripped him of his birth name. In his flight to freedom, he wrote, he was "not only hunting for my liberty, but also hunting for a name."[109] The first life-determining decision he had made after passing north of Cincinnati was to discard both the hated slave name Sandy and the patrimonial legacy of George W. Higgins: "And as for my father, I would rather have adopted the name of 'Friday,' and been known as the servant of some Robinson Crusoe, than to have taken his name."[110] It was as William that he entered the Quaker household, trailing no patronymic, and as William Wells Brown that he departed. In his *Narrative*, he recalled one of the most decisive moments in his life by imparting biblical overtones to the informal naming ceremony conducted by his adopting father: "'I will call thee William Wells Brown.' 'So be it,' said I; and I have been known by that name ever since I left the house of my first white friend, Wells Brown."[111] As a fully consenting adult son, Brown paid his adopting father the ultimate tribute by dedicating his life story to him. That dedication remained in all subsequent editions, even those published in England.

Safe in body and spirit under his hosts' roof, Brown felt free to conjure his past. Memories from St. Louis and Cincinnati washed over him as he entered into vicarious conversation with some of the significant people from his past. First and foremost he addressed his mother and sister, as though by informing them of his liberation he could redeem their suffering (and maybe also ease his survivor's guilt). He then addressed fellow slaves left behind in St. Louis, who he wished could see him in his new state of being. Then, as though by contrast, he called up Captain and Mrs. Price, who he wished could see him now as a free man. They must sorely have wished to get a look at him too, as they bided their time in icebound Cincinnati waiting for news or return delivery of their fugitive property. Even if Price had entertained any thought of continuing up the river to his hometown of Maysville, he would have been hindered by the deep freeze. But that does not mean he was inactive; a man as determined as Captain Price would have spared no effort to retrieve his lawful property.

Brown, reinvigorated and renamed, returned to the road. The food and money from his benefactors sustained him for the next four days, until he approached an inn. No sooner had he entered to warm himself than he overhead conversation in the barroom about fugitive slaves having recently passed through the neighborhood. Fearing that the men were referring to him, he retreated inconspicuously from the inn and took cover in the woods until nightfall. Several more days of flight left him tired and starved, so he stopped at a farmhouse to ask for food. Elbowing aside her begrudging husband, the farmwife let him in, fed him, and gave him a little pocket money for his way. Thus readied for the final push, Brown resumed his journey northeastward. At some point on the third day, peering through the bare woods, he could see the Cuyahoga River and, rising on the far bluff, the small town of Cleveland.

3

Sweet Freedom

One day in spring 1836, a boy stood on the deck of the *Thomas Jefferson* as it steamed into Cleveland's riverside harbor after crossing Lake Erie. As his boat approached the wharf, he observed dozens of moored steamers, schooners, and canal boats laden with cargoes of wheat, flour, salt, and various kinds of cordwood—still the main source for heating as well as construction. Seasick and eager to get a first impression of his new home, he debarked and began to walk up Superior Street, the town's thoroughfare, still unpaved and lacking sidewalks. As he made his way up the poorly graded slope, he passed various shops dealing in dry goods, leather, hats, furs, shoes, and boots, as well as Sanford and Lott's printing office and bookstore, which the next year issued the city's first residential and business directory.[1] He also passed by the leading hotels, several of which were located conveniently close to the harbor. Pigs ran in the streets, and cows browsed wherever they could find grass.

This particular boy was the aptly named James Cleveland, who arrived with his family from their previous home in upstate New York to embark on a new life. The move was a fateful one for Cleveland, who made the city his home for the rest of his life. Sixty years after his arrival, he published a reminiscence of the fledgling municipality of 5,000 residents that recounted a tale of transformative growth so common in nineteenth-century America it sounded generic. Like St. Louis and other nineteenth-century Western boomtowns, the town he encountered in 1836 on the eve of its incorporation as a city would have been unrecognizable to a newcomer after the Civil War.[2] Its wholesale growth had begun very shortly before his arrival, the primary spur to its growth having been the completion of the Ohio and Erie Canal in 1832. In opening navigation between Cleveland and the Ohio River, the canal transformed one of many lakefront towns into a central location on trade routes connecting Cleveland to New York, Boston, and Philadelphia to the east, and to various points south and west via the Great Lakes and the interior river system. From just a small trading port on Lake Erie in 1830, Cleveland developed within several decades into a major commercial center equal in size to Cincinnati.

Ohio had a corresponding history. In the 1830s, it was one of the fastest-growing states in the country. Within a single generation of its admission to the Union, it had a larger population than Massachusetts, the place of origin of many of its settlers, and trends projected its population would soon double that of the Bay State. Migrants poured into all parts of the state, drawn by the lure of cheap, available land and bountiful opportunity. Among them were numerous African American migrants from both Dixie and the East. But as these newcomers soon learned, Northern states were also discriminatory. All sections of the state had so-called Black Laws on their books, statutes written into the state constitution in 1802, soon reinforced by state law, that assigned African Americans to a distinctly inferior caste. By design, the laws set harsh, even punitive terms for migration into the state, denying blacks basic rights of citizenship—suffrage, equal protection before the law, public office—and forbidding them access to white schools. The Black Laws received strictest enforcement where Southern ideas and migrants held greatest sway, as in Cincinnati and southern counties, and least where New England influence was strongest, as in Cleveland and the Western Reserve generally, which was originally settled as an outgrowth of Connecticut.

Life for African Americans was generally insecure, but for some it was also unsafe. Bounty hunters combed the state end to end on the lookout for fugitive slaves. The number of runaways gradually swelled into the thousands in antebellum years, while thousands more passed through on their way to Canada. Those who remained in Ohio lived on a compromised basis in common with all African Americans; freedom was a relative state and equality was nonexistent. Even Cleveland was close enough to the Mason-Dixon line that one might see an occasional runaway-slave advertisement in a conservative local newspaper. During Brown's first summer in town, one such ad was posted for a runaway from Wheeling (then part of Virginia) whose physical description nearly matched Brown's: nineteen-year-old, light-skinned mulatto.[3] All blacks were supposed to register with the authorities and post bond, although the requirement was enforced far more loosely in Cleveland than in Cincinnati. Wherever they lived, fugitives kept their distance from compliance.

ONE FEBRUARY DAY two years before the arrival of James Cleveland, the newly named William Wells Brown tramped up Superior Street toward the heart of the town. Walking the streets of an American town as a free man for the first time, he saw many of the same sights Cleveland would see, but they registered on him differently. He entered the city a fugitive, trailing a troubled past and predisposed to trust no one, at least no white man or woman. He knew no single person in the town and arrived with no particular destination, but he knew what he was looking for: some sign of local African American presence. Whatever he might have heard on his way north, he must have been surprised to find out how tiny the African American community of Cleveland actually was. Its 1834 population numbered no more than fifty, chiefly young people recently arrived. Most were laborers or domestics, and few owned real estate. Small as the community was, it sufficed to serve a fugitive's basic needs: aid, employment, and companionship.

Several people stood out in the fledgling community, and it seems likely that Brown very quickly made their acquaintance: the sailor John Malvin and the barber John Brown. Both of these community leaders were likewise relative newcomers from the South. Malvin was born free in Dumfries, Virginia, in 1795, but was bound to an insufferable apprenticeship. He eventually escaped and embarked on years of travel and adventure. He married in 1829 in Cincinnati and moved between the Kentucky and Ohio sides of the border, doing odd jobs and becoming involved in antislavery activity that included helping a slave family escape from Kentucky. In 1832, he moved with his family from Cincinnati to Cleveland and began a more settled existence. Later that year, he called a meeting of the African American community to organize a school for their children. One member, John Hudson, who owned the canal boat on which Malvin worked, offered a room, and soon thereafter a seasonal school began operating, funded by subscription and run by a part-time teacher.[4] Malvin acted perhaps most immediately to benefit his own children, but he also had a broad appreciation for black literacy, arising out of his illiterate youth. In his late teens, he had observed the intense pleasure taken by people reading a newspaper or book. Impressed by an activity he thought of as *"pretty talking,"* he determined that he would like to *"talk pretty* too, like the white people."[5] His first instructor was an elderly slave who provided his first lessons in reading and spelling by firelight in the man's cabin. As such acts were then illicit in Virginia, the scene was one of whispered tension. Once engaged in reform activity, Malvin came to see a connection among literacy, education, community, and antislavery activity—the same connection that would become a mainstay of Brown's practices as a writer and activist. Moreover, though he was no radical separatist, Malvin understood that connection as situated solidly within the African American community.

John Brown too was born free in Virginia, in 1798, and moved to Cleveland in 1828. He soon took up barbering, the leading profession among African American men in town, and prospered. His shop became a favorite gathering place, serving both black and white clients. Over time, he became the wealthiest African American in the city by virtue of careful saving, an advantageous marriage, and shrewd real estate investments. Despite this socioeconomic trajectory, he was anything but a supporter of the racial status quo. He joined with Malvin in organizing the first African American school, allowed his shop to be used as a stop on the Underground Railroad, and actively participated in organized antislavery activities. He also passed on his activism to his children: His sons John and Charles volunteered for service in the Civil War and his stepdaughter married the talented black journalist and activist William Howard Day.[6]

Malvin and John Brown would have been able to give a fugitive just arrived in the dead of winter lacking means or shelter the most useful advice about where to live and how to make a living. Brown left few personal impressions of the city in his *Narrative*, which all but skips over his several years of residence there. The most important clue he left was that he made his first home in the Mansion House, a well-established hotel located at the bottom of Superior Street, strategically close to the river landing and the stage depot. How he came to work there goes unstated. One possibility is that he simply wandered by or heard that its young manager, Erick M. Segur, was looking for help and, citing his considerable experience as a waiter, offered his service. It seems more plausible, however, that someone directed him to Segur. Most likely it was John Brown, whose thriving barbershop was located on the ground floor of the Franklin Hotel less than a block above the Mansion House.[7] Brown had so often witnessed the efforts to which slave owners would go to retrieve fugitive slaves that he would initially have been wary about exposing himself to white strangers. Although he could not yet read the newspapers that routinely listed transportation lines, he would have known that coaches regularly connected Cincinnati to Cleveland and that at just about any time there was a chance that Price would have a paid agent on one of them.

Brown worked and boarded at the Mansion House until the navigation season began. He presumably performed basic services around the hotel and lent a hand in shuttling passengers and baggage to and from the harbor. Work occupied part, maybe most, of his time these first months in freedom, but he also moved quickly to build a future of a sort not previously possible. Sometime during his first months in town, he became acquainted with an attractive, intelligent, high-spirited young woman of mixed African American and Native American heritage named Elizabeth Schooner.[8] Betsey, as she was familiarly known, was born free in sparsely populated Scipio Center, Seneca County, Ohio, and was living in Cleveland by the time Brown arrived. The likelihood is that, like most other young, unmarried black females, she was working as a domestic with a white family.[9] The two teenagers fell quickly, passionately in love. The nineteen-year-old ex-slave who had privately vowed never to marry while enslaved could now give free expression to his emotions and aspirations. Knowing little about her background and caring little about immediate practicalities, he married her just a few months after their initial acquaintance, in late summer or autumn of 1834.[10] Since black domestics at the time lived with their employers, Betsey presumably changed her life circumstances radically at the time of their marriage.[11]

Marriage would also have placed Brown's life on a fundamentally new basis. Barred during slavery from exercising self-reliance, he took responsibility just months after his escape for the welfare of two—and, in relatively short order, three—people. Too poor to afford a home of their own, the young couple must have shared lodging with another family or taken a room in a boardinghouse. Almost all their peers did, as there were only a handful of black property owners, including John Malvin and John Brown, in town as late as 1840.[12] The names of the young couple appear in no municipal records, and no details have survived about where they lived. The best guess is that they made their home in Ward 1, an area adjacent to the river and south of the Public Square containing the city's largest concentration of African Americans.[13]

By the time their relationship grew serious, Brown had left the Mansion House for work on Lake Erie. Perhaps with the advice or aid of Malvin, he found a position as a waiter on a Lake Erie steamer, one of the relatively few employment categories open to black men in town. "On the lake," as it was listed in city directories, would have matched Brown's background well. Brown served on various ships during his nearly three years in Cleveland, a period in which he gained a close familiarity with a number of the small lakefront cities of western New York, Ohio, and Michigan that had come to life with the surge of maritime commerce.

He traveled six to eight months each of these years on the Great Lakes, observing the ways of people from all over the country, interacting with both whites and African Americans of various backgrounds, and picking up the latest news about goings-on across the region and country.

Accessibility to Canada, land of freedom, was crucial to Brown's early years in the North. Had he been a less daring, self-assured person, he might have given more thought to his escape route to Canada in the event Price sent slave catchers after him. Most of his fellow fugitives either continued north or settled down in or near Cleveland and attended to their own affairs. By all reports, however, Brown did otherwise. Almost as soon as he got situated in Cleveland, he took up service, whether on his own or in concert with other operatives, as a conductor on the Underground Railroad. He bonded with some of the people he helped to reach Canada, accumulating a reservoir of personal narratives and in some instances even visiting them in their new Canadian homes. During hard times, when prospects for scratching out a living were few, or fear for his personal safety weighed heavily, he might have contemplated a new start for himself and Betsey (and, in due course, their family). When so many others were making that decision, he would have had good reason to think life there might be better than in a country in which he would always be vulnerable and subject to discrimination.

Brown left few details in his various memoirs about the particular ships on which he worked during his Cleveland period, but Josephine Brown did, in her brief biography of her father. She stated, for example, that in spring 1834 he went to work on the *Detroit*.[14] If so, it would have been his first berth as a free laborer. A two-deck steamer of that name was built the previous year and was in service in 1834 on Lakes Erie and Huron, connecting Cleveland to Detroit via intermediate points.[15] Its captain was a man with a competitive temper named Baldwin, who might have given him his first experience of steamboat racing on open water. One day in July, a correspondent for the *Cleveland Herald* reported on the ship's pursuit of the *Governor Macy*, which had preceded it out of port by forty minutes.[16] Racing between steamers on American waterways was a common pastime that appealed to a reckless streak in Americans as good sport, but, as everyone knew (and Brown reported in *Clotel*), they occasionally ended in boiler explosions and fatalities.[17] Later that year, a distraught Mercer County man placed a notice in the *Cleveland Whig* calling for information about his two missing sisters, aged sixteen and one, who were last seen on the *Detroit* on September 18, 1834. He had expected the girls to have landed at Huron, Ohio, one of the ports served by the ship.[18] Whether Brown was still working on that ship or had switched to a different one is an open question. Moving from ship to ship to forestall periods of inactivity was common practice among sailors; it might well have been Brown's practice during these years, when only continuous employment would have kept him and Betsey out of abject poverty.

He also served on the *Charles Townsend* in autumn 1835, a new single-deck steamer that navigated between Buffalo and Detroit.[19] He would later write that he took on board many fugitives that season, "dozens" by his count, whom he conveyed to either of those end ports on their way to Canada. They all had personal narratives to tell, each more compelling than the next, but one in particular captured his imagination, that of a man to whom he gave the curious name of Leander. Word of Leander's presence in Cleveland passed through the African American grapevine to Brown, who took action. Anticipating that the man's owner and his local deputies might follow Leander's trail to the *Charles Townsend*, Brown put the skills learned under William Walker to good use by helping Leander disguise himself as a white woman in mourning wearing a black veil.[20] Of the dozens of fugitives he helped to make their way to Canada, the case of Leander was an especially inventive one. On the other hand, given Brown's proclivity for rewriting the past, the story of Leander might just as likely have been an instance—and not the only one—of Brown's recasting of another slave's escape. There was nothing contrived, however, about the service he performed for many individuals and families in their flight to better lives.

Near the end of that season, he found himself left penniless near the port city of Monroe, Michigan, by a captain who absconded with the crew's wages—or so Brown claimed in the European travelogue he published in 1852 while residing in London. Already well connected in this later portion of his life, he had been invited to tour the Bank of England, a visit he archly compared in the memoir preceding the travelogue with his experience several decades earlier of being left high and dry in Monroe. In need of immediate relief, he did what a black man at the time could do to make a living: He set up a barbershop in the small town.[21] With characteristic bravado, he hoisted a red-striped barber pole outside his shop and hung a sign styling himself "Fashionable Hairdresser from New York, Emperor of the West." Whatever skill he had with scissors and brushes he presumably had picked up from his service to Walker; his other major skill was his gift of gab. Within a few weeks, a growing number of customers were coming into the shop, some lingering to trade stories with the emperor, who earned a fast reputation as a good storyteller. One day a customer approached him with a well-timed suggestion: "Emperor, you seem to be doing a thriving business. You should do as other business men, issue your Shinplasters [private paper currency]." Brown thought it over before resolving to stake his fortune as a banker. A few days later, he walked over to a local printing office, where the printer showed him specimens of engraved banknotes he had received from Detroit. Brown looked them over and commissioned a set with his name and particulars imprinted on the notes. With that act, he launched himself into the maelstrom of Jacksonian-era wildcat banking.

Small-denominational paper money issued by wildcat bankers was all the rage across the country in the mid-1830s, when banks were all but unregulated and currency was local. (There would be no national currency until the Civil War.) Brown's shinplasters would have been his first publication—and one of the few of his publications not to remain in circulation for many years. Although none of Brown's bills has survived, the collection of the American Antiquarian Society has a remarkable set of shinplasters and higher-denominational notes from 1830s Michigan.[22] Among these are a few 1836 bills issued in Monroe, simple $1 and $2 notes issued by a local railroad company trying to finance one of the earliest lines in the state. A little later, the Merchants and Mechanics Bank of Monroe issued more elaborately engraved $5 and $10 notes. Reflecting serious professional skill, they featured a variety of scenes of local crafts as well as modes of transportation ranging from Native Americans paddling canoes to trains and steamers navigating the Great Lakes. Brown could not have afforded to finance the expense of their artwork or to risk their higher valuations. But all bankers were chancing the volatility of unregulated fiscal cycles, and all paid when the crash came in the great fiscal Panic of 1837. Brown's day of reckoning came much earlier when a simple run on his notes shortly after their issuance left him "completely 'done *Brown*,'" as he wrote self-mockingly, and drove him to default. It presumably also drove him to return to Cleveland to his family and friends.

Though perhaps partially invented, this episode would have been one of many periods of life in the open for a young man spending many months a year on the lake. His routine was generally the same for each of the first ten years of his marriage. Once the ice broke up in early spring and maritime commerce resumed, he followed the line of employment out onto the lake. He moved from boat to boat, as circumstances required; and as an alternative set of circumstances allowed, he aided fugitives on their way to Canada. Although the life of a mariner required seasonal itinerancy, there was more to Brown's pattern of constant travel than just occupational necessity. Travel was a temperamental preference that continued long after he stepped off his last steamer. Life on the lake made demands on life in the home; how Betsey responded to his frequent absences during the first years of their marriage remains an open question.

VERY SHORTLY AFTER he fled Cincinnati, Brown thought backward to relatives and friends he had left behind in St. Louis. Once settled into a freer, happier existence in Cleveland, he must have kept them frequently in mind. What he actually knew about their circumstances, however, is a mystery, as he maintained a tight public silence on the subject. One can reasonably assume, at least, that if he had previously managed to sustain a line of communication while traveling along the Mississippi River, he must have attempted the same during the extensive time he spent on the Great Lakes. From early on, he had demonstrated an extraordinary talent at gathering intelligence, a trait that made him a superior courier long before he ever considered becoming a writer. As fellow slaves repeatedly tasked him to deliver information to, from, or about loved ones, he must have requested the same once his mother and sister were sold away, and he must have continued to inquire once he became a free man with widespread contacts up North. Yet all that can be said with certainty about his memory of the past is that, once he became an author and public figure, he never referred to his relatives either in print or in speeches as anything but irretrievably lost to him.

For the people he left behind in St. Louis, life had moved on, more agreeably for some than others. William Moore Young, Brown's like-named charge from Marthasville, met his uncle's expectations by going off in May 1834 to Kentucky to complete his education at Cumberland College, a denominational school acceptable to his uncle's strict Presbyterian views. He attended for at least three years, his $40 charge per semester for tuition and board paid from the proceeds of Dr. Young's estate.[23] Meanwhile, the probate of Young's estate crawled through the court before entering its last stages in early 1836. As required by law, its executors placed a series of consecutive weekly advertisements announcing its adjudication in a local newspaper (the *St. Louis Observer*) in late February prior to the final settlement in the court's May session. By that time, brother Leander had been sold off, probably (before Brown's escape) in summer 1833 by order of Sarah, netting the estate $475.[24]

Meanwhile, Sarah Scott Young lived out her life in St. Louis County. At one time in 1834, she briefly considered moving back to Lawrence County, Alabama, to be near her sister, but instead she remained on her 180-acre farm. She spent her final years there, as previously, with much of the manual labor performed by the half-dozen slaves remaining in her possession. On December 1, 1835, she entered into a customary yearlong agreement with a local man for the hire of her "Negro Boy" Peter for $110. That arrangement worked so advantageously that they extended the arrangement for a second year, and a third, in what evolved into an annual ritual.[25] Brown would have known Peter for years as a fellow slave of the estate; they were near in age and had lived in close quarters even though Peter labored chiefly in the fields. Peter remained a part of the Young estate through 1840, the year Sarah (and also William Moore Young) died. Not much changed for Peter, though, as even after Sarah's death he continued to be rented out annually to local farmers by the estate administrator, Hiram Cordell.

So Peter's years passed—until 1844, when his life took an unpredictable twist. Sarah had died intestate, leaving a moderate-sized estate that was contested by competing claimants—local creditors, several Young brothers resident in Missouri, and a larger number of Sarah's family members spread out from Virginia and Tennessee to Louisiana and Texas.[26] In early 1844, St. Louis Probate Court ordered Cordell to sell off slaves in order to make good on debts owed to various creditors. The estate complied by selling off twenty-four-year-old Martha Ann and her seven-year-old son, James, at a public auction held near the eastern steps of the St. Louis courthouse on April 11, 1844. Martha Ann, however, successfully petitioned the court to nullify the sale, claiming she was legally free as a result of the months she had lived with Sarah and John Young in Galena. Meanwhile, the court ordered that a substitute be put up for sale. The unfortunate designee was Peter, who was sold at auction on the Young farm on June 29, 1844, to a man named Andrew Ross for $500. Martha Ann was more fortunate; she and her son filed freedom suits later that year against the estate, which they eventually won.[27]

Of the dozens of people held in slavery by Frances Fuqua Young, John Young, and Sarah Scott Young in Virginia, Kentucky, and Missouri, only a handful were as lucky. Of them, as far as is known, only Brown successfully took ownership over his person by means of flight.

HE WAS ALSO likely the only one to acquire full literacy. How the most prolific African American writer of the nineteenth century acquired his basic skills at the relatively late age of nineteen is of course a subject of critical importance to his life story. Just the same, the phenomenon of

Brown's acquisition of literacy was only one part personal, the other part communal experience. Many of his peers in Cleveland and elsewhere learned to read in their maturity; close at hand was the inspiring model of John Malvin. Whereas Malvin and Frederick Douglass gave rivetingly explicit accounts in their narratives, Brown was generally silent on the subject in his various memoirs, at least until he was living in England in the early 1850s. When he did broach the subject, he gave one of the most rollicking accounts of the "theft" of literacy in all of the fugitive slave literature.

Not long after his arrival in Cleveland, he relates, he purchased a spelling book with his earliest wages but found himself incapable of reading it without instruction. One day while working in a woodshed, he accosted the small sons of his employer, tempting them with a stick of sugar candy purchased for the occasion to teach him his ABCs—a lick for a letter.[28] Over the course of three weeks, he sweet-talked his way to a cursory knowledge of the alphabet. Next came a cursory knowledge of writing, which he likewise accomplished through trickery. Keeping a piece of chalk on hand and waiting for the right moment, he scratched out meaningless markings on a fence board and stopped an unwitting young passerby to ask whether he had written "William Wells Brown." The boy responded tauntingly, "That's not writing," before proceeding to write out Brown's name in large letters and stalking off. Brown immediately did his best to imitate the letters of his name, chalking nearly a quarter-mile of fence boards to accomplish the goal.[29] All in all, it is a wonderfully symbolic story about the young man's quest for personal identity, a name of his own, attained through literacy. But as a trustworthy tale, it testifies more to his accomplishment as a mature writer than to his actual circumstances.

Even as a figurative account of stealing literacy, this story reveals only a partial truth. The full saga of Brown's acquisition of literacy lies in the fluid middle ground between personal striving and communal support, subsuming both. The identity of one of his teachers is known: his wife, Betsey, who was skillfully literate. Brown's close friend Amy Post, a kind-hearted Quaker reformer from Rochester, New York, reported at the time of the breakup of the Browns' marriage that in happier times he had "attributed what little learning he possessed, and much of his intellectual progress to the efforts of his wife."[30] One can only imagine the tender moments of shared literary intimacy between the young couple, a sadly incongruous prelude to the acrimonious, all-too-public disintegration of their relationship a decade later. But he must have had other instructors besides Betsey, neighbors and friends who aided him in what would have been a communal effort to accomplish a communal good. Once he was ready, someone so inclined, perhaps Malvin, did him the service of introducing him to the literature of organized antislavery, and an excited Brown put his new skill to good use by taking out a subscription to one of the earliest antislavery newspapers, Benjamin Lundy's *Genius of Universal Emancipation*. Before long he was also subscribing to William Lloyd Garrison's *Liberator*, the newspaper he would read and contribute to for the better part of two decades.[31] Such papers presented a model of the meeting between literacy and activism, of literacy in action, which, once absorbed, Brown would never abandon.

Winter meant the close of travel and trade on the Great Lakes, so Brown would have passed his last winter in Cleveland close to home, taking odd jobs, spending time with friends and neighbors as well as his family, and working to improve his reading and writing skills. His self-education continued in fits and starts, its method approximating that of another highly motivated young black man Brown met many years later named William Anderson, who wrote modestly but self-respectfully about his autodidacticism: "what little education I have got was obtained in a similar manner that a pigeon gets his food, a little here and a little there."[32] It also resembled the hunger for knowledge of his future friend Lewis Hayden, who struggled in the early years of freedom before earning a good living and a sterling reputation in Boston. When he was three years out of slavery in Kentucky but still only haltingly literate, Hayden expressed his admiration for the polished, eloquent Boston Brahmin Wendell Phillips by making an ironic comparison between their respective writing skills: "you [may] not like my composition it is as good as any of yours when you was but three years old which is my age."[33]

During those first years in Cleveland, Brown would have been working to overcome an age–skill handicap just as severe.

He was also awaiting the birth of his and Betsey's first child. There is some uncertainty, however, about the facts. His normally reliable biographer, William Edward Farrison, claims that the young couple welcomed their first child already in the spring of 1835, a daughter of unknown name who died shortly afterward. But no external records or writings corroborate that claim, and Farrison uncharacteristically provides no documentary evidence.[34] There is no doubt, however, about the birth of daughter Clarissa (known familiarly as Clara) the following February or March in Cleveland, or about this child's survival into adulthood. Her presence not only situated the young family deeper in the community but also helped her father to fill with a living presence the void left by the loss of all his flesh-and-blood relatives.

Even with a child to multiply the attractions of life at home, Brown continued to spend at least half a year on the lake. His travels encompassed the breadth of Lake Erie and included stopovers lasting hours or, at final destinations, days. A port of call that he visited numerous times was Buffalo, the largest city on Lake Erie. After spending extensive time surveying the city and conversing with residents, Brown saw that there was good reason to reconsider his family's prospects. A prime beneficiary of the trade route opened up by the Erie Canal, Buffalo was a much larger city (15,000 residents) than Cleveland and had an African American community nearly ten times larger than Cleveland's. It also had numerous institutional advantages Brown would have found appealing, including a well-established white antislavery society and a more vibrant and activist African American community. After weighing his options, he decided to move his family in the fall of 1836. As things turned out, the family member with the most to gain from the move was Brown.

He soon found Buffalo a more hospitable locale for African Americans than Cleveland. It had no Black Laws, lay at a more secure remove from the South, and had relatively close ties to the antislavery movement in New York City. Just the same, segregation was a fact of life in the city, and its local politics were unfriendly, if not actually threatening. The city's most prominent citizen was Millard Fillmore, a prominent lawyer and, in time, the area's US congressman. A local white antislavery leader who disliked Fillmore dubbed him "His Accidency," but Fillmore was too consequential a figure in local and eventually national affairs to be so easily dismissed.[35]

The Browns lived in Buffalo for nearly nine years. Both parents integrated deeply into the African American community, although in different ways. Brown in time matured into a community activist/leader. Betsey lived a more circumscribed existence, with no extended family nearby and the daily child-rearing burden on her shoulders, but the city provided as much of a home as she would ever have in her desperately unhappy adulthood. The first mention in print of the Browns' residence—in Buffalo or anywhere else—came in the 1844 city directory, which listed the family home at 13 Pine Street. That location put them in the center of the main concentration of African Americans and their supporting institutions on the south-central side of town, within the sector extending east and west of Michigan Street.

Their neighborhood was working class, as one would expect of an African American community, like Cleveland's, made up primarily of male laborers and female domestics. Not surprisingly, it was one of the city's low-rent districts, with municipal tax valuations running only a fraction of assessments in other neighborhoods.[36] But it was the home to their friends and hosted their local religious and educational institutions. The first of Buffalo's African American churches already existed, though without a permanent home. A decade later, the Michigan Street Baptist Church would be built just a few blocks from the location of their house. The neighborhood also hosted an "African School" on the corner of Elm and Eagle Streets.[37] At this time of early public schooling in the United States, the practice of school segregation was common but hardly universal across Northern cities, yet the Browns ran up against it in Buffalo. The rationale for segregating black from white children was spelled out by the superintendent of schools in 1843: "They require greater patience on the part of the teacher, longer training and severer discipline than are called into exercise in the other schools, and generations must elapse before they will possess the vigor of intellect, the power of memory and judgment that are so early developed in the Anglo-Saxon Race. Hence the importance of a distinct and separate organization of the African School."[38] Some of their neighbors sent their children to this school, but Brown withheld Clara through the mid 1840s, despite her obvious readiness. He based his decision on an unwavering principle acquired from the Southern school of hard knocks: He would not allow his children to attend an inferior, segregated school, regardless of where they lived.[39] He applied that principle consistently for the next decade, during which, in large part, it determined his daughters' places of residence as they moved from western to central New York state, from there to Massachusetts, and eventually from Massachusetts to France and England. In Buffalo, whatever schooling Clara got would have come primarily at home from Betsey.

Although Brown never identified any of his Buffalo friends and neighbors in his writings, some can be named on the basis of an extraordinary document compiled later by Betsey. In 1849, four years after the family abandoned the city in distress and two years after Brown separated from her and took the girls to live with him in Boston, Betsey went around their old neighborhood compiling a certificate of good character, defending her reputation against accusations she was an unfaithful wife and a negligent mother. She attached to it a list of sixty-five names of neighbors who, she claimed, could attest to her virtuous conduct. Nearly all, it turns out, were African Americans, and most lived in the immediate neighborhood. An abbreviated listing of her supposed witnesses, cross-referenced against municipal directories for occupation and residence ("h"), provides a shorthanded survey of the Browns' social network: William Hall, truckman, h. Cypress near Pine; William Storum, on the lake, h. 20 Clinton; William Walker, on the lake, h. 22 Illinois; John Bludsaw, laborer, h. Elm near Vine; James Washington, cook, h. William near Michigan; Peter Harris, blacksmith, h. 17 Illinois; Charles Anderson, barber, h. 148 Elm; Richard Jones, white washer, h. 137 North Division; J. Whitfield, barber on the lake, h. 192 South Division; John Mitchell, barber, h. 364 Michigan; John McClean, whitewasher,

h. 180 Elm; Nathan Rosier, laborer, h. 15 Steuben; Richard Turner, on the lake, h. Pine near North Division; Charles Delvecchio, musician, h. North Division near Pine.[40] These people comprised a fairly typical black working-class neighborhood of the antebellum North, and they were the people with whom Betsey and William typically spent time, visiting and hosting, taking walks and outings, raising children, and chatting about everything from family and neighborhood to work and politics. A few would have been Brown's shipmates on Lake Erie.

Two names on the list stand out. One was James Whitfield, who lived a few blocks from the Browns and was listed in the 1844 directory as a "barber on the lake." Brown knew him more intimately as a fellow antislavery activist and a man of uncommon literary skill. Two decades later, Brown would memorialize him as yet one more cautionary tale of a specially talented African American held back by discrimination: "There has long resided in Buffalo, New York, a barber, noted for his scholarly attainments and gentlemanly deportment. Men of the most polished refinement visit his saloon, and, while being shaved, take pleasure in conversing with him; and all who know him feel that he was intended by nature for a higher position in life. This is James M. Whitfield." Brown was by then well aware of Whitfield's literary achievement as author of *America and Other Poems* and excerpted lines from his poignant anti-slavery poem "How Long?": "How long, O gracious God, how long/ Shall power lord it over right?"[41] The other was Nathan Rosier, a middle-aged common laborer (and quite possibly a fugitive slave originally from Maryland) who worked during the 1840s generally as a teamster.[42] More to the point, Rosier and his wife Eliza were hosting the destitute Betsey Brown in their house near the intersection of Steuben and Pollard Streets at the time of her death in January 1852.[43]

Brown's early years in Buffalo followed the pattern of the Cleveland years. In season he worked on the lake, finding employment where he could aboard the city's burgeoning fleet of steamers. Out of season he spent more time at home with his family and in the community with neighbors and friends. He soon had additional incentive to be at home. In June 1839, a second daughter, Elizabeth Josephine (known familiarly by her middle name), was born to the couple—although there is a possibility, if the 1850 federal census is to be trusted, that she was actually born in Detroit.[44] This baby with the magical, haunted name of his wife, mother, and sister would in time become the apple of his eye. Not only was his family growing, so was Brown. He spent more time with his books and newspapers, honing his reading and writing skills, though whether yet with an eye toward public discourse is impossible to say. He simultaneously tightened his ties to the community as he became more involved in activities and organizations promoting local improvement and reform. Gradually self and communal improvement became intertwined, the connecting thread being reform.

How and when did he embark on a path of public service? There seems to have been no specific moment when Brown reached this decision. By contrast with Douglass's dramatic debut at the August 1841 Nantucket antislavery convention, made with Garrison and Phillips present and observing, Brown apparently occupied no stage during this period. He was, for sure, a less extravagantly self-dramatizing figure than Douglass, but it also seems that his path tracked along a long, steady gradient. Once mobilized, however, he never deviated from a life of public service.

In April 1842, Brown contributed his first publicly printed letter to the Albany (New York) *Northern Star and Freemen's Advocate*, a reform-minded African American weekly. The editor was Stephen Myers, who was something of a Brown look-alike: an ex-slave from New York (a state that kept slavery on the books until 1827 and for some years afterward in practice) and ex–steamboat hand who was now channeling his energy into African American reform. Myers and his "much esteemed friend W. W. Brown" had probably already met, and they would subsequently meet many times over the years at Negro conventions and other antislavery gatherings.

The subject of Brown's letter was not slavery but temperance, a lifelong cause. His devotion was partly personal, partly communal. Intemperance was a serious, widely recognized problem in the antebellum African American community, and its redress was an integral part of the overall communal goal of collective reform and advancement. But Brown also had a more intimately personal reason, shame, for what would become a lifelong passion. During his early life, he had been exposed frequently to hard drinking, as were virtually all slaves of his acquaintance. Hard drinking (often accompanied by hard gambling) was a common pastime on the Mississippi riverboats on which he worked, but it was also prevalent closer to home. Most masters of John Young's background did not restrict their slaves from drinking, and many even encouraged their indulgence during periods of leisure, welcoming it as a useful release valve. For this reason, Sunday in particular was widely a day of hard drinking in the slave world, regardless of whether it was also a day of worship. Sabbath observance under the Young family's roof in St. Louis typically brought an abundance of both. Long after the Youngs had turned conspicuously pious, family members—including little William Moore Young—indulged in their favorite drink, mint juleps. Brown watched and—when no one else was watching—joined in the family ritual during his days as a house servant, drinking even more heavily when the family was engaged in prayer.[45] The strong taste for alcohol he developed as a boy soured in freedom when he came to associate it with a deliberate policy of slave degradation by masters. That view in turn had professional consequences for Brown, since it aligned his views with the pairing of antislavery and temperance that figured in the moral-reform underpinnings of both white and black antislavery organizations.

Brown's letter to the *Northern Star* was written in the form of a field report. It summarized the March 31 meeting of the Union Total Abstinence Society, which he served as president and chief recruiter. The society was in a rapid state of growth at the time, one of the largest in New York state, with a membership of more than two hundred.[46] Brown and his colleagues formally resolved to endorse the *Northern Star* as "the promoter and guardian of liberty" and recruited subscriptions to it, following the common linkage between reform movements and their periodical outlets. Pleased with their endorsement, Myers reciprocated with his own: "We shall be pleased to hear from W. W. Brown, as often as convenient."[47]

In 1842, Brown was also moving closer to formal affiliation with the antislavery movement, which by the early 1840s was expanding west-ward from its bases in Boston, New York City, and Philadelphia across New York state, Pennsylvania, Ohio, and the upper Midwest. He kept abreast of developments in the movement thanks to his travels across Lake Erie and close review of the leading antislavery newspapers. A new generation of names—soon to become familiar faces to Brown—was surfacing in news reports: Abby Kelley from Massachusetts; Amy and Isaac Post from Rochester, New York; Joseph C. Hathaway from Farm-ington, New York; the African American Charles Lenox Remond from Salem, Massachusetts; as well as the triumvirate of William Lloyd Garri-son, Wendell Phillips, and Edmund Quincy from Boston. By late 1842, discussions were well underway to establish a new affiliate of the Ameri-can Anti-Slavery Society in New York state. That new organization, the Western New York Anti-Slavery Society (WNYASS), headquartered in Rochester and affiliated with the parent American Anti-Slavery Society in New York City, would soon become Brown's base of operations.[48]

Brown, however, remained unaffiliated with the new organization and all others in 1842, although he took a more active role in the Under-ground Railroad than in any previous year. In that single navigation season, he claimed to have guided sixty-nine fugitive slaves on their way to freedom in Canada. He also claimed to have crossed the border him-self in 1843 to visit the community of Malden in southern Ontario, where he would have updated himself on the lives of people he had helped.[49] The claim is plausible, though unverifiable.

In spring 1843, he joined in the full-scale mobilization of Buffalo's African American community when twenty-four fugitives arrived in town over a two-day period. Larger numbers of fugitives were stream-ing to the North in the 1840s than in Brown's day, but this event was extraordinary. One person in particular came to his attention, a very light-skinned slave woman—such women often caught his eye—named Fanny who had escaped from Maysville, Kentucky, with her four chil-dren. Brown was deeply moved by her plight: an unescorted mother taking in hand her children, the youngest an infant, venturing over the Ohio River, and running northward. The tableau of slaves fleeing across the Ohio River from Kentucky was already one of the most powerful pictures in his personal image archive; the condition of a single mother escaping with children only intensified his identification. Brown made a point of personally escorting Fanny and her family to the steamboat that would ferry them to Canada. As he did, he amusedly reflected to himself about the uproar the spectacle of his walking alongside "a white woman" might have caused in a more racially charged city, such as Philadelphia.

He enthusiastically recounted the story of Fanny and her family in a short public letter, his earliest known antislavery writing. He addressed his account to the editor of the Chicago-based *Western Citizen*, Zebina Eastman, a veteran antislavery man who had been Benjamin Lundy's onetime partner and then his successor in running the *Genius of Universal Emancipation*.[50] Eastman was already aware of Fanny from the runaway ad placed by her owner in his local Maysville paper, which must have crossed the Mason-Dixon line shortly after Fanny via the newspaper exchange system. Having already published for his readers an article detailing the facts in her case, Eastman was eager to print Brown's letter as a happy conclusion to her story. His readers would presumably share in the satisfaction with which Brown concluded his letter: "Mr. Lee need not trouble himself about Fanny, for she has passed through the hands of the Buffalo Vigilance Committee, and when a slave falls into the hands of that committee, he is safe from the slave hunters." Bravado served Brown and his comrades fine then, but it would serve them less well once the Fugitive Slave Law took effect in 1850 during the presidency of Buffalo's first citizen, Millard Fillmore.

4

The Road to Reform

During a career in civil rights spanning four decades, William Wells Brown would participate in countless major gatherings, some organized chiefly by whites, some strictly by African Americans. His initiation into the antislavery movement came at one of the latter, the historic National Convention of Colored Men held in Buffalo the third week of August in 1843. The National Negro Convention Movement had been in existence since first convening in Philadelphia in 1830, with periodic meetings subsequently held in northeastern cities, but momentum had been lost for some time when the call for a national convention went out from New York City in May 1843. As events turned out, it would assemble a rising generation of extraordinarily talented young men who would lead the African American community through the most tumultuous period in its history.

In the weeks leading up to the convention, Brown suspended steamboat work—permanently, as it turned out—to devote his time to helping organizers work out the logistics. The convention was to bring together many of the leading young black activists of the antislavery movement, men then known to Brown only by name: Frederick Douglass, the spellbinding young lecturer for Garrison's Massachusetts Anti-Slavery Society (MASS); Henry Highland Garnet, the powerful, militant minister from Troy, New York; William Cooper Nell, the accomplished factotum for the MASS from Boston; Charles B. Ray, the seasoned New York–based editor and publisher of the second African American newspaper, *The Colored American*; and Charles Lenox Remond, the longtime vociferous advocate of the Garrisonian position from Salem, Massachusetts. There was one person, however, he knew personally—his old friend John Malvin, representing Cleveland.

The convention agenda was so full that the meetings lasted nearly five full days, between August 15 and 20. The delegates debated a broad array of major policy issues facing the African American populace, including colonization to Africa, the Protestant church's relation to slavery, suffrage restrictions, communal self-improvement, agricultural and trade education, and the racial agenda of the Liberty Party, a fledgling third party with an antislavery orientation. On the opening night, an already heightened atmosphere was intensified by the announcement that present among their ranks was a recently escaped slave from Virginia named Dod. The delegates greeted him warmly and by acclamation named him a delegate from his former home. But the most dramatic event of the convention was one that today stands out as a major event in the history of African American oratory. This was the lead address given by the charismatic Garnet, an ex-slave (like his great rival Douglass) from the Eastern Shore of Maryland who had bravely fought through mob violence and repeated discrimination to acquire a serious education. Only twenty-seven at the time of the convention (a year or two younger than Brown), Garnet was already an ordained Presbyterian minister and a widely respected figure in the Negro Convention Movement. Anticipating the special significance of the occasion, Garnet arrived in Buffalo with his text ready.

His path to the speaker's platform, however, was anything but clear. The intricate parliamentary rules laid down for running the convention required that a select five-man committee review the contents of his text. One of its member, editor Charles Ray, objected that some of the statements, if printed, would appear unduly provocative to readers, so he recommended that Garnet's text be submitted for internal editorial review before receiving the convention's imprimatur. Garnet simply bulled his way through such objections, giving his uncensored talk on the second night at Park Street Presbyterian Church. He delivered it with such force it resonated for days afterward, generating impassioned discussions that continued to the convention's end. Subsequently titled "An Address to the Slaves of the United States," it expressed the heartfelt salutation of one ex-slave to his four million brothers and sisters over the "deep gulf" forcibly interposed between them:

> We have been contented in sitting still and mourning over your sor-rows, earnestly hoping that before this day your sacred liberty would have been restored. But, we have hoped in vain. Years have rolled on, and tens of thousands have been borne on streams of blood and tears, to the shores of eternity. While you have been oppressed, we have also been partakers with you; nor can we be free while you are enslaved. We, therefore, write to you as being bound with you. Many of you are bound to us, not only by the ties of a common humanity, but we are connected by the more tender relations of parents, wives, husbands, children, brothers, and sisters, and friends. As such we most affection-ately address you.

Its concluding prescription was provocatively militant: "Let your motto be resistance! resistance! RESISTANCE! No oppressed people have ever secured their liberty without resistance. What kind of resistance you had better make, you must decide by the circumstances that surround you, and according to the suggestion of expediency. Brethren, adieu! Trust in the living God. Labor for the peace of the human race, and remember that you are FOUR MILLIONS."[1]

Though hardly Garnet's intent, his address had its greatest direct impact on the convention delegates. Delivered with aching feeling, it released an outpouring of tears throughout the audience. A white jour-nalist reported his surprise that "for one hour of his life his mind had not been his own, but wholly at the control of the eloquent negro."[2] Ex-slaves such as Brown responded more viscerally, moved by words that unearthed buried pain and revived memories of tender family bonds. Two decades later, Brown remembered it as "one of the most noted addresses ever given by a colored man in this country," so powerful in its effect that "none but those who heard that speech have the slightest idea of the tremendous influence which he exercised over the assembly."[3]

It failed, however, to sway the minds of the majority. Frederick Douglass immediately stood up to respond, objecting to the violence of Garnet's delivery and the militancy of his rhetoric. According to the official convention minutes, Douglass cautioned his comrades to try "the moral means a little longer," while warning that acceptance of Garnet's plea would likely lead to "insurrection" ending in "catastrophe." Garnet responded in turn to Douglass, then Douglass shot back again to him—the two most forceful men in the room locked in a seemingly irresolvable difference of opinion more about antislavery tactics than about goals. An impassioned, many-sided debate spread throughout the church over a resolution to give the collective body's endorsement to printing Garnet's "Address." With feelings running high on both sides and the debate lasting several days, it finally went to a vote, losing 18 to 19. An intense effort by proponents to resume the debate prompted a further exchange of views over the final days of the convention. The intensity of the debate was so great that the convention's president, the respected New Haven minister Amos Beman, stepped down from the chair to express his heartfelt opposition to the inflammatory message of his old friend and former schoolmate.[4] With the convention about to break up, a second vote was called for, and this time, with fewer people left to participate, the resolution lost decisively, 9 to 14. The proposal was returned to Garnet, who did not publish his "Address" until 1848, by which time radical antislavery sentiment had spread widely enough to allow a hearing in print.[5]

The intricate committee structure and parliamentary maneuvering might have frustrated Garnet, but they demonstrated the considerable political sophistication and organizational expertise of the Negro Convention Movement. The leaders of the convention also displayed clear-eyed vision, taking into account not just the agenda of their meetings but also the long-term goals of the movement. Of the several committees charged with reporting on subsequent activities, two in particular had a bearing on Brown's future as a writer-activist. One was the finance committee, which he probably chaired. It reported that the revenue raised during the course of the convention was sufficient to meet the goal of publishing the proceedings. That standard task was carried out later that year. The other was an ad hoc press committee charged with investigating the prospect for establishing a national black newspaper. Although the AASS already had its national organs—the *Liberator* in Boston and the *National Anti-Slavery Standard* in New York City—many of the Buffalo delegates wished to see the installation of a press owned, operated, and conducted by their own people and unencumbered, enabling them to express their own views. The committee reported favorably on that goal. It invoked a common faith in the power of the press but interjected a cautious optimism: "Your committee entertain the common views entertained of the power and influence of the press, for good or for evil; they believe that much of the existing good, as well as of the evil in the world, owes itself to the press as an instrumentality." It also gave an articulate justification for the distinctive good that a black press—and only a black press—might accomplish: "A paper emanating from, and circulating among us, will bring us almost as it were in contact; will make us better acquainted with each other, and with the doings of each other. It will also have the tendency to unite us in a stronger bond, by teaching us that our cause and our interests are one and common." With no such communication structure behind them, this suggestion was, to use a favorite term of Brown's, a preliminary sign of a "rising" people whose rising leadership was conspicuous that week in Buffalo.

The practicality of launching such an initiative, however, severely tested their resources and resolve. The press committee asserted that the African American community was sizable enough to support multiple papers but expressed skepticism it would support any one venture. To be viable, the report stated, a newspaper would require—in language that could only have emanated from a former publisher—*"two thousand punctually paying subscribers."* This was not empty rhetoric. The committee included experienced editors such as Ray and Garnet, who were familiar with the short, unhappy lives of most US periodical ventures and knew that the odds for a black undertaking were far worse. Even the *Liberator* and the *Standard* were struggling, with subscription bases smaller than 2,000 and collections a never-ending headache. On the other hand, the committee made a sober, informed account of the long-term prospects: A viable enterprise would require communal support, and communal support could be generated only by grassroots organization. To maximize the prospect for success, they made a series of linked recommendations: a supervisory committee should be appointed from among the most knowledgeable black print men in the Northern states, including Ray, his former partner Samuel Cornish, Garnet, and the multitalented James Pennington of Hartford; itinerant agents should be appointed in each free state to raise subscriptions; and the place of publication should be New York City, by then the nation's leading publishing center.

In the event, no communal publication of the sort envisioned by the committee materialized in the early 1840s. But the subject persisted at subsequent black conventions. The October 1847 National Negro Convention meeting in Troy made the strongest appeal for a national black press: "Of the means for the advancement of a people placed as we are, none are more available than a Press."[6] Taking up the cause, Garnet argued "the most successful means which can be used for the overthrow of Slavery and Caste in this country, would be found in an able and well-conducted Press, solely under the control of the people of color."[7] When a black newspaper with national ambitions was founded, as happened just a few months later, it came via the solo initiative of one hard-driving man with private backing, Frederick Douglass. Even as a prescriptive set of guidelines, though, the 1843 Buffalo initiative had been groundbreaking. For better or for worse, it designed a useful blueprint not just for the conduct of an African American newspaper press but also for an African American communal literary culture in the antebellum North. The cohort of writers that was about to emerge during an unprecedented era of black literary activity would have to operate within opportunities and constraints similar to those envisioned by the 1843 press committee.

No nineteenth-century African American writer would learn the lesson and respond to it more creatively than William Wells Brown.

"REFORM IS COMMOTION," William Lloyd Garrison liked to say, and Garrison was a master at stirring it up.[8] Wholly immersed within the movement, he was sometimes oblivious of the degree to which reform stirred up commotion inside as well as outside the ranks. When it occurred inside, it had much of the dynamic of a family squabble. The press coverage of the 1843 Buffalo convention is a case in point. Edwin A. Marsh, a white Buffalo abolitionist with ties to the American Anti-Slavery Society (AASS), reported on the convention for the *Liberator*, but his partiality toward its concentrated minority of Garrison supporters slanted his coverage away from the views of authorized convention reporters.[9] Taking white Boston abolitionism as the normative standard for black Buffalo practice, he treated with scorn anyone who contributed to the "share of abuse" he claimed the absent Garrison had received in Buffalo. He saved his most intense hostility for Garnet and his followers, whom he accused of imposing a "gag rule" on the convention—a practice, he claimed, that ran counter to the spirit of democratic openness that characterized meetings of the AASS and the MASS. According to Marsh, Garnet was a danger to his own people, who "in his flights of fancy . . . seemed rather addressing a victorious army, than a gang of crushed and imbruted slaves, despoiled of all rights, and without the means of successful resistance." All that saved the Buffalo convention from authorizing Garnet's insanity was the resistance of the Massachusetts delegation—the Garrisonian allies Remond and Douglass.

Marsh also named a third stalwart who manfully challenged Garnet: "W. W. Brown." At this moment of formal initiation into the antislavery movement, the twenty-nine-year-old Brown participated energetically in the creative ferment of his hometown convention alongside some of his most important future peers. For the first of hundreds of times over the next forty years, he interacted with highly skilled, veteran activists in the intricate maneuvering, strategizing, and public speaking characteristic of nineteenth-century reform meetings, which in Buffalo began with the rules and procedures that governed the convention and ended only when Garnet's address was twice raised and defeated. On that most urgent resolution, he spoke and voted with the Douglass faction against Garnet. Not yet done, he pursued his critique of Garnet out into the open a month later by writing to the national antislavery press and challenging the assertion Garnet made at the Liberty Party convention, also held in Buffalo that month, that only two delegates (Douglass and Remond) demurred from the convention's general endorsement of party principles.[10] Brown made three, and he stated that there were others as well.

Brown's public disagreement—it was only his first—with Garnet was at the time a relatively minor matter. Many of the views expressed at the convention were provisional; and, given the turbulent times to come, all positions taken were lines drawn in shifting sands. Douglass, for example, had just left Buffalo to continue a Western lecture tour when he and a colleague were assaulted by a mob in Indiana. Never one to back down, he defended himself forcefully with a stick against attackers armed with clubs. He suffered a crushing blow that resulted in a compound fracture of his right arm and was fortunate to get away with his life. Douglass was at the time a loyal, respected lecturer for the pacifist Massachusetts Anti-Slavery Society, carrying its banner and doing some of its grittiest work across the Western states. Within a few years, however, he would begin to move away from Garrison and toward a more aggressively interventionist course of black activism and political involvement. A central vehicle of his repositioning was the *North Star*, the independent newspaper he established in 1847 in Rochester.

Brown, by contrast, was just setting foot, after the Buffalo convention, down the Garrisonian path, a route that in four years' time would lead him to Boston at the exact moment Douglass was blazing his separate trail away from the Massachusetts Anti-Slavery Society. A few days after the close of the Buffalo meeting, Brown traveled to Rochester to participate in the statewide New York Colored People's Convention. He played an active role in its deliberations and left as one of two representatives from Erie County responsible for carrying out the convention's goals.[11] Sometime that fall, he formalized his commitment to the movement by signing on as a paid agent of the fledgling Western New York Anti-Slavery Society (WNYASS). His new professional status was recorded formally when the next Buffalo city directory listed him as a "lecturer," one of very few people so listed in a city that supported a wide variety of reform activities.[12] The source of that information was presumably Brown himself, who must have been home for a change when the directory compiler stopped by. He would serve as a paid lecturer, on and off, for various branches of the American Anti-Slavery Society and the Massachusetts Anti-Slavery Society for the next two decades.

He worked for the WNYASS for nearly four years. During that period, Brown devoted the majority of his time, day and night, to promoting, disseminating, and defending the movement's antislavery agenda. The task of itinerant lecturing was nearly all-demanding. It combined elements of all-out political barnstorming and hard-boiled camp meetings conducted for weeks at a time in conditions ranging from uncomfortable to difficult and sometimes primitive. Brown's territory, a largely rural swath of western New York, would have tried the stamina of even the most committed agents. Distances between engagements were considerable, the moods of the populace were unpredictable, and weather might be extreme. Meetings took place every day (including Sundays) and at all hours; most were held in rented public facilities (churches, lecture halls, town and city halls, courthouses, schoolhouses), but from time to time, when other arrangements could not be made, they occurred out of doors, exposing lecturers and audiences to the elements. Lodging was often spare and sometimes depended on the kindness of strangers when local supporters were unavailable or unwilling to share their homes. Hotels and boardinghouses were sometimes an option, but most did not admit blacks, regardless of reputation.

On rare occasions, Brown failed to find housing of any sort, such as one cold night in Attica, New York, when he spent hours pacing in a church sanctuary to keep warm.[13] Such experiences reinforced the underlying reality that racial discrimination was an everyday fact of life for black lecturers, although witnessing actual instances sometimes left their white colleagues in shock. A case in point was the idealistic reformer Reverend Charles Spear, who was mortified to find that his black companion, the onetime North Carolina slave (and Brown's future Cambridge neighbor) Lunsford Lane, was not welcome to join him for an overnight stay at a friend's house in the town of Harvard, Massachusetts. Lane's heroic efforts to purchase freedom first for himself, and then for his wife and children, meant nothing to this friend. Spear reacted tersely in his diary: "He who shuts out my brother, shuts me out also."[14] Nearly a decade later, Spear remained true to his principles by escorting Clara and Josephine Brown across the Atlantic to join their father in London.

Itinerancy was a fact of life, as agents carried the message of reform to anywhere audiences could be assembled. Tours of duty frequently lasted for weeks, sometimes the entire period for which lecturers contracted their services to the host institution. Lecturers generally scouted out receptive locations, sometimes returning to neighborhoods previously visited by their peers to reinforce and spread their message. At other times, they ventured directly into territories considered hostile. One such locale was the town of Fredonia—"the most proslavery place" in New York's Chautauqua County, according to Joseph C. Hathaway—which Brown canvassed numerous times. When no one showed up to hear them one night in June 1846, Brown and Hathaway stood in the village square and sang antislavery songs, such as "Come Join the Abolitionists," until a crowd gradually formed.[15] Audience size and mood were often unpredictable. In most places it took intensive advance work for lecturers and their supporters to fill empty benches with bodies, but even then they could not always anticipate how those bodies might respond to their message. They often faced opposition, and they also understood that in worst-case scenarios hostility might escalate into individual or even mob violence. Violence was so pervasive a fear that *mobbed* became a standard term in the abolitionist vocabulary—a term of dread when mentioned hypothetically, a badge of honor when spoken retrospectively among friends. Agents routinely served as targets for everything from verbal abuse to physical projectiles. During the mid-1840s, hostile listeners pelted Brown with eggs, fruit, vegetables, and stones, though he was never seriously hurt. Unluckier companions, like Douglass, carried a variety of injuries resulting in lifelong scars, brandings, and disabilities.

Travel schedules were hectic; lecturers rarely stayed in one place for more than a day or two before heading out to the next engagement. Popular lecturers like Brown spent far more time on the road than at home, often having to neglect not just their families but also their primary sources of livelihood—the latter, ironically, a problem from which Brown was spared. During a two-week period over November-December 1846, for example, Brown's upstate schedule ran as follows: Hannibal on November 19th, Granby on the 20th, Fulton on the 21st, Volney on the 22nd, Constantia on the 23rd, Amboy on the 24th, Williamston on the 26th, Sand Bank on the 27th, Washington on the 28–29th, Pulaski on the 30th and December 1st, Plattsville on the 2nd, Mexico on the 3d, New Haven on the 4th, and Oswego on the 5th–7th.[16] During the final eight months of that year alone, he participated in 167 meetings.[17] All told during his nearly four years of service with the WNYASS, he conducted or participated in many hundreds of meetings.

Tours were arranged mostly but not entirely in advance by general agents normally stationed at the organization's home base. These coordinating operatives generally dispatched teams of lecturers working in pairs or trios who traveled together for all or part of the tour. The general agents virtually always teamed African American lecturers with white counterparts. Brown was an exception during the various months in 1846–47 when he served for a time simultaneously as the general agent of the WNYASS and the organization's foremost lecturer. These general agents often operated with only limited information, as they sent their agents out in mediated circuits. To spread the word and arouse interest, the movement utilized various means of dissemination. The regional antislavery press generally posted their travel schedules a week or two in advance, and local supporters prepared and posted handbills. Even with the best planning, however, complications caused by weather, illness, faulty planning, or sheer lack of interest necessitated alterations of date, location, or even speaker. An agent unable to improvise was poorly equipped for the work. By contrast, master improvisers like Brown and Douglass typically made the best operatives.

Transportation was only as good as the local networks. On some occasions, particularly over short distances, agents might find transport, along with accommodations, from supporters. More typically, however, they traveled by whatever means was available: train, boat, carriage, horseback, or even sleigh. On any extended campaign, they went equipped with the best available local or regional maps. The New York state "campaign map" used by Brown's lecturing partner E. D. Hudson in 1847 indicates canal, river, and train lines as well as mail routes across the state.[18] Agents also carried the most current railway and steamboat schedules. Conditions improved measurably over the course of the 1840s, particularly as railway lines spread across many parts of the Northeast and even the upper West. Compared to England and France, though, road conditions in the United States remained difficult at best through most of the nineteenth century, and lack of reliability created further problems.

Also a problem was keeping in touch with family and friends as lecturers stretched their lines of communication outside of cities. The wide-ranging Abby Kelley revealed the common frustration in complaining to a fellow agent: "You are aware that I am so much every where and no where that I do not get my letters readily."[19] Family ties often became stretched as thin as communication lines. E. D. Hudson's wife, Martha, expressed the feelings of many spouses left home on their own to hold the family together: "I can assure you that it is not without some sacrifice on my part that I give up my dear Husband to the cause."[20] That confidential revelation to Kelley, of all people, had a particular poignancy, since Kelley herself, from 1845, struggled to balance a young marriage to fellow lecturer Stephen S. Foster with an exhausting commitment to antislavery lecturing and organizing.

The strains on both of them, as on all committed lecturers, tested their dedication to each other and to the movement. Foster, one of the most indefatigable and steadfast of all agents, eventually confided in Kelley (with a verbal conflation not uncommon among white agents),

"You can hardly imagine what a dislike I have to this meandering mode of life. It is the next thing to being a slave."[21] Sydney Howard Gay likewise confided in Kelley the lurking thought that at some moment must have overshadowed most lecturers: "Agents should talk anti-slavery, walk a. s., think a. s., wake, sleep, dream, feast, fast a. s. . . . A man is indeed anti-slavery just so far forth as its principles pervade his being . . . and he makes his life anti-slavery, and not anti-slavery his life."[22] Gay's fine distinctions betrayed his doubts about whether he was up to the task. If so, when did "*the hardness* of the A.S. life," as MASS general agent Samuel May Jr. called it, become too much for some lecturers?[23] Gay knew his limits; he eventually traded a high-pressure career as an AASS activist and editor for a fellow traveler's by taking a well-paying, sedentary editorial position with Horace Greeley's reform-minded but independent *New York Tribune*. Black lecturers such as Brown, Remond, and Douglass were no less likely than their white allies to suffer burnout, but of course they could not escape their skin color or condition.

Brown's private and public lives moved increasingly in opposing directions after he joined the movement. By the mid-1840s, William and Betsey's marriage was disintegrating, as Betsey grew increasingly disaffected by her husband's long absences. With the birth of Henrietta Helen, named after Betsey's mother, on or around August 23, 1842, she now had three small children to care for and, she increasingly felt, no husband to share the burden.[24] What registered as a point of pride with him registered as a source of alienation for Betsey, whose regard for her husband's new profession began in skepticism and over time deteriorated into outright animosity. Overwhelming though it must have felt to them, their discord was not uncommon; the demanding schedules of itinerant lecturers caused strains on the stability of many reform households, black and white. One thinks immediately, on this point as on many others, of the household of Anna Murray and Frederick Douglass. Likewise left to raise a fast-growing family, Anna also suffered from her husband's frequent long absences. Worse yet, gossipy reports came back that Anna had more reason than Betsey to be wary of the consequences of losing sight of her husband for long periods. Douglass was, in the words of one of many admirers of the two men during their tours of the British Isles, more of "a lady's man" than Brown.[25] In this instance, gossip preceded truth.

FREDERICK DOUGLASS'S IMMERSION in the antislavery movement tested the integrity of his marriage to Anna Murray Douglass. Likewise Brown's involvement and his troubled marriage. In truth, Betsey and William each paid a cumulative price for his repeated absences. One major flash point occurred in early May 1844, when Brown left Buffalo to attend his first national convention of the AASS. The society held its annual meeting in New York City as one of the many reform gatherings convened during "Anniversary Week" alongside such organizations as the American and Foreign Anti-Slavery Society, the American Bible Society, and the American Tract Society. Mixing among prominent people, many of whom he had previously known only by reputation, Brown had the heady experience of delivering his first speech to a convention that attracted many of the leading figures in the country, including the New England trio of Garrison, Phillips, and Quincy. His timing, however, was disastrous: Three days earlier, twenty-month-old Henrietta had died in Buffalo. Nothing is known about how the toddler died, whether she had been seriously ill before his departure, or whether Betsey had pressured him to cancel his trip. Since telegraph lines did not yet connect Buffalo and New York City, he might not have received word of her death until after his train from New York had departed for Buffalo. He might not even have arrived home in time for the funeral. All that is certain is that he returned to a house of mourning and a deeply agitated wife. And nothing could have been less calculated to soothe Betsey's grief than the brief obituary in the *National Anti-Slavery Standard*, which misnamed her "Betty" and proudly noted that the little girl had died "while her father was out in the field pleading the cause of the slave."[26] Betsey would have met expressions of intended solace coming from such sources—and possibly even from her activist husband—only with deep resentment, as she grew bitterly hostile to a cause she blamed for undermining her family's well-being.

Despite the situation he faced at home, Brown soon returned to his work. He was back on the road within weeks of Henrietta's death, lecturing at a rate of a meeting nearly every night, participating in antislavery fairs, and selling the movement's publications across the cities, towns, and villages of western New York. The people he was meeting in the countryside, he reported collegially to Amy Post in June, were "wide awake," and so, he was happy to report, were he and his allies.[27] They had to be; only the most resourceful and talented among them succeeded in transmitting the core message about the nation's failure to honor the founding principle "all men are created equal," a message most Americans had little wish or tolerance to consider as applicable to men (never mind women) of all colors. Gradually, out of that tight cadre of committed activists who remained involved for the long term, a small number— some white and a very few black—rose to prominence.

That summer of 1844, Brown was almost constantly on the road, participating in a series of daily meetings—sometimes day and night— that lasted through August. In September, possibly without once touching home base, he undertook his first trip back to Ohio since his escape from Price, turning up the local soil for converts to the cause. He agreed to make the trip despite an eye ailment serious enough to restrict his movement for a time and lead him to consider surgery.[28] The medical problem resolved itself without intervention, however, and he pushed on across parts of the state as an agent on loan to the Ohio American Anti-Slavery Society.[29] Most of his time he devoted to traversing towns and villages already familiar to him along Lake Erie, where antislavery prospects were best in a state notorious for its discriminatory Black Laws. One day, while traveling on the recently built Mad River and Lake Erie Railroad south from the port city of Sandusky to a lecture date in the small town of Republic, Betsey's renamed hometown, he experienced the second-class treatment commonly meted out to black travelers in the state. He was sitting in one of the regular coaches when a conductor confronted him with the company's whites-only policy. His options: Get off the train and transfer to one carrying a Jim Crow car, or move to the uncovered freight car in the rear. When no one came to his defense, he retreated to the freight car, where, in his later written accounts of the incident, he sat on a flour barrel reading Pope's *Essay on Man* or the latest issue of the *Liberator* (the text varied with the account) until interrupted again by a conductor demanding regular coach fare. Brown balked at the demand of equal fare for unequal conditions and engaged the over-matched official in a battle of wits. What was the going rate for freight by the hundredweight? When the conductor insisted on standard fare, Brown countered with the logic of chattel slavery in assessing his person at 150 pounds and insisting on paying bulk rate.[30]

Apparently unconcerned about his vulnerability during this tour, Brown ventured south and southeast across the state, descending danger-ously close at times to the Virginia border. Perhaps he proceeded at first on the assumption that his post-slavery name hid his identity under a cloak of invisibility, but he must have known that his remarks at meetings endan-gered him by exposing his fugitive status. Before long, he found out that no person of color, free or fugitive, had immunity in Ohio. Passing one day through Ulysses S. Grant's boyhood home of Georgetown en route to his next engagement, he learned that the previous night a gang of men had broken into the house of a black family named Wilkinson, assaulted the parents, and kidnapped their teenage son. Moving fast, they crossed the Ohio River into Virginia, ahead of the pursuing father and neighbors. The next morning, Brown visited the Wilkinson house and sat with the bruised mother, noticing blood on the floor; he was still there when the father returned alone. There was nothing he or anyone else could do to retrieve his son, an enraged Brown reported to the press.[31]

By 1844, Brown was already a highly accomplished lecturer, with a spreading reputation. One reason for his success was his fugitive status, which gave his remarks an authority that not even a polished, Northern-born black orator like his sometime-comrade Charles Remond could match. But it took more than skin color or an enslaved past to make an effective lecturer. Dozens of other fugitives took to the lecture circuit during the 1840s and 1850s, but few managed to sustain themselves for long. By contrast, Brown succeeded early and lasted long, never wholly retiring from public speaking. Press reports about him during this Ohio trip indicate he had found his distinctive voice, which held audiences for long stretches and generally earned their respect.

His voice came through clearly one September evening in the kind of setting he occasionally visited, a small Methodist church in Ohio whose doors were open—when most were shut—to the message of reform. Brown ran the meeting, which he began by inviting the resident deacon to recite a prayer for the assembled. The deacon obliged by offering a prayer for the welfare of Henry Clay, a favorite son in southern Ohio then making another run for the White House. No sooner had the deacon finished than Brown stood to deliver a speech in which he coolly took issue with both of the major political parties. That ideological critique of party politics, however, formed no part of the letter he subsequently composed for publication in the New York City antislavery press. With a snide poke at Clay's pose as a Kentucky gentleman farmer, Brown reported to his newspaper audience that "my text was the Farmer of Ashland," an improvised parody of the deacon's prayer:

> Lord! We look to thee to aid us in selecting good rulers. Lord! Let us have men that will rule over us with fear; let us have good rulers . . . Lord! let nothing be said that will hurt anyone's feelings. Lord! may he say nothing about political parties. Lord! thou knowest that some of the Abolition lecturers do say hard things about our Southern brethren. Lord! thou knowest that some of them have attempted to vilify Mr. Clay, and slander him by saying that he is a duelist, and calling him hard names. Lord! let nothing of the kind be said this evening. Lord! thou knowest that Mr. Clay is a good man, and if we do not elect him we will get a worse one. Thou knowest that the Abolitionists are trying to keep out Mr. Clay, but let them not do it. Now, Lord! take charge of thy servant that is going to speak, and let him present nothing but the truth, and let him say nothing about politics, and the glory shall be thine forever, Amen.[32]

Brown's "Farmer of Ashland" recitation is the earliest known display in writing of his storytelling prowess. Though unpracticed, Brown's writing already exhibited some of the standard qualities of his mature rhetoric: its easy mastery of audience address, sly inversion of subject positions, flawless mimicry of the speech pattern and argument of proslavery discourse, and burning anticlericalism of a not-so-true believer.

His words passed smoothly from speech to writing in a pattern that Brown continued throughout his career. The new editorial team of the *National Anti-Slavery Standard*, now including Brown's supporter Sydney Howard Gay, took note of his skill; they recognized they were seeing a distinctly higher order of prose than they generally printed. As Brown continued to send them public letters over the next three years, they printed them with relish, their pleasure occasionally expressed in editorial endorsements. The editors recognized that this eloquent ex-slave had a rivetingly effective way of transmitting exactly the message they wished to disseminate. As long as he kept to that message, he was sure to get lecture dates from the antislavery managers and publication from the editors.

The "Farmer of Ashland" and other public letters of 1844–45 coincide with the earliest handful of Brown's surviving manuscripts, all letters hastily written on cheap paper containing field reports sent off to esteemed white colleagues. The discrepancy between the polished prose and rhetorical mastery of the published talks and the raw penmanship and unfinished grammar of the handwritten letters is striking. Brown habitually dashed off these early, unguarded letters with little regard for formal correctness or stylistic elegance. Their spelling was unsteady, punctuation erratic, paragraphing uncertain, and syntax organized simply by aggregating units of thought on paper more or less as they came to him. At this stage in his development as a public writer, Brown sorely needed an editor and generally got one.

MANAGERS OF ANTISLAVERY SOCIETIES preferred low-maintenance operatives like Brown, whose overall lecturing ability, general reliability, smooth salesmanship, and apparent affability made him a nearly model employee. Even more valuable was his fugitive-slave status. Through the 1840s, he was repeatedly introduced at meetings as William Wells

Brown *fugitive slave*, an honorific he would bear for years before he could replace it with the more desirable titles of William Wells Brown *author* or William Wells Brown *doctor*. Before any but the most skeptical or big- oted audiences, his enslaved past gave him enhanced authority. During his emergence as a model black agent of the movement, his Massachu- setts friend Remond was privately regarded as his foil. Although this long-serving black Garrisonian proved himself an eloquent, dedicated, and loyal comrade, he alienated some of the managers by being prickly and self-justifying. Occasionally he emerged as the subject of internal discussion, some of it snide.

One story—the "horse question," as one exasperated colleague labeled it—exemplifies the complicated relations between Remond and his col- leagues.[33] In 1846, Remond bickered for months with the managers of the MASS over fair compensation for a horse he had purchased in Indiana for transportation over otherwise-impassable roads during the Hundred Conventions campaign in the West, the latest attempt by the antislav- ery movement to disseminate its message across a large geographical area. After the horse died in Pennsylvania on the return trip, Remond unyieldingly demanded fair compensation for what he considered a major expense suffered in the line of duty. He even attended the meeting of the MASS's executive committee in Boston to press his case. Neither side gave ground, resulting in a stalemate that prompted the committee to solicit testimony from Remond's touring companions (even reaching across the Atlantic Ocean to involve the absent Douglass). They too, as it turned out, had bought horses for their use in the campaign but did not charge the organization for what they considered private property. Douglass took the trouble to respond from Scotland and Gay from New York City, although both complied only with reluctance. As neither had anything to say to support Remond's case, he presumably lost.

The story of Remond and the horse has its comic element, but there was nothing amusing about it to Remond. By his calculation, he had given ten years of devoted service to the MASS, yet he found himself in debt with his dignity frayed.[34] Nor would there be anything amusing to Brown several years later when it was his turn to pass before the official eye of the organization. In his case, the subject of investigation was not a horse but an estranged spouse.

Brown—in one of his favorite phrases—was "wide-awake" as usual in service to the cause in fall 1844, but he was less attentive to the state of his marriage. One day in December, he returned to Buffalo to find the mercurial Betsey inexplicably hostile to him ("a change of which I tried in vain to find out the cause," he wrote, years later). Perhaps he should have inquired of his neighbors, who surely were observing a pattern of behavior to which he had been blind. At the time, Betsey was not his only problem; he was also severely short of funds. Whatever salary he was receiving from the WNYASS did not meet the family's needs. Colleagues in the movement were aware of the situation; a private letter exchanged between two of the main fund-raisers discussed the Brown family's poverty and urged that money be raised for them from among the Rochester friends of the movement.[35] There was no special shame in that appeal; funds were periodically raised for other self-sacrificing servants of the movement, most notably and munificently for Garrison. Whatever the outcome of that appeal, Brown continued to labor single-mindedly for the movement through the winter, beating pathways over snow and ice to lecture across the state's western counties. In February 1845, he participated in his first annual WNYASS convention, held in the worst blizzard to hit Rochester in a half-dozen years. He sang an antislavery song to the assemblage, spoke to several resolutions, and conducted himself with the assured competence of one of the organization's central members.[36]

Following that meeting, he headed back onto the road to begin another night-after-night lecture tour across western New York, including an appearance in Syracuse in late February. For March, he was advertised to appear in Port Byron, Seneca Falls, Northville, and a string of locations in Cayuga County.[37] Pushing himself to the limit in harsh cold and primitive conditions, he became ill and had to cut short his tour, returning to Buffalo late one night. Walking into the house unexpectedly, he found Betsey, "in circumstances that filled me with the most painful suspicion," with James Garrett, a friend and fellow traveler who,

Brown noted without irony, made it a practice to borrow his antislavery newspapers. Garrett partnered with antislavery activist Abner H. Francis in a successful Buffalo clothing store but kept his distance from the movement. Brown reluctantly accepted their explanation but afterward demanded of Betsey that Garrett be banned from the house. His suspicion, however, remained aroused, and he kept a watchful eye on Betsey's activities. Sure enough, just weeks later he entered the house at night through the back door and caught them in what he called "circumstances of a still more revolting character."[38]

This time he was ready to demand a break. Standing tall on his male authority, he issued Betsey an ultimatum: Choose Garrett or her family. To force the issue, he arranged in June 1845 to move their family to Farmington, an isolated Quaker farming community about twenty-five miles southeast of Rochester.[39] Brown knew it well; he had lectured there on a number of occasions dating back to January 1844. The main attraction, besides its remoteness from Buffalo, was the presence of his warm friend Joseph C. Hathaway and an actively antislavery Quaker community. Hathaway and his large extended family were mainstays of the community and vigorous supporters of the WNYASS, which Hathaway served from its founding and headed in 1846. Like many other white antislavery activists, Hathaway needed to find creative ways to balance his commitment to the movement and his need to attend to his growing family's source of livelihood, their crops and livestock. For better or worse, Brown had no such choice; his only source of income at this time came from lecturing. Living for the first time since slavery in the midst of farmers, he himself felt no attraction whatsoever to the lifestyle of his past; any possible appeal had been beaten out of him. At this point in his life, he could not even have imagined that he would ever become a rural landowner, despite the fact that property ownership was still a prerequisite to black suffrage in New York.

Hathaway not only appreciated Brown's abilities but also sympathized with his personal circumstances. His family might well have helped the Browns, a family clearly in need, to find local housing and get situated in the community. During their two years in the village, the Browns either lived in their own house or shared quarters with another family, most likely a branch of the Hathaway clan.[40] The two girls attended the local Friends school, which was acceptable to the family because it was integrated. Intelligent and highly motivated, they must have taken to their schooling with enthusiasm. In addition to challenging their minds, school would have been a sorely welcome refuge during this two-year period of serious domestic instability, when their father was generally away traveling for the WNYASS and their mother was acting increasingly irresponsibly. Betsey had made the move reluctantly and never found her own footing in the tightly knit Quaker village. Not even the kindliest intentions from her neighbors would have made her feel anything but alien. To complicate her isolation, there was little or no African American companionship in the immediate vicinity. If there were any black neighbors, they would likely have been fugitives who had arrived in Farmington via the Underground Railroad, but that was a group with which Betsey had little in common, and, given her feelings about the former fugitive at home, one to which she might not have been kindly disposed.

Even worse, her relationship with her husband was going from cold to frozen, as he continued to absent himself from the house for long periods. Eventually her isolation and loneliness drove her to desperation. On several occasions while he was away, she took off impulsively on her own, abandoning the girls to the care of the community. Brown suspected, not without cause, that she went looking for Garrett.

By contrast with Betsey, Brown found Farmington a congenial, supportive community and a spur to his activity. A strategic geographical crossroads for the reform movement, Farmington was one of the most progressive villages in upstate New York. Located along a main east–west stagecoach route, it was easily reached by reform speakers on tour, as well as by fugitive slaves using it as a stopping point on their way north to Lake Erie and Canada. The best-known fugitive to take up residence in the town before Brown was Austin Steward, a fugitive originally from Virginia who had attended school in the village a generation earlier.[41] By the time of the Browns' arrival, Steward was one of the leaders of the Negro Convention Movement in New York state. Brown made his acquaintance at the 1843 Buffalo convention and renewed acquaintance with him subsequently. The town meanwhile maintained close ties to the WNYASS through the Hathaway family and other committed Quakers, as well as to a range of complementary reform movements, including women's rights; no community of its size had an equal number of signatories to the 1848 Seneca Falls Declaration of Sentiments. Some of the leading speakers of the day stopped to address the townspeople. During these years, Douglass, Remond, Lucretia Mott, and Susan B. Anthony (a cousin of Hathaway's wife) all came to town to speak at the Quaker Meeting House, well known throughout the region as a safe house. In time, Brown would partner with all of them on the lecture circuit.

Soon after settling in Farmington, Brown resumed his reform activity, splitting his time at first between the white and black antislavery movements. In the summer and fall of 1845, he attended several black conventions in New York state, including the large black-suffrage meeting held in Geneva in October. Deputed to speak on behalf of Austin Steward, its president, and the other officers several weeks before the meeting, Brown addressed a public invitation letter to ex-Governor William Seward, one of the very few influential national politicians sympathetic to antislavery. Seward responded cordially with his own public letter, sympathizing heartily with the cause but declining the invitation.[42] On the face of it, that exchange was strange. Why was a dedicated employee of the American Anti-Slavery Society—which uncompromisingly opposed all organized political activity as a debased and ineffective means of ending slavery—lobbying a prominent politician for the restoration of black suffrage in New York? Why, for that matter, would Brown engage any politician after consistently opposing the antislavery Liberty Party ever since the Buffalo convention? The paradox typified Brown—unyieldingly loyal to Garrison but intellectually and temperamentally unsuited to any form of orthodoxy. Like it or not, Brown was at the time disenfranchised not simply because he was black but because he was a nonlanded black man. That status would change, however, in late 1846, when Brown became one of the hundreds of African American residents of New York to whom Gerrit Smith, the most beneficent philanthropist in the movement, deeded parcels from the hundreds of thousands of acres he owned in upstate New York. In fact, even after Brown eventually gained citizenship in Massachusetts, he did not cast a vote until after the Civil War. By contrast, Remond earned the scorn of his colleagues when he cast a vote in the 1848 elections. Brown's principled refusal would put him at odds with an increasing number of free African Americans as strife between North and South intensified and slaves were held hostage in the sectional conflict.

Brown's reputation grew during the mid-1840s among both black and white colleagues. He continued as a featured lecturer for the WNYASS through late 1846, but by then he had also come to the attention of the parent AASS and its sister MASS organization. He had a particularly well-placed ally in Sydney Howard Gay of the *National Anti-Slavery Standard*, a regular correspondent of Garrison and Phillips. Brown came to feel comfortable confiding some of his views to Gay, as in stating his opinion about the kind of reaction Garrison and Phillips would receive should they make a long-desired visit to western New York: "Anti slavery folks will welcome them as the Athenians did Demosthenes."[43]

His stature on the rise, Brown became more ambitious about his career prospects. In August or September, he initiated a connection with the MASS, corresponding with its general agent about a salaried position in Massachusetts for the winter of 1846–47, but his timing was poor.[44] The general agent, Loring Moody, eventually took Brown's request to the board of managers, which typically made hiring and retention decisions by weighing a combination of factors, such as ideological purity, personality, needs, and budget. In this instance, however, there was an additional consideration: Moody's own status was uncertain. The board tabled his request for agents, including Brown, then terminated his service and began a search for a new general agent. Meanwhile they hired field agents, though not Brown, on a short-term basis. His time had not yet come, although it was not far off.

So back he went into the field for the WNYASS. Over September–October, he moved across the rural counties of Orleans, Monroe, Cayuga,

Livingston, and Wyoming, his schedule broadcast one or two weeks in advance in the columns of the *National Anti-Slavery Standard* as well as locally. Each night, alone or with others, he delivered a performance to a new audience. Like other agents, he also integrated into his meetings solicitations for movement publications—the *Standard*, almanacs, juvenilia, slave narratives, and miscellaneous polemical works. Those texts came primarily from the AASS book depository in New York City as well as from the Boston depository of the MASS organization, which also operated a high-functioning printing/publishing office.

By the time Brown resumed his work for the WNYASS out of his base in Farmington, one of the fastest sellers in the movement was *Narrative of the Life of Frederick Douglass*, published by the MASS about the time of Brown's move to Farmington. Copies of that work were presumably included among the miscellaneous antislavery materials shipped out from New York to the WNYASS depositories in Rochester and Buffalo, and from there dispensed to agents such as Brown for distribution in the field. At his meetings, Brown almost surely would have been selling copies of Douglass's *Narrative*, a work he read avidly and one that would prove formative in the conceptualization of his own *Narrative*. More broadly speaking, playing the role of sales agent for the movement's publications was a vital component of Brown's work, since he received his compensation principally from collections gathered at meetings, supplemented by donations. This less-than-ideal arrangement was no private matter; Hathaway thoughtfully publicized Brown's tenuous financial situation in the *Standard*.[45]

Brown's backcountry territory was situated far from major cities and half a continent away from the battlefields of the Mexican-American War, but no place in the country lay beyond the range of heated debate about that divisive conflict. By the mid-1840s, Brown regularly entered into this debate in response to the aggressively expansionist policies pursued by the James Polk administration, which raised the stakes of the slavery issue by its confrontational stance toward Mexico. Once armed conflict began in 1846, a growing number of Northerners (as well as Southerners) could no longer disregard a scenario of annexed territories, stretching from Texas to the Pacific Southwest, entering the Union as slave states. With the congressional balance between North and South seemingly at stake, national politics brought the interests of the antislavery movement into greater alignment with those of antiwar factions in the Whig and Democratic Parties, which, for their own reasons, also opposed Polk's gargantuan land grab. As the organized antislavery movement took an increasingly aggressive posture toward the conflict, Brown highlighted it in his meetings during 1846 and 1847. Little by little, even a supposedly apolitical reformer found that his meetings were becoming battlegrounds for the conduct of American policy.

At many stops, he delivered reports of the latest news from the antislavery front. From time to time, he produced an actual newspaper on stage, although it was typically a proslavery paper that he read only to counter its position. Toughened by a lifetime of abuse, Brown not only stood up to attacks on everything from his war views to his skin color but also ventured further than his white comrades by critiquing the racial dimensions of the war. In one graphic instance, at an annual convention of the WNYASS, he offered a resolution that African Americans either refuse to serve in the war or cross over to join the ranks of the racially mixed Mexican army. That argument was labeled so "belligerent," even among allies, as to draw support only from Remond before Brown felt compelled to withdraw his resolution.[46]

His meetings through the fall and winter of 1846–47 continued his assault on the war. One of his most interesting meetings occurred the evening of Wednesday, October 21, 1846, in the small town of Warsaw, seat of Wyoming County. Although it happened to coincide with a session of the district court, he drew a large, animated crowd and wound up overseeing a spirited debate. The meeting culminated in a resolution by the town's leading citizen, the former Whig Congressman Seth Gates, calling for equal suffrage for black males, which received unanimous acceptance. As occasionally happened, that meeting generated such enthusiasm that a second one was called for. Brown accepted the local judge's offer to adjourn his proceedings and use his courthouse for this second gathering, so on Friday evening he lectured in the courthouse to a large audience, including many of the community's professionals. Brown afterward recorded the meeting's outcome in inflammatory language: "This adjourning the county court to hear a nigger, shows some progress in Anti-Slavery. This Mexico war has opened the eyes of the people; they begin to look at the American Union in its true light. The period has, indeed, arrived, the crisis has come, when the wise, the virtuous, the patriotic, and the philanthropic of the United States, and the world, must examine into this Americanism, this slaveholding, woman-whipping, baby-stealing Republicanism."[47]

In November and December, he was off on lecture tours across Wayne, Cayuga, and Oswego Counties, with occasional stopovers to see his family in Farmington. Over the course of a two-day meeting in Mexicoville, Cayuga County, Brown took on Asa Wing, a prominent local lawyer, in a far-ranging public debate that eventually focused on one of the most controversial questions of the day: Did the Constitution protect slavery, as even moderate Americans such as Abraham Lincoln believed? A clearly partisan observer summarized their debate: "The discussion continued until about nine o'clock in the evening; and it is but justice to say that it was very ably and politely handled by both parties. It was admitted by all that Brown did himself great credit, and, I thought, had altogether the best of the argument; and after the meeting the cry was, that the nigger had whipped Wing. One rough man said, no wonder the d———d nigger could whip Wing, for he had the most talented blood in his veins that Kentucky could produce."[48] So it went, as week after week Brown pushed on through the upstate mud to carry his argument.

He continued as a main lecturer for the WNYASS through February 1847, attending the annual convention in Rochester as well as local antislavery fairs. Right after the annual WNYASS convention, he held eight days of meetings in Steuben County, at Avoca, Clisbee's, Mud Creek, and Corning, before going to Bath to stay with friends. He must have made deep inroads with the African American community in Bath, since its "colored choir" insisted on accompanying him to his next destination, Hammondsport, in the Finger Lakes.[49] Shortly afterward, he joined forces with Hathaway, Remond, and E. D. Hudson on a long lecture tour sponsored by the AASS. It might well have marked a change in his professional affiliation; whether he had as yet made a formal decision, his days as a regional lecturer for the WNYASS were over.

The AASS tour took him farther east than he had previously traveled, toward central and eventually eastern New York state. Cutting by sleigh through heavy snowdrifts, he arrived with Remond and Hathaway at West Winfield, a small town twenty miles south of Utica, where they linked up with Hudson, who had made his way from the east through a driving winter storm. The team, minus the ill Hathaway, conducted a few meetings timed to coincide with the local antislavery fair scheduled to open on February 8 and continue through the weekend. Early that day, they went up to the second floor of the building, which was built over a large horse stable and storage area, to inspect the offerings. They found everything in a state of near-readiness for the big fund-raising event—tables handsomely spread out with a display of various crafts, prepared and dry foods, and printed material for sale, proceeds to go to the AASS. By evening, a large crowd had gathered, and, as Hudson reported to his wife, the room was filled with "song and mirth"—that is, until an explosion ripped through the building, shattering glass and causing the floor, unsupported by a crossbeam, to buckle violently on one side toward the street. Hudson, Brown, and Remond were in a portion of the hall where the floor remained intact, but less fortunate people were trapped in rubble or pitched out into the street. Hudson, an accomplished doctor (and a leading prosthetic surgeon during and after the Civil War), rushed down to attend to the injured, noting that miraculously no one had been mortally hurt. Once he had finished that work, he turned his attention to resuscitating the antislavery fair. He performed that labor, he assured his wife, virtually singlehandedly, while Brown and Remond stood by skeptically. "I have worked like a slave," he wrote her, getting precious little help from his team—what with Hathaway sick, Remond "good for nothing in such an affair," and Brown "not knowing what to do."[50] Thanks to his efforts alone, he reported back home, the fair and convention took place that weekend with minimal inconvenience.

The team then split up, Brown now partnering with his take-charge colleague Hudson on a tour of New York state through most of the spring. The pair held meetings at dozens of stops as they traveled eastward toward Schenectady and Albany, then worked their way down the Hudson River Valley as far south as Ulster and Dutchess Counties. They traveled against the backdrop of the heightened political drama following congressional debates on the Wilmot Proviso, a rider to an appropriations bill that would have forbidden slavery in territories annexed from Mexico. Though defeated, it drove a deepening sectional wedge over slavery. All during that lecture tour, Brown was also carrying a personal burden. Following the completion of their tour on May 7, Brown might have made a brief return home to Farmington, but more likely he headed directly to New York City for the annual convention of the AASS, which opened on May 11. He served on the business committee and took an active enough part in the discussions to draw coverage in newspapers and be spotted by Isaac Post's relatives from Long Island.[51] More urgent affairs, though, awaited him at home, just as they had three years earlier.

After prolonged hesitation about how to manage an intolerable domestic situation, Brown was finally ready to put his life on a new footing. He returned to a household beset by recriminations and dissatisfaction. For her part, Betsey was no less restless than he to move on. Having had more than her fill of Farmington, she tried to persuade Brown to move back to Buffalo with her and the girls. The city had always been more of a home to her than Farmington, although perhaps she also had an ulterior motive. Brown paid her no heed.

By the spring of 1847, he was no more inclined to return to a family that included Betsey than to resume residence in Buffalo—a city, for him, haunted with painful associations. Besides, at this moment he had more on his mind than Betsey. He had growing professional ambitions, and by May 1847 they pointed to Boston, the capital of immediate abolitionism in the United States. He had renewed his contact with the board of managers of the MASS sometime that spring, possibly at the time of the annual New York meetings, but no formal offer of a lectureship was yet forthcoming from Boston. Nor would any come until after the board's May 29 meeting, at which it replaced Loring Moody as general agent with the very competent Samuel May Jr.[52] Brown was too eager to wait. Even before receiving the offer of a lectureship, he decided to move to Boston permanently and to take Clara and Josephine with him. He was scheduled to lecture with Hathaway in small towns about twenty-five miles apart in central Connecticut and Massachusetts on May 18–19, probably on behalf of the AASS, but there is no certainty that he fulfilled that commitment.[53] His first priority was the move, which he completed sometime before giving his maiden speech in Boston on May 25.[54]

There remains one other presence in Brown's life to account for. This one, too, pointed him toward Boston. Among the possessions he transported from Farmington was the bulky if incomplete manuscript of *Narrative of William W. Brown*. Although no external documentation survives about its origin, there is good reason to believe that he had been working on it for quite some time, possibly going back to 1846, and had made substantial progress. Very near the end of its published text, Brown mentions that he is sitting within sight of Bunker Hill Monument as he writes.[55] Since the full manuscript was in the hands of an adviser by mid-June and was published the following month, Brown was presumably speaking the literal truth at the time. Even if not, the claim has a nice figurative ring for a winding life story that began on a Kentucky farm, tracked westward to the Missouri frontier, steered countercurrent up the great interior rivers, skirted the southern shore of the Great Lakes, and finally arrived adjacent to the beacon of American liberty.

5

Narrative of a Life, Life of a Narrative

On July 1, 1847, William Wells Brown boarded an afternoon train at
Pleasant Street Station, heading south from Boston to Dedham. As
lines fanned out of the Boston hub during those boom years of railroad
construction, Brown frequently rode the cars to deliver the antislavery
message to villages, towns, and cities across New England and sometimes beyond. His business that day was more strictly personal. His destination was the home of Edmund Quincy, a Georgian–Federal mansion
set back from High Street in a neighborhood of imposing homes. The
Quincy estate backed onto the Charles River, commanding such fine
views that a Quincy friend, the poet and antislavery activist James Russell Lowell, called it Bankside. Brown had seen the interior of big houses
in Missouri and upstate New York, but he had probably rarely seen as
fine a private residence as this. Certainly he had never entered one as a
free man conducting his own affairs.

Brown's host that evening was one of the leaders of both the Massachusetts and the American Anti-Slavery Societies. The organizations
drew heavily for leadership on well-born individuals, but it would
have taken an Adams—and none was then vying—to match Edmund
Quincy for purity of Boston Brahmin blood among the antislavery elite.
By contrast with his cousin Wendell Phillips, Quincy carried his status

heavily. Patrician in manner and erudite in conversation, he comported himself as a well-bred gentleman. Quincy had inherited the property from his father Josiah, just recently retired from the presidency of Harvard, and previous to that a US congressman and mayor of Boston. Once installed in the manse, he lived the life of a man of leisure—except for his unpredictable enthusiasm for antislavery, a passion the rest of his family did not share. Nor did members of his class, who found it alien and even fanatical.

Quincy was one of the most powerful members of the movement, occupying a seat in the unofficial Boston triumvirate alongside Garrison and Phillips—a trio that expanded to a quartet when the formidable Maria Weston Chapman was in town. In addition, he played a leading role in the deliberations of the MASS board of managers, filled in as editor of the *Liberator* when Garrison was ill or absent, and served for years as a lead writer and occasional editor of the *National Anti-Slavery Standard*. By contrast with the ink-stained Garrison, a printer/editor trained at the press, Quincy was a gentleman and a scholar who devoted himself not just to social justice but also to self-cultivation. It showed; he was the most conspicuously literary senior member of the Massachusetts Anti-Slavery Society in the 1840s. On his days in town, he sometimes combined a visit to the society's editorial offices at 21 Cornhill with a stopover at the Boston Athenaeum, where he enjoyed reading the imported periodicals to keep up with the latest literary developments in Britain. Samuel May Jr., the well-born general agent of the MASS, told a fairly typical story about his esteemed colleague. One day in town, he encountered Quincy on the street in a state of excitement. The cause became clear when Quincy presented for May's inspection a copy of a Laurence Sterne first edition bearing the author's autograph, adding with pride of ownership that this had been Sterne's own copy. May's reaction expressed the opinion of the initiated: "a prize truly, and one that few can appreciate as well as E.Q."[1] A lover of the belles-lettres, Quincy also showed a lively interest in Jane Austen and Thomas De Quincey, who he thought might be a relative.[2]

By all accounts, Quincy was an imposing, sometimes overbearing man, although he was all charm and grace the evening Brown showed up uninvited at his house at dinnertime. He liked Brown, he admired his *Narrative*, and he heartily approved of both. Pleasantries aside, their conversation centered on antislavery business. Its main subject: Brown's *Narrative*. Brown had left the bundle of sheets for Quincy several weeks earlier, no doubt requesting editorial review of a manuscript he considered not quite ready to go to press. Why did he entrust it to Quincy, when either Garrison or Phillips, both highly accomplished writers and approachable individuals, might have served as well? Browns' relations with Garrison and Phillips would be cordial and lifelong; with Quincy, they would be more strictly formal and possibly not surviving the Civil War. The best guess is that Brown chose Quincy out of regard for his literary ability and interests. A few years later, considering which of his colleagues was best equipped to write a pioneering history of the American antislavery movement, he publicly proposed Quincy.[3]

The following morning, Quincy dashed off a forthright account about the previous evening's conversation to a trusted friend, Caroline Weston, a member of one of the region's most prominent antislavery families. The manuscript left for his scrutiny, Quincy wrote, took him by surprise. He had completely forgotten his responsibility until the previous day, he explained, when he noticed "a corpulent wall of MS" sitting on his desk. When he picked it up, expecting just to skim through it, he found it so fascinating he read it continuously to the end. His immediate response was to make the comparison of Brown with Douglass— man-to-man, text-to-text—that became a standard reading of these two exemplary black writers for years to come.

First, on the *Narrative*: "It is a terrible picture of slavery, told with great simplicity, with touches at time quite De Foeish. His experience of slavery was much more extensive than that of Douglass. . . . It seemed to me a much more striking story than Douglass's, and as well told. There is no attempt at fine writing, but only a minute account of scenes and things he saw and suffered, told with a good deal of skill and great propriety and delicacy." Second, on the man: "It is a long time since I have seen a man, white or black, that I have cottoned to so much as I have to Brown, on so short an acquaintance. He is an extraordinary fellow. I do not know that his intellectual power is equal to Douglass, but he is of a much higher cast of character. There seems to be no meanness, no littleness, no envy or suspiciousness about him. His mind seems to be singularly healthy and he never seems (and he says he never does) [to] think uncomfortably about his being a black man. He understands everything about the cause, New Org., Third Party, etc, perfectly, and has no twaddle about him. He is the most valuable man we have got since Douglass—and in many respects he is more valuable than he."[4]

The meeting was more than congenial; it was constructive for both men. Quincy found himself in conversation with a collegial black man who rose to all his expectations without pushing him—as Douglass insistently did—outside his comfort zone. Moreover, this particular man was a living link to the martyred editor Elijah Lovejoy, whose murder a decade earlier had incited Quincy to a life of activism. Likewise, he found in the sheath of pages a transfixing narrative that spoke the anti-slavery truth boldly and authentically—as only an ex-slave could—but pronounced it decorously, fit for household consumption. It must have seemed to Quincy as though man and book were made to order. He recommended a few minor "curtailments" and made slight editorial changes to the text, penned a brief public letter to Brown for use as an introductory endorsement, and wished him well.

Brown had his own good reason to take heart at the meeting, during which he jotted down a dedication to Wells Brown and made several of Quincy's suggested alterations. His manuscript, the story of his life, had passed its first crucial test with the highest mark of approval. Whatever anxiety he felt as he entered Quincy's house turned into elation as he returned home with his manuscript largely intact, a written endorsement in hand sure to smooth its way into print, and likely MASS support for publication. Brown knew the reform movement's grapevine well enough to expect that an endorsement from Quincy would pass straight from his lips to Garrison's and Phillips's ears, and from them quickly across town and out to the periphery. That is exactly what happened, and it happened fast.

....

WITH QUINCY'S ENDORSEMENT preceding him, the doors of the Massachusetts Anti-Slavery Society swung open. The society agreed to print the work and to do it in-house, assuring its speedy, controlled production. The society ran a full-service printing office at 25 Cornhill for production chiefly of its house organ, the *Liberator*, as well as of a miscellaneous list of antislavery materials stored in its depository and available through its distribution network. Brown's *Narrative* was slated to join that list.

The most immediate model for the text's production was the first edition of *Narrative of the Life of Frederick Douglass, an American Slave* (1845), also an in-house job and one of the organization's most popular, influential publications. Brown knew its stature all too well; he tried to persuade Quincy that his book needed a distinctive title in order to steer clear of too close an association with Douglass's. He suggested *Personal Narrative of William W. Brown, a Fugitive Slave*, but Quincy parried his wish with the suggestion that they leave the title decision to higher authority.[5] That decision soon came down, but not in the language Brown had preferred. Exchanging one generic title for another might not have seemed a major concern to the managers of the MASS, but the elimination of "Personal" mattered to Brown. He nevertheless consented to the change by July 26, the day he walked into the local district courthouse to deposit the title page with the clerk and claim copyright privilege as "author."[6] Due to the gaping inconsistencies within the US legal system in 1847, he walked out with ownership over his life story but not over his person. Publishing a memoir in these circumstances exposed the author to risk; Douglass had felt so endangered after publication of his memoir that he had immediately taken refuge in England.

Work on production of *Narrative of William W. Brown* began immediately and finished within four weeks, a production schedule so compressed that one can infer urgency on all sides. Brown would oversee many manuscripts through the press over a long, productive literary career, but this initial time he needed guidance. He got it, presumably from well-positioned colleagues. Over that month, a variety of literary professionals set their hands on the manuscript and related tasks. Following Quincy, Garrison probably inspected it sometime during the month, reading it in his customary fashion with an editor's pencil in hand.[7] So must Joseph C. Hathaway, whose high-toned preface to his friend's work indicated a familiarity with its contents.[8] Printers, copyeditors, and proofreaders would have had a more strictly functional go at it, as would stereotypists and finally binders, once the sheets came off the press. All this many-handed involvement was standard procedure, but it does raise a basic question about how a work so produced could be subtitled "Written by Himself"—a question that pertains, for that matter, to the general run of male fugitive-slave narratives. How "himself" was "himself" is always a matter of great moment with Brown, but, in the case of an autobiography issuing through the publishing infrastructure of a tightly run white organization, the question becomes all the more intriguing. Moreover, as will soon become clear, this was no simple autobiography but a William Wells Brown composition that, like all his subsequent works, would crisscross conventional generic boundaries. When one of the boundaries crossed was the line separating autobiography from creative nonfiction, the results were especially provocative. Though stripped of the term from its title, this particular narrative was more intriguingly "personal" than anyone but Brown could have known.

There was one more production task to be done. The blank verso opposite the title page needed to be filled with the author's image. This was standard procedure in the preparation of the more refined fugitive slave narratives, as with the general run of more formal nineteenth-century memoirs. So was the inclusion of an engraved facsimile of the author's signature, positioned right below his portrait but within its frame and corresponding to both the portrait and the printed name of the author on the title page. Text, handwriting, and picture reinforced one another to communicate a message necessary for a presumably skeptical audience: The author was literate, his story was true, and his person corresponded to his text.

The task of producing Brown's likeness fell to a different set of Boston craftsmen, who were engaged on a tight schedule synchronized to the production of the printed text. One day in early July, Brown sat for his earliest known photographic likeness. The "Chase" whose name was inscribed on the engraved page was the skilled "daguerreian artist" Lorenzo Chase, who operated a popular downtown studio at 257 Washington Street. Chase placed Brown in a sitting position, angled his head approximately 45 degrees left of center, and photographed him from just below the shoulders. With that act, Chase unwittingly gave his rather plainly, if respectably, dressed customer a public face that would reach far and wide, eventually carrying across the ocean.

The Chase daguerreotype was then sent off to the nearby 66 State Street shop of Joseph Andrews for engraving, a process then a prerequisite to the printing of images. Whoever directed Brown to Andrews knew he was sending him to one of the leading line engravers in the country. It was most likely Wendell Phillips, who could have recommended Andrews based on personal experience. Andrews had rather recently executed a superb engraving of him that was used as the frontispiece for the 1845 *Liberty Bell*, an antislavery gift book issued annually by the MASS as a fund-raiser. That particular commission was a fairly common one for a high-toned professional like Andrews, who added the term *historical* to his listing among the engravers in the city directory to highlight his specialized talent at engraving historical and other technically demanding kinds of painting. Taking a commission from a fugitive slave or his supporters brought him down a rung from his usual level of operation, but in all likelihood he accepted the commission on the basis of shared principle. Whatever his motivation, he did his customary fine work on the Chase daguerreotype, refining the sitter's physical features and drafting lines to indicate the missing lower portion of his torso and the frame of the chair in which he was seated.

Chase and Andrews combined to bring Brown's image vividly to life. A smattering of reviewers even commented on the "fine likeness" of Brown they produced. There was more to Brown's visual presentation, however, than met the eye. The work they did was technically excellent; the image of Brown as a bright, earnest, self-contained young man comes through vividly. By all indications, William W. Brown looked passably acceptable to his contemporaries, although there were different kinds and degrees of presentability. One can see this difference clearly by comparing the 1847 engraving with the 1852 engraving made in London to illustrate his English travelogue, in which he appeared before the British public as a far more distinguished-looking man of letters (and, not coincidentally, with the wobbly letters of his 1847 facsimile signature straightened and gaps regularized). If in 1847 the scar over his right eye peeked out a bit, the "scissors" across his back most definitely did not. That part of his person Brown had not exposed to anyone but Betsey, whose fingers alone could have traced a path across his scars.

There was also more to the issue of public reception than met the eye. Acceptance of inflammatory works of this kind, touching the explosive subject of slavery, would have split along generally predictable sectional and political lines. So would acceptance of their authors. Even within the ranks of abolitionists, however, there were divisions and tensions. The reaction of Quincy toward the conduct of Brown's peers is a case in point. In the same confidential letter in which Quincy lauded Brown, he savaged Remond and Douglass, two of Brown's closest colleagues. Remond he dismissively referred to as "Toussaint," a mock-heroic comparison between the petty behavior he believed Remond had exhibited during recent MASS meetings and the courageous, self-sacrificing behavior of Toussaint Louverture, leader of the Haitian Revolution. Douglass he slurred even more nastily as belonging to the category of "unconscionable niggers." His latest misdemeanor was the unabashedly high value he placed on his literary services, charging the managers of the *National Anti-Slavery Standard* $2.50 for each letter in a series he was to write for the paper—even though the idea originated with the editors. Though outraged by what he considered Douglass's unrestrained self-regard, Quincy admitted that his coworker's allure was such that the series might yield the paper an additional one hundred subscribers—enough to have defrayed Douglass's salary many times over.[9] About Brown he had no such fears or reservations: Brown was transparently a man true to his word and subservient to the cause. Quincy and his fellow MASS managers staked their organization's credibility on him in authorizing publication of only the second fugitive-slave narrative to appear under their imprint.[10]

······················

THE ORIGINS of *Narrative of William W. Brown* trace back to a remote past that poet Langston Hughes famously conjured in "The Negro Speaks of Rivers" as the mythic cradle of African American experience:

> *I've known rivers:*
> *I've known rivers ancient as the world and older than the flow of*
>   *human blood in human veins.*
>
> *My soul has grown deep like the rivers.*[11]

Fugitive-slave narratives derived figuratively from Hughes's mythic stream running from the Congo and the Nile to the Mississippi, but Brown's had a more literal derivation. Brown must have been swapping personal stories, told in the dialect of his surroundings, with fellow slaves and coworkers ever since he was a preliterate teen at locales stretching from St. Louis to New Orleans. Once enlisted in the antislavery movement in 1843, he began reciting his life story more formally, in anecdotes and episodes, on his antislavery rounds of western New York. Sometime during his final months before moving to Boston, he turned it into a written "narrative," the term then in circulation equally for both oral and printed autobiography (and biography). Narratives of all sorts were in the air: Edgar Allan Poe's *Narrative of Arthur Gordon Pym*, Richard Henry Dana's *Two Years Before the Mast: A Personal Narrative of Life at Sea*, Davy Crockett's *Narrative of the Life of David Crockett*, and related accounts of people from all walks of life. Narratives such as Brown's, however, answered to a cultural politics specific to the lives of black folk, especially those once enslaved. At a time when many whites were predisposed to disbelieve both the teller and the tale, ex-slaves were under particular pressure to prove both their own authenticity and the authenticity of their narratives.

Brown possessed the requisite life credentials and came to the writing of his *Narrative* at a singularly opportune time. By the late 1840s, fugitive-slaves narratives were so numerous they were becoming identifiable as a common body of writing; reviews of one increasingly referenced others, occasionally even the emerging genre itself. Brown was so well versed in the texts and contexts of these narratives that he could recite from memory all the commandments incumbent upon authors—about exemplifying truth, authenticity, sincerity, morality, and integrity. His first decade of literacy had included a steady diet of these texts, a few of which he also peddled during his travels across New York. By the time he set out to compose his life story, he had presumably even assembled an ever-growing collection of newspaper clippings containing stories by and about fugitives, source material, and commentary.

He began his literary career with a remarkably distinctive life story to tell in print. He had traveled to places and witnessed activities that far exceeded the experiential range of the vast majority of both free and enslaved Americans. Quincy had been right to contrast its geographical scale with that of Douglass's story, but there was also a more fundamental difference. While Douglass's heroic narrative was one of self-emancipation culminating in victorious selfhood, Brown's was a story of dislocations and relocations, of shifting identities and equivocal truths. Whereas the strapping Douglass battered his tormentor, the sadistic overseer Covey, into submission in its climactic scene, Brown repeatedly wriggled out of distress, whether by luck or mental agility, during an adolescence lived in constant motion. Even on reaching the depot at the end of his Underground Railroad, in Cleveland, Brown never attained the overall defining unity that Douglass created in his triumphant tale.

The disarray in Brown's life is present throughout the *Narrative*, perhaps most conspicuously in its unceasing parade of personal names. Although he asserted near its conclusion, "I have been known by that name [William Wells Brown] ever since I left the house of my first white friend, Wells Brown," the *Narrative* produces an unsettling succession of names that continues up to the present moment: William, Sandy, William again, William W. Brown as its title character, and William Wells Brown as its author.[12] One now-famous scene highlights the variability of names: the incident in Vicksburg in which Sandy tricks a young black man, his unwitting double, into taking the whipping Walker intended for him. The literary historian William Andrews has given a seminal interpretation of the scene's multiplicity of identities: Sandy as the enslaved adolescent in the story doing his best to survive by his wits, William W. Brown as the adult subject of the memoir apologizing to the reading audience for his earlier indiscretion, and William Wells Brown as the author of record.[13]

The gaping distance between Sandy the teenaged slave and William Wells Brown the author-lecturer typified the divide between life in slavery and life in freedom that onetime-slave writers needed to reconcile. Brown's *Narrative* was unusually adept in bridging these autobiographical gaps, but it managed this feat, in part, because it established an alternative basis for written narrative. It took the liberty of combining into a seamless first-person narration what was specific to him and what was generic to the experience of slavery. His account of the Vicksburg episode is a case in point: What actually happened there was not that Sandy borrowed a substitute back for his punishment but that William Wells Brown borrowed a substitute life for his *Narrative*. As literary historian John Ernest has speculated, Brown might have lifted that episode from a similar story told in an 1830 book about life in early Philadelphia and adapted it to fit his own.[14] Or he might have picked it up more casually as a popular anecdote circulating around the slave community, where jostling for a position of superiority was a psychic necessity. Brown's text, in turn, became a link in a larger pattern, as another ex-slave writer, Jacob Green, long settled in England where he presumably came upon Brown's *Narrative*, incorporated a version of Brown's story into his own 1864 *Narrative*.[15]

This is not the only instance of Brown's practice of incorporating other lives into his own. Another likely appropriation is the horrifying story of a lynching by water in New Orleans that Brown claims to have witnessed during his year with Walker.[16] In this case, he acknowledges in the *Narrative* that he is drawing on an external source in addition to his own observation. The two accounts of the lynching differ in some details but agree broadly about the central story: A white mob pursued an unnamed slave into the river for the alleged crime of stealing a piece of meat. The slave, who could not swim, sought refuge by wedging himself between steamboats moored along the wharf. Terrified of exposing himself to the mob's growing rage, he protested his innocence while threatening anyone who tried to apprehend him. His attempts at self-defense succeeded only in goading the mob to fury, its foremost members taunting, poking, and eventually bludgeoning him with oars. He was already dead by the time one of the assailants retrieved his body from the water on the hook of a pike pole and dumped it onto the deck of the nearest boat. The commotion alerted the captain, who was outraged to see a body left on his boat and demanded it be removed immediately—he didn't care where.

Brown's account departs from the other source by continuing the story of the murder beyond its commission and the captain's reaction. After witnessing the events, he returned to his own boat in shock and spent a sleepless night haunted by images of the crime. Unable to clear his mind, he got up early the next morning to see firsthand what had happened after the corpse had been dragged ashore. It lay just where it had been hauled the night before, undisturbed. Horrified but also engrossed, Brown lingered to observe what, if anything, would happen. Just a few people came near and stopped, but only to gaze. Eventually municipal trash collectors hoisted the corpse into their refuse cart. The narrator chooses not to moralize. The scene represents slavery as it is, the dead man's abandoned body the proof of a system that degrades everyone involved, no commentary necessary.

The secondary source Brown drew on, by a curious coincidence, was an eyewitness account by Lane Seminary student James Thome, later an accomplished antislavery activist and minister, who shortly after the killing returned to Cincinnati and a few months later took part in its historic antislavery debates.[17] Thome claimed his boat had just landed in New Orleans one evening in December 1833 when shouts outside drew him on deck as the attack was progressing. His account combined fairly straightforward reportage of the murder with shrill moralizing about the collapse of a society built on slavery—a fairly common rhetorical practice of the time. Thome's reportage was generally consistent with Brown's, but its rhetorical practice stopped short of doing the one thing that, more than anything else, makes Brown's account so powerful a piece of writing: mobilizing its author as not just a horrified spectator but a potential fellow in suffering.

But even Brown's empathetic reportage falls well short of action. Sandy no more intervenes in this slave's trauma than he did in Cynthia's coercion or, in the very next paragraph of the *Narrative*, in the affairs of a white teenage acquaintance from St. Louis kidnapped into slavery in New Orleans. His concluding remark about that unfortunate white slave, a person his age named Burrill, states the limits of his agency succinctly: "Though I sympathized with him, I could not assist him. We were both slaves. He was poor, uneducated, and without friends; and if living, is, I presume, still held as a slave."[18] So spoke Sandy through Brown. What William Wells Brown could do for all three of these enslaved people— all presumably lost to the larger world in which he now was moving— was incorporate their life stories into his and thereby perpetuate their memory. In effect, these and other lost souls who populate Brown's *Narrative* became rhetorical extensions of the lives of his mother and sister and the many thousand gone.

These scenes gathered from among other lives on the Mississippi demonstrate one of the most fundamental aspects of Brown's literary practice. He was a many-handed, all-purpose collector of sources, which he compiled in any and all forms—printed items in multiple genres, handwritten texts, oral stories, black and white songs—in preparation for integration into his saga. Then, exercising great skill, he refined them into a composite text that did justice to his fragmented experience of reality. Even in penning his form-setting autobiography, he was as much a scissors-and-paste operator as was a newspaper editor like Garrison or Gay, though not always crediting—on the contrary, sometimes obscuring or even hiding—his sources.

Brown had a loose literary model for his practice of appropriation and absorption in Theodore Dwight Weld's *American Slavery As It Is: Testimony of a Thousand Witnesses* (1839), a magisterial compendium of hundreds of eyewitness accounts of life under slavery. Weld held it up to the American public as a mirror on the peculiar institution. Weld and his middle-class household spent many an evening in their parlor clipping their book's contents mostly from Southern newspapers he had picked up as outdated surplus material at the New York Commercial Library.[19] The furthest thing in appearance and content from a Victorian parlor gift book, this cheaply printed volume, with its contents set in small, double-columned newspaper type, sold tens of thousands of copies through the distribution network of the AASS and its affiliates. Assuming the role of prosecuting attorney, Weld delivered the logic of his position in an opening invocation: "Reader, you are empannelled as a juror to try a plain case and bring in an honest verdict. The question at issue is not one of law but of plain fact—'What is the actual condition of slaves in the United States?'"[20] He no sooner asked than answered his question by incriminating the South in its own words in an indictment piling up in the hundreds of pages.

Brown found such riveting confirmation of his experience in Weld's composite testimony that he repeatedly appropriated passages for use in his own books, beginning with the *Narrative*. It was presumably in Weld's book that he first encountered Thome's account of the New Orleans lynching; for once, Brown took care in his *Narrative* to credit a source complementary to his own.[21] That act, however, raises an additional question: Was reading Thome the nearest Brown actually came to encountering the murder? One reason to regard Brown's account with suspicion is the discrepant dating the two men assigned to the event. Brown dates it to his year with Walker, which would place it most likely in 1831; Thome dates it to December 1833, when Brown was present in New Orleans attending Enoch Price's family but not necessarily on the scene. Since no known surviving local newspaper documents the event, one can make only an educated guess about its date. More certainly, a reader can see in such episodes instances in which Brown was honing the "composite method" that would bear his curious literary signature.

BROWN WAS QUICK to organize his new life on reaching Boston in 1847. Finding lodging would have been a relatively simple task. He had previously formed good relations with a handful of local African American activists, most notably the affable, ever-loyal Garrisonian William

Cooper Nell, one of the city's best-networked blacks who might have assisted him in finding convenient, affordable housing. His earliest known address was at West Cedar, a street running below the northern flank of Beacon Hill with clear views of Bunker Hill Monument. What to do with Clara and Josephine, now eleven and nearly eight, required a more complicated decision. As a single parent expecting to be frequently on the road, he needed to settle them in a suitable live-in situation. Arranging an acceptable one for school-aged children would not be possible in Boston, one of the few remaining Massachusetts cities that still segregated its public schools. Although Nell was spearheading an integration campaign, Brown could not afford to wait for results.

He decided instead to board them in New Bedford with the family of Nathan and Mary "Polly" Johnson at their 21 Seventh Street residence. Brown was acquainted with this well-regarded couple from various anti-slavery events, and just about everyone in town knew their reputation as confectioners (Polly's ices and cakes were often used to sweeten requests). Brown came down to lecture in New Bedford as early as June 12 and 13, probably the first of many trips to a city where he lectured repeatedly over the next two years. He returned for the rousing West Indies Emancipation Day celebration of August 1, taking heart at the size and enthusiasm of the local African American community. "The colored people of New Bedford are in advance of the colored people of any other place I have visited in the State," he reported in a letter intended for print.[22] Perhaps that was partially wishful thinking to justify his decision about his girls, but it was also a sentiment he heard from his cordial young friend Jeremiah "Jerry" Sanderson, a local African American barber-activist Brown had met and lectured with on various occasions in New York state as far back as 1844. Sanderson was particularly a booster of the city's public schools, which he claimed were the best in the state. Their quality would have been a crucial consideration in Brown's thinking.

New Bedford was at the time a thriving commercial port city whose prosperity was built chiefly on whaling, one of the largest industries in the country. At midcentury, its fleet of nearly 300 ships proudly led the whaling industry worldwide. Barrels of whale oil lined the harbor as far as the eye could see, and whale parts exited its factories as manufactured goods bound for markets and industries across the country. The port was the fourth largest in the country measured in tonnage, and the ships and whaling-related factories employed thousands of mariners and workers. Herman Melville, who had sailed before the mast of a New Bedford whaler in 1841, memorialized the city in mock-heroic terms in *Moby-Dick* as "a land of oil" whose wealth was "harpooned and dragged up hither from the bottom of the sea."[23] Cannibals, he coyly noted, brushed shoulders with matrons on the city's streets, and scruffy crews comprising sailors from all corners of the globe lingered near the wharves while waiting to push out to sea.

The largest ethnic minority in the city was African Americans, who worked by the hundreds in the whaling industry. Blacks had long found employment openings more commonly on the nation's rivers and oceans than on dry land, a pattern so common it yielded black mariners the generic name "black jacks."[24] This pattern was all the more common in New Bedford, whose ships and factories operated at such capacity that workers, regardless of ethnicity, were keenly in demand. One such person was Frederick Douglass, who came to New Bedford in 1838 with his bride, Anna Murray, days after his escape from slavery and took a string of odd jobs in the city's dockyards and factories before finding his vocation as an antislavery lecturer. The newlyweds made their first home in the comfortable residence of Nathan and Polly Johnson. Their bedroom might even have been the one the Brown sisters occupied a decade later.

Douglass was only one of many prominent fugitive slaves (others included Brown's future acquaintances Harriet and John Jacobs and Henry Box Brown) who settled or took temporary refuge in the city. The year Brown settled his daughters there, a local publisher issued a memoir for a local fugitive minister (*The Life and Sufferings of Leonard Black, a Fugitive from Slavery*) that was only one of more than a dozen written by fugitives who resided in the city.[25] The city's tolerance, however, was only relative. In 1846, Ralph Waldo Emerson and Charles Sumner had rejected invitations to lecture before the New Bedford Lyceum when they heard it had adopted a policy of excluding African Americans from attendance.[26] The city directory attached a discriminatory "c" next to "colored" names until 1849, a pattern of prejudice that carried into employment practices. Even in this fast-growing city with a booming economy, African Americans ran up against some of the same restricted economic opportunities they faced all across the free North. The effect of lingering discrimination drove a conspicuous number of the city's black men to move on in search of better opportunity. The 1849 city directory indicated where some of them went: "California" followed the names of the numerous black homeowners who joined the rush of Forty-Niners. Jerry Sanderson was one of them. In 1854, he struck out for California out of the same professional and economic frustration experienced by other talented young black men of his generation, such as Nell in Boston and James Whitfield in Buffalo. He left behind a young family of five, who joined him only in 1859.

The lure of California also reached into the Johnson household. Although Nathan was a pillar of the African American community and a man of property, he chose to stake his claim in the Golden State as a means of paying back debts. Housing and boarding children, like Clara and Josephine, brought in a little extra revenue but not enough to make a significant difference. Leaving behind his wife and a household containing the Brown girls and several teenagers, he did not return for two decades, by which time Polly was dead.[27] In a pattern that was probably familiar, the girls again lived long stretches without an adult male presence in the house. Virtually no details survive about their residence in the Johnson house, or about the decision made no later than 1850 to move Josephine a few blocks away to the 86 South Sixth Street home of Martha Fletcher, an African American widow variously listed as a confectioner and a laundress.[28] That move presumably did not affect their studies, as both girls made serious progress during these four years. For a time they attended a local public school, but eventually they probably moved on to the Friends Academy of New Bedford, the most academically advanced school in the area. Recently nondenominational, the school also became coeducational in 1846 when Caroline and Deborah

Weston signed a one-year contract to administer it and teach some of its classes, including one in French.[29] Brown knew this prominent family well; the Weston sisters (including Maria Weston Chapman) had a long relationship with the MASS and enjoyed close personal relations with its Garrison–Phillips–Quincy leadership. More to the point, they were steadfast supporters of Brown and his family. They took a special interest in Clara and Josephine and might have helped Brown pay for their private schooling locally, as they did in 1851, when the girls attended a boarding school in France.

Even the best New Bedford schools, private and public, came with their risks. Like African American parents everywhere, Brown knew the unfortunate story of nine-year-old Rosetta Douglass, whose father had sent her in 1848 to Seward Academy in Rochester, New York, expecting she would receive two advantages he had never had as a child: a formal education and equitable treatment. Douglass had done due parental diligence by investigating the principal's racial views and pedagogical practices before sending Rosetta to the academy; nevertheless, he returned from a trip to Cleveland only to find that the school was segregating his daughter from the other children. He promptly transferred her to another school and exposed the academy for keeping his daughter in "prison-like solitary confinement."[30] But for the luck of circumstances, Brown knew the injured child might have been his nine-year-old Josephine.

WILLIAM WELLS BROWN and Frederick Douglass seemed to move in a choreographed pattern between 1847 and 1849—Douglass generally leading, Brown following, adding improvisations. Brown arrived in Boston just as Douglass returned home a free man from a two-year self-exile in Britain. Douglass arrived to a hero's welcome—shouts of "Douglass" reverberated through the 1847 spring meeting of the New England Anti-Slavery Society, a sister organization of the MASS—but he came back a changed man. His independent streak strengthened by foreign travel and his new legal status, he remained in eastern Massachusetts only long enough to consider his options. Then he struck out westward, eventually settling in Rochester, New York, to reestablish himself and renew his work. In effect, Brown entered the lecturer ranks of the MASS just as Douglass left them. Though not explicitly slotted as Douglass's successor, he filled the role of its most successful African American lecturer for the next two years. Then, after proving himself, he again followed Douglass's lead by heading to the British Isles to expand his horizons.

The two years Brown spent in Boston were a time of nonstop activity coupled with extraordinary literary productivity, a pattern that continued to the end of his life. He brought out four editions of his *Narrative*, the last three self-financed and self-published.[31] He brought out two editions of *The Anti-Slavery Harp*, a collection of songs he compiled and edited that went through two additional editions after his departure. He gave hundreds of lectures across New England on behalf of the MASS, one of which he self-published in a highly successful pamphlet circulated in thousands of copies. He also gave two series of lectures in Philadelphia and vicinity on behalf of the Pennsylvania Anti-Slavery Society (PASS). He survived a race riot and a family scandal. At its end, with three works in print and his reputation as a writer and lecturer established and growing, he prepared himself for the most ambitious overseas cultural foray undertaken by an African American.

Brown hit the lecture circuit as an agent of the MASS in June 1847, even before publication of his *Narrative*. The routine was familiar. He lectured alone or in tandem night after night in towns across the region, while also collecting newspaper subscriptions and donations for the society and selling its works. All of this was standard procedure, but now with one difference: he was soon also selling copies of his *Narrative* (and, by summer 1848, also of *The Anti-Slavery Harp*). Cumulative sales of his works at meetings throughout the two years were considerable. He reportedly sold fifteen to twenty copies of the *Narrative*, for instance, on the single evening of August 29 during his first visit to the small town of Upton, in Worcester County. Those sales followed a talk that a listener reported had held the large audience in "breathless silence" for nearly two hours.[32] Other scattered reports about his skill on the lecture circuit circulated in the *Liberator* and local papers, and his reputation spread fast. Presented to the reading public mistakenly in June as "formerly a slave from Mississippi," Brown was by summer's end one of the most anticipated presences across the state at antislavery meetings.[33] By year's end, it was clear the movement was witnessing a new star lecturer.

He teamed on the road during this period with many of the leading antislavery lecturers of the day. Some were familiar faces from past years, such as Douglass, Remond, and Foster. Others were newer acquaintances, such as the implacable Parker Pillsbury, whose unyielding temperament, strident rhetoric, and fierce temper provided a useful complement to Brown's moderate, disarming style of address. Another was Harriet Jacobs's brother John, Brown's occasional partner in 1849 before Jacobs veered off on a different career track by heading out West to try his fortune in the goldfields of California and, after failing to make a strike, continuing on to Australia. He also teamed for a longer period in 1847–48 with the courageous, forceful women's-rights advocate Lucy Stone. At larger quarterly or annual events, he frequently spoke alongside the commanding figures of Garrison, Phillips, and Quincy before audiences generally numbering in the hundreds. On one special occasion, at Harwich on Cape Cod in September 1847, he teamed with Foster and Pillsbury before an audience Pillsbury estimated at 7,000—the largest antislavery gathering to date on the Cape and one of the largest ever in New England. One attendee reported on that meeting: "Wm. W. Brown, the fugitive slave from Missouri, spoke in so affecting a manner that there were few dry eyes in the audience."[34] Some listeners, however, were not so favorably impressed by that day's rhetoric, especially by hard-hitting remarks Pillsbury made at the expense of clergy and public officials. A small number of residents, whether present in the crowd or informed about his remarks from reading the local papers, took serious offense. They would remember these abolitionists the next time they came to the Cape in force.

One of the most notable lectures Brown gave as an agent of the MASS occurred in one of his favorite places in Massachusetts, the historic seaport of Salem. Soon to enter American literature as the hometown and abandoned workplace of the author of *The Scarlet Letter*, it was to Brown principally the home of his good friends the Remonds. Their middle-class home was a model of the kind of household he had never had and that he enjoyed visiting, usually on lecture tours to the North Shore. He was there this time by invitation of the city's Female Anti-Slavery Society, the oldest in the country. His lecture took place on Sunday evening, November 14, as the fifth in that season's six-part series. Phillips and Garrison had delivered two of the previous lectures, but Brown's would have had a special attraction as the only one delivered that year by an African American.

Brown did not disappoint the large multiracial, mixed-gender audience gathered to hear him. He delivered an eloquent talk that followed Theodore Weld's lead in announcing his topic as "Slavery As It Is."[35] Its thesis expressed the rhetorical impossibility of accomplishing that evening's task: "Slavery has never been represented; Slavery never can be represented." The problem was the usual one attendant to communicating atrocities: Those who had not actually witnessed, no less experienced, slavery's organized brutality could not comprehend it—least of all, an audience of Northern women. Though constrained by conventional "fastidiousness," he delivered a forceful indictment of slavery as an assault on not just the nation's ideals, institutions, and international reputation but also on the institution his audience held dearest: the nuclear family. The images he drew of defenseless women preyed upon by their masters, their husbands and brothers powerless to intervene, were well calculated to move his audience. They undoubtedly moved him, too.

Altogether, Brown must have given a remarkably eloquent, forceful lecture that night in Salem, and its text soon reached a broad sectional audience across the North. Plans to publish it had been made in advance by either Brown or the MASS, with an enterprising young fellow traveler named Henry Parkhurst in attendance that night to record Brown's words. An accomplished stenographer often hired by the movement, Parkhurst was advertising himself at the time in Boston newspapers as a "Fonographic Vurbetim Riportur" and vaunting "di acureasi ov hiz Riports," a paradoxical procedure for the scientific rendering of a lecture that called truthful representation into doubt.[36] At its first meeting after the lecture, the MASS board of managers agreed to pay printing expenses for 1,000 copies of the *Lecture*, up to a maximum outlay of $20.[37] By year's end, a network of antislavery outlets was wholesaling the twenty-two-page pamphlet for $.05 for one copy, $.50 for one dozen, and $3.50 for one hundred.[38] Advertisements appeared in the leading antislavery newspapers of Boston, New York, and Philadelphia through the spring and into the summer of 1848, and agents of the society dispensed it far and wide across the North.

While the MASS oversaw the production and distribution of the *Lecture*, Brown took his own initiative in self-publishing a second edition of his *Narrative*. As soon as the first edition of 3,000 copies sold out, probably by November 1847, Brown undertook a new, expanded edition of 2,000 copies to meet the continuing demand. Then luck intervened.[39] He was already very far along in its preparation—too late to stop the press—when his past made a jarring intrusion on his present peace of body and mind. It arrived from St. Louis in the form of a letter dated January 10, 1848, from Enoch Price to Edmund Quincy regarding his runaway slave "Sanford"—the now "said William Wells Brown." Whatever Price knew about Brown (and also about Quincy) presumably came from the copy of the *Narrative* Brown had mailed to him. Whereas Brown had meant the book to shame him, Price drew the conclusion that there was lost property to recoup. He offered Quincy a bargain: He would sell Brown's freedom papers for $325 to any interested buyer—a 50 percent discount, he boasted, off the purchase price he had paid Samuel Willi. Everyone stood to profit.

Although press time on the second edition of the *Narrative* had already come and gone, Brown knew exactly what to do with the letter. He presented it to the public on January 26 in an act that had the theatricality of abolitionist performance at its best. The setting was the annual winter meeting of the MASS. Brown came forward twice that day, afternoon and evening, to exhibit the letter, which he had evidently just seen. The first time he spoke, according to the official report, he appeared "with evident agitation" about the risk he ran of recapture, even though supporters in the audience shouted their readiness to fight off Price's agents should they venture to Boston. Brown rarely lacked for composure, but the unexpectedness of Price's long-distance voice intruding in his neighborhood apparently unsettled him. He was more composed that evening when he again came forward, this time before a very large audience at stately Faneuil Hall, holding up the letter in his hand and talking back to it.[40] He soon had the audience in hand as well, as he and his supporters recited their mutual commitment in a kind of shout-and-response.

BROWN'S SELF-PUBLISHED EDITION of the *Narrative* made its appearance just a week or two after these meetings.[41] The text itself was very nearly a reprint of the original edition except for the last page, but Brown introduced enough significant changes to warrant production of a new set of stereotype plates. He arranged for their preparation at the New England Type and Stereotype Foundry, one of the leading establishments in the city, and paid for them himself—the first of many books over which he would take ownership by hiring printers and publishers subject to his control. The new edition still featured the Chase–Andrews frontispiece illustration, but it now included three additional engravings Brown selected to illustrate key scenes in the text: Sandy treed by O'Fallon's hunting dogs during his first escape, the slave coffle escorted by Walker and Sandy mounted horseback front and rear of the slaves, and the apprehension of Sandy and his mother by slave catchers in Illinois. Though crudely drawn and executed, the engravings provided vivid images of scenes Brown considered central to his life story. He also added a short article on the slave trade he had written for the 1848 *Liberty Bell*, printed the lyrics of "The Blind Boy," and tacked on a lengthy miscellany of printed materials about slavery. One particular excerpt hit home for Brown in a way only those closest to him could have known. This was the account of "white negroes" written by ardent Kentucky slavery defender Robert Wickliffe—another of his Wickliffe cousins, as he liked to say. Wickliffe's provocative idea was to replace slave labor gradually with more reliable white labor imported from the North, a solution to the labor problem that would help North and South simultaneously.[42] How it would deal with the "negro problem" was another question for another day.

The new edition got the expected strong sendoff by the antislavery press, and brisk sales justified Brown's optimistic expectations. Like the first, the new edition of two thousand copies would sell out within six or seven months.[43] The reward for the inexpensively priced and heavily discounted work could not have been very great, but it was enough to motivate Brown to keep the book up to date and in print right up to his July 1849 departure for England. He brought out a third edition in October 1848, this time introduced by a public conversation with his "old master" fifteen years after their last exchange. In printing Enoch Price's letter, followed by his own response, Brown allowed Price to do him the unintentional favor of corroborating the underlying authenticity of his *Narrative*. When that third edition also sold out within half a year, Brown prepared a fourth edition in the late spring of 1849 and assigned it to local publisher Bela Marsh, whose business shared the premises of the MASS at 25 Cornhill and included a printing operation and bookstore dealing heavily in antislavery materials. Marsh made it available for sale at the time of Brown's departure in July for Europe, when he was advertising it as a "complete edition," along with a second work by Brown.[44]

The second work was the other self-published book Brown completed in summer 1848, *The Anti-Slavery Harp*. A cheaply printed forty-eight-page pamphlet, it was a deceptively ambitious foray into American musical culture—and not just because it was the earliest-known African American antislavery songster. A companion of sorts to the *Narrative*, the *Harp* assembled forty-eight songs for individual and group singing culled from a hodgepodge of sources. Thousands of attendees at antislavery meetings from western New York to New England had heard Brown's appealing musicality, as he frequently gave solo renditions of popular antislavery hymns. Musical interludes were a crucial part of the antislavery program, as with church services, and the sound of Brown's rich, sonorous voice singing songs of yearning black spirits and broken families was familiar to friends of the movement. As his friends knew, the spirit emerged from the depths of his own suffering. The song he most frequently performed was "The Blind Boy"—about a helpless boy torn from his mother and left to make his way alone in the world— which resonated with the eternally motherless child in Brown. Listening to him perform the wrenching song brought thousands of Victorian listeners as close as they would come to the pain of broken slave families.[45]

He reprinted "The Blind Boy" along with dozens of other songs and poems in the *Harp*. He had already attached several as musical intensifiers to crucial scenes in his *Narrative*, one of the most music-saturated of all the fugitive-slave narratives. One occurs in a scene in which Walker violently separated and sold a whining baby from its mother on the long march east across Missouri to St. Louis.[46] Brown stage-managed an appropriate emotional response to that generic act of violent separation by immediately printing the poetic text of a slave mother's response. Likewise, he orchestrated the commentary on his own mother's sale in a similarly sentimental fashion with the couplet from a John Greenleaf Whittier poem/song so popular most supporters could recite it from memory: "Gone, gone,—sold and gone/To the rice-swamp dank and lone."

He compiled the book's contents partly from a decade of earlier songsters going back to Maria Weston Chapman's 1836 *Songs of the Free*, whose songs had a ring of orthodoxy absent from Brown's. The more immediate influence came from two other popular songsters he acknowledged in his introduction: *Liberty Minstrel* and *Anti-Slavery Melodies*.[47] The compiler of the former, the talented white musician George W. Clark, was Brown's friend from his western New York years; Brown skimmed contents from the best-known songs of Clark and other compiler/composers, as well as poems and songs by major figures of the antislavery movement, including Garrison, Whittier, and Lowell. Other works he scooped out of the columns of the antislavery press, and several he composed himself. As with other songsters, his collection printed the lyrics but not the notes, instead following the customary practice used by reform groups from temperance to evangelism of attaching each song to a popular melody. He also followed the logic, part commercial and part affective, that he had employed in the second edition of his *Narrative* by illustrating the work with popular images. The most vivid was the engraved cover image of an American eagle attacking a slave mother trying to protect her child; that scene resonated with the most intimate part of Brown's being.

Maximal usefulness of a text designed to do utilitarian good required maximal sales, so attention to distribution was crucial. Antislavery agents dispensed copies of the work along with other publications as they made their assigned rounds. The most colorful in the late 1840s was the intrepid Jonathan Walker, a native of Harwich, Cape Cod, who was famous throughout the movement as the man with the branded hand. The "SS" ("slave stealer") burned into his palm after a failed attempt to help slaves escape to the West Indies soon became a symbol of courage well known to supporters. Walker was working the backcountry of Ohio when he sent back East for copies of the *Harp* that he could sell on his lecture tour: "We have never seen Brown['s] collection of songs. Has he the music of them? Please send them by mail to my address. You will get the publisher to send as many as he can for the sum."[48] Walker was a cog in a well-oiled sales apparatus, as general agents across the Northern states advertised the work in local newspapers and equipped their field agents with copies for distribution on their travels.

The most effective salesman, of course, was Brown himself, who peddled copies at his many talks.[49] Reliable sales figures for the *Harp* are unavailable, as is nearly always true with works published outside the record-keeping system of the mainline book trade. Brown claimed 5,000 copies were sold within the first five months, which may or may not be a salesman's boast, but his work's sustained printing history supports the general claim that it was a very popular work.[50] Employing the same strategy he used with the *Narrative*, Brown kept the *Harp* in print with slightly updated and refreshed printings. He brought out a second edition in April 1849, which in due course also sold out. Following Brown's departure for Great Britain, Bela Marsh, who was overseeing distribution of both the *Harp* and the *Narrative*, foresaw a continuing market for the songster and brought out two more printings in 1852 and 1854—presumably by arrangement with Brown.

Such a work was intended, as its subtitle indicated, "for anti-slavery meetings," and his colleagues undoubtedly put it to good personal and group use. Two surviving copies of the *Harp* bear annotations by their owners that leave testimony about how the book might actually have been used. Samuel May Jr.'s copy of the *Harp*, now at Harvard University, has a number of nineteenth-century markings. The commentator singled out with asterisks three songs he presumably was earmarking for public performance or reprinting: "Emancipation Hymn of the West Indian Negroes" (subtitled "For the First of August Celebration"), "Fling Out the Anti-Slavery Flag," and "Freedom's Banner."[51] A heavily annotated copy also survives at the Historical Society of Pennsylvania; its anonymous owner jotted down alternative lyrics in the margins and singled out several songs with asterisks.[52]

Collecting suitable songs was for Brown a far more intricate task than it was for his friend and colleague George W. Clark. Performing them was even more so. He could no more insulate himself within the confines of the movement as a singer than he could pass down a train corridor without running into racial discrimination. As soon as he stepped out onto the larger American stage, he was subject to the rampant "color-phobia" of the time. A constant performer, he felt himself too often, as he once remarked, "what I most dislike, 'the observed of all observers.'"[53] This was what happened on the evening of May 10, 1849, when he appeared at Convention Hall in New York City to open the meeting of the AASS national convention on a musical note. As happened at other events, even outsiders who could not distinguish his from any other black face noticed his singing. The reporter for the broad-circulation *New York Sun* opened his column by referring to "a coloured man" he plainly did not recognize who opened the meeting with renditions of two songs, "I Am a Slave No More" and "The Blind Boy." The singer's performance was so enthusiastically received, the reporter commented, that he was "encored twice in true theatrical style."[54] The reporter's reaction to the spectacle of Brown as though he were a performer on stage was a common response of the time. In the minstrel-loving 1840s and 1850s, most white Americans viewing a black man singing on a podium would immediately assume a theatrical performance and take the singer for a blacked-up minstrel. This one was simply more talented than most and happened to be authentically black. Or, as the literary scholar Paul Gilmore ironically termed Brown in the language of minstrelsy, Brown just happened to be "de genewine artekil."[55]

Brown, as it happened, loved the musical theater and had an aficionado's appreciation of its culture—not least, its absurdly twisted color code. As curiosity drove him to attend the meetings of political and religious groups for which he had no sympathy, he took in performances of touring minstrel troupes. He could have had his pick among the Ethiopian Melodists, Congo Minstrels, Kentucky Minstrels, Sable Harmonists, and Christy Minstrels—popular groups that performed "true negro music" and "nigga songs" in packed theaters across the country. One of the most celebrated of such troupes, the Ethiopian Serenaders, played the White House and claimed President Martin Van Buren and his secretary of state as their "patrons."[56] Meanwhile, as Brown's *Harp* circulated in antislavery circles, songsters containing the racist lyrics of the broader popular culture flooded the printed-music market.

Brown had a remarkably fine, cultivated talent for mediation, playing the racial/cultural role of man-in-the-middle. In compiling the contents of *The Anti-Slavery Harp*, however, he kept a wary distance from minstrel culture, carefully selecting an alternative set of songs that today look mostly bleached of African content. Although African American slaves inhabit many of them as subjects or objects, Brown selected songs and melodies from a musical tradition more nearly Scotch-Irish than African. This was the hymn- or ballad-based musical tradition of his white Protestant colleagues, familiar to his contemporaries from popular church hymns and religious poetry. A contemporary reader might find a sample poem or song of this sort in nearly every issue of the *Liberator*, a regular column in the newspaper because it conveyed a fundamental appeal to Garrison and the extended congregation of his followers. Brown willingly adapted it to his own compilations and to his performances on the lecture circuit because he understood what would appeal and to whom.

He also seemingly kept his distance from his own musical heritage, muting the musical tradition with which he was most intimately familiar. From childhood, his ears were filled with the words and melodies of Negro spirituals, work songs, and protest songs that surrounded him wherever he went—on the farm, in the city, and on the rivers. The proud black nationalist Martin Delany captured the atmospheric appeal of what white commentators called "pure Negro" songs in his commentary on the sound of black music emanating from the riverboats and wharves in New Orleans: "In the distance, on the levee or in the harbor among the steamers, the songs of the boatmen were incessant. Every few hours landing, loading and unloading, the glee of these men of sorrow was touchingly appropriate and impressive. Men of sorrow they are in reality; for if there be a class of men anywhere to be found, whose sentiments of song and words of lament are made to reach the sympathies of others, the black slave-boatmen of the Mississippi river is that class."[57] One of those voices joining in the chorus of voices from the wharves or decks, or solo singing his private grief, would surely have been that of the teenaged Sandy. The songs of his youth remained part of his inner repertoire that Brown would interject into later works, such as his novel *Clotel*, where he moved freely between African and European traditions. One of the "happy, satisfied, and contented" plantation slaves, for example, responds to his master's request to entertain northern visitors with a ditty:

> *The big bee flies high,*
> *The little bee makes honey;*
> *The black folks makes the cotton,*
> *And the white folks gets the money.*[58]

But that was in England in 1853; in Boston in 1848, Brown exercised greater restraint.

BROWN WAS AS HETERODOX in his religious as in his literary practice. It is far easier to say what he was *not* than what he *was*—other than some form of Christian. He was not, first and foremost, a Presbyterian. He was not, in part, because Dr. Young had been. Everything relating to Young's practice of religion was unacceptable to Brown. His animosity came through in a richly symbolic story he proudly told in the 1860s about the task Young assigned him one spring day of bringing the sacramental wine to church for the Sabbath ceremony. As he walked unsupervised across the property, he stopped to sample the wine but indulged so freely that he feared detection and punishment. To cover up his transgression, he devised a way to substitute one sweet liquid for another by suctioning the sap from a maple-sugar vat into the bottle through his mouth, filling the bottle to the top, and replacing the stopper.[59]

By the same principle, he was also not a member of any of the leading denominations whose creed or practice sanctioned slavery—as most mainline churches did through the 1840s. His disdain did not stop with formal denominations; he also despised missionary and evangelical groups, such as the American Bible Society and the American Tract Society, which refused to disperse their publications among the enslaved population. His spirited debunking of organized religion moved astride the Garrisonian movement, which had a loose reputation as irreligious or sacrilegious. Despite its antisabbatarian and anticlerical tendencies, that charge was more nearly slander than truth. Some of the white leaders were deeply religious, others (such as Thomas Wentworth Higginson, Theodore Parker, and Samuel May of Rochester, a cousin of Samuel May Jr.) were practicing ministers, and the movement was evangelical to its core. The connection between religion and the African American community was at least as tight, and an even larger percentage of its leaders were ministers. What can be said with certainty about Brown is that he was warier of organized religion than most of his colleagues, black and white, in the movement.

A splendid mimic, he took special pleasure in mocking the bigoted pieties of religious groups in speech after speech, book after book. Beginning with the "Farmer of Ashland," he typically exposed their hypocrisy to the public by letting them speak through his mediating voice, rather than by subjecting their theology to critical analysis. He customarily visited churches wherever he traveled, but almost always with a spectator's eye—New York City, Philadelphia, Richmond (after the war), London, Dublin, Paris—much as he did the theater, concerts, lyceum lectures, and exhibitions.

BROWN HAD THREE WORKS in circulation by summer 1848, a busy time
of itinerant lecturing for the MASS. Things seemed to be going well,
with his life stable and his career thriving, when two unforeseen crises
erupted within weeks of each other, destroying any illusion of false security. First without notice, Betsey arrived in Boston on June 30 looking
for her children. After taking the train from Albany to Boston, she went
directly to the Garrisons' house, nicknamed the "abolitionist hotel" for
its open-door hospitality. It rarely hosted guests, however, who bore the
smoking ill will Betsey displayed toward its occupants and their friends.
She arrived in a state of obvious agitation, with a very little child (exact
age unknown) named Paulina in hand. She had given the girl the family
name of Brown, although William did not recognize her as his daughter or offer her a place in his household, a responsibility he presumably
believed to be James Garrett's.[60] Cut off now for a year from her two
older children and probably living without a fixed residence of her own,
she was desperate to see the girls and reunite with them and their father.
All through that period, she had been sending them letters, which never
penetrated the cordon thrown up by Brown and his allies, all apprised
of the family rift. A tight network of white and black abolitionists that
effectively facilitated internal communications presumably also filtered
out unwelcome news. She knew well enough, however, that a sure way to
find William's whereabouts was to go to Garrison.

Garrison walked over to Brown's boardinghouse that evening to
inform him of Betsey's presence. Due to the lateness of the hour, Brown
waited until the next morning to call on her. At first, Betsey refused to
come downstairs to meet him, but Helen Garrison finally persuaded her,
leaving the couple alone, face-to-face for the first time in a year, to talk.
Betsey insisted that Paulina be left in a different room. The meeting was
difficult for both spouses and did little to resolve their personal differences, but it did yield a working compromise to their family impasse:
She would go to visit the girls at the address he provided in New Bedford, then return to Cleveland with Paulina.[61] Probably mistrustful of
her motives, Brown also made a point of going to New Bedford, where

sometime in July he met her and the girls. He gave Betsey enough money to return west with Paulina and then went his separate way. And that finally was that—or so he thought at the time. Instead of returning to either Buffalo or Cleveland, she lingered for weeks in southeastern New England, hovering around Worcester, New Bedford, Boston, and other cities and casting aspersions not just on him but also on a number of the leaders of the movement as false defenders of black families. Brown might have thought he was done with her, but she clearly was not done with him.[62]

Unaware for a time of Betsey's campaign to undermine his reputation, Brown returned to the road as an agent for the MASS and its affiliates. Aside from a short, event-filled trip—his first—to the Philadelphia area, along with Remond, to participate in the PASS's annual convention and give talks, he spent most of the summer partnering in Massachusetts with two white agents, the seasoned Stephen Foster and the young, talented Lucy Stone.[63] A sign of things to come occurred on the Fourth of July at a meeting in East Bridgewater, near Plymouth, when someone apparently trying to make a theological point hurled at Stone a large prayer book that glanced off her shoulder, barely missing her face.[64] They were less fortunate when they returned with Parker Pillsbury to Harwich in late August for a major four-day convention meant to deepen the inroads made the previous year. The weather, though threatening the first day, cooperated, and the team embarked on an ambitious agenda that covered a full range of national and local subjects, including discussions of church, state, and social institutions. The crowds grew from day to day, peaking at 2,500 people for the concluding Sunday afternoon meeting. Because churches were closed to them, they held the meeting in a large grove open to the elements.

They made a team so unacceptably diverse they were bound to draw stares, even howls of outrage: Stone, an Oberlin graduate who fearlessly championed women's rights side-by-side with abolition; Foster, a graduate of Dartmouth and uncompromising advocate of both causes in tandem with his equally uncompromising wife, Abby Kelley Foster; Pillsbury, the granite-tough offspring of New Hampshire soil who had a knack for extreme provocation; and the seemingly constant "fugitive" Brown. As they warmed to their task, they encountered the usual array of skeptics, opponents, and even agitators, who showed up to dispute, challenge, and goad the lecturers. A few of the more respectable skeptics even received the team's consent to mount the speaker's platform to express their views. For the first few days, they sensed no greater degree of opposition than they were accustomed to.

Early warning signs came on Saturday, however, when the first in a series of racial epithets ("Where is the darky?") was hurled at Brown, and the sight of him and Stone together on the platform provoked angry reactions among the audience. Brown helped to contain the situation by closing the meeting with a song, but antagonism simmered.[65] One of the many local ship captains in attendance was reported to have vented the general insult many in the crowd felt these agitators were inflicting on basic American decency and decorum: "Which do this *audience* think would look best, a woman walking with a white man who had a cigar in his mouth, *or* a woman walking with a great black negro?" The reporter who published this account added a scorching commentary on local racial anxiety: "[The captain] talked about women marrying negroes and it might perhaps be inferred from his remarks, that he felt somewhat apprehensive, lest if the slaves should be freed, the women of Harwich would prefer *them*, to such men as himself."[66] There was a local history behind this smoldering resentment that many in the crowd would have remembered. Nine months earlier, a Cape Cod captain named Gideon Wixon, returning north from the James River in Virginia, had steered his vessel into the harbor in Harwich en route to Boston with a cargo containing sixty-six just-liberated slaves. During the several days the ship sat in port, Wixon permitted a small number of residents to come on board and see for themselves the state of the cargo. They found newly freed women, men, and children in such pitiful condition that they raised a collection of clothes, sundry provisions, and a small sum of money.[67]

That particular incident might have been forgotten if it had been only an isolated event on the Cape, but it was not. Though attached to the US mainland by only a slender thread, the Cape was closely connected to slavery through its extensive maritime trafficking in Africans and African Americans—even long after the slave trade had been outlawed. Feelings about real and hypothetical slaves ran high, pulling the populace in increasingly polarized directions. In April 1848, when an armed posse intercepted the coastal schooner *Pearl* near the mouth of the Potomac River outside Washington, DC, and arraigned its cargo of seventy-seven fugitive slaves, many Cape Codders approved. Brown, by contrast, was so moved by that attempted mass escape that he commissioned a painting of it a few years later in London for inclusion in his antislavery panorama.[68]

The explosion in Harwich came on Sunday. Late in the contentious afternoon meeting, by which time Sabbath services had ended, Pillsbury and Foster were lighting into the conduct of the church in debating the resolution "Our Nation's Religion Is a Lie." A ship captain who had just left the Congregational Meeting House a mile away charged the platform in an apparently premeditated plan to assault the lecturers. Dozens of assailants simultaneously made a rush for the three male speakers. Two of them overpowered Brown and threw him high over the back rampart of the platform to the ground six feet below, where he was nearly trampled in the ensuing mayhem before the mob swerved away. Though not seriously hurt, he was severely shaken up, and copies of *The Anti-Slavery Harp*, available for sale from the podium, were tossed every which way and mutilated. Meanwhile, other assailants isolated and surrounded Foster and Pillsbury, punching and kicking them until friends in the crowd managed to pull them free before either was seriously injured. (Abby Kelley Foster would lament the irreparable tear to her husband's new coat but knew she was lucky to get him back home alive.)[69] Stone alone was spared; the mob apparently had enough gallantry not to assault a white woman. That night, the four shaken comrades found refuge with local allies, while news of the riot spread quickly through word of mouth and newspaper accounts across the region. The incident elicited exactly the kind of publicity the antislavery movement sought. Within just a few days of the riot, eleven residents of Harwich alone took out subscriptions to the *Liberator,* as did various other Cape Codders.[70] With no interruption at all, the antislavery work resumed and the team continued their way around the Cape, drawing large crowds at Hyannis.

Brown was expecting to accompany his colleagues in the latest Hundred Conventions tour across southeastern Massachusetts when alarming reports from Boston drew him abruptly back home. By late August, Betsey was broadcasting defamatory charges so widely about Brown and his supporters that she effectively dragged the entire MASS into what its leaders feared was developing into more than a family affair. The manager of its printing office, Robert Wallcut, reported to Samuel May Jr. that he had received a letter from Betsey in New Bedford, "begging, almost screaming for money." He predicted ominously: "We are likely to have more trouble about this matter."[71] His prediction hit so near the mark that the board of managers felt compelled in early September to meet and discuss how to contain the spreading damage. They advised the organization's senior officials to appoint an examining committee to look into "the difficulties subsisting between Wm. W. Brown and his wife Elisabeth [sic] Brown, and for that purpose to seek to have an interview between the parties in their presence."[72] Appearing before that committee would have marked a critical moment for Brown, whose career as a public lecturer was tethered to his reputation for good character, but he was so confident about the outcome that he jumped at the chance to clear his name. Betsey had just the opposite reaction: Her conscience was clear, she was more sinned against than sinning, but she mistrusted everyone connected to the MASS—in this instance, undoubtedly with good reason. The "friends" set to examine her private life were William's allies and supporters, not hers. Only extreme pressure by William could have persuaded her to expose her private life to their scrutiny. As the standoff between them intensified, he had two resources she lacked: a living wage and custody of their children. He must have drawn on at least one and possibly both to apply enough leverage to compel her attendance.

Betsey took the train up to Boston and showed up alone at 21 Cornhill, the operational center of abolitionist activity in New England. She and Brown met privately in the office, but she walked out as soon as he intimated his intention to mention her adultery as the cause of their separation. Samuel May Jr. and Francis Jackson, a senior official of the MASS, somehow managed to coax her to return the next day, and this time she and William met before the committee. No notes were recorded in the MASS ledger entry for that day, presumably a deliberate omission; the only known surviving accounts come in two private letters Brown sent to trusted friends explaining the outcome. He reported first to Garrison, who was away in Northampton taking the water cure, that the meeting cleared his name but accomplished little else. Betsey, he noted, refused to respond to personal questions before the committee and froze up when he threatened to write to Buffalo friends to procure evidence supporting his position.[73] By contrast, he informed Amy Post, who was apprised of the family's tumultuous history, that Betsey had confessed to the affair with James Garrett and had taken responsibility.[74] Shortly after the meeting disbanded, Betsey said that if he would refrain from contacting Buffalo, she would agree to meet again privately with him and Samuel May Jr. and, furthermore, would consent to a joint petition for divorce in exchange for a specified sum of money. They set a date for the following week for that final meeting, but it never took place. Nor did what mattered most to Brown—the divorce. Betsey needed money badly, but she needed even more desperately the preservation of the marriage. An empty shell of a marriage was preferable to no shelter at all for a woman who felt abandoned to the world.

Those two meetings at 21 Cornhill marked the last time William and Betsey ever met. That did not mean, however, that Brown was wholly beyond the range of her voice or influence, not even once they were separated by the Atlantic. Right up to her dying day, Betsey did not go quietly.

BROWN KEPT UP a busy lecture schedule through fall 1848, as the nation went about electing its first president since the successful prosecution of the Mexican-American War. The incumbent, Democrat James Polk, was too ill to run for reelection, and an open race for the presidency became more complicated by the introduction of a third party. This was the new-born Free Soil Party, a short-lived union of discontented Northerners who organized that summer in a national convention in Buffalo. Generating little appeal outside the North and not much inside it, the party ran on a platform featuring moderate opposition to slavery, especially its expansion to the territories, owing more to a concern with the rights of white laborers than with the plight of slaves. Most, but hardly all, radical abolitionists viewed it with scorn, although its platform, like that of the Liberty Party before it, generated animated discussion at meetings. Remond broke ranks by voting for it, earning him the scorn of black and white comrades alike. Garrison was more typical in dismissing it as a party of "white manism." Brown had a more subtly discerning term for it: "The 'anxious seat' in our great Anti-Slavery revival."[75]

Brown's mind was clear about all three political parties: They were all bad, although the two main parties were worst. He had nothing good to say about the Whigs or the Democrats, whose interlocking consensus on the recent southwestern territorial conquests confirmed his longstanding suspicions. The Whig candidate Zachary Taylor, the conquering hero of the Mexican-American War, led the Whigs back to the White House, uniting the two major parties in acceptance of the new continental reach of the Union. But the new facts generated new questions. Which new territories would be slave and which free, and how the sections would coexist, remained subject to debate. As mid-century approached, that debate consumed an increasing amount of national attention.

So, as after previous elections, the Garrisonian abolitionists continued doggedly down their separate path. Brown's led back to Philadelphia for the second time in three months as an agent on loan to the local antislavery society. Eastern Pennsylvania was in need of more star power, and Brown immediately gave it to them. He proved so effective in energizing the antislavery base and spreading its message to the outlying population that the managers of the PASS requested that he stay on through the annual convention in late December. He stayed for nearly three months, his day-by-day, week-by-week travels through the towns and villages of the area as frenetically paced as those through New York state and New England. His itinerary, however, included more stops at black communal gatherings, a reflection of the size of the region's black population. During two early December nights in Philadelphia, he addressed the local African American community in tandem with a new partner whose acquaintance he must just have made, the remarkable Martin Delany—already a distinguished black editor and activist allied for a time with Frederick Douglass at the *North Star* but too headstrong to partner for long with Douglass or anyone else. There is no record of their personal interaction, but two so extraordinarily energetic, intelligent, high-performing men must have quickly grasped their fundamental differences. They began skin-deep in biology; Delany was as dark as Brown was light-skinned, and both were hypersensitive on the subject. The differences, however, descended to the depths of their personalities and ideologies. Even their temperaments were opposed: Delany was impetuous and aggressive; Brown, deliberate and ironic. They quickly realized they had conflicting prescriptions for "the race problem." Brown was an integrationist, Delany a black nationalist. In his biographical sketch of Delany written during the Civil War, Brown would characterize Delany, by then a pioneering explorer of his African homeland, as a charismatic leader who "goes for a 'Negro Nationality.'"[76] That was a path Brown could never wholeheartedly follow.

Those weeks gave Brown the chance to deepen his relationships with a number of the leaders of Philadelphia's well-established African American community, the largest in the nation and the one in which he felt most comfortable outside of Boston. He felt a particular respect for Robert Purvis, the mixed-race president of the PASS and a senior figure in the AASS. A well-born man of affluence and a graduate of Amherst College, Purvis had credentials Brown found admirable, though inimitable. But for another local leader, William Still, he felt a quick affection that grew into a lifelong friendship. By contrast with Purvis, Still was the kind of rising man with whom Brown felt he could stand shoulder to shoulder. Born to ex-slaves who had taken refuge in New Jersey, Still had mostly educated himself and worked his way up from doing odd jobs as a janitor and handyman to positions of increasing responsibility with the Philadelphia Vigilance Committee. Over the late 1840s and 1850s, he would become its most effective black agent, aiding dozens and dozens of fugitives moving north up the Atlantic coast mainline of the Underground Railroad. One was a stranger who came into his office in 1850 with a story whose familiarity gradually led a stunned Still to grasp that he was looking at his long-lost brother Peter, left behind in slavery decades earlier. That amazing saga soon resonated far and wide among midcentury African Americans. Less fortunate ex-slaves like Brown, who heard the story while in England, could only congratulate the Stills on their amazing fortune.

Brown's most intimate new friendship, however, came as a result of geographical serendipity. While lecturing in Bucks County, north of Philadelphia, in late December, he got wind of what he would soon label "the singular escape" of a married fugitive couple just arrived from Macon, Georgia. This attractive young couple had adopted an ingenious ruse for escape whose sheer audacity in defying the gender and racial boundaries of the day actually gave the plan a chance to succeed. Fair-complexioned Ellen Craft made herself over as a white master traveling north for his health, accompanied by his serving man, William. With few questions asked, they made their way north as whites stepped aside to let them pass. After a harrowing rail and sea journey requiring transfers at Savannah, Charleston, and Baltimore, the newly freed couple walked out of the Philadelphia Railroad depot on Christmas Sunday to a new life. Purvis, Still, and other members of the Philadelphia Vigilance Committee soon whisked them off to protective custody with a Quaker family named Ivens, living in the countryside. Shortly after word reached Brown through the committee, he set out to make the acquaintance of these fellow fugitives at their Bucks County hideout. He had known and aided many fugitives since 1834, but his encounter with the Crafts proved special. During those final days of 1848, the young couple touched so powerful a chord in him that he responded by throwing a protective fraternal arm around them as though around younger siblings, and a deep, lasting friendship developed.

His showman's instincts soon kicked in. As Brown observed the effect his unpolished young friends had on the Ivens family circle, he foresaw the sentimental appeal their tale and appearance might have if presented to the general public. He discussed the idea with his friends, and they soon agreed on a plan. They would embark northward as a touring ensemble that would wind up in Boston, a far safer refuge than Philadelphia could ever be. Their plans were already well along by January 4, 1849, when Brown addressed a public letter to Garrison making the Crafts' story public and listing tentative lecture dates.[77] His receptors were as finely attuned as ever; Garrison no sooner printed the story than newspapers across the North picked it up, including normally hostile journals such as the sensationalist *New York Herald*. Before they could set out north, however, Brown had to complete his lecture-a-night commitment in eastern Pennsylvania. He appeared on a frigid night in Attleboro on January 11 and gave so animated a talk that he earned some rave reviews: "I think I never saw a more attentive and interested audience. The old and young, the little boys, the bigots and the liberals, the reformers and the conservatives, were all enlightened and amused by the inimitable manner in which he presented the subject." Brown's platform style pleased the majority but repelled a few listeners. One attendee thought his manner decidedly "sassy": "Friend Brown, perhaps, throws too much humor in his subject, and is too rhetoric[al] for some, but to draw out an audience and to interest and enlighten the public, he is the man. . . ."[78] His final appearances came at a convention held at Franklin Hall in Germantown on January 13 and 14, when he lectured on the shame of slavery in the nation's capital, a subject he would dramatize in *Clotel*. Both nights he also opened and closed the sessions by singing antislavery songs.

Then he was off with the Crafts for the long trip north. Brown advertised their January schedule as including stops at Norwich, Connecticut; Worcester, Massachusetts; Pawtucket, Rhode Island; and New Bedford, but that was only a start.[79] Thanks to effective publicity, their reputation preceded them wherever they went. In a matter of four weeks, two nameless, faceless Georgia fugitives serving out a life sentence were receiving rousing welcomes from large Northern audiences moved to pity and outrage by their story. Brown directed the choreography at this early stage, which also included a featured role for him. He would open the program by giving a set of pointed remarks about some aspect of slavery before transitioning to the story of the Crafts. William Craft would then come forward and give a narrative of their recent escape. Ellen, who at this stage disliked publicity, typically remained seated offstage but even so presented the spectacle of besieged womanhood, her apparent "whiteness" radiating a special appeal to viewers. One commentator disarmingly captured the extraordinary effect she had on viewers by describing her as having "the features and complexion of an Anglo Saxon sister."[80]

Their most important stop was the one closest to an official presentation, when Brown arranged for them to be formally introduced to the assembled membership at the annual convention of the MASS. The program for the evening of January 21, held in Faneuil Hall, was altered to put them front and center before the audience. Following their established procedure, Brown introduced them with a series of remarks before stepping aside to let William tell their story. The convention could not get enough of them that first night, so they returned the following evening; when even that did not suffice, Brown introduced them yet again on the third day of the meeting.

After the MASS convention, the trio went back on the road for an extended tour. Their first stop was a two-day series of meetings in New Bedford. Brown had written ahead to ask friends to attend to logistics, and one of the local newspapers had inadvertently provided advance publicity by reprinting a portion of his letter about the Crafts to the *Liberator*. The city was well prepared by the time Brown came forward at Liberty Hall on a Sunday afternoon to give a solo lecture as a prelude to that evening's gala performance. Taking the actual conduct of slave masters as his subject, he knew full well that he and Ellen would present graphic object lessons to the audience. The hall for the evening meeting began filling at an early hour, although many were unfamiliar with such gatherings in New Bedford. Following their established protocol, Brown was first to take the stage, giving a brief recitation of the Crafts' escape. Ellen and William then came forward, her appearance drawing audible gasps from the audience—the very sight of one so fair offended their preconceptions about white womanhood. Brown invited questions from the audience. Was Ellen actually called a "nigger" down South? What action would they take if their master attempted to capture and return them to slavery? (The question was posed hypothetically, but it became actual a year later, in 1850.) The inevitable skeptic in the house posed basic factual questions about Macon, Georgia, designed to test their authenticity.[81]

The documentary record for that night is unusually detailed. It is blank, however, on one intriguing matter. Were Clara and Josephine present in the jammed house? Or did their father arrange an overnight stay for the Crafts at Polly Johnson's or devise some other way to put his daughters in touch with his friends? He would certainly have wished to arrange their acquaintance. He might well have seen twenty-two-year-old Ellen as a kind of big sister to them—as she might have been a substitute figure to him for his own biological sister. Not until 1855 did either of the Brown sisters mention the Crafts, when Josephine devoted a full chapter in her father's biography to the story of their escape. But she (or her father) sanitized that account of any immediately personal reference, even though Josephine and Clara would undoubtedly have met Ellen in London in the early 1850s.[82]

His tour with the Crafts continued beyond winter and well into spring 1849. They spoke at dozens of cities across Massachusetts, including Worcester, Lowell, Concord, Lexington, Newburyport (to a standing-room-only crowd of 800 to 900), Salem, Dedham (to an overflow audience at City Hall, with Edmund Quincy present but in mourning after the recent death of his three youngest children within a two-week span), New Bedford, Fall River, Roxbury, and of course Boston.[83] One cold, clear winter's night, they stopped to speak in the largest meeting place in Kingston, Plymouth County, where fourteen-year-old Thomas Bradford Drew, raised in the best Yankee tradition, recorded in his diary hearing them speak: "Anti-Slavery meeting in Town Hall this evening. W. W. Brown with 2 fugitives from slavery William and Ellen Crafts [sic] were there who escaped 6 weeks ago." The Drew family, loyal friends of Garrison's, were leading abolitionists in the Plymouth area and sometimes offered overnight hospitality to guest speakers. They might well have boarded these "fugitives," as they would the most recent celebrity fugitive, Henry Box Brown, on his lecture tour a few months later.[84]

BROWN POURED HIMSELF into their tour, but he also had a more adventurous kind of tour in mind. As his thinking matured, he raised the subject with his newest friends in the form of an invitation: Would they join him on an extended tour of the British Isles? Three fugitives from American slavery carrying the antislavery banner across the British Isles would make an attractive spectacle. Even before he had a clear idea of how long he would stay or how he would finance so expensive an undertaking, he was strongly inclined to make the trip, solo if necessary. Moving fast after his great success the previous two years with his books and lectures, he was now eager to spread his wings. What better place to take flight on a voyage of self-cultivation than the British Isles, which Brown had been characterizing for years in song and speech as a haven free of the curse of racial prejudice? When the Crafts declined, preferring to put down roots in Boston, Brown more closely explored his own options.

The timing of his European tour could hardly have been more opportune. Transatlantic travel was in high gear for African American activists, who were welcomed to Europe by various antislavery and clerical bodies in need of experienced, tested allies from American shores. African American lecturers first found themselves welcome in the British Isles following the historic 1840 World Anti-Slavery Convention in London. Remond had attended that convention and stayed on to make a long, successful lecture tour (his sister Sarah followed in the 1850s). By the mid- and late 1840s, a growing number of African Americans, both freeborn and fugitive, crossed the Atlantic to seek aid for their churches, communities, schools, or sometimes simply themselves. They rarely went, however, at the initiative or with the formal encouragement of US antislavery organizations.

Brown made no secret of his plans, which he discussed with his close friends Remond and Nell (the latter the eyes and ears and lead reporter of all activities at the Cornhill office). He probably also sought the counsel of Douglass, whose British experience was recent and extensive. Likewise he consulted his most trusted white friends in the movement, including Garrison and Phillips, who had attended the 1840 London convention and kept up lively correspondences with antislavery advocates across the British Isles. Both of these well-connected allies responded generously with offers of aid—Garrison to provide a door-opening letter of recommendation once the date of departure approached, and Phillips to handle some of Brown's financial affairs, including payment of his New York state real estate taxes. By contrast, Samuel May Jr.'s reaction was somewhat grudging. He expressed his concern about Brown's trustworthiness in a letter to one of his closest English allies, the well-respected antislavery leader John Bishop Estlin, a Bristol surgeon: "He is a very good fellow, of very fair abilities, and has been quite true to the cause. But he likes to make popular and taking speeches, and keeps a careful eye upon his own benefit. The A.S. cause has been everything to him, in point of elevating and educating him, and giving him a respectable position, etc. He owes much to it; and he ought to be true to it.—I do certainly wish him the best success in his visit to your country; he is deserving of a friendly reception and of encouragement. I hope he will fall in with good, judicious and disinterested friends."[85]

May was right about one thing: Brown did keep "a careful eye upon his own benefit." Slavery had taught him to look to his own welfare, and hard, struggling times in the capitalist North had reinforced the lesson. He conducted himself, in other words, as did the vast majority of people not born to wealth or status. May's remark actually revealed more about himself than about Brown. His paternalism toward blacks, free as well as enslaved, was unexceptional among even radical white abolitionists. More problematic yet, his inability to look past skin color was compounded when he looked at women, as in his attempt to communicate the allure of Ellen Craft: "Ellen Craft, the young wife, is a woman who may be called beautiful; she has no trace of African blood discernible in her features—yes, cheeks, nose or hair but the whole is that of a southern-born white woman. To think of such a woman being held as a piece of property, subject to be traded off to the highest bidder (while it is in reality no worse or wickeder than done to the blackest woman that ever was). . . ."[86] His condescension toward Brown was particularly ironic, since Brown would willingly, even gratefully, have met May and his colleagues halfway. He knew better than anyone else how much he owed to the society and he believed unswervingly in its mission. On the other hand, he also knew how hard he had worked to acquire whatever education and cultivation he possessed, and how much latitude he needed to acquire still more.

Brown had lived by his wits for so long that the idea of making his way through the world was second nature. Through winter and into spring 1849, he explored an array of options, without committing himself to a plan until June or early July. He first considered the invitation from Anna and Henry Richardson, warmhearted, affluent Quaker abolitionists from Newcastle upon Tyne, to come on a sponsored lecture tour on behalf of the Free Produce Movement. Their boycott of slave-produced items, especially textiles manufactured from slave-cultivated cotton in the American South, had the support of the main antislavery organization in England (British and Foreign Anti-Slavery Society) and its American sister organization (American and Foreign Anti-Slavery Society). Yet the Richardson family's initiative lacked the immediate credibility that an eloquent ex-slave like Brown could bring to the cause in the British Isles. Brown's closest associates in the MASS considered the trade boycott a foolish panacea; Samuel May Jr. compared it to "bailing out the Atlantic with a spoon."[87] Brown agreed for the most part and politely declined the invitation, a decision made more difficult by his knowledge that Anna and Henry and their sister Ellen had purchased Frederick Douglass's freedom in 1847. What mattered more, as things turned out, was that Brown's rejection did not predispose the Richardson family against him. Once he did arrive in the north of England, they welcomed him warmly into their home. From then on, they numbered among the most steadfast supporters of his activities in England. In time, they would do for him what they had done for Douglass.

A more irresistible invitation came later in the spring from the local branch of the American Peace Society, which planned to send a national delegation to the third International Peace Congress, set to meet in Paris in late August. Nearly half of the American delegation came from Massachusetts, including Elihu Burritt, an idealistic man-of-all-reforms and the peace movement's leading spirit in the United States. His advocacy of an international peace movement followed in the wake of the 1848 springtime in Europe, the revolutionary uprising against traditional authority that swept the Continent from France eastward all the way to the Hapsburg Empire and Poland. Burritt persisted in 1849, despite the powerful wave of military and political reaction that rolled back the progressive changes of the previous year, hoping for a greater showing than the previous year's congress in Brussels. That congress had stressed the need for abolition, but the abolition its leaders had in mind was of war between sovereign nations. Their visionary progressivism had broad scope, however, and Burritt and many of his colleagues so vigorously supported racial progress that they encouraged biracial representation at the convention. It came from an unlikely place, as James Pennington and Alexander Crummell joined Brown in one of the first biracial delegations ever sent abroad to represent the United States.

Brown recognized a unique opportunity to link slavery to world peace on an international stage. He initially considered traveling directly to France by steamship and asked his New York City friend Sydney Howard Gay to check the availability of second-class fares to Le Havre.[88] Whatever information Gay sent him did not meet his needs, so he instead booked passage from Boston to Liverpool. Most members of his delegation planned to continue on to London by train while awaiting their English Channel crossing. Brown probably meant to do the same, until something altered his planning. Very shortly before he embarked for Liverpool, he switched his final destination from London to Dublin. Paris would have to wait.

The change of plan to proceed from Liverpool first to Dublin was a last-minute decision related to his ambition to bring out an Anglo-Irish edition of his *Narrative*. His model was once again Douglass. Back in

1845, Douglass had banked on the popularity of his American edition in thinking he could finance his European tour by reprinting it in Europe. He arranged for its publication with the blunt-spoken, spirited Irish abolitionist printer Richard Webb, one of Garrison's most loyal allies. Webb greeted Douglass in Dublin with great warmth, hosted him in his house, and set him up on a lecture tour across Ireland. Meanwhile, he ran off a new edition of the *Narrative* in his shop from the American stereotype plates, which Douglass had shipped with him. Brown must have received a rosy report from Douglass or some well-informed insider in Boston, so he contacted Webb in June to test his interest in a similar arrangement for his *Narrative*. He could not have known how raw a nerve he was striking. Webb had lost his initial enthusiasm for Douglass, whom he found condescending to well-wishers and meddlesome in publishing matters better left to professionals. Webb probably also made very little money on their venture, even though the new edition by all accounts sold very well. Douglass, considering the market far from saturated, contracted separately with the English printer Joseph Barker for a cheap edition.

When Brown contacted Webb in June 1849, Webb initially responded skeptically. Soured not just on his own account, he informed a friend that Douglass had left Barker a loser on their edition of 5,000 copies. He feared that he would also be left a loser with Brown's *Narrative*, whose prospects he considered less promising than those of Douglass's *Narrative*.[89] After rethinking Brown's proposal, he reluctantly consented, probably figuring his risk was minimized by the fact that Brown was financing the edition and the work was likely to do the cause considerable good. His cautious acceptance reached Boston just days before Brown's scheduled departure. Brown felt no comparable reservations about his edition's prospects, and he arrived as an ever-optimistic author cheering on an ever-doubting printer.

Brown had the stereotype plates of his most recent edition and the Andrews engraving crated in preparation for the voyage. His ambitions for the trip, however, could not be crammed into a single container. He also packed in his personal luggage at least four additional objects he thought might prove useful in paying his way and doing some good: copies of one of the American editions of the *Narrative*, the iron slave collar left with him by a fugitive he had aided in Buffalo in 1843, the leg shackles given him by a slave from Washington, DC, and a set of land-scape sketches he had commissioned from Boston artists. He intended the books for distribution on shipboard to any interested takers, the collar and shackles for lecture tours he was already contemplating, and the sketches for a projected antislavery panorama should he be able to raise the finances. He might even have been working out a plan for shipboard activity, knowing that Douglass had been given permission to stand on the promenade deck of his ship and address anyone willing to listen.[90]

His final weeks were busy verging on frenetic. While making final decisions for his trip, he continued to carry out a full working schedule. He completed nearly six months of lecturing along with the Crafts across eastern Massachusetts. He made his usual appearance at the annual spring convention of the AASS in New York City, crowded with not just the broad base of the organization but also curious onlookers, people hostile to the cause, and the independent press always eager to cover the high drama (or, to some, the farce) of the meetings. This particular year, the attendees encountered an unusually tense atmosphere. Just a week before the various reform conventions, a deadly riot erupted out-side the Astor Place Opera House, where the leading English actor William Charles Macready was playing Macbeth. That evening's mayhem was the culmination of a long-running nationalistic dispute between the vociferous followers of Macready and those of his American counter-part, Edwin Forrest. It exploded the night of May 11 in one of the worst nights of civilian fighting the city had ever experienced. By the time the local militia gained control over the situation, several dozen people were dead and many more injured. Macready was lucky to get out alive.

Antislavery gatherings typically encountered a hostile reception in the mainstream press as an expression of social, political, and religious extremism. At times they were even met with violence in major Ameri-can cities (New York, Philadelphia, and Boston had all experienced large-scale racial violence). But not in 1849 after the Astor Place riot cleared the air. Just the same, the local penny press arrived on the scene as usual to cover the goings-on with its customary skepticism. The reporter for the incendiary *New York Herald* attended some of the meetings seemingly for the sport of it and served up some titillation to a sensation-loving public. His account lingered in particular on public displays of deviancy he must have found more threatening than exhibitions at P. T. Barnum's nearby American Museum: "There were white faces, and yellow faces, and red faces, and black faces, long hair, and short hair, straight hair, and woolly hair, beautifully interspersed throughout the building, both up stairs and down stairs." Panning around the room, he singled out well-known figures of the movement as though identifying specimens in a freak show, including Garrison, Phillips, Douglass, and Brown ("a runaway slave"). He took special interest in Brown, whom he characterized as possessing "the richest fancy and most inventive genius of any man present." He even excerpted the text of Brown's "wag[gish]" remarks as a way of informing the public about the "Bedlam let loose" that day in Gotham: "When I lived down South and my master—and here let me give you a description of my old master, for he made an impression on me I would not like to make upon you—he was a whining, praying, complaining, psalm-singing man who ordered me, every evening at nine o'clock, to go down to the 'niggers,' and call them to prayers. Every night he called them in, and the power the master had, in putting them all asleep by prayer, was remarkable."[91]

Brown's remarks irked the reporter but elicited peals of laughter from the mostly sympathetic audience. Though presented in his customarily meandering, anecdotal fashion, his words spoke adroitly to the day's overarching debate about the role of the Protestant church in supporting slavery in the United States. That was a subject so utterly fundamental in a powerfully evangelical nation that it divided not just abolitionists from slaveholders but one antislavery organization from its sister organizations. One day, in their typical meeting-hopping practice, Brown, Douglass, and other convention participants walked a few city blocks to attend several meetings held by their rival organization, the American and Foreign Anti-Slavery Society, and sat in on the remarks of Henry

Bibb and others on the best means to combat slavery. Bibb argued to his more conservative, religiously orthodox colleagues that the distribution of Bibles to the slaves would transform their lives and thereby undermine the peculiar institution. When challenged about the practicality of his view at his own meeting, he responded that Bibles were already reaching slaves in his native Kentucky and might soon penetrate all parts of the South. Douglass was so amused by that view that he took it back to his own meeting for commentary: "There is a class of men who seem to believe if a man should fall overboard into the sea with a Bible in his pocket it would be hardly possible for him to drown. Mr. Bibb told me in conversation, that he believed if the slave had the Bible, the Lord would help him to read it."[92]

Douglass's remarks, in turn, provoked a white New Yorker named Atwill to mount the speaker's platform and rebut him, point for point, on various key points of contention. Having spent some weeks in Georgia and South Carolina and conversed with a number of plantation owners, Atwill had mastered the subject of slavery in all its aspects. He proceeded to inform Douglass and the whole assembly about the plain facts in the matter. Many slave owners permitted their slaves to read and would certainly not prevent the gift of Bibles to them. To the best of his knowledge, any sizable plantation had at least one literate slave. Not yet finished, he upbraided the radicals in the room on their false, vicious view of the American church as a pillar upholding the peculiar institution of slavery.

In that one building in New York City, on that one day at least, Atwill's claims expressed distinctly minority views, and the majority quickly retorted in earnest. During those few spring days of Anniversary Week, rented meeting halls such as Dove Chapel and the Tabernacle served as places of refuge for the reform-minded faithful of the AASS, who often had to scramble in New York—a city that made no pretense to being a haven for the oppressed—to find personal lodgings and assembly halls. But times were changing, albeit in increments so small they were not easily discernible at any one moment. For years after its founding in 1833, the AASS was a fringe group congregating in New York each spring to greet one another in a spirit of camaraderie, to listen and respond to the views of their multiracial leadership, to counter opponents and shore up morale within the ranks, and to assess the current situation in the nation and plot next steps. Over the 1840s, however, their position began to inch in toward the center of the political spectrum. By the late 1840s, meetings were well attended, the municipal and national press kept a watchful eye on their activities, their literary propaganda reached readers across the North and over the Atlantic, and their central issue was beginning to preoccupy the national political debate. All told, Brown would have some good news to communicate to the friends on the other side of the Atlantic.

Brown headed home promptly at the conclusion of the meetings, with much to do. His trip began memorably: Who should ask permission to sit next to him on the train taking him back up the coast but Macready, who had cut short his tour and was returning to Britain via Boston.[93] The two men could have compared notes on riots as well as the art of performance. Shortly after reaching Boston, Brown resumed a long series of lecture engagements across Massachusetts and possibly Maine. At the most elaborate of them, the annual meeting of the NEASS in Boston, he introduced the hero of another notable fugitive-slave escape. Flanked on the platform by three fellow fugitives (Douglass and Ellen and William Craft), Brown brought forward an ex-slave named Henry Brown, who had recently pulled off an amazing feat of self-emancipation by mailing himself through the US postal service from Richmond to the Philadelphia Vigilance Committee. By the time he was helped out of his full-length wooden box, shaped like a coffin, he was a free man. That night at the Melodeon, Brown "jocularly" gave his new comrade a name— "Boxer"—which by convention's end stuck permanently as "Box."[94] That tag name soon got stuck to him as well by an uncomprehending public that could not distinguish between one black Brown and another.

Brown lectured across Massachusetts and went out to Nantucket in late June before returning to Boston. On July 4, he joined his good friends Nell and the Crafts, as well as dozens of fellow activists, on the special discounted train organized for the annual MASS picnic at the

Grove in Abington. He took his turn speaking at the morning session, which also included addresses by Garrison and Quincy. Meanwhile, William Craft circulated through the crowd, engaging various people on the evils of slavery. Even on this safest home turf, he did not pass without challenge. At one point he got into an argument with a Mexican War veteran who tried to make the case that blacks were better off in slavery than in freedom.[95] After the picnic lunch, the golden-throated Phillips orated for more than ninety minutes on the effects of slavery on the body politic, talking so long—though he was known to go longer—that "Brown of the Box" could not finish his narrative recitation before it was time to board the return train.[96]

Two days later, Brown applied to Secretary of State John Clayton for a passport to attend the Peace Congress in France. (Passports to enter Britain were not necessary.) He listed 21 Cornhill as his address and made his heritage, if not his legal status, unmistakably clear: "I am a native of the state of Kentucky and I am a colored man."[97] The State Department virtually never issued passports to African Americans, free or enslaved, and he must have known it would make no exception for him. He was enough of a committed abolitionist, however, to believe that exposing official discrimination to the general public was a worthwhile act.[98] His instincts proved right, but he could not have guessed his protest would strike so sensitive a nerve; it became and remained for years a lively item in the reform press. Memory of the injustice was still alive a century later when black commentators traced the deprivation of African American travel rights from Brown to the formidable actor-singer Paul Robeson, who was stripped of his passport under the McCarran Internal Security Act for alleged communist activities.[99]

Brown was still awaiting final word from Richard Webb in Dublin during the two weeks before his departure. Two years of intensely social existence in black Boston had earned him many friends to take leave of, but his primary concern was his daughters. Whether he had any thought or even raised the possibility of taking them with him is unknown. At this point, he could not anticipate the duration of his own stay, and even if he had had any thoughts of taking them, he would have needed assistance to pay their passage, no less to send them to private school. Assured that they were comfortably and safely settled, with no fear Betsey would try to take them away, he parted from them in either New Bedford or Boston.

Two nights before his departure, he took his farewell from Boston's black community. A committee of well-placed community leaders, headed by the main planner William Nell and including caterer Joshua Smith and lawyer Robert Morris, organized a spirited sendoff. They rented Washingtonian Hall on Bromfield Street and posted broadsides around the neighborhood, inviting the community to a double celebration: a farewell to Brown and a tribute to Garrison.[100] A number of MASS old-timers attended, gratified to witness Garrison receive due recognition for nearly two decades of unstinting, courageous devotion to the African American community. Brown's friend John T. Hilton, the veteran black community activist and leader who had organized a hero's welcome for Garrison in 1840 on his triumphant return from London, presided over a long program of testimonials, speeches, and musical entertainment. The evening of good feelings began with a testimonial to Garrison from black Boston, which Nell solemnized by presenting him with an engraved silver pitcher paid for by the hard-earned wages of the community. The audience stood and cheered.

Next up on the platform was black civic leader Thomas Paul Smith, Nell's and Hilton's archnemesis in the drive for school integration. Smith shifted attention to Brown, whom he joined with Garrison unevenly at the hip as though linking cause to effect: "Garrison and Brown stand, to-night, in their respective characters, the BENEFACTOR and the REDEEMED."[101] Smith predicted Brown would find greater liberty in France, where he might soon shake the hand of the revered poet and freedom fighter Lamartine. Visibly touched, Brown came forward to accept the tribute of his friends and neighbors, expressing his pride on the linkage to Garrison and his gratitude to the movement: "All that I am now, or expect to be in this world, I owe to the anti-slavery cause." The next day Garrison reciprocated by including a spirited commendation of Brown's service in the ledger of the MASS and dashing off a handful of letters of recommendation designed to open the doors of well-placed friends across the British Isles.[102] The night's celebration also served a practical purpose, as all proceeds beyond expenses went into a travel fund for Brown. It could not have stretched very far, though, as he arrived in Europe full of ideas but short on cash.

He set out from Boston harbor on the *Canada*, newest of the Cunard Line's transatlantic steamships. Commissioned to carry the mail from England, these fast, modern vessels were also transporting a steerage compartment's quota of Irish and German immigrants westward into New York and Boston Harbors—thousands and thousands of people arriving each year in search of an American dream. Once again Brown was traveling counter to the prevailing traffic in quest of a life of greater freedom and opportunity. For years he had joined his white antislavery colleagues in repeating the standard, somewhat perverse mantra in public talks that England—"land of the free, and the home of the brave," as Brown called it—was the land of opportunity for American blacks.[103] Now he was about to test the proposition for himself.

When he arrived at the wharf the morning of July 18, 1849, he had a small entourage. Nell, the Crafts, and other close friends accompanied him and made sure he did not leave empty-handed. Pointing him toward his new home, they gave him copies of *Jane Eyre* and the first volumes of Thomas Babington Macaulay's *History of England* to fill the long hours of seaboard leisure. No one present, not even Brown, had the slightest inkling that five years would pass before they would see one another again. When they did, just about everyone agreed he returned a changed man.

Nelson's Column, Trafalgar Square, London. Courtesy of David Castor.

PART 2

England

6

London, the Biggest Stage

As the *Canada* steamed out of Boston Harbor shortly after noon, Brown took a long look back at the party of friends who had escorted him to the pier. A quick surge of regret overcame him, catching him by surprise. He had worked so hard in planning his journey that he had left himself unprepared for the actual experience of separation from his Boston friendships and associations.[1] One sight in particular arrested his attention: the figure of William Craft waving a white handkerchief over the heads of the crowd.[2] The pain passed quickly enough, and he turned toward the future, ready for one of the greatest adventures of his life. Soon the ship cleared Plymouth, a compromised symbol of freedom that yielded to his imagination the classic two-ship scene of Pilgrim freedom and Virginia slavery in *Clotel*. It moved out into open water and steered toward Halifax, its only port of call before Liverpool. The day was warm and bright, some passengers even resorting to umbrellas for protection from the sun, and Brown enjoyed the sensation of the salt air as the ship pushed farther out to sea.

He was one of 126 passengers traveling on the pride of the Cunard Line, a twin-engine ship launched barely a half-year earlier and vaunted as one of the fastest and largest vessels on the high seas.[3] A steamship like the *Canada* could halve a sailing vessel's usual month-long transatlantic crossing and eliminate some of the unreliability. He must have heard the story of Garrison's travails on the high seas in 1840 en route to the first World Anti-Slavery Convention in England. Spring conditions were typically unpredictable, but Garrison's maritime luck was unusually bad. His packet ship encountered such turbulent winds and seas that he reached London a week late, missing the great controversies that marred the early meetings and fractured the international movement for years. Brown's crossing, on the other hand, was so smooth he barely needed his sea legs during a ten-day trip that went down as the fastest eastbound crossing on record.[4]

The captain was the notoriously gruff Charles H. E. Judkins, a veteran skipper of the line. Judkins had commanded the ship that carried Douglass to England in 1845 and knew as little about Brown as he had initially known about Douglass. When Douglass had asked permission to address his fellow passengers, Judkins not only authorized him to speak from the promenade deck but also summoned the passengers, silencing complainers. By contrast, Brown found that his presence alone aboard the *Canada* communicated enough of a message. Rumors had preceded any initiative he might have taken about a fugitive slave onboard who was embarking as a delegate to the International Peace Congress, the destination of various other passengers, including some Southerners. To stoke the ship's temperature a bit higher, Brown distributed the few copies of the *Narrative* he had carried aboard, which he claimed "produced considerable sensation" among his fellow passengers—the slaveholders in particular.[5]

The only one Brown called out by name was Thomas Chinn, a Louisiana parish judge headed via London and the Paris Peace Congress to fill the post of US consul in Naples. Despite receiving the diplomatic appointment, Chinn trailed a checkered past. He had had impeachment charges brought against him in 1826 by his state legislature for alleged crimes, including vote fixing and theft of slaves from estates passing through his probate court.[6] Complications also seemed to follow him on his travels. In 1835, he visited New York City with his trusted slave "boy" Robin, aged "between 30 and 33." They stayed at the fashionable

City Hotel on Broadway—at least until Robin absconded, compelling Chinn to post fugitive-slave handbills around the city. Robin, he advertised, was "one of the best servants I ever knew. His character has been distinguished for sobriety, truth, and integrity—no servant has ever been or more justly had the confidence of his master than he."[7] If Robin ever went back to Louisiana, it was not voluntarily.

Brown, of course, knew nothing about Chinn's past. In fact, it was less Chinn than the free black servant attending him who caught Brown's roving eye. Still exasperated over discriminatory issuance of US passports, Brown was outraged to discover that this person had what he did not: an official passport. He got so worked up that he made a point of asking to see it and reacted bitterly when he saw the signature of James Buchanan, John Clayton's predecessor as secretary of state: "This proves conclusively, that if a colored person wishes the protection of the U.S. government in going into any foreign country, he must not think of going in any other capacity than that of a boot-black."[8] Such was the cold logic underlying what the literary historian Edlie Wong has called "the racial coordinates of national belonging": A black person could receive the protection of his/her homeland only while traveling in service to a white employer.[9] The incident underscored the basic point that his shipboard coordinates left him belonging legally to neither his native land nor the land he had not yet reached. Whether England would provide a solution to his dilemma of legal statelessness was a question only the experience of Europe could answer. For the time being, at least, he would have had to be grateful he did not need a passport for his entry into France, thanks to the efforts of Peace Congress organizers. For future trips, however, he was on his own.

The Southerners, in truth, were a tiny if vocal minority among a motley group of passengers. They could be found on just about every steamer leaving US ports for England, a matter of irritation to some British antislavery activists eager to find ways to obstruct their free speech, especially from church pulpits. Brown simply steered clear of them, even though he knew they would be unable to touch him the moment the *Canada* docked at an English port. With plenty of time on his hands,

Brown took his typically lively interest in the crowd. Even the newest steamships had cramped quarters that made for intense sociality, so Brown found himself interacting with an interesting array of fellow passengers from the United States, England, France, and Spain. But the largest contingent was an Austrian dance troupe (*Danseuses Viennoises*) returning home after a North American tour. At one point, his amused gaze even fixed on an arresting-looking man sporting "the longest pair of mustaches that mortal man was ever doomed to wear."[10]

Brown was not traveling alone. Accompanying him were fellow International Peace Congress delegates Asa Mahan and Hamilton Hill, president and secretary-treasurer, respectively, of the Oberlin Institute.[11] No American college would have been more likely to send representatives than Oberlin, one of the most socially progressive colleges in the country. Its faculty was stocked with castoffs like Mahan from the Lane Seminary, and it deviated radically from prevailing academic norms. It not only matriculated women and African Americans but also treated them on generally equal terms with white men. The school had meant to send an even larger delegation, but only Hill and Mahan were able to make the trip.

Brown probably knew both men before the voyage from his lecturing tours in Ohio. He would correspond with Hill in 1856, when he was making a cross-country reading tour of his first antislavery play and wished to schedule a reading at Oberlin.[12] As the institution's corresponding secretary, Hill was the contact person for African American families, some poor, intent on acquiring higher education for their sons and daughters. Brown might well have been one of those persons if his family circumstances had been different. Brown and Mahan spent considerable time together on the voyage and later in Paris. During their stopover in Halifax, the two men walked the streets, sightseeing and conversing. As president of the college, Mahan gave the obligatory capstone course in moral philosophy, the subject of one of his major books. Brown was not one to engage in discussion of the finer points of religion or ontology with anyone, no less a learned expert. His conversation with Mahan was more practically directed toward the issues they were traveling to discuss: world peace, abolition of slavery, the counterinsurgency sweeping the Austro-Hungarian Empire.

They arrived in Liverpool on July 28 without major incident, although Brown could have made no such assumption at the time of departure. He had only recently traveled on a Maine steamer from Portland to Bath whose crew had refused him seating at the communal table, leaving him famished by the time the boat docked.[13] He had heard enough stories about the discrimination Douglass had repeatedly met on his home-bound crossing on the *Cambria* to expect that he too might encounter rough treatment. He was more fortunate in his crossing, but getting through customs in Liverpool did not proceed entirely smoothly. No passport was necessary for entry, but Brown caused a stir when an officer scrutinizing his possessions removed a suspicious object from his valise. Bystanders stopped to listen to his explanation, which upset at least a few of his fellow American passengers sensitive to the airing of domestic laundry on foreign soil. It was a slave collar, Brown loudly explained, used by a master to punish one of his female slaves for repeated acts of disobedience. That was of no concern to the officer, and he cleared Brown to continue on his way.

Friends had given him the name of Brown's Temperance Hotel, one of a number of lodgings spread out around Liverpool's Clayton Square, to which he set off by coach. That first stop on British soil he made in conformity with his predecessors Garrison and Douglass, who had likewise chosen that well-known "dry" lodging for their first night in England. Once settled in, he took to the streets to see something of "the great seaport of the world." He had several days to tour before boarding a steamer to Dublin and meant to use that time to satisfy his curiosity. A tirelessly energetic, inquisitive traveler since adolescence, he walked wide-eyed around the booming city those two days—sometimes alone, sometimes with shipmates—taking in the look and feel of a city in an alternative land. One thing that repeatedly caught his eye was the thickness of structures, piers, warehouses, houses built powerfully with wood, concrete, or steel—everything made to last: "Every thing in Liverpool looks old, yet nothing is worn out."[14] He was silent, however, about the city's desperate poverty. During those heady first days in a new land, he saw what he wanted to see, screened out what he did not. A finer-grained, comparative evaluation of English society, political economy, living conditions, and culture would come soon enough.

On his third day in England, he and his set of stereotype plates boarded the steamer *Adelaide* for the trip to Dublin, again crossing against a flow of émigrés, this time people pouring out of famine-stricken Ireland. On reaching Dublin, he headed directly to Richard Webb's house at 176 Great Brunswick (now Pearse) Street, a thoroughfare in a commercial area filled with shops and factories a short walk east of Trinity College. Webb opened his home to Brown with the same warmth he had shown Douglass (and before Douglass, Charles Remond). With Brown, however, he felt greater initial anxiety: Would this particular fugitive be up to the task of professional lecturing on a European stage? How would he comport himself in public? And would his *Narrative* return the expenses laid out for its production? Garrison's letter had gained him entry, but Brown would need to prove his capability.

Brown's anxieties, such as they must have been, he presumably kept to himself; Webb's were communicated in letters to friends. Once he met Brown, he reported, they eased considerably. The two men found an immediate rapport, beginning a warm working friendship that included Hannah Webb, an eager and able partner in her husband's many reform endeavors. Brown probably also met their impressive fifteen-year-old son, Alfred, a future Irish political leader who occasionally assisted his father in the printing shop. The friendship with Webb would last throughout Brown's European residence, a pattern repeated as he traveled from one to another of Garrison's allies, accumulating several dozen influential supporters. Webb found Brown an appealing new presence on the European scene. "He is very intelligent and easy, full of anecdote and staunch to his color," he reported to a common friend. He also fell into the seemingly obligatory Brown–Douglass comparison: Brown was the more personally attractive, amiable man; Douglass, the more forceful, charismatic figure.[15] After noting the trail of bruised feelings Douglass had left behind, Webb was relieved to observe Brown radiated "fellow feeling" for their allies in the cause, a prerequisite for successful maneuvering through Europe's tight-knit reform circles.

He was likewise pleased that the contentious author–printer relationship he had had with Douglass did not repeat itself. One reason was personal; Brown was simply a more accommodating individual, more willing to compromise. He was also a good houseguest who was just the sort of person the news-starved Webbs hungered for. He regaled them with the latest US news and told stories about the cast of characters in the United States they knew chiefly by word of mouth. Some of them were names they had been following for years in the pages of the antislavery press, but Brown also made a point of introducing them to newer names, such as Ellen and William Craft, whom the Webbs would meet once passage of the 1850 Fugitive Slave Law drove a growing number of fugitives to Great Britain. Perhaps anticipating such moments, Brown handed his new friends a recent engraving of Ellen in male dress that he had brought over for selective distribution. Balancing one gesture of respect with another, the Webbs dutifully hung it in the gallery they kept in their drawing room.[16]

The other reason was professional. Brown's *Narrative* amounted to nothing more than a straight printing job for Webb—the sheets to be printed from American plates along with the addition of a new title page and supplementary matter. Webb's liability in the enterprise was strictly limited, inasmuch as he had engaged Charles Gilpin, the leading British publisher of antislavery materials, to oversee its general distribution from London. (Gilpin's name rather than Webb's appeared on the title page as publisher.) Nonetheless, working with Brown was not problem-free. As late as December 1849, Webb was complaining that Brown still owed him nearly $200 for printing costs and, as far as Webb was concerned, had been making himself scarce since their last meeting, in September.[17]

In gaining access to Webb's well-connected circle, Brown began his European adventure on the most solid footing. A short, bald, bespectacled man, Webb hardly looked the part of Ireland's leading abolitionist printer and impresario. But this lapsed Quaker with his can-do personality, quick mind, sharp pen, and radical politics commanded a metropolitan reach extending from Dublin across all of Ireland to England, Scotland, and North America. Born the same month as Garrison, he had a personal as well as generational synchronicity with his revered friend—two printers traversing a corresponding arc from traditional Protestantism to heterodox activism on behalf of antislavery and other human rights causes. Webb had already teamed with his local friends James Haughton and Richard Allen in the late 1830s in organizing the Hibernian Anti-Slavery Society when he met his future ally at the 1840 London antislavery convention. Their unswerving transatlantic friendship/partnership continued through the Civil War. Webb's operating logic subsequently in dealing with visiting Americans was simple: a friend of William Lloyd Garrison's was a friend of his, until proven otherwise. Douglass had been problematic and fractious, but the equally irascible Webb sensed that Brown would be different. For his part, Brown knew that well-connected men like Webb could provide as much legitimation for him in English-speaking Europe as Garrison had done in the Northern states.

Opening night of Brown's European tour took place August 16 at a reception organized in his honor by Webb. Six hundred people, pressed together all the way to the doors, packed the Rotundo concert hall for one of the largest antislavery gatherings held in Dublin in years. Webb, his brother, and several other dignitaries were seated alongside Brown on the platform, with Haughton presiding. Haughton and Webb made introductory remarks about slavery and Brown designed to build excitement for the speaker, but the atmosphere was charged from the moment the speakers seated themselves on the podium. At this inaugural event, Brown kept his remarks safe. Finding his groove quickly, he eased from protestations of lacking the standard "liberal education" to a confident recitation of his life story.[18] He steered many of his remarks close to home, as he frequently would do during his early months abroad. He dwelt on the people in his early life—Elizabeth, Higgins, and Young. He told audience-tested anecdotes, such as the one in which the conductor forced him to move from coach to baggage (though now relocated from Ohio to Massachusetts) and the one in which he tricked his landlord's boys to teach him to read. When he touched on the potentially sensitive subject of current Irish politics, he was careful to align his views with those of Daniel O'Connell, the "liberator of the Irish people," whom Brown obligingly cast as a would-be emancipator of the American slaves. The transcript of his remarks, punctuated by bracketed "cheers" and "sensation," indicated he exercised audience control with the same sure-handed feel he used at home.

To judge from a local reporter's account, Brown captivated at least part of his audience as much by his appearance as by the content of his speech: "Mr. Brown's *personel* is prepossessing; he possesses little of the Nubian or negro cast of head and features; his forehead is good and well developed in its frontal formation, and his figure erect and graceful. His language is strictly grammatical, and his style correct and energetic."[19] If Dubliners were expecting some sort of exotic specimen, they got instead a socially presentable man and cultivated lecturer capable of speaking an intelligent American's version of the Queen's English. (His occasional American idioms were excused as a collective idiosyncrasy.) Given a rousing response at the end of his talk, Brown clearly passed this opening test with flying colors. Webb came away with a heightened appreciation of Brown's capacity as a public man, and Haughton was soon sharing his impression with the American public of having witnessed "a quite superior man."[20]

Brown spent nearly three weeks with the Webbs in Dublin, much of it sightseeing locally. He traveled mostly on his own, while Webb was busily overseeing presswork on the *Narrative* in the printing shop adjacent to his home. There really was not much else Brown could do to help other than to pen a short "Note to the Present Edition" suitable for its Anglo-Irish circumstances. He emphasized several points: He proudly accepted the honor of being selected for the American delegation at the International Peace Congress as a collective honor for his people; defended his work's lack of dates as the mark of an enforced collective ignorance; and—perhaps with his shipboard experience in mind—asserted the necessity of combating the propaganda spread by visiting US slave owners with the antislavery truth. He dated it August

14, 1849, by which time production was already well underway. Webb ran off on his steam-powered press a print run of 1,000 copies, half that of Douglass's *Narrative*. Seizing the moment at the Rotundo meeting, Webb announced its forthcoming publication and took orders after Brown had completed his remarks. By the time the two men set out on the first leg of their journey to Paris, the work was nearly ready for general distribution across Ireland and the British Isles.

WHILE SO MUCH heady novelty was occupying his attention, Brown was unaware of what was transpiring across the ocean, where Betsey was still doing her best to prosecute her case in the court of public opinion. Having no fixed home of her own, she had apparently been moving nomadically with little Paulina between cities—principally Buffalo and Cleveland and possibly also Detroit—since her summer 1848 incursion into Massachusetts. On August 5, she sent an agonizingly unhappy letter to New Bedford shoe manufacturer and antislavery activist Isaac C. Ray, a man in Brown's network of acquaintances. Her subject was simply "Wm.'s villainy as I can call it nothing less." The letter was spurred by an unsettling visit from Charles Remond, who was making a Western swing for the AASS and presumably stopped to see Betsey at Brown's request. Her husband was gone to England, he informed her, and planned to stay indefinitely. Betsey responded to this shocking news in the only way she knew. Composing her thoughts under the influence of great emotion, she launched into a stunning vituperation against Brown, Remond, the leaders of the antislavery movement—anyone and everyone she saw as standing between her and her lost children.[21]

This hastily, impulsively written letter—the only known document to have survived in Betsey's hand and containing her smudged fingerprint in the margin—shoots a rapid-fire clip of invective at Brown and his supporters. The charge she was making was virtually the most serious she could aim at a person with her husband's family history: abandonment. She spared no words. He had run off, cut her off from her children, prevented her letters from reaching them, and failed to provide the promised stream of child support ($25 per quarter) for her outcast daughter. Not satisfied merely to assail his behavior, she also showered her contempt on the "hypocritical friends of the opressed [*sic*]," who served Brown by reinforcing her isolation.

Although Remond had refused to divulge the whereabouts of the girls, she apparently thought Isaac Ray might. She also had a more explicit request to make of this man, whom she probably had met just briefly during her previous year's trip to eastern Massachusetts. Would he advise her how best to prepare for publication the enclosed copy of a certificate of good character? Her reference was to the loose piece of handwritten paper she presumably tucked into the folded sheet of her letter. That page contained a copy of the aforementioned certificate of good character ("her character and reputation stands unspotted") she had had prepared in Buffalo after her desperate summer journey to Massachusetts. This remarkable document, a virtuoso performance of cajolery, ingenuity, anguish, spite, and sheer determination, was her hands-on retaliation for Brown's threat, during their heated encounter in Boston the previous summer, to produce his own indictment of her character. Whether it was a fabrication or a legitimate document is an open question—although there is no doubt she produced it in multiple copies for presentation.

That defense of her character was not all she intended to publish. She claimed she had also prepared for publication a far more offensive-minded text that she called "my Book"—a tell-all account about "my Garrison friends['] treatment to me through out this unfair investigation of Wm's notorious falsehoods." Betsey had not lived all those years with a fugitive-slave memoirist and learned nothing; her book was an act of public service designed to "give the public a true history of these facts from the beginning to the end in order that the public may yet know I have been grossly wronged by the man whom [*sic*] should be called my husband." After storing up anger for so many years, she must have found the act of transferring her personal pain to public words her last, best resort. No such book ever saw the light of day, but that does not mean no such narrative ever existed. Elizabeth Brown was not a woman who typically bluffed.

Ray, she requested, would send by return mail his advice about publication of these two documents. He could trust her not to betray his role, she insinuated, because she was "part Indian" (what value she attached to her "negro" heritage went unstated). The return letter she anticipated was one she presumably never received. Whether Ray ever divulged to anyone the contents of Betsey's letter, whose original remained in his possession for life, is unknown. If he did pass on its contents to Garrison or his friends, they would have known they were drawing gunfire from an unusual direction. They were used to rounds of propaganda aimed at them from the South, churches, press, political and business leaders— not from the wife of one of their most trusted members. Bad enough for coming from within the antislavery community, her aspersions were all the worse for accusing the antislavery movement of the same despicable crime it attributed to slavery: the breakup of a black family. In 1849, at least, there were no immediate public repercussions. In 1850, there would be.

BROWN AND WEBB made for London via Liverpool on August 19, losing no time before continuing by train southward to the great metropolis of the English-speaking world. As the train chugged into the station, Brown gaped through the smoke-filled air at the largest expanse of urban sprawl he had ever seen, picking out St. Paul's Cathedral but little else. He had a ready-made guide in Webb, a lover of London, but little free time for sightseeing. Their main order of business was meeting up the next evening with their contingent of fellow delegates and accompanying visitors, which gathered at Hadley's Hotel, in Blackfriars, to hear about preparations made by the organizing committee for the journey to Paris. The next day, Brown and Webb fell in bright and early with their 600-person-strong entourage on the three-part excursion: by train from London Bridge Station to Folkestone, ferry to Calais, and finally train to Paris.

The plan worked more smoothly for some than for others, like Brown, after the full party arrived in Folkestone on one of the two oversize trains reserved for the delegation. Of the three ferries booked for the group, he boarded one that headed not to Calais but to Boulogne. His group, led by Joseph Sturge, the wealthy, influential founder of the British and Foreign Anti-Slavery Society (BFASS), eventually regrouped in Boulogne and boarded a train bound for Paris via Amiens. They arrived hours late, after midnight, at the end of an exhausting day, but there was Elihu Burritt, still standing vigil in the station to greet the straggling "peace army of invasion" and send its members off in carriages to their lodgings.[22] Brown, like Burritt, stayed at the Hotel Bedford, a favorite place for English-speakers, located near the Madeleine.[23]

He awakened the next day to Paris by daylight and the first day of the congress—too much by half for Brown's ambition to dig deep into Europe. Concentrated sightseeing would have to wait. For the next three days, he poured himself into meetings vital to his belief in national and international justice but also potentially instrumental for his long-term prospects in Europe. The timing of the meetings was not particularly auspicious. They took place while France's armies were deployed in Italy and Hungary, rolling back the previous year's revolutionary accomplishments. Some took that incongruity as a challenge for what needed to be accomplished inside the walls of the congress; others were more skeptical. The eloquent local Protestant minister, Athanase Laurent Charles Coquerel, noted in his remarks the irony of attempting to set down principles of universal peace in a metropolitan capital filled with "the greatest monuments existing in the world to the honour of armies."[24] Worse yet, troops were still stationed around the capital after the revolutionary turmoil of the previous year, even as the delegates were vigorously discussing universal disarmament and international arbitration.

The setting for this major international congress of representatives, an early precursor of the League of Nations assembling from Britain, France, Belgium, the Netherlands, Germany, and the United States, was a curious choice. The organizers had had to compromise in selecting as their meeting place the Salle Sainte Cécile, rue St. Lazare, a music hall better known for the spectacle of its dances (including the hugely popular cancan) than for public events. For its few days of public assembly, however, the hall served its purpose well. Its sprawling interior measuring 120 feet by 300 feet, surmounted by skylights, afforded seating capacity for the expected 1,000 to 1,500 attendees, and the organizers had it gaily decorated for the event with the interlocking flags of the represented nations. For suitable gravitas, the organizers secured the services of France's leading literary figure, Victor Hugo, as president; and for security, the (conditional) protection of the French government. So highly anticipated an event attracted an array of leading European progressives as delegates, including Member of Parliament Richard Cobden (the only English-speaker who dared to address the audience in French); the influential Chartist Henry Vincent; Joseph Sturge and John Scoble from the BFASS; and newspaper editors and religious leaders from across Europe. The American delegation (including two Canadians), though respectably sized at twenty-three men for a transatlantic mission, lacked stature comparable to that of their English and French colleagues. Nor, even with Burritt present, did it have a clear leader; it seemed as diffuse as the US reform community itself.

The meetings took place in half-day sessions between August 22 and 24. In order to maintain control over an event otherwise likely to lose focus, the organizers set the general agenda in advance and arranged lists of speakers for each day's session. In another attempt to maintain control—though in this instance as a necessary concession to the French regime—they forbade discussion of current political issues. Hugo's opening speech, filled with an optimism about the power of technology to erect "an electric wire of concord" to unify a shrinking globe, set the tone for three days of sometimes optimistic exuberance, but the self-imposed censorship over discussion of current politics tempered some participants' expectations.[25] Brown found it dispiriting enough that the entire congress was conducted with "padlocks that the government put upon our lips" but worse that the organizing committee was regulating the sessions to the point of exclusion.[26]

As the last day's afternoon session was drawing to a close, Brown finally lost all patience with the proceedings and approached the podium, intending to address the audience without official clearance. Although a huissier stood guard between him and the podium, his obvious racial difference for once proved advantageous. Coquerel graciously interceded, introducing him cordially as a special representative of the American Peace Society, and Brown took calculated advantage of the opportunity. He chose and paced his extemporaneous remarks astutely, using spare, precise language to make a more direct connection in only five minutes than had yet been made over several days between war and peace, slavery and freedom, meanwhile contrasting recent French abolition with persistent American support of slavery.[27] Standing before the audience in full figure as a fugitive slave, he spoke with enhanced authority, and his remarks, immediately translated into French by the multilingual Coquerel, drew two rounds of animated applause. Brown had made a breach in the protocol so wide that two could pass through, so the other distinguished black delegate, Reverend James Pennington, quickly followed. Although he and Brown had sparred back home over antislavery tactics and allegiances (and would do so soon again in England), he now made common ground with his fellow fugitive by seconding his view of the link between slavery and war and advocating the potential of true, unadulterated Christianity to overcome both.

The special occasion of the Peace Congress gave Brown nonpareil access to a who's who of leading European reformers. Within a few days, he made the acquaintance of the leaders of the British and Foreign Anti-Slavery Society, most significantly Joseph Sturge, a respected Quaker corn merchant from Birmingham who had drafted its constitution a decade earlier, and its operating manager John Scoble—who would soon develop a dislike for Brown so visceral that he tried repeatedly to destroy his reputation. He also made his initial personal acquaintance of Sturge's nephew Charles Gilpin, a senior member of both the BFASS and the British book trade with whom Brown presumably consulted about the forthcoming *Narrative*, since Gilpin was publishing it in cooperation with Richard Webb. Brown took a quick liking to Gilpin, who would remain his trusted publisher for the next three years. He also made a good impression on one of the most idiosyncratic delegates to the Congress, Dr. John Lee, a left-leaning polymath and aristocrat who found Brown the most refreshingly interesting member of the American delegates. Brown also moved fluidly among newspaper editors, religious leaders, and parliamentarians from England and France, the organizers and chief figures of the congress, and members of well-connected anti-slavery families in attendance, such as the Sturges from Birmingham, the Richardsons from Newcastle upon Tyne, the Wighams from Leeds, and his old friends the Westons and Chapmans from Massachusetts. And, in a crucial first step toward gaining a foothold as a lecturer, he received an invitation from his new acquaintance John Morland to visit him in Croydon, near London, shortly after the congress to deliver what would be Brown's maiden lecture in England.[28]

Webb remarked through the US antislavery press that Brown had made the acquaintance of "some of the best people in England" and was already "reaping the good fruits" of his success.[29] He was one of many people who noticed—as European eyes were watching—Brown's conspicuous achievements in Paris. The highlight of Brown's after-hours success occurred at the official soirée honoring the delegates hosted by the French foreign minister and his English-born wife, Alexis and Marie de Tocqueville. Awed by his surroundings, Brown could not help but notice the presence throughout the rooms of "good-looking waiters in white wigs," which prodded him to reflect that had the soirée been hosted in the United States, he could not have gained entry except as one of them.[30] Race and entrée, he noticed that night and repeatedly, mixed differently in Paris than back home. When Madame de Tocqueville ascertained that he was a former slave, she singled him out for personal attention, seating him alongside her on a sofa and engaging him in an animated conversation about his history. Passing observers noticed—the American consul with a particularly nasty look—his special treatment.

Much as he generally disliked such scenes, he took pleasure in the event, but it was a less formal event that he would soon single out for mention in his lectures. This one took place in the Salle Sainte Cécile at the conclusion of the first day's session, following conversations he had held with Hugo and Cobden. One highly interested observer of these conversations was an unnamed Southerner (not Chinn) who had been aboard the *Canada* and, Brown claimed, alluded to him loudly on shipboard as better suited to labor on his master's farm than to pass among good society in Europe. Recalculating his bearings once in Paris, this fellow citizen deferentially approached Brown at the Peace Congress and asked him to intercede in getting an introduction to Cobden. Brown simply walked away. That story, with Hugo sometimes swapped for Cobden, invariably proved a favorite with English audiences on lecture tours, as he knew it would.[31]

BROWN TOURED Paris and Versailles after the congress, accepting the invitation of Maria Chapman to stay with her family in their summer home near the Palais de Versailles. His earliest-known letter—a scratchy field message from Buffalo in 1844—had been written to her; five years later, he was meeting her in the salons of Europe. She noticed the difference as well as he; she sent back glowing reports to the "friends" in Boston about his performance at the congress, nothing that passersby afterward were stopping him on the streets to engage him in conversation, despite the difficulty of communication.[32] One aggravation, however, occurred during his stay in Versailles. At a formal reception given by the English delegates to honor their American colleagues, Reverend William Allen, a prominent educator who had been president of Dartmouth and Bowdoin Colleges, stood up to make remarks exculpating the American government from complicity in slavery. Brown, who just a few days earlier had linked slavery to national and international practices before the Peace Congress, held his tongue then as his fellow Massachusetts delegate carried on, but not later. Soon after his return to London, he vehemently contested Allen's provocations in a public letter to the Parisian newspaper *La Presse*, whose editor, Emile de Girardin, had attended the congress and befriended Brown. He translated the letter and printed it with an endorsement.[33]

That act, which might not even have come to Allen's attention, further elevated Brown's standing with abolitionists on two continents. Back in Boston, a local newspaper reporter attending a meeting honoring the returning Bay State delegates noted Brown's rhetorical victory over Allen: "Brown had studied Constitutional law at the feet of south-ern Gamaliel, and carried his Diploma plainly written on his back, so that he was necessarily a better judge of it than any Doctor of Divin-ity."[34] Five minutes on stage and an impressive public bearing in London, Paris, and Versailles had earned him a favorable reputation among most, if not all, antislavery activists in the shortest possible time. The leaders of the BFASS, however, reserved judgment. Although Brown had arrived in England claiming he was an independent agent bearing no organiza-tion's credentials, they took him immediately for a Garrisonian, their archrival since the 1840 split.

He returned to London on August 31 and took rooms in a board-inghouse at 22 Cecil Street owned by a carpenter–house builder named Evan Jones, who by 1853 or 1854 also owned the house next door at 21 Cecil. The location was so advantageously situated just off the Strand and backing out nearly to the Thames, and the rooms so well served his needs he stayed put throughout his five-year residency in London. The flat put him in easy walking distance of the city's leading museums, theaters, great public buildings, libraries, rail stations, tourist sites, and parks. The central location also served the needs of out-of-town friends like Webb and the Estlins, who sometimes took rooms there during city visits (Webb, his first visitor, dropped by in late September). In time, his daughters would also spend brief spells with him, although they eventu-ally had their own quarters at their boarding school on Gray's Inn Road, near the new railway station at Kings Cross.

By the time of his return to London, the new edition of the *Nar-rative* was available for sale across the British Isles and Ireland. Gilpin had lost no time in getting it ready and announcing it in the London trade paper, a likely sign he meant to sell the book, probably in partner-ship with Webb handling sales in Ireland, through the regular book trade as well as through the network of the reform movement.[35] At the time, Gilpin also had in circulation a new edition of James Penning-ton's popular *The Fugitive Blacksmith*, a narrative similar to Brown's in its account of slavery, escape, and struggle for independence. Those two works together, both published by one of the senior figures of the

BFASS, prompted Britain's leading antislavery newspaper to publish a prophetic joint review of six US fugitive-slave narratives. The reviewer made clear that the British public was witnessing a genuine cultural phenomenon: "A new species of literature has sprung up in the United States, and is making its appearance in this country. Slaves who have escaped from the horrors of American bondage are telling their own tales, with an ability and pathos."[36] Brown did not simply presume on the receptivity of the British reading public; he cultivated it by adding an epigraph to the Gilpin edition consisting of the opening stanza of a song he had composed that expressed a suitably transportable patriotism, which he also sang on lecture tours:

> *Fling out the Anti-Slavery flag*
> *On every swelling breeze;*
> *And let its folds wave o'er the land,*
> *And o'er the raging seas,*
> *Till all beneath the standard sheet*
> *With new allegiance bow,*
> *And pledge themselves to onward bear*
> *The emblem of their vow.*[37]

On September 1, the day after his return to London, Brown made a beeline for the house of George Thompson, the most prominent Garrisonian in the British Isles. As Brown knew, the two men's relationship was long and cordial, going back to Garrison's first trip to England in 1831. It would culminate on April 14, 1865, as the two men, each of whom had once stood up to mob violence and threats of lynching in Massachusetts, joined arms in entering Fort Sumter, retaken several months earlier. On that long-awaited day, the old pacifists assembled alongside other dignitaries in taking a ceremonial hand in restoring the Stars and Stripes (which had been secured in a New York City bank vault) atop the fort for the first time since its evacuation four bloody years earlier.[38] A man as quick to revere as to criticize, Garrison honored his most respected friends by naming sons after them. Thompson joined

Wendell Phillips and Francis Jackson in the Garrison household, as Garrison reciprocally entered Thompson's. Whereas many colleagues in the movement on both continents found Thompson difficult, self-indulgent, and unreliable, Garrison considered him a stouthearted loyalist with the finest oratorical ability among British activists. His many detractors conceded the point that he was the loudest.

Time and again over the years, Thompson proved himself a loyal ally to Garrison's friends. This particular day, he did not need to read Garrison's letter of introduction to guess the identity of its bearer, whom he had been reading about for several years in the antislavery press and in dispatches from Samuel May Jr. He bypassed his servant in personally welcoming Brown into his home and family; in no time, he would lead Brown into the inner Garrisonian-affiliated circles of the European zone. A temperamental opposite of Webb, this boisterous, sentimental public man of affairs, who was currently serving as a progressive Member of Parliament, did as much to launch Brown's boat in England as Webb had in Ireland. Appreciative but discriminating, Brown had an easy talent for allowing other people's generosity to be lavished on him, provided he was allowed to steer his own boat. That role he was not willing to relinquish, not even to men such as Webb and Thompson, for whom he felt sincere regard, even affection. When it came to handling William Wells Brown, a subject that arose from time to time in discussions among white antislavery leaders, it was rarely clear who was taking whom in hand.

Brown had been settled in London for just a few days when he accepted the invitation extended by John Lee to a select handful of French and American delegates in Paris to visit at Hartwell House, his splendid country residence about fifty miles northwest of London. Brown took the train from London to Aylesbury, Buckinghamshire, and hired a coach to drive him the twenty-minute trip to the grounds of one of England's most historic landed estates. Lee had prepared his 1,800-acre estate for the occasion by festooning the trees lining his park's grand avenue with the flags of the nations represented at the Paris Peace Congress. Fresh from Versailles, Brown was soon peering at another of Europe's courtly mansions as the coach swung down the path and turned right toward the imposing northern front of the mansion. The existing structure dated from the seventeenth century, but the estate went back to the family of William the Conqueror and was registered in the Domesday Book. In more recent times, the estate had been let out to the exiled King Louis XVIII, who was still holding the French court-in-exile there at the time Brown was born in a slave shanty in Montgomery County, Kentucky.

John Lee was an amateur bibliophile and a distant relative of the Lees of Virginia, including Robert E. Lee. His tastes and politics could not have been more disparate from those of his American cousins. Trained in ancient languages and cultures at Cambridge, Lee had traveled extensively across the Levant from Egypt to Iraq in his early decades, passing through the region some years before it became a fashionable destination for European tourists and collectors. Lee was a man of fine, scholarly tastes, and, once an ample fortune and Hartwell House were bestowed upon him, he turned avidly to collecting treasures from the exotic places he had visited. He lived, in a manner of speaking, in a neighborhood of great collectors. His Aylesbury friend was Austen Henry Layard, the pioneering archaeologist of Assyria who transferred the excavated treasures from the remains of Nineveh and other great cities to the British Museum, where they formed the basis for the world's leading collection of Assyriology to go along with its nonpareil Egyptology collection. By contrast, Lee carried on a private one-man collecting enterprise, buying treasures from across the Near East and Europe and turning the long galleries of his home into notable exhibit spaces. His collections of Egyptology, law books, and theology books were choice enough to merit their own catalogues; the privately printed *Catalogue of the Egyptian Antiquities in the Museum of Hartwell House*, prepared by his friend, the noted Egyptologist Joseph Bonomi, is itself a superbly fine specimen of bookmaking art.[39] Brown met Layard during the visit to Hartwell House and no doubt saw and heard more about the collections of the ancient world than he had as yet been exposed to. Such artifacts were hardly inert museum objects to Brown and his contemporaries, as they increasingly served as primary evidence for or against contested theories about creation of the species (or creations of species, as proponents of the emergent "science" of race posited).

What was a man of Brown's background doing in a place like Hartwell House and associating with the likes of Lee and Layard? He asked himself that question from the moment he walked through its thick door in the company of a servant who led him to an apartment adorned with paintings by Italian masters. His first full day began early, as he awakened before dawn and ventured outside in his slippers even before the servants were up and about. He traipsed through the sculpted grounds of the park and garden, wishing his "dear daughters" were by his side to enjoy the estate's cultivated surroundings with him. After breakfast, he spent time meandering through the galleries and library, but the highlight of the day was the tour Lee gave his houseguests of model cottages he had had built for the estate's workers. His explanation carried particular significance for Brown, since it took sides in the raging transatlantic debate over a subject of overwhelming interest to him, the organization of labor. That debate, as he understood it, was a triangular one among the proponents of slave labor in the South, free labor in the North, and industrial labor in Britain. The neat, comfortable homes Lee showed off to his visitors provided tangible evidence to Brown of the falseness of all rhetorical claims about the preferential situation of the US slave over the free worker in Britain or America.[40]

The most formal event during his stay was a meeting Lee organized for his guests and local dignitaries for the purpose of ratifying the antiwar resolutions of the Peace Congress. At the local shire hall, Brown sat on the speakers' platform alongside a handful of other delegates and gave a short address (his remarks went unrecorded).[41] Brown's visit to Hartwell House lasted just a few days, but his presence lingered for more than a century. He made so powerful an impression that Lee had Brown's name inscribed on a brick and inserted in the vault of his famed observatory, there to keep company with other revered guests in the Hartwell House firmament.[42] It remained there until the destruction of the observatory in the great house fire of 1963.

UNAFFILIATED AND UNFINANCED on European soil, Brown needed to find means to provide for himself as well as for his daughters back home. Many African Americans who had preceded him to England had failed and wound up as beggars, as Estlin repeatedly warned May, but Brown foresaw a basis for self-sufficiency in a combination of lecturing and sale of his works. That was to prove his formula for financial independence throughout his five years in Europe.

His first lecture engagement in England grew out of a friendly encounter at the Paris Peace Congress. He so impressed English delegate John Morland that he received an invitation to come down on September 5 to speak at Croydon, then a London suburb, and to be Morland's houseguest at Heath Lodge. Brown spent the first portion of the day touring Windsor Castle with a party of friends. Traveling in what would become his customary fashion, with a Baedeker or Murray guidebook, he surveyed the surrounding area as well as the castle. From the top of the Round Tower, he enjoyed the commanding view of the Thames and the surrounding countryside. His primary interest, though off in the distance, was Stokes Park, because of its association with William Penn, whose family had owned it for part of the seventeenth century. Brown had taken so serious an interest in Penn during his 1847 and 1848 trips to Philadelphia that he paid visits to a number of Penn-associated places in the area. It was not Penn's religion that intrigued Brown; he had interacted with a wide-enough array of Quakers since his 1834 stay with the Wells Browns to be able to see the nuances among them as clearly as he could among Presbyterians or Unitarians. In fact, much of what he would see of the British Quakers who made up the stiff spine of the BFASS repelled him. It was, rather, Penn's ideals of religious liberty and pacifism, still fresh in his mind after they had been conspicuously invoked several weeks earlier at the Peace Congress. The last day's session had opened with the formal presentation to Coquerel of an inscribed copy of Penn's 1693 *Essay towards the Present and Future Peace of Europe by the Establishment of an European Dyet*, following which Elihu Burritt, on behalf of the American delegation, came forward to declare Penn an "early friend of peace and humanity" and the spiritual father of their proceedings.[43]

Brown left Windsor ahead of his companions to arrive in time for his meeting at Croydon's old Lecture Hall. His reputation had preceded him, so he could expect substantial support from its small but well-organized antislavery community. To ensure this first appearance on English soil went as smoothly as possible, George Thompson came down from London to make the formal introduction and place the imprimatur of Garrison on him. Brown then came forward and made the usual demurral about his lack of education, provisional status as a fugitive, and limited ability to speak forthrightly in selecting "from the mass of evidence the least disgusting details which the auditory would be willing to listen to."[44] Though real enough, such protestations were part of the style Brown was honing for his British audiences. Besides telling a variety of well-tested personal stories and anecdotes, he appealed to their pride and patriotism as leaders of international abolition. By the conclusion of his remarks in Croydon, he had brought the audience around to strong support of him. The meeting ended with a resolution offering him "a cordial welcome to the shores of England" and the sale of his freshly printed *Narrative*. The keen interest stirred up by his appearance generated fast sales; fifty copies went that night alone.[45]

He was off to a promising start on English soil, and lecture engagements came so quickly he declared himself "overwhelmed."[46] On September 19, with Webb visiting and present, Brown joined Pennington and some other delegates before an audience of a thousand people gathered at Baptist Chapel in Southwick to hear the results of the Peace Congress from its participants.[47] Brown made sure to impress upon the audience that his status as a fugitive slave made him subject anywhere on American soil to arrest and return. In England, he quickly discerned, he could trade on that status. Even the usual stigma and stigmata of enslavement could be turned to sympathetic advantage. Others carried their diplomas in their pockets, he said; he carried his on his back. When he spoke of the Stars and Stripes, he meant something different from those unfamiliar with the whip.[48]

He was one among many honorees that night, but he was the sole one at an official welcome hosted by Thompson on September 27. Brown entered the warm, friendly space of London's Music Hall to an audience of hundreds of supporters gathered to welcome him to England. As sometimes happened, however, he faced vocal opposition—in this instance from an interloper named George Jones, a self-identified Bostonian of English birth. A forward type sporting a black mustache and carrying himself with a military bearing, Jones heckled Thompson as he worked his way through a robust introduction of Brown. The audience called Jones to the platform, where he seated himself beside Thompson and presented his views even before Brown could come forward. Jones bragged that just the day before his departure, he had visited Daniel Webster, the influential but controversial Massachusetts senator whom abolitionists loathed for his compromising deference to the South on slavery. Tone deaf or simply standoffish, Jones took a line before that hostile audience that minimized the severity of slavery. His remarks drew spirited responses from speakers and audience alike. The next day, Brown reported back proudly to Phillips in Boston that he and Thompson had performed good teamwork on Jones: "G. T. skinned a proslavery Bostonian alive last night, all except the feet, and they say that I took the skin off of them."[49] Although Brown occasionally reunited with Thompson at meetings when their paths crossed, he was generally on his own for the next five years.

Wherever he went, Brown dispensed copies of the *Narrative*. He needed to, as his and his daughters' well-being depended on steady sales. That first English autumn proved particularly trying. Weeks after getting settled in London, his funds were stretched so tight that even the slightest miscalculation would leave him straining to make ends meet. That was the case as he prepared for a meeting to be held in his honor in Worcester on October 2. The organizers were so confident of an exceptional turnout they encouraged him to bring a large supply of books for sale. Not yet geographically oriented, he had no idea that reaching Worcester—130 miles from London—would require rail transportation. Having just sent remittances back home for the girls' upkeep, taxes on his New York real estate, and the printer's bill for the third edition of the

Narrative, he was embarrassed to find that he could not afford the train ticket. With Thompson out of town, he knew no one to turn to for a loan. Growing despondent, he was about to cancel when proceeds from sales at a recent meeting arrived. He was more fortunate than he could have known. An audience of 2,000 to 3,000 showed up that night, one of the largest crowds he had ever addressed, with the mayor presiding and the audience enthusiastic.[50]

He sold many copies, probably in the hundreds, during that trip and on subsequent travels those first months. James Pennington provides a good point of comparison. He bragged to a friend in November that he had personally sold nearly 500 copies of *The Fugitive Blacksmith* during a recent lecture tour before audiences numbering as many as 1,200 people.[51] Pennington had the hefty organizational support of the BFASS, but Brown had strong organizational support of his own and likely had comparable success. The first edition presumably sold out by New Year's Day in 1850, when Brown penned a very slightly amended introduction to a new Gilpin printing.[52] That printing also sold out within half a year. In June 1850, he complained to a friend that he was postponing a lecture trip to Bridgewater and Exeter until he could get Gilpin to issue a new printing.[53] If that is any indication, he was careful in his first year not to schedule any lecture tour without an adequate supply of books. Such was also the strategy employed by another US fugitive slave, Moses Roper, a longtime resident of England who made his living there for long periods chiefly by sales of his bestselling, self-published narrative.[54]

In November 1849, Brown made the second of his grand European gestures, the first in England. By then familiar with London institutions, he figured out how best to use the several barbaric instruments of US slavery he had brought with him. One was the slave collar that had attracted attention at customs; the other was a set of leg shackles that had somehow come into his possession from a free African American living in Washington, DC, who had been imprisoned for failure to produce his freedom papers. Brown boxed them together and addressed the package to the keeper of antiquities at the British Museum. Might the museum not wish to put them on display among its timeless exhibitions of the remnants of other civilizations? The museum thought otherwise, its board peremptorily declining Brown's offer. No explanation was given, but Brown would have gotten the message that the museum did not wish to involve itself in the messy politics of international antislavery.[55]

The day the museum board met, Brown arrived in Newcastle as a houseguest of the respected local reformer and businessman John Mawson, another new ally made in Paris. That visit marked the initial stop on his first long trip to the north of England and Scotland, a rite of passage he would repeat through the fall and winter months each successive year. With his monetary supply line tight, he kept primarily to cities where he found concentrations of Garrisonian supporters: Darlington, home of the Peases, a leading Quaker reform family; Newcastle upon Tyne, home of the Mawsons and of the Richardsons (siblings Ellen and Henry, and wife Anna); and Leeds, home of Wilson Armistead, a best-selling antislavery writer. From the start, the trip proved successful and profitable. He quickly began to accumulate friends, contacts, and also cash. Finding his groove, he lectured widely, often to crowds numbering in the hundreds—a tribute not just to his growing reputation but also to effective sponsorship. Typically resourceful as he went from event to event, he sold not only his *Narrative* but also copies of the engraving of Ellen Craft he had given the Webbs.

Newcastle became his first home on the road. His initial public meeting there, with the mayor acting as chair and cordially welcoming him "to the North of England," overfilled the Lecture Room on Nelson Street, with some having to be turned away. After finishing a long, effective talk that combined his personal history with a running, anecdotal incrimination of slaveholding practices, he took questions from the audience. One well-meaning person asked the irritating question Brown and his colleagues repeatedly faced: Did not many slaves prefer slavery to freedom?[56] By chance, an emphatic answer to that question was just then being provided in St. Louis, where his former fellow slave Martha Ann was in the final stage of prosecuting her freedom suit against the Young estate. Although "old master" number two, Samuel Willi, was summoned to the old Courthouse as a witness for the defense, nothing he or any of the other defense witnesses said could prevent a verdict for emancipation.[57]

After a short speaking trip to Darlington, whose Quaker community in particular adopted him warmly, he returned to Newcastle, where on January 3, 1850, he was the guest of honor at a public tea attended by 400 to 500 people at the Music Hall. Visibly moved by the warmth of his surroundings, he confided to his listeners the thought that he might still have a mother, sister, and three brothers alive in slavery. He ended the meeting, as he did many those first months in England, by singing several songs, but not before a woman came forward bearing a purse she had sewn for the occasion filled by the community with twenty sovereigns.[58] From Newcastle he fanned out to other cities in England's industrial heartland—Sheffield, Leeds, Bolton, Manchester—taking his message to both working and middle classes. In a large electroplating factory in Sheffield, where he had spoken the previous two nights, workers took up a collection they presented to him formally in the countinghouse.[59] The gesture alone was meaningful; it stood for the alliance fugitives like Brown knew all too well was missing back home between slaves and white laborers.

While Brown was making his northern tour that first winter, word of his success spread across Britain and over the ocean. Speaking in February on the floor of the US Capitol, Massachusetts Representative Horace Mann, the great champion of the common school movement, singled out Brown's success to support his antislavery position during the historic 1850 congressional debates about the future of slaves and slavery: "His journeys from place to place are like the 'Progresses' of one of the Magnates of that land,—passing wherever he will with free tickets, and enjoying the hospitalities of the most refined and educated men."[60] Mann's words carried little but symbolic import. When those debates concluded in the Great Compromise designed to hold the Union together, the stringent Fugitive Slave Law of 1850 would transform the condition of all slaves, including one fugitive making a name for himself in Great Britain. The new law provided not just legal authority but also enforcement terms for the return of fugitive slaves to their masters. Its impact on Brown was immediate; it effectively fixed him in place.

WHILE IN NEWCASTLE, Brown also took time to conduct a little literary business. He entered into a deal with the publisher of the *Newcastle Guardian*, J. Blackwell, who had printed various sermons for the father of Ellen and Henry Richardson, to bring out an English edition of *The Anti-Slavery Harp*. That initiative presumably came from Brown, who explained his purpose was "to bring before the English people, in a cheap form, a few spirited Melodies against Chattel slavery."[61] Brown claimed—no doubt, with some exaggeration—that 5,000 copies of the first US edition had been sold within months, and he foresaw interest in the work in England too, where his singing was well received.

Meanwhile, he hatched a secondary plan for that initial winter in England, although whether he had time to act on it seems unlikely. In December 1849, he proudly informed his Boston friend William Nell of his newest undertaking, the study of French, with the intent of making a long trip to the Continent.[62] The language was not entirely new to him. He had heard it spoken in his teens in St. Louis and New Orleans, but he worked so exclusively for English-speaking masters and employers that during his first visit to Paris he had only a minimal vocabulary. That new plan explains his renewed campaign to receive a US passport, which finally arrived in late November—courtesy not of the State Department in Washington but of the US legation in London.[63] Its legal recognition of him as a "citizen," a curious discrepancy from his status as a slave at home, mattered nearly as much to him as its practical value in pursuing his plans overseas.

Brown never explained what would take him to France and the Continent, but it seems likely he attempted to make arrangements for the translation of his *Narrative* into French and possibly other Western European languages. In conceiving this plan, he would again have been following in the path of Douglass, whose *Narrative* came out in the Netherlands in 1847 and France in 1848. For her part, Josephine Brown claimed in her biography that her father's work appeared in French and

German editions, but she apparently misspoke.[64] No French or German translation has ever been found.

There was, however, a Dutch translation, which appeared in 1850. Its enterprising publisher, W. E. J. Tjeenk Willink, saw a market for a work popular in the British Isles by an author of some recent celebrity as "a delegate to the Paris Congress," the credential he printed on the title page. Willink hoped to tap into Dutch antislavery feeling at a time when the Netherlands lagged behind its neighbors in still permitting slavery in its colonies, a practice that did not end until 1863. His inexpensive pamphlet edition introduced a bit of novelty by reproducing on a single page all three illustrations of the 1849 Gilpin edition, neatly set out in a circle around the 1847 Chase engraving of Brown. To bolster Brown's credentials, it also reprinted Garrison's letter of introduction and resolutions of black Boston made on the eve of his passage.[65] Since all those documents were already in print, there is no reason to believe that Willink necessarily consulted, much less collaborated, with Brown.

Brown also had personal reasons to tour the Continent, not least, his hunger to explore the larger world. He was in Europe on a one-way ticket and had no definite plans or date for a return to the United States. Not until the Fugitive Slave Law took effect in mid-1850 did he make a conscious decision that a return would place him in imminent danger. His attitude about his personal security had been more relaxed as recently as November 1849, when he published an open letter to Enoch Price in which he exposed him to public contempt, as other fugitive slaves, such as Douglass and Bibb, had done to their former masters. Feeling self-secure, he did not hesitate then to reveal to "old master" his new whereabouts in London.[66] At that moment, he was less immediately concerned about the threat from "old master" in St. Louis than about what he might learn from the old masters of Europe.

PRICE WAS NOT the only menace from the past he mistakenly thought he had left behind. In March 1850, the long reach of Betsey Brown drew him back once again into her life. Still pursuing some semblance of self-righteousness, justice, and sheer security, she finally succeeded in making her case public, as she had long threatened. She chose her forum well in addressing her letter to the editor of the *New York Tribune*. That paper was not just the leading daily in the country but also a powerful force identified with the reformist views of its famous editor, Horace Greeley. There was a good reason why, when Harriet Jacobs was drawn for the first time into the public realm, she addressed her letter to the editor of the *Tribune* to report the murder and decapitation of a slave in her native North Carolina.[67] Despite his broad antislavery sympathies, however, Greeley steered his paper on an independent course and had no more patience for the unyielding dogmatism of Garrisonians than they had for his unpredictability. He—or whichever associate editor took up the story in print—paraphrased Betsey's "long statement of conjugal difficulties, the upshot of which is that, notwithstanding she is a very respectable woman and exemplary wife (which she proves by 'no end' of certificates), her husband has deserted her and her youngest child. . . ." Her accusation went further, and here the paper quoted: "Mr. Brown has become so popular among the Abolition ladies that he did not wish his sable wife any longer." The paper, however, was skeptical of her position: "We know none of the parties, but we suspect Elizabeth is slightly malicious."[68]

The *Tribune*'s skepticism about Betsey notwithstanding, that little gossipy item on its front page did Brown and his allies lasting damage. The toll multiplied as the report circulated nationally through the newspaper exchange system. The following month, a Milwaukee paper reprinted the story under the same title and added its sarcastic two cents about the straying husband, who had "received thousands of dollars wrung from honest laboring men and women by pathetic appeals in behalf of the poor slave, and he has at the same time been living among the aristocracy of abolitionism."[69] Worse was yet to come from a Richmond paper, which approvingly reprinted from a sister paper in Washington, DC, the assault on the character (and therefore the verbal credibility) of "Mr. Brown, the fugitive slave, whose wife advertised him in the New York papers as having left her to starve, while he loafed about the country and spent his substance on other women."[70]

Journalists were not the only ones talking about the Brown family contretemps. So were adversaries within the antislavery movement, as the family scandal soon became subsumed within the larger conflict between competing organizations and ideologies. The brothers Lewis and Arthur Tappan in New York, and John Scoble and Joseph Sturge in London, had been trying to decide ever since Brown's arrival how the BFASS—the leading British antislavery organization but one hostile to Garrison ever since the 1840 London antislavery convention—should handle a major Garrisonian transplant on English soil. What began as a tactical calculation gradually transformed into a moral issue. Lewis Tappan, who in addition to his leadership of the affiliated American and Foreign Anti-Slavery Society (AFASS) ran a pioneering credit agency, apparently found a man of Brown's compromised character a bad risk for the cause. Tappan's problem transferred overseas once Brown moved into Scoble and Sturge's operating arena. From the moment they saw him in operation at the Paris Peace Congress, they struggled to get their bearings, while Tappan goaded them on. Sturge's view was cautiously moderate; Scoble's was belligerent. They were still trying to work out a position on him when Sturge observed to Scoble in late 1849: "We cannot be surprised at W. W. Brown not asking thee to attend any of his meetings, after what he has no doubt heard of us from W. L. Garrison and Geo. Thompson."[71] Sturge was exactly right; Brown had heard an earful and had adopted his zealous associates' view of things.

Once Tappan got wind of Betsey's letter to the *Tribune*, a new urgency entered the discussion about Brown. Tappan apparently mailed to Sturge in Birmingham the clipping from the *Tribune*, along with a secondary investigative letter. That one came from his Buffalo operative, an anti-slavery activist named E. A. Addington, whom Tappan had instructed "to make enquiry about Mr. and Mrs. Brown." Addington did as he was told but could find no conclusive evidence on which to base a definitive judgment. Tappan dutifully forwarded Addington's report inside his own noncommittal response to Sturge, which Sturge in turn forwarded along the chain of command to Scoble in London (while advising Scoble to show it to Gilpin).[72] Sturge threw up his hands ("I suppose it is hardly worth while to pursue the matter further—Some take the side of the wife and some take the side of the husband; it is difficult to know who is most to blame") and advised Scoble and the operating committee of the BFASS to take a "neutral" position. For a time at least, Scoble professed and possibly even practiced a certain "neutral[ity]" toward Brown and his allies.[73] But as anyone dealing forthrightly knew, neutrality was an unviable position in the middle of an acrimonious conflict between the two sides, whose ranks became multiracial as some resident African Americans such as Pennington and Garnet lined up in the BFASS ranks opposite Brown (and later the Crafts) on the Garrison–Thompson side. Following the 1850 passage of the Fugitive Slave Law, and the enormous transatlantic impact of *Uncle Tom's Cabin*, a revitalized antislavery movement in the British Isles escalated both its outfighting and its infighting. Its intensity can be gauged from Brown's term for the conflict within antislavery ranks: "open war."[74]

As soon as Betsey's story reached the US press, setting mouths to talking, Brown countered her charges by going to the press with *his* version of the truth. He chose the safest venue, the *Liberator*, for giving a mostly accurate, mostly candid account of the decline of their relationship. While professing his distaste at airing his private life in public, he held back nothing in placing blame squarely and exclusively on Betsey. She came of poor stock. Her only sister was an unmarried mother, her brother died in prison, and her mother was living in adultery—and now, as the reader was to understand, Betsey was following in their tawdry ways. The sole cause of their marital problems was her infidelity with James Garrett, whom he named and described as previously one of his "best friends," coupled with her increasing irresponsibility toward the children. The second time she abandoned them for one of her extended trips was once too often. In response, he had returned home to Farmington, scooped them up, and taken them to Boston, while omitting to mention his own overture to the MASS for employment.[75]

Brown was not the only one to be alarmed. So were his allies in Boston, whether out of concern for him or fear for the common good. Probably self-delegated to pose the question occupying the minds of many of his colleagues, Wendell Phillips pushed Victorian discretion to the limit by asking Amy Post for a frank account of this sordid affair. As a Quaker woman of remarkable charity and delicacy, she was so disconcerted by Phillips's request that she flinched even on paper in airing her knowledge about "an unpleasant and troublesome subject." Both parties had confided in her, she remarked, and she quietly refused to assign blame. Instead, she responded that she had advised Brown, "for the good of the cause, for his own and family's happiness, and because I thought it his Christian duty, to be reconciled with his wife, to forgive if she needed forgiveness and to endeavor to live in peace and unity." She could not comment knowledgeably about whether Betsey had indeed abandoned her home and family on occasion and did not even broach the subject of the youngest child. In a final gesture, she passed Phillips's core questions down the line: "If you wish testimony regarding her leaving his house, her unkindness to William[,] her cruelty to her children, you can get it from Elias Doty and Abigal Wilson of Macedon[,] Wayne Co." Her husband, Isaac, added his more explicit view in a postscript: "I believe it was notorious that he treated his wife with kindness and bore her *Iritation* [*sic*] with meekness."[76] If Phillips contacted (as seems likely) the people in Macedon, a town bordering Farmington, neither his letter nor their response is known. But the damage was done. In places where gossip of that sort collected, that stain on Brown's character persisted for years.

WORD OF BETSEY's incriminations reached England in the early spring of 1850 just as Brown was making the first of his many visits to Bristol—home of John Bishop Estlin and his daughter Mary, one of the city's most prominent families. The elderly Estlin, an eye surgeon renowned throughout the British Isles, was a pillar of the Unitarian Church. His great, consuming passion late in life, however, was international antislavery, a cause to which he came gradually after an 1832 rest cure on the Caribbean island of St. Vincent. That stay—which brought him into closer contact with slavery than he had ever had as a native son of a once-leading English seaport in the "Guinea trade"—affected him deeply. Estlin supported the BFASS from its founding in 1839 but gradually grew disenchanted by its "culpably cool" posture, especially its (and its sister organization's) lack of activism in the United States; by the late 1840s, he switched his allegiance to Garrison, Phillips, and May.[77] A warm transatlantic friendship with May in particular ensued, as letters, messengers, and publications passed freely between Bristol and Boston. With Mary as his steady supporter, he mobilized Bristol into a center of antislavery activity and established himself as one of Garrison's most trusted operatives in the British Isles. After following Brown's movements across England and Scotland with the keenest interest, he and Mary persuaded their friends to invite him in the spring of 1850 on his southern swing to address the community.

The result was a social tea hosted by the Bristol and Clifton Ladies' Anti-Slavery Society on April 3. Three to four hundred people attended, an exceptional turnout for a local society struggling, like its peers, to remain relevant years after the heyday of antislavery activity in Britain. Brown must have sensed it would be an exceptionally supportive audience at the outset when Estlin, no performer like Thompson, broke with his well-known reticence by taking the chair and introducing him in the warmest terms. Brown moved through a variety of well-tested personal stories but also directed some scorching sarcasm at American defenders of slavery, singling out the American Tract Society for excluding antislavery content from its mass distribution of printed material around the United States. It recently sponsored a prize competition for the best essay against the immorality of dancing, he sneered, but "never published a word against the system of slavery—against the slave dancing at the end of a cowhide."[78] By the time he closed the meeting with "singularly pleasing . . . highly pathetic" renditions of "The Blind Boy" and "The Escape," it was clear the event had been a major success for his hosts.[79]

A local reporter in attendance preferred Estlin's sweeping judgments to Brown's personal anecdotes but missed the point: What gave new life to the local cause was the energizing effect of an actual fugitive drawing on his authentic experience to galvanize the community's hearts and minds against slavery, as no abstract argument could.[80] The meeting was so successful that others soon followed, and Bristol was back in operation as a node in the British antislavery network. A pattern was emerging, as supporters in regional centers in Ireland, England, and soon Scotland realized what a person of Brown's abilities could do to revitalize their local antislavery societies.

Something more personally consequential also occurred that week. Over the course of his stay with the Estlins, the two men formed a reciprocal bond that grew into one of the strongest Brown would form in Britain. Brown felt a special warmth for Estlin, whom he consistently addressed following this first visit as "dear friend."[81] A year later, the relationship expanded to include his two daughters, whom the Estlins considered favored wards. (Estlin affectionately referred to them as the "garls.")[82] Beginning with that 1850 visit, the spacious Estlin house on Park Street became his home base during visits to the west coast of England, just as 22 Cecil Street reciprocated for the Estlins during visits to London.

Their friendship had a curious history, beginning long before either man could even have anticipated they would ever meet. One day in 1848, while chatting with Samuel May Jr. in the MASS office, Brown casually mentioned he would be happy to see copies of the second edition of his *Narrative* added to the box of publications being prepared for shipment to overseas "friends."[83] May consented, and one recipient was John Estlin, whose house served as the west coast postal depot for the Garrisonian network of letters, manuscripts, printed materials, and memorabilia in the British Isles. Once the subject of Brown's planned visit with the Crafts came up in 1849, Estlin warned that "a money speculation for their own benefit" would likely fail.[84] By the time Brown arrived in Bristol, however, as had happened with Richard Webb in Dublin, any initial anxiety quickly turned to admiration.

They talked about many things, ranging from antislavery politics, tactics, and personalities to the practice of medicine. Estlin soon became a mentor and role model for Brown. Like Webb and Thompson before him, Estlin found Brown personable and agreeable and moved to draw him into his intrigues. Quick conversation made it clear the two men stood on common ground in their reverence for Garrison and spite for

Scoble. At the same time, Brown took a serious interest in Estlin's medical practice. He had spent considerable time around a talented doctor in his youth; now he spent time around one of England's finest clinicians, although Estlin's attitude toward medicine and patients differed dramatically from John Young's. In addition to carrying on a highly successful medical practice specializing in but not limited to ophthalmology, Estlin also conducted a dispensary for the poor two half-days a week not far from his home. Brown undoubtedly visited it and drew out Estlin on a range of subjects relating to medicine. Happy to have so extraordinary a student, Estlin gave him medical books to read and "much advice on the profession," which would later prove influential.[85]

In 1853, when Estlin suffered a debilitating stroke, a shaken Brown wrote to a friend in Boston, "I have been upon more intimate terms with Mr. Estlin than with any other person with whom I have become acquainted in this country, except George Thompson, and the more I have seen of him, the more I love the man."[86] Estlin recovered partially, and the two men maintained their friendship and collaboration until the end of Brown's European stay. After receiving news of Estlin's death in 1855, Brown came forward at that year's MASS Fourth of July picnic to eulogize a friend who must also have been in some unspoken sense a father figure.[87]

ESTLIN AND BROWN also discussed one other subject of pressing interest to Brown in 1850. He had crossed the Atlantic with the ambition to exhibit a moving panorama, a giant oil painting consisting of a series of scenes stretching over hundreds of yards of heavy canvas rolled around wooden scrolls. Imagining how he might adapt this popular mid-nineteenth-century forerunner of motion pictures to public service, Brown set out to present graphically the truth about North American slavery to the British viewing public.

The ambitious project he had in mind originated in his personal history on the Mississippi River. He had already told one version of that story in his *Narrative*, but even as he wrote that book he was starting to formulate a pictorial narrative based on his reading of the American landscape. After visiting artists' studios and panorama exhibitions in Boston, he came away frustrated that their work misrepresented life on the Mississippi River as he knew it. An apparently crucial event was his viewing in 1847 of John Banvard's enormously popular *Panorama of the Mississippi Valley*, the biggest spectacle in Boston during its ballyhooed six-month run at Amory Hall.[88] Placarded around the city and advertised daily in local newspapers as a "mammoth" production filling "three miles of canvas," Banvard's panorama was one of the most celebrated American cultural artifacts of the 1840s. In Boston alone, by Banvard's count, a quarter of a million spectators paid a half dollar for the vicarious pleasure of taking a mythic steamboat voyage down the Mississippi River to New Orleans. By a "slight stretch of the imagination," they became part of a nation steaming toward manifest destiny.[89] His painting's fame was such that, even in a country with little history of public support for the arts, Banvard received a medal from Congress and had a commendation bestowed on him by the governor of the Commonwealth of Massachusetts for completing his "Herculean work."

While some viewers, like the correspondent of a leading Boston newspaper, raved over the work as a "proud monument of daring ambition, and genius of American character," the artist and his work irritated Brown.[90] It could not have been easy to listen to Banvard's glorification of a white-dominated manifest destiny that minimized and distorted his own experience of life on the Mississippi. The scene Banvard was inviting his viewers to witness was, in Michael A. Chaney's apt phrase, a "slave pastoral."[91] Banvard's accompanying catalogue set the scene in fine patriotic fashion: "We see extensive sugar fields, noble mansions, beautiful gardens, large sugar houses, groups of negro quarters, lofty churches, splendid villas, presenting, in all, one of the finest views of country to be met in the United States."[92] Just around the historical bend lay the idyllic fantasy of Tara from *Gone with the Wind*. The work was bad enough, but the heroic self-portrait Banvard incorporated into the project made it even more galling: the artist captured in the creative act perched above a broad river, a gun leaning against his chest, with a brush in one hand and a palette in the other.[93] The painter was as false as his panorama.

Brown found Banvard insufferable, but he was only the most famous of the rising cadre of panoramists vying for American market share in the late 1840s. The competition among dueling painter/impresarios grew keener as fellow artists, more than a few with St. Louis ties, vied to paint ever more flamboyantly oversize canvases of the Mississippi. Banvard's chief rival was J. R. Smith, whose leviathan painting of the Mississippi competed with his for audience and critical acclaim in the Northeast. Banvard, however, had bigger ambitions than to go canvas to canvas with the domestic competition, so in September 1848 he packed up his scrolls and steamed for England. In no time at all, he set up metropolitan operations in Egyptian Hall in Piccadilly, exhibiting his Mississippi Valley canvas nightly to large, enthusiastic crowds for months. Although Smith was not far behind Banvard in setting up operations in London and touching off a public rivalry, Banvard scored the ultimate publicity coup when he was invited to give a command performance before Queen Victoria at Windsor Castle.

By the time Brown arrived in England in summer 1849, "panorama mania" was sweeping London. The humor magazine *Punch* lampooned the craze in a cartoon of a painter sprinting across a stage wielding a mop as a brush as the latest proof of the age-old adage "Art [is] long and Life [is] short."[94] US panoramas were all the rage during Brown's first months in London, generating animated cultural commentary: "The introduction of moving panoramas of scenery in this country by the Americans, has been most beneficial to the progress of knowledge. We know of nothing by which so much new and varied information can be obtained in so little time, and in so pleasurable a manner, as by one of these geographical paintings."[95] British pride could not allow the work of Brother Jonathan to go unchallenged for very long in the domain of John Bull, however, and sure enough London was soon talking about its own entry in the international panorama sweepstakes. Since home scenery was too familiar, the new sensation was the first full-length tour of the ancient Nile River Valley, its exotic aura brought back for inspection, like archaeological treasures, to the banks of the Thames. Not just pride of nation was at stake; so, for Brown, was racial domination.

The creator of the highly touted *Grand Moving Panorama of the Nile* was John Lee's Orientalist friend Joseph Bonomi, who, along with two partners, arranged for its exhibition at Egyptian Hall in Piccadilly. Not long after it went on view, an adventurous American expatriate named George Gliddon purchased the original copy from its proprietor and put his mark on it by printing a descriptive catalogue promoting his own distinctive views on the craze for ancient Egyptian civilization. Gliddon had more than money on his mind in taking over the enterprise. As the new proprietor eager to exhibit his trophy, the well-heeled expat walked a fine line "where serious learning bumped into popular entertainment, taking cues from both [Harvard scientist] Louis Agassiz and P. T. Barnum."[96] A noted Egyptologist, Gliddon saw the painting's depiction of the Nile cradle of civilization as conveying a fundamental truth, bordering on pre-Darwinian belief, about what he would later call "types of mankind," the title of a book he copublished in 1854 with Josiah Nott, another true believer in the essential hierarchy of the races.[97] Brown almost surely saw the Bonomi–Gliddon panorama during its London run and heard what one local journalist termed Gliddon's "learned and elaborate lectures, with scientific deductions" on its scenes.[98] He recorded no formal response at the time, but he was already familiar with the views of the emergent "American School" of race theory. A decade later, he made a full-scale retort in *The Black Man* (1863), his timely Civil War–era defense of African and African American heritage.

Brown could no more expect to compete with Banvard and Gliddon for mass popularity in the visual arts than he could with Dickens or Thackeray in the belles letters with his *Narrative*. Yet the outpouring of enthusiasm for such spectacles in London confirmed his longstanding wish to enlist the new medium for presenting the story of slavery to the general public. He had arrived in England carrying preliminary sketches prepared by American artists, according to a journalist who presumably got his information directly from the source.[99] These were the drawings to which Brown referred in the printed catalogue accompanying his panorama as the "series of sketches of beautiful and interesting American scenery, as well as of many touching incidents in the lives of

Slaves"—sketches he had collected back home "after considerable pain and expense."[100]

It took time and money before he could put his plan into execution. Panoramas were elaborate productions entailing very expensive outlays at the first stage for materials and artistic work, at the second stage for shipping and transportation, and at the third for rental of exhibition space, advertising, and attendants. Given his limited means, he kept the size of his composition to less "mammoth" dimensions than those of his celebrated competitors. Whereas some proprietors hired performers and piano accompanists, Brown acted as manager, showman, and vocalist all in one, organizing his tour, narrating his story, and providing his own music. No string of economies, however, could spare him the necessity of raising considerable capital before proceeding, which explains the year's lag between his arrival in England and its execution. Even with a good income from lectures, book sales, and occasional gift offerings, he could not have managed to raise the necessary capital without appealing for loans to close friends of means, such as the Richardsons and the Estlins. Brown rewarded them by allocating space in the back pages of his catalogue to causes dear to their hearts—the boycott on slave produce and the Boston antislavery bazaar, respectively.

The dateline of its production is clearer than the actual details. Work commenced no later than July 1850, a downtime in the lecture season, when Brown commissioned one or more unnamed London artists to paint full-scale oil canvases based on the sketches he provided. During August, he was so preoccupied overseeing production that he decided to pass up attendance at the fourth International Peace Congress, held August 22 to 24 in Frankfurt.[101] Late that month, his new friend Mary Estlin sent one of the Weston "bunch" (as Brown familiarly referred to them) a progress report: "He (W.B.) has 18 drawings of his series complete, and good judges say their execution is equal to those of the 'India route Panorama' which has been drawing crowds daily for several months in London."[102] Work continued through September, as Brown periodically updated his inner circle of supporters, who in turn spread the word through their networks. (Mary Estlin confessed to fatigue after "writing about it to different people in all parts of the kingdom.")[103] By the second half of October, all twenty-four panels were completed, each measuring, by best guess, roughly ten yards wide by two or three high—dimensions suitable for a large or even mass audience spectacle.[104]

Sometime in late October, Anna and Henry Richardson came down from Newcastle to inspect the work and confer with Brown about its exhibition. The three of them, with Thompson and possibly Webb also weighing in, advised Brown to exhibit it first not in London, where competition was too intense, but in Newcastle. Agreeing, he took out ads announcing the work's upcoming exhibition in all the major Newcastle newspapers. Toward month's end, he and the painting were en route to Newcastle, and by October 31 he was exhibiting it twice a day, afternoon and evening, at the city's Commercial Sale Room near the great monument at the head of fashionable Grey Street. He set the admission price for the exhibit and a lecture at the going rate: one shilling for adults, half price for children.[105]

Like nearly all such flammable, fragile artifacts, Brown's panorama has not survived. Its contents, however, are broadly knowable thanks not only to the illustrated advertisements he ran wherever he exhibited but also to the descriptive catalogue he compiled to accompany his lectures. He contracted for the catalogue's production with Charles Gilpin, although Brown would have functioned as its primary distributor, offering copies for sale at his performances at the standard price of sixpence. Altogether he must have sold hundreds or even thousands, and he proudly sent copies home to friends (his personally inscribed copies to Garrison and May survive).[106]

His American landscape deviated sharply from that of Banvard. Its course followed not the linear current of the river but a swerve of lives adhering to no simple, one-directional logic. Comprising a hodgepodge of scenes of slavery spread out across the territorial United States, it opened with a familiar series of tableaux beginning with field labor on a tobacco plantation in Old Virginia, skipped to the slave pens within sight of the Capitol in Washington, DC, and then leaped cross-country to the slave markets of New Orleans. Other scenes of plantation life on sugar and cotton farms followed before finally, near the midway point, he introduced his own story in four views, all featuring his escapes. Two come from the illustrated edition of his *Narrative* (the entrapment by hounds ending his first escape and the capture by horsemen in Illinois ending his second), one from a scene in the *Narrative* depicting his final flight across Ohio, and the fourth the vividly invented scene already mentioned of the *Chester,* the rowboat containing him and his mother, and St. Louis by night. Two more escape views came from illustrated scenes of slavery borrowed from Henry Bibb's heavily illustrated *Narrative,* which corresponded closely to his own.

Six additional views connect him to stories of fleeing or punished slaves. One even carried over from the panorama to the live performance. This was the story of the female fugitive (name not given) who escaped from a boat traveling from Natchez to Cincinnati and gave Brown the slave collar she was wearing in summer 1843 when she was en route to Canada. Brown, in turn, exhibited that collar at the end of each performance as tangible evidence of the barbarity of slavery. Whatever it might take—pictures, texts, songs, artifacts—he brought before the British public to enlist its participation in ending slavery.

BROWN WAS ALREADY in Newcastle exhibiting his panorama when word initially reached him of the recent or imminent arrival of three compatriots from Boston. Only the last two would have been welcome. He could not have been happy to hear that Henry Box Brown had arrived in Liverpool in early November with an antislavery panorama that he had already shown briefly in the United States. In late August, Box Brown had been assaulted in Providence by men intent on shipping him down the coast back to slavery, so he needed to take flight as quickly as possible. England was his refuge, and his panorama his chief prospect for earning his keep. Brown had never had particularly warm personal feelings for Box Brown, but in autumn 1850 he could hardly see the man for his panorama, which portended unwelcome competition. In the short run, one Brown's misfortune was the other's fortune. Box Brown had exhausted his funds in paying for his passage and was unable to pay the hefty customs duty on his panorama. Whereas Banvard, whose fame preceded him, had passed with his panorama duty-free through customs in 1848, Liverpool customs officers were unwilling to cut Henry Brown a comparable deal.[107] His misfortune gave William Wells Brown a brief head start, although in due course it was hardly consequential: The British Isles were big enough to embrace both of their paintings.

Brown was still exhibiting in Newcastle when a letter arrived from a friend in Boston informing him that William and Ellen Craft were en route to England after fleeing Boston just ahead of slave catchers. Their second flight from slavery happened so precipitously that they had been unable to alert Brown themselves. The dramatic turn of events followed quickly upon passage of the Fugitive Slave Law, which facilitated the capture of fugitives living in free states. Just a few weeks after its passage, Ellen's emboldened master dispatched to Boston two trusted white agents, John Knight and Willis Hughes, to return the couple to Georgia. Locating the couple proved simple. William was living in such false security that he advertised his cabinetmaking shop in the *Liberator*. Knight, who had worked side-by-side with him in a carpentry shop in Macon, tracked him to the Boston shop and requested a personal tour of the city.[108] The two agents used other ploys as well to apprehend the couple, as when Knight sent a note requesting Craft (and Ellen, too, if she wished) to stop by his hotel to drop off any letters they might wish him to deliver to their relatives in Macon.[109] Knight and Hughes seriously underestimated not just the Crafts' intelligence and determination but the opposition they might face from both the black and the abolitionist communities. A mobilized citizenry blanketed the city with placards warning against the slave catchers, lawyers hounded the men everywhere they turned with warrant after warrant, and crowds of angry men threatened them with violence.

While the standoff played out, one thing was clear: The Crafts could not remain alone in their home. Ellen went into the protective custody of William Bowditch, a well-connected lawyer loyal to the movement who lived in the outlying town of Brookline. William first barricaded himself in his shop with a gun he hurriedly acquired but did not know how to use. Then he hid out at Lewis and Harriet Hayden's home-turned-fortress in the heart of the black community below Beacon Hill. Afraid to attempt a direct foray against an armed opponent supported by an aroused community, the slave catchers sought the cooperation of local officials, who were legally required to execute their writ, but to little avail. Finally, fearful for their own lives, Knight and Hughes abandoned their mission and returned home. But that was hardly the end of the story for the Crafts or for the black community. Once Ellen's wealthy master appealed to President Millard Fillmore for enforcement of the law and Fillmore signaled his assent to use federal troops to enforce its provisions if necessary, the point was made: Not even liberty-loving Boston lay beyond the reach of slavery.

The Crafts could assume only the worst, and friends aided them in making hurried plans for their escape. At risk of his own arrest for aiding and abetting fugitives, Wendell Phillips accompanied them to the coastal city of Portland, Maine (an act for which the grateful couple would name a son after him). When Phillips turned back for home, the Crafts continued north up the coast into the teeth of blustery winds and bitterly cold temperatures. Already scared for their safety, the Crafts were further dismayed by scattered acts of discrimination against dark-skinned William even across the international border in Canada. After several grinding weeks on the road, they finally reached their halfway haven in Halifax, agitated and exhausted, only to find they had missed the Liverpool-bound steamer by several hours and had to wait a full two weeks for the next. On arriving in Liverpool, they set up temporary quarters at Brown's Temperance Hotel, contacted Brown, and awaited his response before venturing out.

As soon as he received William's letter from Liverpool, Brown invited the homeless couple to join him in Newcastle, no doubt envisioning a joint lecture tour similar to the successful one they had staged in 1848–49. He had excellent reason to hope for the best; he could now build on the powerful lure of their combined reputations. The Crafts' double escapes from slavery were by now well known throughout the British Isles, and the figure of Ellen in particular, so affecting to American audiences as the "white slave," was likely to cast a similar spell on British audiences. In addition, their timing was opportune. The publicity generated by the passage of the Fugitive Slave Law had injected new life into dormant or inactive antislavery societies from Glasgow to Bristol. On November 16, Brown made a special trip from Newcastle to Edinburgh to address a major public meeting held to discuss the new law, which he pointed out affected even people like him who had lived nearly two decades in freedom.[110] He and Henry Garnet, who also spoke that night at length, did good work—a leading Edinburgh newspaper editorialized against the law four days later.[111] The next month, he sent Frederick Douglass's *North Star* a public letter in which he called the law and its consequences "the all-absorbing topic for conversation in this country."[112]

Ellen, it turned out, was far too ill to travel after weeks on the road and the high seas, but once her husband felt confident she was improving and comfortably situated, he took the train to Newcastle. With his old friend William (and soon enough Ellen too) by his side, Brown continued what evolved into his longest, most profitable lecture/exhibition tour of the British Isles. The trio spent nearly half a year touring cities and towns principally across the south of Scotland and the north of England—areas, as Brown knew from his previous year's tour, with some of the greatest concentrations of antislavery sentiment in the British Isles. During January 1851, enthusiastic crowds turned out by the hundreds, even the thousands, to hear the "fugitives" in Edinburgh, Glasgow, Dundee, and Aberdeen. One of the largest crowds they addressed was at Glasgow's City Hall, filled with a supportive audience Brown brought to rousing applause with his ingratiating tribute: "Within the last two or three years, certainly within the last 18 months, large and enthusiastic meetings had been held in the cities of the United States, to welcome to the new world refugees from Hungary, from the banks of the Danube, the Tiber, and the Nile, while here there were three thousand persons assembled to welcome refugees from the banks of the Mississippi."[113] Several weeks later, in Dundee, he gave one of the most successful showings of his panorama before an audience he estimated at 1,600, netting a profit of more than £12. Normally modest about his accomplishments, he could not restrain himself in boasting to Wendell Phillips: "As a Yankee would say, the painting is a *paying concern*."[114] Closer to home, he sent glowing dispatches to the Estlins, which, though no longer extant, survive by reflection in Mary Estlin's relays to common friends: "W.B. . . . is in great spirits at the effect of their *progress* thro Scotland on the A. S. Cause, as well as the success of his own Panorama."[115] And a week later: "W. W. B. has just written in good spirits having got on very well with his painting lectures" and with ambitions to prolong his tour by exhibiting in Carlisle and other cities in northwestern England.[116]

Exhibiting the panorama more than paid his way during those months, but it was only one of his multiple forms of presentation. Some days Brown showed the panorama as a stand-alone exhibit, discounting admission during the day for schoolchildren. Other days he integrated it into lectures he gave alone or jointly with the Crafts. During one stand in Glasgow, for instance, with a large advertisement running in a leading newspaper, he strung together variations on the panorama over three nights. The first night he gave a well-received illustrated lecture on slavery to a large audience at Mechanics Hall. The Crafts joined him in various ways, including the singing of several "negro melodies." The local paper reported positively on the performance: "Mr. Brown is possessed of intellectual powers of no mean order, and has evidently a fine sense of humour, which rendered his observations occasionally not a little amusing, as well as instructive." The second night they employed the same mixed format, with additional variations. The third night Brown gave a more focused talk on the Fugitive Slave Law, a subject the more compelling, he knew, for its presentation by one of the law's actual targets. They presumed on a warm reception but took no chances in advertising that "the lecturers are entirely dependent on the produce of their lectures.[117]

Brown and the Crafts appeared at dozens of professional meetings that winter, but they also took time off to visit local tourist sites and to meet civic leaders, writers, and reformers. By this point, Brown was so well established he had easy access to a network of friends and allies spanning the British Isles. Late February of 1851 found the three friends heading westbound by train and coach for a first visit to the Lake District, hardly a stronghold of antislavery sentiment but familiar to Brown through its association with William Wordsworth, who had died and been buried the previous year at Grasmere. During his first eighteen months in Britain, Brown had been meticulously seeking out places associated with great British writers; meaningful stops on the cultural tour already had included the homes of Scott, Burns, and Byron, one of his favorite writers. In this instance, however, visiting Wordsworth's surroundings took second place to the presence just a few miles away of the multitalented lady of the lakes, the prolific author and pioneering reformer for women's rights and abolition Harriet Martineau. A friend and correspondent of Richard Webb and the Estlins, she had been closely following Brown's progress across the British Isles since his arrival and had tendered a warm invitation to the trio and set up a lecture engagement for them, the proceeds to go "for their benefit."[118]

They arrived after dark at The Knoll, her comfortable cottage in Ambleside, a short walk from Lake Windermere, and entered to a gracious welcome. She was particularly moved to meet Ellen and could barely restrain herself as she listened—hard as it was through her ear trumpet—to the Crafts' account of their ordeal. In the safe confines of her home, they spoke unguardedly to her not just of their hard lives but also of their aspirations, emphasizing their desire for formal education. William had by then acquired a functional degree of literacy, but both of the Crafts, for all their travels, were only two years out of slavery and largely unschooled. They made an incongruous, yet instantly harmonious foursome: two barely literate fugitives, a strikingly sophisticated fugitive/writer, and one of England's most accomplished social thinkers.

The next morning Brown, restless as usual to see his surroundings, set off on a long solo hike across the countryside and up into the surrounding mountains. Part of the way up, he met a farmer who offered to let him ride his donkey to the summit. An experienced horseman but a novice to donkeys, he thought nothing of the difference, but he had gone barely one-eighth of a mile when he lost control of his mount, which slipped on the edge of a chasm. The animal was less panicked than its rider and quickly righted itself on firm footing, but Brown was taking no further chances. Frightened momentarily for his life, he dismounted and climbed the rest of the way up Loughrigg Fell alongside his mount. From the well-situated summit, he had good views of Rydal Mount and Wordsworth's home in one direction, the onetime home of the late poet Felicia Hemans in another, and Lake Windermere to the south. Then he turned back on foot. What he did with the donkey on the return trip, he neglected to say.[119]

Their visit lasted three days and included trips with Martineau to Wordsworth's grave, Hemans's cottage, and other celebrated locations in the Lake District. Brown's description of this visit is one of the most animated in his travelogue, a reflection of his deep and abiding respect for Martineau. He had read her magisterial *Society in America* and two years later would incorporate an excerpt in *Clotel*. The visit ended on a warm, encouraging note, as Martineau, an ardent defender of the rights of women and the enslaved, expressed her intention to look after the welfare of Ellen and William. She was as good as her word. No sooner had they left than she sent out inquiries on their behalf. Just two weeks after the visit, she wrote to inform Brown she had successfully arranged with Lady Byron, whose philanthropic projects included manual training schools, to place the couple at Ockham Industrial School, in Surrey. There they would receive a general education with emphasis on basic reading and writing skills, as well as vocational training (sewing for Ellen and cabinetmaking for William). Although they gratefully accepted the offer, they still had months on their hands before a new term began, so they continued their speaking tour with Brown into the summer.

No one looking for Brown that spring, including the English census takers, would have found him anywhere near London. The winter-long tour of 1850–51 that had begun solo before picking up the Crafts en route and winding across the English–Scottish border now shifted south through Gloucester, Bath, Exeter, Plymouth, Reading, and briefly Wales. They followed the same alternating formats that had worked so well in the north: panorama exhibits, illustrated lectures, accounts of life under slavery and escapes, and lectures on the Fugitive Slave Law. But a new subject arose that spring that soon preoccupied Brown's thinking: the possibility of staging some kind of public protest once they reached London in May at the upcoming World's Fair. Officially known as the Great Exhibition of the Works of Industry of All Nations, the first World's Fair was set to open in early May at the newly built Crystal Palace, with unprecedented crowds of Britons and foreigners expected to visit.

Brown had been disturbed by the presence of US slaveholders in London ever since his outbound journey on the *Canada*, and he feared what might happen once they came to the Great Exhibition, as he anticipated they would, in large numbers: "The slave holders would try to persuade us that they are very good men—a very humane, very philanthropic people."[120] He meant to do his part to prevent their free, unfettered circulation at the Crystal Palace. On June 21, a five-shilling admission day patronized chiefly by people of means, he entered the grounds in the company of a well-organized, multiracial group of close friends.[121] Joining him were Ellen and William Craft, Mary and John Estlin, Hannah and Richard Webb and two of their children, Anne and George Thompson and their unmarried daughters Jenny and Amelia, liberal journalist William Farmer, and several other friends. Too large a group to walk conveniently together, they separated into smaller units, Brown taking the arm of Jenny Thompson and spending most of the day touring with her. To begin the day, however, the entire group purposefully went together to the American department at the end of one portion of the building—hardly the starting place for most non-American fairgoers.

They targeted the centerpiece of the American exhibition, Hiram Powers's celebrated, full-size female nude statue, *The Greek Slave*. In the late 1840s, Powers had sent copies from his studio in Florence on headline tours of the eastern United States, where it was seen by hundreds of thousands of viewers. The Crystal Palace provided him the opportunity to exhibit it on a world stage. Sculpted from white marble, it presented the figure of a young European woman chained and readied for sale in the Ottoman slave market, but to contemporary viewers her iconography suggested a purity of Christian character not even a marauding Muslim master could sully. That interpretation must have been galling to a man like Brown, whose sister looked nothing like the Greek slave and whose experience in no way resembled that depicted by Powers. For him and his friends, *The Greek Slave* eclipsed the American slave from public view.

Brown and his friends (including Ellen, the "white female slave") took a hostile position set off from the crowd. Hoping to incite a reaction, Brown stood alongside Powers's statue holding up a recent *Punch* cartoon of *The Virginian Slave*, which depicted a manacled African American female slave identified by caption as a "companion piece" to Powers's statue.[122] When no bystander dared to challenge him, he simply left the cartoon conspicuously inside the enclosure surrounding the statue. No sooner had they moved down the passage than they saw an American remove it.[123] Anticipating just such an opportunity for a verbal fight, they quickly returned to debate the man, but he refused to be provoked.

They walked next to the American department's exhibition of daguerreotypes, which sparked general discussion among them about the number of US proslavery ministers and statesmen represented. One display, however, must have brought a flash of recognition to Brown's eyes alone: a series of eight copperplate daguerreotypes of the Cincinnati Public Landing. This photographic panorama, today recognized as one of the finest midcentury applications of the new technology to the out-of-doors, was the work of the Queen City's leading daguerreotypists, Charles Fontayne and William Southgate Porter. One sunny day in September 1848, they had set up their equipment atop a riverfront building in Newport, Kentucky, and taken a series of shots of the city stretching along the riverfront and rising up the adjacent slopes. The panorama's reputation soon spread far and wide, and in 1851 two local men, William and Thomas Powell, had the plates carefully packed and shipped to London for exhibition at the Crystal Palace. Happening upon them, Brown would have been looking for the first time since 1834 at the scene of his escape.

Continuing through the halls, Brown and his friends stopped by the exhibition of Colt revolvers. The sight of their group momentarily caused

Samuel Colt, who had come to London to solicit contracts (or a hired employee), to stop his demonstration of the famous revolver's features. That was only one of many shocked reactions that day as the spectacle of Brown and Jenny Thompson strolling arm in arm drew stares. Brown noticed others observing them: "As I walked through the American part of the Crystal Palace, some of our Virginian neighbours eyed me closely and with jealous looks, especially as an English lady was leaning on my arm. But their sneering looks did not disturb me in the least."[124] He was enjoying himself immensely that day, and subsequent days, at one of his favorite places in London.

Brown's overall impression of the Crystal Palace and Great Exhibition was buoyant: "This is the greatest building the world ever saw."[125] Some critics saw on display an uncritical worship of Mammon, concentrated capital, or triumphalist modern science; Brown saw a progressive future of freedom and diversity. Not even the motley array of human types he had moved among on Mississippi River steamboats and New Orleans levees compared with the human spectacle of the exhibition: "All countries are there represented—Europeans, Asiatics, Americans and Africans, with their numerous subdivisions. Even the exclusive Chinese, with his hair braided, and hanging down his back, has left the land of his nativity, and is seen making long strides through the Crystal Palace, in his wooden-bottomed shoes." They came from all corners of the globe and moved across the grounds with an unfamiliar freedom from class: "There is a great deal of freedom in the Exhibition. The servant who walks behind his mistress through the Park feels that he can crowd against her in the Exhibition. The queen and the day laborer, the prince and the merchant, the peer and the pauper, the Celt and the Saxon, the Greek and the Frank, the Hebrew and the Russ, all meet here upon terms of perfect equality. This amalgamation of rank, this kindly blending of interests, and forgetfulness of the cold formalities of ranks and grades, cannot but be attended with the very best results."[126]

Two days later, he was riding home from a return visit when whom should he spot in the omnibus but the Scottish writer and public intellectual Thomas Carlyle, a vocal critic of the exhibition. The sight of the outspoken Scot so affected him that he initially felt uncomfortable sharing a public vehicle with a man whose writings he knew too well. He had read *Heroes and Hero-Worship* and *Past and Present* admiringly, struggled to follow the logic of *Sartor Resartus*, but stopped cold with "Occasional Discourse on the Negro Question" (even before "Negro" became "Nigger" in a later edition), which he saw as a racist screed. Carlyle was an intriguing mystery, part progressive, larger part reactionary: "His heart is with the poor; yet the blacks of the West Indies should be taught, that if they will not raise sugar and cotton by their own free will, 'Quashy should have the whip applied to him.'"[127] Brown so disliked the man for his writings that he could not restrain his contempt for long. He vented his outrage in the London papers, just about the time he was starting the planning for a major public celebration of West Indies Emancipation Day.

Two DAYS AFTER he encountered Carlyle in the omnibus, his daughters finally embarked from Boston for Europe. He had never regarded the separation from them or their homeland as permanent. But as time went on, he gradually reached the conclusion he could not safely return home—Boston had never ceased to be home—as long as he remained a fugitive slave. Following passage of the Fugitive Slave Law in September 1850, he knew slave catchers might show up at his door in Boston just as easily as they had at the Crafts'. His fears were soon proven justified, as Boston, citadel of American abolitionism, experienced three visitations in 1851 alone. In the most notorious instance, which occurred just four months after the Crafts' narrow escape, delegated agents arrested the teenage fugitive Thomas Sims as stolen property and placed him under protective custody. The presiding magistrate was Massachusetts Chief Justice Lemuel Shaw, Herman Melville's father-in-law, who ruled that Sims be returned immediately to Georgia. In a scene repugnant to people steeped in the memory of the Boston Massacre and Bunker Hill, a "slave guard" of several dozen armed policemen marched Sims under cover of darkness to the harbor. Additional fugitive-slave cases soon followed, the most infamous of all the arrest and return of Anthony Burns in April 1854, just months before Brown's triumphant return home. That case moved an irate Henry David Thoreau, addressing the annual MASS Fourth of July picnic that Brown rarely missed, to excoriate Northern complicity in slavery. There was more than enough guilt to go around, he fulminated, from national leaders down to a local press that could not "have gone lower on its belly." The title of his printed remarks was pure outrage: "Slavery in Massachusetts."[128]

Since he could not return home at the time, Brown would have to bring the girls over to him. For the first eighteen months overseas, he had lacked the means, particularly since he meant to place them in boarding school. His situation was no more difficult, however, than that of many other fugitives resident in England who had to choose between family and freedom. One such case in the London news in the early 1850s was that of his sometime-ally, sometime-nemesis Henry Highland Garnet. Garnet had come to England for an extended stay to raise money for his church, but he could not afford to bring along his family. Brown and Garnet occasionally found themselves lecturing side by side in the north of England and Scotland in the fall of 1849 and in 1850, and on some occasions they made common cause; at such times, they might well have discussed their family situations. But the political differences and competing affiliations that had prevented them from forming a personal bond at the time of their initial 1843 meeting in Buffalo still left them wary allies at best. Garnet's difficult circumstances eventually became a subject of discussion among his allies in the BFASS, who regarded him as so valuable an advocate for their boycott of slave-produced goods that they took his case to the press in summer 1851. Within several days, a large contribution came in from a Member of Parliament, but contributions thereafter lagged.[129] Finally, the chief advocate of the boycott, Anna Richardson, agreed to cover the remaining cost of their fare.[130] Brown had sore feelings even about that, snidely belittling Garnet for placing himself "under the care of his mother Mrs. Richardson of Newcastle."[131] What he presumably was feeling was jealousy toward a rival for her attention who slept under her roof.

Brown, by contrast, was finally able to provide for his own daughters by early 1851, thanks to the revenue generated by his panorama exhibits, lectures, and publications. He announced his decision to Wendell Phillips in January while on his lucrative northern speaking tour with the Crafts: "And now my dear Mr. Phillips, I have determined to see my daughters some time during the months of March or April, and as I cannot return to the United States with safety I must get them to this country."[132] He was already starting to attend to the necessary arrangements but needed some coordinated help from friends like Phillips in Boston and his banker, William Coffin, in New Bedford. Because respectable young girls or unmarried women could not be permitted to travel alone, Brown searched his mind for a suitable escort. He decided that the man for the mission was his good friend George Thompson, who, though a sitting MP, was currently renewing ties to American friends (and replenishing his finances) on an open-ended speaking tour for the AASS. Brown's working plan was to coordinate his daughters' departure with Thompson's return to England. To help get them ready for the trip, he enlisted Martha Fletcher, Josephine's landlady, to outfit them and, once the hour approached, to take them to Boston for their departure. The arrangements cost a considerable amount of money, which Brown remitted in various mailings. In January alone, he sent Phillips and May drafts totaling 50 pounds.[133] He requested Phillips to purchase their tickets on the same steamer being taken by the returning Thompson. All too aware of discrimination on the high seas, Brown vacillated about whether to send them first class, fearing that the ship's officers would sequester them in an isolated stateroom, as recently had happened to Garnet. But if the girls could be situated in a women's first-class cabin, he was willing to allow them to take the risk.

The measure of his determination was his concluding thought to Phillips: "If my girls do not come with Mr. T—I must come home if for no other purpose than to get them and return. I do not expect to remain longer in England than when I can return with safety. But I can put my girls in a good school, and that will be of great service to them."[134] Brown hoped to see them in March or April, but Thompson was not yet ready to return. Meanwhile, the girls, now approaching fifteen and twelve, grew increasingly impatient to start their journey. Clara no sooner received a letter from her father in late March than she took the initiative to write Phillips and request a little spending money, to be reimbursed by her father, beyond the standard allotment for food, lodging, and clothes.[135] Phillips had always taken an interest in the Brown girls and must have been impressed with what he saw. Everything about the letter was correct—its penmanship, spelling, address, and manners. Studiously schoolgirlish, Clara was the "good girl" of the family, a trait that extended down to her signature: "Clara B Brown daughter of W W Brown." Whether she (or the more headstrong Josephine) also considered herself the daughter of Elizabeth Schooner Brown is an open question. In all likelihood, neither had had any direct contact with their mother since summer 1848, nor would they once they reached England. Soon afterward, it would be too late.

When Thompson could not be counted on, as was not uncommon, Brown or Phillips moved on to a next-best choice, the Boston reformer Reverend Charles Spear. A crusading opponent of capital punishment and a committed if slightly heterodox abolitionist, Spear was headed overseas to attend the upcoming fifth International Peace Congress to be held in London coincidentally with the World's Fair, and agreed to escort the girls, who might already have been acquainted with him. Once that arrangement was made, Thompson belatedly also committed to the date, so on June 25, 1851, the party of four steamed out of Boston on the *America*, en route to Liverpool. They made the crossing in eleven days, but despite good maritime conditions, it was not an entirely smooth voyage for the girls. Even before they debarked from Boston, the shipping agent of the Cunard Line insisted that the sisters be included on the passenger list as servants due to their color.[136] Then, once on the high seas, an elderly woman from Framingham, Massachusetts, objected to the English captain about the presence in the women's cabin of "two runaway slaves" being taken off by Thompson.[137] The unsympathetic captain could barely maintain his composure while hearing her out. The girls and their chaperones lost no time upon docking in Liverpool; they took rooms for one night only before boarding the next morning's train to London. Waiting to receive them at Euston Street Station was their father, and the family of three was as whole as it could be after a nearly two-year separation.[138]

The reunion, however, was to be short lived, as Brown had ambitious plans for his girls. A Francophile since the 1849 Peace Congress, he had reserved places for them in a boarding school in Calais, which he hoped would equip them with the French language and a strong general education. He must have had an adviser in reaching so specific a decision; the prime candidate would be his trusted friend Maria Chapman, a woman who knew the country well, took a keen interest in his family, and liked to give advice. She could not have persuaded him, however, had he not already reached the conclusion that the girls would be better off there than close to him in London. He had a clear idea of what he wished for them: to acquire the skills for the best possible life available to young ladies of their class and color. By contrast with their workaday mother, they would be teachers.

During their five weeks together, he showed them around London, taking them to the Crystal Palace and as many of the city's attractions as they had time for. He had countless places he wished to show them, but they had desires of their own. At their urging, he took them one afternoon to watch the pomp and ceremony of the queen's prorogation of Parliament.[139] Their interest in the royal family actually matched his; he had followed the royal movements ever since he first saw Victoria and Albert in Dublin shortly after his arrival, when, with "an out-stretched neck and open eyes," he observed their procession from an upstairs perch as it moved down Sackville Street.[140] He probably also took his daughters to at least one of the sessions of the International Peace Congress, which commenced at Exeter Hall on July 22. He was not a delegate this time, but he followed the cause of universal peace with continuing interest. Glowingly proud of his girls, he introduced them—really, showed them off—to many of his friends. Never able to separate the personal from the public, he also presented them more boldly than he ever did in the United States to members of the antislavery movement.

He first exercised this more open-door policy at the second of that year's two major antislavery events in London. The previous one was the mass meeting held July 21 in connection with the congress organized by the BFASS, with senior leaders Scoble, Sturge, and Gilpin present, as well as Garnet, Crummell, and a late-arriving Horace Greeley, whom Sturge summoned to take a seat on the podium.[141] Brown attended but was not invited to sit on the podium or to address the well-heeled, mostly white audience of 3,000 to 4,000. The BFASS had been under attack for months in the progressive press, chiefly the *Morning Advertiser*, for its timid opposition to US slavery and its failure to take active measures against the thousands of US slave owners and their ministerial defenders attending the Great Exhibition. Nothing that happened at the meeting deflected that criticism, which resumed immediately afterward.

By contrast, the meeting of "the American Fugitive Slaves and their friends," which Brown took the lead in organizing, held in the Hall of Commerce on August 1, moved beyond a symbolic commemoration of West Indian emancipation to a demonstration of the actual accomplishments of ex-slaves from the United States and the West Indies.[142] Orchestrating this remarkable event was one of Brown's proudest achievements in England. A "jammed full" audience filled the hall, with Brown in the chair and his daughters and George Thompson among the dignitaries seated nearby on the podium. Many of Brown's friends from the United States and England attended, as did people with whom he was not yet personally acquainted. Present was the liberal historian Thomas Babington Macaulay, whose celebratory, multivolume *History of England* had brought him fame and fortune. Scanning the audience, Brown was surprised to spot Alfred Tennyson, Wordsworth's successor as poet laureate of England. Tennyson, he commented afterward, looked as though he had "been swept in by the crowd, and was standing with his arms folded, and beholding for the first time (and probably the last) so large a number of coloured men in one room."[143]

It was, in fact, a stunning assemblage of people of color, as everyone in the hall would have noticed. Although Thompson was the official honoree on this occasion (and gave the longest address), the event featured remarks by a number of ex- or fugitive slaves from the United States and the British Caribbean. Everything about the look and feel of the night's proceedings distinguished it from the BFASS meeting, but the point was made explicitly when Thompson referred contemptuously to the BFASS as a "nonentity" in the United States and a voice from the floor shouted approvingly, "Where is Scoble?"[144] The most significant moment in the evening's proceedings, though, came as a result of an initiative Brown had set in motion earlier that day. In the days beforehand, he had drafted "An Appeal to the People of Great Britain and the World," a masterful public document that mimicked the language of the Declaration of Independence, only to shift the object of its attack to the other side of the Atlantic. Its purpose, phrased in familiar language, was "to state the ground upon which we make our appeal, and the causes which impel us to do so." The morning of August 1, he had presented his document to a committee of fellow fugitives for their approval. He got it and designated one of them, a recently arrived Baltimorean named Alexander Duval, to read its text to the assemblage.[145]

Duval did, and the meeting quickly adopted it by acclamation—although it is unlikely that many individuals appreciated the significance of what they were hearing. Rarely noticed since 1851, it is one of Brown's most powerful assaults on the makers and chroniclers of American history, two groups merging in the ample figure of Thomas Jefferson. In drafting his original "declaration," Jefferson had aimed its longest section, consisting of a "long train of abuses and usurpations," at the people of Great Britain, which the Continental Congress amended to the figurehead of King George III. Prominent among these abuses was the slave trade, all mention of which (and all mention of slavery, for that matter) was deleted from the final document approved by the Congress. Brown took Jefferson's indictment against the people of Great Britain for violating the colonists' natural rights and converted it to an indictment against the people of America for the decades-long support of violence by one race of Americans against another. His language would have been familiar to American ears, although with a disturbingly seditious twist: "The history of the negroes of America is but a history of repeated injuries and acts of oppression committed upon them by the whites." Whereas

Jefferson had appealed to the enlightened world for aid in fighting British tyranny, Brown turned to the British and European public for aid in fighting US slavery.[146]

The Brown girls sat on the speakers' platform in full view of the audience. They were not there, however, simply to observe the proceedings and admire their father's stage persona. Thompson saw to it that they played a public role. Toward meeting's end, he stood up a second time to tell the story of their ostracism by the vindictive woman from Framingham. One can only guess Clara and Josephine's feelings about their public exposure on a London stage, but there can be little doubt their father must have glowed with pride that they were seated alongside him to witness the triumphant assemblage he considered "one of the most enthusiastic meetings that has been held in England on the subject of slavery for years."[147]

His daughters were his most eagerly anticipated visitors that summer. His least was Enoch Price, who showed up sometime during the six-month run of the Great Exhibition as part of a European holiday. His plan in London was to visit the exhibition and look up the man he still regarded as Sandford Higgins. Brown was probably out of town on a lecture tour at the time, but Price knew Brown's network well enough to leave his calling card with William Farmer, a progressive London journalist inseparable from Thompson, close to Brown, and well apprised of his movements. News that Price had been looking for him startled Brown, who even a year later sought Wendell Phillips's legal opinion whether he was completely safe from the long reach of the Fugitive Slave Law.[148] His correspondence with Phillips was a private matter at the time, but Brown turned the episode into a public joke in 1855, not long after he returned to the United States a free man. While attending an antislavery convention in Cincinnati, he regaled the audience with a variety of saucy stories. One was a wildly invented account of his supposed encounter with Price in London in which he reversed the affront by showing up unannounced at Price's hotel with one of his daughters. Following Brown's intrusion on his privacy, Price supposedly remarked about it to an acquaintance: "Would you believe it, that black rascal talked to me just as though I had been an old school-fellow of his. I never saw such impudence in all my life; and then, to cap the climax, he introduced a yellow gal that he called his daughter."[149] Of all the story's invented details, the most improbable was that Brown would introduce either of his daughters to a living, breathing agent of slavery.

He bade his daughters farewell on August 13, 1851, and received notice within a few days of their safe arrival in Calais. A week or so later, he went over to see for himself how they were doing, returning satisfied. As his second anniversary in London came and went, he settled into a more confined routine, spending more of his time at home in London and devoting himself to an intensive course of reading and writing. He filled his days and nights with the life of the metropolis: attendance at the London Peace Congress, the Crystal Palace, the theater, popular shows and lectures, as well as visits with friends. He attended the wedding of the Thompsons' eldest daughter, at which Thompson saluted him man to man, if not father to father.[150] To supplement his income, he continued his summer practice of writing occasional opinion pieces for the London press. One was a controversial letter to the editor of the London *Times* in which he addressed the vexed status of the growing population of fugitives in England.[151] Many newcomers, he noted, were transplants now at a second remove, coming via Canada, but they were no more likely to find improved economic prospects in urbanized England. The West Indies, he advised, was a more likely place for them—though just six months earlier he was still pursuing his idea of organizing a manual training school in Canada. He also sent a similar public letter to Frederick Douglass that unintentionally mixed self-interest with pointed advice: "There are numbers here, who have set themselves up as lecturers, and who are in fact little less than beggars."[152] With Pennington, Garnet, and Josiah Henson, among others, to contend with on one field of battle, Henry Box Brown on another, and more fugitives arriving by the month, he already had more than enough competition for English attention and support.

He also continued the practice of sending travel letters to Frederick Douglass for publication in *Frederick Douglass' Paper* (successor to the

North Star), one recounting his recent visits to Oxford and Cambridge.[153] He was generally curious to see these great university cities, but he also had more specific reasons. He went to the former hoping to make the acquaintance of the son of the late, great champion of English abolitionism, William Wilberforce, who unfortunately was not there; to the latter, to renew his acquaintance with the brilliant young black churchman and intellectual Alexander Crummell, whom he had probably last seen at the Paris Peace Congress. While in residence in Cambridge pursuing a bachelor's degree at Queen's College, Crummell was receiving international publicity for his academic ambition. Brown not only liked him but also took him as a model of self-advancement. With only slight exaggeration, he extrapolated from Crummell's achievements at Cambridge to a proud comment on other "sons of Africa": "In an hour's walk through the Strand, Regent, or Piccadilly Streets in London, one may meet half a dozen coloured young men, who are inmates of the various Colleges in the metropolis."[154] Their achievements brought special pride to an autodidact frequently self-conscious of his lack of formal education.

BROWN CROSSED the English Channel in January 1852 to see his daughters in Calais and spend leisure time on the Continent. Meanwhile, on the other side of the Atlantic, Betsey Brown's life ended in misery within a few weeks of New Year's Day in Buffalo—once the city of young love and high hopes. The city's surviving death records, which begin only in January 1852, took no official notice of her death. Its only documentation comes in a letter from Nathan Rosier, who owned a house at 15 Steuben near Pollard—just a short walk from the Elm Street house in which the Browns had lived during the early 1840s. Rosier and his wife had cared for Betsey in her final days, but the letter he wrote announcing her death made clear his primary concern was fair compensation for services rendered.[155]

Though only a day laborer, Rosier was well enough informed to know exactly how to get his request for payment transmitted to a man living thousands of miles away. He addressed his request to Arthur and Lewis Tappan, the chief financiers and longtime leaders of the American and

Foreign Anti-Slavery Society in New York City. The brothers were in close contact with their transatlantic colleagues Joseph Sturge and John Scoble of the BFASS; a sluice of publications, funds, and news passed regularly between their shores. One final time Betsey's story flowed through the pipeline. Betsey, Rosier informed one of the Tappan brothers, "has been on my hand more or less for the last four years and is now Dead and Died at my house." That was the first half of the message for Tappan; the other was the actual request: "I therefore make out as moderate as I can for her and the child the sum of $100." Rosier asked Tappan to pass on his monetary claim to Scoble, who should present it to Brown, who in turn should remit payment to him. And what about the poor, unnamed orphan? Rosier's remark was stone cold: "I let the child's grandmother have it as she sent for it." If so, three- or four-year-old Paulina Brown was sent off to live with her maternal grandmother, Henrietta Schooner, by this time remarried to a man named Whetsel and living in Scipio, Ohio (a town where Brown had lectured around 1844).[156]

Rosier's letter had a life of its own. Various hands endorsed the envelope on its way from Buffalo to New York City and on to London. Although Tappan's letter enclosing Rosier's has not survived, its final destination is easily guessed: 27 New Broad Street, London, the offices of John Scoble and the BFASS. Months before Betsey's death, Scoble had passed through Buffalo to interview her en route to conduct a BFASS investigation into reports about the troubled finances of the Dawn Institute, an Ontario-based vocational school and training facility; many of its residents, such as community leader Josiah Henson, were fugitives from US slavery. Scoble sought to corroborate the charges Betsey had brought against William in a letter she sent him, which apparently included a copy of the same certificate of good character she had previously mailed to Isaac Ray, the *New York Tribune*, and no doubt other well-positioned recipients. At the least, Rosier's announcement of her death reinforced Scoble's inclination to trust her word over Brown's.

It probably did more. Not long after receiving Rosier's letter, Scoble took Betsey's underlying charge against Brown's character one degree further by applying it to circumstances: Brown, he let it be known, was spending undue time in the company of another woman. The woman was Ellen Craft, who—Scoble could not have known—was pregnant that spring with her and her husband's first child. Brown exploded on hearing the rumor and moved quickly to hold Scoble to account by bringing suit against him. He could hardly have timed his reaction better: A few months earlier, Scoble had been forced to defend his reputation against libel charges brought by Reverend Edward Mathews, an agent of the American Baptist Free Mission Society (and an ally of Brown's and Thompson's in the internecine antislavery war). That case went to court and Scoble was found guilty. In the controversy between Brown and Scoble, cooler heads persuaded Brown to take the dispute to independent arbitration by a panel of men chosen by the two adversaries. The chief intermediary was George Sturge, brother of Joseph and a longtime ally of Scoble's in the BFASS, who nevertheless insisted on absolute impartiality—all the more necessary because he considered Brown a stranger in a strange land. Sturge acted as the go-between in negotiating rules and procedures; each man was to choose one representative, and those representatives a third.

Brown's choice was intriguing: Charles Gilpin, his publisher but also a man with the closest professional and family ties to the BFASS leadership. Whether an uncommonly astute or simply ingenuous decision to draft a man holding dual allegiance (Gilpin was at the time preparing to bring out Brown's next book), events overtook the legal process. Before the charges could reach adjudication, Scoble removed any grounds for further action by resigning his position and preparing to relocate with his family to the Dawn settlement in Canada West (now Ontario). His decision was unrelated to his recent legal difficulties—so, at least, went the official word in London. But by this point, Scoble had unquestionably become an "embarrassment" to the BFASS leadership, which might well have lost patience with a front-line general whose battles were doing the cause as much harm as good.[157]

Brown must have been relieved finally to be done with Scoble. "That Snake in the Grass," as he once labeled him, had persecuted him for nearly three years.[158] Although their paths would cross again in Canada during the Civil War, he could effectively close the books on that account. But what about Betsey, whose malediction, now hardened into her legacy, had followed him across the ocean? The news of her death must have traveled as fast to him as Rosier's letter did to his adversaries. Brown was so resolved not to comment publicly on her—he left not a single word about her in any of his books or lectures—we can only guess at her continuing effect on his life. At the least, he would have needed to communicate news of their mother's death to the girls, whether in person or by letter. Perhaps he thought, with relief, that her influence on their daughters was done, that they were embarked, like him, on new lives in a freer land. If so, he was mistaken: The ghost of Betsey would live on, manifesting itself in ways neither he nor their daughters could then have predicted.

7

"Almost an Englishman"

One fine morning in June 1850, Brown set out on a leisurely walk along the Strand toward Trafalgar Square. Whatever his intended destination, he lingered in fascination at Nelson's Column, the imposing granite pillar towering hundreds of feet over Westminster. Having little appetite, he later wrote, for military heroics, he found himself gazing less at the crowning figure of the great naval commander that surmounted the column than at the bas-relief of one of the men who served under him—memorialized in full figure at its base. The sight of this "full-blooded African, with as white a set of teeth as ever I had seen," riveted him. The spectacle touched him, a national feat of homage paid by a grateful public to the humble as well as to the great.[1]

Seeing the Trafalgar memorial triggered an equal but opposite association with his experience several years earlier while inspecting a major war memorial in the United States. He was making a lecture tour in Connecticut in spring 1848 when he took time off to visit Fort Griswold, site of the fierce 1781 Battle of Groton Heights that ended in defeat for the patriot army, followed by the massacre of many of its survivors.[2] In 1830, the community erected a commanding 135-foot obelisk, built of locally quarried granite, to perpetuate the memory of their role in the last major Northern battle in the Revolutionary War.

During his self-guided tour, Brown expected simply to pay homage to the fallen. As he scanned the list of soldiers memorialized on the Groton Monument, he was "grieved but not surprised" to see the names of two black soldiers, Jordan Freeman and Lambo Latham, "colonized away" at a safe distance from the names of their comrades.[3] Unequal in life, they were unequal in death—an act of official disrespect at odds with the public commemoration at Trafalgar that so moved him two years later: "My sable brother, as black a man as was ever imported from the coast of Africa, represented in his proper place by the side of Lord Nelson, on one of England's proudest monuments."[4] He took the Groton Monument's discrimination as an insult to all African Americans and was quick to share his injured feelings with his close friend and, in time, brother historian William Cooper Nell. Each man stored that act of omission in his personal archive for future use in a corrective to the official annals of the United States.

The blatant contrast between "American historical injustice to its colored heroes" and English respect preoccupied Brown that June 1850 day as he lingered by Nelson's Column. Still caught up in his thoughts, he resumed his stroll, now knowing his destination must be the national shrine of Westminster Abbey. He entered the church on the south side near Poets' Corner and threaded his way through the monuments, reading their plaques, some accompanied by an official public eulogy. Shakespeare and Dryden, he would later report, he passed by with only a side glance; Addison he noticed more closely, enjoying seeing him dressed in his morning gown as though having just finished a piece for the *Spectator*; and Newton he observed briefly. His attention was fixed that particular day, however, on the great figures of English antislavery memorialized in the historic church—heroic public figures he came to the abolition movement too late to have known personally: William Pitt the Younger, Granville Sharpe, and Thomas Fowell Buxton (who had died four years earlier). Garrison, by contrast, had met Buxton, the leader of antislavery forces in Parliament, at the 1840 World Anti-Slavery Convention in London, although their relationship began on a false note. Buxton had invited the late-arriving Garrison to the communal breakfast but failed to recognize him, having assumed his renowned American colleague must be a black man (a mistake Garrison took as a compliment).[5]

And then, finally, Brown spotted the object toward which he had been walking all along: the tomb of William Wilberforce, leading spirit and personification of English antislavery. Like nearly all members of the MASS inner circle, he had heard the hagiographic story of Garrison's first journey to England, in 1833, as a young, crusading printer/ editor. Shortly after his arrival, Garrison had sought out the elderly Wilberforce and engaged him in a far-ranging conversation about the antislavery movements of their respective countries. Brown had heard, too, how just several months later, Garrison had walked alongside his new friend, George Thompson, in the funeral procession following Wilberforce's body to state burial in Westminster.[6] Large crowds of mourners lined the streets, and, with Parliament suspended in honor of one of its longest-serving former members, some of his colleagues accompanied the casket while others, including the speaker and the lord chancellor, awaited its arrival in Westminster Abbey. Now, seventeen years later, Brown paid homage in person at Wilberforce's monument, a prelude to the impassioned tribute to the iconic figure that he published during his final months in England.

That brief, meditative essay, "Visit of a Fugitive Slave to the Grave of Wilberforce," is one of the most eloquent elegies in the antislavery literature. It mounts a series of ascending steps that begins with the contrasting visits to the Groton and London war monuments, builds to a devotional tour of Westminster Abbey, and culminates in a self-appointed meeting with its holy of holies. Along its wending route through the abbey, he reads, paraphrases, and quotes from the plaques placed by the state on the makers and events of its history. The longest excerpt, naturally, repeats the dignified state benediction placed beneath Wilberforce's seated figure. Brown gives all these official testaments short shrift, commenting neutrally, "Either the orator or the poet have said or sung the praises of most of the great men who lie buried in Westminster Abbey, in enchanting strains." Rarely deferential to the officers or authorities of the state, he reserves the last word to himself, closing with a paean to a life well lived:

> No man's philosophy was ever moulded in a nobler cast than his; it was founded in the school of Christianity, which was, that all men are by nature equal; that they are wisely and justly endowed by their Creator with certain rights which are irrefragable, and no matter how human pride and avarice may depress and debase, still God is the author of good to man; and of evil, man is the artificer to himself and to his species. Unlike Plato and Socrates, his mind was free from the gloom that surrounded theirs. Let the name, the worth, the zeal, and other excellent qualifications of this noble man, ever live in our hearts, let his deeds ever be the theme of our praise, and let us teach our children to honor and love the name of William Wilberforce.

Identifying himself with his surroundings, he closed his benediction by signing it with his Anglicized signature, "W. Wells Brown, London."[7]

Nearly four years passed between the June 1850 day commemorated in the essay and its publication. In all likelihood, Brown composed the essay in 1853, even though part of the description of Westminster came from his 1852 travel book, *Three Years in Europe*. Early in 1854, he sent the text of his essay overseas to Julia Griffiths, a take-charge English activist who had moved to Rochester, New York, in 1849 to work side by side with her dear friend Frederick Douglass. Griffiths included it in the second series of *Autographs for Freedom*, a collection of antislavery writings in which she printed an engraved likeness and facsimile autograph alongside the text written by each of her well-known contributors. In accompanying Brown's selection, the autograph and engraving served not to authenticate personhood, as in the *Narrative*, but to enlist the authority of its prominent author for the antislavery cause. Along with his text, Brown sent an unidentified daguerreotype dating from the late 1840s, one that he presumably carried with him from the United States. Brown (or Griffiths) addressed the photographic plate to the talented American artist John Chester Buttre in New York City for engraving prior to publication, although no one involved in its production in the United States could have known how seriously out of date it was. The Brown it featured, as his essay pointedly demonstrated, bore scant resemblance to the cosmopolitan Brown now living in London.

The essay's contrast between British and American respect for black veterans begs the question: Who was the American Wilberforce? Was it Garrison, arguably Wilberforce's nearest approximation? But how could it be someone who refused to participate in the political process? Or was it some other unforeseen fighter for the freedom of enslaved African Americans? John Brown, whom Melville would brand "the meteor of the war," was still too far beyond the horizon to be visible, and Abraham Lincoln farther yet. In 1854, no less than in 1850, there were no obvious candidates to fill the role of America's great emancipator, and no evident solution to the dilemma that had driven Brown overseas.

THE FIVE YEARS Brown lived in England resulted in a period of productivity unprecedented in African American literary history. He already had his three earlier texts in circulation, which he sold as he made his rounds of antislavery lectures and performances. The most successful was his *Narrative*, which Gilpin reprinted twice in 1850, each time in a print run probably of 1,000 copies, and again as late as 1851 in a one-shilling illustrated edition with a slightly revised text.[8] Gilpin accounted for it on the title page as the "fourteenth thousand," an extraordinary (if unverifiable) figure for a work in this genre, and confirmation that Brown had been correct in thinking his book would prove popular in the British Isles.

Even this inexpensive edition did not exhaust its commercial life. In 1853, the London reprinter and literary pirate William Tegg, sensing a commercial opportunity in what had proven a popular, uncopyrighted text, brought out an unauthorized edition, the final and most curious nineteenth-century edition of the *Narrative* before it subsequently went into deep historical hibernation.[9] Tegg was a well-known but rather disreputable member of the London book trade who seemed to have come to piracy genetically. His father, Thomas, was a notorious London wheeler-dealer who referred to himself as "the broom that swept the booksellers' warehouses" for his wholesaling of remaindered works and, later, his cheap reprints.[10] William Tegg's new edition of the *Narrative*, "with additions" supervised by one Reverend Samuel Green, was a near-reprint of the "extensively" circulated Gilpin edition. Green, however, grafted onto it supplementary material consisting chiefly of excerpts from two other well-regarded fugitive-slave narratives: one, the life story of Josiah Henson, a figure in vogue in the British Isles due to his link to the *Uncle Tom's Cabin* craze; the other, that of Lewis and Milton Clarke. Brown would have had no reservation about having his name associated with the Clarke brothers, whom he knew from Boston and elsewhere, but keeping company in a single volume with Henson was a different story. He heartily distrusted Henson as a stooge of the BFASS and denounced him as taking money under false pretenses for the Dawn Institute.[11]

The *Narrative* in time earned a reputation all across the British Isles, but the central text of Brown's overseas years was his pioneering travelogue, *Three Years in Europe*. He introduced it to the public as the first "history of travels" written by a fugitive slave, although he was well aware there were precedents. He undoubtedly knew *The Interesting Narrative of the Life of Olaudah Equiano* (originally published in 1789), a popular memoir spanning Equiano's claimed childhood in Africa, years of slavery in the West Indies and Virginia, and adventurous adulthood spent on the high seas and in England. The *Interesting Narrative* went through multiple editions on both sides of the ocean, and copies were still on sale from the MASS book depository in Boston as late as the 1840s. Brown's travelogue, however, was the first work of its kind by an African American, and it demonstrated a literary flair that took the British Isles, including some of his friends, by surprise.

The road map for the travelogue's composition and publication is obscure. In its published form, Brown presented the chapters as public letters, the first datelined Liverpool, July 28, 1849, in order to synchronize the book's opening with his landing. It is unlikely, however, that he arrived with the intent to publish a systematic narrative of his travels, since he did not even have a set plan for extended residence. More likely, he followed a travel writer's custom of drafting either journal entries or more polished extracts in a portfolio of some sort, anticipating they might serve some future use. When and how they took shape as a printed book can only roughly be surmised. He certainly arrived with a knowledge of the genre; during his first stay in Paris, he consulted travel and museum guides as he sought out the chief tourist sites, although none would have covered their subjects through the experience and perspective of an African American. At some point, Brown made the intuitive leap that his experience in Europe would make an appealing subject for book-length treatment.

The most likely sequence of composition is this: During his first year in England, he sent back occasional letters to the United States for publication, typically in the *Liberator* or the *National Anti-Slavery Standard*, though with no overriding purpose. These were straightforward field reports about his activities and local antislavery events, not portions of a continuous narrative. His intentions gradually changed as he adjusted his plans for a long-term residence, and by late 1850 he entered into an agreement with Frederick Douglass for publication of a series of long, detailed travel letters in the *North Star*. He chose his venue thoughtfully, as for once he and Douglass had needs that fell into neat alignment. Publishing in the *North Star* was for Brown the chance to appear in the premier black publication of the time; publishing Brown's European letters was for Douglass the opportunity to add one more major voice to an unprecedented array of talented black writers that not even the *Liberator*, for all its achievements, had attracted (or had ever sought to attract). In agreeing to the arrangement, Brown was pleased to join what he later called a "corps of contributors and correspondents from Europe, as well as all parts of America and the West Indies."[12]

In the process of writing the *North Star* letters, Brown came to see a significant advantage in assembling them in a book. He composed the majority of his text over the course of 1851 but lacked the funds for publication. He presumably asked his then-customary publisher Charles Gilpin to underwrite the project, but Gilpin must have demurred. Instead, he managed, but did not finance, its production and sale. Perhaps he was skittish about taking a stake in such an unprecedented venture, but more likely he was making a general withdrawal from new projects as he prepared to stand for Parliament. Long a semipublic figure esteemed by Britain's most prominent progressives, Gilpin came to regard public service as being a more effective means than publishing of pursuing his goals of social justice. Certainly by the time of actual publication, Brown was dealing not with Gilpin but with his appealingly named successors, the brothers W. and F. G. Cash.

Thrown back on his own resources, Brown had little choice but to adopt an alternative scheme of self-publication by way of advance subscription. To set the process in motion, he began mailing out promotional circulars in early 1852 to friends across the British Isles for a work at that point titled *Three Years in Great Britain* and requested they distribute the circular and its accompanying subscription list among their friends. He left blank two columns on the right for subscribers' names and addresses and asked that the lists be mailed back to him by April 1. That date, he figured, would leave enough time for the work to be published on June 1, "if a sufficient number of subscribers can be obtained."[13] The original asking price was 10 shillings, 6 pence (roughly $2.50)—"a high price, this, for a book from a fugitive," Brown admitted to a confidant, while hoping to ease the terms by delaying payment until reception of the work.[14] By the time the book reached the general market in October, however, he had sliced its price to a more reasonable 3 shillings, 6 pence. At the time of publication, he also was fielding an offer from a cheap publisher in London (possibly Tegg) to buy printing rights to a one-shilling edition for $250, a substantial offer but one prohibited by his arrangement with the Cash brothers.[15]

The production of this pioneering travelogue involved a network of partners that originated with Brown in London and spanned the British Isles. Brown presumably delegated oversight to Gilpin, who drew on his extensive commercial ties to go partners with Oliver and Boyd, a well-established Edinburgh publisher. Oliver and Boyd, in turn, delegated the presswork to the printing office of the *Ayr Advertiser* on the west coast of Scotland—an excellent choice, as it turned out, since the

Advertiser printing office did top-quality work on the book. Better still, its publisher, Thomas M. Gemmell, took a decided interest in its success. From the *Ayr Advertiser* office, printed sheets were sent off for binding to London and Edinburgh, the points of distribution of the finished volume. Between the stages of printing and binding, however, one glitch intervened. Brown had assembled his manuscript so carelessly that he neglected to include the text of one chapter (Letter XXIII) when he sent off the manuscript for printing. That chapter recounted the wildly successful February 1851 lecture/exhibition trip with the Crafts to Aberdeen and then to Edinburgh, where they breakfasted with the renowned phrenologist–social reformer George Combe. Making a bad situation worse, Brown instructed that the omitted chapter be printed separately and inserted at the end of the already paginated sheets prior to binding, a mistake he explained in a casual prefatory note printed under the chapter number.[16]

Inside and out, the book broke the mold of Brown's earlier productions, as the price alone would have signaled. Whereas all his earlier works—his fugitive-slave narrative, his Salem lecture, the antislavery songster, and the panorama catalogue—were cheaply printed productions, *Three Years in Europe* was a solidly middle-class volume in design, content, and genre. The publishers produced a handsome volume in attractive brown boards, extra cloth, with the commonplace abolitionist logo of a kneeling slave stamped in gold leaf on the front and back covers as well as on the spine. A clear sign of its intended distinction, it featured a handsome engraving of a cultivated Brown opposite the title page, the work of the accomplished London engraver Richard Woodman, executed from an unknown daguerreotype. An American newspaper called it "a life-like portrait of the author, who, if the picture lies not, is a remarkably fine specimen of a physical man."[17] One might look at the 1847 Boston Brown and at the 1852 London Brown and wonder whether one was seeing the same person. That distinction would have pleased Brown, who had eased deep into London life. But, as in Boston, there was more to his appearance in London than met the unaided eye: the look of cultivated respectability covered the scars on his back and the tensions of being a black man moving chiefly among whites who some-times regarded him as an exotic, or worse.

Brown and his partners did what they could to generate interest by sending review copies to editors across the British Isles. Oliver and Boyd placed ads in a variety of Scottish newspapers and Gilpin (or the Cash brothers) did the same in England. They also had an active ally in Brown, who, according to Gemmell, was "very active himself in such matters" as promotion and invested £10 of his own into the work's advertise-ment in London.[18] Brown also saw to it that presentation copies reached friends on both sides of the Atlantic, although not all responded with the unreserved approval he received in the transatlantic antislavery press. George Thompson, naturally enough one of the first recipients, predicted good sales but expressed uncharacteristic ambivalence about what he saw as his friend's hybrid production: "I wish it contained more antislavery matter, and less of what can be found in our 'guide books' and 'travelling companions.'"[19] Another personalized copy went to the Estlins, who set it in a place of honor among the books in their drawing room.[20]

Other copies crossed the ocean to a variety of white and black friends and acquaintances. One inscribed copy went to Garrison with "love," and a second to William Nell, "with the loving regards, of the Author." As Brown's closest friend back in Boston, Nell was likely to receive it in the spirit in which it was offered. What happened to his copy after his death, however, provided a strange commentary on the life story of a cul-tivated African American in Europe. From Nell, a leading practitioner of African American history, the book took a sharp detour as it passed through a series of unknown hands to—ironically enough—a leading practitioner of Southern supremacist historiography, the early twentieth-century Yale professor Ulrich B. Phillips, and finally from Phillips to Yale University Library.[21] Those two were just several of what must have been many copies Brown proudly shipped to friends and editors back home, extending the range of circulation of a book printed exclusively for distribution in the British Isles and not reprinted in the United States. Just a few weeks after the book's publication, William Farmer reported that it was "having an extensive sale," and probably for some months it did.[22] Whatever the book's specific merits, it rode the wave of popularity generated by *Uncle Tom's Cabin*.

What kind of book was *Three Years in Europe*, and what kind of man was its author? These were the primary questions reviewers raised about a work that, thanks to its novelty, received exceptionally widespread attention. Reviews appeared in newspapers across England, Scotland, and Ireland, as well as in highly respected periodicals such as the *Athenaeum,* the *Critic*, and the *Literary Gazette*. Most reviewers were so unable to separate the book from the author that they typically answered the first question in terms of the second. They did not need to begin this exercise at the same point reviewers of the *Narrative* did; they simply assumed the author and text were authentic. Some were already familiar with his *Narrative*, and most with the reputation he had earned throughout the British Isles as a lecturer. They accepted without question that W. Wells Brown was a fugitive slave—so identified beneath his name on the title page—and took that fact as their point of departure. Many were outspokenly impressed, whether what they saw was a demonstration of his personal achievement or an example of "the negro intellect." Most also complimented its antislavery politics, which caused no commotion in post-emancipation Britain. The *Literary Gazette* expressed the general view in considering it "a bit of genuine writing."[23] But there were dissenters about either the book or its author. The weekly *London Examiner* sounded perhaps the shrillest note of British condescension: "The book . . . is very good—for a chattel, and may be suggestive of some wholesome thoughts."[24] The venerable *Athenaeum* was one of the few publications that liked the book but not the man: "Mr. Brown scarcely makes so heroic a figure as the injudicious flatterers of the black man would have him believe." But even that reviewer excerpted the book to demonstrate its fine literary quality.

George Thompson's ambivalence about the hybrid text was understandable. He was one of many British readers who noticed—although most did not struggle with—its unusual coupling of belletristic travel narrative and antislavery rhetoric. That combination was not all Brown mixed into the text; he also stirred in large doses of memoir and fiction.

The introductory portion of the book consisted primarily of William Farmer's biographical sketch, no doubt prepared with Brown's assistance, which served to intensify interest in the author by providing a duly flattering third-person account of his rise in the world. So did the personal stories, a few newly revealed, that Brown selected from his personal inventory. He related for the first time in print the story of his career as a wildcat banker in Monroe, Michigan, which he contrasted with his visit to the Bank of England in such a way that English readers could relish that story about a fugitive's shinplasters juxtaposed against the "gold coins" of the realm. The *Athenaeum* reviewer plainly did; he excerpted it. The story lingered for some Britons long after they forgot its source. In 1866, newspapers across England and Scotland reprinted a report about a recent conference paper on monetary policy in which an advocate for free trade in banking supported his argument by citing "extracts from a negro who was a barber, and would be a banker, and who took it into his head to issue notes." That policy had worked so well in the western United States, Colonel Sykes asserted, it would surely work in Great Britain.[25]

Neither the *Athenaeum* reviewer nor any other critic, however, commented on one of the book's strangest departures from respectable cultural norms: its wholesale excerpting of published texts for its own use. Public silence notwithstanding, someone must have commented privately on one of its most brazen unacknowledged appropriations: Phrases from Washington Irving's popular *Sketch Book*, an American classic written by an earlier American living in England, came back to life in Brown's description of the great reading room of the library of the British Museum.[26] Whatever other people might have thought, Brown took quiet pleasure in transferring Irving's words about the English-speaking world's most privileged reading room to his own fugitive-slave account of literary London.

If George Thompson thought *Three Years in Europe* disappointingly weighted toward travelogue rather than activism, some recent critics have taken the matter further by calling Brown a self-serving black bourgeois or elitist cultural tourist. The charge is understandable; the book's subtitle, *Places I Have Seen and People I Have Met*, even invites it. Brown held back nothing in serving up an array of famous people he hobnobbed with and places he frequented as conspicuous as they were impressive for a newcomer to the British Isles. As the reader learned, he had met Martineau, Hugo, Cobden, Bright, Tocqueville, Vincent, Combe, the Duchess of Sunderland, and other leading European figures. He had lectured by invitation before the Whittington Club, one of London's few socially and ideologically progressive clubs, and received an honorary membership as his reward.[27] He had shared a dining table, he boasted, with Dickens, Tennyson, the people's poet Eliza Cook, and the esteemed Scottish biographer John Gibson Lockhart. He had met the exiled French socialist Louis Blanc, who gave him a letter of introduction to the popular writer Eugene Sue for use in Paris, and he probably made the acquaintance of the exiled Italian revolutionary Giuseppe Mazzini.[28] He had been hosted at the town and country homes of countless members of the haute bourgeoisie, and even on occasion by their superiors, like John Lee. He had visited castles and museums, frequented theaters and concert halls, and paid homage to the homes of many of Britain's great writers. And now, with visible pride, he recounted his experiences with a wide array of Europe's elite.

That charge, however, fails to square with the single most conspicuous aspect of Brown's conduct throughout his years in England: his nonstop activism. He went to Europe to participate in the Paris Peace Congress, and he stayed on to lecture more frequently and write more extensively against slavery than anyone else in Britain. He traveled 25,000 miles across the British Isles, by his estimate, and gave more than a thousand talks since that first assembly in Dublin in 1849.[29] Following that anxious opening night, he honed his delivery, compiled a growing repertoire of stories and topics, and became a highly polished and versatile performer.

Brown also pursued various other reform-based activities. While readying the travelogue for press, Brown was joining with his closest allies, Estlin and Webb, in the organization of a new antislavery society and journal designed as an alternative to the policies and practices of the

The Last Sale of Slaves (1871), adjacent to the Old Courthouse in St. Louis, by Thomas Satterwhite Noble. Courtesy of Missouri History Museum.

Daguerreotype of the Cincinnati Public Landing, the site of William Wells Brown's escape. One of eight full-plate exposures comprising the riverfront panorama shot by Charles Fontayne and William Southgate Porter in 1848. From the Collection of The Public Library of Cincinnati and Hamilton County.

Banknotes from Monroe, Michigan. Courtesy of American Antiquarian Society.

Public Square, Cleveland, in 1833. Lithograph by Thomas Whelpley, from Whelpley Collection. Courtesy of Western Reserve Historical Society.

Earliest-known likeness of William Wells Brown. Frontispiece engraving for *Narrative of William W. Brown, A Fugitive Slave* (1847).

Wm. W. Brown.

Eng.ᵈ at 116 State St from a Dag.ᵉ of Chase.

R. Andrews Prin.ᵗ

Frederick Douglass

Early likeness of William Wells Brown's great contemporary, Frederick Douglass. Frontispiece engraving for *Narrative of the Life of Frederick Douglass, an American Slave* (1845).

Price, 12 1-2 Cents.

THE

ANTI-SLAVERY HARP:

A

COLLECTION OF SONGS.

BY

WILLIAM W. BROWN.

BOSTON:
PUBLISHED BY BELA MARSH, NO 25 CORNHILL.
1848.

Front cover of *The Anti-Slavery Harp* (1848).

Den in de gran saloon, we take de blushin damsel,
Where eyes shine like de moon, an ebery mouf dey
   cram full.   Chinger, &c.

Dar dance at nite de jig, what white man call cotillion
In hall so mity big it hole haff a million;
Den take our partners out, den forward two an back-e,
Den cross an turn about, an den go home in hack-e.
     Chinger, &c.

Dar too we are sure to make our dorters de fine lad-e,
An wen dey husbans take, dey bove de common grad-e
An den perhaps our son, he rise in glorious splender,
An be like Washington, he country's defender.
     Chinger, &c.

BLACK PINK
or, Love on the Canal St. Plan.

All de way from Wurginny,
My lubly Pink I cum to see,
Oh, my Pink, my lubly flame,
You can't think I am to blame,
 Walk jaw bone, on ginger log,
 Oh, Pink, I'm going de nole nog.

Offensive image of "respectable negro" from popular antebellum songster, *The Negro Singer's Own Book.* Courtesy of American Antiquarian Society.

Cartoon of "panorama mania" sweeping London in 1849. From *Punch*, July 14, 1849, p. 14.

Cartoon of *The Virginian Slave.*
From *Punch*, June 7, 1851, p. 236.

E PLVRIBVS VN

THE VIRGINIAN SLAVE.

INTENDED AS A COMPANION TO POWER'S "GREEK SLAVE."

W. Wells Brown,

William Wells Brown in London. Frontispiece engraving for *Three Years in Europe* (1852).

Minstrel-like scene of "negro dentistry." From London edition of *Clotel* (1853), and reprinted in subsequent works.

CENTRAL HALL,
SOUTH SHIELDS.

FRONT SEATS, 6D.
BACK SEATS, 3D.

On Wednesday Evening the 15th, and Thursday Evening the 16th February,

Doors open at Half-past Seven, LECTURE to Commence at Eight o'clock.

Hunting the Slave with the Negro Dogs.

Death of the President's Daughter.

W. WELLS BROWN,

A Fugitive Slave from the United States (Author of " Clotel, or the President's Daughter ;" "Three Years in Europe " &c.), will Lecture on American Slavery. The subject will be illustrated by new and splendid Dissolving Views, painted expressly for the purpose.

The following, with other Scenes, will be brought before the Audience.

SCENES ON THE COAST OF AFRICA.
The Slave Ship, Branding of Slaves.
Chase of a Slaver by an English Man-of-war
SLAVE MARKET.
THE HEROIC WOMAN.
THE ATTEMPT TO ESCAPE; THE ARREST.
Chasing of Fugitives with Negro Dogs.
STAKING AND THE BASTINADO.
INTERIOR OF UNCLE TOM'S CABIN AT NIGHT.
The Slave-trader & his Victim. The Anxious Mother.
THE TRADER THROWN FROM HIS HORSE—
JOLIFICATION.
ELIZA CROSSING THE RIVER ON THE ICE.
The Mother and her Child in the Forest.
Curious Scene, all sorts of People.
The Broad Brim; the Negro's Friend.
THE MOUNTAIN PASS ; THE TERRIFIC FALL.
The President's Mansion at Washington.
CAPITOL OF THE UNITED STATES.
Mississippi River, Gorgeous Scenery.
THE FLOATING PALACE. THE BURNING BOAT.
The Mother's Escape. Rescue of Eva by Uncle Tom.
TOPSY & EVA. DEATH OF EVA.

The elderly young lady and the servant girl.
Simon Legree and his Gang of Slaves.
THE BLACK DRIVERS AND THEIR VICTIM.
DEATH OF UNCLE TOM.
A Wonderful Escape. The Negro Dogs.
The Red Indian and the Fugitive Slave in the Burning Prarie.
Wm. Wells Brown Caught by Negro Dogs.
THE HAPPY FAMILY BROKEN UP.
Escape of W. Wells Brown & his Mother.
W. Wells Brown & his Mother returned to Slavery.
THE YOUNG SLAVE IN THE ROCKING CHAIR
A New Mode of Obtaining an Education.
Successful Escape of William Wells Brown.
A FUGITIVE AT THE FALLS OF NIAGARA.
THE ESCAPE THROUGH DISGUISE.
A Slave Family in the Forest Worshiping God.
The English Shore.
Meeting of Fugitives in the land of Freedom.
Slaves protected by the British Flag.
The California Gold Fields.
SLAVES AT THE DIGGINGS.

Broadside announcing William Wells Brown's magic-lantern lecture at South Shields the night Ellen Richardson was hosting a fundraising meeting in Newcastle to purchase his freedom. Courtesy of South Tyneside Libraries.

ANTI-SLAVERY MEETING!

The Worcester County North Anti-Slavery Society will hold its Quarterly Meeting in FITCHBURG, on

Saturday & Sunday, 12th & 13th Insts.,

COMMENCING IN THE

LOWER TOWN HALL,

on SATURDAY EVENING, and continuing its Meetings on SUNDAY AFTERNOON & EVENING,

IN THE UPPER TOWN HALL.

Wm. LLOYD GARRISON,

Wm. Wells Brown and Daughter,

together with other Speakers, are expected to be present. The Public are invited to attend.

"LET FREEDOM RING!"

Fitchburg, Jan. 8th, 1856.

Broadside advertising the participation of William Lloyd Garrison, William Wells Brown, and daughter (Josephine) in 1856 antislavery meeting. Courtesy of American Antiquarian Society.

DRAMATIC READINGS.

AT THE SANSOM HALL.

On FRIDAY EVENING, May 15th.

Doors open at 7—Recitation to commence at 8 o'clock. Admission 25 cents.

WM. WELLS BROWN, formerly a Slave among the Border Ruffians of Missouri, will give a Recitation of the new, laughable and highly interesting

MORAL ANTI-SLAVERY DRAMA,

Written by himself, entitled

"EXPERIENCE; OR, HOW TO GIVE A NORTHERN MAN A BACKBONE."

SYNOPSIS OF THE RECITATION.

ACT I. SCENE 1: Thanksgiving Day. Return of a Boston D.D. to the Parsonage; his remarks on his own sermon; thinks his future prospects very fair; his "South-side View of Slavery." Deacon Harris and Lady. SCENE 2: The Doctor, in his study, meets his publisher. Departure of the Doctor on his second visit to the "Sunny South."

ACT II. SCENE 1: A Southern Hotel; the Doctor and the Landlord. The Slave-Trader; sale of the Doctor; he is gagged, chained and carried to the slave market. SCENE 2: Mr. Patterson's plantation; the Doctor's sermon; he refuses to submit, and is whipped in. The Doctor and Dinah. SCENE 3: The Northern man at work in the field. Sam's Toast. SCENE 4: The negro quarters; the Doctor cooking his supper; Sam's remarks. SCENE 5: The repentance; he hates slavery, and thinks he will never go South again if he succeeds in getting his liberty.

ACT III. SCENE 1: The Doctor's release and return home. SCENE 2: Meets his parishioners; sister Harris's congratulations; he resolves to oppose slavery. Marcus, the fugitive slave; his eloquent appeal. GRAND POETICAL FINALE.

On MONDAY EVENING, May 18th, Mr. Brown will give a Recitation of the new, celebrated, and highly interesting

MORAL DRAMA,

Written by himself, entitled

"THE ESCAPE; OR, A LEAP FOR FREEDOM."

Single tickets 25 cts.; to both evenings 38 cts.   2t.

Notice for William Wells Brown's solo recitation of his antislavery plays. *National Anti-Slavery Standard*, May 9, 1857, p. 3. Courtesy of American Antiquarian Society.

Manuscript draft for scene of "negro dentistry" in *My Southern Home*. From the library of Wyatt Houston Day.

"William Wells Brown, M.D., Author of the Rising Son" is depicted at the lower right of this 1883 hand-colored lithograph, *From the Plantation to the Senate,* by Gaylord Watson. LC-USZCN4-26, Prints and Photographs Division, Library of Congress.

BFASS. Estlin provided the financing, Webb the publishing expertise, and Brown the credibility and a small amount of the content. All three assembled in June at his boardinghouse at 22 Cecil Street to plan their move, which resulted in the founding of the *Anti-Slavery Advocate*.[30] Brown was frank in stating that their ambition for this modest penny monthly was to "take the place of the [BFASS's] 'A. S. Reporter.'"[31] That ambition was unrealistic; no marginal publication was likely to undermine the authority of the British antislavery establishment, but Brown, Webb, and Estlin, working with the reformist publisher William Tweedie from London, kept up a stream of criticism of the BFASS for several years.

Even as a member in good standing of the Whittington Club, Brown so fully combined activism with cultured leisure they are not easily separated. A radical organization founded in 1846 as an alternative to the city's many conservative, class-based clubs, the Whittington provided a congenial gathering place for young people from the lower middle class keen to pursue upward mobility. Its presiding spirit and founding president was the radical journalist Douglas Jerrold, who joined with other liberals and reformers to establish progressive principles as the club's guiding mission: admission to both men and women (the latter regardless of marital status), moderate membership fees, inexpensive meals, access to instructive reading matter, and a wide array of cultural activities, including lectures. One particularly valuable feature for Brown was the club library, which was well stocked with foreign as well as domestic books and periodicals. He would have kept good company there; among its more than 2,000 members, the club included a substantial concentration of the most active writers in the city. Brown could hardly have found a more congenial place socially, politically, and culturally to spend leisure hours.

Brown first entered the club just weeks after the Paris Peace Congress as the guest of George Thompson, one of its many vice presidents. In June 1850, with Thompson presiding, he gave an invited lecture on "Slavery in America" that was so well received the club immediately offered him honorary membership.[32] He gladly accepted and probably spent many of his free evenings at the club, whose location on Arundel Street was an easy walk along the Strand from Cecil Street. Since his boardinghouse did not offer meals, he at least occasionally, perhaps regularly, took suppers at the club, where meals were hearty and inexpensive.

Shortly before his departure from London, he gave a second lecture at the club, this one the result of his latest thinking and reading about pan-African history. "St. Domingo: Its Revolution and Its Patriots" presented a triangular view of the African diaspora, encompassing the United States, the Caribbean, and the British Isles as seen from London. Compiling the material for that lecture would have taken some concentrated preparation. "Written orations had not been in my line," Frederick Douglass would recall about a learned commencement address, "The Claims of the Negro Considered Ethnologically," he gave that summer at Western Reserve in Ohio.[33] Nor were they in Brown's, whose US training had prepared him for a more extemporaneous mode of speaking. Little by little, that habit changed as Brown became more solidly a bookman in London.

CLUB LONDON was one of the environments he inhabited; another was street London. Adaptable by temperament and experience, he had found his comfort zone as a Londoner in no time at all after settling in at 22 Cecil Street. From the moment he established quarters there, "the great metropolis," as he labeled the world's most populous city, fascinated him as a bustling, protean environment. He maintained a spirit of curiosity throughout his residence in the city, although his fascination with the city's cosmopolitan life came into focus most conspicuously at the Crystal Palace. Chapter after chapter of vivid, energized reportage in *Three Years in Europe* conveyed his fascination with the most dazzling array of people he had ever observed. An endlessly energetic, inquisitive, sociable man, he came into contact with countless interesting people during these years at antislavery conventions, lectures, public ceremonies, museums, theatrical and concert performances, church services, public lodgings, railway stations; at street crossing; on public transport; in private drawing rooms and at social clubs.

In his *Narrative*, Brown had presented a representative sample of the enslaved community in St. Louis; in *Three Years in Europe*, he sketched an array of fellow black comrades in Britain: a fugitive slave from Maryland reduced to begging near Temple Bar, Africans promenading the grounds of the Great Exhibition, former slaves attending and participating in anti-slavery gatherings, blacks on stage in the city's theaters. He all but omitted the black sailors, servants, craftspeople, shopkeepers, students, professionals, activists, tourists, and beggars he met in the course of his daily movements. And then there were the actual people with whom he consorted, associated, or competed: Ellen and William Craft, Henry Box Brown, Henry Highland Garnet, Alexander Crummell, James Pennington, William G. Allen, Samuel Ringgold Ward, Josiah Henson, as well as the hundreds of fugitives or transplants from North America, the Caribbean, and Africa he met at various events. Ambivalent about his own national status, Brown had this stateless last group in mind especially in 1852 when he wrote advisory articles for the Anglo-American press about the relative merits of England, the United States, Canada, and the Caribbean as potential homelands for people of African descent—articles written with an assurance and authority that belied his own situation.

But as he passed through a city of several million and mixed among the crowds, one person came to stand out in his mind. His name is Joseph Jenkins, and he springs to life in a full chapter that Brown composed during the last year or two of his residence in England but published only in the expanded American edition (1855) of his travelogue. Brown's effervescent sketch of Jenkins, one of the richest portraits in his English writings, is drawn from his continuing meditation on the experience of a black stranger in a strange land. It portrays Jenkins as a jack-of-all-trades—street sweeper, huckster, singer, stage actor, preacher, and ex-slave—adept at any and all of the roles in which life has cast him. The two men meet repeatedly, generally glancingly, around the city as the mobile Brown happens upon Jenkins at one or another of his jobs. In the opening paragraph of the chapter, he describes chancing upon Jenkins so frequently in Cheapside distributing handbills that he comes to identify him in that role. Then he notices him repeatedly in Chelsea sweeping the same street crossing, and in Kensington chanting hymns and hawking religious tracts. As Brown later wrote, he encountered this resourceful individual more than fifty times in the course of his peregrinations around the city. Not just that—he came to consider Jenkins "the greatest genius that I had met in Europe," strong words coming from someone who boasted of having made the acquaintance of Dickens, Hugo, Martineau, Cobden, Blanc, and Tocqueville and who subsequently publicized that fact in a travelogue.[34]

Brown compresses all the details about Jenkins's daily labor on London streets into the opening paragraph, a foreshortened prologue to the main show. That drama begins as he strolls one evening in the East End and notices a placard for "Selim, an African prince," playing the title role in *Othello* at the Eagle Saloon—this during the season of "Uncle Tom mania," when "anything in the African line" attracts crowds to houses of entertainment. Intrigued, Brown ducks in, arriving in the middle of Act 1, Scene 1, and needing time to get his bearings. When the African actor playing Othello shortly enters to shouts of applause, Brown shifts his frame of reference from the audience at the theater to the audience reading his book back home: "Who could this 'prince' be, thought I. He was too black for Douglass, not black enough for Ward, not tall enough for Garnet, too calm for Delany, figure, though fine, not genteel enough for Remond." Such last-name recognition presumed a great deal, but Brown pressed hard on his cultural expectations: His readers would know the distinguished cast of characters in the antislavery movement as well as they knew Shakespeare's and, furthermore, would recognize them as riveting performers able to cast a spell over an audience. This is precisely the effect Jenkins produces this evening at the Eagle, as he is encored to "deafening shouts of approbation."

Although intrigued to decipher this man's identity, Brown claims he lost track of Jenkins once his affairs took him on an extensive tour of "the provinces." Months go by before Brown, by then long resettled into his London routine, wanders aimlessly one Sunday evening near a church where an attendant beckons him to hear a "colored brother" preach. The previous pattern of charismatic performance repeats itself: He follows his curiosity into the theaterlike church and once again encounters the human chameleon, this time in the pulpit, dressed in black and singing and preaching a powerful temperance message to a rapt congregation. Brown claims only belated recognition, as Jenkins comes into focus gradually—first as a familiar voice, then as a familiar face after removing his glasses. Following the service, Brown approaches the pulpit and the two men come face-to-face for the first time. As they do, Jenkins finally casts a return look of recognition on Brown—"I have seen you so often, sir, that I seem to know you"—and the two men walk out into the night engaged in deep conversation. Jenkins does most of the talking, recounting his early history, which Brown transcribes verbatim in the form of a slave narrative: A happy boyhood in the rural Sudan tending to his father's goats ends with his kidnapping and sale into slavery, passage through nine sets of hands as he is sold down the Nile to Cairo, and final purchase by an English gentleman who brought him to England and began his education. When his benefactor died, Jenkins had to give up his schooling and take to the streets to "earn a living as best I could." Several decades later, Brown witnessed the results, as Jenkins, now a paterfamilias, hustled to earn his livelihood and help his sons-in-law earn theirs.

It amounts to an amazing story, spellbindingly told. The whole affair is so uncanny it is tempting to see Jenkins as Brown's long-lost twin, a soul brother separated by slavery at birth and flung out to different ends of the African diaspora. Reunited by serendipity in London, they pursued the same line—Jenkins "as much a trafficker, as skilled in the commerce in blackness and black culture, as Brown was," according to Kennell Jackson.[35] No Joseph Jenkins survives in the annals of the London stage; but the name, if not the person, had a likely origin with Joseph Jenkins Roberts, first president of Liberia and a statesman Brown admired. In fact, Brown modeled Jenkins, at least in part, on a Sudanese native named Selim Aga, whose life story anticipates that of Jenkins. Aga was born near Sudan's Darfur region, sold into slavery by kidnappers, and passed through nine sets of hands before his eventual purchase and liberation by the British consul in Alexandria, who sent him to live with family members and receive a formal education in Aberdeen, Scotland. Brown's source was Aga's slave narrative, which was published in Aberdeen in 1846 and reprinted in London in 1850.[36] Brown was not just familiar but intimate with the text, lifting its opening sentences and putting them, with only the slightest of changes, into Jenkins's mouth.

"Immature poets imitate; mature poets steal," was T. S. Eliot's famous differentiation between mediocrity and genius.[37] Call it what one will, Brown's appropriation of Aga's words is indisputably a high-wire act of theft executed with consummate skill, but there may be more to the matter. It seems likely Brown and Aga actually met in London. Years of genteel comfort in Aberdeen did not strip Aga of his African heritage or identity. He relocated to London in 1849, as he wrote, with the "view of putting an end to the Slave Trade," and likely moved in antislavery circles that intersected Brown's.[38] Multitalented like Jenkins, he even lectured for nearly a year at Egyptian Hall about the Bonomi–Gliddon *Grand Moving Panorama of the Nile*, whose geography he could easily recall from memory.[39] Lecturing for Gliddon, however, was only his night job, an expedient means of earning his living while he devoted himself to basic personal concerns. His greatest ambition, which returned him to his roots, was to redress what he considered the benighted condition of his native Africa by scheming to bring Christianity and commerce to the continent. In 1853, he proposed and advocated a practical solution: an east–west transcontinental railway connecting Africa to the great trade routes of the Eastern Hemisphere. No less a man about town than Aga, Brown likely heard Aga lecture on one or even two panoramas in the early 1850's—the *Grand Moving Panorama of the Nile* or the later *Panorama of the Slave Trade*—for which Aga served as agent in 1853.[40] Brown and Aga had so many common affiliations and interests that Brown's attribution of "Selim" to Jenkins/Othello was presumably no gratuitous gesture but a winking acknowledgment of prior contact.

If Brown slyly paid homage to Selim Aga, he openly admired the other most likely model for Jenkins, Ira Aldridge, the long-reigning "African" prince of actors. Ask any current follower of the stage in England who Aldridge was and the answer typically came back in the form of his nickname, "the African Roscius," the label Brown applies to Jenkins. Brown's visceral regard for Aldridge was a demonstration of an aficionado's attraction to the great performers of the era. Immediately before introducing Jenkins playing Othello, he also mentions his pleasure at attending performances in London of the reigning opera stars, Giulia Grisi and Henriette Sontag and the tragedian William Macready (the same one he met on the train to Boston in 1849). In Paris, too, if he is to be taken at his word, he attended the opera and saw Grisi and her husband, Giovanni Mario, perform in *Norma*.[41]

An African diasporic performer like Aldridge would have excited and intrigued Brown. He claims he saw Aldridge in *Othello*, *Hamlet*, and other popular plays at such topflight theaters as Covent Garden and Royal Haymarket, although it is equally likely he caught Aldridge, who played to far greater success outside the capital, on the provincial stage during stops in their tours of northern England and Scotland. The playful analogy Brown drew in the Jenkins chapter between tragedian and antislavery lecturer, each equipped with mesmerizing capacities, suggests he recognized his like in Aldridge, a performer of great and versatile talents appearing in a wide variety of roles, light and serious, racial and nonracial. During his heyday, though, dominant taste dictated that Aldridge's defining roles were racially based, and preeminent among them was Othello, the role Brown suggestively assigned Jenkins in his command performance.

A connecting line ran through all three of these figures back to Shakespeare's conflicted Moor: the African outsider transplanted to the metropolitan center where, at least for a night, he commands center stage—the trajectory that first landed Brown in London and subsequently put him on display hundreds of evenings across the British Isles. Aldridge and Jenkins would live on in Brown's mind long after he returned across the Atlantic, making their appearance on American soil in 1862 when Brown included complimentary sketches of them in *The Black Man*, his gallery of accomplished African Americans. Before that, however, they played through his mind as he toured the Northern states in the late 1850s performing dramatic works of his own composition, direction, and production.

"THERE SEEMS TO BE no end to his enterprise," the recently arrived black educator Professor William G. Allen reported to Garrison in June 1853 about their mutual friend.[42] Allen was aware of Brown's wide-ranging on-the-ground activities, but it is less likely he knew his friend was also making serious progress on a major new literary undertaking. It was the wildly inventive work now regarded as the earliest African American novel, *Clotel; or, The President's Daughter: A Narrative of Slave Life in the United States*, an intricately composed panoramic account of slavery that Brown began writing sometime in 1852.

No manuscripts from the novel have survived, but one can detect an early stage in its development in two important fictional pieces he published in the second half of 1852. One was a variant on Brown's personal experience, a story about a young "white" slave named George Green who escapes from slavery in Virginia, resides for a period of years in Canada, and migrates to Europe, where he is reunited at story's (and, a year later, novel's) end with the love of his life, another nearly white ex-slave named Mary. Dissembling as usual about literary origins, Brown relegated his role in the story to that of mediator: "Without becoming responsible for the truthfulness of the above narrative, I give it to you, reader, as it was told to me in January last, in France, by George Green himself."[43] He intended it for publication as the closing chapter of *Three Years in Europe* until he realized during its production that he needed to include the misplaced chapter about the visit he and the Crafts had paid to George Combe.

Then, in December 1852, he published in the friendly pages of the *Anti-Slavery Advocate* the story of the sale at auction of a light-skinned young woman named Ellen Carter who was eventually freed and sent north.[44] She was soon adopted into the homes of two of Philadelphia's leading black families, the Purvises and the Fortens, and thrived in freedom. Brown claims he met and interviewed her during a summer 1848 visit to Philadelphia, the ostensible source of the story. In fact, he made the visit but, as with George Green, not the acquaintance.

During the months of his novel's compilation and composition,

Brown was, like all Britain, under the spell of Harriet Beecher Stowe's *Uncle Tom's Cabin*. Displacing even the latest Dickens as the principal topic of literary conversation, the novel smashed every mark for fiction in the British Isles by selling nearly one million copies within months as enterprising British publishers raced to issue editions of a work lacking a UK copyright. Brown read the novel shortly after its publication, reveled in its unrelenting assault on slavery, and immediately incorporated its graphic story into his "illuminated" lectures as he embarked on his speaking tours in the fall and winter of 1852–53. Fully expecting to find audiences agitated by the subject, he hired a London artist to prepare magic-lantern slides representing scenes of slavery drawn from *Uncle Tom's Cabin, Narrative of William W. Brown*, his antislavery panorama, and a mix of other sources. Appearing before audiences in darkened halls, he projected the slide images via powerful candlelight to provide scenic illustrations for his talks. Beginning in November 1852, he gave a series of these multimedia presentations across the country, including such major cities as Newcastle, Leeds, and Bristol.[45] During a February 1853 swing down to the south coast, the crowds were so large he spent weeks traversing the region, lecturing in Andover, Hereford, Southampton, and other towns. On February 3, 1853, when he lectured on *Uncle Tom's Cabin* to a packed audience of 400 listeners at Newport, Isle of Wight, the organizers had to turn away so many people they asked him to give a second talk on the subject.[46] The same thing happened later that month after he crossed back over the English Channel to Hampshire.[47]

Three months later, on the night of May 16, at London's Exeter Hall, he had his first sighting of the celebrity author, who was making a triumphal British tour (with her husband Calvin in tow). Excitement ran so high that Brown claimed the building's 5,000-seat Great Hall could have been filled tenfold. Through connections, he secured a pass that evening and went early. Where he sat is a matter of interpretation, as newspaper accounts placed him in different locations. The reporter for the *Anti-Slavery Advocate* had him seated on the speaker's podium alongside his black colleagues William Allen, Samuel Ringgold Ward, and William Craft as well as Calvin Stowe and the BFASS dignitaries.[48] More likely, he was seated down among the crowd, since the organizers of the BFASS would have had no intention of featuring his presence, least of all of allowing him to speak at one of their most spectacular events.

Anticipation built as the audience awaited the delayed entrance of the most famous author of the day. When she finally entered midway through the speeches and took a seat of honor in the gallery to the right of the podium, the audience erupted. As people stamped, applauded, and shouted, pickpockets used the turmoil to work the tightly wedged crowd. Once the police cleared the room of thieves and the speeches resumed, Brown found the most disappointing talk that of the Reverend Stowe, a tepid stand-in for his wife. Brown cynically dismissed it as typifying the failure of nearly all clergymen, white and black, to use their moral authority to take a principled stand against slavery. By contrast, he found Samuel Ward's the most rousing speech of the night, mounting so vigorous an attack on US slavery that he noticed Calvin Stowe squirming. Brown did his part after the meeting. The next day, he assembled clippings from the metropolitan press and mailed them, along with his eyewitness report, via steamship to Boston. It was the earliest report of Stowe's gala reception to reach the United States, and Garrison lost no time in printing it in the *Liberator*.[49] The ever-watchful Douglass, scanning the international news, gladly followed that lead by reprinting it in his paper, but not without adding an amused comment about the fast company Brown was keeping with literary thieves: Brother Brown was walking in the distinguished footsteps of Benjamin Disraeli by so nearly replicating someone else's flattering description of *Uncle Tom's Cabin* that "we think them enough alike to be twins."[50]

During the downtime of spring–summer 1853, Brown made rapid progress on *Clotel* and by September completed the manuscript. By this point, he positioned the two stories published the year before as bookends, though in the reverse order of their likely composition: the auction of Ellen Carter, now named Clotel, as its opening scene; and the reunion of George Green and Mary in France as its conclusion. In October, he reported to a friend in Boston he was reading proof of "a new work of mine now going through the press," for which he had contracted with the large London trade house of Partridge and Oakey.[51] Although the novel's anticlerical itch might have made it seem an unlikely addition to a publishing list dominated by evangelical Protestant works, the firm must have been willing to overlook that trait for its powerful antislavery message. A year earlier, they had joined the rush of London publishers with their own illustrated edition of *Uncle Tom's Cabin*, just one of a number of their reform-minded works. They may also have done Brown a useful service by referring him to Henry Anelay and James Johnston, the London-based designer and wood engraver, respectively, who had produced the engravings for their edition of Stowe. Whatever the means of introduction, Brown commissioned Anelay and Johnston to execute the woodcut to accompany his novel's minstrel scene of "negro dentistry," and Johnston (apparently alone) to produce its riverboat gambling scene, two of the four high-quality, full-page illustrations Brown assembled for the novel.

By November, while Brown was out on his usual seasonal circuit giving illuminated antislavery talks, *Clotel* was on sale across the British Isles, and inscribed copies were crossing the Atlantic to friends and supporters. The publishers had advertised it widely, and although it excited less interest than *Three Years in Europe*, mostly positive reviews began coming out by December from newspapers and magazines in England and Scotland, and early in 1854 from the US antislavery press. Reviewers of all backgrounds made a common point: *Clotel* belonged in the same family of antislavery literature as *Uncle Tom's Cabin*. Accurate enough as a judgment of the two novels' common subject matter, it failed to account for the fundamental difference between the writers and their writing methods. Brown, by contrast with Stowe, so distrusted the capacity of conventional narrative to do justice to a truthful representation of slavery that he invented an alternative compositional mode of narration that not just alternated nonfictional and fictional elements but blurred, at times even erased, the difference. Even today, as critics trace the encyclopedic borrowing that Brown employed in composing his novel, they are discovering that there was more to *Clotel* than met the conventional novel-reading eye of the day.[52]

....

CLOTEL; OR, THE PRESIDENT'S DAUGHTER opens with a powerful scene that haunted Brown's consciousness, the sale at open-air auction in Richmond, Virginia, of a light-complexioned woman named Currer and her beautiful adolescent daughters, Clotel and Althesa. Even though Brown had repeatedly witnessed public auctions in cities along the Mississippi River—St. Louis, Natchez, New Orleans—this one communicated a symbolic meaning that begs a fundamental question: Where did he get the idea to make the tragic figure of Clotel a daughter of Thomas Jefferson? Brown disliked fellow Kentuckian Henry Clay for his advocacy of black colonization, but he detested Jefferson, as he did his own absentee father, as the personification of the patriarchal slave South. Father of the twins liberty and slavery, Jefferson embodied the contradiction at the heart of the American experiment. Brown had heard numerous stories and rumors about Jefferson's fathering children by his slave "girl" Sally (Hemings), which circulated widely throughout the antislavery movement and the general black community.[53] Jefferson's name was already a byword for hypocrisy in African American circles long before Brown met with a direct descendant of the Hemings family of Monticello named Virginia Isaacs, who in the 1860s married his friend James Monroe Trotter. Brown not only heard such stories, he recycled them. As early as 1848, he reprinted a song called "Jefferson's Daughter" about a presidential child "bartered for gold" in *The Anti-Slavery Harp*. But the president whose presence hovers over *Clotel* was a far more intimately sinister figure.

Brown dealt peremptorily with Jefferson the patriarch in the novel; he referred to him indirectly in the title and a half-dozen times directly in the text, but only as a shadowy reference point of disgrace. When he cited Jefferson's signature phrase from the Declaration of Independence in the novel's epigraph, he modified it by giving the phrase an emphasis verging on accusation as "*Life, Liberty*, and the *Pursuit of Happiness.*" Rather than featuring Jefferson, he allotted the central roles in the novel to the illicit flesh-and-blood children of white patriarchy, particularly the daughters, whom he considered more vulnerable even than the sons. Brown had repeatedly witnessed the tragedy of mixed-race daughters during his travels on the Mississippi, and he had in his mother and sister the most tender contact with its destructive consequences. As he composed the story in his rooms at Cecil Street, Brown must have thanked his good fortune he had two teenaged daughters who, he was confident, would never know the degradation suffered by Clotel and Althesa.

Jefferson's legacy is but the first in an endless series of paradoxes assembled into the novel's panoramic "narrative of slave life." It overshadows the work, as does another, of equal importance, in chapter 21, which not only interrupts the reader's attention to Clotel's attempted flight to freedom but challenges the then-reigning narrative accounts of US history. This attention-grabbing passage portrays the founding moment of the United States as an act of misconception that, like Jefferson's, deeds the future nation its contradictory heritage. The chapter's first paragraph observes the course of the *Mayflower* in 1620 toward safe haven on North American shores; its second paragraph follows the course of "a low rakish ship hastening from the tropics" on its way to Jamestown, Virginia, on that same day—an alteration by Brown of the actual 1619 date. The narrator draws the necessary conclusion: "Behold the May-flower anchored at Plymouth Rock, the slave-ship in James River. Each a parent, one of the prosperous, labour-honouring, law-sustaining institutions of the North; the other the mother of slavery, idleness, lynch-law, ignorance, unpaid labour, poverty, and dueling, despotism, the ceaseless swing of the whip, and the peculiar institutions of the South. These ships are the representation of good and evil in the New World, even to our day. When shall one of those parallel lines come to an end?"[54] When, indeed, the novel asks the British reading public.

Jefferson and the nation's tangled history are two interrelated presences that hover over the novel; a third is the flickering presence of their mixed-race incarnation, the novel's fugitive-slave author. Strange as it might seem to introduce a novel with a memoir, Brown preceded *Clotel* with the latest edition of his life story, now updated as "Narrative of the Life and Escape of William Wells Brown" and adapted for an English readership. Stranger yet, he wrote it in the third person, featuring a central character named "William," occasionally interspersing running quotations, some pages long, excerpted from his *Narrative*. The effect is disconcerting to the reader and destabilizing to the text: Brown quoting Brown about Brown.

If Brown, as in his original *Narrative*, failed to maintain a unified grasp over his personhood, the new "Narrative" explains why. It carries the plot of the autobiography up to the present moment in England but leaves off with the author's life in a state of uncertainty subject to other people's negotiations. It concludes by publishing the text of a letter dated February 16, 1852, which Enoch Price sent to one of Brown's English allies, setting down stark terms of sale for Brown's freedom: the money for the body. By printing the letter, Brown returned Price a tit for a tat; if Brown did not own his own body when he composed *Clotel*, he saw to it that Price did not "own" his text. Texts and bodies, bodies and texts, as interchangeable and exchangeable—such was the underlying logic not just of the "Narrative" but also of its companion novel. Both bodies and text were up for sale in a slave-supported capitalistic society based on unchecked possessive individualism.

First, the bodies. The novel's multifaceted plot follows the downstream course of the expendable lives of the members of the three-woman nuclear family of Currer, Clotel, and Althesa as each one faces her solitary fate following sale in Richmond. Brown's ever-recurrent character, the slave trader Walker, now operating on a national scale, purchases Currer and Althesa at the auction, transports them down the Ohio and Mississippi Rivers, and sells them separately, despite their pleas—Currer to a family in Natchez, Althesa to one in New Orleans. Clotel, seemingly more fortunate, falls to a white admirer in Richmond with whom she enters into a liaison and has a "white" daughter, Mary. But when he grows disaffected and marries a respectable white woman of good family, Clotel is sold to a slave trader and transported to Vicksburg, leaving Mary behind in Richmond to suffer the jealous wrath of her father's wife.

These females lose control over their persons in the most basic ways— beginning, as always, with the looming threat of sexual assault. But they also face other infringements on their persons. Clotel's beautiful long hair is cut to the scalp. Mary is forced to labor in the garden in the heat of day to get enough "seasoning" to darken her skin and make it suit her condition. Currer, who previously oversaw her own small house, family, and livelihood, now labors in her master's kitchen among the domestic servants. Althesa seemingly fares the best, winning the affections of a white doctor who purchases and "marries" her. However, in accordance with the language used by some contemporary feminists to correlate marriage with slavery, he also owns her and, in due course, their two daughters. Because he is a Northerner ignorant of slave laws, he fails to take the necessary legal steps to free either Althesa or their two daughters before his sudden death, exposing the daughters—always the girls, in this novel—to sale by his creditors and thereby perpetuating the chain of degradation by another generation of black Jeffersons.

The situation of slave women is not limited to Americans or "true" slaves. Before her death, Althesa tries to assist a white German immigrant woman living in slavery in New Orleans named Salome (or Sally) Miller, who was kidnapped and sold into slavery many years earlier by her employers. In this instance, Brown drew on the well-known saga of Salome Müller, who, after a generation in slavery, won her freedom (though not her children's) in a case decided by the Louisiana Supreme Court. In a related scene, Clotel flees from Vicksburg by steamboat, along with a fellow slave named William, in an escape many readers would have recognized as modeled on that of Ellen and William Craft. To carry it out, Clotel, with her close-cropped hair and light complexion, masquerades as a white male accompanied by her black servant, William. Her disguise is so effective that in a later portion of her escape, as she rides in a stagecoach across Virginia in hopes of reaching her daughter Mary, she inadvertently attracts the romantic gaze of a young, unmarried female passenger, who asks her father to invite Clotel to their home.

These are bodies in perpetual motion. Instead of resting, much less rooting, in one place, held by domesticity, routine, or simply coercion, the women (and the men) in the novel are in a state of constant migration, crossing state, regional, and even national lines before sometimes doubling back (Clotel most dramatically). At a time when the nation was facing off politically in a fierce sectional contest, Brown took bitter pleasure in erasing geographical divisions, treating even the Mason-Dixon line as permeable. Clotel's tangled life is a case in point. Born and raised in Richmond under her mother's roof in seemingly secure circumstances, she gets transported to Vicksburg after her lover abandons her. After years of servitude, she escapes with William to Cincinnati before they go their separate ways—William continuing north to final freedom in Canada, while Clotel travels across Ohio and Virginia and back to Richmond to rescue her daughter. Arrested there as a fugitive, she is transported to Washington, DC, and held in the slave pens, pending return by sloop to Mississippi. Before her master can execute that plan, she escapes again and tries to run to freedom over the Long Bridge connecting Washington to Alexandria, Virginia. Trapped in a state of indeterminacy between North and South, possible freedom and certain slavery, with slave catchers pursuing her from both ends of the bridge, she jumps to her death in the Potomac.

The novel repeatedly plays on the conflation of human and animal that underlay chattel slavery. The primary difference was their "value": Slaves were worth more than animals. So, in the novel, enslaved bodies are routinely bought and sold at market. Or sometimes they are bartered, as when a slave on a Mississippi riverboat stands as collateral for his master's (losing) bet. In one of the funniest episodes in the novel, a fugitive on the run steals his master's pig and uses the pretext, whenever challenged by a white man on his flight to the Ohio River, that he is returning it to "master." When he reaches his destination, he sells the animal and steals himself over the river. And, in its companion piece, two runaways sharing one horse engage in what they call a "ride and tie" charade as they head toward the Ohio River. One rides the horse with the other bound to it by a trailing rope; then, when the bound man tires, they switch positions—the mounted one always ready, when challenged, with the explanation that he is returning slave (and horse) to master. When they reach the crossing, they set the horse free and head toward Canada.

Where, Brown asks near the beginning of the novel, is "the real negro, or clear black" to be found in the United States when their numbers equal only one-quarter of the slave population?[55] As the novel develops, it refuses to settle on a simple demographic explanation but presses on to a radical conceptualization of race as a full-dress masquerade. Black and white, the novel demonstrates in scene after scene, are so impermanent and shifting that they are not even skin deep. The slave trader Walker employs a trusty servant (based on the teenaged Sandy) named Pompey to prepare his "merchandise" for market by refashioning them: changing their complexion, hair color, age, or whatever it takes to make them look lighter or darker, younger, fitter, and happier to prospective buyers. On the other end of the continuum of slave life, the reunited couple of light-skinned ex-slaves George and Mary simply pass as normatively white at novel's end.

Recoloration works in both directions; whites could be made over as readily as blacks, voluntarily or involuntarily. At a time when an increasing number of white entertainers blackened up with burnt cork to sing, dance, or act "black" on the US stage, whites were actually sometimes taken for blacks. Salome Müller was actually taken as a black in a case of intentional racial reinvention, one that Brown might have had in mind when he wrote a play a few years later about a Northern white minister betrayed during a visit down South and sold into plantation slavery. Brown reinforced the logic of reciprocal racial transformation by producing examples of racial confusion in the novel that, for a change, humiliated white figures of power. He retold the well-known story about how Senator Daniel Webster, a villain to Brown for his vigorous support of the Fugitive Slave Law, was refused entry to a Martha's Vineyard hotel because of his swarthy skin color; and how Ohio Congressman Thomas Corwin, whom he dubbed "one of the blackest white men in the United States," faced an act of prejudice over mistaken identity on a steamboat that echoes comparable refusal of service to Brown. Assembled by the dozen in a cumulative indictment against slavery, such episodes, scenes, and stories expose the categorical instability of species, race, gender, region, and nation, the pillars upholding the peculiar institution of slavery.

Second, the texts. Brown absorbed a crucial lesson from Stowe's example about fiction's enormous power in the fight over slavery, but the underlying logic by which he wrote *Clotel* came less from her novel than from the combination of her back-to-back books, *Uncle Tom's Cabin* and *A Key to Uncle Tom's Cabin* (1853), the novel and the documentary source book she subsequently compiled to counter Southern charges the author had fabricated the novel. Though white as New England granite, Stowe was forced to run the authenticity gauntlet familiar to fugitive-slave authors caught in the genre gap between fiction and nonfiction. Like them, she was guilty until proven innocent by outside corroboration.

Safely insulated in his London surroundings and answering chiefly to himself, Brown, though self-designated "a fugitive slave" on the title page, ran no such gauntlet. He simply ran riot over the dividing line between fiction and nonfiction in composing *Clotel*. In effect, he took the two kinds of works Stowe had produced and spliced them into a hybrid, documentary fiction. Like Theodore Weld, master compiler of *American Slavery As It Is*, he foraged through the archives of contemporary print culture, collecting and adapting excerpts from dozens of books, newspapers, magazines, and learned journals: anthologies of music and poetry, speeches, sermons, travelogues, polemics, fugitive-slave narratives, law codes, biographies, hymnals, literature, the Bible, and advertisements. He was not particular about personalities; he appropriated from friend and foe alike: John Scoble and William Lloyd Garrison, Thomas Jefferson and radical abolitionist Thaddeus Stevens, proslavery ministers and antislavery ministers, old friend Harriet Martineau, Washington Irving, abolitionist authors Lydia Maria Child and Grace Greenwood, frequent lecture partner Parker Pillsbury and dear friend William Nell, and of course Weld. As for the two-ship passage in chapter 21 on New World settlement, he appropriated it from a published speech delivered before the New Jersey Supreme Court by Alvan Stewart, the counsel in an 1845 suit brought to free several of the last remaining slaves in that state and to test the legality of slavery under the state's new constitution.[56] In a curious anticipation of future events, he even borrowed a passage from Boston lawyer William Bowditch, who six months later would handle negotiations for his freedom. Altogether, he borrowed about one-third of the novel's contents from printed sources, including his own, in producing his quiltlike novel.

Brown cared less about the authorship of these materials—for this was a novel that challenged the legitimacy of ownership in a society built on chattel slavery—than about their adaptability to his story. A voracious, purposeful reader, he had been collecting his sources over an extensive period of time. Where he accessed them cannot be precisely delineated; what is certain is that after collecting source materials, he cut, shaped, refashioned, and stitched excerpts by the dozens into his text. An occasional stitch even survives in the novel's sometimes flabby paragraphing.

The ultimate source was Brown himself, beginning with the "Narrative" and culminating in the novel's brief "Conclusion," where he claimed that some of his novel's "narratives" came "from the lips of those who, like myself, have run away from the land of bondage. Having been for nearly nine years employed on Lake Erie, I had many opportunities for helping the escape of fugitives, who, in return for the assistance they received, made me the depositary of their sufferings and wrongs."[57] He chose his key word carefully. Their stories were deposited with him on trust, to be redeemed in kind or to be used, if at all, in principled fashion.

He retold all the stories, both those on deposit and those in his archive, in such a way they became interchangeable with both his own tales and his own person. The chief signifier of the book was actually less Clotel than the shifting presence called "William." In the introductory "Narrative," William is both narrator and subject. In the novel, he is both the narrator and the character William who accompanies Clotel on her escape northward from Vicksburg. Although the immediate source of that episode was the Crafts' escape, the story of William the runaway does not end there. In parting with Clotel in Cincinnati, he continues on a flight path that unexpectedly switches from the story of William Craft to that of William Wells Brown. When William boards the northbound train to Sandusky, he suddenly occupies the personal story Brown repeatedly told on the lecture circuit about his own forced removal to the baggage compartment. In the process, William undergoes a physical transformation from being "a tall, full-bodied negro" before leaving Vicksburg to being a slim person, like Brown, weighing 150 pounds.

And where did that leave William Wells Brown, author of *Clotel*? What limited freedom Brown could offer his black characters in *Clotel* lay chiefly in Europe. So it was for him as well. As the year 1854 began, he remained an indeterminate man who had written a narrative of truth about his native land but had accomplished little in resolving his relation to it.

CLOTEL CHRONICLES many tragic unions: slaves with slaves, fugitives with fugitives, and masters with slaves. It sheds little light, however, on Brown's personal life during these years of freedom and self-cultivation in London. He seems to have observed a self-protective policy of silence on the subject following his bruising public battles with Betsey and later with Scoble. The only known rumor linking him romantically with any woman came from Scoble, but Scoble was a dubious source, and his accusation linking Brown to Ellen Craft was implausible. Brown did retain a close, trusting friendship with Ellen and William Craft for years after his departure from England. When William Craft decided, in 1860, to write the story of the couple's escape, he reached out to Brown for assistance with *Running a Thousand Miles for Freedom*.[58]

Once Betsey died in January 1852, Brown would have been free to pursue romantic relationships. Did he? Never more handsome or more socially engaging than during these years of metropolitan living and personal cultivation, he was, in polite social terms, eligible once again in body and category, though within limits. In publishing a generous notice of *Three Years in Europe* in late 1852 that was more promotional than critical, Garrison described his close friend in terms approaching Hamlet's soliloquy about man as "the paragon of animals": "In manners refined, in language and conduct circumspect, in spirit uncommonly amiable, in speech persuasive and eloquent, in person neat and agreeable, he showed himself to be far superior to the average of white men. . . ."[59] Garrison's compliment lends itself to multiple interpretations, but to judge Brown by his subsequent conduct once back in the United States, his hunger for female companionship seems certain. Within months of his return, he entered into the first of at least three romantic relationships that occurred within five years, all with women twenty years younger than he and one with a white woman.

Would he have dared or chosen to cross the color line in London? Such matches were fairly uncommon if not illicit, but Brown was certainly familiar with interracial couples. He closely followed press accounts of the tribulations of one such couple that trailed him from Boston to London. They were the newlyweds Professor William G. Allen and his young white bride Mary King, who arrived in London on the *Daniel Webster* in April 1853 and in no time sought out Brown, who cordially took them around the city and introduced them to friends.[60] Well aware that Allen was nearly tarred and feathered in New York state once word of their relationship became known and that desperation drove the young couple to take transatlantic flight, Brown undoubtedly observed with close interest their reception in good London society. He would have been watching more than just his old friend; he repeatedly took note of light-skinned women passing through the tight straits of racial scrutiny. With the Allens, however, he would have had to observe carefully beneath appearances, since they maintained a smiling posture in public. They initially had plenty to smile about; like Brown, they found London a haven from US racial prejudice.

Rhetoric of tolerance aside, Brown knew the normative limits of English public acceptance. Ira Aldridge was a fascinating case in point. However well Brown actually knew this lavishly talented, barrier-smashing, self-mythologizing actor, he could easily have intuited the challenges Aldridge faced during three decades of high-risk European living. Just months after arriving in England as an unproven teenaged actor, Aldridge married a white woman named Margaret Gill from Yorkshire. The match was generally a happy one, lasting four decades until Margaret's death in 1864, but it was hardly a simple one, as Aldridge frequently conducted liaisons with other white women. Dramatic to the hilt, his life had the quality of *Othello*, the play with which he was most widely associated. Aldridge drew the analogy himself in fancifully describing his initial meeting with Margaret in his curiously third-person memoir. According to his account, she had been sitting in a private box, watching him perform the title role in Thomas Morton's *The Slave*, when he came up by invitation after the performance: "The actor was formally introduced, and in that short interview commenced an intimacy which, six weeks after, ended in his marriage with a lady who was present, the natural daughter of a member of Parliament, and a man of high standing in the county of Berks. The lady played, to some extent, a modern Desdemona to Mr. Aldridge's Othello."[61]

In fact, the lady was no actress and no daughter of a parliamentarian, but the strict truth was never the point: Aldridge's self-fashioning created a fanciful tale of their pairing that suited his flamboyant image. Facts or no facts, his life was a dramatic production that, in matters of origin, race, sex, and marriage, invoked ready-made comparisons with Othello. Playing in that long-running drama exposed him to the most demeaning ad hominem reviews, such as this judgment—just one of many brutal attacks he received in the English press—of the flesh-and-blood man beneath the costume: "That he was a clever man no one who knew him would dispute[;] his powers of tragedy and comedy alike were most marvelous, he was also an educated man, but at the same time, it shocks a sensitive nature to see a pure blonde with almost angelic features and form, putting on a most bewitching smile and using every art of feminine blandishment to win the notice and deserve the esteem of the true, bred 'African Nigger.'"[62] Sensitive natures of the sort this critic wished to protect were not confined to well-bred whites in London or the provinces; Brown himself had run into them in Harwich, Cape Cod, a few years earlier and at various other places where the purity of white womanhood needed defending.

African American performers like Brown and Aldridge developed a well-honed appreciation for *Othello*, a play guaranteed to generate racial waves on both sides of the Atlantic. Such was the subtext in 1849 when *Punch* shot back a cheeky transatlantic riposte to a New Orleans newspaper's fawning report on William Macready's recent local appearance in the play. Well-favored white women, attended by slaves, flocked to the theater to see the celebrated English actor play the Moor. So reported the city's leading newspaper—the same paper, noted *Punch*, that routinely ran advertisements for runaways and slave auctions. The British paper howled at the "ingenuous" irony of Southern racial codes: "Wherefore praise the Othello on the stage, and advertise the black for sale!"[63] But exposure of American hypocrisy was only half of its critique. The other half concerned the more nuanced issue of the inescapably racial quality of performance itself in a land of codified racial discrimination: How dare a white man in the US South play Othello unless he "'reverse the character' [by] playing the Moor as a white man"? Color switching and racial crossing were as tempting as they were dangerous for mid-nineteenth-century adventurous types; they fascinated Brown and lured Aldridge.

Brown could not match Aldridge for insouciance, impetuousness, or charisma. Perhaps for this reason, rumors about personal and sexual transgressions did not stick to him as they did to Aldridge—or as they did, for that matter, to Frederick Douglass and Henry Box Brown. Effrontery and excess were rarely his style; subtlety, indirection, and role reversal were. Of the many roles he played in London, the one that suited him best was, finally, not Othello but W. Wells Brown—a role largely of his own composition, production, direction, and performance, featuring his irrepressible skill at making himself presentable. Did his personal drama also at this time admit room for a lady, whether a Lady Desdemona or simply an attractive young woman without title? No one actually knows.

MORE CERTAINLY, there were two fast-maturing adolescents in Brown's life. Clara and Josephine spent a year in Calais at a single-gender school boarding with about forty other girls, studying the French language, a general curriculum, and deportment. Although Josephine claimed race was never a problem, the experiment ended abruptly in summer 1852 when their father recalled them to London.[64] They soon passed the entrance exam and entered the large, well-regarded Home and Colonial School, whose mission was the training of young women of the middling classes for careers as primary-school teachers or governesses. Brown chose the school presumably on the recommendation of Mary Estlin, whose uncle was one of its directors. Founded in 1836, the school operated according to the socially progressive, child-centered theories of Johann Pestalozzi, regarding women as ideal figures for instruction and providing a justification for (single) women to embark on teaching as a professional career.[65] That was apparently their chosen path, even if in the beginning it was their father who had done the choosing. They soon accepted that career trajectory, and each excelled in her studies. Josephine so impressed her teachers early on that they offered her a position in the elementary school, which she declined in order to complete the program.[66] As the girls progressed through their course of studies, they must have seemed exemplars of the school headmaster's stated mission: They promised to deliver "glorious results."[67]

They successfully passed their exams after eighteen months and graduated around Christmas 1853, well prepared to enter the public sphere as teachers. Whereas Josephine dismissed the prospect of their getting teaching jobs at white schools in the United States, neither she nor Clara had trouble finding suitable employment in England. Shortly after the New Year, Clara accepted a teaching position at Berden, Essex, about forty miles north of London. Josephine stayed closer to her father by taking a job as an assistant teacher at East Plumstead, Woolwich, a part of Greenwich incorporated into Greater London the following year. Her transition was not quite as smooth as she indicated publicly, since the responsible official at the Home and Colonial School failed to communicate word about her "hue" to the administrators of her new school. No insult, however, was intended and none taken, a sign of the comparatively greater tolerance in Victorian England than in the United States. Brown must have felt great paternal pride as he viewed the outcome of years of striving. His daughters had bypassed the barrier of segregated education and come out whole. Not just that—they came out with the kind of formal education he had never been able to achieve. When Josephine occasionally acted as his corresponding secretary during weekend visits to his boardinghouse, he brimmed with pride at her superior writing skill.[68] He had good reason; she formed her letters and punctuated her sentences more correctly than he was ever capable of doing. She had the same formal polish as other young women and men of her generation born of ex-slaves, who surpassed their parents in formal correctness.

All seemed to be proceeding in England according to a higher plan for the reunited Brown family. One dissonant note survives, however, about these talented young women, whose father's allies frequently held them up in London and the transatlantic press as poster girls for "negro" achievement. In spring 1854, just as the sisters were getting established in their new positions, the opinionated Mary Estlin assembled a variety of letters written by multiple correspondents into a packet to be transmitted to Wendell Phillips in Boston. She kept the originals at home, copying their contents in her own hand for Phillips's inspection. Her cover letter explained her overriding purpose: "You have always I believe felt an interest in Wells Brown and his children: so perhaps you will like to read this letter of Clarissa to her governess, and also my aunt's assessment of the two Miss Browns. My uncle J W Reynolds is Secretary of the training school at which they have been studying."[69] Estlin was striking the main chord: assessment. Six years earlier, it had been their father's turn to pass before the prying eyes of the MASS; now, more informally, it was his daughters' turn.

It would be the bright, self-assured fourteen-year-old Josephine who would soon take up the writing of a pamphlet biography of her father, thereby unknowingly entering her subsequently elusive name in literary history. It was Clara, however, who received higher grades from "Aunt" Reynolds: "Clarissa is the more industrious and painstaking. Her sister is rather indolent. . . . I should rather think her opinion of herself was a little too high from what I hear but they have both excited a good deal of interest and I trust may do well."[70] Mrs. Reynolds's judgment was doubtless a bit prescriptive, but her comparative assessment probably matched the opinion of other people of good breeding that Clara was the better-mannered, more conciliatory, and more respectful of the sisters. These traits come through clearly in the letter Clara wrote to her mentor at the Home and Colonial School, which Mary Estlin transcribed for Phillips. It demonstrates how much—and how little—she had matured since she sent Phillips her schoolgirlish letter from New Bedford shortly before their departure. Now approaching her eighteenth birthday, she evidently still meant, or at least knew how, to please. Her report on the "good children" under her tutelage in Essex says as much about her own goodness. She was careful to mention that she played the piano and still read the Bible every day and other "most proper books." (Josephine, by contrast, mentioned in her only known letter of this time that she read her father's antislavery papers.)[71] It is easy to see why respectable adults would be drawn to Clara. As for Brown, he presumably favored Josephine, the daughter with an independent streak who more nearly took after him.

THE PROSPECT of freedom was never remote from Brown's thinking during these years, but its linkage to a geographical location remained unresolved. During his five years in England, Brown could never quite get a fixed bearing on his geo-racial coordinates. Where was home, America or England? Which way did his conscience point? Giving George Green a seemingly permanent residence in Europe at the end of *Clotel* proved easier than determining his own. Many other people raised questions about his intentions, often beyond his hearing. One person who did in print was the clever African American journalist William J. Wilson, writing as "Ethiop" in *Frederick Douglass' Paper* in early 1854. In paging through Brown's "Visit of a Fugitive Slave to the Grave of Wilberforce" in Julia Griffiths' recently issued *Autographs for Freedom*, Wilson mentioned he had once seen Brown from across the street and now thought, after seeing his engraving, that his face looks "rather more British."[72] His closest friends—the Estlins, Webbs, Thompsons, and Richardsons—wondered repeatedly about his long-term plans, all the more after Clara and Josephine had joined him in England. Composed and agreeable in his daily dealings, he generally kept his innermost thoughts to himself.

He was never absolutely certain himself about his plans and lived in a state of continuing indecision. He might easily have decided to settle permanently in London. He loved the freedom from outright discrimination, took pleasure in the life of the metropolis, and enjoyed his many friends. He could take justifiable pride in being the most accomplished black lecturer and writer in the British Isles. Only Douglass among

African Americans had managed to create a comparably active role in the transatlantic antislavery campaign from his base in London, but no one had matched Brown's ability to issue one critically favored book after another or to find so many innovative ways to engage the general public about reform. Even with all these incentives to put down roots, Brown never resolutely adopted England as a homeland, not even while the operation of the Fugitive Slave Law made it theoretically impossible for him to return to the United States as anything but someone else's reclaimable property.

He must have endlessly debated the ethics, as well as the practicality, of payment to Enoch Price for purchase of his freedom. This was one of the most delicate subjects in the antislavery movement. Was it ever justifiable to pay "blood" or "ransom" money to a slaveholder for manumission of human property? Did not such payment justify the underlying claim of ownership in humans? Few subjects more severely tested individual beliefs or more conspicuously exposed the gaps between white–black positions. It was one thing to argue the question from the abstract heights of principle, another to condemn a flesh-and-blood black man, woman, child, or family to choose between exile and a life of unending toil. The issue separated not only comrade from comrade but also white from black. For Brown, it separated the unconditional freedom he wished for himself from the degradation done to people he loved.

There were, of course, well-known precedents. The most celebrated was Douglass, whose freedom the Richardson family had purchased in 1847 while he was a fugitive in England. These charitable, warmhearted Quaker reformers, like Amy Post in Rochester, were the rare individuals who managed to maintain good personal relationships with allies on both sides of the antislavery combat zone. Garrison himself had gotten caught in the middle of the ensuing controversy over his good friend Douglass, using the columns of the *Liberator* to justify "the ransom of Douglass" against stiff resistance put up even by some of Douglass's white (but not black) friends. In 1851, a similar controversy occurred with the transatlantic arrangement for the purchase of James Pennington (who, curiously, had performed the marriage ceremony for his fellow fugitive

Douglass). The reading public on both sides of the Atlantic received the story of this transaction in the form of an uncomfortable joke. Its perpetrator was a white antislavery minister named Thomas Hooker, who had known Pennington in Hartford, Connecticut. Hooker oversaw an intricate three-way transaction, which began with the collection of a ransom fund by Pennington's supporters in Scotland. Legal restrictions in Maryland against direct manumission required the dodge of a third party who would purchase Pennington from the master's estate using the Scottish ransom fund and then free Pennington. Hooker stepped in to execute the transaction in his own name, after which he crossed the Atlantic carrying the bill of sale. He stopped first at the 27 Broad Street offices of the BFASS to exhibit the document, adding a thought for publication possibly timed to coincide with West Indies Emancipation Day:

> I remarked at the opening of my letter, that Dr. P. was in "a fair way of becoming a man." He is not yet completely one. The title to him still rests in me, and it remains for me, by deed under my hand and seal, to "create him a peer of the realm." I shall, however, defer the execution of this instrument for half an hour, till I have walked up and down the whole length of Main-street, to see how it seems to be a slave-holder, especially to own a Doctor of Divinity. Possibly, during the walk I may change my mind, and think it best to send him to a sugar plantation.
>
> P.S. I have returned from my walk. The deed is executed. Jim Pembroke is merged in Rev. Dr. Pennington. The slave is free—the chattel is a man![73]

Hooker's cavalier attitude pointed up more than a racial divide. It highlighted the vulnerability of fugitives like Douglass and Pennington as negotiations concerning their freedom proceeded behind their backs or over their heads.

Brown was also personally familiar with some fugitives, like his Boston/Cambridge friends Lewis Hayden and Lunsford Lane, who had taken the lead in securing funds for their or their families' manumission. He refused on principle to be one of them. He even went on record in the English edition of his *Narrative* to state his refusal to pay blood money to the likes of Price. When supporters in England offered to come to his rescue after his first years there, however, he did not resist. The first serious attempt to raise money for his release came in 1852, through the initiative of his friend Edward Hoare, the respected vicar of Tunbridge Wells, Kent. Better known as a steadfast keeper of the Anglican faith, Hoare took up advocacy of Brown's case, no doubt with Brown's consent. In January 1853, he made a direct offer to Enoch Price to purchase Brown's freedom, although he refused to meet Price's £100 demand.[74] Feeling his right of ownership strengthened by the Fugitive Slave Law, Price refused anything less than the full amount he had paid for Brown.

The subject of Brown's emancipation did not die; it simply went dormant until early 1854, when his dear friend Ellen Richardson initiated a second round of negotiations. Having previously consulted with Hoare as well as Brown, she organized a meeting at the Friends Meeting House in Newcastle upon Tyne the evening of February 15 to raise a fund for his emancipation.[75] Price had by then sliced his asking price by half, and Richardson sent out printed circulars soliciting a total purse of £60 ($300), any excess to be used to defray passage fare for Brown and his daughters.[76] She exercised great delicacy of phrasing in her appeal:

W. W. B. has thought much on the subject [of manumission], but, till recently, has spurned the idea of being bought. It has been distasteful to him, and he did not wish to put his friends to so odious an expense. Still, his present rambling life is also distasteful, and he longs to have his daughters placed in respectable positions in America, where, as a father, he can watch over them and enjoy their society, and where his own efforts in the great cause of emancipation may be more concentrated in their character, and allow of more domestic quietude. If his British friends can ransom him from the possible horrors of slavery without a compromise of either his principles or their own, he is now prepared to be manumitted, and will be very thankful for the boon, though wishful not to have to stir in the matter himself.

Her language slips and slides between her voice and Brown's silence, his private and public lives, his wishes for his daughters and their silence about their ambitions—all running up against a family history that was far more complicated, and possibly conflicted, than she stated or probably knew.

Brown deliberately absented himself from the February 15 meeting. That evening and the next, he was twenty miles up the Tyne in the port city of South Shields, giving multimedia lectures on US slavery illustrated by magic-lantern slides.[77] While Richardson's appeal for funds circulated among friends across the British Isles, Brown continued his annual winter lecture tour to the north of England and Scotland. He spent most of the second half of February based in Newcastle, as responses to Richardson's appeal quickly came in. Within just a matter of weeks, she and Hoare collected the necessary funds and contacted Price to arrange final steps. Once assured of payment, Price executed a deed of emancipation for Sandford Higgins on April 24 and the next day appeared in the Old Courthouse in St. Louis to certify the act with the court clerk. Encouraged by word of these developments, Brown wrote to William Nell in Boston to alert him he expected to return home in June or July. For some reason, however, he delayed his plans, probably due to complications involving the final payment.[78] Not until July 7 did the Boston representatives of the parties finalize the exchange—William Bowditch, the abolitionist lawyer who had sheltered the Crafts in his Brookline home from the Georgia slave catchers in 1850, acting for Richardson and Brown; Joseph Greely for Price. Greely accepted Bowditch's check for the agreed sum of $300 drawn on the Globe Bank, and Bowditch took possession of the deed of emancipation.[79]

While those negotiations proceeded across the Atlantic, another set was unfolding out of public sight within the Brown family. Richardson had represented the ransom fund as a vehicle for the family's reunification in its native land. Such certainly was Brown's wish, but his daughters, now young women of eighteen and nearly fifteen and equipped with teaching certificates, revealed minds of their own. Clara was so pleased with her work in Essex that she informed her father she intended to remain indefinitely in England. Then Josephine also expressed reluctance about returning home. Brown acquiesced, perhaps because he believed their immediate prospects were more promising in England than in the United States. By the time he was able to book his transatlantic berth, however, Josephine apparently had soured on her teaching position and might already have returned to France to continue her studies, as Brown reported in his last public letter from London.[80]

Brown's friends reacted joyously at news of his impending return to America, but the reaction in the white antislavery community was far from unanimous. One of Brown's former lecturing partners, Charles Burleigh, the mercurial long-haired, long-bearded editor of Pennsylvania's leading antislavery newspaper, editorialized against the payment of ransom money. He turned news of Brown's impending ransom into an object lesson for an absolute resistance to slavery regardless of personalities: "We believe it is full time for the opponents of slave-hunting in the North, to make a stand on the resolution that they will neither buy runaway slaves nor permit their recapture. This issue had far better be made on such a man as Wm. Wells Brown, than on a poor, half-brutalized, ragged hod-carrier. . . ."[81] Gay and Garrison, by contrast, defended the purchase of his freedom in the *National Anti-Slavery Standard* and the *Liberator*. Garrison even presumed to plan on Brown's participation in a large antislavery convention scheduled for Syracuse in late September.[82]

While negotiations dragged on in the United States, commentary about the purchase of Brown's freedom continued in public and private on both sides of the Atlantic, and it was still going on as Brown made his last public appearance in England, on August 1. The occasion was the West Indies Emancipation Day celebration in Manchester, one of the largest antislavery conventions of the year. Town Hall filled to capacity for the evening session, where Brown was not just a featured speaker but also a recurring reference point. His fellow fugitive Samuel Ringgold Ward warned him over the heads of the crowd not to return to the United States: no "piece of brown paper" certifying his freedom would shield him from predatory slave merchants making Northern incursions. His old MASS colecturer Parker Pillsbury, then making an antislavery tour of the British Isles, also made a point of publicizing to the convention Brown's pending return. But during a long day and night of speechmaking, it was Brown who captivated the audience with his sweeping eloquence. He could not have spoken his mind so freely, he added, in a final jibe at the BFASS that upset the chairman and no doubt many other attendees, had he been addressing the annual meeting of an organization afraid to speak the unadulterated truth: "Those who want milk and water, let them go to London at [BFASS-organized] anniversary time, and they will get it there, in homeopathic doses."[83] Looking out for the last time at hundreds of British friends and supporters, he cut through the standard antislavery rhetoric in declaring himself, after five years of crisscrossing the land, "almost an Englishman"—an equal and reciprocal retort to George Thompson's earlier compliment that he "had become almost a countryman of ours."[84] "Almost" and "almost" expressed mutual affection but did not quite add up to a match, as Brown made his formal farewell that evening from the English scene.

HE BIDED his time before booking return passage, presumably because he was still awaiting his deed of emancipation from Bowditch in Boston. By the time it arrived at the end of August, he found the next steamer to Boston already filled, so he booked himself instead to Philadelphia on the *City of Manchester*. With traffic on the high seas running heavy at the time, even that ship, one of the largest steamers on the Atlantic, was booked to its 500-passenger capacity. Space was even tighter than normal in steerage, crammed with very large numbers of Irish and German refugees as well as a sizable group of Roma families.

Whereas his outbound voyage had been smooth and swift, this one was swept up in a prolonged tempest that terrified inexperienced passengers and helped to double the passage time. The rough seas affected the people in steerage far more than Brown, who had the luxury of an upper-level berth and the assurance of familiarity with the seas. He brushed up against steerage passengers during the voyage but kept his emotional distance from them and from the inevitable stowaways who surfaced from hiding places once the ship reached open waters. During the peak night of the storm, he descended to the forward steerage to witness a scene the crew considered laughable: Panicked passengers, some screaming as the ship lurched from side to side, were praying so fervently that Brown compared the scene to a camp meeting. An agitated Roma woman singled him out by his ethnic difference, like Jonah en route to Nineveh, and pleaded with him to intercede with God. Brown drily noted her plea—"O, Master! do get down and help us to ask God to stop the wind! You are a black man; may be he'll pay more attention to what you say"—and moved on.[85]

He had arrived in England a self-proclaimed "stranger in a foreign land."[86] Five years later, he was returning home a changed man to a changed nation. During his absence, the legislative war over slavery had so intensified that the threat of violence was in the air. The key accelerant in the war of words was the May 30 passage of the Kansas–Nebraska Act, which, in abolishing the 1820 Missouri Compromise, opened Western territories—even Kansas, north of the old dividing line—to slavery should local "popular sovereignty" so determine.

Even before the enactment of that earthshaking legislation, the passage of the Fugitive Slave Law had effectively reconstituted the Mason-Dixon line as permeable to both slaves and slave catchers, empowering—so claimed abolitionists—the Southern states to extend their reach into Northern affairs. Brown had that altered state of affairs in mind when he told the August 1 audience in Manchester, "We hear of people speak of free and slave States; but I hold there is no such distinction; for now there are no free States in the United States of America."[87] What now was slavery, and what freedom, was a far murkier question than at the time of his departure. He was returning home legally a free man, and nominally at least no longer a biblical stranger in a strange land, but to what prospects? He could have been no more certain as the *City of Manchester* approached the North American coast than he had been when he had set out across the Atlantic five years earlier.

REDPATH'S

BOOKS for the CAMP FIRES

CLOTELLE.

JOHN ANDREW

BOSTON.
JAMES REDPATH,
221 WASHINGTON ST.

Cover of Civil War–era edition of *Clotelle: A Tale of the Southern States* (1864). Courtesy of American Antiquarian Society.

PART 3

Civil War

8

"Upon an Experimental Voyage"

Brown's arrival in Philadelphia was bittersweet. Shortly after disembarking the *City of Manchester* late afternoon on September 26, 1854, he was back among dear friends and familiar associations. He named some of them in a composite tribute he drafted shortly afterward for the last chapter of his soon-to-appear American travelogue: William Still, by now the lead conductor on the coastal line of the Underground Railroad; Lucretia and James Mott, old friends who in 1848 had specifically asked Garrison to lend him to the PASS; Robert Purvis, the respected patriarch of the African American community; Robert Forten, whose daughter he would soon meet in Massachusetts; and James McKim, the leader of the PASS to whom the box containing Henry Box Brown was addressed. They were but a small minority in a troubled city in which Brown considered "colorphobia" more prevalent than in "the pro-slavery, negro-hating city of New York."[1] Even so, his Philadelphia comrades were his closest friends outside of Boston, and Philadelphia was a city he had always found more welcoming than New York. He would have two more chances that fall to visit at greater leisure, but on this occasion he treated Philadelphia as little more than a stopover. Brief as it was, it gave him enough time to experience the limits of freedom for blacks even in the North. He was walking on Chestnut Street alongside two white shipmates from the *City of Manchester*—neither, he noted mordantly, an American citizen—when a streetcar stopped to collect them but refused him entry.[2] For better or worse, he was back home.

He remained only one night before throwing himself into a routine of antislavery activity so familiar it must soon have felt as though he had never left. The next day, he embarked by train on a quick antislavery swing across New York state. Garrison had presumed on Brown's good will by advertising his participation in upcoming meetings, and he graciously complied. The first stop was the major AASS-sponsored convention in Syracuse on September 29–30.

The drain on Brown's energy showed. A report in *Frederick Douglass' Paper* described him in Syracuse as tired and hoarse due to his not yet having gotten his *"land legs"*—no surprise for someone who arrived at the convention only seventy-two hours after crossing the Atlantic.[3] Garrison and Gerrit Smith were locked that afternoon in a "spirited" debate about the constitutionality of slavery when Brown, just off the train, walked into the room at City Hall. The debate paused as the attendees rose to greet him, although one Syracuse paper needed to inform its readers that this returning Brown was "not Box Brown as is generally supposed."[4] During those two days of camaraderie, he shared a platform with many of his oldest friends and colleagues in the movement. Nell, Remond, Garrison, and Lucy Stone had come out from Massachusetts. Also in attendance was local minister Samuel May (cousin of Samuel May Jr.), whom Brown liked greatly and routinely remembered with inscribed copies of his books. He was also fond of Gerrit Smith, the immensely wealthy New York philanthropist and recently a Free Soil congressman to whom he likewise sent inscribed copies from England. And then, of course, there was Frederick Douglass. Had the two men met on easy speaking terms, they could have reminisced their way clear across the British Isles. Brown arrived, however, nursing a private grudge that shortly afterward would break out into open animosity.

Brown spoke both days on a variety of subjects, proudly interspersing remarks about his daughters' education and success as teachers in England. One of his points sparked an immediate exchange of views that continued for weeks in *Frederick Douglass' Paper*. Fresh from the freedom he had enjoyed in Europe, he argued his core belief that slavery was the root cause of racism: "Get out from the stars and stripes, and prejudice against color is unknown. It is prejudice against condition, not color; only the color is a mark to instance the condition."[5] Drawing on his comparative experience, he insisted that the contaminating effect of slavery had become so pervasive within the United States that a person could escape from slavery but not from racially determined caste. He held up his daughters as the living proof: They had never known a day of slavery at home, yet they had never known a day of true freedom until arriving in Europe. What might happen if they returned home was not a question he chose to raise.

The quick eruption of good feelings at Brown's entrance marked only a brief relief from the acrimony that hung over the sessions. In his capacity as president of the AASS, Garrison had opened the convention's proceedings with a call for good fellowship, stressing that the speaker's platform was open to anyone who supported antislavery principles. From that initial ecumenical gesture of shared purpose, the convention quickly descended into bouts of angry disagreement, as Garrison and his allies clashed repeatedly with both Smith and Douglass on various issues, including the resort to violence in the "Jerry Rescue," the 1851 freeing of the fugitive William Henry (nicknamed Jerry) from the Syracuse jail by a large group of abolitionists. At the Jerry Rescue Commemoration that followed the convention, Douglass taunted Garrison: How did he propose to use moral suasion to liberate future Jerrys from behind the iron bars of jail? Or to slip out of the handcuffs that bound his wrists (which Douglass actually produced for effect)?[6] Seriously challenged, Garrison did his best to defend his pacifist, moralist principles—the same principles, he might have pointed out had he wished to return Douglass's bitterness with his own, under which Douglass himself had operated for years.

These two proud, determined men, once close friends, allies, and confidants, had split in 1853 amid an outburst of pent-up accusations. Ever since Douglass had returned to the United States in 1847, struck

off to Rochester for greater independence, and set up shop with an independent newspaper, pressure on their relationship had been intensifying.
Inevitably, lieutenants and adjutants on right and left were forced to take
sides. Quick to go on the offensive, Douglass lashed out at former allies,
sparing few from his combustible anger. No one could long remain neutral, not even amiable, peace-loving William Nell—"the man whom all
know, but to love him," as one of Douglass's correspondents described
him just as the invective began to fly.[7]

These ugly racial and coalitional cracks in the US antislavery movement were all too familiar to Brown, who judged from the moment of
his return that he would need to steer his course delicately around them.
At first, by contrast with Nell, he avoided an open break with Douglass. He took no openly partisan sides during the debates in Syracuse,
while observing the animosities he had previously been reading about in
London in the transatlantic press. From Syracuse, Brown joined Nell and
Remond on the train to Rochester, Douglass's home turf, where he spoke
on October 4 from the podium at Corinthian Hall—that same distinguished podium Douglass had often filled with sweeping eloquence and
slashing wit. Brown had previous acquaintance with the hall from his
days as a lecturer for the WNYASS, but now he spoke as a seasoned ex-
resident of England. On a night of stormy weather that damped down
the crowd, he gave a wide-ranging talk full of personal stories about his
experiences in Europe and the United States. He also took time during
his visit to renew acquaintances with the strong antislavery community
of the city, which included his old friends Amy and Isaac Post, who
would have wished a full rundown not just about his experience but also
about the girls.

Brown then turned eastward and, other than an overnight stop in
Albany, reached Boston for the first time in five years. He had barely
enough time to get a night's sleep, greet a few old friends, and drop off
whatever luggage he had not previously sent by freight before he was
riding the train again.[8] Although his ultimate destination was the anti-
slavery meetings taking place twenty miles away in Lawrence, he stopped
off in Salem to spend some leisure time with Charles and Amy Remond

and join them on drives to enjoy the autumn colors. A constant companion during his visit was the bright, presumptuous teenager Charlotte Forten, a daughter of the Philadelphia family Brown had just left, who was living with the Remonds while attending the well-regarded Salem Normal School. She looked Brown up and down during this visit, noting in her diary that he was "improved greatly both in appearance and conversation" from her earlier recollection. She got an even better chance to size him up when he returned a month later while lecturing in the vicinity. One cold evening around the Remonds' fireplace, as Brown talked about his European experience, her ears perked up when his conversation turned to Clara and Josephine: "He talks continually about his daughters. They must be prodigies. I feel extremely curious to see them, and hope they are as finely educated and accomplished as he evidently thinks they are." A year later, she would have the chance to meet the one who more closely resembled her.[9]

Then it was back to Boston, where he had multiple chores. The most immediate would have been housekeeping. He was using 21 Cornhill as his initial mailing address, but that would not do for long.[10] He had never owned a house, and, with no family and no fixed place of work, he had no reason to start now. If, as seems likely, he chose to board, where did someone set up house after five years of independent living off London's Strand? Although city directories do not list him until 1856, a good guess would be that he returned to the neighborhood he knew best and felt most comfortable in. The 1856 directory listed him as a "lecturer" boarding at 3 Smith Court, opposite Joy Street in the African American neighborhood flanking Beacon Hill.[11] By no coincidence, that was the same house, just around the corner from the African Meeting House, in which the unmarried William Nell had been boarding since returning from Rochester. Since his closest friend was already there by 1854, it seems likely Brown moved in immediately after his return to the city.

Treated as a returning hero in both the black and the white communities, he kept a busy social calendar those first few weeks. One night that month, he crossed paths with Nell in the neighborhood while returning from dinner at the home of the hearty, successful Boston merchant Charles Hovey, a major benefactor of the MASS. Nell found him in a glowing mood, energized after having "Londonized" with Hovey's sons and regaling the family with stories about his foreign adventures.[12] Hovey had himself recently returned from England, but not even he had the range of reference that Brown brought to Boston-area dinner tables and meetings eager for the latest news from England. On several other nights those first few weeks, he joined Nell for supper at the home of Francis Jackson, another major bankroller of the MASS and its longtime treasurer.

The red carpet was officially rolled out on the night of October 13 for a hastily organized MASS greeting at Tremont Temple's neoclassical Meionaon Room, a meeting hall that served Boston's abolitionists in the same way Exeter Hall did London's. Several Boston newspapers sent reporters for this public celebration, and the hall filled with an enthusiastic multiracial gathering. Francis Jackson chaired the festivities, and William Nell introduced Brown as a man now "beyond *Price*" and a link in the "golden chain" of antislavery spanning the Atlantic. Brown was uncharacteristically immodest on this occasion about his years overseas—"My opportunities for becoming acquainted with the institutions of Great Britain have been greater than almost any other American, white or colored"—and expressed his ambivalence at returning from England to the native soil of John Hancock, John Adams, and James Otis after slave hunters of Anthony Burns and Thomas Sims had trespassed on it. Still preoccupied with thoughts of Haitian revolution and independence, he commented at length on the likely international ambitions of US territorial imperialism, which he feared would soon encompass Cuba and, worse yet, Haiti.[13]

Three days later, he was back on the train, this time accompanied by Garrison, for a series of anniversary activities in Philadelphia. He was in buoyant spirits the evening of October 17 as he stepped up to the pulpit to give an invited address to the African American congregation of the Brick Wesley Church. The building was so crowded that Garrison, who arrived late, had difficulty squeezing his way forward to reach a place of honor reserved for him on the podium.[14] On this special occasion, Brown apparently spoke from a prepared text. He found his theme quickly, sweeping up the congregation in an impassioned voyage through African American history prompted by the Atlantic storm he had recently experienced:

> One morning the clouds cleared away, the sun appeared, and the waves ceased. The captain then came on deck with glass in hand, to take the sun, and find out the longitude and the distance. We, the coloured people of this country, have been out upon an experimental voyage, and for more than two centuries we have been surrounded by the most boisterous weather, with clouds obscuring from our gaze the sun of freedom, and our backs in a leaky condition, seeking a safe harbor. Let us, my friends, stop and take the sun, and see where we are.[15]

What did Brown see from the speaker's podium? High seas, rough conditions, and no clear destination for his fellow passengers. But he took comfort in the communal solidarity of the voyage and what he took to be communal faith in Garrison's leadership. His faith would soon be tested, though, as reconciling those two fundamental allegiances would try his adaptability and principle in the fractious years culminating in the Civil War.

Brown spent the rest of the week in Philadelphia attending the women's-rights meetings before jumping into debates at the annual meetings of the PASS. In another communal welcome, James McKim read a resolution honoring Brown's return before introducing him as the main speaker at the evening session on October 23. McKim, who was Garrison's counterpart in the PASS (and future brother-in-law), warmly introduced Brown to the gathering, congratulating him on his good work for the cause in England, which he had seen firsthand, and on the education of his daughters, who by this time were frequently referenced before antislavery audiences on both sides of the ocean. Pacing the podium thoughtfully, Brown sounded like a man trying to establish a meeting ground between his black "I" and his white majority audience's "you." His wide-ranging talk that evening revealed how difficult a feat it was. To effect a union with his audience, he crossed and recrossed rhetorically shifting grounds: "I stand here as the representative of the slave to speak for those who cannot speak for themselves, and I stand here as the representative of the free coloured man who cannot come up to this convention." Again: "I stand before you . . . tonight, not an African nor an Anglo-Saxon, but of mixed blood." And again: "[I speak] not now as an Anglo-Saxon, as I have a right to speak, but as an African." He asserted that he was a full-blooded citizen of the United States by right, but he complained that, twenty years after escaping slavery, he was still a man without a US passport.

His blackness, he admitted, was a problem, but so was their supposedly unspotted whiteness. His explanation ranged across time and space. The whole country had gotten off to a bad start with the federal Constitution, whose three-fifths clause, tolerance for the slave trade, and provision for return of fugitive slaves contradicted the very principle of liberty it was meant to enact and defend. He had a lifetime of personal stories to draw on to exemplify what this heritage meant for blacks—right up to the recent denial of access to Philadelphia streetcars. As though to strike a balance, he goaded his white audience to consider the limits on their freedom: "Where is the right of free locomotion in the slave States? Go into the Southern states an avowed enemy of slavery, and are you free? I point you to the murdered Lovejoy." And on the limits of their heritage: "If I am not a citizen of the United States, pray, are you? Did your father not come from another country?" Furthermore, he reiterated the taunt he repeatedly heard Europeans utter about Americans' unexamined self-superiority over other nations: "I am ashamed when I hear men talking about the national honour of this country being insulted by the Spaniards, or Cubans, just as if we had any national honour to be insulted! A nation that enslaves and scourges one-sixth part of its people talking about national honour!" His overriding point was basic: Their integrity, freedom, and patriotism as white Americans were inseparable from his as a black American.

His speech was a tour de force, drawing on a breadth of experience spanning slavery and freedom, South and North, America and Europe, and incorporating a free-ranging storytelling facility with a cosmopolitanism he had not previously commanded. As all could see and some remarked, Brown had returned from Europe a broadened man. But what, finally, did his speech add up to? Its conclusion was familiarly, even orthodoxly Garrisonian, tracking far and wide only to return to home base by culminating in a plea for national disunion. The times were finally turning in their favor: "The North is arrayed against the South, and you know it, you are become practically co-workers with us. If you do not go as far as we do, you follow in the wake, and are coming up."[16] This claim was true enough, but what did it all mean if the North, blacks and whites somehow united, uncoupled itself from the South? This was actually a vision bandied back and forth across the Mason-Dixon line over the heads of the majority by radicals of the Right and Left, neither side interested in finding common ground to make peace. The great question remained: What would outright separation accomplish for the nearly four million slaves left to fend for themselves? Brown had been moved to tears by Henry Highland Garnet's cross-border plea in 1843 for armed insurrection, but in 1854 he still did not see Garnet's call to arms as the way forward. Nor did he see any prospect of events that might one day return him to the region of his youth.

BROWN'S WHIRLWIND LECTURE TOURS across New York, Massachusetts, and Pennsylvania were one part of his agenda immediately after his return. The other part was literary. The wave of literary productivity he had experienced in England carried on uninterruptedly over the ocean. He returned with purpose, having carefully strategized about what to leave behind and what to transport. He had abandoned most of his accumulated cultural property: the panorama, magic-lantern slides, stereotype plates of his English and American editions, and all but a few copies of his locally produced books. He did, however, transport selected items that had originated in England. Acting as a transatlantic courier, he carried copies of the proceedings of the Manchester convention for distribution in the United States, as well as mail for friends such as William Craft. He must also have brought as many books as he could afford to transport, as well as the engraved plates from *Clotel* for future use. His most irreplaceable possession, however, would have been a portfolio, scrapbook, or some such case containing manuscripts and clippings. Its contents included the text of the address on Haiti he gave at the Whittington Club in May and now intended for publication, and the text of the Joseph Jenkins chapter and other new chapters earmarked for an expanded American edition of *Three Years in Europe*. Knowing British opinion carried oversize weight in the United States, he also packed an array of the British newspaper and magazine reviews he had clipped to use as endorsements at the back of the travelogue. He was fortunate these were not pilfered when one of his trunks was stolen on board the *City of Manchester*.[17]

Following his arrival in Boston, he lost no time preparing the travelogue for publication. On November 10, the prominent Boston publishing house of John P. Jewett and Company announced that *The American Fugitive in Europe: Sketches of Places and People Abroad* was "in press" and due to be published by month's end.[18] So fast a turnaround time—three weeks from Brown's arrival in Boston to a publication announcement—indicated not just a resolve to publish but also a manuscript in an advanced state of readiness. It also indicated an ambition to reach at least as broad a reading public in the United States as he had in the United Kingdom. Jewett was then the country's leading antislavery publisher, with the proven ability to market his books across the North. The astounding success of *Uncle Tom's Cabin*, all the greater for him because Stowe had turned down a profit-sharing offer for percentage royalties, had bankrolled his operation and also earned him a deep fund of professional capital. At the same time, its runaway popularity also proved a great success for the whole antislavery sector of the publishing industry, an unmistakable demonstration of its growing overlap with mainline commercial publishing after years in which the two sectors kept a wary distance.

Brown took preemptive steps to adapt the book to the American market, though without toning down its tough anti-American rhetoric. The blunt assertion of national difference he had made in the opening chapter of his English travelogue stood unchanged in the American version except for the Americanized spelling: "But no sooner was I on British soil, than I was recognized as a man, and an equal. The very dogs in the streets appeared conscious of my manhood. Such is the difference, and such is the change that is brought about by a trip of nine days in an Atlantic steamer."[19] A dozen new chapters filled out his account of life in Britain, highlighting the breadth of his contacts and his self-dedication to a cultivated life of letters. The effect was to make the point even clearer than in the earlier volume how hard Brown had worked to introduce himself to Western culture.

The new chapters connected him to a broader array of prominent people and places, including Joseph Jenkins, but only one of them changed the book decisively. That was the last chapter, written shortly after his return to Philadelphia, which completed the transatlantic circuit of an Anglo-African-American life. Brown did not concede his return to the United States lightly. "What a change five years make in one's history!" was the fitting opening to this chapter. He could now answer the questions that had preoccupied him when he set out across the Atlantic five years earlier: Who was he? Where was home? What was his mission? He was now home, seemingly on solid ground, in the United States, and he resolved "not to be a spectator, but a soldier—a soldier in this moral warfare against the most cruel system of oppression that ever blackened the character or hardened the heart of man."[20]

He could expect his book to receive aggressive promotion from Jewett, a committed ally of the abolitionist movement with ties to Garrison. Never one to spare expense, Jewett had the book handsomely printed between boards, illustrating it by reusing the steel engraving of Brown originally prepared for the Gilpin edition, and he arranged for joint distribution with his brother's firm in Cleveland and a partner in New York City. He lived up to his reputation as one of the most flamboyant promoters of his time by investing heavily in advertisements, which he ran for months. Playing on its novelty, one of his long-running ads characterized *The American Fugitive* as "a book to be read and pondered, as the production of a colored man, once a slave, the representative of a despised race. God only knows how many William Wells Browns and

Frederick Douglasses may at this moment be grinding in the Southern prison house."[21] He even found a place for it inside the front cover of a New England railroad guide, an appropriate place for a book likely to appeal to the traveling public.[22]

Jewett also spared no expense in distributing review copies to the press. In the days and weeks following publication, reviews poured in from newspapers and magazines across the Northeast and Midwest, some quite revealing. As in Great Britain, many reviewers made race the central issue, as when the *New York Tribune* paid Brown a backhanded compliment by stating he wrote as though he had "Caucasian blood."[23] The publishing trade journal *Norton's Literary Gazette* singled it out, among other new books, as a work "strung together on an ever-visible *black* thread."[24] A reviewer for a Providence newspaper, who had been handed the book by an acquaintance at the Meeting Street Grammar School, wondered how "a man, black or white, who has enjoyed so few opportunities of acquiring a knowledge of men, places and books, can write so well—so correctly, so pleasantly, and so beautifully.[25] The reviewer for an African Canadian newspaper praised the book as "the best, in our judgment, that has yet been written by a colored American."[26] The *Congregationalist*, a Boston religious weekly with a mildly reformist bent, made what was actually one of the most extravagantly perceptive commentaries by setting it side by side with Josiah Nott and George Gliddon's blatantly racist *Types of Mankind*: "It is lively and very readable, and may be perused with much advantage by those who are demonstrating their own baboonity by endeavoring to prove a physiological relationship between that animal tribe and the negro race. If Mr. Gliddon is yet alive in sufficient size to make it pay, we wish Mr. Jewett would mail him a copy."[27]

Once Brown had seen *The American Fugitive* into print, he did the same with his lecture on Haiti, now called *St. Domingo: Its Revolutions and Its Patriots*. His publisher was Bela Marsh, who had kept editions of *Narrative of William W. Brown* and *The Anti-Slavery Harp* in print during his absence. Marsh issued *St. Domingo* as an inexpensive thirty-eight-page pamphlet within days of publication of *The American Fugi-*

tive. Brown was carrying freshly printed copies of both when he set out for a long speaking tour of New York City and Philadelphia in mid-December. On December 20, he delivered a version of *St. Domingo* at the historic African Episcopal Church of St. Thomas in Philadelphia. He followed up that talk with a formal lecture series before the city's well-regarded Banneker Institute, which the *Liberator* called "the first attempt of a colored man to give a course of Lectures, embracing other topics than the anti-slavery subject."[28]

Brown ranged widely in these lyceum-style talks—one night on notable people and places of England and France, another on "The Humble Origin of Great Men," and a third on "Mahomet and Confucius," delivered before the Banneker's literary society.[29] The most politically relevant was "St. Domingo," which set forth an impressive commentary on the parallel but alternative history of slavery and emancipation in the Caribbean. Brown's viewpoint was relentlessly comparative, as when, in the published essay, he provocatively ranked the founding fathers of the two nations:

> Each was the leader of an oppressed and outraged people, each had a powerful enemy to contend with, and each succeeded in founding a government in the New World. Toussaint's government made liberty its watchword, incorporated it in its constitution, abolished the slave-trade, and made freedom universal amongst the people. Washington's government incorporated slavery and the slave-trade, and enacted laws by which chains were fastened upon the limbs of millions of people. Toussaint liberated his countrymen; Washington enslaved a portion of his, and aided in giving strength and vitality to an institution that will one day rend asunder the UNION that he helped to form.[30]

In both the lecture and the printed text, Brown was offering his audience more than a lesson in comparative history. Given Southern territorial ambitions for the spread of slavery, the future of Haiti might one day become part of the future of the United States.

AMID THE BUSY ROUTINE of lectures and authorship in the weeks after his return, Brown apparently initiated a more personal affair. In late November, he accepted an assignment to lecture in Rhode Island. The state antislavery society lacked energy, and the managers of the MASS thought Brown might be the person to galvanize it into renewed activity. Brown accepted their offer, traveling frequently across the state during the last six weeks of 1854, and more occasionally during the first three months of 1855. The routine was the usual in most regards: He lectured wherever crowds could be assembled, stirred up local communities and organizations, and then continued on his way. But one thing might have been different: There is some evidence he struck up a romantic relationship during the course of these travels.

The source is the testimony left by Elizabeth Buffum Chace, a strong-minded antislavery and women's-rights activist who lived with her family in a large house on the Blackstone River north of Pawtucket (today's Central Falls). Brown and Chace knew each other fairly well at this time, since Brown used her as his primary contact person in Rhode Island and stayed at her family's large house when lecturing in the immediate vicinity. The house, as he well knew, was a station on the Underground Railroad, and the Chaces were one of New England's proudest reform families, with Yankee roots running down to Puritan bedrock. Her father, Arnold Buffum, was one of those founding fathers of the AASS whom the young William Nell saw in action that snowy 1832 day through the church window, and Elizabeth was to the manor born and raised.

She and her family had warm feelings for Brown. Her daughter Lillie remembered him "as a handsome and amiable man who enjoyed and added to the minor pleasantry of daily occurrence."[31] But he was enjoying more than minor pleasantry during his visits, according to Lillie's mother. Observing him closely, she became convinced he had formed an attachment to one of her domestics, a sixteen-year-old Irish servant she identified only as "M." in her journal. She allowed the affair to progress only so far before she put an end to it, so her daughter claimed, because she objected not to the racial but to the class differences between the teenaged M. and the forty-year-old Brown. M., she believed, "could not have associated with the people that he did."[32]

Did this romance actually happen, and did it happen this way? Brown never discussed this (or any other romantic) relationship in surviving sources, and no other source corroborates it. But it is not just plausible: It fit the pattern of romantic relationships into which he would enter in the years after his return home as a free man. The Chaces, a wealthy family, did employ servants of Irish or Anglo-Irish background in 1854. Two of them, Mary Macy and Mary Crape, were listed at the time of the 1860 federal census as twenty-year-old residents of the Chace family house. One other fact strengthens the likelihood of an affair with one of these two women. Each fit the female profile to which Brown was repeatedly drawn after Betsey's death: women a generation younger than he and light skinned. Even though M.'s whiteness deviated categorically from this general pattern, nothing in his views or social practices would have made marriage to a white woman implausible or unacceptable. Whiteness was a quality he had lived with his whole life and to which he felt a natural, if complicated, connection.

One other serious matter preoccupied him in late 1854 and early 1855. On November 18, he purchased a copy of Reverend Nehemiah Adams's new book, *A South-Side View of Slavery*—from the MASS book depository, of all places.[33] Why was a flagrant apologia for slavery sold by an antislavery organization? Brown intuitively grasped the reason: The book's fervent defense of slavery made possible the best offense for activists like him. The book was full of high-minded assertions such as the following, sure to infuriate him: "Never, we are constrained to think, could slavery have existed so long amidst such influences of Christianity as prevail in this country, and such efforts of the southern people themselves to abolish it, were it not that God intends to use us as the chief instruments of good to the African race."[34] It was one thing for such propaganda to be produced in the South, the "Sodom of this country"; it was even worse to come out of the mouth of a respected Northern minister.[35] Brown stewed over the book for a year before he figured out the ultimate response, but meanwhile, he held "South-Side" Adams to account on the lecture circuit.

Brown continued to lecture for the AASS in Rhode Island into early 1855, but one night, while home in Boston in early February, he found time to attend a neighborhood event held at the Twelfth Baptist Church on Southac Street. Its purpose was to honor the superintendent of the adult education school on Belknap Street, where a population heavily composed of ex-slaves was taught the basics of literacy and religion. Lewis Hayden, "as their chosen medium," came forward to make the formal presentation, and people in the assemblage called out to Brown to address this audience of his peers. Moved by the occasion, he recited the narrative of his own experience gaining literacy and shared his observations of visiting ragged schools in Edinburgh established to educate the children of the city's poor. Feeling himself in his element, he "struck a chord that vibrated through the experiences of many of his hearers."[36]

Early in 1855, the AASS invited Brown to go on an extended lecture tour of Ohio. He gladly accepted, as it provided a welcome opportunity to return to former haunts. In packing his bags, he presumably took the precaution to include his freedom document, that sheet of paper Samuel Ward had mocked as too flimsy to hold off slave catchers pursuing their trade. He departed Boston by train on or around March 1, stopping first at Springfield to speak at antislavery meetings in towns along the Connecticut River Valley, then using Springfield as the jumping-off point for the long trip westward by rail. The first leg passed via Pittsfield to Albany, a route over the Berkshires familiar from earlier trips. Not ten miles out of Pittsfield, however, without warning, the car in which he was riding derailed in the middle of a late-season snowstorm. Brown was so immersed in reading a volume of Dante that he was caught wholly by surprise. The first violent lurch nearly knocked the book out of his hands; then, as the car plunged off the embankment into a snowbank, he was hurled so forcefully out of his seat that his head bounced off the ceiling. People in his car were thrown in all directions, seats were broken into pieces, and the heating stove was overturned. Chaos and panic set in as passengers realized the doors were jammed shut. A French-speaker got himself jammed into a window too small to exit, another person began shouting the Lord's Prayer, a woman fainted, and no one could get out. Brown, not seriously injured, tried to right the stove; with no exit, there was little more to be done than restore order and try to keep warm until help arrived.[37] Eventually a rescue train arrived and hauled them off to Albany, where he was composed enough to deliver his lecture that night as planned.

The next day, he continued on to Buffalo, where he visited old friends, gave one lecture, promised to give more on his return east, and then set off for Cleveland. Although his assigned territory was actually eastern and southern Ohio, he lingered long enough to make the acquaintance of William Howard Day, whom he found to be one of the most impressive African Americans of the rising generation. Day, whose early education included training in a printing office, had graduated from Oberlin Institute in 1847 as the only black student in a class that included Lucy Stone. Although not a Westerner by birth, he chose to remain in Ohio and found work as a reporter for the *Cleveland True Democrat*. He gave his best energies, however, to the antislavery movement and quickly emerged as one of the West's leading activists. In 1853, he founded the first African American newspaper in the West, the *Aliened American*.[38] By the time Brown arrived there, a city he remembered as having only a fledgling African American community now had its own independent newspaper and communal institutions. He found Day thoroughly impressive and took pride in his achievements as reflecting on the entire community's.

Continuing southeast, he reached Salem, "the centre of radical antislavery in the Buckeye State," by March 19 and spent several weeks lecturing in its general vicinity. He then crossed the state on the "new and rather rickety railroad" via Dayton to Cincinnati, his primary destination, reversing the track of his flight twenty-one years earlier on the Underground Railroad. He had a full agenda in Cincinnati, including giving a lecture at a black church and playing a central role in a major antislavery convention, but he arrived with one overriding desire: to return to the Public Landing to see whether he could retrace his first steps toward freedom on that frigid New Year's Day in 1834. Although the city had since grown fivefold, to nearly 200,000 residents, he easily located the spot on which he made landfall by taking his bearings from recognizable nearby buildings. As he walked along the wharf, he could clearly see across the river the "mean looking buildings in Covington, and its deserted streets," contrasting Covington's squalor to Cincinnati's booming waterfront as an accurate picture of the cost slavery exacted on all whites as well as blacks. That afternoon, he returned through the back lots of the city to see whether he could locate the marsh where he had taken refuge until sundown, but the expanding city had paved it over with brick houses.[39] Alluding to a book that seemed a frequent companion, he noted that the experience of playing Robinson Crusoe in search of footsteps along the river bank left him with "strange feelings." Wherever he went in Cincinnati, the message was the same: The city had changed, and so had he.

He poked around Cincinnati a bit but used most of his preconvention time to fill lecture engagements up the river. One day in early April, he boarded an Ohio River steamer for the first time since escaping from Enoch Price's *Chester*. Traveling southeast around the big bend in the river, he dipped deep into keenly contested territory, now buzzing with antislavery activity and border-crossing slave catchers, but that was not the reason he found the trip so unsettling: "[I] lost my dinner, or rather failed to get it, because I would not eat with the *servants*." He got off at the port city of New Richmond, Ohio, where he spoke that evening before a large audience. Afterward he spent the night as the guest of Thomas and Susanna Donaldson and their family, frontline abolitionists originally from Swansea, Wales, who welcomed him warmly into their fine riverfront house. The next day, with spring just coming on, he sat in their pleasant parlor writing in his notebook as he observed flatboats and rafts descending the river. From his chair, he could even see slaves toiling in a field on the Kentucky side.[40]

During this emotionally charged month in southern and eastern Ohio, Brown saw just about every shade of slavery. While upstate, he met no fewer than eight fugitives at various way stations along the

Underground Railroad.[41] Wherever circumstances allowed, he drew them out in conversation in his customary inviting fashion. One family particularly intrigued him. A blonde, blue-eyed mother and a child in arms, they were "white slaves"—she the daughter of her master, her even fairer infant the son of the same man, who had sold away her husband "to get him out of the way." A second family recounted another recognizable history. The husband had escaped from Virginia and established a farm in Canada. Now he had come back to rescue his wife, whom the master refused to sell. He hid nights inside the hollow of a tree until he could make contact with her and lead her away; Brown now met them on their flight to Canada. While staying with the Donaldsons, he met yet another family with a familiar history—a fugitive father and little son who ran away after their wife and mother was forcibly separated from them.

There was also one enslaved person whom he read about but never actually met: a teenager named Rosetta Armstead, currently incarcerated in town while her freedom suit was making front-page news in Cincinnati and across the antislavery network. Although such cases were typically too common to generate broad publicity, hers was newsworthy due to the identity of her master, a Kentucky minister named Henry Dennison—better known as the son-in-law of former president John Tyler than for his own accomplishments. Although Brown did not get to see her, he did spot her "claimant" in town. He also observed a person more to his interest, her distinguished lawyer Salmon Chase, a former US senator from Ohio well respected by most abolitionists as one of their few defenders in Washington. Chase had recently played a major role in founding the new Republican Party, and, after failing to win the party nomination for president in 1860, served Abraham Lincoln as secretary of the treasury before Lincoln nominated him to succeed the reactionary Roger B. Taney as chief justice of the Supreme Court.

By the time Brown addressed the Cincinnati convention, he was in a rollicking good mood, regaling the crowd as usual with a repertoire of personal stories, some more inventive than others. One was the story, perhaps arising out of Cincinnati associations, about taking his daughter to Enoch Price's hotel in London. Another was a sly parable about antislavery commitment that pitted him in a competition with Nehemiah Adams over moral resolve. Shortly after his escape, when he still feared looking "the white man" in the face, he had stopped in a Massachusetts town to deliver an antislavery talk but found the local clergyman initially unwilling to open his church for the talk. As slight followed slight, Brown added them to the inventory of charges he planned to press against the church and its ministers as soon as he got a platform. Gradually the minister relented, opening up his church, then his house, to Brown. The seduction continued: The minister and his wife seated him in a comfortable rocking chair, addressed him with civility, offered him tea, added an extra lump of sugar. For each kindness received, Brown deleted an item from his list: "What a good woman. I'll cut some of the hard things I was going to say about her church," "What a good man, I'll scratch a little more off," until he was finally ready to erase everything and, like Nehemiah Adams, declare total absolution. But when their daughter went to the piano to play for him, he snapped back to his senses, the girl's presence reminding him of his sister's absence.[42]

This was his third trip across Ohio, each made at a decade-long interval, giving him a clear comparative perspective. This particular trip registered on him as an exhilarating reckoning with his past. Now legally and personally free, he felt as though he had banished the ghost of his earlier self, something more recent fugitives had not yet done. He took heart at what he was witnessing: The entire antislavery enterprise was thriving in Ohio, with new branches of the Underground Railroad running in every direction and, as he joked, shares of the joint stock company selling "above par."[43]

Brown's reputation as a lecturer had never been higher. One of the two dueling African Canadian newspapers called him "the most powerful speaker among the antislavery coloured men of the States" and hoped he would soon come to Canada to lecture.[44] That was an exaggeration at any time when Frederick Douglass was active, but it might have buoyed Brown's feelings at a moment when he was embroiled in a nasty feud with Douglass that eventually erupted into public view. In the months after his return, Brown apparently had complained to Boston friends that Douglass had tried to prejudice a female friend in England (probably Anna or Ellen Richardson) against his mission shortly before he arrived in that country. The two rivals exchanged charges and countercharges through the mail before Douglass took the fight public in his newspaper. Professing friendship for "our distinguished brother" but not for the AASS, he called on Brown in early March to state frankly the grounds for his animosity.[45] Brown immediately responded by publicly calling out Douglass man to man: "Let me say to you, Frederick Douglass, that my difference with you has nothing to do with the American Anti-Slavery Society, and no one knows that better than yourself," before giving a full accounting of Douglass's allegedly devious conduct.[46] Douglass published "A Reply" immediately beneath Brown's letter, and there the matter came to rest—at least in public.

But the conflict between the two men was so deep-seated that it lingered for months. When they unexpectedly crossed paths in Boston one night in November 1855, Brown ignored Douglass's greeting and walked on.[47] Even as England receded as a battleground worth contesting, their differences remained live and substantive, reflecting the deepening split in the black community during the mid-1850s, when a radicalizing minority of disaffected people, mobilized by the increasingly strident character of national politics, drifted away from white antislavery organizations to black activism of a sort personified, in different ways, by Douglass, Delany, and Garnet. The acuteness of African American resentment against seeming friends and allies occasionally exploded in outcries of grievance. One bolt of lightning flashed across the Atlantic from England, where the black Samuel Ringgold Ward and the white Parker Pillsbury, engaged as lecturers for groups at cross purposes, attacked each other nearly as mean-spiritedly as they did the common enemy. Ward's counterattack to Pillsbury's repeated aspersions against his antislavery politics was ferocious: "I ask, once more, is not this the animus of the overseer?"[48]

In the heat of the moment, Ward implied little to nothing had changed. But a great deal had, and one unmistakable sign was Ward's freedom to publish his unexpurgated views in an independent black press. *Frederick Douglass' Paper* was open not just to him but also to the broadest possible range of black opinion. The rising black intelligentsia of the 1850s made free use of it, as Brown had in England. After he returned, however, his relations with Douglass were so compromised that the paper was no longer open and friendly to Brown. The loss of the main organ for black expression would have severely restricted most of his African American contemporaries, but to Brown it made little practical difference. During the late 1850s, he would find one alternative pathway after another for speaking his mind to the public.

BROWN'S SCHEDULE through summer 1855 was packed with tours of Massachusetts, New Hampshire, and Maine, where he claimed audiences were less prejudiced than anywhere else in New England. He was still in the middle of his monthlong tour of Maine when he received word that Josephine had arrived in New York, having returned from England on the *Baltic*, which docked on August 8.[49] The only surprise to Brown would have been that only one daughter actually arrived when he was expecting two; in a public letter dated August 6 from Maine, he spoke of "the return of my daughters."[50] No details have survived about the passage, although the passenger manifest singles out Josephine in one curious way: She was the only passenger, male or female, listed by her given name rather than by an honorific, initials, or as someone's companion—whether as a result of race, gender, age, or some combination. The celebrity among her fellow passengers was the gun manufacturer Samuel Colt, whose display her father had visited in 1851 at the Crystal Palace. Colt was by 1855 one of the leading weapons manufacturers in the world and had recently built a Thames-based factory in London that produced guns for the huge European market. An equal-opportunity merchant with no vested interest of any sort in slavery, he also sold guns to both North and South right up until the attack on Fort Sumter. Only when the *New York Tribune* and the *New York Times* accused him of treason did he desist.[51]

All of Josephine's comings and goings at this point in her life have long seemed obscured by a transatlantic fog. On a handful of occasions in 1854–55, Brown had told the public that she was then living in France, a report that, though unconfirmed, was probably true. Why in mid-1855 she chose to leave France a second time, just a year after she chose to leave England, can only be conjectured, but these movements foreshadowed the restlessness she would shortly display back home. Once she informed her father about her intentions, Brown presumably asked his English contacts to help her make the necessary arrangements, which would have included finding a suitable escort for the voyage. As she had gone out in 1851 escorted by Charles Spear and George Thompson, so now she came back in the company of Horace Greeley, who was returning home from a long stay in France and England.[52] Greeley might simply have been offering a gentlemanly courtesy, but he knew Brown by reputation and surely had crossed paths with him at antislavery events in New York and London. More curiously, he presumably knew he was bringing home the daughter of Betsey Brown, who five years earlier had sent his newspaper an accusatory letter about the girl's father.

When Josephine stepped off the train in Boston two days after landing in New York, it was not her father, not yet back from Maine, who greeted her but the ever-loyal William Nell. He, for one, was well pleased to see her. In place of the immature girl he had last seen in 1851 now stood a fully grown young woman, though still only sixteen—"quite tall, accomplished, and well-appearing." Brown cut short his trip and returned to Boston a day or two later. The reunion was to all appearances joyous. On seeing father and daughter together, Nell was struck by their close relationship: "Her father seems remarkably devoted and she as cordially reciprocates."[53]

Charlotte Forten also noticed a tight bond when father and daughter paid a visit to Salem a week later, arriving by chance on Forten's eighteenth birthday. She was more than a bit curious to take the comparative measure of this faintly exotic creature about whom she had heard so much: a young lady of color nearly her age, liberally educated and trained as a teacher, and raised like her to move in good middle-class society. She was cautiously predisposed to take a favorable view: "I think

I shall like her. Her father's fondness for her is rather too demonstrative. I guess she is a sensible girl. I enjoy talking with her about her European life. She is pleasant and communicative, and though coming lastly from England, has, I think, lived in France too much to acquire a great deal of that reserve which characterized the manners of the English."[54]

Having Josephine back home put barely a crimp in Brown's busy lecture schedule. Although he had taken her to the Remonds in Salem to introduce her to his friends, his ulterior purpose was to use their comfortable house as a base of operations while giving lectures on the North Shore. Two days after they met Forten, Brown lectured in nearby Manchester to a full house at the Congregational Church, with Josephine present, on a biblical text (Matthew 12:12) that had a particular immediacy for an ex-slave: "How much better is a man than a sheep?"[55] She also joined him on some of his fall travels in Massachusetts and Vermont, occasionally taking a turn speaking. But that was certainly not all she was doing that fall. One other task was the search for a teaching job, the logical position for a young woman of her background, education, and training. She apparently did not have the same result she had had in England, although how hard she exerted herself is an open question.

Meanwhile, back in London, her older sister Clara had embarked on a different course. On October 8, when Brown and Josephine were probably on a speaking tour in Vermont, Clara married a Swiss watch engraver named Fritz Alcide Humbert. The wedding took place at St. Anne's Church, Westminster, in a ceremony performed by the Anglican rector, Nugent Wade.[56] Clara had led her father to believe she and her new husband would soon be coming to live in the United States, but almost immediately after the wedding she corrected that impression to say they would remain abroad indefinitely.[57] In time England became her permanent home, and she never returned to the United States, even for a visit.

Brown was delighted to have even one daughter near his side, and that fall Josephine paid him a special kind of homage. He must have watched with pride as the daughter who had learned her ABCs in the family's Buffalo home and later served as his occasional secretary in London now used her literary skill to take a hand in writing his biography. *Biography of an American Bondman*, she claimed, originated as a response to repeated inquiries by her French schoolmates about her father's life in slavery. She stated in its preface that she wrote the first ten of its twenty-four chapters in France; the remainder she presumably composed in Boston.[58] But the printed name of the author, "By his Daughter," undoubtedly missed the mark by half. It took at least two hands to compose this book, and one—probably the dominant hand—was her father's.

To judge from her book, Josephine had comparatively little firsthand information about her itinerant father's early life. From the start, she indicates she is telling her father's life story "as I had heard the incidents related," but the chief sources, from beginning to end, are his published works, not his oral recollections. The account she composes of her father's life is a mostly paraphrased or loosely quoted retelling from published sources—the portion covering slavery, mostly from his *Narrative*; the portion covering the arc of freedom from Cleveland to Great Britain, from the introductory biographical sketches in *Three Years in Europe* and *Clotel* and sizable excerpts from the English and American versions of the travelogue (the latter possibly in manuscript). She also had access to some of his private papers, including his St. Louis court documents, as well as his personal copy of the 1848 edition of the *Narrative*. According to biographer William Edward Farrison, who acquired this unique Brown artifact in the mid-twentieth century, Josephine incorporated some of her father's handwritten changes to chapter 1 into her text—unless, as may well be true, Brown did it himself.[59]

One of the most interesting features of the book is its epigraph from Nehemiah Adams's *South-Side View*: "Let us not insist that the slaves shall never be separated, nor their families broken up." Whoever selected it—Josephine, or more likely Brown, who at the time was preoccupied with Adams—quoted it only to contest its untruth. Whoever it was, father and daughter would have passionately agreed between themselves that the peculiar institution did incalculable damage to the families of the enslaved.

Brown lost no time going through the familiar routine of arranging for its publication. He contracted with Robert Wallcut, manager of the *Liberator* printing office, who minimized expenses by assigning the manuscript to in-house printers. The work came out shortly before Christmas as a no-frills, unillustrated, 104-page pamphlet. It carried the unofficial endorsement of the MASS and circulated, like Brown's *Narrative* and *The Anti-Slavery Harp*, through the antislavery network. Garrison published a duly flattering review in the *Liberator*, and Brown did what he could to disseminate copies during his lectures. At some unspecified date, he bought a dozen copies from the MASS book depository, but he must have distributed as many copies as he could to help the book along.[60]

"The Bondman and His Daughter," as labeled by the *Liberator*, spent considerable time together that first winter. Nell spotted them sitting on Christmas Day in the office at 21 Cornhill. On observing Nell writing a letter to Amy Post, Brown directed Josephine to send Post a copy of the book.[61] Father and daughter spent much of the first half of the winter together on the lecture circuit across eastern and central Massachusetts. At City Hall, Fitchburg, on January 12–13, 1856, they joined forces with Garrison on the podium for the Worcester regional antislavery convention. A few nights later, Josephine, for once appearing under her own name, gave an invited lecture in the Millbury Lyceum on "The Bards of Freedom"—a subject of compelling interest to her father as well.[62] She soon reunited with him to lecture in Town Hall in South Reading, impressing a listener with her "very prepossessing" appearance and "chaste and clear elocution, which acted like a spell upon that large audience." No sooner, however, did that reporter predict that "she promises to be an effective pleader for those in bondage" than her name disappeared from the antislavery record, then and forever.[63] Her plans had changed, and soon so would her life.

WHAT HAPPENED to Josephine Brown has long been a subject of confusion. Shortly after publication of *Biography of an American Bondman* and her lyceum talk, she seems to have disappeared from public view. Historians looking for the author of this pioneering work of African American biography have been unable to discover a trace. Brown's biographer, William Edward Farrison, made the educated guess that she set off for Europe about that time and never returned home.[64] That was a plausible enough surmise; she was multilingual, felt freer of the constraints of racism in Europe than in the United States, possessed professional and personal skills that might have secured her a comfortable existence, and had many friends and contacts, including a married sister. But Farrison made his surmise without giving any source, and no evidence of her presence in Europe has turned up.

He apparently looked the wrong way. The evidence is sketchy, but it indicates she remained in the United States, where her life took a sharp wrong turn in 1856–57 and possibly never righted itself. In August 1857, William Nell confided startling news to Amy Post that was just beginning to circulate through rumors: "By the bye the friends of Wm. Wells Brown are pained at what seems to be the degeneracy of his daughter Josephine; She has lost her good name; please (as I know you will) make judicious use of this which I am afraid is more than idle rumor. He has appropriated much money and devotion upon his daughters and I grieve for his feelings; but she may yet redeem herself." And a few days later: "Please [do] not mention to Sarah P. Remond [sister of Charles] when she visits Rochester or indeed to any one else what I whispered concerning the Daughter of WWB. No one need to know who told you, though Mr. Brown himself has just now for the first time spoke [sic] on the subject to me. I am very sorry—he feels sad about it and deserves better."[65] What act had Josephine committed that could have elicited such strong terms from Nell as "degeneracy" and as requiring her "redemption," and what state of mind could have compelled Brown to hide his feelings for months from even his closest friend?

The most plausible answer seems to have been an act or pattern of promiscuity. Even prostitution is not out of the question. In September 1856, several US newspapers published a nearly identical report about two female teenagers dressed as sailors who were picked up by New York City police on lower Broadway for vagrancy or solicitation. One account added that they had until recently lived in a "house of ill-fame."[66] Was the one who identified herself as fifteen-year-old Josephine Brown from Canada actually Brown's Josephine? That question has no definite answer. But later there comes indisputable confirmation of her loss of respectability in the black community—the source was her distant peer Rosetta Douglass. The favored daughters of the two esteemed leaders had never met, but Rosetta had certainly heard scandalous rumors about Josephine that had been circulating in the black community for some time.

Rosetta raised the whiff of Josephine's scandal in 1862, when she was undergoing her own trials as a middle-class black woman trying to chart an independent course through the tight-laced straits of conventional morality. Still unmarried at the relatively late age of twenty-three, she had felt stifled while boarding with the middle-class Thomas Dorsey family of Philadelphia, a period in which, according to her father's biographer, "Mrs. Dorsey was trying to teach Rosetta that a world that gave excessive value to respectability expected a black girl to appear twice as virtuous as a white one. If she did not, she would be the victim of the racist assumption that black people were sexually promiscuous."[67] Stubborn like her father, Rosetta would have none of the Dorseys' meddling and eventually moved to an uncle's house in Salem, New Jersey, while preparing in the local normal school for a teaching career. Instead of gaining relief, however, she found herself snared in a new round of family surveillance and nasty innuendo about her behavior. Her patience exhausted, she complained bitterly to her father about their interference in a hastily written letter that told a story of confused identities tracing back to Martha Fletcher's home in New Bedford, Josephine's residence before her departure for Europe:

> Uncle's wife was repeatedly asking me questions about my former habits[;] she had heard I was not altogether what I should be, I was driven from my house on account of my growing intimacy with men, and again on account of my quarrelsome disposition toward my mother, that There was some minister come from Rochester who was acquainted knew [sic] of you having been obliged to send me away and

some Lucy Oliver from New Bedford had said I was in New Bedford living at one Martha Fletcher's but had gone astray from there and my father had come and removed me, he had taken much pains with my education having taken me to England for that purpose. This part of the story I knew who was meant Wm Brown's daughter I supposed the girl meant.[68]

The convoluted syntax and unexplained shifts in perspectives would not have confused her father one bit. Even had he not once lived in New Bedford and known most of the people named, he would have gotten the point, and so would other African American fathers and mothers with no connection to the locality: No self-respecting daughter must conduct herself like Josephine Brown, whose very name had become a byword for promiscuity in their community. To be compared to or mistaken for the daughter of William Wells Brown was one of the worst insults Rosetta Douglass, or any other respectable young black woman, could possibly receive.

The actual exchange between Brown and Josephine has left no record, but the gravity of Josephine's action can be guessed by the severity of the consequent reaction, a lifelong break between a stricken father and a beloved daughter. Brown must have felt many emotions—bewilderment, anger, betrayal, grief—but the one that seems to have governed his public behavior was shame, shame so powerful he delayed telling his best friend for months. That emotion must have eased with time, but the pain did not. A man who had suffered—and never stopped suffering—the enforced separation of his childhood family and the disintegration of his marital family now drove his daughter out of his life. They would not meet again until the prodigal daughter returned to her father's home in Cambridge at the very end of her life, in late 1873–74, in final-stage tuberculosis. Even then, she might not have been certain she would find his door open.

"This life is a stage, and we are indeed all actors," Brown would write in his serialized novel *Miralda*, a heavily revised version of *Clotel* published in 1860–61. The stage was so fundamentally a part of his life that he could have been referencing himself side by side with Shakespeare. He had frequently been on the stage since joining the antislavery movement in 1843—lecturing, singing, debating, and exhibiting—and by the mid-1850s he was a consummate performer. Talented actors surrounded him, most especially his fellow lecturers, skilled masters of the spoken word and the stage gesture. And chief among them, front and center in his imagination, was Joseph Jenkins, a master performer who prefigured his creator's easy movement back and forth between the lecture platform and the stage.

In 1856, Brown rounded a performative circuit by assuming two roles: dramatist and performer of his own stage work. The subject of his newest composition was "South-Side Adams," whom he had been denigrating on the lecture circuit for months. It was bad enough that Nehemiah Adams belonged to the circle of Northern churchmen who defended slavery, but he earned special contempt as a vested Bostonian. Brown completed the play early in 1856 and by late March was ready to perform it as a one-man recitation.

Although he never published *Experience; or, How to Give a Northern Man a Backbone*—the play's most frequently cited title—and no physical trace has survived, its three-act plot and something of its reception are retrievable from newspaper reports.[69] Brown turned Adams's Northern defense of slavery against itself by composing a send-up about a Boston minister named Jeremiah Adderson, who goes to the South expecting to inspect slavery but instead experiences it. During his stay in the South, his hotel manager conspires with a slave trader to kidnap him and hauls him off for auction as a white slave. A plantation owner purchases him and loses no time setting him to hard labor in the fields. Act 2 situates him in the slave quarters. Although no reviews describe these intermediate scenes, it is not hard to imagine Brown exploiting the incongruity of a smug, high-minded Northern minister sharing the plight of plantation slaves. In Act 3, Adderson, now repentant and reformed, wins his release through friends and returns to his congregation a changed man who concludes, "The Abolitionists are not so far out of the way after all."[70] The tone of that line likely captured one aspect of the spirit of a play Brown advertised as "laughable and highly interesting."[71] Audiences were expected to laugh at Adderson's predicament, and to judge from press reports they did, but finally also to take pity, if less on him than on the fugitive slave who accompanies him north and delivers the play's closing oration. Brown was not about to give even a reformed man like Adderson the last word.

Brown meant *Experience* to drive home the menace of the Fugitive Slave Law to Northern households. Every man and woman was a potential accomplice or victim in a nation of permeable borders and shifty racial definitions. While still composing the play, he got a whiff of public opinion when, in the midst of the annual MASS meeting, he went unsuspectingly with "many other blockheads" to hear Senator Robert Toombs of Georgia speak at Tremont Temple. He was prepared for Toombs's well-known proslavery views ("he said that it was the duty of the Caucasian to look after and rule the Negro, and the God of justice would protect the southern people in so doing"), but not for the respectful reaction Toombs received from an audience that included some of Boston's bluest blood. It stunned him, reinforcing his resolve to deliver his countermessage as widely as possible. The next night, he told the assembled society: "We want to make Massachusetts so hot that no Senator Toombs, or any body else, will come into the State to lecture in favor of Slavery." To accomplish that, he and his colleagues needed to forget about political parties and concentrate on influencing public opinion: "If we cannot change public opinion, it is useless to do any thing in the way of antislavery. But I believe we can do it; and I am satisfied that all we can do is to labor to change public opinion; do that work, and do it well."[72]

He weighed his options of how best to present his new play in order to influence public opinion. The most obvious way would have been to publish it, even though US copyright did not extend to dramatic works at the time Brown wrote it. (Not until August 1856 did Congress liberalize the existing 1831 federal statute to include dramatic rights, in response to pleas from playwrights and theater managers intent on maximizing profits.) He rejected that option, as well as the possibility of handing it over to a professional manager for formal staging in Boston, presumably because he was unwilling to transfer authority over so polemical a work to anyone else's hands.

A third possibility appeared right before his eyes in Boston, where the talented young Mary Webb, nicknamed "the Black Siddons," gave a series of dramatic readings adapted from *Uncle Tom's Cabin* as part of her late 1855–early 1856 tour of the Northeast.[73] Audiences of up to 1,300 people turned out to hear her recite *The Christian Slave* in Massachusetts, and reviews were generally appreciative. Brown likely saw a performance and could have drawn inspiration from her example. More likely he drew on his own earlier practice with his panorama by turning it into a performance piece. Beginning in April 1856, he took it on the road, giving one-man recitations at many of the same sites where he was scheduled to give formal lectures. Within weeks, he knew he had a hit on his hands. The pattern was soon predictable: Local communities that had engaged him to lecture invited him to stay on another night or two to recite his play. He could do good for himself as well as for the public, especially since he had a direct proprietary interest in his recitations that he did not have in antislavery lectures he gave as a salaried agent. He followed the general practice he had employed in exhibiting his panorama, charging admission at the door or, where lead time allowed, selling tickets through booksellers and reform organizations. Tickets went for 10 to 25 cents, a normal price range for stage performances, but for once he had no accompanying texts to sell at the performances.

During 1856 and early 1857, he performed the play on zigzagging jaunts across New England, New York and Pennsylvania, out across New York to Ohio, and possibly even as far as towns and cities in Michigan, where antislavery activity was growing fast in the years preceding the Civil War. He played to receptive audiences just about everywhere he performed, with favorable reports coming back from viewers in Boston, Worcester, Salem, Lynn, Providence, New York City, Philadelphia, upstate New York, New Jersey, western Connecticut, and northern Vermont. Some of the engagements seem to have been officially sponsored, such as the performance he gave May 26, 1856, at Tremont Temple the night before the NEASS began its annual convention there—tickets to be had at 21 Cornhill, John Jewett's bookstore, and Lewis Hayden's clothing store (a favorite shopping and gathering place for black Bostonians).[74] That reading went over so well that Garrison called the play "first rate" and the audience "highly appreciative and delighted" by his performance.[75] A week later at Groveland, near Newburyport, a listener reported, "Our people were fairly taken off their feet with delight. I have never seen a Groveland audience so highly entertained."[76]

For half a year, Brown combined recitations with official lecture engagements, but in November 1856 he resigned from his MASS lectureship to devote himself primarily to recitations and self-scheduled lectures.[77] By this time, he had enlarged his prospects by writing a second, more adventurous five-act play called *The Escape; or, A Leap for Freedom.* There were so few lulls between speaking engagements during those busy months that he must have composed it rapidly at odd hours snatched at home and on the road. By the time of his resignation, even though he had not yet published *The Escape*, he had lined up more than twenty invitations for dramatic readings.[78]

He made a particular point to schedule speaking engagements at Oberlin College (its official name since 1850) during his western tour in winter 1857. Shortly before leaving Boston, he contacted Hamilton Hill, his fellow delegate to the Paris Peace Congress who served as Oberlin's secretary-treasurer, to offer to give both a lecture and a recitation.[79] The request was not an unusual one for Brown, but he had a personal reason he did not reveal to Hill. By contrast, Nell, who seems to have been informed about everyone and everything, knew his friend's intentions for his visit to Oberlin; he dispatched an updated bulletin to Jerry Sanderson, who had relocated from New Bedford to California, about the latest chapter in their mutual friend's romantic life: "Wm Wells Brown is smitten with a Miss Jackson student at Oberlin."[80] Nell neglected to mention the young woman's first name, an omission that makes positive identification today tenuous at best. An attractive match for Brown on paper would have been the future educator Fanny Jackson (later Coppin, for whom Coppin State University is named), but she did not officially matriculate at Oberlin until 1860, and there is no proof Brown had previously met her at her home in Newport, Rhode Island. The Oberlin College archives list several other female students named Jackson in attendance in 1856–57, both in their late teens from Ohio, but none is identifiable as the object of Brown's interest.[81] All that can be said with certainty is that the relationship, however serious it might have been, did not last beyond 1857.

Beginning with that Western trip, Brown alternated readings of the two plays, although he later told Garrison he considered his new one "far superior."[82] He was right to think so. *The Escape* had superior imaginative complexity, social commentary, and personal investment—the result of an ever-returning stream of memories of youth flooding his sensibility. Now a full generation removed from slavery, Brown was revisiting a past he thought he had abandoned but that had never really left him. Painful memories returned of his rural Missouri boyhood, John and Sarah Young and the phantom George W. Higgins; the Young household with its domestic servants and visiting clergymen; and the slave trader William Walker. The underlying logic of his imaginative life repeated itself one more time: Art and life aligned so interchangeably that, in revisiting his Missouri past, Brown scavenged a hodgepodge of autobiographically based characters, scenes, and situations from the *Narrative, The Anti-Slavery Harp*, the panorama, *Clotel*, and *The American Fugitive* for his latest work.

The play opens on a Missouri farm owned by Dr. and Mrs. (Sarah) Gaines, a mismatched couple loosely modeled on John and Sarah Young. From the start, Dr. and Mrs. Gaines present themselves as models of good breeding and rectitude. Gaines prides himself on his father, who fought with Washington in the American Revolution; vaunts his medical expertise; and tries on the rank of colonel for size. His match in most regards, Sarah prides herself on her FFV (First Families of Virginia) heritage and Christian forbearance toward her inferiors, who range from slaves to husbands. Well matched in their self-pity, they are quick to blame others for their discontent. Dr. Gaines faces competition for patients from Dr. Jones (perhaps a reference to Young's dealings with the more popular Dr. John Jones back in Marthasville), condescends to do business with the slave trader Walker to raise the cash needed to keep up appearances, and runs into resistance to his lascivious wishes from his wife and servants. Sarah, meanwhile, frets over the ingratitude of her servants, friends, and husband. Her first husband (of blessed memory) was the better man of the two, but she seems to think him better gone. She has grievances against nearly everyone and is quick to express them. Husband and wife agree on one thing: Their most serious problem is domestic. Each finds the other insufferable, as they live their lives at cross purposes. They quarrel incessantly over the smallest detail, but for this childless couple the determining conflict, the one that threatens the integrity of their union, is the racial incarnation of original sin.

The snake in the garden enters with their new neighbor, Major Moore, in Act 3, Scene 3. Moore knows Gaines from their service in the most recent session of the state legislature and has come to pay his respects as one country gentleman to another. He prides himself on mastery of the art of ingratiation, especially with women: "If you wish to gain the favor of a woman, praise her children and swear that they are the picture of their father." On entering the parlor, he tries it out on her by paying a compliment to the boy standing behind her chair:

MAJOR M. How do you do, bub? Madam, I should have known that this was the Colonel's son, if I had met him in California; for he looks so much like his papa.

MRS. G. [*to the boy.*] Get out of here this minute. Go to the kitchen. [*Exit* Sampey, R.] That is one of the niggers, sir.

MAJOR M. I beg your pardon, madam; I beg your pardon.

MRS. G. No offence, sir; mistakes will be made. Ah! here comes the Colonel.[83]

Dr. Gaines is a serial predator; his current prey is an attractive, intelligent, light-skinned slave woman named Melinda. She resists, but when he learns she is already secretly married to an equally well-spoken slave named Glen from a neighboring farm, he kidnaps her to a remote farm he owns and threatens to use force if necessary. She continues to resist, and then so does Sarah, who in learning of his intention conspires to preempt it by taking steps to sell Melinda down the river (while Gaines, who has purchased Glen, plans to skin him alive with the whip and sell him away). All these actions by the masters provoke counteractions by their slaves, who eventually take flight north toward Niagara Falls, with Gaines and his posse in close pursuit. Brown concludes his play seemingly happily, like his panorama, as the fugitives pass safely into Canada.

The play draws on elements of fugitive-slave narratives, freedom suits, and conventional stage melodrama, but it has the distinctive iconoclasm of Brown's zaniest work. As a confirmed Garrisonian in his antislavery politics, Brown knew where the boundary line of approved policy passed between right and wrong, but in creating the topsy-turvy world of *The Escape*, as in *Clotel*, he set all ideological positions in flux. Opposites not only coexist but depend on one another for their identity: gentry and slaves, North and South, heaven and hell, Queen's English and slave dialect, decorum and minstrelsy.

Brown so flagrantly paired off normative opposites that it is not hard to understand why audiences roared with laughter. One particular object of his contempt was Sarah Gaines, the play's incarnation of white Southern womanhood. A pious soul, Sarah yearns for heaven, which in her mind mirrors earth as a place where genteel is segregated from uncouth, rich from poor, and white from black. In Act 1, Scene 4, she asks the visiting itinerant preacher Reverend Pinchen, just back from a dream visit to heaven, whether he spotted her beloved first husband, Mr. Pepper. She no sooner inquires than her body servant Hannah interjects the identical question about *her* first husband. The minister admits to Sarah he didn't notice Mr. Pepper and parries Hannah's inquiry, "No, Hannah; I didn't go among the niggers." Later, in Act 2, Scene 2, the same minister engages the slave trader Walker in a professional exchange between seeming opposites that ends by conflating the saving of souls with the sale of slaves as allied profit-making enterprises.

The richest comic doubling links master and slave. Cato serves Gaines as manservant, but he also serves the play as the seemingly obligatory minstrel figure, back by popular demand, whose reason for being is to entertain the audience by providing comic relief to his master (most graphically in the "negro dentistry" scene Brown imported from *Clotel*). Gaines knows the fool he is dealing with, or thinks he does; and so perhaps did at least a portion of Brown's audience, which sat down each evening primed with racist beliefs inculcated by a culture suffused with derogatory representations of blacks. Knowing the racial stereotypes with which he had to contend, Brown stage-managed the situation to cue the audience, behind Gaines's back, that there is more to Cato than meets the eye. Midway through the play, in Act 3, Scene 2, he has Cato reveal his desire to fly to Canada in a crucial soliloquy, which Cato then performs in a minstrel-derived song consistent with his two-faced character:

> *Come all ye bondmen far and near,*
> *Let's put a song in massa's ear,*
> *It is a song for our poor race,*
> *Who're whipped and trampled with disgrace.*
>
> *CHORUS.*
>
> *My old massa tells me, Oh,*
> *This is a land of freedom, Oh;*
> *Let's look about and see if it's so,*
> *Just as massa tells me, Oh.*
>
> *He tells us of that glorious one,*
> *I think his name was Washington,*
> *How he did fight for liberty,*
> *To save a threepence tax on tea. [Chorus.]*
>
> *But now we look about and see*
> *That we poor black folks are not so free;*
> *We're whipped and thrashed about like fools,*
> *And have no chance at common schools. [Chorus.]*[84]

Cato presents his song as a work of his own invention, although Brown composed and published the lyrics a decade earlier as "A Song for Freedom" in *The Anti-Slavery Harp*. He intended it at that time as a takeoff on the wildly popular minstrel song "Dandy Jim of Caroline," whose chorus projected the smiley face Cato shows to his master:

> *For my ole massa tole me so,*
> *I was de best lookin Nigger in de County O,*
> *I look in de glass an I found it so,*
> *Jus what massa told me O.*

In having Cato step out of the shadow of Dandy Jim, Brown was presenting a slave to antebellum Americans as the strangest of creations, his own man.

As a one-man recitation in which a black actor read and sang the full complement of roles before live audiences, *The Escape* was one of the most daring productions of its time. It was also daringly personal. Night in and night out, Brown impersonated the people who had made his young life a living hell: Dr. Gaines, Sarah Gaines, Walker, and Reverend Pinchen. But the key to his performance was his impersonation of Cato, the character who most nearly resembled him. Cato's overall situation as live-in amanuensis to Gaines doubles Brown's relationship to Young: an all-purpose servant placating old master while biding his time until circumstances allow for escape. When the moment finally arrives, Cato springs into action. He steals his master's coat, assumes his identity, and strikes out for freedom. Just as Sandy gulled Enoch Price in New Orleans, Cato cons Dr. Gaines by acting out the well-known slave adage "Got one mind for white folks to see,/ 'nother for what I know is me."[85] The saying fits, but the change of identity is so extreme that Cato can barely recognize himself: "I wonder ef dis is me? By golly, I is free as a frog. But maybe I is mistaken; maybe dis ain't me. Cato, is dis you? Yes, seer. Well, now it is me, an' I am a free man."[86] The first thing he does as a free man, like Brown on the open road in Ohio, is to change his name.

The spectacle of William Wells Brown, dressed in respectable coat and cravat, playing Cato constituted one of the most curious casting decisions of the early American stage. It was at once both wholly plausible (featuring Sandy, the slave boy) and wholly implausible (featuring William Wells Brown, the man of letters)—and so, many times over, was his impersonation of the entire ensemble, performing both whiteness and blackness. Given the pervasive racism of the 1850s, Brown needed to tread the stage carefully, to make sure his mostly white audience would take the play as he hoped when they might so easily have gotten mired in their prejudices. Wherever he took his drama on the road, he was self-consciously competing for credibility against minstrelsy, the reigning form of race-based popular entertainment when white minstrel troupes fanned across the country and even over the ocean. That aficionado of racial entertainment Mark Twain fondly and even reverently remembered his first minstrel show, a formative experience he dated to the early 1840s in Hannibal. A half-century later, he still retained a passion for what he called "the real nigger show—the genuine nigger show, the extravagant nigger show—the show which to me had no peer and whose peer has not yet arrived, in my experience."[87] One week after Brown recited *The Escape* or *Experience* at Howard Hall in Providence, Rhode Island, the Christy Minstrels took to the same stage for a three-night engagement.[88] That celebrated troupe was the one Twain took his mother to see in St. Louis, sitting with her in the front row and easing her fear of perceived impropriety by assuring her that "the best people in St. Louis" would be in attendance.[89]

Profoundly personal, *The Escape* was simultaneously profoundly national. It effectively transformed Brown's psychodrama into a national drama of race, as suited a nation tearing itself into antagonistic halves over slavery. Acutely sensitive to what the times demanded, Brown gave the public a topsy-turvy spectacle of race, class, and section that ingeniously captured the strained contortions of a society coming loose from its foundation. Selectively popular in its day but hardly ever staged since the Civil War, *The Escape* ranks with *Uncle Tom's Cabin*, *Clotel*, and Herman Melville's *Benito Cereno* among the greatest race dramas of the fractious 1850s.

....

ONE SOLITARY writer-performer could do little to affect "the cultural drama of race," as literary historian John Ernest has called it, in late antebellum America, but Brown dutifully played his role, touring the North intermittently for four years.[90] The work was hard and at times must have been risky. There is no surviving report that he faced violence at any performances, but even routine travel presented hazards. During a speaking tour of upstate New York in winter 1858, bad traveling luck caught up with him when the train in which he was riding hit a broken track between Syracuse and Utica and derailed. His car pitched over the embankment, flipped, and burned as Brown slithered out the window. Though badly bruised and banged up, he resumed his tour.[91] A few weeks later, he gave a series of recitations in the vicinity of Cortland, where one of his largest audiences was at nearby New York Central College, whose faculty previously included William G. Allen.[92]

During those years, Brown was in effect attempting something no African American writer had yet accomplished: earning his living primarily, if not exclusively, as a literary/cultural professional. Not even his major white peers had much prospect of making their living by writing alone—especially by writing for an audience seeking more than entertainment. Melville's now-famous complaint, "Dollars damn me," had wide currency in his day, but the odds against African Americans were immeasurably greater. No documentation survives about the proceeds from Brown's recitations, but the frequency of his engagements indicates the plays' popularity. Nell, at least, provides one insight into Brown's early success. In summer 1857, he informed Jerry Sanderson: "Wm. Wells Brown is seated in the [MASS] office in good health and spirits and sends love to Jerry[;] he is flourishing by reading his antislavery Dramas."[93] And in an update a few months later: "Wm. Wells Brown is beginning to reap a harvest from his antislavery Dramas."[94] In one of the few extant comments on the success of his plays, Brown explained to a leading Ohio abolitionist, "There are some places where it would take better than a lecture; people will pay to hear the Drama that would not give a cent in an anti-slavery meeting."[95] His harvest continued on and off nearly up to the Civil War as he alternated readings with lectures.

Brown took one more initiative with *The Escape*: He published it, though not until June 1858, a full eighteen months after its first recitation. The deal he arranged resembled the same cost-saving one he had made for *Biography of an American Bondman* with Robert Wallcut, who had it printed in the *Liberator* office and issued as a paperback pamphlet for twenty cents a copy. Its delayed timing raises questions: Why only then and why only that play? The explanation he provides in the Author's Preface is enigmatic: "By the earnest solicitation of some in whose judgment I have the greatest confidence, I now present it in a printed form to the public."[96] So was the unsecured copyright statement on the overleaf of the title page, a claim corresponding to no recorded deposit. Ultimately, the only judgment Brown ever consistently followed was his own.

He presumably made a modest profit from sales of the book, which would have been available for purchase through the antislavery network and at performances. Nineteen copies survive in US libraries and others are in private collections, a substantial remnant for a cheap paperback. The most notable copy is at Brown University—a heavily annotated one bearing signs of considerable usage. It belonged to one of a group of young (mostly female) friends from Northampton, Massachusetts, born in the mid- and late 1840s who were preparing to stage an amateur performance of the play.[97] The owner jotted down their names and their intention to perform it above the title on the first page but left no date. Given its thematic contemporaneity, the girls must have performed it sometime between 1858 and 1861 in Northampton, where Brown lectured at least once in 1859 and again in 1860.

This amateur theatrical would have been a singular exception to Brown's rule, but its exceptionality makes an important point about his management of *The Escape*. For all its theatricality, the play was never professionally staged. As its (supposed) copyright owner, Brown controlled production rights, which he maintained tightfistedly. By contrast, most other literary professionals would have done what the accomplished playwright/actor/stage manager Dion Boucicault did with his popular race play *The Octoroon*. He produced it at his theater, the Winter Garden in New York City, premiering it on December 5, 1859—a date that coincided, to Boucicault's great luck, with the furor surrounding the execution of abolitionist John Brown. Professional playwrights and stage managers like Boucicault knew that more money was typically to be made by staging than by publishing dramas, but Brown chose the less popular way.

He continued to perform his plays well into 1860. During those spring months of national agitation, he added a third play to his repertoire, which likely was a revised version of *Experience*, updated to respond to the latest political developments. In this unprinted drama whose text and title have not survived, Jeremiah Adderson is reincarnated as a Northern Democratic politico allied with New York City's corrupt Tammany Hall political machine. He gives a proslavery speech so well received that he is elected as a delegate to the Democratic Party National Convention, meeting in Charleston to select a candidate to stand against the Republican candidate, Abraham Lincoln, in the most important election in memory. Full of himself, he disseminates copies of his speech widely before setting out on an inspection tour down the Mississippi River en route to Charleston. He never arrives, succumbing to the same fate as Adderson did in *Experience*. According to the only known review, the intent was to hold up the would-be politician to the laughter of the audience, although it would not have been unlike Brown also to hold the audience to a scrutiny that escaped the reviewer.[98]

IN 1858, a new presence entered Brown's life, bringing the prospect of personal happiness and fulfillment that had eluded him since the early years of his marriage to Betsey. She was Annie Elizabeth Gray, a strikingly attractive, light-skinned young woman of cultivated sensibility and progressive views who offered Brown, still grieving over the loss of Josephine, a kind of companionship he had not previously known.[99] Annie was born in 1835 to a free family in Baltimore the year after Brown escaped from Enoch Price. Her mother, Harriet, was also born in Maryland; her father, William, was born in Virginia, just three years before her future husband. After starting their family in Baltimore, they moved north around 1840 to Cambridge, Massachusetts, where Annie grew up and attended school. The 1850 census listed her father as a waiter, a common profession among black males, but William Gray improved his circumstances over the next decade, saving money and buying at least three houses in a mostly working-class neighborhood of East Cambridge still known as Cambridgeport. Gray also had higher aspirations, involving himself and his family in the antislavery and temperance movements. Raised in reformist circles, Annie thus acquired an early commitment to racial improvement that remained central throughout her life.

William Nell knew the Gray family and remembered Annie fondly from her childhood. It was precisely for children like her that he had led the fight for school integration, even though he was himself childless well into his fifties. For that matter, Annie's whole family was well known not only in the black community but also within the circles of the MASS. In a quite unusual gesture toward a black family, the *Liberator* printed a death notice for Annie's infant sister Sarah, who died in Cambridgeport on the same day in spring 1849 when Brown lectured there with the Crafts.[100] The Grays subscribed to the *Liberator* and were active in the movement, so it seems likely Brown met Annie at a Boston-area antislavery or temperance meeting.

Their relationship had progressed far enough by spring 1858 that Annie occasionally went to hear Brown give readings of his plays. She was his special guest one evening in mid-April when he performed *The Escape* in the North Shore city of Lynn. He had written ahead to enlist the aid of Garrison, then paying the city a visit, in delivering a package containing 300 handbills to the Sagamore Hall manager for distribution at the door. Although Brown normally stayed overnight when traveling to an out-of-town reading, on this occasion he departed from custom by arriving shortly before and leaving directly after the performance in order to get Annie home at a timely hour.[101]

Their relationship intensified during 1859, when Brown was also paying increasing attention to the course of national politics leading up to the decade's climactic event: John Brown's October 16–18 attack on the federal arsenal at Harpers Ferry. He and Annie would have had many chances to see each other that year, but the only one recorded was on August 1, West Indies Emancipation Day, during the New England Convention of Colored Citizens at Tremont Temple in Boston. Brown played a central role in organizing this meeting, which attracted prominent black leaders from all across the country as well as a small delegation from Canada. The attendees included people he had known for years from earlier black conventions and antislavery organizations: Charles Remond, William Nell, and Lewis Hayden, who were always particularly active on their home turf; the successful caterer George T. Downing from Newport, who was chosen to preside; his good friend William Still from Philadelphia; and Reverend John Sella Martin, a fugitive slave of great oratorical ability. Martin had ministered at the Michigan Street Baptist Church in Buffalo before accepting a pulpit in Boston, where Brown later noted that Martin soon developed "a popularity not surpassed by any of the preachers of Boston.[102] Other attendees included Reverend Jermain Wesley Loguen, a pivotal figure in the Syracuse depot of the Underground Railroad and leader of the Jerry Rescue; Lewis Clarke from Canada (who had made an unexpected appearance in the Tegg edition of Brown's *Narrative*), and, as a member of the business committee, Annie E. Gray of Cambridge.

Reporters were in attendance to cover the event at Tremont Temple's Meionaon Room, as were a number of white and black spectators. The only white person authorized to speak was William Lloyd Garrison, present by special invitation, who stated his pride at being "a black man" as though he was one person of color congregating among his fellows. His inclusion might have been a courtesy extended to him in his hometown, but following the close of the convention, the *Liberator* expressed (probably his) pinched criticism of the convention's failure to give credit where credit was due: "We do not see in the proceedings of the Convention that distinct recognition and grateful appreciation of the Anti-Slavery movement which the occasion naturally suggested, and which might have been justly expected. . . ."[103] There was no lack of touchiness inside the hall, as well.

Brown opened the proceedings by singing his well-known song

"Fling Out the Anti-Slavery Flag," to the melody of "Auld Lang Syne," before the convention got down to business. He immediately expressed his ambivalence at the brand of racial politics it seemed likely to endorse: "I confess that I am unfavorable to any gathering that shall seem like taking separate action from our white fellow-citizens; but it appears to me that just at the present time, such a meeting as this is needed. The colored people in the free States are in a distracted and unsettled condition. The Fugitive Slave Law, the Dred Scott Decision, and other inroads made upon the colored man's rights, make it necessary they should come together that they may compare notes, talk over the cause of their sufferings, and see if anything can be done to better their condition."[104] Speaker after speaker came forward to note improvements in the social, educational, and cultural lives of free African Americans; life for them, if not for their brothers and sisters under the Mason-Dixon line, seemed to be advancing. Not until the second day did the issue of voluntary emigration to Africa arise, but when it did, it came forcefully and elicited strong reaction. Brown made clear his unequivocal opposition to black emigration to Africa; it was not a return but a rupture. He held the majority view among the congregants, but there was also serious support for the idea voiced by articulate men such as John Sella Martin, who believed African Americans might bring badly needed religion and civilization to their African brothers and sisters.

The emigration debate took place under the looming shadow of the absent Henry Highland Garnet, its powerful, influential proponent. After working for the Richardson family's Free Produce Movement, often at odds with Brown, Garnet left England in 1853 to minister to a congregation in Jamaica for several years before returning to the United States. In the late 1850s, he played a leading role in founding and presiding over the African Colonization Society, preaching the case for black presence not only in the United States but also in the Caribbean and Africa. Though revered in many quarters, the brash, outspoken Garnet accumulated his share of enemies. Douglass was one; the two men were on edgy terms for decades. Brown was another, though on a more occasional basis over the 1850s. A new outbreak of antagonism occurred during the weeks following the Boston convention when Garnet took offense at antiemigration remarks made by Brown and others. On August 30, Garnet publicly responded to them in an acrimonious meeting at Joy Street Church on Beacon Hill, singling out Brown in remarks that took on a personal character. Brown soon countered, and the two men took to *Frederick Douglass' Paper* to argue their differences in public.

That summer, though, the person Brown had most in mind was Annie. In June, he had lectured on "Love, Courtship, and Marriage" at Joy Street Church, but months passed before he proposed.[105] On April 12, 1860, they were married at Boston's Twelfth Baptist Church—the "Fugitive Slave Church," as its parishioners familiarly called it, on Beacon Hill. Officiating was its pastor and Brown's close friend Reverend Leonard Grimes, one of black Boston's most revered figures. Though freeborn in Virginia, Grimes had come under the long institutional whip of slavery by spending two years in prison for helping a family of seven escape to Canada. He learned his lesson well enough to migrate to New Bedford and join the Underground Railroad. He later moved to Boston, took his ministry, and did all in his power to aid fugitives—most famously, Anthony Burns. But mostly he ministered to his congregation, which included some of Brown's closest friends (though not Brown).

Days after the ceremony, the newlyweds were on their way to Pennsylvania. Brown wished to introduce Annie to his many friends in Philadelphia, but he also tacked on a side trip to Harrisburg, where he lectured on "Practical Christianity" and, on successive nights, gave readings of his plays. After their return north, they set up house next door to her family on Webster Avenue, near the corner of Hampshire Street, in Cambridgeport. They resided in that modest house, owned by William Gray, for eighteen years, allowing Annie to maintain daily contact with her parents and siblings and to have companionship during the long stretches when her husband was on the road. Before long, she would have additional company at home: Several months after their wedding, she was pregnant.

As the historic election of 1860 approached, Brown was unimpressed with all three major-party candidates. He jokingly told his fellow picnickers at the MASS Emancipation Day picnic on August 1 that federal elections were the devil's work. The "satanic majesty" of olden times was a smooth talker who took Jesus up to the mountaintop and tempted him, "Worship me, and I'll give you this." Now, Brown went on, "the same individual, every four years, takes the whole American people, (women and negroes excepted) (laughter and applause), shows them the White House at Washington, and says, 'Worship me, and I'll get you in there.'"[106] Even the most skeptical among the picnickers, however, sensed that the drama over the issue of slavery, decades delayed by one temporizing compromise after another, was approaching a climax; and most of his listeners differed with him in looking to the political process for its resolution.

The Democratic Party could come to no easy consensus, as the front-runner, Stephen Douglas, proved too moderate on slavery to satisfy the party's emboldened core of extremists, who eventually split from the majority, organized a rump convention, and selected the diehard Kentucky senator John Breckenridge to represent their interest against both Douglas and the dark-horse Republican nominee, Abraham Lincoln. Brown, meanwhile, skirted the political intrigue. In August, he went to Vermont to read his newest play, and he continued to read and lecture through the fall. On November 6, the day the nation went to the polls, with early indicators predicting a Republican victory, Brown, as in every previous election cycle, cast no vote. He had no more patience for Lincoln than for the rest of the scoundrels—Northern doughfaces and Southern fire-eaters alike.

At this time of high national drama, Brown, still pursuing cultural as well as political means to fight slavery and racism, decided the time was right to rewrite *Clotel* to address it chiefly to a black audience. The original version had been written and marketed primarily for a British market, and, mainly for that reason, had almost no impact in the United States. The timing of the new work's publication was notable. Over the six months of national crisis stretching from Lincoln's election in November 1860 to his inauguration in March 1861, Brown serialized the novel as *Miralda; or, The Beautiful Quadroon: A Romance of Ameri-*

can Slavery Founded on Fact. It appeared in Thomas Hamilton's *Weekly Anglo-African*, an ambitious New York–based journal of news, opinion, and original writing that attracted the work of the leading African American journalists and writers of a generation that had come of age with the black press. Hamilton featured each installment of the novel on the *Anglo-African*'s front page, and the work reached a broad Northern audience. It even reached Brown's old home. The St. Louis–based correspondent of the paper boasted that he distributed 100 copies in that city alone.[107]

Miralda was a greatly simplified, conventionalized adaptation of the original work. Brown stripped away much of *Clotel*'s borrowed source material, presuming an African American audience would need no external proof of the destructiveness of slavery or of the hypocrisy of the people and institutions that supported it. He also changed the names of central characters. Currer, Clotel, and Althesa were now Agnes, Isabella, and Marion (and Clotel's daughter Mary became Miralda). Of greater significance, he changed both the name and the skin color of George Green ("as white as most white persons") by recasting him as the "perfectly black" Jerome, whom he gave a commitment to racial progress that George had lacked.[108] He also made a related change to the novel's conclusion. Whereas George and Mary pass as a happy white couple in England, Jerome and Miralda live proudly as a black couple in Europe and even manage to convince her slave-owning father to free his slaves and accept their union. Further than that, however, Brown would not go. Even in a novel of racial pride and uplift published in the weeks leading up to the Civil War, he did not see how life in the United States could be a viable option for the couple.

It *was*, however, for his family. In February 1861, William Wells Brown Jr. was born in Cambridgeport, entering a world torn by dissension. In the days and weeks surrounding his birth, one Southern state after another seceded from the Union. Even while the president-elect was still residing in Springfield, Illinois, threats made on Capitol Hill passed quickly into acts of secession at state capitols across the Deep South. On January 7, 1861, outspoken Senator Robert Toombs of Georgia delivered a contentious farewell to his colleagues in the US Capitol as he prepared to attend his state's secession convention: "We want no negro equality, no negro citizenship; we want no negro race to degrade our own; and as one man [we] would meet you upon the border with the sword in one hand and the torch in the other." His fellow Georgia senator, Alfred Iverson, used even more curious fighting words in making his farewell: "You may whip us but we will not stay whipped. We will rise again and again to vindicate our right to liberty."[109]

As Lincoln took office on March 4, he tried hard to carve out a middle position, appealing to "the better angels of our nature" in his first inaugural address. The appeal failed miserably. Thomas Hamilton, editor of the *Weekly Anglo-African*, eloquently expressed the bitter disappointment felt by much of the black community as he, like readers around the country, scoured Lincoln's printed text for clues about the new administration's priorities. The terse, plainspoken language of the speech, he noted, had earned "Honest Abe" his nickname and shown him to be "a man of warm and generous impulses, uncorrupted by the chicanery of parties, fresh from the people, out of the bosom of the Great West"—a politician cut from a different US-made cloth than were previous presidents. But for all Lincoln's fine personal qualities and blunt talk, he remained the leader of a strictly one-color political party: "The Republican party is for the white man. We must rely on ourselves," concluded Hamilton.[110]

Brown was lecturing in eastern Massachusetts when the "irrepressible conflict between opposing and enduring forces," as William Seward had named it in 1858, finally exploded. On April 12, 1861, South Carolina militiamen trained their cannons on the lightly defended federal arsenal at Fort Sumter, igniting civil war. The North immediately responded by mobilizing. In an emergency community meeting convened at the Twelfth Baptist Church on the night of April 23, one speaker after another, including some of Brown's closest colleagues—Lewis Hayden, Robert Morris, George T. Downing, John Sella Martin—argued for black support of the war effort. Brown stood virtually alone in advocating restraint. Why should the African American community support a government that had not yet earned its trust or fight in a campaign that did not name abolition of slavery as its goal? Training and preparing their fellow blacks to fight, he argued, was a worthwhile endeavor, and he assured them he was no "peace man," but knowing the actual mission was indispensable.

His appeal for patience, caution, and clarification persuaded few, antagonized many. Hecklers interrupted him, and one outraged protester even denounced him as a "slaveholder."[111] Cooler-headed insiders would have known that in the winter of 1860 Brown had led a petition drive on behalf of black Boston that submitted a memorial to the General Court, "praying that the word 'white' may be removed from the militia laws of the Commonwealth," but his petition did not make it out of committee.[112] The sticking point, curiously, was the legislature's rejection of a presumptive states' rights argument; opponents prevailed by arguing that Massachusetts had no constitutional right to enact enlistment criteria that conflicted with those of the nation. That position was an outrage to Brown, denial to African Americans of a right as fundamental as citizenship, suffrage, or equality of schooling.

As it turned out, the debate over black enlistment in the Union Army was at the time largely theoretical. Northern whites were generally unreceptive, often downright hostile, to acts of racial inclusiveness, even as the nation mobilized for war. If the specter of black men armed and uniformed descending upon their territory conjured diabolical nightmares to white Southerners, it also presented a disquieting prospect for most white Northerners, including Lincoln. When the commander in chief appealed for 75,000 volunteers in response to Fort Sumter, he meant, expressly and exclusively, white soldiers.

9

The Black Man at War

By returning to the United States in 1854, Brown had voted with his feet. He believed he had definitively resolved the homeland question over and against the views of emigration "missionaries" such as Henry Highland Garnet and Martin Delany. In writing *St. Domingo* that year, he had expressed pride in the achievement of Haitian independence and self-rule, but he was not prepared to endorse the only black-led nation in the Western Hemisphere as a desirable home for North American blacks. As civil strife intensified in 1860–61, however, he gradually recalculated his bearings. Lacking faith in the new president and his professed war goals, he no longer saw the future of "the black man" as limited to North America. "This war," he argued—even after the 1863 enactment of the Emancipation Proclamation—"was begun with the purpose of restoring the nation as it was, and leaving the black man where he was."[1] What business was it of black Americans to support it?

Most of his friends, blacks and whites, supported the war effort, but at a moment when one had to choose sides, Brown cast his lot with an organization promoting emigration of North American blacks to Haiti. The leader of the new emigration drive was James Redpath, an impetuous Scottish journalist-activist who had become involved neck-deep in radical abolitionism soon after moving to the United States. He migrated west to Missouri and "Bleeding Kansas" during the vigilante skirmishing in the mid-1850s and allied himself so wholly with John Brown that, but for circumstances, he might have joined Brown's raiding party at Harpers Ferry. Switching directions after that failed attack, he made several trips to Haiti, ingratiated himself with the country's leaders, and emerged as the head of the Haitian Emigration Bureau in 1861.

A born operator, Redpath orchestrated a full-fledged emigration campaign out of his rented Boston office, backed by official Haitian support. He used all means at his disposal: he solicited the support of the leading progressive black and white newspapers in the country; he purchased the *Weekly Anglo-African* from Thomas Hamilton's short-lived successor, renamed it *Pine and Palm*, and turned it into an advocacy organ; and he hired a team of lecturers to proselytize in the field. One was John Brown Jr., but most of the others were black men respected and influential in their home communities. They included Reverend James Theodore Holly of New Haven, who internalized the message so deeply in 1861 that he took his young family and a group of settlers to live in Haiti; the dynamic Chicago-based abolitionist H. Ford Douglass, a captain in the Union Army at the time of his death in 1865; the witty New York columnist William J. Watson; Henry Highland Garnet; William Wells Brown; and—his biggest coup—Frederick Douglass, a longtime opponent of emigration but in 1861 suspicious about Lincoln's resolve. Redpath paid his lecturers $20 a week plus a $5 bounty for every emigrant recruited, and he assigned each one to a particular territory, although it would not have been principally payment that brought men like Brown, Douglass, and Garnet to line up on Redpath's side.[2]

The Confederate attack on Fort Sumter had no determining effect on Brown. As convoys of militia rode southward that spring toward Washington, DC, in response to Lincoln's appeal to put down the rebellion, Brown set out westward on a promotional speaking tour lasting from May to June. All that time, his name was appearing on the masthead of the pro-emigration *Pine and Palm* as one of its "special contributors." His recruitment tour took him through Troy, Albany, Schenectady, Syracuse, Rochester, Buffalo, and smaller communities along the Erie Canal corridor, where he delivered a lecture on "Past History and Present Prospects of the Republic of Hayti."[3] In Troy, the onetime home base of Henry Highland Garnet, it culminated in a call to action: "Now if we may go to California, Oregon, and other places to better our conditions and to give an inheritance to our children, why should we not go to Hayti?"[4]

For the first time since he had started down the AASS road in Buffalo in 1843, Brown veered away from many longtime abolitionist friends and allies who had abandoned their previous principles as apolitical pacifists to stand behind Lincoln in support of the war. The single-track–minded Garrison made one of the greatest pivots of his life in 1860–61 and carried with him many of his allies, such as Samuel May Jr., Edmund Quincy, and Robert Wallcut, although not the more radical flank of Wendell Phillips, Parker Pillsbury, and the Fosters. Closer to home, a groundswell of support in the black community grew quickly in the tense days and weeks following the fall of Sumter. One packed meeting after the next took place at churches in Brown's former Beacon Hill neighborhood, and excitement reached such a pitch that young black Bostonians clamored by the hundreds to sign up for combat duty. No federal recruitment officers, however, were waiting outside to take names.

Meanwhile, events ran their course. On July 21, as Northern picnickers waited outside Washington for news about the expected opening victory, the Union Army was routed near Manassas at the first Battle of Bull Run. Four days later, with few dissenting votes, Congress passed the Crittenden–Johnson Resolution. An act of expediency drawing on broad agreement that the fragile confederation of Northern states required stability, it declared the overriding purpose of the war the reunification of the states and ruled out "overthrowing or interfering with the rights or established institutions" of the South—a euphemism for slavery. The bill's proponents saw the measure as vital to the war effort by keeping the pivotal border states of Missouri, Kentucky, and Maryland in the Union. Brown could not have been reassured to observe his home states pacified on such terms.

But he had a far more pressing concern right at home. On the day the Congress approved the Crittenden–Johnson Resolution, five-month-old William Wells Brown Jr. died in Cambridgeport of either cholera or dysentery.[5] Those diseases were rampant in Boston that summer; four fatal cases of cholera among children were reported that week alone at the city clerk's office. Just a few weeks earlier, the three-month-old son of John Sella Martin had also succumbed to one of them, and they would soon sweep like the plague through the military camps.[6] How the stricken Brown family handled its sudden loss can only be imagined. All that is known for certain is the bereaved parents buried their baby in Annie's family plot at Cambridge Cemetery.

Just as when little Henrietta died in 1845, Brown did not linger long at home to mourn his namesake. The next day's *Liberator* announced that he was making his first trip in many years to Canada to lecture on "the elevation of the colored population," and sure enough, within a few weeks he was off on a two-month barnstorming tour of black settlements in Ontario, his mission to help fill the next emigrant ship bound for Haiti with as many black Canadians as he could muster. Annie would have had to manage at home without him, although she at least, by contrast with Betsey, had a supportive family network to help console her for the tragic loss. She also had one other comfort that might soon have eased her grief: By the time her husband left for Canada, she was pregnant with their second child.[7]

Brown seems to have dealt with his loss by immersing himself in his work. Putting to use his multiple powers of persuasion, he contributed a lively series of seven articles on the lives of African Canadians for Redpath's *Pine and Palm*. In addition, Brown agreed to write "a series of biographies of distinguished colored Americans" for the paper, the first indication he was beginning work on the ambitious project that eventually became *The Black Man*.[8] He initiated that series with a lively sketch of Madison Washington, leader of the 1841 rebellion on board the slave ship *Creole*. The following week, he published a sketch of the accomplished late-eighteenth-century intellectual Benjamin Banneker, a personal hero.[9] Those biographies, however, were all he sent to *Pine and Palm*; possibly he was saving the rest for the book, which eventually included those two sketches, slightly altered, with dozens more he had yet to write.

En route to Canada, he paused in Troy and Syracuse to give talks on loosely related subjects. Attuned to the latest news from the battlefront, he singled out for praise the first major act of Civil War heroism by an African American. This unlikely hero was a free black sailor named William Tillman, who was serving as a cook aboard the merchant schooner *S. J. Waring* in early July when it was commandeered off the Jersey shore by the Confederate privateer *Jefferson Davis*. Facing sale into slavery if the ship reached Charleston, Tillman singlehandedly overpowered or killed all the Southern officers, captured the crew, and freed the Union prisoners. By the time the ship safely moored in New York Harbor, liberal newspapers such as the *New York Tribune* praised him for his heroism, and the illustrated *Harper's Weekly* featured him ascending to the deck brandishing a hatchet.[10] In a public letter to President Lincoln, Gerrit Smith called him "the black sailor who stands, as yet, at the head of all the heroes of the present war."[11] To many Northerners, however, a black man wielding a hatchet generated threatening associations. A reporter for the local *Syracuse Daily Courier and Union* was among the latter; he covered Brown's lecture and bashed him for what he regarded as the sheer effrontery of his remarks.[12]

Brown then crossed the border to start his tour in Toronto, home of the largest African Canadian community. He gave four lectures there before a community he estimated at 1,500 strong and described as representing "every shade of color from purest white to midnight darkness." The work of promoting emigration proved problematic from the start; he found that little to no groundwork had been laid and there was scant enthusiasm for his opening talks, but he pressed on.[13] Over the next six weeks, he traveled to many of the African Canadian centers clustered in relative proximity to the US border—Hamilton, London, St. Catharines, Chatham, and Dresden. Wherever he went, he delivered the Haitian Emigration Bureau's message formally and informally—conducting multiple organized meetings in each locality, going out to farms and villages to meet prospective settlers, mingling extensively with residents, and inquiring more generally into the conditions of life for black individuals and families in their current homes.

His Canadian letters followed the pattern of local journalism he had favored in dispatches he filed from Cincinnati in 1855 and Cleveland in 1857 during AASS-sponsored lecture tours. Zesty field reports filled with sharp-eyed observations, they drew on his endless curiosity about the human scene. He conversed with people wherever he encountered them: in their places of work, outdoor markets, stores, meeting halls, churches, courthouses, and newspaper offices. In many instances, he paid visits to their homes. To broaden his knowledge, he rifled through local publications and consulted with community leaders. By the time he left each locale, filled with personal impressions and informed by his sources, he was well prepared to scrutinize it in print with the skill and sometimes the detachment of an urban anthropologist.

His relish for these encounters was palpable; their lives resembled what his had once been. In an open-air market in St. Catharines, a few miles from his onetime milepost of freedom, Niagara Falls, he counted thirty-seven black vendors selling everything from poultry to fresh produce in a scene that brought vividly back to his senses the markets of the South. Moving from stall to stall, he got into a breezy, free-flowing conversation with an old "Aunty" sporting a familiar broad-brimmed straw hat. They exchanged salutations—"Good morning, Aunty," "How de do, honey"—before slipping into conversation so pleasurable he rendered it word for word:

> "You speak as if you came from the eastern shore of Maryland."
> "God love yer heart, honey, I jess is—is you from dar, too?"
> "No," I replied, "I am from old Kentucky."
> "Yer don't say so—well, den, well, gib me yur han; dar is plenty here
> from ole Kentuc," and she gave me a hearty shake of the hand,
> that made my fingers ache.
> "Is yer jess come to de promis' lan'?"
> "Yes, Madam, I came here last night," I replied.

"You was house servant, down dar, I spose."

"Yes."

"Well, you see, honey, you is got yer freedom now, you must make
good use ob it. Did you leave any wife and chillen back dar?"

"No, madam, I had no wife when I came off."

"Now I tell yer, honey, yer must be on yer '*p's*' and '*q's*' here—many
dese women ain't no count, and you mustn't go and get a wife de
fust week yer is here, like some ob um. Wait a little while, honey,
till yer knows who's who."[14]

So it went as he made his way about the streets and markets of St.
Catharines, engaging in repartee with its residents. When a second resident took him for his master's son ("as you is light and well dressed"),
Brown responded that he was his uncle's. That Sunday night, he heard
one of the most renowned African Canadian fugitives, the now-free
Anthony Burns, preach from the pulpit of the black church. Afterward
he went forward, as the congregation requested that Brown take a turn
himself.

As he traveled west from Toronto, he encountered growing numbers
of refugees from US slavery. For the most part, he liked what he saw:
self-respecting people who avoided liquor, applied themselves to their
work, and sought the best conditions for their families. Some had accumulated capital; others, land they put under cultivation. Much as he
approved of the self-help attitude and material progress of black Canadians, he disliked what he observed of white Canadians. To his mind, they
made up a class of people lower than their peers in London, Dublin, and
Edinburgh, their primary failing being their penchant for a systematic
bigotry as mindless as it was offensive to his sense of justice. They closed
their schools to the children of their black neighbors, discriminated
against them in their employment practices, and generally treated them
as second-class citizens. They put up buildings that looked comparatively
flimsy. But they built hotels that featured one particular excellence he
could testify to: "In point of size, strength, physical development, and
fleetness, I think that the bedbugs of Canada surpass anything of the

kind I have ever before met. . . . Indeed, I am almost of the opinion that they have a particular liking for the colored man."[15] One night, he was visited by rats "the size of a woodchuck" that congregated on his blanket.[16]

A trip to Canada meant a reunion of sorts for Brown. Given his far-flung social network, he could not go anywhere without meeting familiar faces, some delightfully unexpected. He enjoyed renewing acquaintance with Reverend Samuel H. Davis, a good friend from Buffalo days who had chaired the 1843 National Convention of Negro Men at which Brown joined the movement. He also renewed acquaintance with local black leader Reverend L. C. Chambers, who invited him to speak at his Methodist church in London (Ontario). Most of those he met he had known in cities across the Northeast and Midwest, but others went back with him to the far side of the Mason-Dixon line. In London, he met a former slave he had known from the South; Brown held him up to the public as a model of industry for his sixty acres under cultivation, multiple barns, and comfortable house. He also reacquainted himself in London with two women he had known nearly thirty years earlier in St. Louis, Rose Breckenridge and Julia Clamorgan, who both had married into one of the city's distinguished free black families. Taking him even deeper into his youth was a nostalgic visit to a woman, unfortunately unnamed, who had been a favorite playmate on the Young farm in Marthasville until they were separated about the time Brown moved to St. Louis. He found her near Chatham, now the matron of a household consisting of four children, the oldest twenty and the youngest small enough to sit on his lap. And near her lived a woman Brown remembered as once "the handsomest quadroon" in St. Louis, now wrinkled and bent over.[17]

Occasionally a reunion revived old nastiness. In Chatham, a town with a majority of African Canadians, sparks flew as he renewed acquaintance with Martin Delany, who had embarked in 1859–60 on a major settlement expedition to the Niger Valley in Africa. They had probably not seen each other for years, but their respective novels, *Miralda* and *Blake*, had both been published in the pages of Thomas Hamilton's *Weekly Anglo-African*. No time at all passed before their mutual dislike broke out into verbal sniping. In one of his *Pine and Palm* letters, Brown made fun of Delany's high-handed pretense, noting he crowned himself in one of his handbills as "Dr. M. R. Delany, chief of the Niger Valley Exploring Expedition, Member of the International Statistical College (H. R. H. Prince Albert, president), London, Member of the National Society for the Promotion of Social Science of Great Britain"—and the list of honorifics went on. He went after Delany even more unsparingly in sketching him as an extremist: "Considered in respect to hatred to the Anglo-Saxon, a stentorian voice, a violence of gestures, and a display of physical energies when speaking, Dr. Delany may be regarded as the ablest man in Chatham, if not in America. Like the Quaker, who when going to fight pulled off his coat, and laying it down, said, 'Thee lie there, Quaker, till I whip this fellow,' so the Doctor, when going to address an audience, lays aside every classic idea of elocution and rhetoric, and says, 'Remain there till I frighten these people.'"[18]

WHY SHOULD WE NOT go to Haiti? Brown had asked rhetorically in Troy. The question boomeranged at him in Canada at a recruitment meeting he led at a Baptist church in Dresden, site of the Dawn Institute, when a skeptical listener called him out: Why did the distinguished lecturer, who had come to enlighten "*our dark minds*" on "the beauties of Haytien emigration," not set an example for his people? Struck right between the eyes, Brown responded evasively, according to a hostile reporter: "No, I have a pretty little young wife, and she is opposed to my going there; but if she would go there, I would go." The reporter had a retort for that disingenuous explanation and for another attempt at humor by Brown about unequal power relations between husbands and wives: "I would beg leave to remind him that there are few, if any in these parts, who are disposed to do as he is accused of doing, that is, leaving their first wives to get pretty young ones." John Scoble yet lived! In fact, he resided right in the neighborhood after emigrating from England in 1852, which probably explains not just this remark but also the overall contentious reception Brown received that day. Another skeptic came at him from a different direction by challenging his personal knowledge of his subject:

"Whilst Mr. Brown was speaking, some one asked: 'Were you ever in Hayti?' To which he replied, 'Yes, I was there two months'; but he did not tell a single thing which he saw or heard while there."[19]

Hiding behind Annie's skirts was one way to handle a position that was indeed delicate. Another way was to take cover behind James Redpath, whose position was even more exposed. A white man encouraging blacks to leave their homes in North America for greener pastures on Caribbean islands triggered virtually automatic resistance from some activist blacks, such as Martin Delany and James McCune Smith, as well as longtime white abolitionists who for years had fought to make the case for black rights at home. One of the fiercest critics of the Haitian Emigration Bureau was the strong-minded Mary Ann Shadd Cary, longtime editor of the black Canadian *Provincial Freeman*. Brown plainly admired her, but that autumn the admiration was hardly mutual. "The most intelligent woman I have met in Canada," as he labeled her, took dead aim at a movement she saw as challenging her life's cause, the establishment of an African Canadian homeland.[20] For months she fired away roundly at the emigration leaders, mostly at Redpath ("But what has Mr. Redpath done?") but also at "a few agents, using the name of Brown," who sowed dissatisfaction among her people.[21] Why should her fellow black Canadians follow the "south star" Redpath and his agents were dangling before their eyes when the "north star" would do? Years later, Brown would praise Cary's toughness—"Had she been a man, she would probably have been with John Brown at Harper's Ferry"—but in 1861 he found himself on the receiving end of her anger.[22]

Brown was vulnerable to charges of inconsistency and worse that year, but the criticism he received on tour and in the press had little noticeable effect on his work for the bureau. All that fall he continued to walk a knife-edge between old and new allies, but he sincerely believed he was advocating a policy that would help some people move forward with their lives—even if, as critics noted, he failed to adopt for his own family the advice he routinely dealt out to others.

He returned home from his Canadian tour by mid-October. He had barely had time to settle back in before he found himself outnumbered and outflanked at yet another community meeting, this time in Boston, called to debate the increasingly unpopular question of Haitian emigration. Brown did what he could to defend its historic and practical legitimacy, but he made little headway against a vocal majority led by his former allies Leonard Grimes and Robert Morris. For once he apparently performed his public role unconvincingly. The Boston correspondent for the *Anglo-African*, by this time purchased from Thomas Hamilton and reestablished under new, antiemigration ownership, even reported that although he argued his case eloquently, "Boston refused to hear or even believe that his heart was in his speech."[23] A few days later, he was back on the road for another monthlong trip, this time promoting Haitian emigration across eastern New York and New Jersey. During this tour, President Lincoln put a little wind in his sagging sails. If Congress had been unsympathetic with its compromising agenda, Lincoln proved even more insulting when in November 1861 he countermanded the order of his St. Louis–based commander of the Western Department, General John C. Frémont, to emancipate slaves in Missouri.

Brown was back home again in early December, his service to the cause by now nearly spent. Although he published a letter in *Pine and Palm* defending himself against antiemigration statements attributed to him, his days as an emigration spokesman were all but over.[24] By year's end, the movement was well past its peak, having run up against mounting criticism and waning support. The heady description James Theodore Holly had given of his large outbound party of émigrés as "a Mayflower expedition of sable pioneers in the cause of civil and religious liberty," once inspirational to his followers, lost all credibility as conditions in Haiti proved far more difficult than in North America and disease ravaged the settler community. News about the deaths of settlers, including Holly's own mother and child, arrived back north and gave force to antiemigration arguments, as did returning settlers telling stories of deprivation, disease, and hardship.

What most decisively reversed the tide on the emigration movement, though—more than shifting antislavery alliances, horror stories from the Caribbean, or organized resistance from the black community—was surging support for the war. The longer the fighting continued, and the broader its scope, the more it transformed into a war over slavery—even if, by a slippery reversal of victim and victimizer, reactionaries in North and South alike devised explanations that faulted slaves for causing the war. Calls for the emancipation of slaves, once the shouts of so-called extremists, increasingly emanated from cities across the North. At long last, after cautiously feeling his way forward as circumstances in Washington and progress on the battlefield developed, Lincoln sent a message to Congress, in March 1862, advocating gradual emancipation and compensation to slaveholders. On April 16, he signed the Compensated Emancipation Act, the long-awaited congressional bill abolishing slavery in the District of Columbia.

A week later, Brown sided with the overwhelming majority in a meeting at the Twelfth Baptist Church in opposing emigration. The immediate object was Liberia, but the "we don't want to go now" resolution expressed the gathering antagonism to emigration generally (a view even Brown acknowledged when he admitted in hindsight, "It would have been better for [the emigrants] and for Hayti had they remained home").[25] Now solidly back in step with the old movement, he joined the annual southbound delegation for Anniversary Week in New York City, which he had skipped the previous year. Introduced by Garrison as the first speaker at the AASS annual convention, Brown gave a rousing speech on the current state of the American union, bringing the audience to its feet. Playing off white against black in the contrapuntal style he frequently employed to challenge expectations, he paraded before his audience two of the most pressing questions of the day: "What shall be done with the slave, if freed?" and "What shall you do with the slaveholders?" Brown gave an elaborate response to the first but fired off a snappy riposte to the second:

The only recommendation I have to make in regard to that is, that you shall take the slave from the slaveholder, and let the slaveholder go to work and labor for himself, and let him keep out of mischief. [Applause.] If the slaveholders had had the opportunity of laboring for themselves, for the last forty years, we should never have had this rebellion. It is because they have had nothing to do but to drink and walk about and conduct mischief, while the black man was toiling for their support, that this rebellion has taken place.[26]

Brown remained in New York overnight to take part in the business meetings, as he typically did. Longtime participants recognized a historic shift, now accelerating, that was bringing about a closer alignment between their long-established position on abolition and the emerging position of the federal government. That closer alignment with the establishment, however, caused incipient cracks to form in the decades-old coalition of abolitionists. Whereas Garrison wished to draw a clear line between the abolitionist concerns of the AASS and the philanthropic concerns of groups organized to aid and educate the freed slaves, the hard-driving Stephen Foster called for adoption of a more aggressive, comprehensive agenda. Brown did not take a recorded position in that debate, nor would he align himself in the immediate future with one faction or the other. He was present, however, to hear the feminist activist Ernestine Rose urge the AASS to publish his convention speech and distribute copies to members of Congress. She even offered to contribute to printing expenses, but the society had more pressing demands.[27]

Shortly afterward, Brown returned home by train, possibly in time for the birth of daughter Clotelle on May 8, 1862. In dedicating the 1867 edition of *Clotelle* to Annie, Brown whimsically claimed that Annie chose the unusual name after reading his novel *Clotel* and taking the title character to heart—no matter that, in 1862, no such title existed. Why would they name their daughter after a "tragic mulatta" when they planned to raise her in as free and secure a home as a respectable, middle-class black family like theirs could provide? The naming revisited the old chicken-and-egg question that Brown's work repeatedly posed: Which came first, Clotelle Brown (1862) or *Clotelle* (1864/1867)? Who could tell one from the other any more than one could tell life from literature when, for William Wells Brown, sequential cause and effect failed to explain the course of events?

While a savage war increasingly dedicated to the abolition of slavery dragged on hundreds of miles away, Clotelle's parents apparently had the means to offer her a life of comparative comfort. Their home on Webster Avenue situated them in a working-class neighborhood of relative stability and security. Local schools were integrated and creditable. Annie's parents and her three younger siblings lived next door, and her oldest brother lived close enough to pay visits. Their nearest neighbors included a fairly large number of other African Americans, mostly transplants from the South, as well as immigrants from Nova Scotia, Scotland, England, and Germany. The majority of the population, however, was composed of Irish immigrants. Some of the men were craftsmen and common laborers, and others worked at nearby factories in Cambridge and Boston.

Brown remained mostly close to home during the late spring and summer months leading up to the issuance of the Preliminary Emancipation Proclamation in September. One night in June, he and William Nell went out to hear Frederick Douglass speak before the Emancipation League on the future of blacks in the United States. Old animosities vanished as the three men engaged in a "free and easy exchange" after the lecture; they all felt, at long last, the forward tug of historical momentum.[28] Some other nights, Brown attended social and cultural events in the black community of the sort that Nell typically organized. Most typically, however, when not at home, Brown occupied the podium at meetings held in churches, town halls, and meeting halls in Boston and surrounding areas to speak on current events. On rare occasions, he also performed one of his plays, although for the most part he abandoned dramatic performances during the Civil War.[29]

His mood bounced up and down with the course of events on the battlefield and in the national capital. At his most optimistic, a note of prophecy entered his discourse as he honed his message about the new day coming for African Americans. At the annual MASS picnic on August 1, marking West Indies Emancipation Day, he began his remarks by outlining the long historical arc of racial ideology. He reminded his fellow abolitionists of an 1860 Democratic Party election cartoon depicting a vessel containing a single black man among a boatload of whites: "The boat was sinking and the picture represented the black man on top, and these words were put into his mouth—'No matter where the boat goes, this nigger is on top.'" Miracle of miracles, that was exactly what was happening: "Little did they dream . . . that those words would become literally true, that no matter how they might flounder, or what became of their political boat, the colored man would come out on top." Brown had just recently met a slave, presumably fresh from the South, who responded forthrightly to his question about why there had not been a slave insurrection: Why rise up, he said, when "the white people are killing each other off; we have nothing to do but sit still, and wait until the good time comes."[30]

But Brown was not speaking to a mostly white audience to endorse that or any other view advocating race war or elevating one race over the other. Instead, he turned his commentary to the occasion for that day's picnic, measuring the potential benefit that emancipation would bring to the United States by the actual benefits that emancipation had brought to Jamaica over the previous three decades. Optimistic for once about political outcomes, he asserted that the quickest, surest way to accelerate the coming of emancipation was to open the Union Army to black volunteers. Break down existing barriers, he predicted in his closing remarks, and recruits would surge from all directions: "black men will rush from the North, and black men, formerly slaves, will rush from Canada, and, more numerous than all those, there will rise up in the Southern States black men with strong arms. . . . There are thousands and tens of thousands of black men at the South, with strong arms and willing hearts, ready to strike for freedom, and lay down their lives, if need be, for freedom, if you will give them the opportunity."

BROWN HAD HAD HISTORY on his mind at the black church in Philadelphia in 1854 when he envisioned that he and his audience were embarked on an "experimental voyage," and again the next year when he called for a history of US abolitionism to be written by Edmund Quincy.[31] The nation, not just the movement, needed such a work, he had said, but now there was another history the nation needed more urgently. By 1860, he was publicly asserting the national imperative of a history of America's black people. At that spring's anniversary meeting of the AASS in New York City, he stressed that an acknowledgment of African American history was sorely missing even where one might most expect it: "History has thrown the black man out. . . . You look in vain to [George] Bancroft and other historians for justice to be colored."[32] The Bancroft he had in mind was the preeminent US historian of their generation, author of the well-known, widely respected *History of the United States*—a magnum opus in eight volumes (and counting) that did no better justice to black presence in the United States than did John Banvard's three-mile-long panorama.

The record needed redress and someone had to intervene, Brown liked to say about such omissions. Fortunately, someone had actually tried and in fact was still trying: his close friend and frequent confederate William Nell. For his path-breaking, self-published *The Colored Patriots of the American Revolution* (1855), Nell publicized his indebtedness for information to conversation and correspondence with a circle of black and white friends, men of a generation, including Brown, Remond, Garnet, Pennington, Delany, Bibb, Whitfield, James McCune Smith, Robert Purvis, Robert Morris, Lewis and Milton Clarke, Wendell Phillips, Gerrit Smith, Senator Charles Sumner, Theodore Parker, the poet John Greenleaf Whittier, and other well-placed individuals.[33] But when he tried to publish an updated edition in the early 1860s, he failed to secure funds and eventually gave it up. Even before he did, though, Brown passed him by.

Whether stepping on Nell's toes or hoisting himself on his friend's back, Brown took the initiative in early 1862 to write the first of his major books on African American history. He seized that challenge more combatively than Nell was predisposed to do, presuming a necessary battle between opposing historical narratives. To build up an African American historical tradition, he needed to tear down existing white ideologies and narratives that had promulgated false views. In his preface, he called out "the calumniators and traducers of the Negro," men who propagated views of African "natural inferiority" so prevalent in the

1850s that they required rebuttal. He did not even need to single out the core group of these well-known race commentators, the men whom historian George Fredrickson called "the scientific triumvirate which attempted to convince educated Americans that the Negro was not a blood brother to the whites": Samuel Morton, father of race "science" in America; and George Gliddon and Josiah Nott, Morton's disciples and the coauthors of *Types of Mankind*.[34]

Closely linked to them was Louis Agassiz, the distinguished Harvard paleontologist who argued for separate creations of the different races. He had gone on a foraging tour of South Carolina plantations in 1850 with his local host, amateur ethnologist/physician Robert Gibbes, to gather evidence among good ethnographic specimens of unadulterated Africans to prove his theories. To document their findings, Agassiz and Gibbes arranged for the local daguerreotypist to take photographs of seven specimen slaves from a neighboring plantation; some of the men and women were forced to pose naked. After Agassiz's return north, Gibbes added identifying information and boxed the daguerreotypes—to this day, one of the most graphic representations of slavery in existence—and shipped them off to Agassiz for private study in Cambridge (just a few miles from the location of the Browns' future home).[35] Gibbes was so encouraged by Agassiz's visit that he also invited Morton to Columbia (South Carolina): "Can you not take a run South during April and see flowers enjoy fine air and study races?"[36]

This was one group of men whose ideas of African inferiority and differential origins of the species Brown needed to counter. Another, as mentioned, was the emergent generation of American historians led by Bancroft, with their alluring new narratives of US expansion, progress, and exceptionalism. The self-proclaimed grandson of Daniel Boone—so anointed in the book's introductory "Memoir"—saw the field of US history differently, bulldozing existing Anglo-Saxon structures and clearing ground to make room for African Americans. Brown had had his fill of them, as he had of landscape artists like John Banvard.

He had already made serious progress on his book project when, on May 28, 1862, he addressed the annual convention of the NEASS.

He spoke that evening from a carefully prepared text that reversed the normal direction of midcentury racial accusation: "It does not befit the whites to point the finger of scorn at blacks, when they have been so long degrading them." Instead, Brown pointed a black finger back at them. Early Anglo-Saxons had rated low for cultivation and intelligence with their conqueror Julius Caesar, he noted, and still did with such modern historians of England as David Hume and Thomas Babington Macaulay. Not so long ago, Brown said, he had stood on the Roman-era walls surrounding an English city and inspected the work of the enslaved ancestors of Montgomery Blair, Lincoln's prejudiced postmaster general. How, he wondered aloud, could the legacy of such a degraded people be compared favorably with the noble heritage of ancient black Egypt?[37] That address, soon reformatted for print, would serve as the core of the upside-down essay on race with which Brown was planning to open his new book.

He made good progress during the first half of 1862 and by late summer was far enough along to arrange for its publication. If he attempted to reach a deal with a trade publisher like John Jewett (by then bankrupt), he found no takers. Instead, as in London when trying to get *Three Years in Europe* into print, he took steps to self-publish the work, although in this instance without resorting to advance subscription. On September 4, while sitting in the printing office of the *Liberator*, he addressed a request for support to Gerrit Smith. Brown had recently visited Smith's Peterboro estate in central New York and must have expected he could draw on Smith's generosity. Dozens of African American writers and publishers before him, seeking aid for their endeavors, had left footprints at Smith's door, but Brown's pride led him to make the untrue assertion that this was the first such request he had ever made. Claiming to be seriously short of cash, he offered to compensate Smith in advance copies of the work. Smith sent five dollars.[38]

Even without a major sponsor, however, Brown managed to raise enough money to see the project quickly into print. He had the printing plates produced at the Boston Stereotype Foundry, the shop on whose top floor Ralph Waldo Emerson found Whitman in 1860 reading proofs of the newest edition of *Leaves of Grass*.[39] Brown paid the firm $300 and retained control over the plates for as long as the book remained in print.[40] To expand sales coverage, he worked out a joint New York–Boston arrangement, Thomas Hamilton to handle distribution from New York and Robert Wallcut from Boston. Brown had sent Gerrit Smith a tentative table of contents along with his request, but in the ensuing two or three months he added new sketches and updated others to keep pace with fast-changing events on and off the battlefield. The additional pages boosted the projected price from $.75 to $1, at a time when the wartime "paper famine" was inflating production costs.[41] Early notices for the forthcoming book began to appear in the antislavery press in late October, followed by the first advertisements in late November. A few came from unexpected places, such as the organ of the free-love community of Oneida, New York, which announced the book as due to appear on December 1 and identified its author as "one of the leading minds among the colored men of this country."[42] Once the work was in print, just about everyone who reviewed it agreed on one significant point: *The Black Man*, as advertised, was "the Book for the Times."[43]

There was an obvious reason for the accolades: Brown's publishing luck—or foresight—was solid gold. The run-up to the book's publication coincided with the outpouring of emotion, ranging from outrage to euphoria, unleashed by Lincoln's September 22 issuance of the Preliminary Emancipation Proclamation. Lincoln had bided his time painstakingly since signing the emancipation bill for the District of Columbia, as circumstances frustrated his ability to take any further initiative. Disastrous defeats on the battlefield had piled up through spring and summer of 1862. His senior officer corps was in disarray, with commanding officer Major General George B. McClellan verging on incompetence on the battlefield and insubordination off. Critics from all sides sabotaged Lincoln in the press, and politicians right and left issued threats. But on September 22, five days after Lee's Army of Northern Virginia retreated back over the Potomac after the unprecedented bloodbath at Antietam, Maryland, Lincoln issued his long-delayed executive order: As of January 1, 1863, slaves in all unoccupied states still in active rebellion against the Union would be free. One of the states granted exemption was nominally loyal Missouri, the state in which Brown might have believed his brothers were still living in slavery.

Abolitionists reacted for the most part with hallelujahs. Douglass exulted on his magazine's front page: "We shout for joy that we live to record this righteous decree."[44] Ralph Waldo Emerson responded appreciatively that the president's policy of "extreme moderation" in taking action, which had so tested the patience of his would-be supporters, suddenly made perfect sense. With one stroke of the pen, Lincoln had at long last stepped out as the national commander: "He has been permitted to do more for America than any other American man. He is well entitled to the most indulgent construction."[45]

Many liberal critics now agreed, but not Brown. Although he devoted his fall speaking tour across the northeastern states to praising the president's decisive act, he privately seethed over Lincoln's imperious conduct. Long a skeptic who reacted instinctively to nearly all politicians with distrust, Brown harbored a special animosity toward Lincoln for his rough handling of a group of Washington, DC, black leaders whom he had summoned to the White House on August 14. They were there, he summarily let them know, to be lectured and solicited, not listened to. After reading to them from a prepared text about the irreconcilable differences between the races, he sounded out their willingness to serve as leaders of a voluntary African American resettlement colony planned in Central America. Brown's occasional lecture partner, the talented African American poet Frances Ellen Watkins Harper, laughed off this scheme: "The President's dabbling with colonization just now suggests to my mind the idea of a man almost dying with a loathsome cancer, and busying himself about having his hair trimmed according to the latest fashion."[46] Brown was in a less forgiving mood, brooding over that meeting up to the moment he finalized the introductory essay for *The Black Man*, which treated Lincoln with backhanded derision.[47]

THAT OPENING POLEMIC, "The Black Man and His Antecedents," cleared space; the fifty-three biographical sketches filled it with the raw material for an alternative history of African Americans about which nearly all white and most black Americans were ignorant. Brown based his book on one of the central historical developments of his lifetime: He was part of a singularly accomplished generation of African Americans up from slavery or enforced inferiority who had made their collective mark on society. In short biographical sketches, he paraded a roll call of accomplished "black men" (three of whom were women) before black and white reading publics in what was the most extensive, though hardly the first, survey to date of black achievement.

Operating as a pioneering writer in a nascent field with self-appointed authority to name and anoint, he exercised his power broadly. He knew many of these people personally, had struggled side by side with them in a common cause. Old conflicts, jealousies, and misalliances wore away in the neutral zone of *The Black Man*, exposing bedrock solidarity among people he now treated as brothers and sisters: Douglass, Garnet, Nell, Sanderson, Remond, Bibb, Delany, Still, Grimes, Robert Morris, John Sella Martin, James Pennington, James McCune Smith, Alexander Crummell, Samuel Ringgold Ward, Frances Ellen Watkins Harper, Robert Purvis, George Downing, Charlotte Forten. From his earlier years, he zestfully cited the talented poet/barber James Whitfield of Buffalo, the admirable Ira Aldridge, and the impossible Joseph Jenkins. Reaching farther back in time, he reverently named the great insurrectionary leaders of the past—Denmark Vesey, Nat Turner, Joseph Cinque, Madison Washington—as well as Haitian Revolution leaders Toussaint, Dessalines, and Rigaud. He also named people he regarded as historical forebears, such as Crispus Attucks, Phillis Wheatley, and Benjamin Banneker. For some unknown reason, however, he skipped over the brilliant polemicist David Walker, author of the insurrectionary 1829 *Appeal* "to the Coloured Citizens of the World." Brown often passed by Walker's Joy Street house on Beacon Hill, and he was friendly with his son, Edward. Scanning the horizon for black talent, he "discovered" the fine young painter Edward Bannister working in the Studio Building in Boston and predicted greatness for him.[48] And, in the most bizarrely inventive selection, he named a chapter after "a man without a name," whom any close reader of his *Narrative* would have recognized as a variant of William Wells Brown.

The composition of the work was an attention-grabbing demonstration of what Brown did best: free-ranging, fact-filled compilation laced with thought-provoking stories, perceptive judgments, and sly improvisations. Frederick Douglass reviewed the book with amazement in the Emancipation Proclamation issue of his journal: "It is hard to repress the enquiry whence has this man this knowledge? He seems to have read and remembered nearly every thing which has been written or said respecting the ability of the negro—and has condensed and arranged the whole into an admirable argument—calculated both to interest and convince."[49] Whence indeed! In his preface, Brown partially anticipated that question by attributing his feat to his access to French and English archives—a strange and misleading claim about a work that included only two European figures (and one, Joseph Jenkins, a fiction).[50] Instead, as in writing *Clotel*, he had at hand a wide array of printed sources, many with little or no immediate connection to their subject until Brown made them fit.

Brown brought an excitement to *The Black Man* that was palpable. Author and readers alike sensed that *The Black Man* modeled black history in the making, even participated in it. Douglass immediately grasped its utility, declaring, "It should find its way into every school library—and indeed, every home in the land—especially should every colored man possess it."[51] An extravagant statement when men like Brown and Douglass struggled even to get their children into white schools, it nevertheless conveyed an excitement that passed reciprocally between author and reader, who could each stand proudly under its broad title.

They could, at least, in theory. In actuality, membership in Brown's "talented fifty-three" soon became a subject of heated debate in the African American community in the months following publication. An aggressive columnist for a new African American newspaper serving San Francisco's sizable black population rebuked Brown for his poor judgment. Brown, who did nothing if not read the press, took close note. After absorbing as much criticism as he could stand, he lashed back at all the critics, though singling out the San Franciscan as chief "blunderer."

They reminded him of a former friend with whom he had been back in touch after a long lapse. "'Ah,' said he, 'you were thinking of me just now, but you could not think of me when you were writing the book.'"

Meanwhile, other black critics scolded him for a variety of faults: not writing a synthetic history of African Americans, not systematizing his table of contents by date, not going over his text more closely. An author's thin skin could take only so many bruises before he retaliated. Brown did in "'The Black Man' and Its Critics," one of the era's most scorching critiques of the African American cultural field. Snapping off an impassioned self-defense against the "negro critics" and printing it in the *Anglo-African*—a good place to seek refuge, since its publisher was also the lead distributor of his book—he bared his prickly side to his critics. He unleashed even more anger, however, at the black reading public, which he accused of preferring trashy white scandal sheets to serious black periodicals: "The *N. Y. Herald* has more subscribers and readers today, and gets a larger support from the colored people of California and the other States, than *Douglass's Monthly*, *The Anglo-African*, and *The Pacific Appeal* put together."[52] Likewise, he accused his people of practicing reverse literary discrimination in their failure to patronize black-authored books, such as William Nell's *The Colored Patriots of the American Revolution* and Martin Delany's *The Condition, Elevation, Emigration and Destiny of the Colored People of the United States*. He worked himself up to a suitably disgusted aphorism: "No black man's ability was ever 'recognized' by his own people until it had been first discovered and acknowledged by the whites."

Brown was guilty of overreaction. The communal infighting was unpleasant, even nasty, but it was also a sign that the book had struck a live nerve with the public. A young but fast-growing black intelligentsia and reading public, with its writers, books, journals, and print infrastructure, had tastes and opinions that Brown could not unilaterally dismiss. He also was exaggerating and distorting the negativity. Douglass had issued high praise for the work in his journal, and another national black newspaper took Brown as living proof of "the positive ability of black men as authors."[53] Brown believed he had written a historically important book, and reviews for the most part confirmed his view. So did strong sales, which required a number of editions over the 1860s. That was as much popular success as any book written against the grain of Bancroft's *History of the United States* was likely to earn.

ON JANUARY 1, 1863, Brown awakened to a day he had dreamed of his whole conscious life. Celebrations were planned across the Union, although no one knew exactly when to expect Lincoln to sign the Emancipation Proclamation, while some people doubted whether he even would. Bostonians planned two separate celebrations on a grand scale near the Common, one at the Music Hall on Winter Street, the other at Tremont Temple on Tremont. Just a few blocks separated them, but that day it measured the social gulf dividing the city's white elite from its black residents.

The city's men and women of property and standing, some formerly with commercial and social ties to the South, attended the gala at the Music Hall. Presiding over this ornate affair was Edmund Quincy's brother Josiah, former mayor of Boston and father of a senior officer in the Union Army. New England's literary lions came out that evening in force. Henry Wadsworth Longfellow, Ralph Waldo Emerson, Oliver Wendell Holmes, John Greenleaf Whittier, and Harriet Beecher Stowe were present, with Emerson and Holmes even giving recitations. So were the old-line abolition mainstays Garrison, Phillips, Quincy, and May, as were many of their former antagonists, recent converts now swept up in the gathering momentum for abolition. The setting had the appearance and atmosphere of a gala, the building finely appointed and an orchestra hired to play celebratory selections from Beethoven and Mendelssohn. Late in the evening, when Josiah Quincy announced that Lincoln had signed the document, the attendees erupted in cheers: hurrahs first for Lincoln, next for Garrison—who would have been the most welcome white Bostonian had he chosen to go instead to Tremont Temple.[54] The formalities concluded with a thunderous rendition of Beethoven's Fifth Symphony.

The vigil at Tremont Temple began earlier, at 11:00 a.m., and continued, with intermissions, well into the night. For hours, Brown moved among his closest friends and colleagues, who filtered into and out of the building as the day stretched on. With Nell presiding over the morning session, attended by a large multiracial crowd, Brown came forward to read the full text of the Preliminary Emancipation Proclamation. Later in the morning session, he took the podium a second time to address the prospects of blacks as citizens in the new society, speaking fighting words: Though long a man of peace, he wished to see the freedmen armed and positioned to defend themselves against former masters. He knew slave masters too well to expect they would back down except under compulsion backed by force of arms.[55]

As no word had yet arrived from the White House, the evening meeting commenced at 7:30 and continued uninterruptedly well into the night. People who had waited years could wait a little while longer. Leonard Grimes offered prayers, while Frederick Douglass, John Rock, the fiery young white abolitionist Anna E. Dickinson, and other black citizens gave speeches, some harking back to slavery but most looking forward to a new day. With each passing hour, though, more and more people were beginning to doubt the president's resolve. Finally, Judge Thomas Russell, an old, trusted friend of black Boston, walked into the hall, excitedly carrying a draft of the Emancipation Proclamation that he had scooped off a table in the telegraph office. Jubilation erupted across the hall, with people screaming for joy, rapping canes on the floor, dancing in the church aisles, and throwing loose objects into the air. Frederick Douglass rose to his feet and began to sing—with the full house joining in—"This is the day of jubilee."[56] The celebration eventually spilled out of the building, resuming closer to home at the Twelfth Baptist Church and continuing into the early morning hours.

Lights flared bright late into the night in cities across the Union down to occupied Dixie, cities Brown knew well: Boston, New York, Philadelphia, Buffalo, Rochester, Cleveland, Cincinnati, Detroit, St. Louis, New Orleans. When Brown sought to memorialize the joy of Emancipation Night a few years later, however, he set the scene in the sprawling refugee camp and hospital complex of Washington, DC, a city he had never visited but, he knew, a beacon to freedmen streaming north by the thousands from Southern farms and towns. Brown recorded men and women singing and dancing jubilantly in the late-night buildup to the Day of Jubilee and the New Year—at which moment "a sister" broke out in song-and-response with "the vast assembly":

> *Go down, Abraham, away down in Dixie's land,*
> *Tell Jeff. Davis to let my people go.*
>
>   *Our bitter tasks are ended, all our unpaid labor done;*
>   *Our galling chains are broken, and our onward march begun:*
> *Go down, Abraham, away down in Dixie's land,*
> *Tell Jeff. Davis to let my people go.*
>
>   *Down in the house of bondage we have watched and waited*
>   *long;*
>   *The oppressor's heel was heavy, the oppressor's arm was strong:*
> *Go down, Abraham, away down in Dixie's land,*
> *Tell Jeff. Davis to let my people go.*
>
>   *Not vainly long have we waited through the long and darkened*
>   *years;*
>   *Not vain the patient watching, 'mid our sweat and blood and*
>   *tears:*
> *Go down, Abraham, away down in Dixie's land,*
> *Tell Jeff. Davis to let my people go.*
>
>   *Now God is with Grant, and he'll surely whip Lee;*
>   *For the Proclamation says that the niggers must be free:*
> *Go down, Abraham, away down in Dixie's land,*
> *Tell Jeff. Davis to let my people go.*[57]

Brown barely had time to descend to earth after the late-night rejoicing before boarding the morning train for the long trip to New York

City. He had committed himself to speaking that night at the Bridge Street Church in Brooklyn, which would be concluding its three-day celebration of black freedom with a gala array of speeches, prayers, and singing. He encountered a heightened atmosphere all the way down the coast, but nothing like what he experienced in New York City. The *New York Tribune* reported the New Year's mood of the city as festive beyond past years' standards, as "the people seemed to breathe more freely than before, as though a load had been lifted from their hearts, for they expect to see peace, freedom and union follow the abolition of Slavery."[58] Actually, as events the following months would dramatically show, the *Tribune* spoke for only one portion of the metropolitan populace. One New Yorker's cause for celebration might be another's for protest in a city bitterly divided over the war and simmering with resentment. An abolitionist family related to Horace Greeley celebrated Emancipation Day by draping their house in red, white, and blue bunting, only to step out later that day and find their front door and steps smeared with pitch.[59]

Brown stayed on in New York for two full weeks and participated in "rejoicing meetings" in New York City, Brooklyn, and Jersey City, including one at Henry Highland Garnet's home congregation, the historic Shiloh Presbyterian Church at the corner of Prince and Marion Streets in lower Manhattan.[60] The most elaborate was the joyous Emancipation Jubilee held on the night of January 5 in the Great Hall at Cooper Institute (now Cooper Union). The *Tribune* reported that the building was filled with the city's leading professionals and dignitaries, "many of them glad even to enjoy a place to stand."[61] The setting for that night's festivities would have resonated with attendees who recalled Lincoln's memorable debut appearance in New York, which had taken place in February 1860 in the same Great Hall not long after it opened to the public. The major speech he made that night, affirming the federal government's constitutional authority to regulate slavery in the nation's territories, culminated in the ringing aphorism "Right makes might," although at the time there was not the slightest unanimity anywhere in the country about what made right. For the people gathered in the same hall three years later, the Emancipation Proclamation was a powerful new beginning.

On that wartime night of celebration, the long, angular man occupying the podium was the charismatic Henry Highland Garnet—"tall and commanding in appearance, has an eye that looks through you, and a clear, ringing voice," as Brown had just described him.[62] Garnet presided over the jubilee as much in spirit as in person. He opened the formalities by reading the brief, businesslike text of the Emancipation Proclamation before giving a heartfelt commendation of Lincoln as "an advancing and progressive man" who had at last made good on his promise and, in the process, earned the trust of his nation. That reverent tribute, coming from the militant Garnet, expressed a more accepting assessment shared by many African American leaders who just a year earlier had doubted the principles and resolve of the commander in chief.

In a celebratory night of orchestral music, communal singing, and inspirational addresses that went on until midnight, Brown took his turn as one of a half-dozen well-known speakers, most of whose remarks (including Brown's) failed to survive in the historical record of the night. A snippet has survived, however, of the remarks of Lewis Tappan, a founder of the AASS and the American and Foreign Anti-Slavery Society. In an earlier period, Tappan had been Brown's nemesis, having authorized an investigation of Brown's troubled first marriage. Now, in the course of surveying the history of antislavery—a role few could fill more ably than the seventy-four-year-old veteran—he paid tribute to the author of *The Black Man*: "This is just the book for the hour; it will do more for the colored man's elevation than any work yet published." Brown did with that high praise what he did with any quotable phrase: He added it to the list of endorsements printed at the end of the book's second edition.[63]

During the weeks of celebrations for African Americans and their supporters, many of their fellow citizens were experiencing a hard winter of discontent. The war was not going well, rumors of impending Confederate cross-border attacks kept the citizenry tense, and casualty figures, by now mounting out of the tens into the hundreds of thousands, were appalling. Exuberant commentaries on emancipation appeared those weeks in the metropolitan press alongside grim reports from the battlefield. Newspapers carried daily accounts of battles, sometimes accompanied by lists of casualties—columns of the dead normally reported by regiment and company but occasionally set out in rows of newsprint approximating the rows in makeshift cemeteries in remote, unfamiliar places such as Murfreesboro, Tennessee. Beneath the text of the Emancipation Proclamation, *Harper's Weekly* featured the question weighing on the minds of millions of Northerners: "Have We a General Among Us?"[64] For that matter, fellow citizens vented so wide an array of complaints about the proclamation that Brown mockingly inventoried them: "'It will destroy the Union.'—'It is harmless and impotent.'—'It will excite slave insurrection.'—'The slaves will never hear of it.'—'It will excite the South to desperation.'—'The rebels will laugh it to scorn.'"[65]

Brown returned home to Cambridge in mid-January, exhilarated by the whirl of previous days and the heady reviews of his book. Late that month, he took his usual role in the events surrounding the annual winter convention of the MASS, this time probably along with Annie, who made contributions in her name to the organization.[66] On the opening evening of the convention, a few blocks from the Music Hall where Brown was addressing his colleagues, the popular young actor John Wilkes Booth was headlining as Othello at the Boston Museum. One local newspaper thought the role was made to order, matching Booth's "intensity of passion which is his greatest attribute" to the tragic Moor's "impetuous nature."[67] At the very hour of his performance, a passionate discussion was taking place at the convention, where some speakers interjected a sober second look at the course of the government's policy following the Emancipation Proclamation. Charles Remond expressed particular skepticism about whether the president's word was creditworthy at a moment when race hatred was running all but rampant across the North, even in Boston. Brown, by contrast, took a guardedly optimistic stance, emphasizing the inclusion of African Americans in state and national militias.[68]

He struck a main note, although he could not yet have known that

the recruitment of black troops, long urged by blacks and their supporters, was already in the works at the time he spoke and that Boston
would be a central location. In signing the Emancipation Proclamation,
Lincoln had opened the door he had previously barred, finally allowing
African Americans to serve in the Union Army. Choosing his words
carefully in the proclamation, he limited their activity to "garrison[ing]
forts" and "man[ning] vessels," so narrow a mission that it was impracti-
cal from the moment he signed his name. An expanded set of war goals
that now prioritized the end of slavery would alone have necessitated
an expanded military obligation for African Americans, but the army's
halting progress over a widening geographical area dictated their full and
immediate combat service (and, before long, the enormously controversial imposition of a draft).

Authorization passed down the chain of command in January from
Lincoln to Secretary of War Edward Stanton to Massachusetts's abolitionist governor, John A. Andrew, who was determined to put his
state's black men at the vanguard of the Union's troops. Once Andrew
received the go-ahead from Stanton, he appointed Major George Luther
Stearns to hire a team of prominent African Americans to help fill the
ranks of the first black Northern regiment. Stearns, like the men he
recruited, faced obstacles, not the least being the clash of wills between
most Union politicians and officers and the overwhelming majority
of the African American community, about allowing the new recruits
to serve under black officers. Despite that fundamental disagreement,
however, Stearns succeeded in signing up an impressive recruiting
team of African American leaders from Massachusetts and across the
North, starting with Douglass and soon gaining the services of Brown,
Remond, Delany, Downing, Garnet, and others. They, in turn, aided
by local leaders, took their advocacy to black communities to persuade
young black men they were enlisting not in a white man's army fighting
a white man's war but in a revolutionary battle for freedom. The official
name designated for the new cavalry regiment conventionally linked
state and numeral as the Fifty-fourth Massachusetts Volunteer Infantry Regiment, but everyone connected to it knew the name had the

potential—and its strongest supporters would say the obligation—one day to be a term of black pride.

Brown began his recruitment effort in Massachusetts within a month of his return from New York. On February 18, he addressed a packed Liberty Hall meeting of African Americans in New Bedford, home to the state's second-largest black community. Presiding over the meeting was local minister William Jackson, a veteran of the Underground Railroad who would soon join the recruits as their regimental chaplain. Supporting Jackson were a white colonel, a number of local men who had already enlisted, and a band to enliven the enlistment tempo. When Brown took his turn, he spoke soberly. He stressed he knew well the history of military discrimination and had even discussed it with the oldest black residents of the Commonwealth, but he believed the elimination of the hated exclusionary "white" from state documents was just a matter of time.[69] The stipulation that commanding officers be white was a stinging insult to black manhood, but Brown claimed that this alone was not sufficient reason to close off enlistment. Blacks already had their poets and preachers but now needed their fighters, for "the time had come for the black man to vindicate his own character."[70]

Several of the impressive people Brown met at the meeting had already internalized that message. One was a former hand on a New Bedford whaler named James Henry Gooding, a city resident who had signed up four days earlier and served the meeting as a vice president. An excellent writer whom Brown later memorialized as "the accomplished Goodin [sic]," he began a correspondence with his hometown New Bedford newspaper, filing updates from the field.[71] Gooding also began a correspondence in September with the man in Washington he called "Excellency," to register the regimental grievance of receiving unequal pay for equal service—a particular sore point for men who had generally known no pay or lesser pay in return for their labor. A second impressive individual was a fugitive slave from Virginia named William Carney Jr., who in 1859 "confiscated himself" and settled in New Bedford. Like Gooding, Carney enlisted early and distinguished himself in combat. He became a national hero when, in the frenzy of fighting at

Fort Wagner, South Carolina, he caught the regimental banner from a wounded comrade and, despite his own nearly mortal wounds, carried it back to safety. Two decades later, he belatedly received the Congressional Medal of Honor for that act.[72]

In March, Brown set up a recruiting office on Prince Street in the midst of Garnet's congregation in lower Manhattan. A local reporter noted: "He is sending off men daily to Massachusetts, to fill up the 5th [*sic*] Regiment."[73] One of Brown's proudest enlistments was a native of Bermuda named Robert J. Simmons, the rare black recruit with formal military training. Brown thought so highly of Simmons that he made a quick point of introducing him to Francis George Shaw, the father of the regiment's commanding officer. Once in combat, Simmons also impressed one of the regiment's officers, who referred to him as "the finest looking soldier" in the unit.[74] When the regiment shipped out, Brown followed Simmons's movements closely: He rose to noncommissioned officer and served heroically at Fort Wagner before dying from his wounds while a prisoner of war in a Charleston hospital.[75] Brown signed up other men for Simmons's company and remained in New York for a period of weeks, giving talks at local churches and joining colleagues at recruitment meetings across the area.

He was on hand also to witness the results of sustained recruitment. The ranks of the Fifty-fourth Massachusetts filled steadily over March and April as recruits arrived from across the Northern states and assembled for basic training at Camp Meigs, in Readville, a short train ride from Boston. On May 18, one of the first fine days of a cold, wet spring, Governor Andrew formally presented to commanding officer Colonel Robert Gould Shaw the regimental banner, along with flags representing church, state, and nation. Ten days later, the unit shipped out of Boston Harbor, but not before parading in full uniform before a crowd of 20,000 supporters lining a route that passed from the railway depot across the center of Boston—past the Common, the State House, the Exchange—to the wharf. That route, as numerous commentators noted, retraced the inglorious steps taken by Thomas Sims and Anthony Burns on their enforced deportation from Boston—although who should be present in the crowd to witness the parade but Sims, back in Boston a free man after escaping weeks earlier with his family from Mississippi.[76] The parade proceeded peacefully despite dread of mob violence, a fear so realistic after a recent attack on an abolitionist gathering that riot police were on alert. By 1:00 p.m. the unit was on board the *De Molay*, weapons and equipment stowed, ready for the momentous voyage down the coast past Charleston to the Union stronghold of Port Royal, South Carolina.

Brown attended the parade and chronicled the regiment's sendoff in one of the proudest chapters of his Civil War military history.[77] He also attended the anniversary meetings of the NEASS, which by chance coincided with the official sendoff of the Fifty-fourth. Seizing the moment, the NEASS leaders no sooner convened the morning meeting than they suspended it to allow everyone to go out and watch the Fifty-fourth march by. That glorious evening, a medley of speakers took the podium, including Brown, Douglass, and Harriet Jacobs, who mounted the stage with two young African American orphans she had brought from northern Virginia for adoption. Many longtime activists used the historic occasion to give retrospective assessments of the long fight for freedom, but Brown wished to talk more about black empowerment and was still glowing with excitement as he exclaimed, "We have had, to-day, a sight such as I never expected to see in the free States." Speaking as the people's historian, he commented on the long sweep of time: "We have lived a humbled life, having no historians except the abolitionists. We have been oppressed at the South, and despised at the North. The literature of the country has ignored us, except when it has abused us. But a new time has come. We are now beginning to be a people."[78]

Those were brave words to characterize a people about whom the chief military question of this new day was "Will they fight?" Even Colonel Shaw had his doubts about the fighting capacity of his men, doubts that nothing short of actual battle could ease. To confront his misgivings head-on, he insisted on drawing a tough combat assignment. After participating in marginal engagements in the Low Country of Georgia and South Carolina, the Fifty-fourth was ordered to join with other cavalry units on July 18 in a frontal attack on Fort Wagner, one of the islands protecting Charleston Harbor. The fort was so well defended by parapets and breastworks, and the assault was so expected that the assignment was effectively suicidal. To prove their manhood, the Fifty-fourth took the lead in charging the well-entrenched, elevated Confederate fort, leaving themselves exposed in the open sandy terrain to heavy Confederate artillery and musket shot. Four hundred men—nearly half of the regiment—were killed or wounded, including Shaw, who had breached the fort and was urging his men forward when he was shot dead. As the survivors retreated raggedly behind their lines, the bodies were left where they fell, and the Confederate officers made a point of throwing Shaw's body into a mass burial pit along with what they and Southern newspapers repeatedly called "his niggers." Brown's later account of the battle turned the insult into a compliment: "They buried him with his niggers!" became the opening verse of a song he printed honoring all the Union dead.[79]

News of the decimation of the Fifty-fourth filtered northward in subsequent days and weeks, a major news story featured in newspapers across the North but read with particularly keen interest in Boston. The unit's pyrrhic bravery was predictably a prime topic of conversation when the MASS gathered at its annual August 1 picnic at Abington. Brown made a point of commending the black troops of Fort Wagner and Port Hudson for combating prevailing views of "the essential inferiority in the black race." He also memorialized Shaw, who, Brown told the crowd, had made him a personal pledge to ensure the fair treatment of his men and had sealed it with the sacrifice of his own life.[80]

Even in that pastoral setting in Abington, it was impossible to separate talk of the bravery of the Fifty-fourth from the gruesome recent events in New York City. Just ten days after the momentous Union victory at Gettysburg, riots broke out in Manhattan over the implementation of the new mandatory-conscription measures legislated by Congress and signed by Lincoln to fill the Union ranks. For three tumultuous days, marauding working-class mobs overran entire portions of Manhattan in the city's single worst outbreak of civil insurrection. First they attacked the institutions, property, and people associated with the new draft law and the offending Republican Party. Then they spread out to carry their assault to the city's conspicuously wealthy, Germans and Jews, as well as such prominent antislavery proponents as James McCune Smith and Horace Greeley, whose *Tribune* office was torched. In no time, riots broke out all across the larger city and spread to its periphery.

What began as a working-class attack on a draft system perceived to treat rich and poor unequally swerved in midcourse toward vicious race warfare, as gangs of mostly Irish men (and sometimes women) ravaged black institutions and individuals. They burned down the Colored Orphan Asylum at Forty-Third Street and Fifth Avenue, ransacked the Colored Sailors' Home at 2 Dover Street (while the proprietor and his terrified wife and children took refuge on the roof of the five-story building), and assaulted African Americans indiscriminately on the streets and in their homes.[81] In the course of their mayhem, they murdered at least eleven black people, and, in one particularly grisly incident on Clarkson Street, hanged a laborer named William Jones from a tree and set his body ablaze. Their battle cry was a variant on a Confederate theme: Blacks were responsible for the war and therefore accountable. The metropolitan police were so badly outmanned that Lincoln had no recourse but to send in troops still bloodied from the Battle of Gettysburg to help restore order. It is not hard to imagine, however, that many of the city's besieged black residents would have felt more secure if the arriving soldiers had been their own. They could not have known that the city's police superintendent, who was himself maimed in the riots, had intervened a week earlier with Secretary of War Stanton to forestall the parade planned in New York for the newly organized Fifty-fifth Massachusetts Regiment.[82]

One common argument mounted by opponents of emancipation held that slaves, once set free of their bonds, would rise up in retribution against their former masters. Lincoln took this fear seriously enough to address it in the Emancipation Proclamation, where, in the process of freeing enslaved people, he lectured them to exercise restraint: "And I hereby enjoin upon the people so declared to be free to abstain from all violence, unless in necessary self-defence." In New York City, his lecture could hardly have been more misdirected. Or in other Eastern cities, including Boston, where Governor Andrew hastily left Harvard commencement exercises in Cambridge on July 14 to marshal local troops to control an antiwar mob in Boston. His best option might have been to summon the Fifty-fifth, still stationed at Camp Meigs, but instead he mobilized other units for fear of further antagonizing the rioters.[83] Like fellow blacks around the country, Brown observed the draft riots with incredulity verging on horror. On August 4, he sent an outraged letter to the editor of the *Boston Daily Advertiser* contrasting the patriotic courage of the men of the Fifty-fourth Massachusetts with the craven cowardice of the New York rioters.[84] There was not much else he could say or do about an event that awakened his lurking doubts. Few events in his life more severely tested his faith in racial harmony.

BROWN KEPT a frenetically busy schedule through the second half of the war years. He was now a middle-class man who needed to provide for his young wife and daughter, especially once he began the summer custom more typical of the wealthy of taking them out to the country to avoid the city heat. His income, as in past years, came from a combination of lecturing and book sales, but his prospects were now improved as the war spurred unprecedented interest in lectures and books dealing with all aspects of race. Sometimes he traveled as a lecturer for either the MASS or the AASS on a contractual basis; at other times, he managed his own tours. In both capacities he sold copies of his book.[85]

He also operated as a literary entrepreneur. In summer 1863, he updated the first edition of *The Black Man* by adding four new biographical sketches, chiefly of distinguished Civil War fighters recently in the headlines. Before issuing it, however, he took care to dispose of the remaining copies of the old edition. Some, at least, he shipped off to William Still in Philadelphia, asking his friend to do his best to market them, while he presumably also tried to sell copies via other well-placed colleagues in Boston and elsewhere.[86] The new enlarged edition was ready for sale by August and listed Robert Wallcut of the *Liberator* office as the sole publisher. That arrangement did not last long, because by

September Brown gave control over sales to James Redpath, who was still operating out of his 221 Washington Street offices (also now home of the *Liberator* and the MASS), though at present, after resigning his connection with the Haitian Emigration Bureau, he was Boston's primary radical book publisher. The partnership brought together two like-minded radical abolitionists intent on transacting some public good by literary means. Redpath added his own title page, featuring a pine tree (now without a corresponding palm) and an ornate illustration of President Fabre Geffrard of Haiti, one of the book's subjects, and he promoted it aggressively along with his biggest seller, a collection of speeches by the suddenly popular Wendell Phillips. Always the high-powered salesman, Redpath managed to catch the attention of the press a second time for *The Black Man*, getting a new round of reviews in newspapers in various cities and even in the publishers' trade journal.[87] He also had success in getting the book onto the shelves of major retailers and kept the book alive until he retreated from publishing in summer 1864, at which time Brown took over active management.

Brown also collaborated with Redpath in January 1864 on the third incarnation of *Clotel*, now called *Clotelle: A Tale of the Southern States*. Redpath filed the copyright and probably financed its publication, which he issued in a series of dime novels he called Books for the Camp Fires. Redpath marketed the series to Union troops with more time than money on their hands, hoping to provide them inexpensive popular literature with high-quality, socially progressive content a cut above pulp fiction. The series opened with a volume of stories by his popular new author, Louisa May Alcott, followed by *Clotelle*.

Redpath agreed to the deal even though he disliked the book. He wrote confidentially to Alcott, one of his most trusted authors, that it was "the only book of a second rate character" he would publish in his new series.[88] In all likelihood, he weighed more heavily the interest the book might kindle among soldiers than its inferior literary quality. That was an ambitious wish when so many members of the Union Army, from senior officers down to enlisted men, were hostile to the commander in chief's goal of emancipation. How many copies actually made it into the hands of soldiers, and what use they made of the book, are unanswerable questions.

BROWN'S DOUBTS about the administration's conduct of war and peace flared intermittently during the election year of 1864. At that spring's contentious annual convention of the NEASS, at which the Garrison and Phillips camps faced off, Brown spoke forcefully on behalf of black people: "We have heard much debate respecting Mr. Lincoln. I enter but little into it. The colored people of the country rejoice in what Mr. Lincoln has done for them, but they all wish that Gen. Frémont had been in his place."[89] Brown's renewed preference for the immoderate Frémont over Lincoln allied him loosely with Wendell Phillips, who had supported the breakaway Republican convention that was meeting in Cleveland to nominate Frémont for the presidency. Garrison, by contrast, had for months thrown the editorial support of the *Liberator* behind Lincoln, while his critics complained that the once fiercely independent paper had become merely a mouthpiece for the Republicans. For more than three decades, Garrison had kept his physical, moral, and editorial distance from the entire political sphere as though from a plague, but in early June 1864 he made his allegiance clear when he attended the Republican presidential convention in Baltimore, a city that had jailed him for libel in 1830 and long a stronghold of secessionist sympathizers. Despite doubts swirling around Lincoln's prospects going in, he received the party's endorsement for a second term, and Garrison received a boisterous hero's welcome from the delegates. Continuing south for his first trip to the nation's capital, the proud iconoclast who for years had championed "disunion" on the masthead of the *Liberator* found himself sitting face-to-face in the White House with the president.

Black Boston had its own views of the growing split between Garrison and Phillips. William Nell, a close, loyal friend to both men and a frequent mediator, tried his best to keep peace among the city's abolitionists. Brown, too, observed with discomfort the widening, increasingly ugly break between two men he esteemed as comrades and close friends, but there was no compromising his own mistrust of Lincoln's resolve. By contrast, he felt nothing but admiration for Governor Andrew, who had pressed for black enlistment and, once discrimination followed, exerted his influence to ensure their equal payment. So, on June 20, Brown gratefully chaired the open meeting held at the Twelfth Baptist Church during which Nell, acting on behalf of the community, presented Andrew with a portrait by the talented young painter William Simpson (another of Brown's fifty-three subjects).[90]

Brown displayed deeper anger at the mass meeting held at the Twelfth Baptist Church to observe the "day of national humiliation and prayer" proclaimed by Lincoln for the first Thursday in August. The morning meeting was given over to prayer, but Reverend Grimes opened the floor during the afternoon meeting to a discussion of national affairs. The mood in the church was gloomy, as many people were anxious about the war's direction and depressed by the awful reports of black death tolls reaching Boston from the field. Brown stepped up to the speaker's platform after Reverend H. H. White of the Joy Street Church, who took the hopeful view that the brave men who were dying by the thousands were making a blessed sacrifice for attainment of eventual good. Brown took a bitterly oppositional view toward what he disparaged as White's "bloodthirsty" God and Lincoln's hopelessly "imbecilic administration."[91] He went so far as to admit he was having second thoughts about recruiting men for the bloody war. He had never really made peace with the "half loaf" concession—as he called it the day after the Fifty-fourth deployed—of consenting to black soldiers serving only under white commanders.[92] Perhaps he felt black commanders were more likely to bring their men home alive.

Later that month, he accepted a commission—it would be his last—from the AASS to conduct a lecture tour across northern New England on the "entire emancipation of the slaves and the recognition of the rights of men without regard to color."[93] The trip took him back to many small cities he had visited in earlier tours, though now under strikingly different circumstances. Whereas he had previously found Maine a relatively race-tolerant locale that, he once predicted, "would be the first anti-slavery State in the Union," the long, grueling war had changed racial views for the worse.[94] Now he encountered a grudging animosity even among these truest of Yankees, whose attitudes had calcified since many of their young men were engaged in deadly combat on remote battlefields from Gettysburg to Virginia's Wilderness. "The cry everywhere," he reported from Bangor to a comrade, is "'this is a war for the damned nigger.'"[95] For someone who had spent thirty arduous years in the field, the message could hardly have been more discouraging.

Brown's service to the AASS ended by early September, but after a short period at home he was back on the road in early October with the Massachusetts delegation to the meeting of the National Convention of Colored Men in Syracuse, the most important Negro convention in years. "National" now carried new significance as delegates attended from such previously inaccessible states as Mississippi, Louisiana, North Carolina, Tennessee, and Virginia. The sessions took place under the specially exhibited battle flag of the First Louisiana, one of the first black regiments commanded by black officers. The unit had performed commendably in a long series of battles at Port Hudson, Louisiana, as part of the siege of Vicksburg, which culminated in Union control over the Mississippi River down to the delta. Captain James Ingraham brought the flag to the convention and recounted the story of his regiment, a tale of bravery already familiar to the several thousand attendees from various printed sources, including chapters Brown added to updated editions of *The Black Man*.

Despite major advances on the battlefield, however, the mood both inside and outside the convention was tense. For all the accelerating progress brought by the war, some things had barely changed. One of the National Negro Convention Movement's central figures, the controversial but respected Henry Highland Garnet, arrived shaken at the convention's opening session after drunken white hoodlums had assaulted him outside his hotel and stolen his cherished gold cane, a gift from his appreciative congregation.[96] The brazen attack on a one-legged black minister brought home to everyone a basic fact of life: No congregation of black people could meet anywhere, even in the North, without running the risk of insult or even assault. The fear of a race riot in Syracuse was then running so high that a vocal minority argued for relocating the convention—Garnet suggested Troy; Brown's old friend John Malvin, his home city of Cleveland. In the end, Douglass and others who refused to be intimidated carried the day, although not until the indomitable local Underground Railroad operator Reverend Jermain Wesley Loguen secured a pledge of police protection.[97]

In an act of homage to Garnet for his many acts of devotion to the black community, most recently his ministry to hundreds of fellow displaced black New Yorkers following the draft riots, convention leaders took up a collection to replace the stolen cane.[98] In matters of substance, however, Garnet faced rough handling at a freewheeling convention during which the delegates debated the future of black Americans in a post-slavery environment. Simmering disputes about emigration and colonization, not yet a dead issue, inevitably gathered around his head, as did a power struggle, chiefly with his old antagonist Douglass, for control over the convention as president. But three days of intense debating, infighting, and bargaining by black leaders representing different generations, regions, and ideologies yielded some hard-earned agreement about the path forward. Out of the discussions and debates came the crucial decision to found the National Equal Rights League to carry on the fight for equal civil rights, including suffrage. In the years to come, this long-lived organization would play a central role in the national political fight for equal civil rights. Not until the founding of the National Association for the Advancement of Colored People (NAACP) in the early twentieth century would it be eclipsed.

Brown formally addressed the convention early in its deliberations, but for the most part he participated at the committee level. He would have been conspicuous as a noted historian circulating among men consciously living and making history. More than half a dozen of his fellow delegates figured in *The Black Man*, and many more would appear in a later book. At some point in the convention, however, he must have gathered that he had a potential rival. James Pennington, his adversary on both sides of the Atlantic, tried to persuade the Business Committee to appoint a small group to take preliminary steps toward writing a history of the Civil War. Failing to gain its consent, Pennington tried to take his idea to the floor but was unable to squeeze his proposal into an already full agenda. Six months later, as Richmond was besieged and teetering, he sent a public letter to the black press suggesting the establishment of an Anglo-African Historical Association to "collect, authenticate, and preserve in a substantial form the facts connecting colored soldiers with the present war." His language sounded almost indistinguishable from that of Brown: "We who act in the living present should have our own history in the archives of the present. We have no right to trust to the whites to write our history. Hitherto our enemies have written our history. In so doing they have made us hideous. Let us now write it ourselves."[99] The initiative, however, went nowhere.

Brown continued from Syracuse on a lecture tour of western New York that lasted several weeks before he returned home to Cambridge near the end of 1864. From there he watched and waited as the great, concluding events of the war hurtled the nation forward into uncharted territory: the decisive reelection of Lincoln; the death of reactionary chief justice Roger B. Taney and his replacement by the radical Republican secretary of the treasury Salmon Chase; congressional (though not yet final state) passage of the Thirteenth Amendment, outlawing slavery; the rebellion-crushing skein of victories by Sherman at Atlanta, Savannah, Charleston, and Columbia; the fall of Petersburg and, finally, of Richmond to Ulysses S. Grant; the unconditional surrender by Robert E. Lee to Grant at Appomattox; and the assassination of President Lincoln at Ford's Theatre—all in a headlong rush of five frantic months.

Celebrations came fast those final months of 1864 as emancipation spread across the nation's shadowy middle border. Maryland freed its slaves in November, and Brown took a turn at the speaker's podium in Cambridge City Hall on December 6 to welcome that event.[100] Missouri soon followed, but Kentucky, native state to both Brown and Lincoln, lagged until ratification of the Thirteenth Amendment. Most Kentuckians, however, could already see the inevitable outcome of the war. In November, after Lincoln's reelection a Louisville newspaper commented on the state's failure to resolve its issues: "The question now is, not how shall we save slavery, but how shall we raise our bread, and bake it after we have raised it. Where shall we get the labor?"[101]

In the epochal year of 1865, Brown frequently took a turn on the public stage. On New Year's Day, he attended the second anniversary of the Emancipation Proclamation at Tremont Temple, and later in the month he was back, as he had been nearly every year since 1847, for the annual meeting of the MASS. This meeting, however, was like no other he had attended, as the proud organization William Lloyd Garrison had founded and led for nearly thirty-five years began to veer beyond his control. The radicals, led by Wendell Phillips, were out to take over the organization—some, it seemed, even thirsty for Garrison's blood. Early on, Brown's old lecture partner Stephen Foster called for the once-powerful and still-imperious Maria Weston Chapman to be removed from the board of managers, but that was only a start. Other radicals (Abby Kelley Foster, Parker Pillsbury) went after the rest of the old guard (May, Quincy, Chapman, Henry Wright, and even George Thompson) on point after point of policy and procedure. Strangely enough, it was the fumbling, elderly transcendentalist Bronson Alcott, father of Louisa May, who made one of the unkindest cuts to Garrison in calling him a great antislavery teacher before adding, "But if he should fail to go forward as before, he will cease to be your teacher, and you will select some other."[102] Everyone understood he was alluding to Phillips.

Brown was uncharacteristically silent at the meetings, disinclined to choose publicly between old friends until forced to do so—but soon enough that would happen. On February 13, he sponsored and presided over the joyous celebration of 2,500 people at Tremont Temple set off by congressional passage of the Thirteenth Amendment.[103] The scene in the Capitol on January 31 had been one of high drama. Black residents of Washington, historically forbidden admittance, packed the House chamber alongside members of the Supreme Court and cabinet secretaries and watched with high anxiety as the administration barely eked out the necessary two-thirds majority. Other cracks running through the citadel of American slavery and racism broke out in February, as Chief Justice Salmon Chase admitted Brown's Boston friend John Rock as the first black lawyer to plead before the Supreme Court, and Henry Highland Garnet became the first black to preach a sermon in the House of Representatives—on Lincoln's fifty-sixth and last birthday.[104] Meanwhile, back in Boston, Governor Andrew awarded former fugitive slave Lewis Hayden a gavel made from the whipping post of Hampton, Virginia, for presentation to the local Prince Hall Grand Lodge of Masons.[105]

On April 23, as Abraham Lincoln's body lay in state at Independence Hall in Philadelphia, on its transcontinental journey to burial in Springfield, Illinois, Brown was the first speaker at a mass meeting held at Tremont Temple to discuss the crisis of the times. The mood was grim for loss of the man Walt Whitman would soon memorialize as "the sweetest, wisest soul of all my days and lands," but there was no solemnity whatsoever in Brown's remarks as he talked personally for thirty minutes about his life in slavery, even lacing his speech with plantation stories that set the audience laughing. By contrast, the two major speakers who followed him, Phillips and Thompson, spoke more strictly to the occasion: Phillips to deliver a diatribe against the concessions he feared the new president, Andrew Johnson, would make to the South, Thompson to eulogize Lincoln as the nation's great conciliator. The differences among the three men and their positions could not have been starker.[106] Thompson had been Brown's close friend and ally during his London years, but now his politics seemed retrograde. Even Phillips, the only white abolitionist Brown ever held up as the equal of Garrison, occupied a footing alien to his own.

CHANGE WAS IN THE AIR; the end of the war posed a final challenge to the antislavery movement. In May, at the annual conventions of both the AASS in New York and the NEASS in Boston, the movement's leaders and members confronted the necessary question: Where did the effective abolition of slavery leave the antislavery movement? Edmund Quincy gave a simple, logical answer: The end of slavery meant the end of the antislavery movement—so he signed off at the end of the twenty-fifth volume of the *National Anti-Slavery Standard*.[107] Maria Weston Chapman, Samuel May Jr., and Oliver Johnson (editor of the *Standard*) likewise planned their exits.

It was Garrison, however, who alone had the authority to speak for much of what had been the white vanguard of the antislavery movement, and he answered in the most definitive way possible by deciding to close down the *Liberator* at year's end. An exhausted but vindicated man, now in his sixties, Garrison had waged a thirty-five-year struggle against the colossus of slavery through his weekly paper, which had presented the longest-running argument in print against the peculiar institution and its far-flung assault on life, liberty, and equality. A complex embodiment of self-effacement and unrelenting willfulness, Garrison had long since built his life story into an object lesson for steadfast, heroic allegiance to the overriding American ideal of liberty. As the course of events in 1865 gained momentum, he declared the victory won, resigned his leadership of the antislavery movement, and, on December 29, 1865, after a long debate argued in public as well as at his family home, printed his final issue. The last item on its ultimate page was an advertisement for "printing material for sale," consisting of assorted fonts, composing sticks, and stones—"the usual material of a newspaper office."[108]

Annie Brown still had an active subscription in her own name at the time Garrison closed down operation, a decision neither she nor William supported.[109] As African Americans, they could hardly consider abolition the solution to the racial problems that transcended slavery or to the enormous challenge, clearly just beginning, to build a robust black community, North and South, on the basis of freedom. By May 1865, Brown had already been allying himself with the new radical cohort led by Phillips that took over the AASS and the *Standard* and made maximalist demands of the Johnson administration. He sided openly with Phillips at the May 31 annual meeting of the NEASS (from which Garrison was conspicuously absent) in Boston, arguing that nothing short of radical reconstruction, rigorously prosecuted, would protect the freedmen of the South against a resurgent slavocracy.[110] At the MASS Fourth of July picnic in Framingham, he opened the proceedings with bitter fighting words: "The great millennium," so long sought, had not come.

The new president was returning to power the same Southern recidivists whose uncompromising aggression had caused the war. Hopes for black suffrage were fading, chattel slavery was evolving into wage slavery, and the overall prospects for the black man were dim and getting dimmer.[111] The question before the people was fundamental: What were the New South and the New North to be in an era of freedom?

One possible indicator might have been the fate of the members of the Fifty-fourth Massachusetts, the brave men who carried their regimental colors into battle for two years across South Carolina, Georgia, and Florida. In summer 1865, the unit, severely tested but widely regarded as redeemed, completed its service in the area of Charleston, South Carolina. In late August, the regiment steamed back north to temporary quarters on Gallops Island in Boston Harbor while awaiting release. During those slow days of imposed waiting before embarking on the next phase of their lives, many of the veterans proudly purchased their weapons as keepsakes.[112] Brown was appointed to head their reception committee, a signal honor for him to help welcome back the regiment he had helped to send out.[113] On Saturday, September 2, the regiment arrived at Commercial Wharf for the beginning of the official procession across Boston. Brown stood with the honorary Shaw Guards, summoned into duty for the occasion by Governor Andrew, to receive them. Their route into the city resembled the route on which they had marched out of it two years earlier. Thousands of Bostonians again lined the route as the regiment passed the reviewing stand at the stairs of the State House, where Governor Andrew and other officials were waiting. The regimental historian later memorialized the proud moment as the Fifty-fourth marched on, "welcomed at every step, with the swing only acquired by long service in the field, and the bearing of seasoned soldiers."[114]

The men of the Fifty-fourth dispersed to their homes and new lives, but the welcome that awaited them was not necessarily the one they had expected, nor were the glowing accounts of their return wholly accurate. A more sobering report came from the talented young African American painter Nelson Primus, who was working in Boston as a waiter while he struggled to launch his artistic career. Primus was just then getting acquainted with black Boston, in part by attending the Twelfth Baptist Church, where on recent Sundays he had heard talks given by Brown and the *Anglo-African's* current editor, Robert Hamilton.[115] He wrote home to Hartford that the regiment's return generated "a great deal of excitement," but, after getting paid, many of the men were robbed, and others got drunk and wound up in fights with fist or knives.[116] Heroism faded fast when confronted by the hard reality of lingering resentment and prejudice. Even for battle-tested veterans, building on the hard-earned accomplishments of the war was going to present an enormous challenge.

very truly your friend,
Wm. Wells Brown.

William Wells Brown in early 1870s. Frontispiece engraving for *The Rising Son* (1873).

PART 4

"The World Does Move"

10

"Help Me to Find My People"

"Help me to find my people" was the plea out of the mouths of count-less freedmen in the months following the Civil War. Relatives des-perate to reattach missing pieces to their families circulated notices by the hundreds through the *Anglo-African* in New York, the *Christian Recorder* in Philadelphia, and a new generation of black newspapers that mush-roomed across the South in the months and years after the Civil War.[1]

One man posted a notice seeking information about his long-lost younger brother:

Information wanted of the whereabouts of Wesley Brooks, youngest son of Isaac and Sylvia Brooks. He was sold 30 years ago to Natchez, or some-where near the Mississippi River. His father and mother, brother Samp-son and sister Mary, are dead. His brother John D. and sister Barbara are alive. Reply to J. D. Brooks through the columns of the Anglo African.[2]

And an elderly mother posted word she was looking for her scattered children:

Information wanted of the children of Hagar Outlaw, who went from Wake Forest. Three of them, (their names being Cherry, Viny, and

Mills Outlaw) were bought by Abram Hester. Noah Outlaw was taken to Alabama by Joseph Turner Hillsborough. John Outlaw was sold to George Vaughn. Eli Outlaw was sold by Joseph Outlaw. He acted as watchman for old David Outlaw. Thomas Rembry Outlaw was sold in New Orleans by Dr. Outlaw. I live in Raleigh, and I hope they will think enough of their mother to come and look for her, as she is growing old and needs help. She will be glad to see them again at her side. The place is healthy, and they can all do well here. As the hand of time steals over me now so rapidly, I wish to see my dear ones once more clasped to their mother's heart as in days of yore. Come to the capital of North Carolina, and you will find your mother there, eagerly awaiting her loved ones.

Hugh Outlaw, if you should find any or all of my children, you will do me an incalculable favor by immediately informing them that their mother still lives.[3]

Some of those who had fled slavery many years earlier took decisive action by going back to their former homes to look for loved ones or by making inquiries through intermediaries. The roads were now passable and new channels of communication opened for possible reunions. When Frederick Douglass returned as early as fall 1864 to give a lecture in Baltimore—site of his enslavement for part of his childhood and adolescence—by his side was an emancipated sister he had not seen in three decades.[4] Although he did not then continue on to his native Eastern Shore, which he would visit three times in the 1870s, his soldier son Lewis did the family honor. Stationed at war's end with a detachment of the Fifty-fourth Massachusetts in the neighborhood of his father's old home, Lewis was granted leave to visit his father's people.[5] Another one-time slave from the Eastern Shore, Henry Highland Garnet, lost no time after the war in making his first return to the plantation from which his family had made a group escape twenty-nine years earlier.[6] Likewise, Harriet Jacobs, who had spent part of the war doing relief and educational service among the freedmen in northern Virginia, paid a return visit in 1867 to her people in Edenton, North Carolina.[7]

Even Ellen Craft, still living in England, reached across the Atlantic shortly after war's end to locate her long-lost mother, from whom she had been cut off since her 1848 flight from Georgia. Putting her transatlantic connections to good use, she addressed a request for aid to a well-placed friend in the North—quite possibly Garrison in Boston—asking that her contact use his connections to make inquiries about her mother, Maria Smith, in Macon. That person, in turn, relayed Ellen's request through channels to the twenty-seven-year-old Union "boy general" James Wilson, whose forces, moving east, had mopped up Confederate positions in Alabama and Georgia all the way to Macon. Wilson quickly ascertained the good health and whereabouts of Ellen's mother, and he swiftly initiated the dispatch of return letters to the North and across the ocean to London.[8] Months later, Ellen's mother was en route to England for a reunion that had elements of the fictional Green family's European reunion in *Clotel*, except that, in a final twist inconceivable to Brown in 1853, the reunited Craft family permanently returned and resettled in Georgia.

And what about Brown? He, too, had had no contact with his family since his 1834 escape. Like John D. Brooks, he had a sibling sold down to Natchez in the early 1830s, and, like Hagar Outlaw, he might have imagined how a mother (part Hagar, part Rachel) would yearn for reunification of her far-flung family around her. But not at war's end and not for a long time afterward did Brown, as far as is known, return to St. Louis or send an emissary. Four years would pass before he went back, and when he did, it was as part of a lecture tour out West. He must already have known that there was no family to find—not there and probably not anywhere else down the Mississippi.

His situation differed from those of John and Hagar in one key regard. Even before the war, Brown had access to multiple channels of communication connecting Boston and St. Louis. He could have made inquiries through the *Liberator*, which periodically received local reconnaissance from a correspondent based in St. Louis; he would have had only to ask Garrison to activate the connection. Furthermore, he had contact with former residents of St. Louis, like Julia Clamorgan and

Rose Breckenridge, who would have apprised him of the latest news. For that matter, as news carried both ways, word about him (whether as Sandy or as William Wells Brown) would long since have reached St. Louis. Copies of his *Narrative*—not least, the one he sent Enoch Price—reached St. Louis by the late 1840s, and in subsequent years so did many copies of his more recent works. Had his brothers been alive, they might well have known who and where their youngest brother was.

Brown's literary characters displayed a quality in common with their creator: They were quick-change artists who reinvented themselves whenever circumstances required. In or around 1864, Brown once more reinvented himself. The previous year, he had informed William Still in one of his "by the bye" transitions that he had been reading medicine for some years and had given some thought to going into practice. His interest, he explained, went as far back as his friendship in England with Dr. Estlin, who had given him good medical books and expert professional advice. Ever since his return to the United States in 1854, he had been reading medical literature sporadically, but in the previous three years, he had devoted "all my spare time" to reading medicine, conversing with physicians, and attending medical lectures—all strictly "for the love of it." Meanwhile, he dispensed "medical advice [and medicine] to all my neighbors who are green enough to ask for it." Apparently quite a few of his male friends did, and so did some of Annie's female friends, all treated without charge.[9]

He presumably read medicine with some unnamed, established physician in Boston. In following this widely accepted nineteenth-century path to professional training, Brown was unknowingly repeating the practice of his father, who had read medicine with Dr. Young in the early 1810s. Brown's mentor might have been one of Boston's leading black practitioners—John Rock or John V. de Grasse, a brother-in-law of George Downing—but his familiarity with professional men also included any number of prominent white practitioners who might have taken him on. By late 1863 or 1864, he began practicing medicine on a part-time basis. Not until the war was reaching its conclusion, however, was he ready to open a new department in his professional life. In a letter dated February 17, 1865, the Boston correspondent to the *Anglo-African* reported that "Dr. W. W. Brown" had been warmly applauded on taking the chairmanship of a great meeting of 2,500 people at Tremont Temple to celebrate passage of the Thirteenth Amendment.[10] A few weeks later, Brown placed his first advertisement in Boston newspapers, introducing himself to the public as a "dermapathic and practical physician" using the latest medical techniques, with an office at 140 Court Street in Boston.[11] Later in the year, he advertised himself as using a new German cure to treat a wide array of diseases, including consumption, paralysis, rheumatism, neuralgia, gout, scrofula, and specifically female ailments.[12]

His patients, in all likelihood, came at first mostly through word-of-mouth referrals in his neighborhood and extended social network. The majority presumably came from the black community, but his clientele probably diversified as he branched out into more nearly full-time practice in his Boston office. An English visitor stopped by to see Brown at his medical office on January 2, 1866, and found him well established, with "a large practice," although he gave no details about Brown's clientele.[13] The identity of at least one early patient is known: Helen Garrison, wife of William Lloyd. On the last day of 1863, she had suffered a major stroke that paralyzed her left side. She recovered slowly and partially, not taking her first, tentative steps until March and not walking any distance until early summer. Although her improvement was fairly steady, the Garrisons hoped to accelerate her recuperation by turning to Brown to apply his new dermapathic "cure" to her condition. The family watched one day in August as he applied to her spine and extremities the tentacles of an instrument he had imported from Germany, a *Lebenswecker* ("life resuscitator," or "artificial leech"). Fine acupuncture-type needles running along the end of the foot-long rod broke the skin like the teeth of a reaper, and toxic oil was applied through the wounds to cause blistering, the first stage toward rejuvenating healing. At first the family thought their matriarch had improved, but as weeks passed without significant effect, they gradually came to doubt the efficacy of the treatment.[14] As far as is known, they did not return to Brown for further treatment, then or later. Other chemical methods of treatment he used apparently included the ingestion of homemade medicines, produced perhaps from recipes he had learned as far back as his service to Dr. Young.

It is easy to dismiss Brown's medical career as amateurish verging on charlatanism—a criticism not unrelated to the dismissive view of twentieth-century critics of his unorthodox, eclectic literary practices. From today's perspective, the case against William Wells Brown M.D. is basic: His training does not meet modern standards, his theories and practices would now be deemed unscientific, and he failed the professional disciplinary practice of keeping a strict office schedule whenever other preoccupations took him on the road. His practice was, in the worst sense of the term, "eclectic," although that was also true for most practitioners at the time. On the other hand, patients never ceased to go to him for treatment, and he never ceased to attend to them. No formal complaint, as far as is known, was ever made against him, and if his sense of responsibility in other matters was impeccable, it seems likely he also took his medical practice seriously. He certainly did his title. Although modest in most regards, he attached the honorific "Dr." to his name on all his later books and was regularly referred to as such in public until the end of his life, when his death certificate listed his profession as "physician."[15] Both his eulogists and the general public used that title respectfully.

THE OTHER LABEL that was attached consistently to him during his last two decades was "author." News reports from the early and mid-1860s began to tag him less as an ex-slave than as an author. A white paper in Syracuse, for instance, covering the 1864 National Convention of Colored Men identified him as "the author of a romantic autobiography and other works."[16] The label fit his profile increasingly when, beginning in 1865, his work for the first time could be sold nationally. His first book to cross the Mason-Dixon line freely was *The Black Man*, for which he had always harbored nationwide ambitions. He had had to bide his time, however, as during wartime, Northern books and periodicals ran up against a nearly impenetrable wall at Southern borders. Once federal forces expanded their hold across the entire Confederacy in the war's final months, Brown took to scanning the map with a proprietary eye. In February 1865, he made his entrepreneurial ally William Still one of his insinuating propositions: "By the bye," would one of Still's friends (or would he) be interested in purchasing the stereotype plates of the book and, with them, the proprietary right to future sales? The lay of the land for a venturesome young black man was promising: "There is a demand coming in from the South. The book has never been circulated there. They want copies in New Orleans, Vicksburgh [*sic*], and other places."[17] There is no evidence Brown found any takers for those locations through Still, but he definitely located one for Savannah.

A title page of an African American book bearing the imprint of Savannah, 1865, was (and is) eye-catching. Just months earlier, General William T. Sherman had conquered the city in time to present it to Lincoln as "a Christmas gift" for 1864, but this proud Southern bastion would have been an unlikely place for an African American publishing venture. Brown's partner in the edition was a rising community activist named James M. Simms, an ex-slave from Savannah and the sort of ambitious man Brown typically admired. Simms had purchased his freedom in 1857 and started a local school, but he ran afoul of the authorities and suffered a public whipping for teaching black children to read. He soon abandoned Savannah for Boston, where in 1864 he must have come to Brown's attention.[18] Simms returned home in February 1865, shortly after Sherman imposed military control over the city; most likely, he had already reached an arrangement with Brown to bring out a new edition of *The Black Man*. In the months following his return, Simms would embody an exemplary success story of the sort told many times over in the book. He quickly established himself in postwar Savannah as a religious leader, newspaper publisher, and politician. But first he brought out *The Black Man* for an audience of his peers.

The actual place of production was Boston. The text consisted of gatherings of printed sheets from the second Boston edition, fitted with a new Savannah title page prepared in Boston, which reused the symbol of the pine tree from the Redpath edition. The binding consisted of the same or leftover cloth boards used for the fourth edition, which Robert Wallcut had issued in late 1864.[19] Once the work was ready, Brown presumably authorized shipment of the bound volumes down the coast to Simms, who must have left Boston too early to correct the misspelling ("Symms") of his name on the title page. Brown might have put Simms on some kind of sales-commission basis, but whatever the exact agreement, each man could expect to put a penny in his pocket while providing the freedmen of the South with models of black achievement.

Simms lost no time getting the book into circulation; one surviving copy has an inscription dated July 16, 1865, a gift presented by one African American friend to another on Edisto Island, South Carolina.[20] To judge from surviving copies, which are located primarily in Southern libraries (and at least several of which carry the stamp of the Georgia Equal Rights League on the spine), that edition must have reached readers mostly south of the Mason-Dixon line.[21] By contrast with their contemporaries in the North, those readers probably would have been overwhelmingly African American, many of them social, political, and religious leaders of communities making transformative strides as they progressed through Reconstruction. A book "for the times" that had been written in the midst of civil war, as it turned out, also spoke forcefully to the immediate postwar situation. It offered inspiration in addressing a question of gripping relevance: How would millions of African Americans—nearly four million recently freed and now repositioned wherever they were—rebuild their lives in a newly reconstituted nation?

SLAVERY WAS DEAD, but freedom was tenuous and equality was barely even theoretical. After fighting slavery for more than two decades, Brown rededicated himself after the war to working for black civil rights and community reformation. Although from this point forward he made his living primarily from his medical practice, he continued to devote considerable time and attention to a life of activism. He maintained old allegiances, such as to the AASS, led by Wendell Phillips until its dissolution in 1870, and he formed new ones in the years to come, on both local and national levels. That pattern continued to the end of his life.

By war's end, Brown had mixed views of Lincoln, but he never felt anything other than contempt for his successor, Andrew Johnson. His suspicions began almost immediately after the assassination and intensified as Johnson entered into bitter battles with Congress over the terms of Reconstruction for black and white citizens of the South. In 1865, Brown told the MASS Fourth of July picnic in Framingham that the situation was "darker" than a year earlier and the outcome was dubious: "The prospect is, that the black man is to be ground to powder." He forecast dire results unless Congress took control over national politics: no voting rights, white minority rule, lawlessness with resort to violence, and loss of black property claims.[22] He might have been speaking rhetorically to this particular assembly, but his grim forecast proved disturbingly accurate.

The politics of the new president, a conservative Tennessee Democrat and onetime slave owner, were largely unpredictable at the time of his sudden entrance into the White House. Clarification, however, came quickly and definitively as Johnson sided on issue after issue with the former rebels, and against the radicals in Congress and their abolitionist supporters. Who owned property the Union Army had confiscated from Confederate rebels and now occupied by freedmen needing land for residence and sustenance? Johnson's unyielding answer: the old owners. Who should administer the rebel states, whose final status remained indeterminate? Johnson: the former elite; Congress: anyone but. Should male freedmen be given the vote? In a swift sequence of moves and countermoves, Congress answered emphatically by legislating the Fifteenth Amendment, which Johnson vetoed and Congress overrode. So it went, with one major issue after the next regarding the future of the South and the rights of the freedmen as Johnson's presidency spiraled into acrimonious disagreement between a conservative executive and a radical reformist legislature. The showdown culminated in 1868 in Johnson's impeachment by the House and, but for one vote, near-dismissal by the Senate.

In the immediate aftermath of the war, as the contest to determine the future character of the nation shifted from Southern battlefields to state legislatures and Congress, Brown monitored the evolving situation carefully. He was mostly a spectator in 1866, sticking close to home in Cambridge and devoting the majority of his time to his medical practice and occasional writing. As typically happened, however, the combination of opportunity and commitment drew him back out into the field.

In early 1867, he accepted appointment as general agent for the Freedmen's National Memorial, an initiative organized by the African American community to commemorate Lincoln, the Great Emancipator. The idea was born in 1865 even before Lincoln's body was in the ground. In an April 20 public letter to the black community, Martin Delany, then a major stationed in Charleston with the men of the 104th Colored Troops, called for a monumental statue to honor "The Father of American Liberty." To keep the project wholly black, Delany proposed its financing come from a self-imposed one-cent tax on the head of every African American, including those most recently free, and he called out Henry Highland Garnet, James McCune Smith, and Daniel Payne, president of Wilberforce University, the nation's earliest historically black college, to support the initiative.[23] These leaders, bolstered by other prominent men and women and common people from all walks of life, joined in supporting this major initiative, which for a time began to gain momentum. The noted sculptor Harriet Hosmer produced a bold, elaborate model designed to illustrate the progressive history of Southern blacks from slavery to freedom, and collection of funds began.[24]

Brown came to the enterprise relatively late but took special interest in a project that embraced not just a core principle but also his ideal of truthful public art. Its purpose was to celebrate Lincoln and African Americans together, the emancipator and the emancipated—a linkage reminiscent of the public coupling made between Garrison and Brown as "benefactor" and "redeemed" on the eve of his departure for Europe. Douglass expressed the principle well in calling for black people's "incorporation into the American body politic," but the monument initiative necessarily extended that view to include the incorporation of the black body in public art—this at a time when blacks were rarely if ever portrayed positively in visual terms.[25] Not even Brown, with his relentless search for effective means of visual and verbal representation, had made serious progress in this regard. His engravings of kneeling slaves, minstrel-type figures, and defensive women and children fell short of the heroic ideal of black personhood Hosmer and her supporters had in mind. Her bold, elaborate design featured four stages in African American historical development, beginning with the conventional kneeling slave and rising to the figure of an armed African American soldier standing tall—but too tall and too armed a black man, for some people's taste.

Brown's advocacy for the memorial took him for the first time to Washington, DC, a city more Southern than otherwise. Known to him only by report and reputation, he had long associated it, as in *Clotel*, with auction stalls, slave pens, and sleazy politicians. Expecting little, he was pleasantly surprised to encounter a "really free" city whose public transportation, facilities, and government buildings were open to blacks to a degree he had rarely encountered even in Northern cities. Although he was there primarily on monument-related business, he also toured the city enthusiastically. He paid visits to black establishments around town, scrutinized Thomas S. Noble's acclaimed *The Slave Mart* hanging in the Capitol rotunda, visited the Freedmen's Bank, enjoyed a reading by the African American poet J. Madison Bell, and visited with community leaders. Taking advantage of the new access given to blacks on Capitol Hill, he also spent some hours attending sessions of Congress. One memorable session he attended was dominated by a marathon oration by Senator Willard Saulsbury of Delaware, a Democratic lawmaker notorious for an 1863 drunken rant from the Senate floor in which he called Lincoln an "imbecile." On this occasion, Brown noted, Saulsbury "happened to be sober."[26]

He observed a surprising new progressivism breaking out in the capital, but he saw something starkly different when he ventured out for the first time into the countryside of Virginia and Maryland, two states previously not accessible to a fugitive slave and not welcoming to a free black with his reputation. His conversations and encounters with the newly free population led him to draw forbidding conclusions about postwar conditions on the ground. Freedom for the freedmen was hanging in the balance; only the decisive intervention of the federal government could protect new liberties and prevent old injustices.[27] By the time he returned home from this Southern swing, he had gained a more urgent sense of the necessity of government intervention.

One wonders what the men and women he encountered in Virginia and Maryland thought of the Lincoln memorial project. Some of these hard-pressed people must have confronted him: Where were black communal priorities when tens of thousands of black people still lacked food and shelter and had no access to education? Opposition to the project spanned the region. When Brown gave a promotional talk for the monument after returning to Boston, he ran into immediate resistance. The local correspondent of the *Standard* found Brown's total projected figure, now up to $250,000, "startling" and wondered whether it was defensible when "immense suffering" was occurring among the freedmen: "The monument can wait; the starving cannot wait."[28] A more focused objection came from a thoughtful black South Carolinian who thought the money could be better spent on the educational future of the freedmen themselves: "Gather together, then, the funds. Build a college—an institution—a university, or whatever may be its name, and let it be the monument of him who is to be the future idol of a freed race."[29]

Brown labored on behalf of the project intermittently through 1867, making stops not only in cities with large African American populations like Philadelphia, New York, and Boston but also in smaller cities across the Northeast. In May, he stopped by the Philadelphia office of the *Christian Recorder*, an African American weekly allied with the African Methodist Episcopal Church, to hand the editor a photograph of Hosmer's design and to inform him that $25,000 had to date been raised.[30] During a November speaking tour that took him back to familiar places in New York state, he paused while in Canastota, a village only nine miles from Gerrit Smith's house, to appeal to his old friend for support. Not much aid would be forthcoming from that quarter (Smith endorsed Brown's letter on the back: "I will do a *little*–but not now"), but that was the least of the project's problems.[31] As its critics complained, the price was excessive, with little more than 10 percent raised in two years, which may explain why Brown and his colleagues broadened the project's subscription base by appealing to wealthy white benefactors like Smith. In addition, intricate organizational complications and inexpert guidance doomed the project to languish for years. Not until 1876 was a scaled-back version of the renamed Freedom's Memorial to Abraham Lincoln constructed in Lincoln Park, Washington, DC—rising just as the grand, visionary plan of Reconstruction collapsed in inglorious heaps in Southern capitals from Richmond to Austin.

The memorial was only one of Brown's public concerns throughout 1867. He also lectured on temperance, suffrage, black military conduct, and Radical Reconstruction—related subjects in his mind. On April 23, he delivered a "bold" lecture at Liberty Hall in Philadelphia to 200 people on the dangers to blacks of alcohol and tobacco use, a concern of increasing importance as he and other African American leaders turned their attention to the education and deportment of free-willed individuals. Even when he stressed the obligation of personal morality, his speaking style rarely employed the fire-and-brimstone rhetoric typical of black clergy. A local reporter, amused by the personal stories he mixed into his instructional discourse that night, remarked afterward, "He is a travelling repertory of anecdotes."[32]

On May 7, Brown entertained the annual convention of the AASS with one of those anecdotes, which allowed rare public entry into his guarded private life. The meeting took place at New York's Steinway Hall, a new 3,000-seat theater on Fourteenth Street near Union Square sometimes used for public meetings and concerts. In the course of momentous debates over the proper role of Washington in overseeing Reconstruction, Brown gave the audience a rollicking account of an encounter that never happened but that slyly enacted one of his recurrent fantasies:

> While at the South not long ago, I had a very interesting interview with my old master. It was indeed very interesting to both of us. We had not met for thirty years. He congratulated me on my position, and I congratulated him on his. (Laughter.) We compared opinions and

talked over all the ground. Every once in a while he would give a long sigh, especially when I spoke of the progress of freedom in the land. At last he said, "Well, it may be that this thing will last; but I don't know as it will." Then he went back to reckon up some old scores that stood between us. . . . "You remember when you ran away that you stole one of my coats." Well, I had to plead guilt to the coat; but said I, "You had two coats, and I had none; and you was not willing to apply the Scripture doctrine to the coat, so I did." (Laughter.) Said he, "I have heard a great deal about your travelling in Europe and this country, and read a book you sent me, and bought another I saw advertised, and you said a great deal there about justice and all this sort of thing. Now, I think you ought to pay me for that coat." (Laughter.) "How much is the coat worth?" "It cost me thirty-five dollars." Said I, "Your memory is good on that subject, after thirty years." "Well," he said, "I remember it." Said I, "Are you poor?" "Well, no; still I want justice done. And I think you ought to pay me a little interest on the coat." I told him I could not do anything of the kind. "Well," said he, "you seem to have been among people who talk a great deal about justice and Christianity, and you must pay me for that coat. If you don't I will meet you at the day of judgment and demand pay for the coat." I looked at him. He seemed very serious. He had got into one of his religious moods, and he preached me a short sermon, closing by demanding pay for the coat. "Well," said I, "I shall have to say to you what the Irishman said to the priest. A woman in Ireland lost a pig, and she found out after some days who stole it. So she went to the priest and told him about it. The priest sent for the man, and said to him: 'Mrs. Malone says you have stolen her pig. Did you steal it?' 'Faith, and your reverence, I did.' 'You must give it up.' Now Pat had killed the pig and half devoured it. So he said, 'Faith, and what if I don't return the pig?' 'If you don't, you will have to answer for it in the day of judgment. What will you say then?' 'And will Mrs. Malone be there?' 'Yes.' 'And will I be there?' 'Yes.' 'And will the pig be there?' 'Yes.' 'Then I'll tell Mrs. Malone to take her pig.' So I said to my old master, that if he was there, and I was there, and the coat was there, he might take his coat." (Laughter and applause.)[33]

"Old master" somehow never failed to show up at Brown's doorstep, or Brown at his, but for this occasion neutral ground in the heart of New York City served them equally well. Brown had been addressing this friendly national gathering during more than a quarter century of kaleidoscopic change, but the core element of the story he told that May 1867 night was exactly what it had always been. Once again, he and old master locked heads in a battle of wits, this time in a story spun for an appreciative but uninitiated New York audience enchanted by the verbal ingenuity with which Brown bettered his mortal antagonist. The flesh-and-blood reality was more complicated: He got the coat, but old master got Brown's relatives and was never going to give them back. Psychologically for Brown, the past was never past; it lingered endlessly on the margin of consciousness.

BROWN CLAIMED in the preface to *The Negro in the American Rebellion* (1867) that he wrote the book because no one had as yet taken up the challenge: "I waited patiently, before beginning this work, with the hope that some one more competent would take the subject in hand, but, up to the present, it has not been done. . . ." That statement was Brown's usual test of a too-literal reader's credulity. In fact, he had followed the war news with intense interest throughout the conflict, possibly with a sense of responsibility. He had no son to give to the fighting, but he watched over the movements of all black units, particularly those with men he had recruited, with a nearly paternal regard. After the war ended, he was still joking about the glory reflected on him as he went about his daily affairs in Cambridge. He told a Philadelphia audience early in 1867 that he came in for a look of new respect on neighbors' faces as soon as word of his units' military exploits reached home: "Colored stocks went up; wool had a rise."[34]

He had begun writing the book, originally more specifically entitled *The Negro in the Great Rebellion*, in the fall of 1866, but he was probably stockpiling sources as soon as African American units entered the conflict in force.[35] He drew his material primarily from four kinds of sources: the torrent of war news coverage pouring out of the press, the slew of Civil War histories and other kinds of war-related books issuing even in the course of the fighting, battlefield accounts he received fresh from returning veterans or their intimates, and an array of materials saved up from previous books. He even singled out by way of acknowledgment in the preface the aid of one particular recent book as a source for his own book's opening chapters—namely, the patrician bibliophile George Livermore's chronicle of the Founding Fathers' views toward African Americans at the time of their military service in the wars of 1775 and 1812.[36]

Brown was familiar with Livermore, a well-to-do Cambridge resident (long removed from his native Cambridgeport) who had a loose acquaintance with leading members of the African American community. For many years, Livermore had been no more a radical abolitionist than had his hero Lincoln, but he too came gradually to equate the "great civil war" with the complete elimination of slavery. Enlisting his friend Senator Charles Sumner to press his case with the president, Livermore laid claim to the pen with which Lincoln signed the Emancipation Proclamation. His claim, according to the *New York Tribune*, was "founded upon his 'historical research' as to the opinions of the founders of the Republic respecting negroes as slaves, citizens and soldiers, a copy of which was presented to the President while he was engaged in writing the Proclamation."[37] To rephrase the *Tribune's* logic in broad historiographical terms: Lincoln did not read William Wells Brown or William Cooper Nell on the subject of black Americans, but he did read Livermore. And he did make him a present of the treasured pen.

Had Livermore lived (he died in 1865), he might even have scooped Brown in writing an updated history that carried his chronicle into the Civil War. In his practice as an amateur historian, Livermore drew on advantages beyond Brown's reach. He had excellent access to people in power from federal and state capitals to learned societies, libraries, and universities. He had an honorary MA from Harvard, even though he groused to a confidant it should have been a DD.[38] He possessed one of the finest private libraries in the country, thanks to his large fortune. It was particularly strong in rare Bibles, including a Gutenberg, an

Eliot Indian Bible (the first English Bible printed in the New World), a Mormon Bible (inscribed to Joseph Smith), and even a Confederate Bible salvaged from a blockade-runner. Broad and deep as it was, his collection contained precious few books by people of color, though with one noteworthy exception: a personally autographed copy of Nell's *The Colored Patriots of the American Revolution*.[39] Livermore put it to good use, consulting it closely in compiling his more antiquarian estimate of the standing of African Americans in the new nation.

Brown, like Nell, practiced a different kind of history. His was a dynamic, popular history written close to ground level from odd angles, created from a grab bag of sources and populated mostly by common people performing heroic actions. Brown's history-making pen put black men in the center and relegated everyone else to the periphery. Even Lincoln (like Jefferson in *Clotel*) was mostly marginalized; he did not even come in for a good bashing comparable to the one he had received from Brown in the introductory essay of *The Black Man*. Lincoln made an appearance in Brown's chapter on the Emancipation Proclamation, but only as the author of the document whose words were detached from his person and embodied in the chants, stories, and figures of the objects of emancipation. His major appearance came chiefly in the role of the assassinated president; only martyrdom made Lincoln truly palatable. Grant, Sherman, Lee, and their subordinates likewise left few footprints in Brown's history.

Brown replaced these standard figures with a black set of military heroes: William Tillman, who commandeered the *S. J. Waring*; Robert Small, an enslaved South Carolina sailor who shanghaied a Confederate transport, piloted it through the heavy fortifications of Charleston Harbor, and crossed through the Union naval blockade to safety; William Walker, a sergeant in the South Carolina 3d Colored Volunteers who led his unit into mutiny to protest discriminatory payment for black troops and was court-martialed and executed by a reluctant firing squad; and André Cailloux, an intrepid officer with the Louisiana Native Guard killed while leading the charge at the Battle of Port Hudson. Of all the black units in the field, *The Negro in the American Rebellion* paid particular attention, of course, to the men of the Fifty-fourth and Fifty-fifth Massachusetts Regiments, tracking and highlighting their collective accomplishments and singling out various individuals for praise. One in particular was the multitalented Lieutenant James Monroe Trotter, a future musicologist and recorder of deeds in Washington who settled after the war in Boston, became Brown's close personal friend, and received an inscribed copy of the book in 1878.[40]

Brown was venturing into one of the hottest, most competitive subject areas in contemporary American publishing. The war dominated public interest as had no event in the nation's history, and some of the same industrial and technological developments that made field combat so massively deadly also made war publications readily transmissible to a mass audience. Enterprising authors and publishers joined forces in planning publication projects as early as 1862–63, when not even the sharpest-eyed historian could clearly predict its outcome. The popular historian John S. C. Abbott was early in the field in 1863 with the first volume of *History of the Civil War in America*, a runaway bestseller issued in the hundreds of thousands of copies even before the name of the war was fixed. Another major narrative came from the pen of Horace Greeley, who had an opinion and often a book about everything that passed before his roving gaze. Greeley embarked in 1864 on what became his bestselling *A History of the Great Rebellion* at the behest of two unknown subscription publishers who came knocking on his door. He eventually accepted their offer, but only after two events incited him to act: the Emancipation Proclamation and the New York draft rioters, whose 1863 attack on the Colored Orphan Asylum outraged his abstract sense of justice and whose incineration of the *Tribune* office made it personal.[41] These books and others—some heavily illustrated for a popular audience and sold by subscription agents working assigned territories across the country—proved enormously popular. Civil War titles flew off of retail shelves and out of peddlers' packs in the tens, even hundreds of thousands while the conflict raged, and sales continued strong for years afterward.[42]

Brown distinguished himself among this busy crowd of historians by being the first to take up the subject of black military service in the late phases of the war. *The Negro in the American Rebellion* was another of his timely books that had a seemingly ready-made appeal for a particular kind of progressive publisher, as might be expected for an author coming off the success of *The Black Man*. Confident about his prospects, Brown contracted for the book with the dynamic Boston publishing house of Lee and Shepard. Founded in 1862 by two talented young bookmen, the firm was already one of Boston's finest. William Lee had worked his way up with the firm of Phillips and Sampson, Charles Shepard with John Jewett, and both men had strong ties to the antislavery movement and reform. At the time Brown engaged them, they were building a publishing list that reflected their views.[43] One of their most successful authors was the scabrous social satirist "Petroleum V. Nasby," whose syndicated columns attacking ignoramuses, racist populists, bigots, Copperhead Democrats, and in time the Johnson administration, made him a household name (Lincoln, a keen admirer of his satiric dexterity, was said to have wished to swap talents and jobs with him). Just a year after publishing Brown's book, Lee and Shepard published a biography of Martin Delany by a young African American from Charleston who signed herself Frank (i.e., Frances) A. Rollins, and they soon afterward published multivolume sets of the speeches of Charles Summer and Wendell Phillips.

Lee and Shepard marketed Brown's book energetically. They placed an advance notice in the publishing trade journal through their New York City contact Frederick Beecher Perkins (nephew of Harriet Beecher Stowe and father of the writer Charlotte Perkins Gilman), who also placed a copy at the Mercantile Library in New York and sent one overseas to London (possibly to the British Museum).[44] Lee and Shepard handled it strictly as a subscription book, not to be retailed by bookstores around the country. This business model for book publication and distribution surged after the Civil War as enterprising publishers sought untapped markets for popular new books in a hinterland so sprawling that millions of literate Americans lived without access to bookstores. Some of these new publishers used flamboyant sales methods, as the

Hartford-based American Publishing Company did in featuring Mark Twain dressed up as a Native American on one page in the salesman's display copy of *Innocents Abroad*.[45] Lee and Shepard resorted to no such pyrotechnics; they calculated that the subject alone was novel and timely enough to capture a sizable audience. Brisk sales and a long life in print would confirm their judgment.

Lee and Shepard shipped boxes of books to their subscription agents all across the country. These people, familiar with their sales regions, knew where to concentrate their canvassing and how to leverage the endorsements of community leaders, such as ministers, to gain maximal access. Some of these agents undoubtedly had canvassed for Lee and Shepard previously, but in order to make inroads in the black community, the firm posted newspaper ads calling specifically for "One Hundred Intelligent Colored Men" to sell Brown's book.[46] In some instances, they used white agents who subcontracted local canvassing to black salesmen better positioned to place the book with black readers. In Philadelphia, for instance, their seasoned white salesman T. B. Pugh hired a black man to handle door-to-door sales, explaining his reasoning in terms Lee and Shepard must have heard repeatedly: "I would advise you to get colored men to canvass that book wherever you can, as it is in keeping with the work, and besides it is a novelty. I find that an intelligent colored man makes a more successful canvasser (these times particularly) than a white man, inasmuch as no one at first suspects the object of his visit, and his path is much *more* smooth."[47]

One of the firm's more active field agents was a civilian named Edward Little, attached to the US quartermaster's staff in New Orleans, who had seen a newspaper notice of the book's publication and wrote the company to offer his services. Little guessed it would "prove popular among the colored people of the city"—a city where Brown's previous commercial experience was chiefly in the sale of people.[48] The company accepted Little's offer and responded with their conditions of service and a sample copy. Little, in turn, agreed, but only on the conditions that he be given "exclusive agency" in the city and that the book not be sold in bookstores.[49]

A similar publisher/agent arrangement operated in St. Louis. The local agent there was a man named Estes, who subcontracted one or more employees to help him canvass the area. The book remained in circulation there for at least a year, hawked door-to-door by both black and white salesmen. At least a smattering of the doors on which they knocked must have been opened by people, black or white, who had known the adolescent Sandy. Then, in 1868, a seasoned white agent named Brainard took delivery of a consignment of two boxes in the city, noting that the books in one box had arrived slightly mildewed—although not enough, he thought, to prevent their sale. Having heard that an African American minister named Dickson had previously canvassed the city, Brainard worried he would not be able to compete with someone so rooted in the community. Yet he assessed the market in the white community to be sizable enough that he decided to accept the assignment.[50]

The book also reached a third area associated with Brown's earliest years, the rural Missouri River Valley stretching well west of St. Louis toward Jefferson City and Boonville, a town associated with Daniel Boone's sons. The agent claiming this swath of mostly rural sales turf was a black Civil War veteran from Massachusetts named Guice, one of the many veterans who canvassed the backcountry with one Civil War history or another. Though proudly hailing from the Bay State, Guice must have been living in Missouri when he enlisted in Company A, Fifty-sixth US colored Troops, part of the first black regiment organized in Missouri. Composed of a combination of ex-slaves and freeborn men mostly from Missouri, the unit trained in St. Louis before mobilization but served primarily in garrison duty, mostly in Arkansas. It saw limited combat but met its match in disease, which wiped out half its men.[51]

Guice came to his assignment relatively late. In 1869, he picked up a copy of the work from an itinerant agent, liked what he saw, and, thinking the book would be attractive to African Americans, offered his services to Lee and Shepard. They agreed, initially calling for payment on receipt of shipment. Guice refused, replying from experience that blacks had so often been cheated by "sharpers" that they would not agree to payment until they held the books in their hands, not just the sample dummies shown by agents. The company made a special exception for him and sent the actual books. A seasoned salesman, Guice opined that the book would interest only the black portion of the community but held up high hopes for success among them. His forecast was pragmatically bullish: "I think I can sell immense sums of them in districts where their children can read."[52]

One means Guice used to drum up interest among potential subscribers was to recite selections he guessed would be particularly effective. On one occasion, his selection caused a reaction that startled him. His auditor was a middle-aged black man, a "tolerable scholar" to whom he read a passage about the African slave rebel Madison Washington from chapter 4 ("Slave Revolt at Sea"). The man stunned Guice with the violence of his reaction upon hearing Guice pronounce the name of Thomas McCargo: "He bursted into tears, a man stout of stature and of 36 winters age," and insisted Guice repeat the name. Guice did not indicate what it was about the name of McCargo—a name that apparently lived in infamy in some black circles as owner of many of the enslaved Africans on board the *Creole*—that had triggered this outburst, but the man subscribed on the spot and then persuaded neighbors to do the same.[53] Despite his initial optimism, however, Guice could report back to Boston only scant success: "But the business don't pay. My expenses were heavy, and license $6.00. The colored people are not quite far enough educated and very poor 'to boot' and the white people had no use for such a book in this section of country prejudicial to educational advancement of negro race." Already short of funds to care for his own family, he reluctantly gave up the endeavor and sent back most of the books.[54]

Little, Estes, and Guice were a few of the identifiable footmen in the small army of salespeople Lee and Shepard deployed coast-to-coast to sell the book. There was even a Pacific Coast operation centered in San Francisco, where a black newspaper ran an ad for local agents.[55] In Boston, where the firm presumably needed least help, they nevertheless got some from the author, who was as usual engaged in promotion by keeping an eye out for likely sales agents. One new recruit was Nelson Primus, the aspiring young painter. Primus, who had had his heart set on going to Europe to pursue his art studies, confessed to his mother his ambivalence about accepting Brown's offer: "Mr. Wells Brown has got out a book called Negro in the rebellion, something lately out, he wants me to take the agency of that, do you think it would sell well on there, if so I will bring it on with me when i come on. . . . i will try to do the best that i can."[56]

At a time when popular subscription bookselling was at its historical peak, Brown kept fast company with his fellow Missourian Mark Twain. Brimming with self-confidence and ambition, though just a novice, Twain had arrived in the East to pursue his livelihood. For a time during the late 1860s, each of these ambitious writers fielded an army of salespeople hawking his work. Twain, who had briefly enlisted in the Confederate Army in 1861 before deserting to seek his fortune out West, had at his disposal a mostly white army peddling his first book, *Innocents Abroad*, around the country. That army did him prouder than any in the recent war. Sales were so brisk that Twain boasted to his good friend William Dean Howells that subscription bookselling was the fast road to success: "Anything but subscription publication is printing for private circulation."[57] Brown could not have made Twain's flip boast that his book was flying out of backpacks like Bibles, but Lee and Shepard's door-to-door, coast-to-coast canvassing mechanism served him exceptionally well. The first printing sold out by the end of June, and a second was immediately prepared and sent out.[58] Their salespeople kept the book actively in the field well into the next year, while sales by mail continued considerably longer. As late as 1876, they continued to list it among their published works.[59] At some point afterward, Brown and Annie took over sales of the book themselves, preparing a new title page in 1880 and filling orders by mail up to the time of his death.

The arrangement with Lee and Shepard was so lucrative that Brown also contracted with them for publication of the fourth and final version of his long-lived novel, now called *Clotelle; or, The Colored Heroine*. Lee and Shepard published it in July 1867 in a thin hardbound volume alternately praised for its handsome binding and disparaged for the tiny font used to reduce printing costs. Despite its radically altered format from the 1864 Redpath dime novel, the new edition might easily have been taken as a reprint of its predecessor except for the four new closing chapters, which delivered an updated message of courage and heroism to a post-emancipation audience.

The new chapters not only extended the story to the postwar period; they also effectively rounded the circle of African American life Brown himself had traveled. Clotelle and her husband Jerome, once slaves in New Orleans and Natchez, respectively, return home to the United States from their fugitive haven in Europe and head directly to New Orleans after the city falls to the Union Army. Jerome enlists in the Louisiana Native Guard, originally a black Confederate militia now reconstituted as a black fighting unit of the Union Army, but dies unnecessarily at Port Hudson while carrying out a white officer's foolhardy orders. Following his death, Clotelle matches his bravery by volunteering her services as an army nurse, even working behind enemy lines as an "Angel of Mercy" at Andersonville Prison, tending to Union prisoners of war and engineering a prison break. At the novel's end, she is operating a freedmen's school on the Natchez farm where she had once been held in slavery. And with that, she emerges as "the colored heroine" of the novel's subtitle, a suitable match for the role models sketched in *The Black Man*.

In 1873, a man named Oliver Fairbanks wrote to Lee and Shepard on the official stationery of the Andersonville Prison Survivor's Association to inquire whether copies of the work were still available.[60] He presumably had a personal reason for making a connection between actual experience and fiction. So did Brown in prefacing the novel with the slippery claim that Clotelle and Jerome were "real personages," but there is no question that he knew self-sacrificing people like them who had returned South on service missions. He was well acquainted, for instance, with Harriet Jacobs, who returned to Union-occupied northern Virginia to teach and care for ex-slaves; and Ellen Craft, who a few years later provided similar relief work in her native Georgia. Brown felt particular admiration for another of these black Samaritans, Virginia-born Louise de Mortie, who migrated from Boston to New Orleans in 1863 and oversaw the city's colored orphanage. Her initial reason for staying in the city, according to one newspaper account, was her reunion with an aunt she had not seen since childhood, but her main concern was attending to the orphanage. Though warned of the imminent danger to her own well-being during the fall 1867 yellow-fever epidemic, she stood by her children resolutely and succumbed to the disease.[61]

The logic of the final *Clotelle*, a novel fifteen years in the making that had migrated with Brown over the ocean and that spanned the Civil War, was the logic of his friends' lives: It was time for black Southerners to come home, if only as aid workers or missionaries. Soon enough, the South would beckon Brown, too.

AFTER ABANDONING fundraising efforts for the Lincoln memorial project in late 1867, Brown devoted an increasing amount of his time in Boston and on the road to the temperance movement, which he regarded as a critical means for promoting self-improvement in both the black and the white communities across the country. The work brought him down to the grassroots level of individual and communal self-help as not even antislavery had. It appealed to his core optimism about the possibility of transformational change, but it required that every individual do as he had in his early years: take full responsibility for his actions. At the same time, temperance work elevated him to positions of authority he had never held in exclusively white-led antislavery societies. Riding his reputation as an accomplished professional—writer, doctor, and lecturer— he was installed in early 1868 as president of the National Association for the Organization of Night Schools and the Spread of Temperance among the Freed People of the South. In May, as the impeachment trial of Andrew Johnson for high crimes and misdemeanors reached its culmination in the US Senate, Brown issued an "Appeal to the Public" to promote his new organization. Its goal was to send as many "missionaries" as the association could subsidize to direct fieldwork down South. Its ambitious mission would require a large operational fund—$10,000 was Brown's goal.[62]

He kept to a more limited travel schedule in the second half of 1868, but he did go to Utica to attend the New York State Convention of

Colored Men. On New Year's Day in 1869, he hosted the annual Emancipation Day celebration at Tremont Temple, just as African Americans' dream of voting rights advanced to the edge of reality. A blizzard that day blanketed Boston under fifteen inches of snow and limited the number of celebrants, but those who braved the storm heard some of the most renowned orators of the day: Frederick Douglass, Leonard Grimes, Frances Ellen Watkins Harper, Wendell Phillips, and Brown. Other speakers were new to the civil rights movement. After Brown gave an opening address congratulating his fellow celebrants on the recent election of Ulysses S. Grant as the eighteenth president, a black student from Harvard named Emanuel Sullivan read the Emancipation Proclamation, and the talented Richard T. Greener, who was on the fast track to becoming Harvard's first black graduate, gave a formal address stressing the necessity that suffrage be given to "the black man." Did Greener mean to include the black woman?[63] Some speakers did; others pointedly did not.

Brown did not, and he made clear his position during a long speaking trip later than month. The trip eventually took him to Chicago, the farthest west he had been in decades, and gave him his first acquaintance with the fast-growing prairie city, then engaged in a heated rivalry with St. Louis to be the primary gateway city to the West. He probably timed his trip in order to take part in an important women's-rights convention organized by his prewar antislavery comrade Susan B. Anthony. He still had warm memories of her from their intensive lecturing tour of New York state and Ohio in fall 1857, especially of the evening when they and several other members of their team stopped for dinner at the Bennet House in Cleveland. When he was refused service alongside his colleagues, they all rose from the table, joined him in the parlor, and refused to return to the dining room until they could all be seated at the same table.[64]

At the 1869 Chicago women's-rights convention, however, Brown found himself positioned on the opposite side of the table from Anthony and her distinguished feminist colleague Elizabeth Cady Stanton. Dividing them, and roiling any hope for consensus as attendees clashed during several days of vigorous debates, was the fraught issue of suffrage expansion. They were convening just as the Fifteenth Amendment, granting suffrage free of consideration of "race, color, or previous condition of servitude," but with no mention of gender, was moving quickly toward adoption in Congress. With suffrage expansion looking likely, the impressive multiracial coalition of men and women who had marched arm in arm for a generation under a common antislavery and women's-rights banner was beginning to splinter, as became painfully clear in Chicago. Stanton forcefully told the convention that she opposed the amendment as creating unnecessary distinctions: "It was not a question whether the negro or the woman should have the right of suffrage, but whether the nation should be reconstructed upon the broad basis of impartial suffrage."[65] That bold, visionary statement notwithstanding, she expressed an underlying nativist bias privately in correspondence with her cousin Gerrit Smith that revealed how complicated any plan for national reconstruction might be: "I admire you more than any living man though you do persist in putting Sambo, Hans, Patrick, and Yung Tung above your noblest countrymen."[66]

The next day, in a room with a majority of women, Brown eased his way into the debate by stating he was there to add "a little *color* to the convention," before sparring with Anthony about whether priority should be given to race, gender, or neither. His view was clear: "He looked upon the negro question as the great question before the country, the one underlying the reconstruction of the Southern States and the restoration of harmony between the two sections, and he should oppose any coupling of the negro question with any other issue, simply because both were of vital importance, and must stand or fall on their own merits." Under current circumstances he supported passage of the Fifteenth Amendment as the strategically requisite act. His primary allegiance, unambiguously, was to race.

Four days later, he gave a lecture on African history at Chicago's Farwell Hall that proved no less controversial. The talk was a variant of one he had been giving in recent months in New York and New England that drew on Afrocentric views present in the 1862 prefatory essay to *The Black Man* and current in black intellectual circles. His audience that night, which included a large contingent of the city's African American community, was generally receptive. He evidently upset some of his white listeners, however, with remarks challenging rigidly separate views of black and white racial origin. A debate soon ensued in the local and national press about the speaker, his remarks, and blacks in general. The *Chicago Tribune* praised "the eminent colored orator and author" for his "very able" address, but his colleague for the *Chicago Times* charged Brown with distorting history by claiming Hannibal as a black African. Brown, in turn, rebuked its reporter for attributing views to him he had never made about Hannibal as being a Negro, or more broadly for darkening whites and blanching blacks. The argument he did make about racial origins, he protested, was strictly environmental. To support his thesis, he singled out the varying skin color of the Jewish people, an ethnicity that practiced strict endogamy but whose skin color ran a racial rainbow.[67]

The crux of Brown's debate with the *Times* reporter was less historical accuracy about the African past than acceptable racial views in the present. When the reporter slipped into what Brown dismissed as "the old doctrine of the South"—in Brown's paraphrase, "the only progress the negro has ever made is found in such civilizing tendencies as connected him with slavery among a superior race"—Brown countered with the handy revisionist argument he had used in the prefatory essay to *The Black Man* about the faulty hierarchies of white and black history. That exchange soon provoked additional coverage in the national press, mostly hostile and sometimes vicious toward Brown. A Cincinnati newspaper labeled him "one of the negro pets of Boston" and disparaged his views as those of a misguided "miscegenist" ignorant of both Anglo-Saxon and Negro history.[68] A correspondent for a Memphis newspaper leveled an even stronger ad hominem attack, which was actually a pretext to making a categorical dismissal of all black pretensions to learning. This expert took his stand on the authority of racial ethnology: Blacks had smaller brain capacity than whites and constituted "the lowest in the scale of the human species."[69] The logic put Brown in a double bind: His views could not be right even if they were right.

The highlight of his western swing was his return to St. Louis after a thirty-five-year absence. He presumably had secured lecture engagements—his reputation as an activist by now reached coast-to-coast—but he also must have arrived with a more strictly personal agenda. What is certain is that when he stepped off the train, he walked out of the station into a transformed city of 300,000 people, now the nation's fifth largest after New York, Philadelphia, Brooklyn, and Chicago. At the time of his visit, a local booster was building on the city's geographic centrality to advocate westward removal of the national capital to St. Louis. Six months after Brown's visit, twenty-one states and territories took the idea seriously enough to send representatives to a meeting at the city's impressive new Mercantile Library to consider the possibility.[70]

Brown must have had a Rip Van Winkle experience as he walked the sprawling, industrializing city. Old landmarks Sandy had known well, such as the old French section with the Chouteau mansions, were gone or slated for demolition; and the once-pristine Chouteau Pond, spoiled by industrial waste, had been drained to prevent the spread of disease.[71] The unpaved, ramshackle waterfront was now modernized and systematized. Plans were underway to build a great span over the Mississippi River, whose passage had been largely the monopoly of the ferry company owned by Samuel Wiggins and his family. Train tracks crisscrossed the city. Meanwhile, the old generation that had run municipal affairs had passed into history—the Chouteaus and O'Fallons; Senator Thomas Hart Benton, to whom Isaac Mansfield had once attached himself; and Daniel Page, the early mayor to whom Brown had drawn scandalous attention in his *Narrative*. (Page died only weeks after Brown headed back East.) New names and ethnicities surged into positions of leadership: the German-born Carl Schurz in politics, the Hungarian-born Joseph Pulitzer in journalism, and the Yankee migrant William Greenleaf Eliot (grandfather of the poet) in education and civic affairs.

Times had changed dramatically, but even in postwar St. Louis, the hub of a state that contributed nearly 100,000 soldiers to the Union Army, much of the daily political and social small talk was pronouncedly racial, often racist. As Congress debated the Fifteenth Amendment in the early weeks of 1869, passed it on February 26, and sent it on to the individual states for ratification, the city's newspapers editorialized nonstop on the racial issues of the day. The *St. Louis Times* editorialized that passing the suffrage amendment would also enfranchise the fledging Chinese communities on the Pacific Coast. That, however, was deemed the lesser threat to white supremacy: "Are a few thousand intelligent and self-supporting Chinamen to be denied the same privileges that are conferred upon the million vagabond and half-barbarian negroes on the Atlantic coast?"[72] In the weeks surrounding Brown's visit, the venerable *Missouri Republican*, the paper to which Sandy was carrying Elijah Lovejoy's type when he was attacked, ran a series of editorials mocking suffrage expansion. It was also one of multiple local papers that derided the initiative to integrate the invitation list to Grant's inaugural celebration as brazen presumption: "Until now negroes have never appeared at the Inauguration ball, except as servants, but the sable Rubicon is crossed and our black Caesars and Pompeys are to be guests."[73] Less gratuitously, it repeatedly joined the chorus of Democrats lamenting the nagging injustice of enfranchising blacks while disenfranchising rebel whites.

That was only half the story in a border city home to a very large radical Republican population. St. Louis had served as the military administration center for General Frémont's operations in the West, and it was currently home to the Western Sanitary Commission, the benevolent organization that had taken charge of collections for the Freedmen's Memorial. Thomas S. Noble's postwar paintings of slave sales and markets represented a newly popular commentary on the demise of a long-divisive institution that many St. Louis residents were happy to see dead and buried. Part of the press, such as the *Missouri Democrat*, took up the cause of black enfranchisement with one degree or another of support. That newspaper had once employed the young James Redpath during his early period of activism in the West, and it was currently adding to its editorial staff his friend William W. Thayer, one of the partners in the failed radical antislavery publishing firm of Thayer and Eldridge.

Did Samuel Willi and/or Enoch Price figure among the new civic majority after the war? Brown went looking for an answer. He could have located "old master" as easily in St. Louis as "old master" could have located him in Boston or London. Though elderly, both Willi and Price were still hearty, active men visible around the city. Willi had amassed some property and was one of the founders of the Missouri Historical Society, organized in 1866 "for the purpose of saving from oblivion the early history of the city and state." At its January meeting, Willi agreed to join a small committee charged with photographing the archaeological mound in whose vicinity Pierre Laclède and Auguste Chouteau had founded the original settlement, and he chaired its February meeting.[74] The septuagenarian Price remained well known locally as a member of the Mississippi River steamboat fraternity, although his active days on the river were well behind him. He still enjoyed travel, however, going down to New Orleans to visit relatives or east to visit his daughter at her home near Gloucester, Massachusetts (where he would die in 1882).

No known detailed account survives of Brown's meeting with "old master," but squibs appearing in newspapers around the country make clear that Brown did indeed make personal contact with at least one of the men. Knowing who was coming to visit, his host made an occasion of Brown's visit by inviting several dozen neighbors to meet him. The meeting was apparently convivial, and Brown went away, according to reports, convinced they were "reconstructed."[75] Whether Brown's word choice or the reporter's, "reconstructed" raised more questions than it answered—not only about "old master" and his St. Louis neighbors but also about Americans in general.

Once back in Boston, Brown accepted an agency advocating for the "Suffrage Amendment" for the American Anti-Slavery Society. His lecture partners for this Connecticut-based tour included his former comrade Charles Burleigh, who as editor of the *Pennsylvania Freeman* had argued in 1854 against the payment of "ransom money" to secure Brown's legal emancipation; and James M. Simms, his partner in the Savannah edition of *The Black Man*.[76] For the most part, however, he was at home during 1869, splitting his attention between his medical practice and moving back and forth between the white and the black communities of eastern Massachusetts promoting temperance.

His involvement in temperance took a novel turn in 1870 when he abandoned his lifelong aversion to the political process and lined up behind his close friend Wendell Phillips, who was making an unlikely run for governor of Massachusetts. On August 17, Brown called to order the convention of the new Prohibitory Party, which nominated Phillips as their candidate for governor.[77] Phillips ran as a third-party candidate for an improbable coalition supporting temperance, women's suffrage, and labor rights. The interests of his constituency conflicted nearly as much as they overlapped, and Phillips, an upright patrician with little feel and no patience for the give-and-take of politics, showed little skill in mobilizing alliances or building support. Not surprisingly, his candidacy went nowhere, and even onetime friends and allies, now soured on the man they believed had betrayed Garrison and true abolition, scoffed at his poor showing. Edmund Quincy reported to Irish abolitionist Richard Webb, "I am happy to tell you Wendell Phillips has been handsomely snubbed at the election last week."[78]

Right in the middle of the campaign, however, Brown's attention was suddenly diverted from politics. On October 1 in the family home, Clotelle Brown died of typhoid fever. For a second time, William and Annie gathered their family and friends at Cambridge Cemetery to bury a child.[79] An obituary in the renamed New York *National Standard*, written by someone who knew the family well—quite possibly Brown's onetime antislavery lecture partner and currently the paper's editor Aaron M. Powell—memorialized the eight-year-old as "a sprightly, beautiful child, of more than ordinary promise. She was fondly loved, not alone by her parents, but a large circle of friends, to whom her early death will be indeed a sore bereavement."[80] An earthquake later that month shook buildings in Cambridge, but William and Annie must have felt their private universe had already been shaken to its foundation.[81] Their marriage survived, it perhaps closed more tightly around them, but they lost their last hope for a family heritage. Although Annie was only thirty-six, she had no more children of her own. Instead, she had nephews and nieces living nearby to whom she could devote herself. Brown had no such consolation.

Grieving at home, he sent a public letter on October 8 to Powell to apologize for his absence from an upcoming meeting on "caste" to be hosted by the Reform League at New York's Cooper Institute. But formal mourning did not last long; as always, there was work to be done. Late in October, he traveled to Syracuse to participate in a New York state black suffrage convention, presided over by Henry Highland Garnet. The convention considered but rejected the possibility of disbanding such conventions; more urgent action still needed to be taken, they insisted, when hotels even in New York City and across the state proscribed blacks, and the Democratic Party did all it could to interfere with black voting nationwide. Under such circumstances, the only correct vote for blacks was a vote for a Republican candidate.[82] Brown was also active in suffrage organizations these months. He was elected an officer of the Sons of Temperance at the meeting of Boston's Grand Lodge on October 19, and he continued his role in the Good Templars and as president of the National Association for the Organization of Night Schools and the Spread of Temperance among the Freed People of the South (NAONSSTFPS). An evolving commitment to the mission of that more familiar organization would soon point him back to the region of his birth.

ANNIE KNEW she had married a traveling man; he rarely stayed home for long. Perhaps she could more easily bear his prolonged absences—though perhaps not—because the cause that most often took him on the road after the war was one she heartily shared. "Sister Annie" was as involved as "Brother Brown" in temperance reform during the last two decades of their marriage. For much of it, they worked as a team in the Boston area—conferring, planning, and sometimes even leading together as officers. Periodically, however, his high positions in national and international temperance organizations required that he travel farther afield. Those trips he made alone.

One of them took place in 1871, when, after presiding over a September 7 meeting of the John Brown Division of the Sons of Temperance at Joy Street Church, he set out on a grueling speaking tour of Kentucky on behalf of the NAONSSTFPS. The trip marked his first return to his native state since Dr. Young moved his operation westward in 1817, and it brought him into close contact with the kinds of people he had known as a youth. Local residents housed and boarded him, and many attended his talks. He found the Bourbon State fertile soil for the message he had come to deliver: clean living, self-help, abstinence from liquor, and communal improvement. Local ministers, such as the influential AME Reverend Jehu Holliday of Louisville, shepherded him around their communities, enlisting their congregants to aid him in his work. A reporter for a Louisville daily spotted "the well-known colored author" in town and followed his movements as he delivered talks and dispensed free books for general education. Impressed by what he witnessed, he concluded that Brown was successful with the black population because he led by way of familiar example: "Being a self-made man, and a native of the South, the doctor's influence is very great with his people, and his lectures here have been highly appreciated by them. The meetings have been large and enthusiastic."[83] He gave some talks in Louisville, others in the surrounding countryside, with plans to extend his work to the middle part of the state.

The work in which Brown was engaged was gratifying, but it was also dangerous. During 1871, newspapers across the country reported regularly on race-based attacks occurring throughout much of the Old South. Many were the work of the newly formed Ku Klux Klan, a white-supremacist organization founded in Tennessee shortly after the war that spread quickly into Kentucky and other states. The attacks presented such a serious danger to public order that Congress held hearings in the late 1860s and in 1872 published a stunningly graphic set of volumes documenting what many saw as a reign of terror. Brown was too well acquainted with the fathers of the men beneath the white sheets to ignore frequent reports about racial attacks. Although violent incidents were prevalent that year across Kentucky, ranging from verbal warnings to whippings and hangings, they were clustered particularly in his native Bluegrass Country.[84] Unintimidated by the stories and reports, Brown stuck to his plan.

Anxiety about nearby KKK activity was in the air when Brown

boarded the eastbound train out of Louisville on the afternoon of September 25. Roughly midway between Louisville and Lexington, he exited at the tiny town of Pleasureville, intending to give a talk nearby to freedmen. In a pattern that was becoming all too common, however, he failed to reach his destination. Brief reports of his kidnapping and near-lynching by the Klan went out almost immediately via telegraph to newspapers around the country, but once safely back home, Brown gave a much fuller account to the *Boston Daily Advertiser*.

He claimed he arrived alone at Pleasureville depot at 6:00 p.m. and was met by a local black man responsible for escorting him the five miles to the designated meeting place. When their expected carriage failed to arrive, the two men set out on foot, his companion assuring him they were safe. After they had walked a distance but still had not encountered the carriage, eight to ten white men suddenly rode up and surrounded Brown, while his escort disappeared into the shadows. Three of the men dismounted, bound Brown's arms behind him, and connected the free end of the rope to one of their horses. Then they remounted and set a pace so brisk that Brown struggled to keep up. This would have been the second time in his life he had been tracked down and bound up in such fashion, but this time the situation was life threatening.

The men made no secret of their intentions. While passing one house on their way, he overheard them say, "Lawrence don't want a nigger hung so near his place," before continuing on. When his hat flew off, they taunted him that he would soon have no need for it. He grasped his extreme danger but could do nothing while bound to a horse. After proceeding for a while along a side path, they were stopped by an agitated man who ran out of a house to tell them their acquaintance inside was dying. Jim, it turned out, was suffering an extreme bout of delirium tremens and needed immediate intervention. Brown had treated the condition—mind and body—many times with injected drugs and quickly seized on the opportunity. He convinced his uneducated, superstitious kidnappers that he was a practitioner of black magic and could conjure away the man's ailment. Playing on their gullibility to distract them, he secretly injected the man with a strong dose of morphine, which silenced and incapacitated Jim for hours. He then convinced the gang's ringleader that he could also cure his severe sciatica. After isolating him, Brown found a way to inject him too into unconsciousness. Once the sole remaining guard, by then intoxicated, fell asleep, Brown slipped out the door, reversed his way back to Pleasureville depot in the dark, caught the morning train to Cincinnati, and told his story to the local press.[85]

Most newspapers implicitly endorsed Brown's account by printing his initial report without comment, while some others, such as his home paper in Cambridge, explicitly accepted its veracity. The *Advertiser* even provided corroboration several weeks later, when it reported that the escort who had set Brown up had received his due reward when a group of his fellows captured and whipped him.[86] A few newspapers, however, questioned its authenticity—chief among them the *New York Herald*, with which Brown had a long history of mutual disdain. The previous year, the *Herald* had published a grudgingly admiring report on Brown, while conflating him with Henry Box Brown and noting his disdain for the paper.[87] As soon as it got wind of the KKK story, the *Herald* printed a dismissive commentary about Brown's "miraculous escape" from "a convenient hanging tree."[88]

There is good reason to believe the story was fundamentally true, if told with some embellishment. Trains did run directly from Louisville to Pleasureville, and indirectly from Pleasureville to Cincinnati via either La Grange or Lexington.[89] Brown was a public figure operating in the open and might well have presented a conspicuous target while traveling around an area in which "hanging trees" were conveniently located. A white professional's respect for him in Louisville might have been an uneducated white countryman's outrage. If so, the attack on him would have been only one of numerous race-based attacks in the area. Another had occurred half a year earlier when four white men boarded a train at North Benson, four stops past Pleasureville on the same branch of the Louisville, Cincinnati and Lexington Railroad, and assaulted a black railway mail clerk.[90] In a more deadly assault that took place two nights after Brown's ordeal, three black men accused of arson were dragged out of jail in Winchester, Tennessee, and summarily lynched by a group of ten disguised white men.[91] Brown could easily have read of that particular KKK atrocity in the Boston press once he reached home, although he could not have recognized the town as the fledgling community in which his father had played an important civic role after leaving Mt. Sterling around 1814.

Such attempts at intimidation as took place in North Benson, Pleasureville, and Winchester were among the many acts of terrorism occurring across the South as armed vigilantes resorted to threats—often backed up by violence—to reimpose white supremacy. The instinctive inclination to shift the burdens of life to an inferior black servant caste had not died; it simply adapted to fit new rules and circumstances following the expiration of slavery. In his brush with the KKK, Brown got a whiff of what was happening and took quick action, reporting it to the press though not the authorities. By the time he did, he had abandoned the field and returned to the safety of Massachusetts. He arrived home in Cambridge in late September chastened but undaunted. More trips to the South, including Kentucky, would follow over the subsequent decade.

Why would an esteemed professional man, sharing a comfortable home with a loving partner and enjoying the respect of his community, continue to venture solo down South to face humiliation and risk danger? The obvious answer is that he believed vital work remained to be done and he could do it. Annie must have agreed and given her consent, but she must also have feared for his safety each time he returned to the field. But the never-ending wanderlust of Brown's life may have another, irreducibly personal explanation. In a strangely discordant chapter of *The Negro in the American Rebellion* that seems generically out of place even in one of his scruffiest books, he told a somewhat updated version of the story of his own escape to freedom. In this latest incarnation, "William" was a Kentucky-born quadroon named George Loomis, son of his master. Closely matching Brown's path to freedom, George had escaped decades earlier from slavery in Missouri via Ohio, where he accepted the name of his benefactor and settled in Canada but returned to the United States to take up arms (passing as a white man) with the Union

Army. After serving with General Grant at Vicksburg, George happened into the cottage of an old black woman in Mississippi and entered into a conversation about origins. At a certain point, they exchanged looks of recognition and George realized he was seated opposite his long-lost mother, sold down the river and out of his life decades earlier.[92] So this fablelike chapter ends in revelation—a fantastic stroke of fortune for George but a bittersweet illusion for its teller. Miraculous reunions happened to other survivors of slavery looking to find their people, but they did not happen to the real-life "William."

Brown would never stop searching for a sustainable lifeline to the world of his past. Elusive since his escape in 1834, its pursuit would grow all the more complicated as the Old South of his youth changed before his eyes into the New South of Jim Crow. That would happen under the banner of national reunion—but reunion, as became increasingly clear over the 1870s and 1880s, in place of reconstruction.

11

My Southern Home, Revisited

In 1871, a twelve-year-old Boston schoolgirl named Pauline Allen won an essay contest for black high school students on "The Evils of Intemperance and Their Remedies," along with a $10 gold prize.[1] The contest sponsor was the Congregational Publishing Society, but its initiator was Boston's leading black temperance advocate, William Wells Brown. It would not take much imagination of the sort relished by both Brown and Pauline Hopkins (the adopted name under which she gained fame as one of the leading African American writers of her generation) to see him personally handing her a gold coin—a fit act of literary patronage by one generation of its successor. By decade's end, Hopkins reciprocated by beginning the process of incorporating her predecessor's work into her own, adapting it for life in the twentieth century.

Young Pauline was well acquainted with William and Annie, whom she liked and admired. She had known them nearly all her conscious life, but the relationship also had overlapping familial and communal dimensions. The Brown, Gray, and Hopkins families were reputable strands in Boston's tight-knit black community, which numbered no more than 2,500 people after the Civil War. Like Annie and William and dozens of other couples, Pauline's mother and stepfather were married in the Twelfth Baptist Church in a ceremony conducted by Reverend Leonard

Grimes; in all likelihood, Annie and William attended that ceremony on Christmas Day of 1864. According to Pauline's recollections, her step-father had had a relationship with Brown close enough that he often cited examples of Brown's witty conversation. One consisted of a favorite story Brown repeated—as he retold all favorite stories—about how in the 1840s he verbally disarmed a hostile, western New York crowd that had come prepared to pelt him with rotten eggs.[2] The point of the story, by the time Pauline Hopkins fancifully retold it in the early twentieth century, had come to lie as much in its transmission as in its content. Through family lore and retrospection, a story about field activism in slavery times came back to life as a piece of entertaining lore connecting post-Emancipation blacks to a receding past.

The witty, nimble Pauline Hopkins, whose storytelling style spun fact into fiction and back again, bore an uncanny resemblance to Brown. His imprint is heavy on her work. She probably kept some of his books on her bookshelves, and she certainly knew many of them well enough to draw from them with ease. In a series of "do unto others" acts of appropriation worthy of Brown, she lifted characters and passages from his works for use in her own and reformulated them for a generation that knew slavery chiefly via oral and written tales. One of the characters she resurrected was the St. Louis slave trader Walker, whom Brown had already fixed in the public mind as a figure, like Simon Legree, deserving of notoriety. Hopkins gave his reputation an additional touchup by typecasting him in her fine serial novel, *Hagar's Daughter* (1901–2), as a repulsive St. Louis slave trader come east to transact business. Her physical descriptions of his background, person, and enslaved assistants come right from the pages of the *Narrative of William W. Brown* and various editions of *Clotel*, which she adapted to serve a plot line about the sale of white or near-white women that also drew heavily on various editions of *Clotel*.

During Brown's lifetime, however, the most powerful cultural connection between these two pioneering African American writers came through their performative work. Each had written a landmark race drama that explored the character of blackness for a reluctantly mixed-race nation. As Hopkins's biographer, Lois Brown, has noted, their plays linked up in a color-coded conversation about freedom, slavery, and equality running from antebellum to postbellum times. Hopkins's was a popular musical drama, *Peculiar Sam; or, The Underground Railroad* (written in 1879 but not published), which extended the fugitive-slave story at the center of Brown's *The Escape* into postwar times in Canada.[3] That plot was already familiar to audiences of both races by the late 1870s—her enslaved characters take flight from a Deep South plantation, stop overnight at a station of the Underground Railroad, and finally find freedom in Canada—but the play itself was genuinely experimental and socially progressive. Hopkins self-consciously established its theme of personal and communal reinvention in the opening scene when her title character, a clever, independent-minded Mississippi slave named Sam, tries out "de new step" in the field before admiring friends, as no doubt the actor playing Sam (by no coincidence, the famous black minstrel Sam Lucas) performed it on stage to the pleasure of the audience. One step in the play leads to the next, and by the time the evening is out, the newest steps Sam works out lead his family and friends via the Underground Railroad to Canada. In the play's final act, which jumps the plot forward to 1871, the characters are safely, comfortably resettled in Canada and leading lives they could previously only dream of: secure in their marriages, formally or informally educated, upwardly mobile, and politically empowered (Sam, now a US senator-elect resettled in Ohio, is even about to join black colleagues in the multiracial, Reconstruction-era Congress).

Hopkins apparently wrote the play as a performance piece for the prodigious Sam Lucas. With Lucas flanked by a troupe of talented black actors, singers, dancers, and musicians, *Peculiar Sam* successfully toured the broad region of the upper Midwest, New York state, and New England that Brown had covered twenty years earlier with *The Escape* and *Experience*. Her play's audiences, like his, were composed mainly of white people curious to witness the sights and sounds of black performance and amenable to (or dismissive of) the message of self-empowerment, even while a drama of intimidation, disenfranchisement, and segregation was spreading over the South. Brown had left open the possibility for improvisation, as the mood suited him, in his nightly performances, but Hopkins gave such free rein for onstage improvisation that her drama had elements of a live revue. Each night the performers introduced an array of popular songs and dances that corresponded loosely to the play's script. Nearly all these antebellum standards—"Home, Sweet Home," "My Old Kentucky Home," "Suwanee River," "Good By, Old Cabin Home," "Way Over Jordan," "Virginia Rosebud"—were so familiar that the audiences could sing along (some people still can today). On some nights, the cast lingered after the main show to perform a medley of plantation songs; on other nights, they performed concerts of sacred music more typically performed by popular 1870s black touring groups such as the Fisk Jubilee Singers.

The music to which the troupe sang and danced, ranging from minstrelsy in dialect to sacred song in elevated diction, corresponded to the dual linguistic code both Hopkins and Brown employed as playwrights to signal their characters' social class and complexion. All the characters in *Peculiar Sam* except the tragic mulatto heroine—the soprano Virginia who plays Sam's love interest—speak dialect through the first three acts, but in the final act, in postwar Canada, the younger generation cross over into Standard English. Those linguistic codes signify not just the characters' level of education but also their attitudes toward their recent history. The older generation, though comfortably settled into freedom and security in their new Canadian home, still feels nostalgia for the jasmine-scented memory of their old Southern home. Sam's mother, Mammy, speaks longingly for many people of her generation in confessing that the familiar old songs, memories, and associations carry her "way back to dem good ol' times dat'll neber return."[4] To reinforce that sentiment, someone other than Hopkins penciled a marginal notation onto the play's manuscript for the performance of "Good By, Old Cabin Home" alongside one of her expressions of nostalgic yearning.[5] More regressively yet, Mammy's husband, Caesar, adds that he would even be happy to be buried alongside old master's family. By contrast, the younger generation moves eagerly into the new world of freedom, which the script implies Sam, as a legislator, may help shape from inside the halls of Congress.

What nostalgia could twenty-year-old, New England–born Pauline Hopkins possibly feel for plantation life, dialect humor, or minstrel entertainment during these years when even Mark Twain expressed popular white taste in mooning over "the real nigger show"? Perhaps a more appropriate question might be the contrary: What revulsion must she have felt about the North investing itself ever more deeply in racial stereotypes and reactionary politics as it entered with the South into an increasingly reactionary national reunion? Given the prevailing materials, attitudes, and audiences of her time, she was doing her best to craft a story of redemption from slavery that would strengthen black family life, increase communal pride, and transmit a positive, living heritage.

Across Boston, what was the reaction of sexagenarian William Wells Brown to the cultural and political turn toward an emerging system of racism no longer tethered to slavery? As a theater-lover and veteran performer of extraordinary accomplishment, Brown would have had access to a rich array of stage and musical entertainment during the last years of his life, a period in which Boston overflowed with concerts, musical theater, minstrel shows, and other forms of live entertainment. It seems likely he attended a performance of *Peculiar Sam* during its 1880 run in Boston, a series of performances in which Hopkins, a talented vocalist, took the stage alongside Lucas and company. At any of these performances, he would have heard a rendering of such songs as Stephen Foster's standard minstrel tune "My Old Kentucky Home," with its plaintive lamentation for hard times when "darkies have to part":

> *The head must bow, and the back will have to bend,*
> *Wherever the darkey may go;—*
> *A few more days and the trouble all will end,*
> *In the fields where sugar canes grow.*
> *A few more days for to tote the weary load,*
> *No matter 't will never be bright;—*
> *A few more days 'til we totter on the road.*

Weep no more, my lady,
Oh! Weep no more today!
We will sing one song for the old Kentucky home,
For my old Kentucky home far away.

Hopkins's play gave this popular minstrel standard emphatic significance: The fugitives sing it at the end of Act 3 in call-and-response fashion just as they prepare to cross over the symbolic river to freedom.[6] When the play resumes, the characters are leading new lives in Canada.

Land of sad darkies and lamentations for the weary load—this was hardly the old Kentucky home William Wells Brown experienced in youth or recollected in old age. If, like Mammy and Caesar, he had left behind a formative portion of his heritage, he was too ironically constituted to consider unreflecting nostalgia a legitimate response to loss—not for him, and not for his white or black neighbors. But even Boston-based Dr. Brown was not immune to the tug of the past, as changing life circumstances in his last years also spurred him to reconsider his old Southern home and left him searching for a usable history. What it might be for him, and what it might be for African Americans in general as they moved farther from slavery but into a not-yet-discernible future, became the central preoccupation of his final years.

Brown returned a third time in the early 1870s to the challenge of composing a popularized account of black historical experience, this time a work broadened to include Africa along with his enduring interest in the Caribbean and the Americas. His growing attention to Africa, a recurring subject of his lectures for the previous decade, coincided with increasing Western interest in, and subsequent colonization of, the "Dark Continent." Disinclined to be an explorer or settler himself, Brown was content to play fellow traveler, following the published expeditionary accounts by contemporary explorers and missionaries, such as Martin Delany, Robert Campbell, David Livingstone, and John Leighton Wilson, who pushed into interior parts of Africa previously unknown to Westerners.

The result was his longest, most comprehensive book, *The Rising Son* (1873). A reviewer familiar with Brown's earlier histories, and his presumed ambition to be "the Negro historian of the age," commented (skeptically) after seeing the new book's advertisement: "We understand that Dr. Brown proposes in his forthcoming work . . . [to] begin at the Genesis and come down to the Revelation of all and everything that pertains to the negro."[7] That observation had an element of truth. It was almost as though Brown, working in his Cambridge study, was attempting to assemble as much information as he could find about any and all aspects of the black African diaspora, sift through it, and organize his material into a composite account fit for a broad reading public. The reviewer, however, mistook Brown's intentions in writing this history. From the start, Brown conceived the book as encyclopedic rather than biblical, more reference work than systematic master narrative. Brown asserted in its preface that he had availed himself of "all available information" but found himself hemmed in by scarcity. That was undoubtedly an accurate assessment about the state of information and knowledge about peoples originating in Africa, but it was also misleading. His table of contents suggests not an attempt at exhaustive, sweeping historical synthesis but instead a miscellany of topics supposedly of interest to contemporary readers about Africa, the Caribbean, and the Americas as seen from a black perspective.

This was a book purportedly for readers to learn something about topics ranging from ancient Africa to current race relations, but it offered them no discernible path for guidance. For most of its readers, the most interesting part would have been the last section, "Representative Men and Women," a compilation of sketches of eminent blacks whose ranks had grown during the intervening decade from fifty-seven in the second edition of *The Black Man* to seventy-eight. Brown's range of contacts was so broad he could draw on personal acquaintance for many of the sketches, but he also relied on information from any and all sources, printed or oral. In some instances it was inaccurate, as in his acceptance of Ira Aldridge's deceptive assertion that he was born in Africa rather than New York City, but most of the portraits were informative and perceptive. By 1873, the time had come for a few old-timers, such as Joseph Jenkins, to be replaced by a rising generation of highly accomplished, mostly self-made men and women, including Lewis Douglass, Charles Purvis, and Charlotte Forten. All these representative figures came before the reader as living proof of Brown's core belief: "An ignorant man will trust to luck for success; an educated man will make success. God helps those who help themselves."[8]

The book followed Brown's basic operating principle: Blacks should take their heroes, as he did, wherever they found them. Hannibal, Toussaint, and Joseph Cinque were interwoven with Nat Turner, Harriet Tubman, Robert Small, and the men of the Fifty-fourth Massachusetts. Although most of these role models started humbly, all performed distinguished service, whether as ministers, diplomats, orators, politicians, lawyers, doctors, journalists, businessmen, educators, social workers, or artists. Brown was careful to present them as worthy exemplars, but he could not restrain himself from sprinkling a dash of spite into sketches of a few people he had come to dislike, such as Charles Remond, whose abilities were "overrated" and whose printed speeches "attracted little or no attention"; and James Pennington, whose alcoholism he exposed. Although his mode of presentation was characteristically informal, he paid punctilious respect to the cultural norm by printing each person's formal name, with the middle initial intact. He made only one exception—and many readers would have known why—for the folk heroine known as "Moses" (Harriet Tubman).

Sometimes he made surprising choices. One of the most curious inclusions was the gifted Jamaican journalist and writer Henry Garland Murray. Brown had apparently met Murray the previous year during his visit to Boston and came away impressed by a fellow performer with a "gift" for podium storytelling that resembled his own: "His ludicrous stories, graphically told, kept every face on a grin from the commencement to the end. He possesses the true *vivid avis* of eloquence."[9] A selection basis that included people like Murray was noticeably casual, following no set of formal criteria or standard list of black notables. It simply brought an open-minded acceptance to the measure of lives as they occurred. Equally striking in a work of history, it flattened the plane of time, presenting the lives of Hannibal, Toussaint, and "Moses" as though chronologically and experientially coexistent. A history conceived according to these standards was one that proceeded not by systematic movement over time and space but by repetition and gyration.

Role models might show up in the most unexpected places. In his chapter on the 1863 New York City draft riots, a subject too infuriating to let pass, he offers an alternative cast of role models that, in turn, suggests an alternative view of black history.[10] His discussion of this atrocity reaches a climax when the white mob that has already murdered, lynched, and dismembered black residents surrounds a building serving as a last haven for hundreds of refugees. Brown takes the reader inside, where eight "athletic black women, looking for all the world as if they had just returned from a Virginia corn-field, weary and hungry, stood around the room" armed with tin dippers containing boiling soap and water scooped out of the boiler nicknamed "the King of Pain." A self-identified "writer" (loosely, Brown's surrogate) interviews one of these sweaty "Amazons" and records it:

"Do you expect an attack?" we asked.

"Dunno, honey; but we'se ready ef dey comes," was the reply from the aunty near the stove.

"Were you ever in slavery?" we continued.

"Yes; ain't been from dar but little while."

"What State?"

"Bred and born in ole Virginny, down on de Pertomuc."

"Have you any of your relations in Virginia now?"

"Yes; got six chilens down dar somewhat, an' two husbuns—all sole to de speclaturs afore I run away."

"Did you come off alone?"

"No; my las ole man brung me 'way."

"You don't mean to be taken back by the slave-catchers, in peace?"

"No; I'll die fuss."

"How will you manage if they attempt to come into this room?"

"We'll all fling hot water on 'em, and scall dar very harts out."

"Can you throw water without injuring each other?"

"O yes, honey; we's bin practicin' all day."

The first white intruder is the one who proves her point.

The book's black populism treats the "aunty" and her comrades as exemplary race figures in whom self-defense and collective defense merge. They join the ranks of other black role models catalogued in the rest of the book, although their true peers, according to the book's underlying populist logic, would be the black folk featured in Brown's many writings. Brown never lost his sympathetic eye and ear for the people with whom he had grown up, and he even suggests they may at times have special status. In this New York episode, the aunty's plain-spoken, unyielding self-assertion stops the rioters dead in their tracks, but it also relegates the stiff, correct-speaking writer, a man of indeterminate race, to the second-tier status of idle curiosity and spectatorship.

The aunty's presence looms so large it not only crowds out the white rioters and the writer-reporter but also obscures what may be the strangest feature of the episode, the sudden absence of William Wells Brown. Shifty as always, he bears no fixed relation to either the aunty or the writer, no less the rioters. By the end of the chapter, he loses even his narrative voice, ceding the narrative function to the unnamed writer. That strange moment is reminiscent of the book's equally weird third-person "Memoir of the Author," the sixth and last such (auto)biographical introduction, though the first allegedly written by someone who supposedly once sat on his lap as a small boy. Brown's role in the composition of this latest version of his life story, an amalgam of bits and pieces of information from his earlier writings, remains an open question.

What kind of historian not only failed to unify his subject matter but even lost his voice in the course of its narration? The great African American writer Charles Chesnutt later had a blunt answer: a not-very-good one. Chesnutt made his remarks after reading the 1880 version of Brown's long-lived *The Negro in the American Rebellion*. It dissatisfied him, frustrating his desire for a systematic, coherent narrative in the same way that all of Brown's books did: "It only strengthens me in my opinion that the Negro is yet to become known who can write a good book. Dr. Brown's books are mere compilations."[11] Chesnutt's judgment is indisputable; they were all compilations, the histories most blatantly. The truly good book Chesnutt was looking for, a genuinely synthetic history of African Americans, was published in two volumes the year before Brown died: *History of the Negro Race in America from 1619 to 1880*, by George Washington Williams, the onetime minister of the Twelfth Baptist Church who had moved on to new fields, including politics, diplomacy, and the pursuit of history.

But Chesnutt's judgment missed the point of Brown's writing. An amateur rather than a professional historian, he was not attempting to write a unified, objective overview of black history that would wind up in the libraries of American colleges, not even of first-generation black institutions such as Fisk, Howard, Lincoln, and Wilberforce Universities. He was writing a history of the black experience for common readers, a topic that was so close to its lived experience it had few precedents in fact or in writing. What it had was the personal experiences of people like Brown and the other accomplished individuals—stories in the making representing the history of a people in the making. Even its language of record was as yet indeterminate. Although Brown wrote in Standard English, the logic of his book allowed an exemplary character, like the New York aunty, to thrive in her comfort zone with dialect. Rather than impose one on the other, Brown allowed room for their coexistence.

Brown had high hopes for this ambitious book and ran an advertisement for months borrowed from the review in the *Christian Recorder*: "Let every colored man in the country buy this Rising Son, and read its forty-nine chapters; and the fiftieth too, if he have the time. There is much in it that will repay the most complete perusal."[12] He expected to bring out the book with Lee and Shepard, the publisher of *The Negro in the American Rebellion* and *Clotelle*. A deal for a third Brown book would have made good sense. Their previous collaboration had been profitable, Lee and Shepard had been thriving in the intervening years, and the new title was a good fit for their list. By late summer of 1873, a price had been set at $2.50 and Brown had the manuscript nearly ready for the printer, although, as usual, he was tying up loose ends until the last moment.[13] He expected the work to be ready for publication by October 1, good timing to make the firm's fall list.[14] Then something scotched the deal.

The most likely explanation is that the outer shock waves of the financial Panic of 1873 caused Lee and Shepard to pull back. Such severe financial instability rocked the US economy following the September bankruptcy of Jay Cooke and Company that the New York Stock Exchange closed for ten days. Banks and railway lines went out of business, shops shuttered their operations, and no industry, including cash-strapped publishing, was spared the effect of severe credit contraction. One likely casualty was trade publication of *The Rising Son*, although it is also possible Lee and Shepard simply lost interest and withdrew their offer.

The unexpected reversal severely taxed Brown's patience, causing him to vent his frustration in a testy letter to his Philadelphia confidant William Still. After days of cooling his heels, walking the project between two publishers at their solicitation, he chuckled, "The little Devil that's in me got stirred up," and he noted that he was giving some thought to putting "New Citizen and Era Company's name on my book as Southern publishers."[15] Instead, after losing all patience, he walked the project back home, arranging for the stereotype plates to be manufactured at his own expense and self-publishing it as a book to be sold only by subscription. Out of the turmoil of the Panic of 1873 (or perhaps simply the bad breaks of business) arose the family publishing house of A. G. Brown and Company, Annie G. Brown president. That household partnership would be Brown's publisher of choice for the rest of his life.

The loose use of Annie's name was an inside joke of a sort the couple enjoyed, but it was also a sign of their domestic order. An intellectually lively woman who mixed easily among Brown's cultured friends, she had taken a serious interest in his writing since early in their relationship. Now she assumed a more active professional role by helping him manage mail orders for the new book and tending to other odds and ends around the office. While she was his partner at the home office, William Still served as his partner out in the literary field. One of the country's most experienced black literary professionals, as well as a thriving businessman, he had taken a sympathetic interest in Brown's work even before 1854, when Brown presented him and his wife, Letitia, with an inscribed copy of *The American Fugitive*.[16] With *The Rising Son* he played an active role by offering to promote the book and agreeing to commission sketches of notable African Americans. Two "lives" he took charge of were those of Mary Ann Shadd Cary, the former African Canadian newspaper editor now working as a school principal in Washington, DC; and Fanny Jackson, once possibly Brown's romantic interest during her studies at Oberlin and now a well-respected black educator and motivational speaker in Philadelphia.

In October, when Still inquired how the book was faring "in these hard times," he was pleased to hear that his friend had amassed 400 orders from the South and 800 more from the Boston book trade.[17] Meanwhile, he did his part in Philadelphia by taking delivery of a shipment for distribution. Checking back with Brown in November, he was glad to hear more encouraging sales news and responded collegially as one veteran activist and reformer to another: "It would hardly seem possible for it not to be well received by thousands of our people—not our people only—but other people the country over."[18] But as the year closed out amid worsening financial conditions, Brown grew bitter about the results; he had nearly sold out the first printing but still found himself in arrears by nearly $200.[19] Sales sagged so badly through the depressed winter of 1873–74 that Brown probably suspended operations, but by spring he reported that he had agents in California, Colorado, and Indian Territory (Oklahoma), all doing their best to generate a new round of sales.[20] Whatever ambition he might once have had about a bestseller was gone; his best hope now was for a steady seller with a long life.[21]

All through these roller-coaster months of fiscal and psychological volatility, the two old friends and comrades engaged in an occasional correspondence that quietly contained one of their era's most significant conversations about black history and book culture. The two men could speak not only freely but reciprocally after Still came out with his own major contribution to black history, *The Underground Railroad* (1871), a kind of fraternal twin to *The Rising Son* in postwar African American historiography. To write his pioneering book, Still had drawn heavily on his extensive experience as a conductor on the Underground Railroad, but he also employed the methodology that had served Brown well: He assembled reams of documentary information from a network of contacts and an archive of printed sources and cobbled together the results piecemeal in a loosely organized narrative. Although he lacked Brown's wit and inventiveness, he compiled a pioneering book of solid substance, communal memory, and serious historical significance. Duly proud of his nearly 800-page achievement, he called it his "monument," a living signpost connecting past to present via the black road to freedom.[22] Likewise, he saw Brown's book as another monumental work connecting blacks to their past: *The Rising Son*, he complimented his friend, would shed its "effulgent rays" on a new generation of readers.[23]

The exchange of mutual esteem was reassuring, but these two enterprising men repeatedly shifted their discussions to the practical issue of how best to get their works to the black reading public at a time when the postwar book trade showed declining interest in works by and about blacks. Each man put his book's message of black self-reliance into practice via self-publication. After a year, Still tore up the contract with his original publisher, the Philadelphia house of Coates and Porter, to take full managerial control; and Brown, who already had considerable experience from earlier books, did the same. Each set up a private distribution apparatus, assembling a team of all or mostly black sales agents (likely with some overlap) and equipping them with a dummy copy of the work, sales instructions, and an assigned geographical territory. Still had great expectations for his book, telling anyone who would listen that it would sell 100,000 copies—until the Panic of 1873 forced him to temper his expectations. Brown had somewhat more reduced prospects but was making the same higher calculation: Their reward would come not just in a healthy profit but also in the satisfaction of transmitting a living black heritage printed and bound to the doorsteps of the rising generation.

....

BROWN WAS CLEARLY DEPRESSED in the winter of 1873–74, but he had more reason for low spirits than just faltering sales of *The Rising Son*. His prodigal daughter Josephine had come home to die.

The evidence surrounding Josephine Brown's "missing" years is so sketchy that only a tentative narrative can be given, although its broad pattern seems clear enough. After being banished from her father's life, Josephine had gone out to live on her own. In the undocumented period of fifteen years following her departure from Boston, she might well have spent some time with her maternal grandmother, the nearest surviving relative likely to accept her. Henrietta Schooner Whetsel was then living in Republic, Ohio, where she ran a large household that would presumably have been open to a granddaughter, even an errant one with whom she had had little or no contact in recent years. Her household at the time included the last of Betsey's daughters, Paulina, who was listed at Henrietta's house in the 1860 federal census. Thus, Josephine would have come to know her half-sister, who remained in her grandmother's household at least up to her teenage years, after which her whereabouts are unknown.

At some unknown date, Josephine moved to New York City. There, on her thirty-first birthday, June 12, 1870, she married George Dogans, a "mulatto," according to the 1860 and 1870 federal census reports, and a few years older than she.[24] He was born free in Alexandria, Virginia, and trained as a butcher across the Potomac in Washington, DC—the locations marking the long span that Clotel had tried to cross in her tragic flight from the city's slave pens to freedom. Little is known about their marriage, which apparently was childless and short lived. On October 16, 1872, Dogans died of "croupe" in New Bedford, Josephine's hometown in girlhood and now again in married life.[25] Not very long afterward, she must have married a second time, since she next appears in the Massachusetts public records with the family name of Campbell. Those official records register the final act of her short, unhappy life: She died of consumption at age thirty-four on January 16, 1874, and was laid to rest in a shared grave in Cambridge Cemetery alongside Clotelle, the half-sister she had never met.[26] The records give her place of death only as

Cambridge, but she quite possibly died in her father's house at 15 Webster Avenue. He and Annie presumably nursed her during her last days before accompanying her body to one of the family plots across town.

When William Jr. and Clotelle died, their parents provided details to the press. Not so for Josephine, nor presumably did they spread word to their community. Whoever reported her death to the authorities took care to remove her maiden name: The Cambridge city registrar listed the deceased woman as E. Josephine Campbell; the cemetery recorder, as Josephine E. Campbell. So listed, she had in death more nominal connection to her long-deceased mother, Elizabeth, than to her father. What name, if any, was carved on her gravestone is unknown, since no headstone today marks the grave and none has for decades. Once burial space grew scarce in the twentieth century, the cemetery made arrangements that older headstones of graves not categorized "perpetual care" be removed to make room for a more recent generation able to pay full price. The same indignity awaited her father, whose grave was left unmarked for decades until a local African American civic group redressed the omission on September 23, 2001.[27]

Brown never discussed Josephine, alive or dead, in public during her last years, but her early death must have been one of the most terrible strokes of a life both stunningly fortunate and horribly afflicted. Her death, as it turned out, was only the first in a series of tragedies, near and afar, that befell him over the first half of 1874. On March 11, one of Brown's longtime heroes, Charles Sumner, died in Washington, DC. Brown had never enjoyed the kind of close personal relationship with the vain, temperamental Sumner that Lewis Hayden and Joshua B. Smith (Boston's "prince of caterers") did, but he consistently esteemed Sumner as one of the few unflinching allies of African Americans in the nation's capital.[28] As other old friends of "the Negro" abandoned the fight for equal rights for one reason or another, Sumner steadfastly labored to push through Congress a major civil rights bill that would prohibit discrimination in public accommodations, transportation, and jury duty—just the kind of unequal treatment that even Northern blacks like Brown routinely encountered. Sumner's proposed bill, long in creation and slow in adoption, preoccupied him to the end. Just hours before his death, his servants mistook his animated rambling about the "bill" as delirious concern about his household expenses. Even later that day, when Frederick Douglass looked in on him, Sumner recognized him and implored him to fight for the bill's adoption.[29] The Civil Rights Act did in fact become law in 1875, but in such unfavorable times a potentially historic piece of legislation received scant enforcement and had only a short, ineffective life before being ruled unconstitutional in 1883.

Numerous ceremonies marked Sumner's passing in Boston during the following weeks, a curious outpouring of public grief for a man with a talent for alienating friends and supporters alike. Even Brown admitted that Sumner had no sense of humor, only a finely honed sense of sarcasm more useful for skewering enemies than for cultivating and retaining allies. His death, at least, had the effect of providing a rare occasion for reuniting the city's polarized civil rights community across party, factional, and racial lines. Brown was a member of the host committee, along with William Nell, Lewis Hayden, James Monroe Trotter, and Robert Morris, at a major commemoration of black Boston that took place at Faneuil Hall on April 14. Brown's moving reading of "Our Lost Leader," written for the occasion by local poet Elijah Smith, led the audience up to the rhetorical altar to pay communal respects to the champion of "civil rights."[30] The formal oration was given by eloquent US Congressman Robert B. Elliott, a black leader from Beaufort, South Carolina, whose presence was seen as living testimony to the efficacy of Sumner's advocacy.

The symbolic role of race representative transferred from Elliott to Brown at the city's largest Sumner commemoration, on May 17 at the Music Hall, the spacious Boston auditorium where many of the attendees had congregated the evening of January 1, 1863, to celebrate the Emancipation Proclamation. Garrison spoke briefly before deferring to Brown, who came forward ex officio as a former slave to give the eulogy. Brown kept his remarks brief, contrasting Sumner and Daniel Webster as model republican and arch-compromiser: "Webster saved the Union with a million of slaves, but Sumner saved the Union with not a slave in it." His concluding comment—"The good that men do lives after them"—was appropriately eulogistic, but, as events would show, terribly shortsighted.[31] The harsh reality was that Congress had little appetite for radical reform and few candidates to succeed Sumner. Elliott's career was an example of changing times, now for the worse. After a robust tenure in the US Congress fighting for civil rights legislation, he served a term in the South Carolina State House, rose to Speaker of the House of his state's majority/minority General Assembly and later to state attorney general, but he was driven out of office in 1877 when the Democrats cleaned house following the collapse of Reconstruction.

The succession of commemorations for Sumner was just ending when Wendell Phillips went looking for Brown on May 25 to break the news that their esteemed friend William Nell had just died following a series of strokes. He found Brown in the basement of Tremont Temple participating in the convention of the international Good Templars. Brown could not have been caught completely by surprise, because he knew Nell had been bedridden for a week, but the report still stunned him, leaving him feeling his own mortality as he relayed the news to William Still: "Thus the old guard, one after another fall, and leave us with the assurance that we, to [sic], are on the downward road."[32]

Brown joined Garrison, Phillips, and progressive journalist Charles W. Slack in delivering eulogies at the funeral of his onetime closest friend at Park Street Church, the congregation once led by the renowned radical theologian Theodore Parker. The old friends had drifted apart somewhat since their marriages, settling in different cities and finding fewer occasions for civic collaboration. Nell had gradually retreated from activism after the Civil War, facing long hours at the Boston Post Office and new domestic responsibilities following his late marriage in 1869, yet Brown never lost respect for a man he regarded as one of the pillars of black Boston. Three days later, Brown joined the community at Joy Street Church to honor Nell's legacy, particularly his roles in the 1850s in integrating the city's schools and in pioneering African American historical writing. Fittingly enough, several members of the younger generation to whom Nell had devoted himself came forward to eulogize him. Edward Walker, son of the renowned pamphleteer David Walker, whom Nell had known as a boy, gave one of the lead eulogies. And Annie Brown, who had known Nell since girlhood, recited a poem written for the occasion by Elijah Smith. The practical goal of the evening, however, was to honor Nell in the way Nell had sought to honor Boston Massacre hero Crispus Attucks: to fund a monument commemorating his contributions to the municipal good.[33] Attucks's name and prostrate figure eventually appeared prominently on the large collective monument placed on Boston Common in 1888, but Nell's name gradually faded from general memory. Not until 1989 did the community place a marker on his grave in Boston's Forest Hills Cemetery.[34]

Worse news was yet to come. Sometime and somehow—no evidence survives—that summer, Brown must have received notice that his only remaining child, Clara Humbert Sylvester, had died in Leeds, Yorkshire.[35] It is impossible to know, in the absence of any surviving correspondence between father and daughter, how often Brown had stayed in touch with her once she decided in 1855 to make her life in England with her husband. But her life, too, took a sharp, unexpected turn when Fritz Alcide Humbert died within a half-dozen years of their wedding. Left unprovided for, Clara moved north not later than 1861 to the fast-growing industrial zone of Salford, a center of Manchester's thriving textile industry, where she took up work as a governess.[36]

After working for a time in that profession, she at some point turned to a different skill set—one that would have met with the severe disapproval of her music teacher and mentors at the Home and Colonial School—when she ventured out as an entertainer singing and acting on the popular stage. She had already amassed some fair experience when, in 1871, she married a fellow musician named George Wainwright Sylvester, a white bachelor, in Bradford, Yorkshire.[37] In registering herself as "a widow and vocalist," she understated her age by seven years, probably to close the gap with a male partner ten years her junior. During the four years of their marriage, the couple made the rounds of provincial stages as musical comedy entertainers. Clara, whom the London theatrical paper described as "a lady of colour," provided vocals and guitar, while Sylvester played the piano and violin.[38] Her father would hardly have approved of this daughter's turn to the stage—all the Browns from this ill-fated marriage, it turned out, had more than a bit of the performer in them—but it is by no means certain he was ever informed. By the time he finally got back to England, in 1877, he was likely to see only her grave.

BROWN'S REACTION to these latest deaths was to do what he had done after earlier tragedies: He kept moving forward. He needed all his resilience during those trying months as he poured himself into his work as a doctor and civic activist. Beyond his private grief, things were not going well in the larger world, as newspaper reports filtering northward told of an accelerating deterioration of racial conditions down South. Tempers flared on the evening of September 2, when he joined many leaders of the black community at Twelfth Baptist Church for what newspapers across the country called an "indignation meeting," organized to protest "the recent murders and outrages upon the peaceful colored citizens of the South."[39] The mood that evening was bitter, with anger to spare over not just physical assaults and discrimination against blacks in the South but also inaction in Washington, with the civil rights bill stalled in Congress and lax federal enforcement undermining black voting and property rights.

The host and organizer of the protest meeting was the brilliant young minister (and future historian) George Washington Williams, newly installed successor to Leonard Grimes as pastor of the Twelfth Baptist Church; the chief speaker was Brown. He did not talk long, but his remarks amounted to a sweeping indictment of the loss of federal nerve. He lambasted the entire federal government, but most particularly President Grant, for failure to hold Southern whites to account for physical attacks on blacks, voter suppression, theft of property, and other illegalities. He noted mordantly—in a remark well calculated to strike a nerve—that the only white person ever hanged down South was a rebel brought to judgment by General Benjamin Butler during the Union occupation of New Orleans. The underlying problem was fundamental: "There seems to be a feeling that the colored man has got about all he needs in this country, and what he will get in the next twenty-five years will be gained by hard work."[40] An emotional meeting ended with adoption of a series of resolutions whose targets stretched so wide—the recently formed, violently supremacist White League, the Congress, and the presidency—they exposed a prevailing feeling of futility. Speakers bickered over whether or not to include the Republican Party, the supposed last best hope for African Americans, in the long list of irresponsible do-nothings. In the end they did, leaving themselves with no further alternative for appeal.

Brown's remarks raised a fundamental question: Were blacks, now supposedly legally free and equal citizens, to improve their condition through their own unaided agency? Or were they to seek their advancement with the help of active enforcement of existing and future laws by the federal government? Although he called for federal intervention, his general politics contradicted the logic of his appeal. Ever since striking out on a life of activism in the 1840s, he had never trusted the major political parties. He did not trust the Whig and Democratic Parties that occupied the White House in the 1850s, the Republican Party of Lincoln in 1860, or the Republican Party of Grant in 1872 (or, for that matter, the oppositional Liberal Republicans of Horace Greeley). To the extent any organized political group earned his support and vote, it was third parties organized on narrow reform foundations, such as temperance—hardly a practical option for either election or governance.

A lifetime of disillusionment with the political system might have led a person of Brown's accomplishments and alternatives to limit his sphere of activity or even withdraw from public life. He saw retreat all around him in the 1870s, and not just from the federal government. While some members of his cohort retired from activism, Brown rededicated himself to public service. Although he needed to earn a living by his medical practice, he remained a committed activist and reformer on the local and national levels, focusing on temperance. With the energy and determination of a younger man, he traveled widely across North and South, conveying to audience after audience—ranging from workers of all races

to the black intellectual elite of Boston's Banneker Club—the message
that he was proud to be a "total abstinence" man and so should they be.[41]

Wherever he spoke, the message was blunt: Liquor destroyed individual lives, spread like a blight within families, and gradually under-
mined whole communities. Nothing deviated farther from his vision of
a good society—with black and white citizens fully, equally, and virtu-
ously empowered—than a "republic of rum." Alcohol respected no color
line; it afflicted blacks as it afflicted whites, and it infected all regions of
the country. Although he promoted temperance extensively in both the
black and the white communities, he believed the stakes were greater
for the black community because intemperance, as he liked to say, was
"the second slavery of the South."[42] People who had come to freedom
only recently, and still dragging a legacy "taught from early experience
to consider themselves members of an inferior race," needed to cultivate and practice self-restraint. Long before Booker T. Washington and
like-minded self-help advocates, he argued for the fundamental necessity
of temperance to the black community as part of the overall self-help
agenda: "A large portion of the coloured men and women in the Northern states are recently from the South and need the Temperance pledge
and the spelling book more than they need advice on politics."[43] Dili-
gently practiced, temperance would be the "main spring" of the elevation
of the race in the years following emancipation.

This ideal of a multiracial temperate society repeatedly ran up against
the realities of postwar racial relations. Just several weeks before he set
out on his near-fatal 1871 trip among the freedmen of Kentucky, he took
part in the twenty-eighth annual session of the Sons of Temperance,
a major fraternal organization reporting a nationwide membership of
nearly 100,000 people, which met September 6 in Boston.[44] The agenda
consisted largely of internal matters, but Brown succeeded in turning
attention to a delicate subject: the effective segregation of temperance
lodges in parts of the South. The immediate issue that came before the
meeting was the request by black Templars in Maryland to form a local
lodge within the state's Grand Division. As the only credentialed black
person at the Boston meeting, Brown took the lead in advocating their

case before the assembly. He appealed so powerfully to "social equality" that his speech received repeated shouts of approval and rounds of applause, and his message of a biracial organization that did biracial good carried the day. Some progressives remembered that address for years afterward—long after segregation became the organizational practice across most of the South.

A reporter attending the meetings noted Brown took the position that he "stood between the races and had no prejudices against either."[45] This was essentially the article of faith he had expressed a generation earlier, the evening in 1847 when he went to Edmund Quincy's house to collect the manuscript of *Narrative of William W. Brown*, and it remained a guiding principle he struggled to live by his whole life. As a reformer, doctor, and citizen, he tried to practice racial comity; as a writer, he devised ingenious strategies to mediate black–white racial intersections and exchanges. But what he was attempting to accomplish was the impossible; no positions were more untenable in nineteenth-century America than racial neutrality or hybridity.

Over the course of the 1870s, he allied himself with a number of temperance societies whose ideology and practices corresponded to his own. His earliest work remained with the organization over which he had presided since 1868: the National Association for the Organization of Night Schools and the Spread of Temperance among the Freed People of the South, to which he was reelected president in 1873.[46] Some of that organization's leaders—William Still, Henry Highland Garnet, John Mercer Langston—resided in the North, but many came from the South, predominantly ministers with local congregations and immediate knowledge of community exigencies. The organization sought to address basic needs of freedmen—schoolbooks for both juvenile and adult learners, salaries for their teachers, funds for facilities and their upkeep, as well as expense money for field agents—but an organization with limited means had to parcel out its aid. As the South evolved toward institutional segregation, the movement suffered from diminishing resources and foundered at some point after 1873.

By the time it did, Brown had shifted affiliations. He transferred his main allegiance to the International Order of Good Templars, a fast-growing multinational society that spread from its home base in the United States to the United Kingdom and across the breadth of the British Empire. Both he and Annie were active members prominent in the organization in the Boston area, and Brown was appointed a representative in early 1874 in time to serve at that year's international meeting, which took place May 26–30 in Boston. As the date approached, he went into operation quickly. Hours after the British delegation disembarked in Boston Harbor on May 20, he and Annie drove by buggy to the delegation's hotel to meet the dynamic Joseph Malins, a young, self-educated workingman who had risen quickly to become the leader of the movement in the United Kingdom and founding editor of its weekly newspaper. That evening, they took him along to a meeting at the small affiliated lodge in Newton, about six miles west of Boston.

Although this was their initial encounter, Malins was well aware of his host's reputation. Brown's name, as events would show, still circulated among well-placed people across the British Isles in temperance as well as antislavery circles. That evening was so memorable that both Brown and Malins would refer to it fondly for years. Malins also took a quick liking to Sister Annie, who he reported to his British readers was "a most lady-like person and refined speaker . . . and G.W.V.T. [Grand Worthy Vice Templar] of this State. She is a lady of colour, though several removes from the pure negro race."[47]

The quick rapport between Malins and Brown carried into the Boston meetings, at which "the Negro Question" came home to Brown with unexpected vehemence. Malins faced off there, for the first of many times during the late 1870s and 1880s, with Colonel John J. Hickman of Louisville, the leader of the US delegation and an advocate of segregating the organization's lodges. Although the question of race occupied only a small part of the agenda, it cast a shadow over the proceedings. Brown complained to a friend that, as nearly the only black person in attendance, he was receiving "wolfish looks" from Southern representatives.[48] Even an intended compliment, reported after the meetings, came as a backhanded slap when one of the North Carolina participants remarked about him: "He was a gentleman and a scholar, so far as we saw, and knew his place, and did not offer offense in any manner."[49]

One supremely ugly incident stood out. Meaning well, Malins invited the senior Canadian representative, a Mohawk physician named Oronhyatekha ("Burning Cloud"), to pose for a symbolic triracial photograph alongside him and Brown. Oronhyatekha's response, according to Malins's retrospective account, startled them: "No, Brother Malins, I don't mind coming down to have my portrait taken with a white man, but I will never come down so low as to be photographed with a Nigger."[50] Brown was probably not present to hear that reported remark, but once apprised of it, he never forgot or forgave Oronhyatekha. The insult festered for years and provoked reciprocal slurs uncharacteristic of Brown: Oronhyatekha, who actually had a medical degree from the Toronto School of Medicine, was an incompetent "root doctor" and Native Americans were "treacherous."[51]

THE TOUGH INFIGHTING over "the negro problem" within the International Order of Good Templars that occurred at the 1876 meeting in Louisville, Kentucky, led Malins and his supporters to withdraw from the general movement and form the breakaway Right Worthy Grand Lodge of the World (RWGLW) under his leadership. Predictably enough, their opponents immediately challenged their interpretation of events and accused Malins of personal aggrandizement, but Brown, who had been unable to attend the Louisville meetings, dismissed such charges as nothing but hidebound Southern propaganda. Malins and his colleagues were, in his eyes, champions of race progress. Immediately after reading newspaper accounts of the Louisville meetings, he wrote to express his deep gratitude to George Gladstone, a Scottish minister whom he had met in Boston and who in Louisville had forcefully advocated black inclusion: "In behalf of the race here I tender you their undivided thanks for the good and true words spoken for those who could not speak for themselves."[52] As Gladstone and Malins knew, Brown had as good a claim as anyone to speak as a representative of African Americans across the country. But with representative status came responsibility; anguished letters were reaching him from freedmen living in towns and cities across the South, asking, "what shall they do."[53]

Brown did what he could that summer, engaging in a range of activities. He was the invited speaker the evening of September 19 at the state convention of black Republicans meeting in Utica. Their chief business was endorsement of the party's slate of candidates for state and national office, but field reports and newspaper accounts of a state of terror down South split their attention.[54] Brown's view of the Republican Party, then running the moderate Rutherford B. Hayes to succeed President Ulysses S. Grant, was one of wary suspicion (with good reason, as Hayes would agree to remove federal troops from the South and thereby end Reconstruction as the price for breaking the deadlocked election against Democrat Samuel J. Tilden). The next day, Brown took the eastbound train, arriving in western Massachusetts in time to give a fiery address in North Adams at the meeting of the state's Grand Lodge. He listened to the long defense of Colonel John Hickman made by his lieutenant, Samuel Hastings, before mounting the platform and taking careful aim at his native Kentucky: By what right did Kentucky, of all states, invoke the principle that only people of "pure white blood" might join the temperance order when it was "about the last State in the American Union that should make such a claim"? Uncharacteristically worked up, he heaped up aspersions. He told his audience the story about "the Indian Good Templar" who had slandered blacks and added an irate judgment: "Of the two races the negro is infinitely above the Indian in this country, and if either had cause to object it should have been myself, for I was the person referred to."[55]

A month later, he had new, perhaps unanticipated business at home in Cambridge. Despite his longstanding ambivalence, he stood for public office in the 1876 general election. He allowed himself to be nominated for one of the three state senate seats representing Middlesex County by the only party he could take seriously, the Prohibitionists, although it is by no means clear he exerted himself in the few days leading up to the general election. The results were dismal: He polled a remote third, with only 142 of about 7,000 votes cast, to the Republican and Democratic candidates from Cambridge.[56]

A more suitable opportunity soon came his way. In December, a Good Templar from Yorkshire recommended in a public letter that the RWGLW bring Brown to Great Britain to combat malicious untruths currently being circulated there by Colonel Hickman and his followers.[57] Brown's name was then current in the British Isles, where Malins's *Good Templars' Watchword* had recently run a front-page profile of him.[58] At year's end, however, there was no practical plan to utilize Brown's special stature as a black advocate. But a quick solution emerged early in the spring of 1877 when Glasgow replaced Philadelphia as the site for that summer's RWGLW meeting, the new organization's first international convention since the split in Louisville. With the "negro question" roiling the surface of temperance debate during these months, and Malins keen to prevent Britain from being "missioned" by interlopers, he and his colleagues invited Brown to Glasgow.

"The leader of the coloured population of the United States on the Good Templar question," as a leading Scottish daily called him, needed no coaxing.[59] He had apparently had England on his mind ever since the showdown at Louisville. Soon after reading about that unexpected outcome, he had expressed his personal sentiment to Gladstone: "I spent several years in Europe, mostly in England and Scotland, and I should like to see the old country once more. . . ."[60] As his departure date approached, his British colleagues invited him to extend his stay with a sponsored lecture tour around Britain. Brown accepted enthusiastically, knowing he would have an ideal opportunity not just to serve the movement but also to reacquaint himself with friends and places from a generation earlier.

He embarked from Boston on June 9 on the Cunard steamer *Parthia*. Ten days later, he walked out onto the Liverpool dock to a welcoming committee headed by the Right Worthy Grand Templar James Yeames, an English minister who served as the first leader of the RWGLW (and who would later emigrate to Boston and become the Browns' close family friend). The local lodge welcomed Brown with a reception, but he used most of his time in Liverpool to educate himself about the state of the liquor trade in the United Kingdom, a hard-drinking nation like the United States. One day he went to Drunken Court to see for himself how justice was meted out. He came away unimpressed, reporting he saw nothing but the injustice of the victimizer blaming the victim for vicious behavior: "There was nothing more ridiculous than to condemn a poor, weak drunkard who could not control his appetite, and send him off for drinking that which you have licensed for sale."[61] That statement summarized his view of public policy on both sides of the Atlantic: Government would do better to prohibit the sale of alcoholic beverages than to punish the intemperate.

Before heading north to Glasgow, Brown made several intermediate stops by request. One was a temperance session at Nottingham; the other, a lecture at South West Lancashire, where he was honored with another public reception. On that occasion, he gave a speech on race that was generally well received, although dissenters occasionally interrupted him.[62] If he needed any instruction about differing views on race in imperial England, he got it that evening. In general, however, he would find British audiences welcoming and supportive, as they had been a generation earlier. His reputation as "a released slave, a talented speaker, author of several works on the color line practices of America" and his credentials preceded him, and he soon proved his persuasive ability.[63]

He reached Glasgow by June 25 and quickly launched himself into the meetings.[64] In mounting the speaker's platform at City Hall and sitting alongside Gladstone, Yeames, and several other dignitaries, Brown recalled that he had spoken from that same platform twenty-six years earlier during his successful panorama tour. As he took his turn to speak, the audience rose "en masse" to greet him, a demonstration probably less of respect for past work than for leadership expected in dealing with the conflict that had split the movement.[65] For many of the attendees, Brown conveyed an authenticity that transferred to them all. They might not know much about the politics and practices of racial segregation across the ocean, but they trusted that their black American visitor did and would give informed advice about how to address troubling issues, such as the incorporation of African Americans into accredited Southern lodges.

Brown realized he had an authority he could trade on, and he did so wherever he went. In Glasgow he proudly listed not only his accomplishments within the movement but also Annie's ("the only coloured woman in America," he proudly noted, "who had held the high and honourable position of Grand Worthy Vice Templar for a white Grand Lodge").[66] Furthermore, knowing the general convergence of antislavery and temperance sentiment in the RWGLW, he was also careful to introduce the names of Garrison and Phillips, who were well respected in Britain for their advocacy of both causes. Brown might well have had an ulterior motive to use their names in Glasgow, since he wished to promote the candidacy of Boston (successfully, it would turn out) to host the next year's international sessions.

He remained in the British Isles for two busy months, keeping a tight travel and lecture schedule. The leaders of the organization had advertised his services for local lodges and organized a master schedule that had him participating in temperance meetings and delivering lectures in cities across the United Kingdom. Brown plunged avidly into the tour, excited to have a renewed opportunity to bring his energies to people and places familiar to him. At some venues, he found himself appearing alongside interesting accompaniment. In Middlesbrough, North Yorkshire, he spoke at a large afternoon gathering at Central Temperance Hall, where he was joined by the Wilmington Jubilee Singers, a touring troupe of ex-slaves from North Carolina.[67] White minstrels had been crossing the ocean for decades, but by the 1870s African American troupes, most notably the Fisk Jubilee Singers, had begun to carry the sound of black music to Europeans. In Bristol, he was advertised to speak along with the grandson of William Wilberforce (Reverend Ernest Wilberforce, future chairman of the Church of England Temperance Society) at the Templars' grand soiree.[68] At various other events, Malins, Gladstone, and/or Yeames accompanied him, as years before he occasionally had had George Thompson or Richard Webb by his side.

Brown's practiced rhetoric worked as well as ever in Britain. Interest generally ran high, as he found, for instance, at Burslem, Staffordshire, where the subject of US racial exclusion proved a matter of great concern even to a white middle-class temperance audience seated in a town hall in the English Midlands. He came forward that evening after a generous introduction by a local dignitary to address an obviously receptive audience, some of whose members even remembered an antislavery talk he had given there a generation earlier. He described himself as half black and half white and noted that he and Colonel Hickman hailed from the same city in Kentucky, although "he did not want them to make a mistake and think that the Colonel was any relation of his." He quickly put the purpose of that night's meeting into perspective. If there was, as he had been apprised, divided sentiment in England about segregation in the Southern lodges, "it is not on account of wont of sympathy, but it is because the British people have had presented to them a false issue." Brown announced that he was there to help the audience understand the history of racism in the South and thereby distinguish between false and true statements by temperance leaders. To judge from the frequent printed mentions of laughter and applause in the reporter's text, it did not take him long to bring the audience over to his point of view.[69]

One notable stop during his tour was Newcastle upon Tyne, where he took time to visit old friends, including Ellen Richardson. She was disappointed his busy schedule prevented him from staying longer, but even a brief visit brought her keen pleasure. She saw in "Dr. Brown," as she referred to him, the living proof of her faith in human equality.[70] As luck would have it, a few days earlier she had breakfasted with Garrison, who was making a tour of Great Britain that almost exactly coincided with Brown's. Their itineraries and their purposes, however, were entirely distinct. Garrison was traveling via New York City with his son Frank at the request of his family, who hoped an ocean voyage and reunion with old friends might restore mental and physical vigor to their elderly, widowed father. Richardson was delighted to see the revered leader of US antislavery come to her hometown and pressed Garrison for news about her cherished friends Brown and Douglass.

For Richardson, the one missing presence that summer was Douglass, for she could not think of one remarkable fugitive slave she and her family had helped without thinking of the other. It was as though she was completing a circle of beloved friends from her past when, in a subsequent letter to Douglass notable for its depth and sincerity, she described her pleasure in renewing acquaintance with Garrison and Brown and informed him how she had pressed Brown for news about "F. Douglass." And, in one further curious comment, she conveyed to Douglass her impression of the more mature Brown: "I was pleased to hear something more and that was that he bore his dignity with more *humility* than in earlier days."[71]

These were her associations. Brown's during this rendezvous visit can only be guessed. In London, he must have stopped by to see George Thompson, as Garrison did, now in failing health with only months to live. While in Bristol, where he lectured, he presumably visited with Mary Estlin, who had moved out of the fine Park Street house but still lived nearby in Clifton. He also paid visits to new friends. One was the impressive Quaker activist Catherine Impey, who hosted him in Street, Somerset, an act of hospitality Brown would reciprocate when she came to Boston on RWGLW business the following year.[72] By that time, she had taken over fundraising duties for the RWGLW's support of mission work in the US South.

He departed Liverpool on August 30, after a successful tour that concluded with his agreement to do fieldwork in the South for the organization, a role his British colleagues believed no African American could do better. They agreed to stake Brown financially for his service, assigning Impey to be his contact person on behalf of the organization's Negro Mission. Once the mission was operational, she would also serve as liaison for the transatlantic flow of money and field reports. Thus began a commitment that would return Brown to the South intermittently over the next three years.

HE RETURNED HOME a reinvigorated man, carrying not only a commission but also an oversize memento of his trip. That was the "magnificent" photograph album (now lost) the organization gave him as a parting tribute at the dock in Liverpool. It lay open for inspection below the speaker's platform of Twelfth Baptist Church during the large, formal reception on September 27 honoring Brown for his devoted service.[73] Between tributes, Brown gave the multiracial audience an hour-long account of his mission. Meanwhile, word about his trip spread fast around the country via the black and the white presses, often accompanied by commentaries that aligned with racial and/or party lines. The *Christian Recorder*, the Philadelphia-based AME newspaper that reached black readers across the South, praised him enthusiastically, noting that "from John O'Groat's house in the North to the Land's End in the South, his receptions were of the nature of ovations," and recounted his position on the temperance war point for point.[74]

He lost no time taking up his new assignment. In November, he was already "working up the cause of temperance" in Richmond, ex-capital of the Confederacy and home to a large, struggling black population.[75] That relatively brief visit was the first of a series of trips he made between 1877 and 1880, during which he immersed himself more deeply in the life of the South than he had since his escape. Returning "home," he found the South a giant paradox: the scourge of slavery eradicated but race prejudice remarkably persistent, even contagious. There was work to be done among both whites and blacks to alter this state of affairs, but Brown understood that, given current social and political conditions, once he crossed the Mason-Dixon line, his sphere of operation was necessarily limited to work among fellow blacks. Malins highlighted this polarized situation by publishing a temperance map of the United States that portrayed the racial exclusionary line within lodges as running exactly along the Mason Dixon, a phenomenon he derided as "A Black Picture of the Sunny South."[76]

Brown's most intensive fieldwork took place during a string of visits that stretched from February 1879 to February 1880. Now thirty-five years older than when he had first set out on the antislavery trail, Brown must nevertheless have felt as though he was revisiting old times. Roads were primitive, towns were distant, surrounding populations were hostile, and even the weather was trying after years of acclimation to the North (though now it was summer heat rather than winter cold that most interfered with his work). The work was quietly, modestly heroic. Brown pushed forward across large tracts of Virginia, West Virginia, and

Tennessee with dogged persistence, going wherever his services seemed most necessary. Often he had no choice but to ride on horseback to reach destinations where trains or coaches were unavailable, putting up with substandard fare in private homes when public lodgings refused him entry, struggling to organize lodges where resources were few and infrastructure was often insufficient, and maneuvering between rivalries within both the black and the white temperance communities.

He witnessed repeated instances of the resistance black communities were facing from sullen whites in trying to gain a foothold in the new South. While in Tennessee, he was particularly struck by the searing resentment among its displaced white aristocracy:

> The older whites, brought up in the lap of luxury, educated to believe themselves superior to the race under them, self-willed, arrogant, determined, skilled in the use of side-arms, wealthy—possessing the entire political control of the State—feeling themselves superior also to the citizens of the free States—this people was called upon to subjugate themselves to an ignorant, superstitious, and poverty-stricken, race—a race without homes, or the means of obtaining them; to see the offices of State filled by men selected from this servile set made these whites feel themselves deeply degraded in the eyes of the world. Their power was gone, but their pride still remained. They submitted in silence, but "bided their time," and said: "Never mind; we'll yet make your hell a hot one."[77]

One sudden outbreak of that resentment occurred as Brown was standing in front of the Knoxville House. Two well-dressed men were engaged in conversation when suddenly one took his cane, knocked off the other man's hat, and swore at him, "'Don't you know better than to speak to a white man with your hat on, where's your manners?'" The white man, Brown learned on inquiry, was a real estate agent; the black man, a former state legislator.[78]

His primary concern, though, was always the black population. In late 1877, he had labored in Virginia to spread his message and organize an infrastructure of lodges. He had focused his work in the littoral region of the state, an area formerly of large-scale plantation slavery whose towns and cities now had exceptionally large African American concentrations. He also spent extensive time in the ex-Confederate capital of Richmond, a city with which he had had no familiarity when he wrote *Clotel*. He worked hard to get to know the black community and to build up an infrastructure of lodges. By the time he left, he felt serious progress had been made.

But when he returned to Virginia in winter 1879, he found the state "in a terrible condition." The problems were familiar—white resistance, poverty, ignorance, organizational infighting, and backsliding—but he retained his temperamental optimism about what he could reasonably accomplish. He intended to concentrate on the basics, as he was quick to state publicly. His fellow blacks needed to face down King Alcohol, to raise money for funding their lodges, and to sort out allegiances between competing temperance affiliations. He was there to help accomplish these goals, he told them, but he could do nothing if they did not adopt a policy of total abstinence—the one and only means of elevation for each individual, family, and community. Individuals and their communities must be responsible for their conduct. They must also take charge of raising the money necessary to purchase charters for their lodges rather than depend wholly on outside philanthropy. Realizing that this was not always possible in communities with high rates of unemployment and limited means, he did his best to reduce lodge startup expenses by contributing some of the necessary materials from northern lodges and paring other costs. But he required at least partial payment from even the poorest groups looking to start lodges, because "I think it best they should pay something where they can, for people appreciate a thing more highly if they have to pay something for it."[79]

He was all business in the field reports he sent off to England for consideration and publication, but he also took time to dig deep into the rich, familiar soil of the South for his personal education and pleasure. What he observed left him with deep ambivalence about the progress these mostly impoverished, uneducated people were making. He repeatedly characterized their situation as "improvident." Their pasts had prepared them poorly for freedom, and the failure of the Freedmen's Bank had made their financial planning, if possible, worse. The overreliance on one-crop farming—chiefly tobacco—had depleted the soil and left many people, black and white, impoverished and unemployed. In Petersburg, he saw back in use one of the most reviled signs of the past, all too familiar to him, a whipping post. When he asked a black resident his opinion about it, he got a seasoned response: "Well, sar, I don't ker fer it, kase dey treats us all alike; dey whips whites at de pos jes as dey do de blacks, an dats what I calls equality before de law."[80] He found their religion loud, boisterous, and ignorant—the false religion of an uneducated people worked up by uneducated ministers. His overall impression was that they were in serious need of "elevation," to use one of his key terms.

He also took care to collect stories and gather notes on his impressions for a book already fast taking shape in his mind. As when recruiting in Ontario in 1861 for Haitian emigration, he made time to meet local folk and inquire about their lives. He plainly took pleasure in walking around rebuilding Richmond. On Saturdays, he visited the outdoor markets, which he loved for their splashy displays of dress, manners, song, and dialect. He walked the market stalls, stopping to converse with hucksters and customers and to listen to the music. On Sundays, he visited a gamut of churches, black and white, Protestant and Roman Catholic, making mental notes on the range of pastoral performances.

One Sunday he paid a visit, along with many other curious people, to Richmond's Sixth Mount Zion Baptist Church. His curiosity already aroused, he arrived early to witness the gathering drama as the city's white elite, including members of the legislature, occupied seats in the center, with blacks all around the sides and in the upstairs galleries. The object of attraction was the city's famously old-school Baptist preacher, John Jasper—like Brown, up from slavery and illiteracy. The day's announced sermon had already spread his name around the country: "De Sun Do Move," a scorching homily on the duty of obedience based on a literalist reading of Joshua 10:12–13. Jasper had recently taken that sermon on the road in a widely publicized, generally successful tour of Northern churches, but response to his fundamentalist preaching in Richmond was mixed, even in the black community. The state's leading black paper, the *Virginia Star*, expressed the view of most educated blacks: "Brother John will find that either the stopping of the STAR or the moving of the sun is a task that demands more moral and intellectual strength than he possesses."[81] Brown had just as little attraction as the editor to Bible-thumping fundamentalism, but his account of Jasper's spirited reading of Joshua rendered a begrudging admiration for a rhetorically gifted man who knew how to command an audience from the pulpit: "The preacher, though wrong in his conclusions, was happy in his quotations, fresh in his memory, and eloquently impressed his views upon his hearers."[82]

Several months of energetic labor in eastern Virginia led Brown to consider the state's Grand Lodge as "strong and in good condition," so in April 1879 he pushed on to West Virginia. Here, too, he had to work from the ground up to build an organizational infrastructure, a task complicated by the sparseness of the state's black population. He centered his time and effort on Wheeling, where he eventually succeeded in organizing the state's Grand Lodge. He began his work in the state, however, farther east in Charles Town, the county seat, seven miles from Harpers Ferry, where John Brown had been tried and executed nearly twenty years earlier. He was thrilled to discover the aura of John Brown still pervasive, and he may even have contributed an additional tale to the John Brown mythology. In the public letter he filed from Harpers Ferry, he wrote that he had met in Charles Town the black babe-in-arms, now a twenty-one-year-old woman, whom the freedom fighter kissed on the forehead as he was led out of jail to the gallows—a story that circulated nationally after the execution and was commemorated by a Currier and Ives engraving. Brown proudly reported through the press that the young woman was now the Worthy Vice Templar of Charles Town's new John Brown Lodge.[83]

This is another of Brown's life sketches that satisfies as either fiction or history, but as both? John Brown's recent biographer categorically dismisses the story of the babe-in-arms as apocryphal, citing eyewitness accounts that the bound and guarded prisoner had no freedom of movement as he exited the jail for the waiting wagon.[84] Brown presumably did not dig very deeply into the facts; what mattered to him was the legend of John Brown, who had been a living, looming presence in his life for years. On the night following the execution, he had given a lecture in Providence on "The Heroes of Insurrection."[85] During the late 1860s, he had served as president of Boston's John Brown Lodge, the local affiliate of the Sons of Temperance. In the early 1870s, he had devoted a short chapter to Brown in *The Rising Son*. And shortly before his own death, he would have the honor of shaking the hand of the widowed Mary Brown at a commemorative ceremony in Boston.[86] For Brown, author and activist, the young woman in Charles Town was usefully part of the mythology gathering around the "Old Hero."

On May 23, Brown informed Catherine Impey that he planned to organize a few more lodges before heading home in another week. He moved up his return, however, on hearing the shocking news that William Lloyd Garrison had died in New York City on May 24. He was already back in Boston on May 26, even before the body's arrival, in time to attend the commemorative service at the Twelfth Baptist Church and to offer communal resolutions praising Garrison, a man he had never ceased to admire as the backbone of the antislavery cause and a fighter for equal rights to his dying day.[87] On May 28, he attended the funeral, which, though originally intended by the family to be private, was instead organized as a public memorial and held at the First Church in Roxbury. That afternoon, Brown sat jammed among the 1,500 mourners, many of them comrades with whom he had shared some of his most cherished memories as a movement activist. In one sense, however, he was left an outsider, as the family did not invite him to be either a pallbearer or a speaker.

Four months later, once the summer heat had passed, Brown returned to the field. So many requests for his services poured in from community leaders in the South—from Alabama, Tennessee, Kentucky, and Georgia, where a lecture at the chapel of the new, predominantly black Atlanta University was offered—he could only pick and choose.[88] He spent the majority of his time in Tennessee and perhaps also got to Alabama, which would have been as far south as he traveled in his late years. But his optimism faded over the winter of 1880 as his efforts yielded diminishing returns and his strength gave way. Returning home in February, sick and frustrated after months of bone-wearying touring and unending discrimination, he vented his disgust to Impey: "With all the hotels and other places of accommodation closed against me— made to pay for a first-class ticket, and forced for the poorest possible excuse, into a second-class car; often going hungry, because niggers are not allowed in the most common eating-houses; walking long distances from depots (railway stations) on account of the rules not permitting niggers to ride in public conveyances; frequently waiting in the cold for a train, and not allowed in the railroad waiting rooms, and other obstacles too numerous to mention; made me feel rather blue in the South."[89] Feeling "rather blue in the South" was his last personal experience of his native region. He would never return in person, although he was already very far advanced in a new book that would revisit the South—old and new—on terms he got to dictate.

BROWN WAS JUST COMPLETING his final temperance mission down South when a correspondence about the deteriorating living conditions of Southern blacks was resuming between two members of his once-enslaved Kentucky cohort.[90] Time and distance had separated these trusted old friends, fellow activists going back to "the earliest days of the Antislavery Cause." Its initiator was Lewis Clarke, one of the flying Clarke brothers who had escaped slavery in Kentucky about the time Brown took flight from Missouri. Clarke was at that time living unhappily in Oberlin, Ohio, the rare town with a reverential memory of the antislavery past. His correspondent was Lewis Hayden, a highly respected citizen of Boston and one of Brown's dearest friends. Clarke, Hayden, and Brown shared common personal histories of Kentucky birth, escape from slavery, belated acquisition of literacy, and continuing advocacy of equal rights. Now, as they all moved through their seventh decade, Clarke noted that their ranks were thinning: "There are a few of the old vetrons still alive hare and thare thoe they are getting verry scurs and few and fair between but as a general thing they stand firm and sturdy on the old principle of Human rits. . . ."

At a time of nationwide cultural nostalgia for a supposedly simpler, happier bygone era that swept up even white antislavery veterans yearning for the heroic camaraderie of their early manhood, Clarke expressed only a flinty outrage about the racial injustices of the present. In reconnecting with Hayden, he took them both on a grim reckoning with the long, hard slog out of slavery. What, in the end, did four decades of black activism and historical change amount to? What, after all the years of struggle, was black life in the South worth? He was so depressed he even raised a counterfactual scenario that might once have been unthinkable or unmentionable: Would things have been different if "you and I and [Lunsford] Lane and Brown and Dougless [*sic*] should not of left but should of staid thare and fight it out"? But that was only momentary frustration crowding out the solid sense he and they could all agree on: "A good run is better than a bad stan[d]."

A consensus about the past, however, did not amount to agreement about the present. A "good run" worked for slaves in the past, but would it serve the South's six million blacks in the present? Clarke was one of many black leaders who split with Douglass in winter 1879–80 over this now-pressing question. Whereas Douglass urged his brothers and sisters to stay and fight for their hard-earned rights, Clarke advised migration to the North. Waves of emigrants had already begun striking out to new territories, such as the Exodusters, whose migration to Kansas was receiving national attention. Not even the West was far enough from US racial hatred for Clarke, who was contemplating moving with his family to Australia, a land where "thare is no prejious."

The ongoing public debate among black intellectuals and activists about the viability of black life in the South echoed anguished family and community discussions held in cabins, schools, churches, shops, and editorial offices across the region. Times were brutally difficult. To many black people, it felt as though they were being dragged into a renewal of warfare by other means, even if, as Brown acerbically commented, "the war was all on the side of the whites."[91] Poor, despairing freedmen continued to write to Brown; surely a person so widely read and connected who had lived and traveled extensively in the South could give them trustworthy advice. He undoubtedly replied to many of them privately, one by one, as their letters reached Cambridge, but by the late 1870s he was also readying for publication a sweeping meditation on the South, *My Southern Home* (1880). Disheartened by his own recent experience, he offered hard advice to his Southern brothers and sisters:

> Some say, "stay and fight it out, contend for your rights, don't let the old rebels drive you away, the country is as much yours as theirs." That kind of talk will do very well for men who have comfortable homes out of the South, and law to protect them; but for the negro, with no home, no food, no work, the land-owner offering him conditions whereby he can do little better than starve, such talk is nonsense. Fight out what? Hunger? Poverty? Cold? Starvation? Black men, emigrate.[92]

Brown's call for migration seemingly matched Clarke's: The South had become an inhospitable home for millions of African Americans subjected to the imposing reign of Jim Crow. At the time of this writing, however, a surge of memory, reinforced by his recent visits, was carrying him back powerfully to the South—or, more exactly, to a South that by 1880 was as much a product of his memory and writings as an actual place. A rich blend of contemplation and experience, *My Southern Home* charted a return not just to his native region but also to its full-scale treatment in writing for the first time in nearly a generation since *Clotel* and *The Escape*. In 1880, once again, Brown was recalculating his bearings.

So was the nation. The shift in the national mood toward a politics of reconciliation was accompanied by a postbellum vogue for cultural nostalgia, "true-life" local-color writing fit for a newly united citizenry hungry to retrieve its connection to an authentic rootedness. No region of the country better sated this need than the South, and no imaginative mode proved better than the plantation tales of a new generation of white Southern storytellers like Thomas Nelson Page and Joel Chandler Harris, whose first collection of Uncle Remus tales was published in New York City in 1880. Old-time Southern blacks had their place in such writing, and these writers knew what it was and assigned it.

My Southern Home addressed both Brown's and the nation's need for a reckoning with the past. He counted on that in advertising the book as "the great inside view of the South. It runs back for fifty years and gives the state of society in the olden times."[93] Always a writer with a knack for entertainment, he designed it well for popular appeal to both black and white readers, creating a wide array of vivid generic scenes and illustrating them more profusely than he had any of his earlier books. This was especially his practice in the long opening section about life in the Old South, in which he served up a loosely organized succession of tableaus designed to play to (and on) readers' expectations: coon hunting by night, high jinks played by slaves on masters, minstrel scenes of slaves vying with one another for status, outlandish displays of racist preaching, high-stakes riverboat gambling, traditional African dancing in New Orleans's Congo Square, cornhusking by night, Emancipation Day observed in a South Carolina slave cabin. To judge from reviews, most readers took such scenes for "the real thing." A reporter for the *New York Times* rendered a typical white reaction: "A colored physician, who began life on a farm near St. Louis as a slave, gossips very acceptably about the old days of 'coon hunts, negro jollifications, whippings, and trackings with blood-hounds, which form a staple of slave reminiscences."[94] Black readers like Pauline Hopkins, who borrowed and remade passages from it for *Hagar's Daughter,* would have taken a different view of the book's "jollifications" and "reminiscences" of slavery and reached their own conclusions about what constituted "acceptability," but they too generally read it as an expression of authentic memory about the past, as well as commentary about the present.

These scenes of olden times in the South, however, had less connection to actual places or unmediated memory than to Brown's compositional gamesmanship. As had been his practice since *Narrative of William W. Brown,* what he was offering the public was a movable feast lifted from scores of printed texts, well supplemented by popular songs and recycled engraved images. The process of serving up his doctored view of the past begins in the opening scene, a set piece familiar to both readers and theatergoers of an antebellum St. Louis–area farm populated by a large workforce of slaves presided over by their masters, Dr. and Mrs. Gaines. The physical description of the house and grounds comes, however, not from the author's direct recollections of the Youngs' property outside St. Louis but from his description nearly thirty years earlier of Clotel's conjugal cottage near Richmond, Virginia—a description that he had lifted and reformatted from Lydia Maria Child's 1842 short story, "The Quadroons." Likewise, the book's corresponding frontispiece engraving of the "Great House at Poplar Farm," the name given to the Gaines's property, was a generic work Brown probably picked up in some printing office that bore no relation to any specific home in Missouri, Virginia, or (as in Child's story) Georgia. It returned to the reader's eye nothing but his or her expectations of what a great house should look like.

Story after story from Brown's earlier repertoire comes back to life in *My Southern Home* in postbellum incarnations, which by 1880 had acquired life histories of their own related to but increasingly independent from his own. A typical example was the minstrel tale of "Negro dentistry" about Sam, the "Black Doctor" who pulls the wrong tooth. That curiously favored story, concocted long before Brown turned to medicine, was one he told on the lecture tour in England about himself as assistant to Dr. Young, in *Clotel* about an earlier version of Sam, and again in *The Escape* about the central character, Cato. In addition to retelling this story—kept at a safe remove from himself, about a minstrel character—Brown illustrated it with the same slapdash engraving he had used nearly thirty years earlier in *Clotel*. (The plates are identical, except for the scratched-out page number, indicating Brown probably owned, stored, and reused the original.) In like fashion, he recycled most of the engravings he had first used in *Clotel* to illustrate corresponding plantation-era episodes in *My Southern Home*. Some of the other illustrations, such as the prints he used to represent Sarah Gaines, the Reverend Pinchen, and the slave trader Walker, were just generic images that he must have selected from the drawers of a Boston printing office.

The scene of Sam as the Black Doctor is the nearly unique instance in which a manuscript documenting Brown's compositional practice survives.[95] It consists of a draft text jotted on several small sheets of cheap paper, marked with deletions and corrections, and written in an unidentified hand (perhaps Annie's). The manuscript is undated, but it was very likely written in the late 1870s as a trial draft for a scene in chapter 3 of *My Southern Home.* Although the entire scene derives from Act 1, Scene 2, of *The Escape,* it introduces new details and language that exactly match the text of *My Southern Home,* as when Dr. Gaines is described sarcastically as "saluting [Cato] in his usual kind and indulgent manner" before tasking him. Perhaps the most revealing detail is the substitution of Cato for Bill as the black dentist's name. Once again, with a flick of the pen, Brown routinely shifted persons, perspective, and phraseology from text to text as he searched for language that did at least temporary justice to the slippery nature of experience.

These old stories about racial relations in plantation times, stories that had served him well in his antislavery work, signified differently in postbellum times. He meant them, as always, to entertain and instruct his readers, but the audience of black and white readers he was addressing in 1880 had changed dramatically since the 1850s, when he had put slavery on trial in *Clotel* and *The Escape.* In 1880, it was the Old South he was putting on trial in an attempt to dispel the spreading myth about Southern chivalry, happy darkies, and the mildness of the peculiar institution, a myth he regarded as the misbegotten offspring of Jim Crow.

He portrayed the customs and pastimes of the Old South with such verve and humor that a reader, such as the *New York Times* reviewer, might initially be lulled into a false sense of the book's participation in that myth. Its series of high-spirited stories about the characteristic activities of the Old South cast so appealing a charm over Southern life that an unwitting reader is brought only gradually to the revelation of its dark underside, the system of racial exploitation and intended dehumanization that made routine existence possible for whites. In extending his book's coverage to the postwar South, Brown took no chances it would be misunderstood. Its final chapters mount so searing an indictment of organized violence and repression against black people that no reader could mistake its call for migration as anything but the conclusion that the South, no wonderland past or present, was beyond redemption.

Despite its despair about the New South, *My Southern Home* is actually a testament to Brown's continuing faith in his people—particularly those, like Cato in *The Escape*, the fighting aunty in *The Rising Son*, the Crafts, and countless others, who came up from the South and brought with them their enduring resiliency, creativity, and fortitude. Their resourcefulness in countering the threat of dehumanization was the very quality on which he drew to undermine the latest regime of racism. His retelling of his old stories refreshed with a stock of new ones—such as the wonderful episode in chapter 9 in which he presented gangs of slaves singing and joking while taking part in the corn-shucking harvest—celebrated the spirit of black creativity. They kept alive the songs, tales, and dialect repartee that Brown, looking backward, believed had animated and sustained life in the black South. As confident about his own powers as he was dismissive of those of a younger generation of writers and entertainers, black and white, to create a true picture of the South, he intended *My Southern Home*, as Pauline Hopkins did *Peculiar Sam*, as a legacy for a younger black generation that did not know slavery. In the process of composing it, he created for himself a lifeline attaching his present life as close as was still possible to his long-lost Southern home.

The book closes with a characteristic anecdote about identity politics—Brown's last printed joke and one appropriate for a lifelong searcher for a language of truth. The issue was terminology: "In this work I frequently used the word 'Negro,' and shall, no doubt, hear from it when the negro critics get a sight of the book. And why should I not use it? Is it not honorable? What is there in the word that does not sound as well as 'English,' 'Irish,' 'German,' 'Italian,' 'French'"? The joke immediately follows:

> "Don't call me a negro; I'm an American," said a black to me a few
>   days since.
> "Why not?" I asked.

"Well, sir, I was born in this country, and I don't want to be called
out of my name."

Just then, an Irish-American came up, and shook hands with me.
He had been a neighbor of mine in Cambridge. When the young
man was gone, I inquired of the black man what countryman he
thought the man was.

"Oh!" replied he, "he's an Irishman."

"What makes you think so?" I inquired.

"Why, his brogue is enough to tell it."

"Then," said I, "why is not your color enough to tell that you're a
negro?"

"Arh!" said he, "that's a horse of another color," and left me with a
"Ha, ha, ha!"[96]

The moral of the story closes the book: "Black men, don't be ashamed
to show your colors, and to own them."

The point of the joke was the central tenet of his life's faith: black
pride. When all else seemed to be in flux, that quality alone gave African
American identity a firm basis that spanned time and region.

IT IS NOT KNOWN whether Brown sought a commercial publisher for *My
Southern Home* after the fiasco with *The Rising Son*. In any event, the
publisher of record was A. G. Brown and Company, with William and
Annie handling production and sales, as they did with *The Rising Son*.
They marketed it as a subscription book available through their sales
agents around the country, as well as via mail order out of their 28 East
Canton Street office—their residence and Brown's medical office at the
time.

They collaborated in their home operation during the last four years
of Brown's life. By 1880, their list grew to include Brown's last three
books. Lee and Shepard had kept *The Negro in the American Rebellion*
in print for nearly a decade, listing it as late as their 1876 centennial
catalog.[97] Sometime between 1876 and 1880, Brown purchased from
them the unsold copies and the stereotype plates and in 1880 ran off

an additional printing, with a new title page listing A. G. Brown and Company as publisher.[98] Likewise, he and Annie kept *The Rising Son* in print, running off new printings as necessary. The total sales figure of 13,000 copies they listed on the 1882 "thirteenth edition" (by which the publishers meant thirteenth printing, each presumably consisting of a cautious 1,000 copies) sounds plausible and would indicate that, market volatility and Brown's frustration notwithstanding, the book had taken hold with the public and proven a fairly successful steady seller.[99]

The income from the three books was undoubtedly an important source of livelihood, supplementing Brown's medical income. He and Annie also earned some onetime income from the sale of Gray family property in Cambridge following the death of Annie's mother in April 1875. Harriet Gray's estate included the three adjacent lots on Webster Avenue, where the family had been living since the 1850s. During the two decades William and Annie lived in the house at 15 Webster Avenue, Brown assumed the role of big brother, dispensing advice and help to Annie's younger siblings. He sent Horace J. Gray, for instance, down to Philadelphia in 1865 to meet William Still, presumably for help in finding employment, but Horace soon proved himself the family member least dependent on Brown's connections. A highly capable, intelligent man, he would make a fine career as deputy collector in the Boston office of the Internal Revenue Service, where he worked under Brown's friend Charles W. Slack.

Brown played a more active role in assisting William H. Gray, who received the territory of Delaware for subscription sales of Still's *Underground Railroad* and probably also handled regional sales of *The Rising Son*.[100] When that arrangement no longer was lucrative, he decided to seek his fortune out West, settling in Oakland, California. Before he did, he signed over power of attorney to Brown in 1875 to supervise his affairs back East.[101] One of the most interesting transactions Brown made on behalf of his brother-in-law was to sell a property on Webster Avenue to—of all people—Wendell Phillips.[102] What possible reason could the wealthy Phillips, owner of a fine house in Boston, have in purchasing a modest property in a working-class neighborhood? The transaction, it turns out, was an expression of Phillips's friendship for Brown, the contract giving William Gray the right to reclaim the house by repaying the $500 purchase price with interest within two years, as he did. In all likelihood, Gray accepted the money as a loan from Phillips in getting a start in Oakland, one of several such arrangements Brown brokered for him.

Annie inherited one of the houses on Webster Avenue through a complex deal with her siblings, and in time she decided to sell it. But she ran into complications when she learned there was an outstanding claim on the property by an elderly man, long since relocated to Wisconsin and mistakenly thought ≠≠by his family to be deceased. She resolved that obligation by making a nominal $1 payment in return for a quit-claim deed, which, once received on September 12, 1882, cleared her and Brown to sell the property. They did that same day—to a resident of Boston for $1,005.[103]

By that time, the Browns had been living in Boston for four years, their ties to Cambridge long since attenuated as Annie's family, one of the city's most respected black families, had dispersed from the old neighborhood. Once settled in Boston, however, the couple began a roughly biennial pattern of moving from one rented house to another. Only people in close touch would have been able to keep up with their changing addresses: 7 Decatur in 1878–79 in the South End, 28 East Canton in 1880–83(but his medical office moved to Hanover Street in 1882), and in 1883 or 1884 over the Mystic River to 89 Beacon Street in Chelsea—the final address of a man who had led a roaming existence.

"THE WORLD DOES MOVE" was Brown's commentary on the long-delayed ceremony that took place in January 1883 in the town cemetery of Framingham, Massachusetts. After protracted discussions, city officials finally instructed that a granite memorial be placed to mark the grave of Peter Salem, a onetime slave who had gained his freedom and earned a century-delayed respect for his military service at Concord, Bunker Hill, and subsequent battles of the Revolutionary War.[104] The act spoke directly to Brown's sense of honor and justice. It was as though, in commemorating this one veteran, the town was correcting the erasure of all the Peter

Salems, Crispus Attuckses, Jordan Freemans, and Lambo (Lambert) Lathams whom he and William Nell, as civic activists and historians, had worked to restore to the nation's historical record. Sometimes the issue came down to the correct transcription of the personal name, as Latham's descendant bitterly noted in commenting on the distortion of his great-uncle's given name as Sambo on the Groton Monument.[105]

Movement typically signified progress to Brown. One of the best symbols of the progress he had in mind was the last illustration incorporated in *My Southern Home*, which he deliberately positioned very near its conclusion. The emblem was one he (or a printer acting on his instruction) selected from the wide array of ornaments a nineteenth-century shop had on hand for use in illustrating printed works. Many well-stocked US printing shops of the day would have contained a standard ornament of two white hands clasped firmly in a grip, sometimes with the national eagle flying imperiously above. By contrast, Brown employed a variant ornament much less commonly used because much less normatively accepted: the figure of a firm black–white handshake. The Boston Type Foundry, which had stereotyped *The Black Man*, had one in its inventory and supplied copies to the trade before the Civil War.[106] Given the state of national affairs in 1880, as "redemption" brought the Old South back to life with a renewed grip on national power, Brown's incorporation of that ornament in his closing thought was nothing but a leap of faith. It signified the unwavering faith, however, of a man, part-black and part-white, who had dedicated his life to uniting those warring elements in himself and in his fellow Americans.

Throughout his life, Brown presented the figure of a man in motion. Even during his last two years, as he approached his eighth decade, he continued to perform the activities he had pursued for decades: public speaking, organizational activism, medical care, and writing. His mind remained razor sharp, his zest for public service continued strong, and he showed few signs of slowing down—at least not until the spring or summer of 1884, when the effects of bladder cancer began to drain his energy. In February, he had lost one of his dearest friends and role models when Wendell Phillips passed away. He had dedicated *The Negro in the American Rebellion* to Phillips, the only white man so honored other than Wells Brown; and he regarded himself, as he said publicly at the Faneuil Hall commemoration, as more intimately acquainted with Phillips than was any other black man.[107] He even noted proudly that he was in possession of fifteen letters from his admired friend.[108]

The deep emotion he displayed at Phillips's memorial service reflected the sense of loss that came with the end of an era. Brown was dealing with it in his own way. There is slight but persuasive evidence—James Monroe Trotter, a family intimate, referred to it as just completed at the time of Brown's death—that he had written a summary account (now lost) of the antislavery movement called *History of the Anti-Slavery Workers*.[109] As early as 1855, Brown had called for a history of the movement and floated the name of Edmund Quincy as the man to write it, but in the more retrospective years of his life, he came to see this as yet another literary challenge he needed to meet himself. The title, if indicative, suggests he had in mind a book that followed the logic of *The Black Man* by sketching a host of exemplary figures rather than a narrative history, although he would surely have included both black and white figures. The impulse to write such a work matched that of one of his most frequent antislavery lecture partners, Parker Pillsbury, who in 1883 published his own retrospective account, *Acts of the Anti-Slavery Apostles*—an exercise, as its title indicates, in hagiography. Pillsbury, however, seriously slighted African American agency, including Brown's, a common feature of white antislavery historiography for many decades to come. By the early 1880s, Brown knew all too well that if anyone would do justice to the movement as he had known and lived it, it would have to be a black man—and, to follow the logic he repeatedly invoked, who better than he?

He was generally active through the first months of 1884, but his health declined noticeably by autumn. On October 22, he attended the splashy seventy-fifth birthday party of Francis William Bird at the posh Revere House in Boston. Brown had a longstanding respect for Bird, a radical antislavery congressman close to Garrison. When he planned a lecture stop during his spring 1849 tour with the Crafts in Bird's hometown of Walpole, he counted on Bird's involvement in "getting up" arrangements, and in subsequent years he frequently consulted with Bird on issues ranging from temperance to civil rights.[110]

That afternoon at the Revere House, he met, perhaps for the last time, not just Bird but many other people with whom he had stood side by side over the years: Lewis Hayden, who seemed even more than Brown to go from funeral to funeral those days; Charles W. Slack, the self-made editor/publisher of the progressive *Commonwealth*; Thomas Drew, a well-known dentist who had been just a boy when his family hosted Brown during an antislavery lecture tour in southeastern Massachusetts in 1849. Brown apparently was too weak to address the group but not to join in its concluding act of singing their generation's favorite antislavery anthem, "John Brown's Body."[111]

During the next two weeks, the nation was caught up in the final stage of the bitterly contested presidential race between the Democrat Grover Cleveland and the Republican James Blaine. A Democrat had not held the White House since before the Civil War, but the old antislavery coalition that had long served as a bastion of the Republican Party was in steep decline. Boston's new African American newspaper, the *Boston Advocate*, would deliver a belated obituary in 1885 in concluding, "The grand old Republican party of Garrison, Lincoln, Phillips, Sumner, Garnet, Morris, Wm. Wells Brown, Greeley, and the illustrious Grant, is no more."[112] Its editor considered his community's newfound independence from automatic support for the party of Lincoln a welcome development.[113] Cleveland and Blaine were two more presidential candidates for whom Brown would have had little enthusiasm, but his mind was elsewhere. He might not even have been conscious as fellow citizens went to the polls on Tuesday, November 5. At last light, about 4:30 p.m. on November 6, 1884, he died at his and Annie's home in Chelsea, age approximately seventy.

The nation at the time was caught up for days with the counting of electoral votes in a contest too close to call. During that period, ceremonies took place around Boston to mark the passing of one of the most respected members of its black community. The Brown family held a private service at the house on Sunday morning and from there proceeded to the public service at the Zion AME Church on North Russell Street in Boston. The church was filled with many of the leading black and white activists and civic leaders of Boston, as well as family and friends. The casket, covered with floral wreaths donated by the Grand Lodge of the Good Templars, was brought in and placed near the chancel as the noon service began.

The speakers spanned his last forty years and the races, as Brown would have wished. Several of Boston's leading black ministers delivered sermons or remarks on behalf of the community; other speakers came from the ranks of his fellow activists. Samuel May Jr., the longtime general agent of the MASS, spoke personally from their long acquaintance and praised Brown's nonstop devotion to spreading temperance through the South. James Yeames, an English transplant to Boston who had worked closely with Brown during his 1877 tour, reminisced about Brown's popularity in the British Isles and noted that word of his death would come as a shock to homes across England, Ireland, and Scotland. Charles W. Slack, who himself had only months to live, surveyed Brown's wide-ranging achievements and gave personal reminiscences of a man for whom he had the highest respect. Lewis Hayden, who among all the speakers understood best the amazing trajectory of Brown's life, reminisced about a dear friend who had led a parallel life to his own.[114]

Following the service, the family took the body for burial in the family plot at Cambridge Cemetery, a thirty-five-acre field across the road from sprawling Mount Auburn Cemetery, one of the nation's first garden burial grounds. Although plots were still readily available and hardly unaffordable at $75 to $150, the family buried him in the same plot as Annie's mother, Harriet, who had died in 1875.[115] Cambridge Cemetery was decidedly the lesser of the city's burial grounds; Mount Auburn contained the remains of Charles Sumner, scientist Louis Agassiz, sculptor Horatio Greenough, and poets Henry Wadsworth Longfellow and James Russell Lowell. But even modest Cambridge Cemetery would soon become the resting place of a handful of America's distinguished writers—Brown first, followed by William James (1910), Thomas Wentworth Higginson (1911), and Henry James (1916).

News of Brown's death spread quickly across the English-speaking world. Obituaries appeared in most of the Boston newspapers and were quickly picked up by newspapers across the country, almost all careful to credential him as a physician. A Buffalo newspaper remembered him as "one of the leading colored citizens of the United States and at one time a Buffalonian" who in the day had organized a vigilance committee to aid runaway slaves.[116] A St. Louis newspaper reprinted the long obituary from the *Boston Herald*, to which it added the title, "An Emancipator's Death," but without addressing his life as a slave in St. Louis. Major white newspapers all across the country picked up the story—most, like the *New York Times*, as reprints from Boston dailies. All the major black newspapers in the country ran obituaries, and some paid tribute (whereas few white newspapers did) to his literary accomplishment. A few major black papers, like the *Christian Recorder*, recognized him as the most prolific black writer of his era and acknowledged his impact on their readership.

Obituaries likewise appeared in newspapers across the British Isles, from London (the *Times*) to points all around the periphery—Liverpool, Bristol, Exeter, Leeds (where Clara had died), Huddersfield (birthplace of his son-in-law George Sylvester), Edinburgh, Aberdeen, and many other cities. The English Good Templars made a point of commemorating him at their annual convention in Stockholm in July 1885.[117] Most of his old friends overseas received the news speedily enough, but, curiously, not Ellen Richardson, who wrote Douglass in late 1885 that she had only recently been notified.[118]

Old friends left revealing personal remarks about a man whose habitual modesty and guarded reticence generally shielded his inner person from public view. Feminist leader Lucy Stone fondly remembered her cool-headed lecture partner from the riot at Harwich as "one of the most genial of men . . . [who] in the most trying circumstances always kept serene." She judged his reaction to that day's assault as his characteristic response to life's indignities: "But he came up smiling, though hurt and bruised. It was always the way with him."[119] Charles W. Slack, who knew his conversation well enough to quote it, honored him by citing his own mantra: "Mr. Brown wrote, he was in the habit of saying, 'to give a faithful account of his people and their customs without concealing their faults.'"[120] Parker Pillsbury left no known personal tribute to a man he had esteemed, but his nephew Albert E. Pillsbury did. The younger Pillsbury—at the time a Massachusetts legislator and later the state's attorney general and the drafter of the original constitution and bylaws of the National Association for the Advancement of Colored People—claimed Brown was one of the first three blacks (along with Douglass and Remond) he ever met in his New Hampshire childhood and fondly remembered him for "the twinkle of his eye, which always signaled the utterance of a particularly good thing."[121] Benjamin T. Tanner, the distinguished editor of the *Christian Recorder,* who had followed his literary career closely and critically, commented, "Probably no other colored man has left so many books bearing his name as has Dr. Brown. His services in behalf of this race have been of the highest order."[122]

James Monroe Trotter emphasized at a commemorative meeting in January 1885 that Brown had led a consistently self-sacrificing life, even passing up the offer of a college position.[123] But what, materially speaking, did a life of high-level service, countless lectures, many books, and an active medical practice (carried on, according to Slack, with "fair success") amount to?[124] The sum total was apparently not appreciable. Jessie Forsyth, an energetic temperance worker and editor who worked closely with him and Annie in Boston and knew them very well, noted his scant financial reward: "This determination to stand by his own people often stood in the way of his personal interest, and it is to the credit of this noble and large-hearted man that, after having devoted his life to the cause of humanity he died poor."[125]

Commemorative assessments of this sort offer only soft evidence, but their common conclusion accords with the documentary record. Brown's death left Annie in a precarious financial situation. Whatever estate he bequeathed was not large enough to require probate. It included no real estate and probably no other major appreciable assets. He had never owned a house before meeting Annie, nor did he and Annie own one during their twenty-four-year marriage, except the inherited property she quickly sold. His death left her in 1884 with only the rented house in Chelsea where she apparently planned to remain. But her plans changed as a result of the death in January 1885 of her younger sister Henrietta A. Calvin, who left behind her husband Thomas and their toddler Viola. Perhaps when Annie went "abroad" to the countryside on her customary summer vacation in 1885, she took along her little niece.[126] Certainly not later than 1886, Annie moved in with her brother-in-law in Boston, assisting with housework, attending to Viola, and moving with them each time they changed residence. For some time, she also remained active in the temperance movement, filling high positions in local lodges and carrying on the legacy she had created with her husband. She was present and elected an officer, for instance, at an 1886 session of the Joseph Malins Lodge of the International Order of Good Templars at 465 Washington Street, a building she would live to see named in honor of her husband.[127]

She probably also kept up her husband's literary legacy the best she could. She continued to sell copies of his last three books by mail order, but probably with only limited success and for a limited time. She undoubtedly lacked his knowhow and connections, which may explain why she was unable to usher the manuscript of *History of the Anti-Slavery Workers* into print. She had, however, an additional limitation, which in time would have made it impossible for her to attend to any business affairs: deteriorating eyesight that finally left her nearly or entirely blind. It was indirectly the cause of her awful death. About 1:00 p.m. on September 4, 1902, she was adjusting the stove in the family home in Roxbury when her apron caught fire. She had the presence of mind to throw it off, but she did not realize her other garments were also in flames. Her shrieks alerted her niece Viola, who rushed downstairs but too late to save Annie from an agonizing death. Her burns were so extensive, one newspaper reported, she was unrecognizable.[128]

At the time of her death, Annie had considerable standing in the community for her temperance and charity work. The major newspaper of Cambridge knew her well enough to identify her both in her own right and as Brown's widow, but a major Boston paper reporting the accident identified her only by name and race.[129] Her funeral, like Brown's, took place at the Zion AME Church on North Russell Street, with handsome floral arrangements contributed by friends. Afterward, she was interred in Cambridge Cemetery in a shared grave with William Wells Brown Jr. and her sister Henrietta. Her brother-in-law presumably paid for a headstone, although the current marker for the two sisters (only) is of more recent date.[130]

The most tangible legacy Brown left Annie would have been his library—what must have been an extraordinarily rich and extensive collection of books, journals, manuscripts, clippings, scrapbooks, albums, notes, business records, photographs, engravings, and letters. Measured against the length and breadth of his literary oeuvre, reading, and career, it was undoubtedly one of the choicest African American collections of its time. Annie, his longtime literary partner who supposedly named their daughter after one of his literary progeny, would undoubtedly have kept close watch over it as long as she lived. But with no children to survive her and no local institution likely to show interest in preserving the collection of a black man, its existence was presumably bound to hers.[131]

What happened to it? Did it go up in flames alongside Annie that terrible day in 1902? Newspaper accounts of the tragedy report that a fire company was called to the house but mention no serious structural damage. If so, the archive—such as it was—might have survived the blaze. Even if it did, its fate for the last century has been as elusive as has proper recognition for its creator.

Epilogue—Afterlife

In May 1955, William Wells Brown was featured on the front cover of the official journal of the National Medical Association, the black "sister organization" of the American Medical Association. Staff artist Naida Willette Page did the drawing, rendering Brown realistically after the frontispiece of *Narrative of William W. Brown*. In an issue containing articles ranging from clinical topics such as the development of the Salk polio vaccine to the social fallout following *Brown v. Board of Education*, the editor devoted the medical-history section to a well-informed assessment of "William Wells Brown, M.D.," paying homage to a man already three generations eclipsed in standard histories of American literature. Surveying Brown's accomplishments as a writer, activist, and physician, he found Brown deserving of historical respect: "He was a man of great courage ability and resourcefulness, and the vicissitudes of his career make as fascinating a story as one may find in American biography."[1]

So, by a similar measure, does the story of his literary reputation. The editor remembered Brown as "America's first Negro man of letters," and any observant student of the standard bibliography of American literature, a long-term project begun shortly after the Civil War, could have seen that the entry for Brown and his books ran to more than a page.[2] What little surviving public regard there was for Brown after his death, however, remained for many decades the legacy primarily of the African American community, which clung to the names and accomplishments of its distinguished ancestors throughout the era of official racial segregation.

In 1900, however, there came a potential breakthrough moment for the collective memorialization of nineteenth-century African American life. The occasion was the Paris Exposition, the centennial World's Fair at which dozens of mostly Western nations prepared to present their best features to the world. So did the African American community—led by thirty-two-year old W. E. B. Du Bois, special agent Thomas Calloway, and a team of black educators and leaders who collected an unprecedented array of African American artifacts with the intent to showcase their people's accomplishments. Though housed on the rue des Nations outside the US national pavilion, the Exhibit of American Negroes, Du Bois proudly declared, would offer the public "an honest straightforward exhibit of a small nation of people, picturing their life and development without apology or gloss, and above all made by themselves. In a way this marks an era in the history of the Negroes of America."[3]

One of his key collaborators was Daniel Murray, a black assistant librarian at the Library of Congress, who undertook to compile a comprehensive bibliography of published works by African Americans and managed to assemble two hundred books and many more pamphlets for the exhibit. Like Du Bois, Murray envisioned things on a grand scale: He undertook his share of the project with not one but two national capitals in mind, predicting that after the exposition closed in Paris, the collection of books would be placed "on exhibition and for consultation for all time" in the new Jefferson Building of the Library of Congress.[4] That aspiration, however, went unrealized; the books returned to Washington but to no public display. Many wound up in the collections of Howard University.

Murray's preliminary list included five of Brown's works. Although Murray excluded such major titles as *Narrative of William W. Brown*, *Clotel*, *The Escape*, and *My Southern Home*, Brown was one of the best-represented writers on the list. By the time of the exposition, however, his life's work was already part of the growing erasure of African American print culture. All of his books were out of print, not to return until the years of the civil rights movement. Although copies of all of them survived in the collections of numerous libraries, historical societies, and private collectors, what use they got was presumably marginal and what memory of Brown remained was individual and tangential.

His memory survived, nevertheless, in the minds of numerous African American educators, professional people, writers, journalists, broadcasters, and community leaders. Just as Brown had mastered the art of retooling his books for changing times, so his works continued to speak meaningfully to successive generations. More to the point, they helped people, often communicating through the black press and early electronic media, to respond to the challenging social history of their times. They surfaced, for instance, repeatedly in attempts to systematize and transmit a body of African American knowledge. In 1899, when a teacher at a new black normal school in Washington, DC, asked for recommendations for black history texts "that would stimulate our students to greater endeavor," the editor of the black newspaper to which she appealed recommended *The Black Man*, among a dozen inspiring titles.[5] In newspaper quizzes that circulated in the black press over the years, Brown's name would frequently be the answer to questions of general black knowledge: Who wrote the first black play? The first history of African Americans? *Clotel*?[6] On the eve of World War II, as tank units conducted military exercises in Boston Common, a journalist put present-day mobilization into perspective by recalling the early history of black combat service as recorded in *The Negro in the American Rebellion*.[7]

Clotel had a particularly interesting history throughout this transitional period. Though little known in the United States during Brown's life, it became the best known of his works in the decades after his death. In 1963, it even served as the basis for a stage adaptation called *Clotield*, by Pearl M. Graham, that provoked strong reaction in the black press when produced in Long Beach, California.[8] The primary draw of the play, as of the novel in the African American community at the time, was its tantalizing exposé of Thomas Jefferson and the ensuing mixed-race family history. Memory, however, often proved tricky. Although to one columnist *Clotelle* was "the most thrilling romance ever written," most black critics preferred what was often called the "unexpurgated" *Clotel*, the earliest version of the novel, some mistaking Brown's subsequent excisions and removal of Jefferson as signs *Clotelle* had been censored.[9]

Cursory attempts to revive his reputation began by midcentury. In 1944, a journalist dedicated his column for Negro History Week to three major black writers he considered generally neglected: Brown, Douglass, and Charles Chestnutt. Brown, he believed, was "practically unknown to most Negroes," but his many accomplishments deserved a better hearing: "Brown is not a great writer, but since he is a pioneer in so many fields, he deserves to be better known at least among his own people. And bear in mind—Brown is always interesting."[10] In 1948, a bright graduate student at Hampton Institute, supported by a network of black faculty advisers and sufficient library collections, wrote an informative master's thesis on Brown.[11] In 1952, the trailblazing disc jockey and radio host Bass Harris dedicated an hour-long show on Los Angeles's KMPC to the cultural accomplishments made decades earlier by Brown, the actor Ira Aldridge, and the vaudevillian Bert Williams.[12] Early anthologies of African American writing rarely went to press without excerpts from Brown's writings, but with little appreciation for his artistry.

Then, at a crucial historical turning point in both African American cultural development and US race relations, along came William Edward Farrison, founding head of the English Department at the historically black North Carolina College at Durham (today North Carolina Central University, part of the University of North Carolina system). Farrison devoted nearly three decades to researching and composing his pioneering biography of Brown, which he finally published, in 1969, in the series of "Negro American Biographies and Autobiographies," edited by John Hope Franklin, his onetime colleague at NCC. Farrison's landmark work, which spanned the years from Jim Crow to civil rights, was itself a participant in the drama of race history it chronicled. A victim of the times, Farrison probably could not get access in person to some of the genealogical collections in Southern institutions for researching the histories of the Young and Higgins families, so he resorted to correspondence with library archivists.[13] That same year, he revived not only Brown's life but also his work, with the first reprinting of *Clotel* in more than a century.

Not even Farrison, however, was wholly impressed with the aesthetic qualities of Brown's work, nor was his fellow generation, or the next, of African American critics and scholars. Regard for Brown's writings was generally dutiful, rarely enthusiastic. Blyden Jackson expressed a general view in 1989 when, in his then-authoritative history of African American literature, he asserted that *Clotel* inaugurated a black novelistic tradition but "cannot pretend to be great fiction, novelistic or otherwise. Everyone agrees on that."[14] The discomfort caused by even Brown's greatest work was symptomatic of the more general complaint about his entire oeuvre, which the African American poet-critic Robert F. Reid-Pharr has diagnosed precisely: "The reality that Brown never establishes the authorial control that is so very apparent in the novels of twentieth-century (Black) America, continues as almost an embarrassment within some quarters of Black American and American literary and cultural criticism. The *first* Black American novelist must be, so the positivistic logic of literary development would have it, the *worst* Black American novelist."[15]

Brown was in no position to exercise the same kind of magisterial command of the past, say, that Toni Morrison has brought to such late-twentieth-century masterpieces as *Song of Solomon* and *Beloved*. Whereas Morrison has engaged in overarching acts of imaginative reclamation, retrieving a past whose forward progress was already known, Brown lived and wrote on the other end of the historical spectrum. Entangled in cataclysmic change, unguided by literary scholarship and tradition, and mistrustful of white contemporaneous models, Brown improvised a piecemeal, conditional literary treatment of a historical experience that was still entirely in process.

Two centuries after his birth, Brown the writer is gradually coming into clearer focus. One may characterize him as he characterized a contemporary he considered an ideal colleague in the antislavery movement:

"Were we sent out to find a man who should excel all others in collecting together new facts and anecdotes, and varnishing up old ones so that they would appear new, and bringing them into a meeting and emptying out, good or bad, the whole contents of his sack, to the delight and admiration of the audience, we would unhesitatingly select James N. Buffum as the man."[16] Alternately writer, actor, and mixed-media artist, Brown is the performer pouring out his sack's contents before the eyes of twenty-first-century audiences. Perhaps it has taken a generation of postmodern readers, accustomed to the fluidity of texts in the computer age and the practice of sampling, to appreciate the improvisatory performance art, mastered in earlier times and under different circumstances, that Brown has been offering.

More congruent to Brown's writing than Morrison's has been that of 2012 US Poet Laureate Natasha Trethewey, whose poetry weaves complex patterns of meaning out of fragments of memory, family, history, and regionalism in ways that recall Brown's blended life's work. In "Miscegenation," she recounts how her parents (white father, black mother) violated Mississippi law in 1965 by traveling to Cincinnati to marry before returning home to Mississippi. A year later, en route to Canada, they "followed a route the same/ as slaves, the train, slicing the white glaze of winter, leaving Mississippi."[17] A wayfarer in a now-well-grounded African American literary tradition, Trethewey seeks to bring reconciliation, if not closure, to her tangled family history.

A century and a half earlier, Brown ran the route of the Underground Railroad, leaving Missouri, heading north. Traveling nonstop over the years, he devoted his life to a pioneering quest, like Trethewey's today, the goal of which was always more or less clear: to make a home in the world. His writing is its final address.

ACKNOWLEDGMENTS

William Wells Brown once complained that the state of African American literary culture was so forbidding that prospective biographers should beware: "Let anyone attempt to write biographies of our 'great men,' and he will at once see how soon he will run ashore for material. Any fool can find fault with a book, but a dozen cannot write one."

I've occasionally wondered whether attempting to write a comprehensive biography of a man lacking a central archive was a fool's errand. But the aid of colleagues, friends, and family has helped turn an improbability into a practicality. Acknowledging their support gives me great pleasure.

For institutional support, I owe repeated thanks to my home institution, Southern Methodist University; and to my home unit, the English Department; as well as gratitude to my esteemed colleague Steve Weisenburger for his constant intellectual support and friendship. My progress was greatly facilitated by a trio of superb research and technical assistants at SMU, beginning with Elizabeth Tshele (who by project's end blossomed into NoViolet Bulawayo) and concluding with Christopher Stampone and Sarah Sage. I would also like to thank Yochi Gordon for her aid in photocopying the final text.

The American Antiquarian Society supported me for a year as a Mellon Senior Fellow, providing me time and resources for conducting core research. This book joins the shelves alongside hundreds of others made possible by the AAS's nonpareil collections and staff. I feel gratitude to this model institution of letters and wish to thank in particular Paul Erickson, Vince Golden, Elizabeth Pope, Gigi Barnhill, Thomas Knoles, David Whitesell (now at the University of Virginia), Ashley Cataldo, Jackie Penny, and most especially Lauren Hewes, whose expertise in visual culture, warmly shared, improved my understanding of WWB's multimedia art. I also had the advantage of productive conversations with a continuous infusion of fellows and researchers. I owe particular thanks to Amy Hughes for sharing her work on printing ornaments, and Michael Winship for alerting me to the WWB-related correspondence in the Lee and Shepard Papers.

At a later stage, the National Humanities Center supported me as a John Hope Franklin Fellow, and that period, extended by a fellowship from the National Endowment for the Humanities, allowed me opportunity to do much of the writing. I owe thanks to the hospitality and congeniality of the entire staff of NHC, as well as to the many fellows who answered questions and gave advice. I wish to acknowledge in particular the aid and camaraderie of librarians Eliza Robertson, Brooke Andrade, and Jean Houston, as well as of project specialist Marianne Wason.

The first home of the project was Missouri, where I had the good fortune my first day on site to meet Gary Kremer, executive director of the State Historical Society of Missouri, who steered me to Mike Everman, prince of Missouri state archives. Mike guided me through the invaluable St. Louis court records and put me in touch with well-placed archivists whose collections and advice proved vital to my work: Dennis Northcott, Lynn Morrow, Bill Glanker, Dusty Reese, and Cathie Schoppenhorst. On my last day in Missouri, with Cathie leading the way by early survey maps, Mike, his wife Diane, my wife Riki, and I walked the grounds of the old John Young estate in Marthasville in an attempt to reattach WWB's boyhood life to its local roots. Mike also introduced me to three scholars expert in Missouri history whose knowledge proved essential to my work: Lea VanderVelde, Julie Winch, and Adam Arenson. I owe special thanks to Lea for hosting Riki and me in Iowa City and spending invaluable hours discussing Missouri freedom suits and speculatively reconstructing the early history of WWB's life in slavery.

I also owe thanks to librarians and archivists across the country who guided me through their collections—in particular, Ann Sindelar at the Western Reserve Historical Society; Patricia Van Skaik at the Public Library of Cincinnati and Hamilton County; Cynthia Van Ness at the Buffalo and Erie County Historical Society; James Holmberg at the Filson Historical Society; Paul Cyr at the New Bedford Free Public Library; Nancy Finlay at the Connecticut Historical Society; Judy Phillips at the Franklin County Archives, and Virginia Ellington in the Local History Room of the Franklin County Public Library, both in Winchester, Tennessee; Thomas Hutchens at the Heritage Room of Huntsville Public Library in Alabama; John Allison at the Morgan County Archives in Decatur, Alabama; and Mimi Miller at the Historic Natchez Foundation. I also had the good fortune to be put in touch with a collegial group of New York State researchers who guided me to local sources and shared files and information: Karl Kabelac, Charles Lenhart, Christopher Densmore, Judith Wellman, and Nancy Hewitt.

I received expert help at many institutions across the British Isles and Ireland. I would particularly like to thank Dawn Dyer at Bristol Central Library, Donald Simpson at Newcastle City Library, Stephanie Clarke at the Central Archive of the British Museum, Phaedra Casey at Brunel University Archives, Susan Snell at the Library and Museum of Freemasonry, and Lucy McCann at Rhodes House Library. In addition, I would like to thank John Charlton and Sean Creighton for sharing their expertise in British antislavery activity.

The book's final home was Boston–Cambridge, where I received expert guidance at many institutions, including from Sean Casey, Kimberly Reynolds, and Henry Scannell at the Boston Public Library; Alyssa Pacy at the Cambridge Room of the Cambridge Public Library; Charlie Sullivan and Kit Rawlins at the Cambridge Historical Commission;

James Shea at the Longfellow National Historic Site; and Marie Daly at the New England Historic Genealogical Society.

I have benefited from the support of great scholars who have performed extraordinary service in making WWB available to the twenty-first century. I owe special thanks to John Ernest, whose scholarship illuminated the way; and to Robert Levine, whose work on WWB and his peers is exemplary and who answered my many questions with unfailing professionalism. Geoffrey Sanborn and Dawn Coleman opened their substantial files on WWB's sources, and Radiclani Clytus shared his extensive knowledge of WWB's use of visual media. I also owe an incalculable debt to Reginald Pitts, literary detective par excellence and my frequent collaborator, who led the way down paths and opened doors on Betsey, Clarissa, and Josephine Brown I could not have accessed on my own. The book is significantly the better for Reg's leads; inaccuracies are mine.

I also owe thanks to dozens of people, too many to individualize, who have responded to my countless inquiries. To name just a few, I wish to express my gratitude to William Ambrose, Christopher Bishof, Richard Blackett, Marty Blatt, Randall Burkett, Scott Casper, Lara Cohen, Matt Cohen, Don Doyle, David Fahey, Suzanne Flandreau, Ed Folsom, Eric Gardner, Ted Genoways, James Green, Richard Harrison, April Haynes, Jim and Lois Horton, Martha Jones, Chris Kent, James Klotter, Cheryl Knott, Leon Jackson, Phillip Lapsansky, Jess Lepler, Barbara McCaskill, Meredith McGill, Joycelyn Moody, Claire Parfait, Alasdair Pettinger, Jeremy Popkin, Arnold Rampersad, Jerry Rose, Ellen Ross, Adriaan van der Weel, Al von Frank, Heather Williams, and Kristin Zapalac for answering questions and suggesting connections.

Cheryl Hurley and Henry Louis Gates Jr. put me in touch with the distinguished collector/dealer Wyatt Houston Day. I wish to express my gratitude to Wyatt for opening his house and collections to me and giving me permission to publish a sheet of his WWB draft manuscript.

Friends and relatives hosted me on long road trips: Cindy and Larry Goldman (no reservation required), Steve Cohen and Linda Nathan (keepers of The Barn), Andy Shulman and Robin Wish (multiple trips), and Libby Keller and David Savitz. Along the way, I also made new friends, among whom I wish to single out Lois and T. J. Anderson. Bonding with them has been one of the most memorable rewards of this project.

I had the good fortune of finding in Susan Schulman a determined agent who believed in this project from the beginning, and in Alane Salierno Mason a marvel of an editor—savvy about its strengths and deficiencies, sure-handed in shaping its narration, and unvaryingly genial and generous in her guidance. WWB has emerged a tauter, more sharply defined figure for her deft handling. Copyeditor Kathleen Brandes caught many factual and grammatical inaccuracies and streamlined the prose.

At project's end, I can see that this undertaking has been all along a family affair. It gives me special pleasure to acknowledge and thank my children—Yoni, Noam, and Tamar—for hosting me, taking on research assignments, providing technical assistance, and sharing in the spirit of this book. My ultimate thanks and gratitude belong to Riki, who knows—as I know—how fully and wholeheartedly this book is *our* book.

NOTES

Introduction

1. *The Souls of Black Folk* (Chicago: A.C. McClurg and Company, 1903), p.1.

2. Julia Griffiths, ed. "Visit of a Fugitive Slave to the Grave of Wilberforce," *Autographs for Freedom*, 2nd series (Auburn, NY: Alden, Beardsley and Co., 1854), p. 71.

3. "Welcome to William Wells Brown," *National Anti-Slavery Standard* 15 (Oct. 28, 1854): 2–3.

4. James L. W. West III, *Making the Archives Talk: New and Selected Essays in Bibliography, Editing, and Book History* (University Park: Penn State University Press, 2012), p.1.

Chapter 1

1. Frederick Douglass, *Narrative of the Life of Frederick Douglass, an American Slave* (Boston: Anti-Slavery Office, 1845); William Wells Brown, *Narrative of William W. Brown, A Fugitive Slave* (Boston: Anti-Slavery Society, 1847); Henry Bibb, *Narrative of the Life and Adventures of Henry Bibb, An American Slave* (New York: By the Author, 1849); Booker T. Washington, *Up from Slavery* (Garden City, NY: Doubleday and Company, 1901).

2. Deed books in the local county courthouses indicate that the master of William Wells Brown (hereafter, WWB) owned no land in Fayette County but had

extensive holdings in Montgomery County. His master's father and some of his master's brothers, by contrast, were well established in Lexington and surrounding Fayette County.

3. "Memoir of the Author," *The Black Man, His Antecedents, His Genius, and His Achievements* (New York: Thomas Hamilton; Boston: R. F. Wallcut, 1863), p. 11.

4. Clark journal entry of May 25, 1804, cited in Lowell M. Schake, *La Charrette* (Lincoln, NE: iUniverse Star, 2003), p. 117.

5. He purchased land in Winchester as early as September 1815. Deed between George William Higgins and Thomas Shelton Carpenter, Jan. 13, 1819, Book F, pp. 146–47, Franklin County Court House, Winchester, TN.

6. Higgins Family File, Local History Room, Franklin County Public Library, Winchester, TN; Ann B. Chambers, "Dead Towns in Jackson County, Alabama," *Jackson County Chronicles* (Oct. 11, 1979), in Wendell Page, comp., *Jackson County Archives*, vol. 1 (Scottsboro, AL: Jackson County Historical Association, July 1991), p. 8.

7. William H. Jenkins and John Knox, *The Story of Decatur, Alabama* (Decatur: Decatur Printing Co., 1970), p. 85. On his financial affairs, see Estate File of G. W. Higgins, #1303, Morgan County Probate Loose Files, Morgan County Archives, Decatur, AL.

8. "W.W. Brown in Ohio," *National Anti-Slavery Standard* 15 (April 7, 1855): 2.

9. *Life and Times of Frederick Douglass* (Hartford, CT: Park Publishing Company, 1881), p. 13.

10. *Massachusetts, Town Vital Collections, 1620–1988*, Marriage Record for WWB and Anna E. Gray, April 12, 1860, Boston, Registration entry 574.

11. Family Record of Richard M. and Matilda Young of Quincy, IL: Young Family File, Filson Historical Society, Louisville, KY.

12. Young died in Spotsylvania County on February 26, 1778: Will Book E, pp. 33–34, Virginia County Records, Library of Virginia, Richmond.

13. Leonard Young published accounts of all these events in the *Kentucky Gazette* in the following issues: Sept. 27, 1794; Aug. 26, 1797; and Jan. 5, 1813. Matilda was raised in Virginia, according to the runaway notice. So, in all likelihood, were most or all of the Young slaves.

14. Benjamin Young advertised for two male runaways in the *Missouri Gazette* (July 21, 1819). Aaron and John Young were both named in the 1833 freedom suit of James Wilkinson: Case 102, Circuit Court Case Files, Office of the Circuit Clerk, City of St. Louis, Missouri, Missouri State Archives–St. Louis.

15. Young Family File, Filson Historical Society, Louisville, KY.

16. He first appears on the tax rolls for Shelby County in 1804, but a letter from his father seeking advice about the possibility of a medical career for him in Lou-

isville places him in Shelby County a year earlier: Leonard Young to Jonathan Clark, April 3, 1803, Clark-Hite Papers, Filson Historical Society, Louisville.

17. *Kentucky Marriages: 1801–1825* (Bountiful, UT: Heritage Quest, 1999), p. 754.

18. *Kentucky Gazette* (April 3, 1810).

19. Two indenture bonds are dated March 4, 1811 (Deed Book 5, pp. 437–39); the third is dated Aug. 1, 1814 (Deed Book 6, p. 532): Montgomery County Recorder's Office, Mt. Sterling, KY.

20. Young became the manager of the Missouri Auxiliary Bible Society at some point after his move to Missouri: *Missouri Republican* (Oct. 24, 1825): 1.

21. The tax rolls of both Shelby and Montgomery County consistently list him as owning a carriage and horses: Kentucky Historical Society, Frankfort, KY.

22. On his apothecary shop, *Kentucky Gazette* (May 23, 1806). A hemp factory served as the corner marker of one of his town lots: Deed Book 7, pp. 276–78, Montgomery County Recorder's Office, Mt. Sterling, KY. The town history indicates he sold a hemp and bagging factory in 1815: Carl B. Boyd Jr. and Hazel Mason Boyd, *A History of Mt. Sterling, Kentucky, 1792–1918* ([Mt. Sterling, KY]: C.B. Boyd Jr., 1984), p. 202.

23. *Narrative of William W. Brown*, p. 13.

24. A family Bible was listed among the objects from her estate purchased by a neighbor: Sarah Young Probate File (1609), Probate Estate Files, St. Louis Probate Court.

25. The Young–Hitt family Bible is not in the public realm, but in 1956 a relative of the family copied its list of Young family members and slaves and sent it to the Kentucky Historical Society: Young Family File, Folder 5, Kentucky Historical Society, Frankfort, KY.

26. Will Book E, pp. 412–16, Fayette County Clerk's Office, Lexington, KY.

27. Sarah Scott Young was born into Virginia gentry. Her wealthy father (Major Francis Scott, of Charlotte County, VA) owned thirty-eight slaves, according to the 1810 federal census.

28. *Narrative of William W. Brown*, p. 13. Henry Bibb recited a nearly matching family background—white father, mixed-race mother, six siblings by multiple fathers: *Narrative of Henry Bibb*, p. 14.

29. Douglass, *Narrative of Frederick Douglass*, p. 1.

30. St. Louis Circuit Court Record Book 24, p. 150, April 25, 1854, Office of the Circuit Clerk, Missouri State Archives–St. Louis.

31. The document is dated December 21, 1828, and appears at the end of Young's probate file, John Young Probate File (1021), Probate Estate Files, St. Louis Probate Court.

32. William Edward Farrison, *William Wells Brown: Author and Reformer* (Chicago:

University of Chicago Press, 1969), pp. 3–5; Nell, *The Colored Patriots of the American Revolution* (Boston: Robert F. Wallcut, 1855), p. 223.

33. Will Book, 1765–1791, Part 2, p. 434, Charlotte County Courthouse, Charlotte Court House, VA.

34. Case 1809-001, Chancery Records, Library of Virginia, Richmond.

35. Speech of William Wells Brown," *National Anti-Slavery Standard* 21 (May 26, 1860): 4. WWB was mistaken; the Wickliffe and Higgins families were well acquainted but not related.

36. Much of this information comes from the family history given by their descendant, Mary Ford Higgins Rodes, in her certificate of application for membership in the Kentucky Historical Society: Higgins Family File, Folder 1, Kentucky Historical Society, Frankfort.

37. Deed of land sale, Jan. 8, 1808: Deed Book 4, pp. 341–42, Montgomery County Recorder's Office, Mt. Sterling, KY.

38. Typed transcripts survive in the Mt. Sterling Public Library, Kentucky Historical Society, Filson Historical Society, and John Fox, Jr. Genealogical Library (Paris, KY). The Filson's copy was deposited by May Stone, a descendant whose accompanying letter states she saw the circular letter at her great-uncle's house in Indiana. May Stone to Mrs. Thurston, May 19, 1935, Higgins Family Papers, Filson Historical Society.

39. Transcript of H[iram]. H. Higgins to William J. Higgins, Oct. 16, 1872. H. H. Higgins, born in Mt. Sterling in 1802, was a well-known architect in his adopted hometown of Athens, where he pursued various projects, such as Founders Hall at the local college, in the Greek Revival style. A general by war's end, he is the highest-ranking Confederate soldier in the local cemetery, a fact of continuing significance to some Confederate heritage organizations.

40. *Narrative of William W. Brown*, p. 75.

41. John Young Higgins (1830–1902) was the tenth of the family's twelve children: Higgins Family File, Local History Room, Franklin County Public Library, Winchester, TN.

42. C. Vann Woodward and Elisabeth Muhlenfeld, eds., *The Private Mary Chesnut: The Unpublished Civil War Diaries* (New York: Oxford University Press, 1984), p. 42.

43. *The Black Man*, pp. 86–88.

44. The Clarke brothers not only appeared entirely white but may actually have been. Mario Valdes, a producer for the PBS investigative program *Frontline*, in 2009 found a trail of deliberately buried evidence indicating that Milton had summoned a justice of the peace shortly before his death to record an affidavit

attesting to his actually having been white; Lewis and Milton Clarke File, Cambridge Historical Commission, Cambridge, MA.

45. On the Younger connection, see William S. Bryan and Robert Rose, *A History of the Pioneer Families of Missouri* (St. Louis: Bryan, Brand, and Co., 1876), pp. 235–36. Younger was listed on the same page as Young in the 1813 tax records for Montgomery County, KY, Kentucky Historical Society.

46. Deed Book D, pp. 219–20, St. Charles Recorder's Office, St. Charles, MO.

47. Ibid., pp. 555–56.

48. Ibid., p. 104.

49. Deed Book 8, pp. 74–76, Montgomery County Recorder's Office, Mt. Sterling, KY.

50. Power of Attorney signed April 12, 1817; Deed Book 8, p. 151, Montgomery County Recorder's Office, Mt. Sterling, KY.

51. *Memoir of William Wells Brown* (Boston: Anti-Slavery Office, 1859), p. 4.

52. *Missouri Gazette* (June 21, 1817). Hattie M. Anderson characterized the *Gazette* as taking "a leading and active part in advertising the marvels of Missouri Territory" to potential settlers: "Missouri, 1804–1828: Peopling a Frontier State," *Missouri Historical Review* 31 (Jan. 1937): 17.

53. James Neal Primm, *Lion of the Valley: St. Louis, Missouri* (Boulder, CO: Pruett Publishing Company, 1981), p. 107.

54. Harriet M. Anderson, "The Evolution of Frontier Society in Missouri, 1815–1828," *Missouri Historical Review* 32 (April 1938): 34.

55. Rufus Babcock, ed., *Memoir of John Mason Peck D.D.: Forty Years of Pioneer Life* (Philadelphia: American Baptist Publication Society, 1864), pp. 126–28, 34.

56. Indenture between John Young and Benjamin Sharp, March 12, 1818: Deed Book A, p. 457, Warren County Historical Society, Warrenton, MO.

57. His probate file refers to hundreds of volumes, naming several dozen by title. The phrase about his poems appears in his will: John Young Probate File.

58. *History of the Pioneer Families of Missouri*, p. 520.

59. *Missouri Gazette* (July 17, 1818).

60. "Memoir of the Author," *The Black Man*, pp. 11–12.

61. John Young Probate File.

62. Cumberland College in Princeton, Kentucky, the denominational home of Cumberland Presbyterians; tuition receipts are in Sarah Young's probate file.

63. "The Colored People of Canada," *Pine and Palm* 1 (Oct. 19, 1861): 2.

64. *Narrative of Frederick Douglass*, pp. 6–8.

65. *Narrative of William W. Brown*, pp. 15–16.

66. Josephine Brown, *Biography of an American Bondman, by His Daughter* (Boston: R. F. Wallcut, 1856), p. 7.

67. *Memoir of William W. Brown*, p. 8.

68. On the charges registered against Young's reputation, *Missouri Gazette* (Oct. 23, 1818): 3; on the countercharges orchestrated by Young, *Missouri Gazette* (Jan. 27, 1819): 3; on State of Missouri v. John Young, Dec. 1821, St. Charles Circuit Court Case Files–Criminal, St. Charles Historical Society; on Benjamin Young's runaways, *Missouri Gazette* (July 21, 1819).

69. "Emancipation Day in Boston," *Liberator* 33 (Jan. 16, 1863): 12.

70. *Narrative of William W. Brown*, p. 17.

71. *St. Louis Enquirer* (April 12, 1820).

72. *History of the Pioneer Families of Missouri*, pp. 502–3.

Chapter 2

1. Major Amos Stoddard quoted in Stan Hoig, *The Chouteaus: First Family of the Fur Trade* (Albuquerque: University of New Mexico Press, 2008), p. 8.

2. Primm, *Lion of the Valley*, p. 108.

3. Quoted in Primm, *Lion of the Valley*, p. 110.

4. James Essex diary, Caleb Green Collection, Missouri History Museum Archives, St. Louis, MO.

5. Dickens quoted in Adam Arenson, *The Great Heart of the Republic: St. Louis and the Cultural Civil War* (Cambridge: Harvard University Press, 2011), p. 15.

6. Hoig, *The Chouteaus*, pp. 27–28. The Chouteau mansion was torn down in 1841, making room, as one resident noted, "for more modern buildings better suited to the commercial extension of the place" (Arenson, *Great Heart of the Republic*, p. 16).

7. Young also bought land from O'Fallon: Jan. 10, 1832, Deed Book T/158, City Recorder's Office, St. Louis.

8. *Narrative of William W. Brown*, pp. 38–39.

9. Patricia Chadwell, *Missouri Land Claims* (New Orleans: Polyanthos, 1976), p. v.

10. The executor of her estate placed an advertisement for their sale in the *St. Louis New Era* on Oct. 1, 8, 15, and 22, 1846. A copy of the ad is in her probate file: Sarah Young Probate File.

11. Report of sale of slaves filed in probate court by estate executor Hiram Cordell on Dec. 12, 1846: Sarah Young Probate File.

12. "Letter from Wm. W. Brown," *National Anti-Slavery Standard* 7 (Nov. 12, 1846): 95.

13. James D. Birchfield, Albert Boime, and William J. Hennessey, *Thomas Sat-*

terwhite Noble, 1835–1907 (Lexington: University of Kentucky Art Museum, 1988), pp. 35–42.

14. Quoted in Primm, *Lion of the Valley*, p. 142.

15. "Note to the Present Edition," *Narrative of William W. Brown* (London: Charles Gilpin, 1849), p. iv.

16. "Memoir of William Wells Brown," *Three Years in Europe* (London: Charles Gilpin, 1852): pp. ix–x.

17. J. T. Sharf, *A History of St. Louis City and County* (Philadelphia: L.H. Everts and Co., 1883), p. 951.

18. John Young to Finis Ewing, Aug. 22 and Oct. 12, 1825: Finis Ewing Papers, Tennessee Historical Society, Nashville.

19. Diary entry for Sunday, Aug. 27, 1826: Collection Box 2-2, Stephen Hempstead Collection, Missouri History Museum Archives.

20. William Carr Lane to Mary Lane, Jan. 9, 1827: William Carr Lane Papers, Missouri History Museum Archives.

21. Sale by Joseph and Vienna White to John Young, Feb. 1827; recorded in resale of this plot by John and Sarah Young to Stephen Hempstead, June 23, 1828: Vol. O, pp. 253–54, City Recorder's Office, St. Louis.

22. Melville to Evert Duyckinck, March 3, 1849, in *The Letters of Herman Melville*, ed. Merrell R. Davis and William H. Gilman (New Haven, CT: Yale University Press, 1960), p. 79.

23. He attended, for instance, to passengers carried off a New Orleans steamer critically ill with smallpox: diary entry for June 8, 1826, Collection Box 2-2; Stephen Hempstead Collection, Missouri History Museum Archives.

24. The book is listed in the inventory of Sarah Young's estate: Sarah Young Probate File.

25. Dolly signed her statement with a cross, the typical practice of an illiterate: Dolly v. John Young, July Term, 1828, Case 7, Circuit Court Case Files, Office of the Circuit Court, Missouri State Archives–St. Louis.

26. On Dolly, see *The Black Man*, p.17.

27. "The Colored People of Canada," *Pine and Palm* 1 (Oct. 19, 1861): 2.

28. Her lawyers phrased their request for habeas corpus as follows: "Your petitioner has reason to believe and does believe, that because of her application for freedom, the said John Young will treat her with great severity and that he will remove her out of the jurisdiction of this Court before the trial of the said Court instituted to establish her right to freedom": Dolly v. John Young, Case 7.

29. Sarah Young's presence in St. Louis is confirmed by her purchase on April 26 of a tract of land in the common field of St. Louis. Her name alone appears as

purchaser, a sign that John Young was likely at the time still living in Galena: Deed Book O/467, City Recorder's Office, St. Louis. An outstanding bill for Sarah Young's medical treatment "after her return from Fever-Run" was filed by Doctor William Carr Lane and is present in John Young's probate file (1021).

30. Another witness for the plaintiff was Thomas Cohen, the well-placed friend of James Essex, who was summoned to appear before the court in its August 1829 term: Dolly v. John Young, Case 7.

31. Martha Ann v. Hiram Cordell, November Term, 1844, Case 9, Circuit Court Case Files, Office of the Circuit Court, Missouri State Archives–St. Louis.

32. *Narrative of William W. Brown*, p. 31.

33. Ibid., p. 73.

34. Ibid., pp. 21–23.

35. Ibid., p. 35.

36. Thomas C. Buchanan, *Black Life on the Mississippi: Slaves, Free Blacks, and the Western Steamboat World* (Chapel Hill: University of North Carolina Press, 2004), p. 8.

37. Lee Sandlin, *Wicked River: The Mississippi When It Last Ran Wild* (New York: Pantheon, 2010), pp. xii–xiv.

38. Buchanan, *Black Life on the Mississippi*.

39. Ibid., p. 8.

40. *Narrative of Frederick Douglass*, p. 64.

41. *Narrative of the Life and Adventures of Henry Bibb*, pp. 29–30.

42. On the history of the Clamorgan family, see Julie Winch, *The Clamorgans: One Family's History of Race in America* (New York: Hill and Wang, 2011).

43. Julie Winch, ed., *The Colored Aristocracy of St. Louis* (1858; Columbia: University of Missouri Press, 1999), p. 45.

44. William Wells Brown, "The Colored Population of Canada," *Pine and Palm* 1 (Oct. 19, 1861): 2.

45. Rachel v. William Walker, November Term, 1834, Case 82, Circuit Court Case Files, Office of the Circuit Court, Missouri State Archives–St. Louis.

46. Lea VanderVelde, *Mrs. Dred Scott: A Life on Slavery's Frontier* (New York: Oxford University Press, 2009), p. 290.

47. *Narrative of William W. Brown*, p. 81.

48. Walter Johnson, *Soul by Soul: Life Inside the Antebellum Slave Market* (Cambridge: Harvard University Press, 1999), p. 121.

49. *Narrative of William W. Brown*, p. 46.

50. Ibid., pp. 46–48.

51. *Clotel; or, The President's Daughter* (London: Partridge and Oakey, 1853), p. 244.

52. The chronological sequence of occupations given in the *Narrative* suggests an earlier date, but Lovejoy did not buy a share of the newspaper until August 1830.

53. *St. Louis Observer* (Oct. 1, 1835).

54. Merton L. Dillon, *Elijah P. Lovejoy, Abolitionist Editor* (Urbana: University of Illinois Press, 1961), pp. 60–72.

55. *Liberator* 32 (Dec. 5, 1862): 194.

56. Paul Simon, *Freedom's Champion: Elijah Lovejoy* (Carbondale: Southern Illinois University Press, 1994), p. 13.

57. *St. Louis Times* (Feb. 11, 1832).

58. *Narrative of William W. Brown*, p. 27.

59. *St. Louis Observer* (Nov. 5, 1835).

60. *Narrative of William W. Brown*, pp. 29–30. This account of Brown's fight and subsequent beating follows closely the account he gives in the *Narrative*. It is not out of the question, however, that McKinney bore a personal animosity toward Brown not mentioned in the *Narrative*. A man with a nasty streak frequently hauled before the court for his violent behavior, as well as the defendant in a freedom suit *(Julia v. McKinney)*, McKinney was an associate of Isaac Mansfield. By the time of this altercation, Mansfield probably had begun acquiring members of Brown's family from Young but seemed to have no interest then or later in acquiring Brown. If anything, he may already have harbored a special spite for Brown, as he indisputably would later.

61. Primm, *Lion of the Valley*, p. 317.

62. The codicil to Young's will mentions his purchase of land from Bledsoe: John Young Probate File.

63. John Simonds Jr. to George Sibley (St. Louis), Jan. 4, 1829, Sibley Papers, Missouri History Museum Archives.

64. The only Colburn listed in the 1836 St. Louis Directory is a Mrs. M. Colburn, "widow."

65. *Narrative of William W. Brown*, pp. 24–26.

66. Why Young fell into financial decline can only be answered speculatively. The most likely answer is that he was invested in a model of agricultural livelihood that was becoming outdated. Likewise, his medical practice faced extensive competition, including that of the better-placed William Carr Lane. The new or growing fortunes in the city were increasingly based on commerce, manufacturing, and supplying the army.

67. *Narrative of William W. Brown*, p. 32.

68. Mansfield as witness: Land sale by Albert Gallatin to Sarah Young, April 26, 1828, Deed Book O/467, City Recorder's Office, St. Louis.

69. The Jan. 25, 1826, issue of the *Missouri Republican* listed him among the address-ees of unclaimed letters in the St. Louis Post Office.

70. O[rville] D. Filley to Marcus Filley, July 11, 1830, Filley Family Papers, Missouri History Museum Archives.

71. *Missouri Republican* (Jan, 25, 1827): 3.

72. As a Jacksonian operative, *Missouri Intelligencer* (Sept. 10, 1831): 2; as candidate for state legislature, *Missouri Intelligencer* (Oct. 1, 1831): 2.

73. Brown misspelled his name as "Swan" in *Narrative of William W. Brown*, pp. 42–43.

74. Lavinia Titus's freedom suit in Illinois is referenced in Sam v. Alexander P. Field and Elijah Mitchell, July Term, 1832, Case 49, Circuit Court Case Files, Office of the Circuit Court, Missouri State Archives–St. Louis.

75. Swon was involved in the sale or purchase of four slaves in 1834–35 alone; the receipts are in the Slaves and Slavery Collection, Folder 3, Missouri History Museum Archives.

76. Isaac Franklin to Rice C. Ballard, Jan. 9, 1832, Series 1.1, Folder 4, Rice C. Ballard Papers #4850, Southern Historical Collection, Wilson Library, University of North Carolina at Chapel Hill.

77. *Narrative of William W. Brown*, pp. 65–66.

78. Ibid., pp. 64–65.

79. No handbill has been located, nor, more surprisingly, a runaway-slave advertise-ment in a St. Louis newspaper. In all likelihood, Young and Mansfield surmised their slaves would head directly to Illinois and thus placed their ads at a printing shop in Illinois. Unfortunately, copies of newspapers from the most likely sites for such ads—Galena, Peoria, and Springfield—are not extant for 1832.

80. Mention of Wiggins, who for many years owned monopoly rights to the Mis-sissippi River ferry, offers strong support for the authenticity of this portion of Brown's account: *Narrative of William W. Brown*, pp. 72–73.

81. *Narrative of William W. Brown*, p. 74.

82. *Missouri Republican* (March 13, 1832).

83. *St. Louis Times* (Jan. 5 and Feb. 9, 1833).

84. *Narrative of William W. Brown*, pp. 77–79.

85. Execution Book S, pp. 273–74 and 274–75, City Recorder's Office, St. Louis.

86. Last Will and Testament of John Young, 1834 estate account settlement; both in John Young Probate File.

87. Receipt from Samuel Willi to Robert Renick, John Young Probate File.

88. Brown listed his sale price varyingly as $650 and $700. The former is more likely the actual price, since it was the one that Enoch Price cited as the price he paid in an 1848 letter to Edmund Quincy. Brown reprinted that letter as a prefatory

document to the third Boston edition of *Narrative of William W. Brown* (Boston: Anti-Slavery Society, 1848), p. viii.

89. This biographical sketch draws heavily on notes compiled by Ruth Ferris: Ruth Ferris Collection of River Life and Lore, St. Louis Mercantile Library at the University of Missouri–St. Louis.

90. The Prices were listed at that location in the city directories of 1836 and 1840. No directory was printed in the early 1830s, but the 1830 federal census lists their residence as being in the middle ward, which included Sixth Street. It listed the occupants of their household as two white adults and two female slaves, one under ten and the other (probably Maria) between ten and twenty.

91. The likely owner of Uncle Frank was John B. Sarpy, Pierre Chouteau's right-hand man in managing his fur company. Sarpy's family had been well established in St. Louis, going back to the French period. WWB misspelled their family name as Sarpee. For information on the family, see Walter Barlow Stevens, *St. Louis: The Fourth City, 1764–1911*, 2 vols. (St. Louis: S. J. Clarke, 1911), vol. 2, pp. 668–69.

92. *Narrative of William W. Brown*, pp. 91–93.

93. *A Description of William Wells Brown's Original Panoramic Views of the Scenes in the Life of an American Slave* (London: Charles Gilpin, 1850), p. 29.

94. *New Orleans Bee* (Nov. 30, 1833): 2.

95. The story of Milton and Delia's reunion had a strange role reversal, as it was Delia, already freed, who eventually helped to secure money for the emancipation of several of her siblings, including Milton: *Narrative of the Sufferings of Lewis and Milton Clarke* (Boston: Bela Marsh, 1846), pp. 74–75, 81–82.

96. *Narrative of William W. Brown*, 3d ed., p. viii.

97. *New Orleans Bee* (Jan. 14, 1833).

98. *Missouri Republican* (Dec. 20, 1833).

99. *Narrative of William W. Brown*, pp. 90–91.

100. *New Orleans Courier* (Dec. 3–7, 1833).

101. Price cited these extraordinarily high prices in his 1848 public letter to Edmund Quincy; *Narrative of William W. Brown*, p. viii.

102. *National Anti-Slavery Standard* 28 (May 18, 1867): 3.

103. *Cincinnati Directory for the Year 1831* (Cincinnati: Robinson and Fairbank, 1831), p. 182.

104. Edward Tracy, quoted in Richard H. Abzug, *Passionate Liberator: Theodore Dwight Weld and the Dilemma of Reform* (New York: Oxford University Press, 1980), p. 74.

105. Letter from Theodore Weld to Lewis Tappan, March 18, 1834, printed in *Genius of Universal Emancipation* 5 (May 1834): 69.

106. *New York Evangelist* 19 (May 14, 1834): 74.

107. *Cincinnati Advertiser and Ohio Phoenix* (Jan. 8, 1834).

108. *Narrative of William W. Brown*, p. 104.

109. Ibid., p. 98.

110. Ibid.

111. Ibid., pp. 105–6.

Chapter 3

1. Russell Duino, "The Cleveland Book Trade, 1819–1912: Leading Firms and Outstanding Men" (PhD diss., University of Pittsburgh, 1981), pp. 40–41.

2. James D. Cleveland, "The City of Cleveland Sixty Years Ago," *Annals of the Early Settlers Association of Cuyahoga County*, vol. 3, no. 1 (Cleveland: Williams Publishing Co., 1892), pp. 693–95.

3. *Cleveland Herald* (Aug. 9, 1834): 3.

4. John Malvin, *The Autobiography of John Malvin* (Cleveland: Leader Printing Co., 1879), p. 27.

5. Ibid., p. 9.

6. Much of the information in this sketch comes from *The Encylopedia of Cleveland History, http://ech.case.edu/ech-cgi/article.pl?id=BJ9*, accessed 11/14/2010.

7. Edmund H. Chapman, *Cleveland: Village to Metropolis* (Cleveland: Western Reserve Historical Society, 1964), p. 28.

8. On her self-professed claim to Native American heritage: Elizabeth Brown to Isaac C. Ray, Aug. 5, 1849, Box 1, Folder 15, Slavery in the United States Collection, American Antiquarian Society, Worcester, MA.

9. David W. Demming, "A Social and Demographic Study of Cuyahoga County Blacks, 1820–1860" (Master's thesis, Kent State University, 1976), pp. 108–10.

10. No municipal records of any sort survive for the family.

11. Demming, *Cuyahoga County Blacks*, p. 113.

12. Ibid., p. 85

13. Ibid., p. 11.

14. Josephine Brown, *Biography of an American Bondman*, p. 45.

15. United States Enrolment for the Great Lakes, http://www.maritimehistoryofthe greatlakes.ca/enrolment/Enrolment.asp?EventID=871.

16. Reprinted from the *Cleveland Herald* of July 5, 1834, in the *Annals of Cleveland, 1832–1834*, vols. 15–17, Part 1 (Cleveland: WPA, 1938), p. 247.

17. *Clotel*, pp. 67–68.

18. The young man, John Henry Depka, thought that the girls might have landed at Huron, Ohio, and he requested that lakefront cities from Cleveland to Detroit copy his notice: *Annals of Cleveland, 1818–1935, 1835–1836*. vols. 18–19, part 1 (Cleveland: WPA, 1938), p. 80.

19. He remembered it as the *Townsend* in the catalogue that accompanied his panorama: *Original Panoramic Views*, p. 28. For information about the *Charles Townsend*, see United States Enrolment for the Great Lakes, http://www .maritimehistoryofthegreatlakes.ca/enrolment/Enrolment.asp?EventID=282. The 1837 Cleveland city directory list a *Charles Townsend* in operation on Lake Erie.

20. *Original Panoramic Views*, p. 28.

21. *Three Years in Europe* (London: Charles Gilpin, 1852), pp. 97–104.

22. Banknotes Collection, Michigan Private Currency, Box 1, Folder 22, American Antiquarian Society.

23. Receipts from Cumberland College are in Young's probate file: John Young Probate File.

24. Court documents filed in St. Louis on April 30 and May 3, 1833, list Leander as part of Young's "inventory"; he was valued at $450. Leander's name no longer appears among the ten slaves legally delivered over to Sarah Young in a document dated November 1, 1833. An account ledger indicates he was sold in July 1833. All documents are in Young's probate file: John Young Probate File.

25. Agreement between Sarah Young and William Sublette, Dec. 1, 1835, Book 1, Folder 8, Sublette Papers; and receipt from Sarah Young to W. H. Sublette, Sept. 12, 1838, Book 2, Folder 3, Sublette Papers, Missouri History Museum Archives. Young had previously hired out Peter to his overseer, D. D. Trice, to work on one of his farms for the calendar year 1832. Their detailed agreement is preserved in Young's probate file, no doubt due to nonpayment: John Young Probate File.

26. She left behind not only an unapportioned estate but also a simmering family dispute. Sarah and John Young had taken into their Marthasville home two very small children: William, son of brother Benjamin; and Sarah Ellen Renick, daughter of his deceased sister. Young left a $500 legacy to Sarah Ellen in his will on the condition that she remain under his wife's custodianship; however, Sarah Ellen left the Young farm for her father's home, very likely at Sarah Young's initiative. Sarah Young refused at the time of her niece's departure to pay her legacy, an omission the Renick family did not forget. They sued the estate for its payment—adducing strong evidence that Sarah Young was responsible for her niece's departure—and won; Sarah Young Probate File.

27. Sarah Young Probate File; Martha Ann v. Hiram Cordell (Case 9).

28. The literal truthfulness of the story is undercut by the fact that Segur was still a bachelor at the time Brown worked for him: *Historic Sites of Cleveland: Hotels and Taverns* (Columbus: Ohio Historical Records Survey Project, 1942), p. 454.

29. *Narrative of the Life and Escape of William Wells Brown*, the introductory sketch to *Clotel*, pp. 25–29.

30. Amy Post to Wendell Phillips, June 20, 1850, Anti-Slavery Collection, Boston Public Library.

31. *Narrative of William W. Brown*, pp. 109–10.

32. William Anderson to William Nell, April 1860, Anti-Slavery Collection, Boston Public Library.

33. Hayden to Phillips, Feb. 21, 1848, MS Am 1953 (693), Wendell Phillips Papers, Houghton Library, Harvard University.

34. Farrison, *William Wells Brown*, p. 63.

35. Elwin H. Powell, "Street as School: Ideas and Assembly in Buffalo, Seen Through the Diary of George Washington Jonson (1835–1849)," *Urban Education* 18 (January 1984): 424.

36. *Buffalo Courier and Economist*, supplement (Aug. 14, 1843).

37. Ibid. (Aug. 17, 1843).

38. Quoted in Mark Goldman, *High Hopes: The Rise and Decline of Buffalo, New York* (Albany: State University of New York, 1983), p. 91.

39. Josephine Brown to Samuel May Jr., April 27, 1853, Anti-Slavery Collection, Boston Public Library. May published the letter without her consent in the *Liberator* 24 (May 26, 1854): 82.

40. Elizabeth Brown to Isaac C. Ray, Aug. 5, 1849.

41. *The Black Man*, pp. 152–53. The poem was published in *America and Other Poems* (1853), but the more likely source for Brown's text would have been *Autographs for Freedom*, ed. Julia Griffiths (Boston: John P. Jewett and Company, 1853), pp. 46–54.

42. Rosier was born in Montgomery County, Maryland, and moved no later than 1844 to Buffalo, where he lived for a number of years. He relocated with his family to Chatham, Canada West, between the mid-1850s and 1860. The overriding reason fugitive slaves migrated to Canada after 1850 was fear for their safety after passage of the Fugitive Slave Law. Émigrés streamed out of such Northern cities as Boston and Buffalo; Rosier might have been one. Sources for this sketch: Buffalo city directories, 1861 Canada Census, and Freedman's Bank Records—all courtesy of Reginald Pitts.

43. Nathan Rosier to "Mr. Tappan," Jan. 29, 1852, MSS Brit Emp 518 C22/48, British and Foreign Antislavery Collection, Rhodes House, Oxford University.

44. The 1850 federal census lists her as Elizabeth J. Brown, born in Detroit.

45. *Narrative of William W. Brown*, pp. 37–38.

46. *Northern Star and Freemen's Advocate* (Jan. 2, 1843), in *Black Abolitionist Papers, 1830–1865* (Sanford, NC: Microfilming Corporation of America 1981). 17 reels. Reel 4. [Cited hereafter as BAP.]

47. *Northern Star and Freemen's Advocate* (April 7, 1842), in BAP, Reel 4.

48. *Liberator* 13 (Jan. 6, 1843): 2.

49. *Narrative of William W. Brown*, pp. 109–10.

50. "The White Slave," *Chicago Western Citizen* (June 8, 1843), in BAP, Reel 4.

Chapter 4

1. "An Address to the Slaves of the United States," in *Pamphlets of Protest: An Anthology of Early African-American Protest Literature, 1790–1860*, ed. Richard Newman, Patrick Rael, and Philip Lapsansky (New York: Routledge, 2001), pp. 160–64.

2. Howard H. Bell, "National Negro Conventions of the Middle 1840's: Moral Suasion vs. Political Action," *Journal of Negro History* 42 (Oct. 1957): 251.

3. *The Black Man*, pp. 149–50.

4. Carleton Mabee, *Black Freedom: The Nonviolent Abolitionists from 1830 Through the Civil War* (New York: Macmillan, 1970), p. 61.

5. Garnet self-published it in a short volume along with David Walker's "Appeal," in effect binding together two of the most powerful black nationalist addresses of the century: *Walker's Appeal* (New York: Printed by J. H. Tobitt, 1848).

6. *Pamphlets of Protest*, p. 167.

7. Robert S. Levine, *Martin Delany, Frederick Douglass, and the Politics of Representative Identity* (Chapel Hill: University of North Carolina Press, 1997), p. 29.

8. Quoted in Henry Mayer, *All on Fire: William Lloyd Garrison and the Abolition of Slavery* (New York: St. Martin's, 1998), p. 316.

9. E. A. Marsh, "The Colored Convention," *Liberator* 13 (Sept. 8, 1843): 142. George Washington Johnson contemptuously referred to him as "little Edwin A. Marsh": entry of Aug. 12, 1843, Johnson diary, Buffalo and Erie County Historical Society, Buffalo.

10. *National Anti-Slavery Standard* (Oct. 5, 1843): 70. His spelling was unrealiable; he misspelled Douglass's first and last names.

11. *Albany Weekly Patriot* (Oct. 3, 1843), in BAP, Reel 4.

12. *Walker's Buffalo City Directory* (Buffalo: Lee and Thorp, 1844), p. 65.

13. Josephine Brown, *Biography of an American Bondman*, p. 55.

14. Entry of Oct. 14, 1842, Diary of Charles Spear, Anti-Slavery Collection, Boston Public Library.

15. "The Cause in Western New York," *National Anti-Slavery Standard* 7 (July 30, 1846): 34.

16. "Anti-Slavery Meetings," *National Anti-Slavery Standard* 7 (Nov. 26, 1846): 103.

17. "Annual Meeting of the Western New-York Anti-Slavery Society, *National Anti-Slavery Standard* 7 (January 14, 1847): 130.

18. This 1841 foldable map is in the Hudson Family Papers, University of Massachusetts Library, Amherst, MA.

19. Kelley to E. D. Hudson, July 23, 1844, Hudson Family Papers, University of Massachusetts Library, Amherst.

20. Martha Hudson to Abby Kelley, Feb. 13, 1845, Box 1, Folder 23, Abby Kelley Foster Papers, American Antiquarian Society, Worcester, MA.

21. Samuel S. Foster to Abby Kelley Foster, March 2, 1855, Box 2, Folder 8, Abby Kelley Foster Papers, American Antiquarian Society, Worcester.

22. Sydney Howard Gay to Abby Kelley, Oct. 6, 1843, Box 1, Folder 17, Abby Kelley Foster Papers, American Antiquarian Society, Worcester.

23. Samuel May Jr. to Samuel Foster, March 2, 1857, Box 2, Folder 11, Abby Kelley Foster Papers, American Antiquarian Society, Worcester.

24. The only reference to Henrietta's birth (or existence) is in the *National Anti-Slavery Standard* 4 (May 30, 1844): 207. Few life-cycle records from this period in Buffalo survive, and Brown kept silent about his family in his published writings during these years of young married life. The three-year gap between her birth and Josephine's leaves ample room for the possibility of additional births or at least pregnancies in the family.

25. R. J. M. Blackett, *Building an Antislavery Wall: Black Americans in the Atlantic Abolitionist Movement, 1830–1860* (Baton Rouge: Louisiana State University Press, 1983), p. 134.

26. *National Anti-Slavery Standard* 4 (May 30, 1844): 207.

27. WWB to Amy Post, June 23, 1844, Isaac and Amy Post Family Papers, University of Rochester (NY) Library.

28. WWB to Amy Post, Sept. 3, 1844, Isaac and Amy Post Family Papers, University of Rochester Library.

29. His agency in Ohio began September 8: *National Anti-Slavery Standard* 5 (Nov. 21, 1844): 99.

30. Brown told this favorite story repeatedly on the lecture circuit and twice in print (*Clotel*, pp. 172–74; *The Negro in the American Rebellion*, pp. 370–73), as well as to his daughter Josephine, who retold it (*Biography of an American Bondman*, pp. 56–59).

31. "Kidnapping in Ohio," *National Anti-Slavery Standard* 5 (Nov. 7, 1844): 90.

32. "Letter from Wm. W. Brown—A Methodist Preacher's Prayer," *National Anti-Slavery Standard* 5 (Sept. 26, 1844): 66.

33. Sydney Howard Gay to Wendell Phillips, March 5, 1846, MS Am 1953 (593), Wendell Phillips Papers, Houghton Library, Harvard University.

34. Charles Lenox Remond to Executive Committee, Massachusetts Anti-Slavery Society, Jan. 6, 1846, MS Am 1953 (1036), Wendell Phillips Papers, Houghton Library, Harvard University.

35. Pliny Sexton to Isaac Post, Dec. 7, 1844, Isaac and Amy Post Family Papers, University of Rochester Library.

36. *National Anti-Slavery Standard* 5 (March 6, 1845): 158.

37. *National Anti-Slavery Standard* 5 (Feb. 20, 1845): 151; and (Feb. 27, 1855): 155.

38. "To the Public," *Liberator* 20 (July 12, 1850): 111.

39. The *National Anti-Slavery Standard* published a notice of the move for friends of the movement: "W. W. Brown's address for the future will be Farmington, Ontario county, instead of Buffalo. Liberator please copy": 6 (June 20, 1845): 11.

40. The Hathaways made no secret in the community that they were housing fugitive slaves. Joseph C. Hathaway even published an account in the national press of offering to shelter a runaway from Virginia: *National Anti-Slavery Standard* 2 (May 5, 1842): 190.

41. Steward discussed his years in the village in his fugitive slave-narrative, *Twenty-Two Years a Slave, and Forty Years a Freeman* (Rochester, NY: William Alling, 1857), pp. 115–18.

42. *National Anti-Slavery Standard* 6 (Oct. 30, 1845): 85.

43. WWB to Gay, June 22, 1846, Box 3, Sydney Howard Gay Papers, Columbia University Library.

44. Entry for meeting of Nov. 23, 1846, p. 220, account ledger of Massachusetts Anti-Slavery Society, Anti-Slavery Collection, Boston Public Library.

45. See, for instance, his call for WWB's support in the *National Anti-Slavery Standard* 6 (May 14, 1846): 195.

46. *National Anti-Slavery Standard* 7 (Jan. 14, 1847): 130.

47. *National Anti-Slavery Standard* 7 (Nov. 12, 1846): 94.

48. *National Anti-Slavery Standard* 7 (Dec. 17, 1846): 114.

49. *National Anti-Slavery Standard* 7 (Feb. 11, 1847): 146.

50. E. D. Hudson to Martha Hudson, Feb. 14, 1847, Hudson Family Papers, University of Massachusetts Library, Amherst.

51. Mary Robbins Post to Isaac and Amy Post, May 1847, Box 3, File 3, Isaac and Amy Post Family Papers, University of Rochester Library.

52. Notes of meeting of May 29, 1847, account ledger of Massachusetts Anti-Slavery Society, Anti-Slavery Collection, Boston Public Library.

53. Those engagements were advertised a week in advance in the *National Anti-Slavery Standard* 7 (May 13, 1847): 199.

54. His speech was given at the NEASS convention; *National Anti-Slavery Standard* 8 (June 3, 1847): 2.

55. *Narrative of William W. Brown*, p. 105.

Chapter 5

1. Samuel May Jr. to Ade, n.d., Anti-Slavery Collection, Boston Public Library.

2. Edmund Quincy to John Bishop Estlin, May 25, 1852, Anti-Slavery Collection, Boston Public Library.

3. *National Anti-Slavery Standard* 15 (April 7, 1855): 2.

4. Edmund Quincy to Caroline Weston, July 2, 1847, Anti-Slavery Collection, Boston Public Library.

5. Ibid.

6. Copyright Record Books, District Court of Massachusetts, Reel 12 (Vol. 64), p. 308.

7. Garrison was the most likely author of his paper's puff for the book: "We predict for it an excellent sale, having read it with deep interest as written by himself": *Liberator* 17 (July 23, 1847): 118.

8. Hathaway accompanied Brown to the Boston area in May 1847 and remained active there into the early summer. His dateline of Farmington, however, raises the alternative (if less likely) possibility that he penned his letter before the move, based on his reading of the preliminary text.

9. Quincy to Weston, July 2, 1847. The editor of the *National Anti-Slavery Standard* put a smiling face on the subject, asserting that Douglass's letters "will be received with universal satisfaction"; 8 (Aug. 12, 1847): 43.

10. The precedent for the publication by the MASS of the narratives of Douglass and WWB was the AASS's disastrous publication of *The Narrative of James Williams, an American Slave* (1838). Doubts raised about its authenticity forced the AASS to withdraw it from circulation.

11. "The Negro Speaks of Rivers," *The Collected Poems of Langston Hughes*, Arnold Rampersad and David Roessel, eds. (New York: Alfred A. Knopf, 1995), p. 23.

12. *Narrative of William W.* Brown, p. 106.

13. William L. Andrews, *To Tell a Free Story: The First Century of Afro-American Autobiography, 1760–1865* (Urbana: University of Illinois Press, 1986), pp. 144–51.

14. William Wells Brown, *My Southern Home*, ed. John Ernest (Chapel Hill: University of North Carolina Press, 2011), pp. 203–4, n5.

15. Jacob Green, *Narrative of the Life of J.D. Green, a Runaway Slave, from Kentucky* (Huddersfield, UK: Henry Fielding, 1864), pp. 8–9.

16. *Narrative of William W. Brown*, pp. 59–61.

17. Theodore Weld, *American Slavery As It Is: Testimony of a Thousand Witnesses* (New York: American Anti-Slavery Society, 1839), pp. 158–59.

18. *Narrative of William W. Brown*, p. 62.

19. Trish Loughran, *The Republic in Print: Print Culture in the Age of U.S. Nation Building, 1770–1870* (New York: Columbia University Press, 2007), pp. 356–57.

20. Weld, p. 7.

21. *Narrative of William W. Brown*, pp. 59–61.

22. *Liberator* 17 (Sept. 3, 1847): 143.

23. Chapter 6, *Moby-Dick*.

24. W. Jeffrey Bolster, *Black Jacks: African American Seamen in the Age of Sail* (Cambridge: Harvard University Press, 1997).

25. Kathryn Grover, *The Fugitive's Gibraltar: Escaping Slaves and Abolitionism in New Bedford, Massachusetts* (Amherst: University of Massachusetts Press, 2001), p. 6.

26. *National Anti-Slavery Standard* 6 (Jan. 22, 1846): 134.

27. The 1850 federal census lists the residents of the Johnson household as Polly, Clarissa, and two teenagers.

28. The 1850 federal census lists Elizabeth J. Brown, age ten and born in Detroit, as living with Martha Fletcher at this address. The 1845, 1849, and 1852 city directories give Fletcher various occupations and residences.

29. *Historical Sketch of the Friends Academy Prepared for the Centennial Year* (New Bedford, MA: Fessenden and Baker, 1876), pp. 21–22.

30. The story quickly spread through the antislavery press of the US and the UK after Douglass published an exposé: "H.G. Warner, Esq., (Editor of the Rochester Courier)," *North Star* 1 (Sept. 22, 1848): 2.

31. For the argument that Brown also financed the first edition of the *Narrative*, see the fine introduction by Claire Parfait and Marie-Jeanne Rossignol, trans., *Le Récit de William Wells Brown, Esclave Fugitif* (Mont-Saint-Aignan, France: Publications des Universités de Rouen et du Havre, 2012), p. 29.

32. "W. W. Brown in Upton," *Liberator*, 17 (Sept. 17, 1847): 151.

33. *National Anti-Slavery Standard* 8 (June 24, 1847): 15.

34. *Liberator* 17 (Oct. 1, 1847): 158.

35. *Lecture delivered before the Female Anti-Slavery Society of Salem* (Boston: Massachusetts Anti-Slavery Society), p. 4.

36. See, for instance, his advertisement in the *Boston Chronotype* (Aug. 7, 1847): 4.

37. Notes of meeting of Nov. 23, 1847, account ledger of Massachusetts Anti-Slavery Society, Anti-Slavery Collection, Boston Public Library.

38. *Liberator* 17 (Dec. 31, 1847): 211.

39. On the size of the first edition, see *Liberator* 18 (Feb. 8, 1848): 22; on the size and cost of the second edition, see Samuel May Jr. to John Bishop Estlin, Dec. 15, 1847, and Jan. 13, 1848, Anti-Slavery Collection, Boston Public Library.

40. Massachusetts Anti-Slavery Society, *Sixteenth Annual Report* (Boston: Massachusetts Anti-Slavery Society, 1848), p. 88; *Liberator* 18 (Feb. 4, 1848): 19.

41. "Narrative of William W. Brown," *Liberator* 18 (Feb. 11, 1848): 22.

42. *Narrative of William W. Brown* (Boston: Anti-Slavery Society, 1848), p. 141.

43. The calculation for the size of the second edition comes from subtracting the known size of the first edition (3,000) from the advertised size of the combined sale of the first and second editions (5,000): *Liberator* 18 (Oct. 20, 1848): 166.

44. *Liberator* 19 (July 20, 1849): 116.

45. It deeply moved Garrison, who jotted syllabic accents above the first line of the song as a mnemonic device to facilitate internalizing the song's rhythm. His copy of *Clotel*, which reprinted the song, is in the Anti-Slavery Collection, Boston Public Library.

46. *Narrative of William W. Brown*, pp. 49–51.

47. *The Anti-Slavery Harp: A Collection of Songs for Anti-Slavery Meetings* (Boston: Bela Marsh, 1848): p. 3.

48. Walker to Stephen Foster, March 13, 1849, Box 1, Folder 33, Abby Kelley Foster Papers, American Antiquarian Society, Worcester, MA.

49. He also gave many copies to friends. The copy of the second edition he inscribed to Anna Davis is in the collections of the Library Company of Philadelphia.

50. He made this claim in the note to the first English edition of *The Anti-Slavery Harp* (Newcastle: J. Blackwell and Co., 1849).

51. The markings are probably though not necessarily in May's hand. This well-preserved copy is at Houghton Library, Harvard University.

52. Historical Society of Pennsylvania, Philadelphia.

53. *Three Years in Europe*, p. 51.

54. Reprinted in the *National Anti-Slavery Standard* 8 (May 18, 1848): 201.

55. Gilmore, "'De Genewine Artekil': William Wells Brown, Blackface Minstrelsy, and Abolitionism," in *The Genuine Article: Race, Mass Culture, and American Literary Manhood* (Durham, NC: Duke University Press, 2001), pp. 37–38.

56. On their patronage: *New York Commercial Advertiser* (Oct. 21, 1847): 3.

57. Martin Delany, *Blake; or, the Huts of America*, ed. Floyd J. Miller (Boston: Beacon Press, 1970), p. 100.

58. *Clotel*, p. 138.

59. "Memoir of the Author," *The Black Man*, p. 18.

60. Paulina Brown is listed in the 1860 federal census as age twelve, information not reliable enough to be wholly trustworthy.

61. WWB to Amy Post, July 16, 1848, Box 3, File 7, Isaac and Amy Post Family Papers, University of Rochester Library.

62. WWB to "My Dear Friend" [Garrison], Sept. 15, 1848, Anti-Slavery Collection, Boston Public Library.

63. Leaders of the PASS had wished as early as July 1847 to bring WWB to Philadelphia: Lucretia Mott to Maria Weston Chapman, July 28, 1847, Anti-Slavery Collection, Boston Public Library.

64. *Liberator* 18 (July 14, 1848): 110.

65. "Anti-Slavery Convention at Harwich," *Liberator* 18 (Sept. 15, 1848): 145.

66. Ibid.

67. "The Sixty-Six Slaves at West Harwich," *Liberator* 17 (Nov. 5, 1847): 177.

68. *Original Panoramic Views*, p. 12.

69. Dorothy Sterling, *Ahead of Her Time: Abby Kelley and the Politics of Anti-Slavery* (New York: W. W. Norton, 1991), p. 247.

70. *Liberator* Day Books, vol. 2, pp. 128–29, Anti-Slavery Collection, Boston Public Library.

71. Wallcut to Samuel May Jr., Aug. 25, 1848, Anti-Slavery Collection, Boston Public Library.

72. MASS ledger, notes for Sept. 5, 1848, Anti-Slavery Collection, Boston Public Library.

73. WWB to "My Dear Friend" [Garrison].

74. WWB to Post, Sept. 30, 1848, Isaac and Amy Post Family Papers, University of Rochester Library.

75. *Pennsylvania Freeman* 5 (Dec. 28, 1848): 2.

76. *The Black Man*, p. 175.

77. "Singular Escape," *Liberator* 19 (Jan. 12, 1849): 7.

78. *Pennsylvania Freeman* 6 (Jan. 25, 1849): 2.

79. "Singular Escape," 7.

80. *Liberator* 19 (March 2, 1849): 35.

81. "Anti-Slavery Meetings in New Bedford," *Liberator* 19 (Feb. 16, 1849): 27.

82. Josephine Brown, *Biography of an American Bondman*, pp. 75–81.

83. On Newburyport reception: *Liberator* 19 (April 27, 1849): 67; on Quincy's family tragedy, *Liberator* 19 (March 30, 1849): 51.

84. Entries of Feb. 3 and July 24, 1849, Thomas Bradford Drew diary, Massachusetts Historical Society.

85. Samuel May Jr. to John Bishop Estlin, May 21, 1849, Anti-Slavery Collection, Boston Public Library.

86. Samuel May Jr. to John Bishop Estlin, Feb. 2, 1849, Anti-Slavery Collection, Boston Public Library.

87. May to Estlin, May 2, 1848, Anti-Slavery Collection, Boston Public Library.

88. Brown to Gay, June 5, 1849, Box 3, Sydney Howard Gay Papers, Columbia University.

89. Webb to Friend, July 8, 1849, Anti-Slavery Collection, Boston Public Library.

90. *National Anti-Slavery Standard* 6 (Dec. 18, 1845): 113.

91. Reported in *National Anti-Slavery Standard* 10 (June 14, 1849): 9.

92. *National Anti-Slavery Standard* 9 (May 24, 1849): 206.

93. Wendell Phillips made propagandistic use of the incident by publicizing it: *Liberator* 19 (June 8, 1849): 90.

94. Jeffrey Ruggles, The *Unboxing of Henry Brown* (Richmond: Library of Virginia, 2003), p. 49.

95. *North Star* 2 (Aug. 24, 1849): 3.

96. *National Anti-Slavery Standard* 10 (July 12, 1849): 27.

97. WWB to John Clayton, July 6, 1849, Record Group 59, Passport Applications, 1795–1905, Reel 30, National Archives, Washington, DC.

98. The antislavery press publicized the discriminatory policy of the Department of State immediately following its back-to-back rejections of applications by Brown and Peter Williams of Philadelphia: *National Anti-Slavery Standard* 10 (Aug. 16, 1849): 46; (Aug. 23, 1849): 50–51; (Sept. 6, 1849): 58; (Sept. 20, 1849): 65.

99. "New Gotham Newspaper Sponsors Drama of Press," *Baltimore Afro-American* (Nov. 3, 1951): 20.

100. A copy of the broadside with the handwritten addition, "*This* Evening," is in the Anti-Slavery Collection, Boston Public Library.

101. "Presentation and Farewell Meeting," *Liberator* 19 (July 27, 1849): 118.

102. Entry for July 19, account ledger of Massachusetts Anti-Slavery Society, Anti-Slavery Collection, Boston Public Library.

103. *Three Years in Europe* (London: Charles Gilpin, 1852), p. 9.

Chapter 6

1. *Three Years in Europe*, p. 2.

2. *North Star* 4 (Jan. 16, 1851): 3.

3. Francis E. Hyde, *Cunard and the North Atlantic, 1840–1973* (London: Macmillan, 1975).

4. *Three Years in Europe*, p. 6; Stephen Fox, *Transatlantic: Samuel Cunard, Isambard Brunel, and the Great Atlantic Steamships* (New York: Perennial, 2004), p. 116.

5. "Letter from Wm. Wells Brown," *Liberator* 19 (Nov. 2, 1849): 175.

6. http://louisdl.louislibraries.org/cdm4/document.php?CISOROOT= /LWP&CISOPTR=1454&REC=1, consulted Sept. 16, 2011. WWB told a revisionary version of this story in 1860 with a certain Judge Gwinn [*sic*] of Mississippi replacing Thomas Chinn. He presumably was thinking of the sitting US

senator from California, William M. Gwin, an ardent defender of slavery who once held public office in Mississippi: "Speech of Wm. Wells Brown," *Liberator* 30 (Aug. 17, 1860): 130.

7. *Emancipator* n.s. 1 (Sept. 1835): 3.

8. *Liberator* 19 (Nov. 2, 1849): 175.

9. Edlie L. Wong, *Neither Fugitive Nor Free: Atlantic Slavery, Freedom Suits, and the Legal Culture of Travel* (New York: New York University Press, 2009), p. 248.

10. *Three Years in Europe*, p. 3.

11. Robert Samuel Fletcher, *A History of Oberlin College, From Its Foundation Through the Civil War*, 2 vols. (Oberlin, OH: Oberlin College, 1943): 1: 281–82.

12. WWB to Hamilton Hill, Dec. 26, 1856, File 7/1/5, Oberlin College Library.

13. *Liberator* 19 (Nov. 2, 1849): 175.

14. *Three Years in Europe*, p. 8.

15. Webb to "Friend," Aug. 3, 1849, Anti-Slavery Collection, Boston Public Library.

16. Details about the Webbs come chiefly from Richard S. Harrison, *Richard Davis Webb: Dublin Quaker Printer, 1805–72* (Cork, Ireland: Red Barn, 1993).

17. Richard Webb to "Mrs. Hateful W. Perkins" [probably one of the Weston sisters], Dec. 11, 1849, Anti-Slavery Collection, Boston Public Library.

18. "Slavery in the United States of America: Lecture of Mr. William W. Brown, a Self-Emancipated Slave," *Liberator* 19 (Sept. 14, 1849): 146.

19. [Dublin] *Freeman's Journal* (Aug. 17, 1849); the report was largely reprinted in the *National Anti-Slavery Standard* 10 (Sept. 13, 1849): 62–63.

20. "Letter from James Haughton," *Liberator* 19 (Oct. 12, 1849): 162.

21. Elizabeth Brown to Isaac C. Ray, Aug. 5, 1849, Box 1, Folder 15, Slavery in the United States Collection, American Antiquarian Society, Worcester, MA.

22. "Elihu Burritt's Account of the English Delegation to Paris in 1849," *The Herald of Peace and International Arbitration* (Sept. 1, 1904): 264.

23. *Galignani's New Paris Guide for 1851* (Paris: A. and W. Galignani and Co., 1851), pp. 589–90.

24. "The Peace Congress at Paris," *London Times* (Aug. 25, 1849): 5.

25. Hugo's speech was printed in English in the official *Report of the Proceedings of the Second General Peace Congress, Held in Paris* (London: Charles Gilpin, 1849), pp. 10–14.

26. *Three Years in Europe*, p. 53.

27. WWB's remarks were published in several newspapers in English and French, but the most nearly accurate text can be found in the *Proceedings of the Congress*, pp. 77–78.

28. *Three Years in Europe*, p. 96.

29. *National Anti-Slavery Standard* 17 (Oct. 18, 1849): 83.

30. *Three Years in Europe*, pp. 50–51.

31. Both stories are in *Three Years in Europe*, pp. 50–52, 34–35.

32. *National-Anti-Slavery Standard* 17 (Sept. 20, 1849): 67.

33. WWB also sent the text to Garrison, who printed it on the front page of the *Liberator* 19 (Oct. 12, 1849): 161.

34. "Peace Meeting in Boston," *Liberator* 19 (Dec. 7, 1849): 196.

35. *Publishers Circular* (Sept. 1, 1849): 294.

36. The others were the narratives of Douglass, Bibb, and Lewis and Milton Clarke: *Anti-Slavery Reporter* (Oct. 1, 1849): 154.

37. *Narrative of William W. Brown* (London: Charles Gilpin, 1849), p. ii. WWB first published the song (to be sung to "Auld Lang Syne") in *The Anti-Slavery Harp*.

38. Mayer, *All on Fire*, pp. 578–80.

39. Lee's inscribed copy is in the collections of the British Library, London. The most informative source on Lee is H. A. Hanley, *Dr. John Lee of Hartwell* (Buckinghamshire [UK] Record Office, 1983).

40. *Three Years in Europe*, pp. 89–91.

41. "The Peace Congress," *Christian Inquirer* 4 (Oct. 13, 1849): 3.

42. *Three Years in Europe*, p. 93.

43. *Proceedings of the Congress*, pp. 56–57.

44. "Meeting to Welcome the Fugitive Slave, Mr. William Wells Brown," *Standard of Freedom*, 2 (Sept. 8, 1849): 6.

45. Richard Webb to "Mademoiselle," Sept. 19, 1849, Anti-Slavery Collection, Boston Public Library.

46. "Letter from Wm. Wells Brown," *Liberator* 19 (Nov. 2, 1849): 175.

47. *British Friend* 7 (Sept. 1849): 230.

48. "American Slavery—Wm. Wells Brown," *North Star* 2 (Nov. 2, 1849): 2.

49. WWB to Phillips, Sept. 28, 1849, MS Am 1953 (327), Wendell Phillips Papers, Houghton Library, Harvard University.

50. *Three Years in Europe*, pp. 110–16; *Worcester Herald* (Oct. 6, 1849): 2.

51. Pennington to P. Bolton, Nov. 13, 1849, MSS Brit Emp 518 C26/85, British and Foreign Anti-Slavery Society Collection, Rhodes House, Oxford University.

52. "Note to the Present Edition," *Narrative of William W. Brown* (London: Gilpin, 1850).

53. WWB to J. B. Estlin, June 4, 1850, B 32045, Box 2, Estlin Family Collection, Bristol Central Library, Bristol, England.

54. Moses Roper to John Scoble, May 9, 1844, MSS Brit Emp 518 C21/52, Rhodes House, Oxford University.

55. WWB to Keeper of Antiquities, Nov. 19, 1849, Original Letters and Papers, Vol. 43, Nov. 1849–May 1850; on the Board's refusal, Committee CE/24, Vol. 24, p. 7905, record for Dec. 8, 1849. All in Central Archives, British Museum.

56. *Newcastle Guardian* (Jan. 5, 1850).

57. Martha Ann v. Hiram Cordell, Case 9.

58. "Soiree to William Wells Brown, in Newcastle," *Newcastle Guardian* (Jan. 5, 1850): 5; [Auburn, NY] *Northern Christian Advocate* (March 20, 1850): 1, in Fulton Historical Newspapers Archive.

59. *Sheffield and Rotherham Independent* (Feb. 9, 1850): 2.

60. "Speech of Horace Mann, of Massachusetts, on the Subject of Slavery in the Territories, and the Consequences of a Dissolution of the Union," Feb. 15, 1850, in *Making of America, http://quod.lib.umich.edu/cgi/t/text/text-idx?c=moa;idno=ABJ4844.0001.001.*

61. *Anti-Slavery Harp* (Newcastle on Tyne: J. Blackwell and Co., 1850).

62. William Cooper Nell to Amy Post, Dec. 23, 1849, Isaac and Amy Post Family Papers, University of Rochester Library.

63. Nell, *Colored Patriots*, pp. 323–25.

64. Josephine Brown, *Biography of an American Bondman*, p. 5.

65. *Levensgeschiedenis van den Amerikaanschen slaaf W. Wells Brown*, trans. M. Keijzer (Zwolle, Netherlands: W. E. J. Tjeenk Willink, 1850).

66. "William W. Brown to His Master," *Liberator* 19 (Dec. 14, 1849): 199.

67. To protect her anonymity, she signed herself "A Fugitive": *New York Tribune* (July 25, 1853).

68. "A Stray Husband," *New York Tribune* (March 12, 1850): 1.

69. "A Stray Husband," *Milwaukee Daily Sentinel* (April 11, 1850): 2.

70. Richmond Enquirer (Nov. 15, 1850), excerpting the *Washington Union* (n.d.), Raymond English Anti-Slavery Collection, 1834–1886, George Thompson's Anti-Slavery Scrap Books, Box 6, REAS/6/3 (1850–51), John Rylands University Library, University of Manchester, UK.

71. Sturge to Scoble, Dec. 5, 1849, MSS Brit Emp 518 C112/29, British and Foreign Anti-Slavery Society Collection, Rhodes House, Oxford University.

72. Sturge to Scoble, July 18, 1850, MSS Brit Emp 518 C112/46, British and Foreign Anti-Slavery Society Collection, Rhodes House, Oxford University.

73. *Special Report of the Bristol and Clifton Ladies' Anti-Slavery Society; during Eighteen Months, from January 1851 to June, 1852; with a Statement of the Reasons of Its Separation from the British and Foreign Anti-Slavery Society* (London: John Snow; Bristol: W. Whereat, 1852), p. 26.

74. WWB to John Bishop Estlin, June 4, 1850.

75. "To the Public," *Liberator* 20 (July 12, 1850): 111–12.

76. Amy and Isaac Post to Wendell Phillips, June 21, 1850, Anti-Slavery Collection, Boston Public Library.

77. The term comes from his acquaintance and earliest biographer, William James, *Memoir of John Bishop Estlin, Esq., F.L.S., F.R.C.S.* (London: Charles Green, 1855), p. 16.

78. Quoted in Blackett, *Building an Antislavery Wall*, p. 148.

79. *Bristol Mercury* (April 20, 1850): 6.

80. Ibid.: 8.

81. WWB to Estlin, June 4, 1850.

82. Richard D. Webb to Maria Chapman, May 29, 1853, Anti-Slavery Collection, Boston Public Library.

83. May to Estlin, March 7, 1848, Anti-Slavery Collection, Boston Public Library.

84. Estlin to Samuel May Jr., April 26, 1849, Anti-Slavery Collection, Boston Public Library.

85. WWB to William Still, July 10, 1863, Box 9-G, Folder 17, Leon and Beatrice M. Gardiner Collection, Historical Society of Pennsylvania, Philadelphia.

86. "Memorial of the Late Mr. Estlin," *National Anti-Slavery Standard* 16 (Dec. 29, 1855): 4.

87. *National Anti-Slavery Standard* 16 (July 21, 1855): 2.

88. *Original Panoramic Views*, p. iii.

89. Advertisement (1847) for Banvard's panorama, Broadsides Collection, American Antiquarian Society, Worcester, MA.

90. *Boston Evening Transcript* (Feb. 6, 1847): 2.

91. Michael A. Chaney, *Fugitive Vision: Slave Image and Black Identity in Antebellum Narrative* (Bloomington: Indiana University Press, 2008), p. 120.

92. *Description of Banvard's Panorama of the Mississippi River* (Boston: Joseph Putnam, 1847), p. 32.

93. John Francis McDermott, *The Lost Panoramas of the Mississippi* (Chicago: University of Chicago Press, 1958), pp. 34–35.

94. "The Monster Panorama Manias," *Punch* (July 14, 1849): 14.

95. "Panorama of the Nile," *Colburn's New Monthly Magazine* 87 (Sept. 1849): 130.

96. Ann Fabian, *The Skull Collectors: Race, Science, and America's Unburied Dead* (Chicago: University of Chicago Press, 2010), p. 110.

97. Josiah C. Nott and George R. Gliddon, *Types of Mankind* (Philadelphia: Lippincott, Grambo and Company, 1854).

98. "Panorama of the Nile," *Illustrated London News* (July 28, 1849): 55.

99. "General Intelligence," *Christian Register* 29 (Nov. 2, 1850): 175.

100. *Original Panoramic Views*, pp. iii–iv.

101. Mary Estlin to Emma Weston, August 28, 1850, Anti-Slavery Collection, Boston Public Library.

102. Ibid.

103. Mary Estlin to Anne Weston, Oct. 4, 1850, Anti-Slavery Collection, Boston Public Library.

104. A reporter for the *London Inquirer*, apparently getting his information from WWB, estimated its length at 200 to 300 yards, a safer guess than advertisements claiming it as 800 yards. The *Inquirer* article was picked up and reprinted in Boston by the *Christian Register* 29 (Nov. 2, 1850): 175.

105. Advertisements for the panorama's exhibition ran on the front page of the *Newcastle Courant* in early November.

106. Garrison's, at the Schomburg Center for Research in Black Culture, New York Public Library; May's, at Kroch Library, Cornell University, Ithaca, NY.

107. On Banvard's free pass on the £48 duty, "Compliment to an American Artist," *Scientific American* 4 (Nov. 18, 1848): 66 (American Periodical Series Online).

108. William Craft, *Running a Thousand Miles for Freedom*, ed. R. J. M. Blackett (Baton Rouge: Louisiana State University Press, 1999), pp. 58–62.

109. "Slave-Hunters in Boston!!" *Liberator* 20 (Nov. 1, 1850): 174.

110. *Scottish Press* (Nov. 16, 1850): 3.

111. *Scottish Press* (Nov. 20, 1850).

112. *North Star* (Jan. 16, 1851).

113. *North British Mail and Glasgow Daily Advertiser* (Jan. 7, 1851): 1.

114. WWB to Phillips, Jan. 24, 1851, MS Am 1953 (327), Wendell Phillips Papers, Houghton Library, Harvard University.

115. Estlin to Anne Weston, Feb. 13, 1851, Anti-Slavery Collection, Boston Public Library.

116. Estlin to Miss Weston, Feb. 21, 1851, Anti-Slavery Collection, Boston Public Library.

117. *North British Mail and Glasgow Daily Advertiser* (Feb. 12, 1851): 4.

118. Deborah Anna Logan, ed., *The Collected Letters of Harriet Martineau*, vol. 3 (London: Pickering and Chatto, 2007), p. 189.

119. *Three Years in Europe*, pp. 200–2.

120. *Yorkshire Gazette* (March 29, 1851): 6.

121. One paper claimed that the restrictive admission price kept attendance down to 5,000 people, "who were almost exclusively of the aristocratic world": *Morning Advertiser* (June 23, 1851): 4.

122. "The Virginian Slave," *Punch* (June 7, 1851): 236.

123. William Farmer, "Fugitive Slaves at the Great Exhibition," *Liberator* 21 (July 18, 1851): 116.

124. *Three Years in Europe*, p. 211.

125. Ibid., p. 209.

126. William Wells Brown, *The American Fugitive in Europe* (Boston: John P. Jewett and Company, 1855), p. 195.

127. *Three Years in Europe*, pp. 216–19.

128. "Slavery in Massachusetts," *Liberator* 24 (July 21, 1854): 116.

129. The appeal was published in the liberal *Morning Advertiser* on June 20, 1851, with updates on June 23 and 24.

130. Anna Richardson to John Scoble, Aug. 4, 1851, MSS Brit Emp 518 C21/27, Rhodes House, Oxford University.

131. WWB to Phillips, Aug. 8, 1851, Ms Am 1953 (327), Wendell Phillips Papers, Houghton Library, Harvard University.

132. WWB to Phillips, Jan. 24, 1851, MS Am 1953 (327), Wendell Phillips Papers, Houghton Library, Harvard University.

133. WWB to Wendell Phillips, Jan. 28 and March 28, 1851, MS Am 1953 (327), Wendell Phillips Papers, Houghton Library, Harvard University.

134. WWB to Phillips, Jan. 24, 1851.

135. Clara Brown to Wendell Phillips, March 31, 1851, MS Am 1953 (327), Wendell Phillips Papers, Houghton Library, Harvard University.

136. Josephine Brown, *Biography of an American Bondman*, p. 73.

137. "Celebration of West Indian Negro Emancipation and Welcome to George Thompson, Esq., M.P.," *Liberator* 21 (Sept. 5, 1851): 141–42.

138. "Arrival of George Thompson in London," *Liberator* 21 (July 25, 1851): 118.

139. WWB to Wendell Phillips, Aug. 8, 1851.

140. *Three Years in Europe*, pp. 17–19.

141. Horace Greeley, *Glances at Europe* (New York: Dewitt and Davenport, 1851), p. 84.

142. WWB's term for the occasion: WBB to Wendell Phillips, Aug. 8, 1851.

143. *Three Years in Europe*, p. 238.

144. London *Morning Advertiser* (Aug. 2, 1851): 3.

145. On Duval, who arrived in England carrying endorsements from Garrison and May, see C. Peter Ripley, ed., *The Black Abolitionist Papers*, vol. 1, *The British Isles, 1830–1865* (Chapel Hill: University of North Carolina Press, 1985), pp. 256–57 (n. 2) and 268–69.

146. WWB reprinted it in *Three Years in Europe* (pp. 246–50) from its original appearance in "Celebration of West India Negro Emancipation, and Welcome to George Thompson, Esq., M.P.," *Liberator* 21 (Sept. 5, 1851): 141–42.

147. WWB to Phillips, Aug. 8, 1851.

148. WWB to Phillips, Sept. 1, 1852, MS Am 1953 (327), Wendell Phillips Papers, Houghton Library, Harvard University.

149. *Cincinnati Gazette* (April 26, 1855): 2.

150. William Farmer turned the wedding into a public affair with his open letter to Garrison: "Marriage of Mr. George Thompson's Eldest Daughter," *Liberator* 21 (Sept. 12, 1851): 146.

151. "Fugitive Slaves in England," London *Times* (July 4, 1851): 5.

152. "Don't Come to England," *Frederick Douglass' Paper* (July 25, 1851): 118.

153. "Letter from William Wells Brown," *Frederick Douglass' Paper* (Oct. 2, 1851); reprinted as Letter XIX in *Three Years in Europe*, pp. 227–35.

154. *Three Years in Europe*, p. 233.

155. Nathan Rosier to "Mr. Tappan," Jan. 29, 1852.

156. Evidence that Paulina did make the move appears in the 1860 federal census, which listed her as a resident in her grandmother's Ohio household and categorized her as a twelve-year-old "mulatto" born in Canada. I thank Reginald Pitts for informing me of this source and others documenting Henrietta's life story. 1860 Census, Ancestry.com.

157. The primary documentation is the correspondence between George Sturge and John Scoble: Sturge to Scoble, May 26, June 7, June 10, and June 12, 1852 (MSS Brit Emp 518 C113/28-31); Rhodes House, Oxford University. On Scoble's worsening relations with the BFASS leadership, see Howard Temperley, *British Antislavery, 1833–1870* (Columbia: University of South Carolina Press, 1972), p. 242.

158. WWB to Wendell Phillips, Aug. 8, 1851.

Chapter 7

1. "Visit of a Fugitive Slave to the Grave of Wilberforce," in Griffiths, ed., *Autographs for Freedom*, p. 70.

2. Among the survivors was a young first sergeant named Stephen Hempstead, who remained to raise a family locally but migrated in 1811 to St. Louis, where he became a prominent member, along with Dr. Young, of the First Presbyterian Church.

3. William Cooper Nell, "New England Anti-Slavery Convention," *North Star* 1 (June 16, 1848). It is impossible to say whether the term here was originally WWB's or Nell's or simply in general circulation, but WWB used it as his own in "Visit of a Fugitive Slave to the Grave of Wilberforce," p. 71.

4. Ibid.

5. Mayer, *All on Fire*, p. 155.

6. Ibid., p. 163.

7. "Visit of a Fugitive Slave," p. 76.

8. *Illustrated Edition of the Life and Escape of Wm. Wells Brown from American Slavery* (London: Charles Gilpin, 1851).

9. *Narrative of William W. Brown* (London: William Tegg and Co., 1853).

10. Quoted in James J. Barnes and Patience B. Barnes, "Reassessing the Reputation of Thomas Tegg, London Publisher, 1776–1846," *Book History* 3 (2000): 45.

11. Blackett, *Building an Antislavery Wall*, pp. 136–37.

12. *The Rising Son; or, The Antecedents and Advancement of the Colored Race* (Boston: A. G. Brown and Company, 1873), p. 439.

13. This description of the four-sided circular is based solely on inspection of photographic images. The location of the actual document is not currently known.

14. WWB to Wendell Phillips, Sept. 1, 1852.

15. George Thompson to William Lloyd Garrison, Sept. 24, 1852, Anti-Slavery Collection, Boston Public Library.

16. "This letter is rather out of its proper place here. I had mislaid the MS., and my distance from the printer prevented the matter being rectified. In another edition, the transposition can be effected": *Three Years in Europe*, p. 305.

17. "The American Fugitive in Europe," *Indiana Democrat*, quoted in *Liberator* 24 (Dec. 15, 1854): 198.

18. Thomas M. Gemmell to Oliver and Boyd, Oct. 9, 1852, Oliver and Boyd Archive, Acc. 5000/207, National Library of Scotland. A handful of charges for ads placed in Scottish newspapers in mid-October survive in the advertising portion of the archive (Acc. 5000/55). An earlier letter from Gemmell to the firm, dated June 11 and quite possibly relating to the printing of *Three Years in Europe*, is missing.

19. Thompson to Garrison, Sept. 24, 1852.

20. Inventory of Estlin family antislavery library prepared by Clare Taylor: Samuel J. May Anti-Slavery Collection (4601), Box 13, File 13.0735, Kroch Library, Cornell University, Ithaca, NY. That handsome, red-leather-bound copy is in the collections of Dr. Williams's Library, London.

21. Garrison's is in the Boston Public Library; Nell's is in the Beinecke Rare Book and Manuscript Library, Yale University. Nell's copy has the nameplate of Phillips inside its front cover and the bookplate of the James Weldon Johnson Memorial Collection of Negro Arts and Letters inside its back cover.

22. Farmer to William Lloyd Garrison, Nov. 1, 1852, Anti-Slavery Collection, Boston Public Library.

23. *Literary Gazette* (Oct. 2, 1852): 1056.

24. *London Examiner* (Oct. 30, 1852).

25. *Nottinghamshire Guardian* (Aug. 24, 1866): 5.

26. *Three Years in Europe*, pp. 108–09.

27. Christopher Kent, "The Whittington Club: A Bohemian Experiment in Middle Class Social Reform," *Victorian Studies* 18 (Sept. 1974): 31–55.

28. On Louis Blanc's letter, see *The Black Man*, p. 128.

29. *The American Fugitive*, p. 32.

30. John Bishop Estlin to William Lloyd Garrison, June 7 and 11, 1852, Anti-Slavery Collection, Boston Public Library.

31. WWB to Wendell Phillips, Sept. 1, 1852.

32. "Mr. Brown's Lecture," *Whittington Club and Metropolitan Athenaeum Gazette* (June 22, 1850): 171–72; *Three Years in Europe*, p. xxiv.

33. Douglass, *Life and Times of Frederick Douglass*, in *Frederick Douglass: Autobiographies*, ed. Henry Louis Gates Jr. (New York: Library of America, 1994), p. 814.

34. *The Black Man*, p. 266.

35. Kennell Jackson, "Introduction: Traveling While Black," in *Black Cultural Traffic: Crossroads in Global Performance and Popular Culture*, ed. Harry J. Elam Jr. and Kennell Jackson (Ann Arbor: University of Michigan Press, 2005), p. 3.

36. [Selim Aga], *Incidents Connected with the Life of Selim Aga, a Native of Central Africa* (Aberdeen, Scotland: W. Bennett, 1846).

37. T. S. Eliot, *The Sacred Wood: Essays on Poetry and Criticism* (New York: Alfred Knopf, 1921), p. 114.

38. Selim Aga, *Africa Considered in Its Social and Political Condition, with a Plan for the Amelioration of Its Inhabitants* (London, 1853), p. 8.

39. James McCarthy, *Selim Aga: A Slave's Odyssey* (Edinburgh: Luath Press, 2006), p. 120.

40. Aga, *Africa Considered*, p. 12.

41. *The Black Man*, pp. 128–29.

42. "Letter from Prof. Wm. G. Allen," *Liberator* 23 (July 22, 1853): 116.

43. *Three Years in Europe*, p. 304.

44. " A True Story of Slavery," *Anti-Slavery Advocate* (Dec. 1852): 23.

45. *Newcastle Guardian* (Nov. 13, 1852): 1; *Bristol Mercury* (Dec. 25, 1852); *Hampshire Independent* (Feb. 5, 1853); *American Baptist* (March 25, 1853): 45.

46. *Anti-Slavery Advocate* (March 1853): 45.

47. *Hampshire Telegraph* (Feb. 26, 1853).

48. *Anti-Slavery Advocate* (June 1853): 68–69.

49. "Letter from William W. Brown," *Liberator* 23 (June 3, 1853): 97.

50. "Letter from William W. Brown," *Frederick Douglass' Paper* 6 (June 10, 1853).

51. "Extract of a Letter from William Wells Brown," *Liberator* 23 (Nov. 4, 1853): 175.

52. On WWB's borrowings, see Geoffrey Sanborn, "'People Will Pay to Hear the Drama': Plagiarism in *Clotel*," *African American Review* 45, nos. 1–2 (Spring-Summer 2012): 65–82; Robert S. Levine, ed., *Clotel; or, The President's Daughter*, 2nd ed. (Boston: Bedford/St. Martin's, 2011), pp. 6–8 and passim; Dawn Coleman, *Preaching and the Rise of the American Novel* (Columbus: Ohio State University Press, 2013), pp. 174–96; Lara Langer Cohen, "Notes from the State of Saint Domingue: The Practice of Citation in *Clotel*," in *Early African American Print Culture*, ed. Lara Langer Cohen and Jordan Alexander Stein (Philadelphia: University of Pennsylvania Press, 2012), pp. 166–77; Christopher Stampone, "'The abolition of slavery would be brought on by the amalgamation of races': Textual Sources and Synecdochic Representation in William Wells Brown's *Clotel*" (unpublished essay).

53. They were, we now know, more than rumors; six or seven children were born to Jefferson and Sally Hemings. See Annette Gordon-Reed, *The Hemingses of Monticello: An American Family* (New York: W. W. Norton and Company, 2008).

54. *Clotel*, p. 183.

55. Ibid., p. 55.

56. Alvan Stewart, *A Legal Argument before the Supreme Court of the State of New Jersey* (New York: Finch and Weed, 1845), p. 9.

57. *Clotel*, p. 244.

58. Geoffrey Sanborn, "The Plagiarist's Craft: Fugitivity and Theatricality in *Running a Thousand Miles for Freedom*," *PMLA* 128, no. 4 (Oct. 2013): 907–22.

59. Notices of New Publications," *Liberator* 22 (Nov. 19, 1852): 186.

60. "Letter from Prof. Wm. G. Allen," *Liberator* 23 (July 22, 1853): 116.

61. Quoted in Bernth Lindfors, *Ira Aldridge: The Early Years, 1807–1833* (Rochester, NY: University of Rochester Press, 2011), p. 93.

62. Lindfors, *Ira Aldridge: The Vagabond Years, 1833–1852* (Rochester, NY: University of Rochester Press, 2011), p. 176.

63. "Othellos in New Orleans," *Punch* (March 31, 1849): 133.

64. Josephine Brown to Samuel May Jr., April 27, 185[4], Anti-Slavery Collection, Boston Public Library.

65. Jane Martin, *Women and the Politics of Schooling in Victorian and Edwardian England* (Leicester, UK: Leicester University Press, 1999), p. 57.

66. William Farmer, "Education of Colored Refugees in England," *Liberator* 23 (Jan. 14, 1853): 7.

67. *Educational Paper of the Home and Colonial Society* 2 (April 1859): 41; Home and Colonial Society Reports 814, British and Foreign School Society Archives at Brunel University Archives, Uxbridge, UK.

68. WWB to Mary Estlin, July 30, 1853, Anti-Slavery Collection, Boston Public Library.

69. Parker Pillsbury to Phillips, June 1, 1854, Ms Am 1953 (528), Wendell Phillips Papers, Houghton Library, Harvard University.

70. Mrs. Reynolds to Mary Estlin, n.d.

71. Clara Brown to Miss Jones, March 27, 1854.

72. "From Our Brooklyn Correspondent," *Frederick Douglass' Paper* 7 (Feb. 10, 1854).

73. "Rev. J. W. C. Pennington, D.D.," *Anti-Slavery Reporter* (Aug. 1, 1851): 140.

74. WWB mentioned the negotiations at least three times in fall 1853—once in the introduction to *Clotel*, pp. 51–52, and twice in lectures: *Kentish Mercury* (Sept. 3, 1853): 4; and "Slavery in the United States," *Hereford Times* (Dec. 17, 1853): 6.

75. WWB had lectured extensively in Kent in October 1853 and might well have consulted with Hoare about his ransom: *Anti-Slavery Advocate* (Oct. 1853): 104.

76. MSS Brit Emp 518 C35/110, British and Foreign Anti-Slavery Society Collection, Rhodes House, Oxford University.

77. Broadside, Central Library, South Shields, UK.

78. On likely date of arrival, see "William Wells Brown," *Liberator* 24 (May 26, 1854): 82.

79. WWB took physical possession of the legal documents relating to his purchase following his return to Boston and authorized Josephine to print them: *Biography of an American Bondman*, pp. 96–98.

80. "Letter from W. W. Brown," *Liberator* 24 (Sept. 22, 1854): 151.

81. "Wm. Wells Brown and J. B. Gough," *Pennsylvania Freeman* 11 (April 20, 1854).

82. William Lloyd Garrison to Samuel May, Sept. 11, 1854, Anti-Slavery Collection, Boston Public Library.

83. *Report of the Proceedings of the Anti-Slavery Conference and Public Meeting, Held at Manchester, on the 1st of August, 1854* (London: William Tweedie, 1854), p. 35.

84. On Thompson's remark, see *Report of the Proceedings*, p. 15.

85. *The American Fugitive in Europe*, pp. 309–10.

86. Ibid., p. 303.

87. "Celebration of W. I. Emancipation at Manchester, England," *Liberator* 24 (Sept. 1, 1854): 138.

Chapter 8

1. *The American Fugitive in Europe*, p. 312.

2. *National Anti-Slavery Standard* 15 (Nov. 4, 1854): 1, in BAP, Reel 9.

3. *Frederick Douglass' Paper* 7 (Oct. 6, 1854): 2.

4. *Syracuse Chronicle*, quoted in *Liberator* 24 (Oct. 13, 1854): 161.

5. William Nell, "Anti-Slavery Meetings at Syracuse and Rochester," *Liberator* 24 (Oct. 27, 1854): 171.

6. "'Jerry' Rescue Celebration," *Syracuse Journal* (Oct. 2, 1854), in BAP, Reel 8.

7. William J. Watson, "Frederick Douglass in Boston," *Frederick Douglass' Paper* 6 (Aug. 12, 1853): 3.

8. William Nell to Amy Post, Oct. 17, 1854, Isaac and Amy Post Family Papers, University of Rochester.

9. Brenda Stevenson, ed., *The Journals of Charlotte Forten Grimké* (New York: Oxford University Press, 1988), pp. 103, 111.

10. *Liberator* 24 (Oct. 13, 1854): 163.

11. *Boston Directory, 1856* (Boston: George Adams, 1856).

12. Nell to Post, Oct. 17, 1854.

13. [William] N[ell], "The Reception at the Meionaon," *Liberator* 24 (Oct. 20, 1854): 166.

14. William Lloyd Garrison to Helen Garrison, Oct. 19, 1854, Anti-Slavery Collection, Boston Public Library.

15. W[illiam] S[till], "Welcome to William Wells Brown," *National Anti-Slavery Standard* 15 (Oct. 28, 1854): 2–3.

16. *National Anti-Slavery Standard* 15 (Nov. 4, 1854): 1.

17. *The American Fugitive in Europe*, pp. 310–11.

18. *Liberator* 24 (Nov. 10, 1854): 179.

19. *The American Fugitive in Europe*, p. 40.

20. Ibid., p. 315.

21. *Liberator* 25 (Jan. 5, 1855): 3.

22. *Pathfinder Railway Guide for the New England States* (Boston: George K. Snow, 1854), Railway Guides Collection, American Antiquarian Society, Worcester, MA.

23. *New York Tribune* (Dec. 12, 1854): 6.

24. *Norton's Literary Gazette* n.s. 1 (Dec. 15, 1854): 625.

25. "Wm. Wells Brown," *Providence Daily Tribune* (Dec. 14, 1854): 2.

26. "Sketches of Places and People Abroad," *Provincial Freeman* (Jan. 27, 1855), in BAP, Reel 9.

27. Quoted in *Liberator* 25 (Jan. 12, 1855): 5.

28. "William Wells Brown at Philadelphia," *Liberator* 25 (Jan. 26, 1855): 14.

29. Ibid.

30. William Wells Brown, *St. Domingo: Its Revolutions and Its Patriots* (Boston: Bela Marsh, 1855), p. 37.

31. Lillie Buffum Chace Wyman and Arthur Crawford Wyman, eds., *Elizabeth Buffum Chace, 1806–1899: Her Life and Its Environment*, 2 vols. (Boston: W. B. Clarke Co., 1914), vol. 1, p. 142.

32. Ibid., p. 143.

33. MASS account ledger, Ms. B.1.23, pp. 4–5, Anti-Slavery Collection, Boston Public Library.

34. Nehemiah Adams, *A South-Side View of Slavery* (Boston: T. R. Mavin and B. B. Mussey and Co., 1854), pp. 209–10.

35. "Anniversary Meeting of the New York City Anti-Slavery Society," *New York Herald* (May 9, 1856): 1.

36. W. C. N., "Presentation Meeting," *Liberator* 25 (Feb. 16, 1855): 27.

37. WWB, "Letter from the West," *National Anti-Slavery Standard* 15 (March 31, 1855): 3.

38. "The Aliened American," *Aliened American* 1 (April 9, 1853): 2.

39. "Letter from W. W. Brown," *National Anti-Slavery Standard* 15 (April 21, 1855): 3.

40. Ibid.

41. WWB, "W. W. Brown in Ohio": 2.

42. "Anti-Slavery Convention at Greenwood Hall," *Cincinnati Gazette* (April 26, 1855): 2.

43. "W. W. Brown in Ohio—The Underground Railroad," *National Anti-Slavery Standard* 15 (April 7, 1855): 2.

44. *Provincial Freeman*, quoted in *National Anti-Slavery Standard* 16 (May 26, 1855): 3.

45. "William Wells Brown," *Frederick Douglass' Paper* 8 (March 2, 1855): 2.

46. "To Frederick Douglass," *National Anti-Slavery Standard* 15 (March 10, 1855): 3.

47. William Nell to Amy Post, Nov. 30, 1855, Post Family Papers, University of Rochester.

48. Ward, "The Modern Negro—No. II," *Frederick Douglass' Paper* 8 (April 13, 1855): 2–3.

49. *National Anti-Slavery Standard* 16 (Aug. 11. 1855): 2.

50. "Letter from Wm. W. Brown," *Liberator* 25 (Aug. 17, 1855): 132.

51. William Hosley, *Colt: The Making of an American Legend* (Amherst: University of Massachusetts Press, 1996), p. 96.

52. Robert C. Williams, *Horace Greeley: Champion of American Freedom* (New York: New York University Press, 2006), pp. 180–81.

53. Nell to Amy Post, Aug. 12, 1855, Isaac and Amy Post Family Papers, University of Rochester.

54. *Journals of Charlotte Forten Grimké*, p. 138.

55. "William Wells Brown," *Liberator* 25 (Aug. 24, 1855): 134.

56. *Liberator* 25 (Nov. 16, 1855): 183.

57. William Nell to Amy Post, Nov. 11 and 30, 1855, Isaac and Amy Post Family Papers, University of Rochester.

58. Josephine Brown, *Biography of an American Bondman*, p. 4.

59. Farrison, *William Wells Brown*, p. 272, n. 17.

60. MASS account ledger, Ms. B.1.23, pp. 4–5, Anti-Slavery Collection, Boston Public Library.

61. Nell to Amy Post, Dec. 25, 1855, Isaac and Amy Post Family Papers, University of Rochester.

62. "The Bondman and His Daughter," *Liberator* 26 (Jan. 25, 1856): 14.

63. Ibid.

64. Farrison, *William Wells Brown*, p, 275.

65. Nell to Post, Aug. 23 and 26, 1857, Isaac and Amy Post Family Papers, University of Rochester.

66. *Lowell Daily Citizen and News* (Sept. 30, 1856): 2; *Trenton State Gazette* (Sept. 29, 1856): 2. Both in America's Historical Newspapers.

67. William S. McFeely, *Frederick Douglass* (New York: W. W. Norton, 1991), p. 220.

68. Reginald Pitts directed my attention to this letter: Rosetta Douglass to Frederick Douglass, Sept. 24, 1862, Box 3, Reel 1, General Correspondence, 1841–1912, Frederick Douglass Papers, Library of Congress.

69. The unpublished play apparently had various titles. A reviewer who had seen Brown perform it in Connecticut called it *The Doughface Baked* (*National Anti-Slavery Standard* 16 (April 19, 1856): 3); Charlotte Forten recorded it in her diary as *The Kidnapper Kidnapped* (*Journals of Charlotte Forten Grimké*, p. 164).

70. This synopsis draws on three reviews: "Wm. Wells Brown," *Liberator* 26 (Aug. 1, 1856): 124; "Dramatic Readings," *National Anti-Slavery Standard* 17 (May 9, 1857): 3; "Mr. Brown's Drama," *National Anti-Slavery Standard* 16 (May 10, 1856): 2.

71. "Dramatic Readings": 3.

72. *Liberator* 26 (Feb. 8, 1856): 22.

73. Newspapers across the region advertised her readings—as, for instance, the *Liberator* 26 (Feb. 15, 1856): 27.

74. "Don't Fail to Hear It!" *Liberator* 26 (May 23, 1856): 82.

75. *Liberator* 26 (June 13, 1856): 95.

76. D. A. W., *Liberator* 26 (June 13, 1856): 95.

77. "Anti-Slavery Dramas," *Liberator* 26 (Nov. 21, 1856): 186.

78. Ibid.

79. WWB to Hill, Dec. 26, 1856, File 7/1/5, Oberlin College Library, Oberlin, OH, BAP, Reel 10.

80. William Cooper Nell to Jeremiah Sanderson, Dec. 17, 1856, BANC MSS 75/70, Box 1, Jeremiah Sanderson Papers, Bancroft Library, University of California, Berkeley.

81. *General Catalog of Oberlin College, 1833–1908* (Oberlin, OH, 1909), pp. 508–11. Fanny Jackson's original file has apparently gone missing: Alumni Records, RG28/2 Box 208, Student File of Fanny M. Jackson, Oberlin College Archives, Oberlin College Library.

82. WWB to WLG, April 12, 1858, Garrison Family Papers, Sophia Smith Collection, Smith College Library, Northampton, MA.

83. William Wells Brown, *The Escape; or, A Leap for Freedom* (Boston: R. F. Wallcut, 1858), pp. 27–28.

84. Ibid., p. 24.

85. Quoted in Harry J. Elam, Jr., "The Black Performer and the Performance of Blackness," in *African American Performance and Theater History: A Critical Reader*, ed. Harry J. Elam Jr. and David Krasner (New York: Oxford University Press, 2001), p. 294.

86. *The Escape*, Act 5, Scene 3, p. 40.

87. Quoted in "The Minstrel Show," *The American Stage: Writing on Theater from Washington Irving to Tony Kushner*, ed. Laurence Senelick (New York: Library of America, 2010), p. 84.

88. *Providence Journal* (May 26, 1857): 2.

89. "The Minstrel Show," pp. 88–89.

90. John Ernest, ed., *The Escape; or, A Leap for Freedom* (Knoxville: University of Tennessee Press, 2001), p. xlii.

91. "A Narrow Escape," *Liberator* 28 (Feb. 19, 1858): 30.

92. W. H. F., "Wendell Phillips, C. C. Burleigh and Wm. W. Brown in Cortland, N. Y.," *Liberator* 28 (March 5, 1858): 39.

93. Nell to Sanderson, July 1, 1857, BANC MSS 75/70, Box 1, Jeremiah Sanderson Papers, Bancroft Library, University of California, Berkeley.

94. Nell to Sanderson, Oct. 1, 1857, BANC MSS 75/70, Box 1, Jeremiah Sanderson Papers, Bancroft Library, University of California, Berkeley.

95. WWB to Marius Robinson, Nov. 29, 1857, Schomburg Center for Research in Black Culture, New York Public Library.

96. *The Escape*, p. 3.

97. The most likely owner was Delia D. Cook, the first name listed on the page. The 1870 federal census lists both her and her sister Nettie as single women living in

Northampton (Delia as a French teacher); the 1850 census lists David and Mary Hunt as born in Northampton in the late 1840s. Another of the girls, Caroline Hopkins, died in Northampton in 1864. The copy is in the Harris Collection of American Poetry and Plays, John Hay Library, Brown University, Providence, RI.

98. "Letter from West Randolph," *Liberator* 30 (Aug. 31, 1860): 137.

99. Pauline Hopkins said she was "noted for her beauty" in "Famous Men of the Negro Race: William Wells Brown," *Colored American Magazine* 2 (Jan. 1901): 235.

100. *Liberator* 19 (April 27, 1849): 67.

101. WWB to Garrison, April 12 and 17, 1858, Sophia Smith Collection, Garrison Family Papers, Series III, Box 111, Folder 25, Smith College Library, Northampton, MA.

102. *The Black Man*, p. 245.

103. "New England Convention of Colored Citizens," *Liberator* 29 (Aug. 26, 1859): 134.

104. "New England Colored Citizens' Convention," *Liberator* 29 (Aug. 19, 1859): 132.

105. W[illiam] C[ooper] N[ell], " Colored People in Boston," *Liberator* 29 (June 17, 1859): 94.

106. "Speech of Wm. Wells Brown," *Liberator* 30 (Aug. 17, 1860): 130.

107. "Affairs in St. Louis," *Weekly Anglo-African* 2 (March 2, 1861): 2–3.

108. *Clotel*, p. 222; *Miralda; or, The Beautiful Quadroon*, *Weekly Anglo-African* 2 (Jan. 19, 1861): 1 [chapter 18].

109. Quoted in Opinionator blog of Adam Goodheart, "The South Rises Again—and Again and Again," *New York Times* (Jan. 27, 2011), http://opinionator.blogs .nytimes.com/2011/01/27/the-south-rises-again-and-again-and-again/#more -78437.

110. "President Lincoln's Inaugural," *Weekly Anglo-African* 2 (March 16, 1861).

111. "Meeting in Boston," *Weekly Anglo-African* 2 (May 4, 1861).

112. Massachusetts Legislature. Senate Documents, 1860, Senate No. 71 (Feb. 25, 1860).

Chapter 9

1. "New England Anti-Slavery Convention," *Liberator* 34 (June 3, 1864): 90.

2. John McKivigan, *Forgotten Firebrand: James Redpath and the Making of Nineteenth-Century America* (Ithaca, NY: Cornell University Press, 2008), pp. 71–72.

3. *Pine and Palm* 1 (May 18, 1861): 2.

4. "Lecture on Hayti," *Pine and Palm* 1 (Aug. 31, 1861): 4.

5. Reports differ: *Cambridge Chronicle* 16 (July 27, 1861): 3; *Liberator* 31 (Aug. 2, 1861): 123.

6. Martin to Gerrit Smith, July 2, 1861, Gerrit Smith Papers, Special Collections Research Center, Syracuse University Libraries, Syracuse, NY. In BAP, Reel 13.

7. Clotelle Brown was born May 8, 1862.

8. *Pine and Palm* 1 (July 13, 1861): 2.

9. They appeared under the series title "Celebrated Colored Americans": *Pine and Palm* 1 (Aug. 17, 1861): 2; and (Aug. 24, 1861): 2.

10. *New York Tribune* (July 22, 1861): 4; "The Schooner 'S. J. Waring,'" *Harper's Weekly* 1 (Aug. 3, 1861): 485.

11. "Letter to the President from Gerrit Smith," *New York Tribune* (Sept. 9, 1861): 6.

12. *Pine and Palm* 1 (Aug. 24, 1861): 2.

13. "The Colored People of Canada, I," *Pine and Palm* 1 (Sept. 7, 1861): 2.

14. "The Colored People of Canada, II," *Pine and Palm* 1 (Sept. 14, 1861): 2.

15. "The Colored People of Canada, III," *Pine and Palm* 1 (Sept. 21, 1861): 2.

16. "The Colored People of Canada, VII," *Pine and Palm* 1 (Dec. 7, 1861): 2.

17. "The Colored People of Canada, V," *Pine and Palm* 1 (Oct. 19, 1861): 2.

18. "The Colored People of Canada, IV," *Pine and Palm* 1 (Sept. 28, 1861): 2.

19. Parker T. Smith, "Letter from Canada," *Christian Recorder* 1 (Oct. 26, 1861): 166. Smith also challenged the leadership of other prominent African Americans. In 1863, he publicly called on Frederick Douglass, who already had two sons in the Union Army, to enlist at the head of a black regiment: "Letter from Frederick Douglass," *Anglo-African* 2 (Aug. 1, 1863): 1.

20. "The Colored People of Canada, IV": 2.

21. "Haytian Emigration," *Weekly Anglo-African* [n.s.] 1 (Sept. 28, 1861): 2.

22. *The Rising Son*, p. 540.

23. "Haytian Emigration in Boston," *Weekly Anglo-African* [n.s.] 1 (Nov. 16, 1861): 1.

24. *Pine and Palm* 1 (Dec. 14, 1861): 3.

25. "The Colored People of Boston on Colonization," *Liberator* 32 (May 2, 1862): 71; *The Rising Son*, p. 238.

26. "Speech of Wm. Wells Brown," *Liberator* 32 (May 16, 1862): 77.

27. "Business Meetings," *Liberator* 32 (May 16, 1862): 79.

28. Nell to Amy Post, June 10, 1862, Isaac and Amy Post Family Papers, University of Rochester.

29. He was so favorably received in Poughkeepsie in March 1862 that he stayed a week to give lectures on four nights and perform a play the local newspaper called "Life at the South" (most likely, the play he had premiered in August 1860): "Tour of William Wells Brown," *Liberator* 32 (April 4, 1862): 54.

30. "Celebration of the First of August," *Liberator* 32 (Aug. 15, 1862): 131.

31. On Quincy, see *National Anti-Slavery Standard* 15 (April 7, 1855): 2.

32. "Speech of William Wells Brown," *National Anti-Slavery Standard* 21 (May 26, 1860): 4.

33. Nell also named them in an 1855 advertising circular promoting the book: Broadsides Collection, American Antiquarian Society.

34. George M. Fredrickson, *The Black Image in the White Mind: The Debate on Afro-American Character and Destiny, 1817–1914* (Middletown, CT: Wesleyan University Press, 1987), p. 75.

35. The long-forgotten cache of daguerreotypes was discovered in 1976 in the attic of Harvard's Peabody Museum of Archaeology and Ethnology.

36. Robert W. Gibbes to Samuel Morton, March 31, 1850, Samuel George Morton Collection, Box 4, Folder 25, Historical Society of Pennsylvania, Philadelphia.

37. "Speech of William Wells Brown," *Liberator* 32 (June 13, 1862): 96.

38. Smith jotted that sum on the back of the letter: WWB to Smith, Sept. 4, 1862, Gerrit Smith Papers, Box 5, Special Collections Research Center, Syracuse University.

39. Ted Genoways, *Walt Whitman and the Civil War: America's Poet During the Lost Years of 1860–1862* (Berkeley: University of California Press, 2009), pp. 28–29.

40. WWB to William Still, Feb. 2, 1865, Box 9-G, Folder 17, Leon and Beatrice M. Gardiner Collection, Historical Society of Pennsylvania, Philadelphia.

41. *Liberator* 32 (Nov. 28, 1862): 191.

42. [Brooklyn] *Circular* 11 (Nov. 27, 1862): 167.

43. *Liberator* 32 (Nov. 28, 1862): 191.

44. "Emancipation Proclaimed," *Douglass' Monthly* 5 (October 1862): 721.

45. "The President's Proclamation," *Atlantic Monthly* 10 (Nov. 1862): 639.

46. "Mrs. Francis E. Watkins Harper on the War and the President's Colonization Scheme," *Christian Recorder* 2 (Sept. 27, 1862): 153. In BAP, Reel 14.

47. Internal evidence suggests he worked on the opening essay for *The Black Man* virtually until publication. He appropriated portions of the long paragraph about Macaulay (pp. 35–36) from Edward Wilmot Blyden's *Liberia's Offerings,* which was published in New York in or around November 1862. For the slur on Lincoln, see p. 34.

48. Romare Bearden and Harry Henderson, *A History of African-American Artists: From 1792 to the Present* (New York: Pantheon, 1993), pp. 41, 43; *The Black Man,* pp. 214–17.

49. *Douglass' Monthly* 5 (Jan. 1863): 771.

50. *The Black Man,* p. 6.

51. *Douglass' Monthly* 5 (Jan. 1863): 771.

52. "'The Black Man' and Its Critics," *Anglo-African* 3 (Aug. 8, 1863): 1.

53. "The Black Man," *Christian Recorder* 2 (Dec. 27, 1862): 206.

54. Mayer, *All on Fire*, pp. 545–46.

55. "Emancipation Celebration at Tremont Temple," *Boston Herald* (Jan. 2, 1863): 4; "Celebration of New Year's Day," *Boston Daily Advertiser* (Jan. 2, 1863): 1.

56. "Celebration of New Year's Day": 1.

57. William Wells Brown, *The Negro in the American Rebellion* (Boston: Lee and Shepard, 1867), pp. 118–19.

58. "City Items," *New York Tribune* (Jan. 3, 1863): 2.

59. In Iver Bernstein, *The New York City Draft Riots: Their Significance for American Society and Politics in the Age of the Civil War* (New York: Oxford University Press, 1990), p. 25.

60. The term is WWB's: *The Negro in the American Rebellion*, p. 111.

61. "Great Emancipation Demonstration," *New York Tribune* (Jan. 7, 1863): 3.

62. *The Black Man*, p. 150.

63. "Opinions of the Press," *The Black Man*, 2nd ed. (New York: Thomas Hamilton; Boston: R. F. Wallcut, 1863), p. 312.

64. "Have We a General Among Us?" *Harper's Weekly* 7 (Jan. 17, 1863): 34.

65. *The Negro in the American Rebellion*, p. 62.

66. *Liberator* 33 (Feb. 20, 1863): 31; *National Anti-Slavery Standard* 23 (Feb. 21, 1863): 3.

67. *Boston Daily Advertiser* (Jan. 28, 1863): 1.

68. "Annual Meeting of the Massachusetts Anti-Slavery Society," *Liberator* 33 (Feb. 6, 1863): 22.

69. "War Meeting of Colored Citizens," *New Bedford Mercury* (Feb. 19, 1863): 2.

70. James Henry Gooding, *On the Altar of Freedom: A Black Soldier's Civil War Letters from the Front*, ed. Virginia M. Adams (Amherst: University of Massachusetts Press, 1991), p. xxviii.

71. *The Negro in the American Rebellion*, p. 127.

72. On Carney's early life, see Grover, *Fugitive's Gibraltar*, pp. 253–54.

73. *Christian Recorder* 3 (March 28, 1863): 50.

74. Luis F. Emilio, *A Brave Black Regiment: History of the Fifty-Fourth Regiment of Massachusetts Volunteer Infantry, 1863–1865* (1894; New York: Arno, 1969), p. 93.

75. *The Negro in the American Rebellion*, p. 209.

76. On Sim's grand reception at Tremont Temple, see "The Sims Meeting," *Liberator* 33 (May 15, 1863): 78.

77. "Fifty-Fourth Massachusetts Regiment," *The Negro in the American Rebellion*, pp. 85–91.

78. "New England Anti-Slavery Convention," *Liberator* 33 (June 5, 1863): 60.

79. *The Negro in the American Rebellion*, pp. 202–3.

80. "West India Emancipation Anniversary," *Liberator* 33 (Aug. 7, 1863): 126.

81. On the harrowing escape of William Powell and his family from the rooftop, see "Colored Sailors' Home," *Liberator* 33 (July 24, 1863): 118.

82. Bernstein, *New York City Draft Riots*, p. 27.

83. Thomas H. O'Connor, *Civil War Boston: Home Front and Battlefield* (Boston: Northeastern University Press, 1997), p. 140.

84. "Look on this Picture, and on That," *Boston Daily Advertiser* (Aug. 4, 1863): 2. The title, a loose borrowing from *Hamlet*, was one of WWB's favorite lines from Shakespeare.

85. As, for instance, at the Emancipation Day picnic in 1863: "West India Emancipation Anniversary": 126.

86. WWB to Still, July 10, 1863.

87. *American Publishers' Circular* 2 (Nov. 16, 1863): 47.

88. Redpath to Alcott, Jan. 23, 1864, Louisa May Alcott Papers, University of Virginia Library, Charlottesville.

89. "New England Anti-Slavery Convention," *Liberator* 34 (June 3, 1864): 89.

90. "Presentation to Governor Andrew," *Liberator* 34 (July 1, 1864): 107.

91. "Mass Meeting in Boston," *Anglo-African* 4 (Aug. 13, 1864): 2.

92. *National Anti-Slavery Standard* 24 (June 13, 1863): 2.

93. *Liberator* 34 (Aug. 19, 1864): 135.

94. "Letter from Wm. W. Brown," *Liberator* 25 (Aug. 17, 1855): 132.

95. WWB to Parker Pillsbury, Aug. 24, 1864, MS Am 1953 (1001), Folder 7, Wendell Phillips Papers, Houghton Library, Harvard University.

96. William Cheek and Aimee Lee Cheek, *John Mercer Langston and the Fight for Black Freedom, 1829–65* (Urbana: University of Illinois Press, 1989), p. 428.

97. [Letter of William Howard Day], "National Convention of Colored Men," *Anglo-African* 4 (Oct. 8, 1864): 3.

98. *Proceedings of the National Convention of Colored Men, held in the City of Syracuse, N.Y.* (Boston: Rand and Avery, 1864): 12.

99. "An Anglo-African History of the Present War," *Anglo-African* 4 (April 1, 1865): 4.

100. *Liberator* 34 (Dec. 9, 1864): 198.

101. "The Destruction of Slavery in Kentucky," *Louisville Journal*, quoted in *Liberator* 34 (Dec. 16, 1864): 201.

102. "Massachusetts Anti-Slavery Society: Thursday Afternoon, Friday," *Liberator* 35 (Feb. 3, 1865): 18–19.

103. "Affairs about Boston," *Anglo-African* 4 (March 11, 1865): 2.

104. Eric Foner, *The Fiery Trial: Abraham Lincoln and American Slavery* (New York: W. W. Norton, 2010), pp. 313–17.

105. *Liberator* 35 (Jan. 20, 1865): 11.

106. *Boston Daily Advertiser* (April 24, 1865): 1, in America's Historical Newspapers.

107. E. Q., "The End of the Twenty-Fifth Volume," *Liberator* 35 (May 12, 1865): 74.

108. *Liberator* 35 (December 29, 1865): 208.

109. *Liberator* Subscription Book, Anti-Slavery Collection, Boston Public Library.

110. "New England A.S. Convention," *Liberator* 35 (June 16, 1865): 94.

111. "Anti-Slavery Celebration at Framingham," *Liberator* 35 (July 14, 1865): 112.

112. Emilio, *A Brave Black Regiment*, p. 317.

113. "The Return of the 54th Mass. Regt," *Anglo-African* 5 (Sept. 16, 1865): 3.

114. Emilio, *A Brave Black Regiment*, p. 319.

115. Nelson Primus to his mother, July 10, 1865, Box 2, Primus Family Papers, Connecticut Historical Society, Hartford.

116. Primus to his mother, Sept. 21, 1865, Box 2, Primus Family Papers, Connecticut Historical Society, Hartford.

Chapter 10

1. For an eloquent, comprehensive analysis of this phenomenon, see Heather Andrea Williams, *Help Me to Find My People: The African American Search for Family Lost in Slavery* (Chapel Hill: University of North Carolina Press, 2012).

2. *Anglo-African* 4 (July 15, 1865): 3.

3. Williams, *Help Me to Find My People*, p. 157.

4. *Liberator* 34 (Dec. 2, 1864): 195.

5. McFeely, *Frederick Douglass*, pp. 235–36.

6. Garnet to Gerrit Smith, Oct. 23, 1865, Box 20, Gerrit Smith Papers, Special Collections Research Center, Syracuse University.

7. Jean Fagan Yellin, *Harriet Jacobs: A Life* (Chapel Hill: University of North Carolina Press, 2004), pp. 210–11.

8. "Ellen Craft and Her Mother," *Liberator* 35 (Aug. 4, 1865): 122.

9. WWB to Still, July 10, 1863.

10. "Affairs about Boston," *Anglo-African* 4 (March 11, 1865): 2.

11. *Liberator* 35 (March 3, 1865): 35.

12. *Boston Herald* (Dec. 1, 1865): 1.

13. "My American Tour," supplement to *Manchester Weekly Times* (May 26, 1866): 162.

14. William Lloyd Garrison Jr. to Ellen Wright, Aug. 6 and Sept. 7, 1864, Garrison Family Papers, Sophia Smith Collection, Smith College Library, Northampton, MA.

15. Death Records, Suffolk County, Massachusetts Archives, Columbia Point, Boston.

16. "The National Convention of Colored Men," *Syracuse State League* (Oct. 15, 1864).

17. WWB to Still, Feb. 2, 1865, Historical Society of Pennsylvania, Philadelphia.

18. Whittington B. Johnson, *Black Savannah, 1788–1864* (Fayetteville: University of Arkansas Press, 1996), p. 128.

19. On the reuse of the printed sheets and binding, see Phillip Lapsansky, "Afro-Americana," in *The Annual Report of the Library Company of Philadelphia for the Year 1989* (Philadelphia, 1990), p. 25.

20. This copy is in the collections of the Library Company of Philadelphia. Its original owner, Reverend J. Moultrie, later became a Charleston-area salesman of William Still's *The Underground Railroad*: Still to Moultrie, June 30 and July 7, 1873, William Still Letterbook, 1873–74, AmS 47, Leon and Beatrice M. Gardiner Collection, Historical Society of Pennsylvania, Philadelphia.

21. South Caroliniana Library, University of South Carolina–Columbia, has one copy with the stamp; a second is in private hands.

22. "Anti-Slavery Celebration at Framingham, July 4th, 1865," *Liberator* 35 (July 14, 1865): 112.

23. "Monument to President Lincoln," *Anglo-African* 4 (May 13, 1865): 1.

24. Kate Culkin, *Harriet Hosmer: A Cultural Biography* (Amherst: University of Massachusetts Press, 2010), pp. 101–9.

25. Quoted in Kirk Savage, *Standing Soldiers, Kneeling Slaves* (Princeton, NJ: Princeton University Press, 1997), p. 117.

26. "Letter from Washington," *National Anti-Slavery Standard* 27 (March 2, 1867): 3.

27. *National Anti-Slavery Standard* 28 (June 15, 1867): 3.

28. *National Anti-Slavery Standard* 27 (March 23, 1867): 3.

29. "The Lincoln Monument," *National Anti-Slavery Standard* 27 (May 4, 1867): 2.

30. "The Freedmen's National Monument," *Christian Recorder* 7 (May 4, 1867): 70.

31. WWB to Smith, Nov. 6, 1867, Box 5 ("B"), Gerrit Smith Papers, Special Collections Research Center, Syracuse University.

32. *Commonwealth* 5 (May 4, 1867): 2.

33. "Speech of William Wells Brown," *National Anti-Slavery Standard* 28 (May 18, 1867): 3.

34. "Letter from Philadelphia," *Commonwealth* 5 (Feb. 23, 1867): 1.

35. *National Anti-Slavery Standard* 27 (Oct. 6, 1866): 2.

36. *An historical research respecting the opinions of the founders of the Republic, on Negroes as slaves, as citizens, and as soldiers* (Boston: John Wilson and Son, 1862).

37. *New York Tribune* (Jan. 16, 1863).

38. *Tribute of the Massachusetts Historical Society to the Memory of George Livermore* (Boston: Massachusetts Historical Society, 1866), p. 11.

39. *Catalogue of the Valuable Private Library of the Late George Livermore, Esq.* (Boston: Libbie, 1894), p. 142.

40. Trotter's copy is in the Charles D. Martin Collection, James E. Shepard Library, North Carolina Central University, Durham.

41. Horace Greeley, *Recollections of a Busy Life* (New York: J. B. Ford and Co., 1868), pp. 420–21.

42. Alice Fahs, "The Market Value of Memory: Popular War Histories and the Northern Literary Marketplace, 1861–1868," *Book History* 1 (1998): 107–39.

43. Shepard's canceled check for his subscription to the 1865 volume of the *Liberator* is in Box 11, Folder 4, Lee and Shepard Papers, American Antiquarian Society, Worcester, MA.

44. Perkins to Lee and Shepard, June 5, 1867, Box 8, Folder 3, Lee and Shepard Papers, American Antiquarian Society.

45. Salesman's canvassing sample of *Innocents Abroad*, Subscription Book Collection, American Antiquarian Society.

46. *National Anti-Slavery Standard* 27 (April 13, 1867): 3.

47. T. B. Pugh to Lee and Shepard, Feb. 25, 1867, Box 8, Folder 5, Lee and Shepard Papers, American Antiquarian Society.

48. Little to Lee and Shepard, June 22, 1867, Box 7, Folder 1, Lee and Shepard Papers, American Antiquarian Society.

49. Little to Lee and Shepard, July 13, 1867, Box 7, Folder 1, Lee and Shepard Papers, American Antiquarian Society.

50. J. S. Brainard to Lee and Shepard, Oct. 24, 1868, Box 2, Folder 1, Lee and Shepard Papers, American Antiquarian Society.

51. Michael Tow, "Secrecy and Segregation: Murphysboro's Black Social Organizations, 1865–1925," *Journal of the Illinois State Historical Society* 97 (Spring 2004): 31.

52. Henry N. Guice to Lee and Shepard, Oct. 2 and 20, 1869, Box 5, Folder 2, Lee and Shepard Papers, American Antiquarian Society.

53. Ibid.

54. Guice to Shepard and Lee, Nov. 18, 1869, Box 5, Folder 2, Lee and Shepard Papers, American Antiquarian Society.

55. *Elevator* (April 10, 1868): 4.

56. Nelson Primus to his mother, March 22, 1867, Box 2, Primus Family Papers, Connecticut Historical Society, Hartford.

57. William Dean Howells, "My Mark Twain," in *Literary Friends and Acquaintance*, ed. David F. Hiatt and Edwin H. Cady (Bloomington: Indiana University Press, 1968), p. 269.

58. *National Anti-Slavery Standard* 28 (July 6, 1867): 3.

59. *American Bookseller* 1 (June 1, 1876): 408.

60. Oliver B. Fairbanks to Lee and Shepard, June 10 and 19, 1873, Box 4, Folder 3, Lee and Shepard Papers, American Antiquarian Society.

61. WWB eulogized her in "Death of Madame Louise de Mortie," *National Anti-Slavery Standard* 28 (Oct. 26, 1867): 3.

62. *National Anti-Slavery Standard* 28 (June 27, 1868): 3; *Independent* 20 (July 2, 1868): 3.

63. *National Anti-Slavery Standard* 29 (Jan. 9, 1869): 1.

64. WWB, "The Western Convention," *Liberator* 27 (Nov. 6, 1857): 179.

65. "The Women. Progress of the Female Suffrage Movement in Chicago," *Chicago Tribune* (Feb. 13, 1869): 4.

66. Ann D. Gordon, ed., *Against an Aristocracy of Sex, 1866 to 1873*, vol. 2 in *The Selected Papers of Elizabeth Cady Stanton and Susan B. Anthony* (New Brunswick, NJ: Rutgers University Press, 2000), pp. 212–13.

67. The *Tribune* reprinted WWB's letter to the editor of the *Times*, "Was Hannibal a Negro? Controversy Between a Brown Negro and a White Story-Teller—The Negro Ahead," (Feb. 21, 1869): 2.

68. "The Cause of It," *Cincinnati Daily Enquirer* (Feb. 23, 1869): 4.

69. "Was Hannibal a Negro?" *Memphis Daily Appeal* (March 21, 1869): 1, in Chronicling America, Library of Congress.

70. Primm, *Lion of the Valley*, pp. 273–75.

71. Just before WWB's arrival, a local paper reported that the Chouteau mansion was to be demolished and replaced by an elaborate jail complex: "The New County Jail," *St. Louis Democrat* (Feb. 15, 1869): 2.

72. *St. Louis Times* (Feb. 19, 1869): 1.

73. "'Bal d'Africaine,'" *Missouri Republican* (Feb. 28, 1869): 2.

74. *Missouri Democrat* (Jan. 8, 1869): 4; *Missouri Republican* (Feb. 5, 1869): 5.

75. *Commonwealth* (March 13, 1869): 3; *Independent* 21 (March 18, 1869): 4; *National Anti-Slavery Standard* 29 (March 20, 1869): 2.

76. *National Anti-Slavery Standard* 29 (March 27, 1869): 2.

77. "Prohibition in Massachusetts Politics," *Zion's Herald* 47 (Aug. 25, 1870): 404.

78. Quoted in James Brewer Stewart, *Wendell Phillips: Liberty's Hero* (Baton Rouge: Louisiana State University Press, 1986), p. 296.

79. *Cambridge Chronicle* (Oct. 8, 1870): 3.

80. *National Standard* n.s. 1 (Oct. 15, 1870): 5.

81. *Cambridge Chronicle* (Oct. 22, 1870): 2.

82. "Colored Voters' Convention," *New York Tribune* (Oct. 27, 1870): 5.

83. *Louisville Daily Commercial* (Sept. 23, 1871), reprinted in *National Standard* n.s. 2 (Oct. 8, 1871): 3.

84. Anne E. Marshall, *Creating a Confederate Kentucky: The Lost Cause and Civil War Memory in a Border State* (Chapel Hill: University of North Carolina Press, 2010), p. 58.

85. "A Night in the Hands of the Ku-Klux," *Boston Daily Advertiser* (Sept. 29, 1871): 2.

86. *Boston Daily Advertiser* (Oct. 18, 1871): supplement to 1.

87. "'Box Brown' on the *Herald*," *New York Herald* (May 2, 1870): 6.

88. *New York Herald* (Sept. 28, 1871): 6.

89. *Appleton's Railway and Steam Navigation Guide* (July 1871): 214–15.

90. Hambleton Tapp and James C. Klotter, *Kentucky: Decades of Discord, 1865–1900* (Frankfort: Kentucky Historical Society, 1977), p. 383.

91. "Three Negroes Lynched at Winchester," *Boston Daily Advertiser* (Sept. 29, 1871): 1.

92. "A Thrilling Incident of the War" (chapter 36), *The Negro in the American Rebellion*.

Chapter 11

1. "Pauline E. Hopkins," *Colored American Magazine* 2 (January 1901): 218. A portion of the manuscript, written in Hopkins's neat, elegant lettering, survives in the Hopkins Papers, John Hope and Aurelia E. Franklin Library, Fisk University, Nashville, TN.

2. Pauline E. Hopkins, "William Wells Brown," *Colored American Magazine* 2 (January 1901): 235–36.

3. The manuscript libretto is in the Hopkins Papers, Fisk University, Nashville, TN. The play was originally published in Eileen Southern, ed., *African American Theater* (New York: Garland, 1994). See also Lois Brown, *Pauline Elizabeth Hopkins: Black Daughter of the Revolution* (Chapel Hill: University of North Carolina Press, 2008), p. 117.

4. *African American Theater*, p. 140.

5. Ibid., p. 128.

6. Someone other than Hopkins entered a stage direction for its singing near the climactic end of Act 3 in the margin of Hopkins's manuscript text: *African American Theater*, p. 138.

7. "The Negro Again," *Christian Recorder* 11 (Sept. 25, 1873): 4.

8. *The Rising Son*, p. 417.

9. Ibid., p. 549.

10. Ibid., p. 385.

11. Richard H. Brodhead, ed., *The Journals of Charles W. Chesnutt* (Durham, NC: Duke University Press, 1993), p. 164.

12. *Christian Recorder* 11 (Jan. 8, 1874): 4.

13. William Still to Mary Ann Shadd Cary, Sept. 9, 1873, William Still Letterbook, 1873–74, pp. 453–55, Historical Society of Pennsylvania, Philadelphia.

14. William Still to Mary Ann Shad Cary, July 30, 1873, William Still Letterbook, pp. 280–82.

15. Still quoted Brown in his own Sept. 9, 1873, letter to Mary Ann Shadd Cary.

16. The Stills's copy of *The American Fugitive* is in the author's collection.

17. Still to WWB, Oct. 28, 1873, William Still Letterbook, pp. 585–86.

18. Still to WWB, Nov. 7, 1873, William Still Letterbook, pp. 616–17.

19. Still to WWB, Dec. 23, 1873, William Still Letterbook, pp. 690–91.

20. WWB to Still, May 27, 1874, Box 9-G, Folder 18, Leon and Beatrice M. Gardiner Collection, Historical Society of Pennsylvania.

21. Advertisements for *The Rising Son* at the end of the 1880 edition of *My Southern Home* claimed it had gone through ten prior "editions"—each, if to be believed, probably of 1,000 copies.

22. Still to WWB, June 14, 1873, William Still Letterbook, p. 75.

23. Still to WWB, Oct. 28, 1873, William Still Letterbook, p. 585.

24. They married June 12, 1870: Marriage of George S. Dogans and Josephine Brown, June 12, 1870, Certificate no. 5517 for 1870, New York County, Municipal Archives of the City of New York.

25. The death record misspells his name as "Dougans": Massachusetts, Death Records, 1841–1915.

26. Death Records, Clerk's Office, Cambridge City Hall; Commonwealth of Massachusetts; *Massachusetts Death Records, 1841–1915*, 266: 62, Massachusetts Archives, Columbia Point, Boston; Records, Cambridge Cemetery. The location of the sisters' grave is Range 7, Grave 16.

27. Program for WWB Memorial Ceremony, Cambridge Room, Cambridge Public Library.

28. For Smith's title, see Nell, *Colored Patriots*, p. 112.

29. David Donald, *Charles Sumner and the Rights of Man* (New York: Alfred A. Knopf, 1970), pp. 586–87.

30. Broadsides Collection, American Antiquarian Society, Worcester, MA.

31. "Eulogy of Charles Sumner," *Boston Globe* (May 18, 1874): 2.

32. WWB to William Still, May 27, 1874.

33. "A Monument to the Late William C. Nell Proposed," *Boston Globe* (June 3, 1874): 8.

34. Dorothy Porter Wesley and Constance Porter Uzelac, eds., *William Cooper Nell: Selected Writings, 1832–1874* (Baltimore: Black Classic Press, 2002), pp. 58–60.

35. England and Wales Deaths 1837–2007, Vol. 9B, p. 297. The registry gives her date of death only as the second quarter of the year.

36. 1861 English census.

37. England and Wales Marriages, 1837–2008, Book 9, p. 355.

38. "Provincial Theatricals," *London Era* (Dec. 25, 1870). Reginald Pitts provided this reference.

39. Quoted in John Hope Franklin, *George Washington Williams: A Biography* (Chicago: University of Chicago Press, 1985), p. 18.

40. "The Southern Outrages," *Boston Daily Advertiser* (Sept. 3, 1874): 1.

41. On his talk to the Banneker Club, see *Boston Globe* (Dec. 27, 1873): 8.

42. Quoted in *Springfield Republican* (Nov. 9, 1884): 4.

43. WWB, "The Elevation of the Coloured Race," *Good Templars' Watchword* 10 (Nov. 5, 1883): 705–6.

44. Samuel F. Cary, *Historical Sketch of the Order of the Sons of Temperance* (Halifax, Nova Scotia: W. Theakston, 1884), p. 8.

45. "The National Division of the Sons of Temperance," *Boston Journal* (Sept. 7, 1871): 1.

46. *Boston Evening Transcript* (Jan. 13, 1873).

47. "The British Delegation to R. W. G. L.," *Good Templars' Watchword* 1 (June 11, 1874): 239.

48. WWB to William Still, May 27, 1874.

49. Quoted in David M. Fahey, *Temperance and Racism: John Bull, Johnny Reb, and the Good Templars* (Lexington: University of Kentucky Press, 1996), p. 73.

50. Joseph Malins, *The Unlawful Exclusion of the African Race* (Birmingham, UK: G.L. Printing Office, 1877), pp. 25–26.

51. *Good Templars' Watchword* 4 (July 11, 1877): 462.

52. "Interesting Letters on the Negro Question," *Good Templars' Watchword* 3 (July 26, 1876): 505.

53. "G. L. Massachusetts," *Good Templars' Watchword* 3 (Oct. 11, 1876): 675.

54. "Convention of Colored Men at Utica," *Hartford Daily Courant* (Sept. 20, 1876): 3.

55. "Dr. Wells Brown on the Colour Question," *Good Templars' Watchword* 3 (Nov. 1, 1876): 724–25.

56. *Lowell Daily Courier* (Nov. 29, 1876): 1.

57. "The Negro Question," *Good Templars' Watchword* 3 (Dec. 13, 1876): 839.

58. *Good Templars' Watchword* 3 (Oct. 25, 1876) 705–6.

59. Malins, *The Unlawful Exclusion of the African Race* p. 64; *Scotsman* (June 20, 1877): 5.

60. "Interesting Letters on the Negro Question": 505.

61. "Dr. Wm. Wells Brown," *Boston Journal* (Sept. 28, 1877): 1.

62. "Arrival of Dr. Wells Brown," *Good Templars' Watchword* 4 (June 27, 1877): 421.

63. "Good Templars," *London Mercury* (June 26, 1877): 6.

64. "G. L. Special Session," *Good Templars' Watchword* 4 (June 13, 1877): 394; "Local News," *Liverpool Mercury* (June 18, 1877).

65. *Scotsman* (June 27, 1877): 4.

66. "Independent Order of Good Templars," *Glasgow Herald* (June 27, 1877): 4.

67. [Durham, UK] *Northern Echo* (Aug. 20, 1877): 4.

68. *Western Daily Press* (Aug. 25, 1877): 5.

69. "Temperance Meeting at Burslem," Supplement to *Staffordshire Sentinel* (July 24, 1877): 8.

70. Richardson to Frederick Douglass, Nov. 14, 1882, Reel 3, Frederick Douglass Papers, Manuscript Division, Library of Congress.

71. Richardson to Frederick Douglass, Jan. 22, 1878, Reel 3, Frederick Douglass Papers, Manuscript Division, Library of Congress.

72. David M. Fahey, ed., *The Collected Writings of Jessie Forsyth, 1847–1937: The Good Templars and Temperance Reform on Three Continents* (Lewiston, NY: Edward Mellen, 1988), pp. 331–32.

73. "Public Reception of Dr. Wm. Wells Brown," *Christian Recorder* 15 (Oct. 4, 1877): 2.

74. "Dr. Brown's Reception," *Christian Recorder* 15 (Oct. 4, 1877): 2.

75. "General Mention," *Christian Recorder* 15 (Nov. 22, 1877): 2.

76. Joseph Malins, "A Black Picture of the Sunny South," *Christian Recorder* 16 (June 13, 1878): 3.

77. William Wells Brown, *My Southern Home: or, The South and Its People* (Boston: A. G. Brown and Company, 1880), pp. 179–80.

78. Ibid., p. 183.

79. "Our Work in the Southern States," *Good Templars' Watchword* 6 (May 3, 1879): 244.

80. *Boston Evening Traveller* (March 11, 1879).

81. *Virginia Star* (May 11, 1878): 2.

82. *My Southern Home*, p. 205.

83. "News from Bro. Dr. W. Wells Brown," *Good Templars' Watchword* 6 (April 16, 1879): 309.

84. David S. Reynolds, *John Brown Abolitionist: The Man Who Killed Slavery, Sparked the Civil War, and Seeded Civil Rights* (New York: Alfred A. Knopf, 2005), pp. 394–95.

85. *Liberator* 29 (Dec. 16, 1859): 199.

86. *Washington National Republican* (Oct. 30, 1882): 1.

87. "Wm. Lloyd Garrison," *Boston Herald* (May 27, 1879): 2.

88. *Good Templars' Watchword* 6 (Oct. 29, 1879): 713.

89. Quoted in Fahey, *Temperance and Racism*, pp. 116–17.

90. Lewis G. Clarke to Lewis and Harriet Hayden, Jan. 3, 1880, Charles Chapman Collection, Box 14-1, Folder 2, Moorland–Spingarn Research Center, Howard University, Washington, DC.

91. *My Southern Home*, p. 166.

92. Ibid., p. 248.

93. *Christian Recorder* 18 (Sept. 16, 1880): 4.

94. "New Books," *New York Times* (Nov. 8, 1880).

95. The two sheets of cheap paper, with three sides containing trial text for *My Southern Home* and one filled with notes on Napoleon, are in the Wyatt Houston Day Collection of Books & Manuscripts by African American Authors, Nyack, NY.

96. *My Southern Home*, pp. 252–53.

97. *American Bookseller* 1 (June 1, 1876): 408.

98. A copy of the 1880 printing is in Butler Library, Columbia University.

99. The New York Historical Society has an updated "edition" of the work with a tipped-in "Publishers' Note to the Thirteenth Edition."

100. William Still to William H. Gray, Sept. 2, 1873, William Still Letterbook, pp. 419–20.

101. Deed Book 1403, pp. 441–42, Middlesex Probate and Family Court, Cambridge, MA.

102. Deed Book 1437, pp. 108–9, Middlesex Probate and Family Court, Cambridge, MA.

103. Deed Book 1610, pp. 142–44, Middlesex Probate and Family Court, Cambridge, MA.

104. "Honor Done to a Colored Man," *Christian Recorder* 21 (Jan. 25, 1883).

105. Nell, *Colored Patriots of the American Revolution*, p. 138.

106. Boston Type Foundry, *Specimen Sheets from the Boston Type Foundry* (Boston, 1856), American Antiquarian Society.

107. *Boston Journal* (Feb. 9, 1884): 3.

108. *Boston Herald* (Feb. 9, 1884): 2.

109. James Monroe Trotter, "William Wells Brown," *Boston Globe* (Jan. 15, 1885): 2.

110. WWB to Bird, April 19, 1849, Francis William Bird Papers, Houghton Library, Harvard University.

111. "Hon. F. W. Bird," *Boston Journal* (Oct. 23, 1884): 1.

112. "Is the Negro Inferior?" *Boston Advocate* (Sept. 19, 1885): 1.

113. *Boston Advocate* (July 4, 1885): 3.

114. "William Wells Brown," *Boston Herald* (Nov. 10, 1884): 2.

115. On the cost of cemetery plots, "Our Cemetery," *Cambridge Press* (June 16, 1866): 2.

116. *Buffalo Evening Republic* (Nov. 10, 1884): 2.

117. "Notes of a Temperance Scamper," *Liverpool Mercury* (July 6, 1885).

118. Richardson to Douglass, Nov. 2, 1885, Reel 4, Frederick Douglass Papers, Manuscript Division, Library of Congress.

119. *Women's Journal* 15 (Nov. 15, 1884): 368.

120. *Commonwealth* 23 (Nov. 15, 1884): 3.

121. "William Wells Brown," *Boston Evening Journal* (Jan. 15, 1885): 4.

122. "William Wells Brown, M.D.," *Christian Recorder* 22 (Nov. 27, 1884): 2.

123. *Boston Journal* (Jan. 15, 1885): 4.

124. On his medical practice, see his friend Charles Slack, *Commonwealth* 23 (Nov. 15, 1884): 3.

125. Fahey, *The Collected Writings of Jessie Forsyth, 1847–1937*, p. 85.

126. "South End Notes," *Boston Advocate* (Aug. 29, 1885): 3.

127. *Boston Advocate* (March 6, 1886): 3.

128. "Burned to Death," *Cambridge Chronicle* (Sept. 13, 1902): 14.

129. Ibid.; "Woman Fatally Burned," *Boston Herald* (Sept. 5, 1902): 9.

130. Range F, Grave 51. Thomas Calvin paid the cemetery $30 as recently as 1920, though not necessarily for upkeep of this grave: Cambridge Cemetery Records.

131. There was brief discussion in the black community shortly after his death about forming an African American historical society in the Boston area and collecting relevant materials, but nothing apparently came of it: "An African Historical Society," *Boston Advocate* (June 27, 1885): 3; "Historical Society," *Boston Advocate* (July 4, 1885): 1.

Epilogue

1. "William Wells Brown, M.D., 1816–1884," *Journal of the National Medical Association* 47 (May 1955): 207.

2. Joseph Sabin, *Bibliotheca Americana* (New York: Joseph Sabin, 1868), 2: 562–63.

3. Quoted in Eugene F. Provenzo Jr., *W. E. B. DuBois's Exhibit of American Negroes: African Americans at the Beginning of the Twentieth Century* (Lanham, MD: Rowman and Littlefield, 2013), p. 1.

4. Murray folded the circular letter (dated Jan. 22, 1900) containing this phrase into copies of his bibliography, *Preliminary List of Books and Pamphlets by Negro Authors for Paris Exposition and Library of Congress* (1900). A copy is in the collections of the American Antiquarian Society.

5. "The Round Table," *Colored American* (May 13, 1899): 2.

6. These quizzes appeared commonly in the black press. Several examples: "Negro History Week Quiz," *Atlanta Daily World* (Feb. 11, 1953): 3; "Do You Know These Things?" *Norfolk Journal and Guide* (March 27, 1937): A9.

7. Mabe Kountze, "War Views from Boston," *Chicago Defender* (Oct. 7, 1939): 13.

8. "Play Features Jefferson and His Negro Mistress," [New York] *Amsterdam News* (Nov. 9, 1963): 30.

9. *Indianapolis Freeman* (Feb. 24, 1906): 3; "Some Facts Touching Racial Relations Many Years Ago," *Baltimore Afro-American* (Aug. 17, 1912): 7; "Rare and Priceless Literary Items Return to Popular Use," [New York] *Amsterdam News* (Dec. 2, 1944): 9A.

10. Walter P. Davis, "With a Grain of Salt," *Norfolk Journal and Guide* (Feb. 19, 1944): B8.

11. Mattye Breckinridge Gaye, "A Biography of William Wells Brown" (Master's thesis, Hampton Institute, 1948).

12. "Bass Harris Plans Unique Broadcast," *Los Angeles Sentinel* (Aug. 28, 1952): B3.

13. Farrison to Reference Librarian, June 18, 1949, Folder 3, Higgins Family File, Kentucky Historical Society; Farrison to Librarian, June 18, 1949, Young Family Letters File, Filson Historical Society.

14. Blyden Jackson, *A History of Afro-American Literature*. Vol. 1, *The Long Beginning, 1746–1895* (Baton Rouge: Louisiana State University Press, 1989), p. 326.

15. Robert F. Reid-Pharr, *Conjugal Union: The Body, the House, and the Black American* (New York: Oxford University Press, 1999), p. 38.

16. *Three Years in Europe*, p. 267.

17. "Miscegenation," *Native Guard* (Boston: Houghton Mifflin, 2006), p. 3.

TEXT CREDITS

Letters: William Cooper Nell to Sanderson, 17 December 1856, Nell to Sanderson, 1 July 1857; BANC MSS 75/70, Jeremiah Burke Sanderson Papers, The Bancroft Library, University of California Berkeley; Materials from the Antislavery Collection courtesy of the Trustees of the Boston Public Library/Rare Books; Letters to the Estlin Family courtesy of the Estlin Family Collection, Bristol Central Library; Materials from the British Museum Central Archive by kind permission of the Trustees of the British Museum; Milton Clark file courtesy of the Cambridge Historical Commission; Program for WWB memorial ceremony courtesy of the Cambridge Public Library Archives and Special Collections; ALS Nelson Primus to his mother courtesy of The Connecticut Historical Society, Hartford, Connecticut; Materials from the Clark-Hite Papers, Higgins Family Papers, and Young Family file courtesy of the Filson Historical Society; Higgins Family Papers courtesy of the Family History Collection, Franklin County Historical Society, Franklin County Library, Winchester, Tennessee; Materials from the Raymond English Anti-Slavery Collection courtesy of the University of Manchester; Inventory of Estlin Family Antislavery Library courtesy of the Kroch Library, Cornell University; Quotations from the Thomas Bradford Drew diaries courtesy of the Massachusetts Historical Society; Materials from the Ruth Ferris Collection of River Life and Lore courtesy of the St. Louis Mercantile Library, University of Missouri; Materials from the St. Louis Circuit Court Case Files courtesy of Missouri State Archives; Materials from the Charles Chapman Collection courtesy of Moorland-Spingarn Research Center, Howard University, Washington,

INDEX

Page numbers in *italics* refer to illustrations.